THE BACH FAMILY

1. Johann Sebastian Bach
Pastel by Gottlieb Friedrich Bach in the possession
of Paul Bach, Eisenach

KARL GEIRINGER

IN COLLABORATION WITH

IRENE GEIRINGER

THE BACH FAMILY

*Seven Generations of
Creative Genius*

LONDON

GEORGE ALLEN & UNWIN LTD

RUSKIN HOUSE   MUSEUM STREET

First published in 1954

*Printed in Great Britain
in 12 pt. Fournier type
by T. & A. Constable Ltd.
Hopetoun Street, Edinburgh.*

To the Memory of
MARY CONOVER MELLON
whose eager quest
for the adventures of the mind
was a source of stimulation
to the Author

*

PREFACE

BOOKS and articles on members of the Bach family are so numerous that a complete bibliography would fill several volumes. Nevertheless it does not seem to have occurred to previous authors to write the history of the whole clan from the first manifestations of musical talent in the 16th century to its last occurrence in the middle of the 19th. This has been attempted in the present book, and the magnitude of the task will, it is hoped, be accepted as an excuse for the inevitable shortcomings of the work.

From the outset the writer was aware of the complexity of problems confronting him, since, with the exception of Johann Sebastian's works and a small number of modern reprints, the majority of the material needed was only available in European libraries. Moreover, the whereabouts of the invaluable Bachiana of the former Preussische Staatsbibliothek, Berlin, were not known in 1947, when the present research was started. A tremendous amount of slow and painstaking spadework had to be done before the author was in possession of a representative collection of photostats and microfilms, on which to base his study. However, most obstacles were eventually overcome, and the writer believes that the book offers in each of its sections material new to the English reader. In the case of Sebastian's relatives a great amount of works accessible only in manuscript or in contemporary prints was dealt with, among them various compositions not considered by former research students. An attempt was also made to outline the careers of the different Bachs against the religious, social, and political backgrounds of the time. With regard to Sebastian it was felt that a substantial part of the book ought to be devoted to this most representative member of the family. The author aimed at including the results of recent German research, in particular from publications issued in honour of the Bicentenary of 1950. Various details have now been cleared up which contribute to an interpretation somewhat different from that given in the classical biographies of Spitta, Schweitzer or Terry. In this connection mention should be made of the frontispiece to this book, the miniature portrait of Sebastian painted by his kinsman, Gottlieb Friedrich Bach, which the artist's great-grandson gave to the author for first publication.

As the amount of music quotations included in the present book was naturally restricted, the author plans to present before long an Anthology of music by members of the Bach Family.

The list of persons and institutions to whom the author feels indebted is a very extensive one. In the first place he should like to express his deepest appreciation to the Bollingen Foundation for their generous financial assistance which enabled him to obtain the necessary material from foreign countries. Moreover, he found European experts most co-operative and interested in his project. Without their unfailing assistance and patient labours this book would never have been written. In particular he wishes to express his thanks to Mr. Paul Bach, Eisenach; Mrs. Mia Bach, Witten/Ruhr; Mr. Ernst Brinkmann, Mühlhausen; Professor Victor Burr, Director of the Universitätsbibliothek, Tübingen; Dr. A. Corbet, Bibliothécaire de la Bibliothèque du Conservatoire Royal, Brussels; Dr. Martin Cremer, Director of the Westdeutsche Bibliothek, Marburg/L.; Dr. Conrad Freyse, Director of the Bach-Museum, Eisenach; Professor Wilibald Gurlitt, Freiburg/B.; Dr. Rudolf Höcker, former Director of the Oeffentliche Studienbibliothek, Berlin; His Honour, the Mayor of Jena; A. Hyatt King, Esq., Department of Printed Music, British Museum, London; Dr. Hedwig Kraus, Director of the Collections of the Gesellschaft der Musikfreunde, Vienna; His Honour, Mayor Mögk of Meiningen; Dr. Herbert Pée, Curator of the Kunsthalle, Hamburg; Dr. Roland Philip, Vienna; Mrs. Fritz Rollberg, widow of the late Bach scholar, Eisenach; Dr. Friedrich Schäfer, Kirchenarchivrat, Eisenach; B. Schofield, Esq., Keeper of the Department of Manuscripts in the British Museum, London; Dr. Friedrich Smend, Professor of the Kirchliche Hochschule, Berlin; Stadtarchivar Fritz Wiegand, Erfurt. In this country the author received most valuable help from Dr. Huntington Cairns, Director of the National Gallery, Washington, D.C.; Dr. Archibald T. Davison of Harvard University; Dr. George S. Dickinson of Vassar College; Dr. Paul H. Lang and Dr. Daniel G. Mason of Columbia University; Mr. Philip Vaudrin, New York. Unfailing assistance was given by Dr. Harold Spivacke, Mr. Edward Waters, Mr. Richard S. Hill and Mr. William Lichtenwanger of the Library of Congress, Washington, D.C., as well as by Mr. Richard Appel, chief of the music department of the Boston Public Library. Various officials of the Widener, Houghton and Isham Libraries of Harvard University, the Sibley Musical Library of Rochester, N.Y., and the New York Public Library proved most helpful too. Dr. George B. Weston, Professor emeritus of Harvard University, very generously made the treasures of his Friedemann Bach

Collection available to the writer. Thanks are also due to Lord Hilling-don and the Oxford University Press for permission to reproduce the portrait of Johann Christian Bach by Thomas Gainsborough from *Johann Christian Bach* by Terry. For basic advice regarding the evaluation of the Bach painters he has to thank Mr. Thomas M. Messer, Assistant Director of the American Federation of Art, and Dr. Else Hofmann, New York. Linguistic advice was generously contributed by Mrs. Mabel E. Blandford and the late Walter F. H. Blandford, as well as by Mr. Klaus G. Roy, Librarian of the College of Music of Boston University. Dr. Henry S. Drinker of Merion, Penna., very kindly translated some poems into English; moreover his outstanding translations of Bach Cantatas and Chorales were used throughout this book. The author's brother, Dr. Ernest Geiringer, rendered valuable help in checking historical data. Great patience and understanding were displayed by the publishers, to whom sincere thanks are due for their splendid co-operation.

Dr. Irene Geiringer (Mrs. Karl Geiringer), who has assisted the author in his previous literary efforts, extensively collaborated in the writing of the present book, particularly with regard to the biographical sections.

KARL GEIRINGER

BOSTON, MASS., *October* 1953

CONTENTS

ILLUSTRATIONS

SKETCHES

ABBREVIATIONS

---

*The numbers appearing in brackets after certain Bach names are those
established by J. S. Bach in his 'Origin of the Musical Bach Family' (cf. p. 6)
In the discussion of the music lower case letters indicate a minor key, capitals
a major key (a=A minor; A=A major, etc.)*

AfMf	Archiv für Musikforschung.
BG	J. S. Bach's Collected Works published by the Bach-Gesellschaft. Leipzig, 1851-1900.
BJ	Bach Jahrbuch. Leipzig, 1904-
BWV	Thematic catalogue of the works of J. S. Bach in Wolfgang Schmieder, 'Thematisch-systematisches Verzeichnis der musikalischen Werke J. S. Bach's.' Leipzig, 1950.
DDT	Denkmäler deutscher Tonkunst. Leipzig, 1892-1931
EDM	Das Erbe deutscher Musik (continuation of *DDT* since 1935).
F	Thematic catalogue of the works of Wilhelm Friedemann Bach in Martin Falck, 'Wilhelm Friedemann Bach.' Leipzig, 1913.
fl.	Abbreviation for the German *Gulden* (florin), which was, similarly to the present pound sterling, subdivided into 20 *Groschen* (gr.), each *Groschen* comprising 12 *Pfennige* (pf.)
gr.	*Groschen*. One-twentieth of a German *Gulden*.
MQ	Musical Quarterly.
P.	J. S. Bach's organ works as published by C. F. Peters in 9 vols.
pf.	*Pfennig*. One-twelfth of a German *Groschen*.
Schn.	Thematic catalogue of the works of older members of the Bach family in Max Schneider, 'Thematisches Verzeichnis der musikalischen Werke der Familie Bach,' in *BJ*, 1907.
SIMG	Sammelbänder der Internationalen Musikgesellschaft.
Sü	Thematic catalogue of the works of Johann Christoph Friedrich Bach compiled by Georg Schünemann in *DDT* 56.
T	Thematic catalogue of the works of Johann Christian Bach in Charles Sanford Terry's 'John Christian Bach.' London, 1929.
th.	*Thaler*. 1½ of a German *Gulden*.
Wq	Thematic catalogue of the works of Carl Philipp Emanuel Bach in Alfred Wotquenne, 'C. Ph. E. Bach, Thematisches Verzeichnis seiner Werke.' Leipzig, 1905.
ZfMw	Zeitschrift für Musikwissenschaft.

PART I

THE RISE OF THE BACH FAMILY AND THE FIRST GREAT ACHIEVEMENTS (-1700)

A

INTRODUCTION: ORDEAL IN GERMANY

THE story of the Bach musicians is unique with regard to achievement as well as duration. In seven successive generations Bachs were active as church or town musicians, and even the immortal genius rising out of their midst was succeeded by sons who played a highly significant part in the art of their time. And of so tough a fibre were the Bachs made that they managed to rise from the humblest beginnings in a period of the greatest national distress.

It is hardly possible to paint too dark a picture of the ordeal which the German people had to endure in the first half of the 17th century, when the Thirty Years War was fought in their land. 'Fields lay waste and desolate. Burnt castles and villages in ashes were scattered far and wide. The towns groaned under the scourge of undisciplined and predatory garrisons, who wasted the property of the citizens, and availed themselves to the utmost of the licence of war. The destruction of the crops and the constant succession of armies which overran the exhausted country were inevitably followed by famine. The crowding together of men in camps and billets spread diseases which proved more fatal than even fire and sword. All vices flourished under the protection of anarchy and impunity, and men became as savage as the country itself.' This description by the German poet, Friedrich Schiller,[1] is, if anything, still too moderate in tone.

There are other historians[2] who have most bloodcurdling tales to tell. Certainly the German people had reached a tragically low level by 1648, the year in which the peace of Westphalia was concluded. In the more fortunate provinces the population had dropped to half its former strength, while in other states, for instance Thuringia, which will occupy us in particular, not more than one fourth was left. Those who had miraculously survived were physically and spiritually exhausted, and naturally the children they produced during the later war-years and the immediate post-war period also showed a lack of vitality.

From such a generation no great creative achievements could reasonably be expected. Indeed, the German literature of this period produced

[1] 'Geschichte des dreissigjährigen Krieges,' written in 1791-92.
[2] Cf. Hermann Gebhardt, 'Thüringische Kirchengeschichte,' Gotha, 1882.

3

hardly anything of lasting value. There were few gifted poets or writers, and those who did show a distinctive talent spoiled a genuine capacity for expression by crude and unsavoury details. Even the German language itself had, as it were, been given up by the people, who were anxious to interlard it with as many French and Latin idioms as possible, in order to give it style. In the fine arts things were hardly better; 'lacking talents, lacking independent artistic ideas, lacking opportunities for expression, German art could in no way compete with the creative work of the neighbouring countries.'[1]

It is a strange and heartening phenomenon that in these disastrous years music remained alive, composers of indisputable talent appeared, and although they were often badly hindered by the exigencies of war, there was never the arid desert which was to be found in other domains of art. A 17th-century writer, Johann Flitner, even went so far as to speak of a 'seculum musicum.' A baffling paradox indeed!

A key to its solution may be found in the close interdependence of music and religion. Wherever destruction and ruin were not complete, religion retained something of its former power. The little spiritual force that subsisted in the survivors of the war and the nearest post-war generation found its expression in religious life. The worse conditions became in the outside world, the more fervent grew the longing for the peace and inner security to be derived from a life in Christ. In such an atmosphere music, the most transcendental of all creative manifestations, was a spiritual necessity, a medicine the German people simply could not do without. In particular the Protestant Church, with much of its original driving force still intact, was responsible for a continuous flow of new and important musical works. Wherever a church was spared from destruction, the parishioners did their utmost to have services which, with the help of music, would enable them to triumph over their wretched and hopeless material existences. This does not mean, of course, that the long war and its after-effects did not cause grave damage to musical life as well; the injuries inflicted were serious, but by no means fatal.

This is most vividly revealed when we turn from the large cities, which had naturally greater resources, to the small Protestant communities, where cantors, organists, and town musicians did an amazing job against tremendous odds. In particular, music flourished in the province of Thuringia and a local historian[2] could remark proudly in 1684:

[1] Cf. Wilhelm Lübke and Max Semrau, 'Barock und Rokoko,' 14th ed., Greifswald, 1913.
[2] August Boetius, 'Merkwürdige und Auserlesene Geschichte von der berühmten Landgraffschaft Thüringen,' Gotha, 1684.

'Music is diligently cultivated in churches and schools. The Thuringians know what the ancient claimed, that he who does not love singing, does not possess balance either in mind or body. Here they build in villages not only string instruments such as violins, basses, viola da gamba, clavicymbals, spinets, citterns . . . because also the peasants play them, but one finds even in insignificant parishes organ works with an amazing number of stops and variety of equipment. [Moreover] such families as the *Lindemann, Altenburg, Ahle, Brigel* and *Bach* have through their compositions given a great name to the province of Thuringia.'

When this report was written, members of the Bach family had indeed already tended the musical soil of their homeland for a long time. Yet the Bachs were to continue work in this field through more than another hundred years, and they were to leave the other musical families far behind, rising to a distinction which even the enthusiastic chronicler was unable to foresee.

A MILLER—A JESTER—A PIPER
(VEIT—HANS—CASPAR BACH)

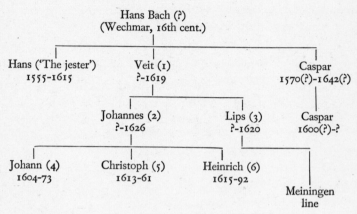

Numbers following a name are those of Sebastian's Genealogy.

DURING the 18th century the Bach musicians became fully conscious of their family's unique history. In 1727 a Cantor of the Thuringian town of Gehren by the name of Bach proudly claimed in a letter that 'the genealogy of the world-famous Bach family could be traced back to the year 1504.'[1] Whether the Cantor really possessed a document of this kind, we do not know. If he did, it was not accessible to his great kinsman, Sebastian Bach, who wrote eight years later the history of the clan entitled 'Origin of the Musical Bach Family.' The Thomas Cantor's chronicle[2] went back only to the later part of the 16th century, beginning with these words:

[1] The writer of this letter was Johann Christoph Bach (No. 17 in Sebastian's Genealogy). Cf. Fritz Wiegand, 'Johann Sebastian Bach und seine Verwandten in Arnstadt,' Arnstadt, 1950. In the district of Coburg, Franconia, the name of Bach can be found as early as the year 1000, according to Mr. Paul Bach, Eisenach.

[2] There are two copies of the *Ursprung der musicalisch-Bachischen Familie* in existence. One belonged to Philipp Emanuel Bach and was sent by him, in 1774, with some additions and corrections, to Johann Nikolaus Forkel, the first Bach biographer. The other was probably copied by Sebastian's kinsman and secretary, Johann Elias Bach, who gave it to his brother, Lorenz, whose descendants preserved the document. Complete editions of the 'Origin' are available in English translations by Ch. Sanford Terry, London, 1929; and by David and Mendel ('Bach Reader'), New York, 1945.

6

'Veit Bach, a white-bread baker in Hungary, in the 16th century was compelled to escape from Hungary because of his Lutheran faith. After converting his property into money, as far as this could be done, he went to Germany, and finding security for his religion in Thuringia, settled at Wechmar near Gotha, and continued his trade there. What he most delighted in was his little cittern which he used to take with him to work to play while the mill was grinding. A pretty noise the pair of them must have made! However, it taught him to keep time, and that apparently is how music first came into our family.'

We wish Sebastian's report were somewhat more explicit, for it leaves one essential point unclear. We do not know whether *Veit* was a native of Hungary or a German baker of Wechmar who on the traditional journeyman's tour had found conditions in Hungary favourable and remained there. The latter theory was adopted unquestioningly by the majority of scholars, who point out that the name of Bach can be traced in various places of Thuringia all through the 16th century and that a man called Hans Bach (maybe Veit's father) is mentioned as city guardian of Wechmar in 1561. Recently a dissenting voice was heard, however, in Germany.[1] If Veit emigrated from Germany, it claims, he could not have stayed too long in Hungary; how was it possible for him to acquire in so short a period the apparently considerable property mentioned by Sebastian? And why did the chronicler describe him as baker in Hungary, without mentioning the Thuringian origin? Doesn't it seem more likely that Veit was born in Hungary and inherited property from his father? His family might still have been a German one, for at that time many people of German origin were living in Hungary. On the other hand, a possible mixture of the German and Magyar races in Veit's or in his wife's ancestry might have been one of the factors determining the rich artistic heritage Veit bestowed on his descendants.

The question is unanswered yet.[2] Two significant facts emerge, however, from Sebastian's narrative. Veit, for the sake of his faith, gave up a settled existence, thus proving the deep affinity to the Lutheran religion which was to characterize so many Bachs, and Thuringia was the section of Germany he decided on. Perhaps he did so because the Bachs residing there were kinspeople, but whatever were his reasons, there is no doubt

[1] Cf. W. Rauschenberger, 'Die Familien Bach,' Frankfurt a.M., 1950.
[2] J. M. Korabinsky's assumption in 'Beschreibung der . . . Stadt Pressburg,' Pressburg, 1784, that Veit Bach had his domicile in Pressburg (Bratislava) has not been proved so far.

that the country suited him. Many generations of Bachs following him felt the same attraction and they stayed on in this part of Germany, just moving from one Thuringian town to another, establishing Bach centres in Gotha, Arnstadt, Erfurt, Eisenach, and so forth. Maybe a certain lack of initiative in the Bachs was responsible for this, as was also the traditional conception of the time that the son should inherit the father's position. But these were not all the decisive factors. Partly it was love of Thuringia that made the Bachs cling to it up to our own time.

It is a beautiful country, this Thuringia. In the south-west and north-east, a central basin is bordered by the huge, dense forests of the *Thüringerwald* and Harz Mountains, which even in our days are among the most popular vacation resorts in Germany. Nature is kind to the Thuringians; a moderate climate and fertile soil bring forth crops not excelled by those of any other German province. The inhabitants are stolid and introvert, and an abundance of legends testifies to their strong imagination. In Thuringia stands the Kyffhäuser mountain in which the Emperor Friedrich Barbarossa is believed to be waiting with his crusading army until such time as the ravens give him the signal to return to the German people. The highest mountain of the Harz, the Brocken, famous for the peculiar mist formations on its summit, is held to be the meeting place of all witches. Near Eisenach there stands the *Hörselberg* in which Venus is reported to have kept Tannhäuser in bondage, until he left her and appeared in the Wartburg while the Minnesingers' song contest was being held. But the name of Eisenach's Wartburg conjures up yet another picture. Here it was that Luther, under the assumed name of Junker Jörg, stayed whilst working on his epoch-making translation of the Bible; and this is by no means the only place in Thuringia connected with the reformer. In Eisenach he went to the Latin school, the same institution which Sebastian Bach was destined to attend almost two hundred years later. In Erfurt Luther studied at the University and entered the Augustinian monastery. No wonder that Thuringia became one of the pillars of the new Reformation, and that some of its ruling princes were among the leaders of the movement.

So Veit Bach settled down in Thuringia, where simple plough-boys were apt to appear on Sundays in their choir-loft to sing or perform on instruments 'with more art than many a learned musician,'[1] where even in the churches of the tiniest hamlets 'vocal music was adorned and

[1] Preface to the 116th Psalm written in 1623 by the Jena official, Burkhardt Grossmann (formerly Prussian State Library, Berlin, Mus. aut. G 930).

embellished by at least five or six violins.'[1] In this land, steeped in music, the baker's musical proficiency increased, and his beloved cittern became so much a part of his existence that he did not confine himself to playing it in hours of leisure but also took it to his mill.

Veit was not the only Bach of his generation to feel so strongly inclined towards music. About the same time there lived *Hans* Bach, possibly a brother of Veit, who, though a carpenter by trade, became fiddler (*Spielmann*) and court jester to the widowed Duchess of Württemberg in Nürtingen. The little we know about him is revealed in two portraits which were preserved to posterity through Emanuel Bach's[2] collection of family treasures. In the earlier of the two portraits, an etching formerly in the State Library of Berlin, we see a middle-aged man, wearing the large ruff fashionable at the time, and carrying a fiddle in his left hand, a bow in his right. His hair is cut quite short, except for a carefully modelled 'quiff' in the middle of his forehead, which was probably meant to produce a comical effect, and he has a pointed beard and moustache. On his right shoulder are displayed the jingling bells of the jester. The music he performed was apparently of a light character. At least that is what the verses[3] on a panel above his head imply:

> Hans Bach, the fiddler, has a style
> That when you hear him, you must smile;
> It is indeed unique and weird,
> In keeping with his Hans Bach beard.

The other portrait, a copperplate engraving owned by the Bibliothèque Nationale in Paris, depicts an older man, dressed in about the same style, and bears an inscription in Latin: 'Hans Bach, famous and amusing court jester, jocular fiddler, a diligent, upright, and religious man.' As a symbol of his real trade, eighteen different carpenter's tools are engraved around the inscription (Ill. IV).

The fact that two different portraits were engraved of Hans Bach, one of them by the well-reputed Wilhelm Schichard, subsequently a University professor in Tübingen, reveals that the portrayed was by no means a common court jester. It is also noteworthy that although jesters, like jugglers, ranked at that time among the 'infamous' (*unehrlich*) professions,

---

[1] Cf. Michael Altenburg, preface to 'Erster Teil newer lieblich und zierlicher Intraden,' 1620.

[2] Emanuel Bach erroneously assumed the portrayed to be Johannes (Hans) Bach (2), the great-grandfather of Sebastian, who died in 1626. Actually the Hans of the pictures died in 1615 and his exact relationship to Sebastian is not known.

[3] Translation by Henry S. Drinker.

the church register mentions that Hans 'this diligent and faithful servant of Her Ducal Highness was given an honest funeral.' Thus Hans Bach had, thanks to his fine character and excellent work, succeeded in rising out of the lowest stratum of society and had earned general respect.

While the miller-baker Veit was an amateur musician, and Hans combined the positions of a fiddler and jester with that of a carpenter, another Bach, by the name of *Caspar* (born around 1570), perhaps a younger brother of Veit, served in the Thuringian city of Gotha as a town piper (*Stadtpfeifer*). Caspar lived in Gotha in the high tower of the town hall,[1] as was the custom for the town piper; for, according to the instructions given to him, in addition to his duties as a town musician (cf. p. 15), he had to 'strike the hours, look out day and night for riders and carriages, watch closely all roads on which more than two riders were approaching, and also report whenever he observed a fire nearby or in the distance.' He stayed in Gotha until 1620, when he was called in the same capacity to the city of Arnstadt. This Thuringian town was to play a highly important part in the Bach chronicle, and, save for short intervals, to harbour musicians of the clan for almost two centuries.[2] Caspar came to a city sadly depleted through an epidemic of plague in the preceding year, in which around a third of the population had perished. Even when health conditions improved, the war, which had broken out in 1618, created an atmosphere of tension. The watch duties of the piper were now of the greatest importance and Caspar may have experienced plenty of anxious moments while living in the tower of the castle. In 1633 he was at last able to resign his position and to buy a house of his own, which still stands to-day. He continued, however, to work as musician, though not as watchman, both for the town and for the city's patron, the Count of Schwarzburg-Arnstadt, in whose band he played the *dulzian* (bassoon). The music-loving sovereign showed himself very generous in promoting the training of another Caspar, probably the town piper's eldest son (born around 1600). He sent the youth, who apparently showed great talent, to the courts of Bayreuth and Dresden, paying for Caspar's instruction by renowned masters, and liberally equipping him with the necessary clothes and instruments. In return Caspar had to sign a pledge that he would practise assiduously on various instruments and subsequently

[1] The Genealogy relates that he resided at the castle of Grimmenstein, which cannot be correct as the castle was demolished in 1567.

[2] The name of Bach occurs for the first time in the Arnstadt church register of 1613, when a Johanna Elisabeth Bach from the village of Ichtershausen married the cooper, Andreas Hartmann. Cf. Wiegand, *l.c.*

enter the Count's service. This plan never materialized, however. Maybe the Count did not engage young Caspar because the war situation was interfering more and more with musical activities, maybe the promising young artist died at an early age; whatever the explanation, there is no trace of him in Arnstadt. Nor were old Caspar's other descendants privileged to carry on the father's work. Four of his younger sons died before him, in the years 1632 to 1637, and the town thus lost a number of musicians.[1] After experiencing so much unhappiness in Arnstadt, old Caspar seems to have felt the urge to leave it for the time being. There were many kinsmen living in nearby villages and he may have joined one such group and supported himself as a musician. Thus his death, which occurred between 1642 and 1644, is not noted in the Arnstadt register.

It was to Caspar Bach that a son of Veit by the name of *Johannes* (2), born around 1580, was apprenticed when the lad's 'evident talent' (Genealogy) induced him to adopt the profession of a musician. Johannes stayed with his master even after the traditional term of apprenticeship was served, but at last he moved back to Wechmar. He was frequently called to nearby places like Gotha, Erfurt, and Arnstadt, when the town musicians needed reinforcement, and he had an excellent reputation all through the district. In addition to this he worked as a carpetmaker,[2] and when his father Veit died in 1619, Johannes seems to have taken charge of the mill as well. But, only seven years after his father's death, this busy life was cut short when Johannes succumbed to the plague which ravaged the district. He left three sons, each of whom was destined to found an important musical dynasty.[3]

The Genealogy also mentions a brother of Johannes, describing him as a carpetmaker but omitting his name. It is generally assumed that this was *Lips* Bach, who appears in the Wechmar register as the son of Veit,

---

[1] Three of them, Melchior (1603-34), Johannes (1602-32) and Nicol (1619-37), are described in the death-register as musicians; the fourth, who died in 1635, as a blind man. This latter, by the name of Heinrich, may well be the 'blind Jonah' whom the Genealogy mentions as the subject of many adventures.

[2] This is how the funeral sermon for his son, Heinrich Bach, by J. G. Olearius, 1692, describes him. The Genealogy on the other hand mentions his work as a miller.

[3] The information in the Genealogy regarding his marriage, taken over uncritically by some Bach biographers, including Ch. S. Terry, is slightly misleading. It states that on his return after Veit's death, Johannes married Anna Schmied, an innkeeper's daughter. This marriage would have taken place in 1619. On the other hand, the important sons of Johannes mentioned in the Genealogy were born in 1604, 1613, 1615. If he married Anna Schmied in 1619, she can only have been his second wife, while the sons we know of were children of a first marriage. It seems more likely, however, that he moved to Wechmar much earlier.

and died in 1620. The family tradition claims that the three gifted sons of Lips were sent to Italy by the Count of Schwarzburg-Arnstadt for their musical education, but so far no evidence to support this claim has been unearthed. It is not until a century later that we find solid historical evidence of this branch of the family, the so-called 'Meiningen line,' which was to produce some very fine artists.

THE FOUNDER OF THE ERFURT DYNASTY
(JOHANN BACH)

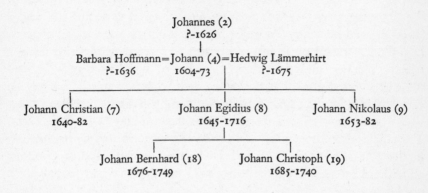

AT the time when Johannes Bach (2) died, Wechmar was no longer a good place in which to live. War had come to Germany, and as Thuringia was crossed by two strategically important roads, one to Nürnberg and one to Würzburg, troops marched again and again through the lovely land and drained its resources. Moreover, it did not take long for the plague to catch up with war. The little community of Wechmar suffered dreadful epidemics in 1626 and 1635; in the latter as many as 503 victims were listed, among them the widow of Johannes, who himself had been felled by the first outbreak of the Black Death nine years earlier. If ever a time was inimical to the muses, this can be said of the years when the three sons of Johannes started on their careers. Nevertheless they all chose music as a profession. The eldest, *Johann* (4), born in Wechmar in 1604, loved accompanying his father on musical expeditions. At an early age he showed such skill that the town piper of the city of Suhl, a man by the name of Johann Christoph Hoffmann, persuaded Johannes to entrust the lad to him for instruction. For seven years young Johann stayed at Suhl as apprentice and journeyman. He became attached to his master's daughter, Barbara, and ultimately married her, when he was financially able to do so. As a rule it was a tendency of the Bach family and, as a matter of fact, of the times, to marry young, but the disastrous conditions then prevailing in Germany forced Johann to wait until he was 31 years old. In spite of excellent qualifications, Johann was unable for some considerable time to find a permanent position; he drifted from Suhl to Schweinfurt, thence to his native village, and off again to various places, only to return six years later to Wechmar. He may have been connected with the army, for in a subsequent declaration for income tax he admitted possessing some money in cash, which he 'had previously earned from the officers.'[1] At last in 1635 he was called to the city of Erfurt. The events that were responsible for an opening in the town band were so typical of the time that they deserve mention here. Since 1631 Erfurt had had a Swedish garrison within its walls; but although the Swedes had come to help the Protestant cause and had orders to treat the Erfurt citizens in a friendly manner, the soldiers could not be restrained from brutality and the city suffered greatly at the hands of its Swedish allies. One day an Erfurt citizen by the name of Hans Rothlander invited a Swedish soldier to his house and induced the town musicians to play at his little party. The soldier drank too much and dozed off; when roused by his hostess, he thought he was being attacked. He jumped up and killed or wounded all within his reach. Thus the town band was depleted and Johann Bach got his chance.[2]

In spite of the grim reasons for his appointment, Johann must have been glad of the opportunity. Erfurt, with a population of 60,000 (a number that was to drop to 15,000 before the end of the century!), was one of the cultural centres of the country. It had always been a progressive town. One of the earliest organs in Germany was erected in the 11th century in its church of St. Paul, and its University, founded in 1392, formed one of the bastions of Humanism. But since the outbreak of the Thirty Years War the city had suffered enormous damage, both economically and morally. How its funds were depleted may be seen from the following summary. In 1622 Erfurt had to pay 200,000 fl. (cf. note 2, p. 20) for the army of Duke Frederick of Altenburg; in 1625 the war taxes paid to the Elector of Mainz amounted to 60,000 fl.; one year later the citizens gave 50,000 fl. to General Merode to ward off the billeting of his army, and in 1630 they were called on to supply 50,000 pounds of bread and 7000 thalers to the Emperor's general, Tilly. When ultimately the Swedish garrison occupied the city in 1631, it stayed there for five long years. The respite offered by its departure was all too short. Hostilities were soon resumed and in the following years various armies invaded

---

[1] Cf. Otto Rollert, 'Die Erfurter Bache,' in 'J. S. Bach in Thüringen,' Weimar, 1950.

[2] The Genealogy claims that Johann was appointed director of the town band. Rollert, *l.c.*, states, however, that although Johann Bach held a very influential position in the band, its nominal head was a man by the name of Christoph Volpracht.

Erfurt. Even after the end of the Thirty Years War the ill-fated city's troubles were not over. In 1664 it again suffered a heavy bombardment and, a few years later, occupation by an imperial army.

Through these turbulent years up to his death in 1673, Johann Bach remained at his post, the duties of which were manifold. In these dangerous times the town musicians had to 'keep watch seriously and diligently,' and when their suspicions were aroused, 'to blow with the greatest force so that all the people might take heart and grasp their guns.'[1] Many of the town musicians' activities helped the citizens 'to take heart.' The populace woke up to the sound of a chorale (a Protestant hymn tune) played around 3.30 a.m. by the pipers from the tower to signal the beginning of the day; they heard another sacred melody when they sat down to their noonday meal; and when a chorale sounded for the third time in the day, they knew it was time for bed. Great art was displayed in the arrangement and performance of these chorales. Johann Kuhnau, for instance, described the work of the Leipzig pipers in 1700 in these words:[2] 'when our town pipers blow a hymn tune from the tower on their sackbuts, we are all immeasurably stirred and imagine that we hear the angels singing.' There is reason for assuming that the playing of Johann Bach and his colleagues was on the same high level. Aware of the morale-building effect of music, the Council, in 1657, added a balcony to the City Hall, on which the band performed regularly on Wednesday and Saturday afternoons. In all these performances Johann Bach and his kinsmen played so decisive a part that eventually the name of Bach became a synonym for town musician, and maintained this meaning even at a time when no member of the family was living in Erfurt. The minutes of the City Council expressly refer to the 'local privileged band of town musicians or so-called Bachs,'[3] and once a man by the name of Tobias Sebelitzky was threatened with a fine of 5 th. if he engaged for his daughter's wedding musicians who did not belong to the town band as 'no others but the Bachs . . . were privileged to perform.'[4]

This decree is also interesting as proof of the authorities' endeavours to protect their town musicians. Playing at christenings, weddings, and funerals made up the larger part of their work and of their income too, and the rates for such performances were strictly regulated by the Council.

[1] Falckenstein, 'Civitatis Erfurtensis Historia Critica et Diplomatica,' Erfurt, 1740.
[2] Johann Kuhnau, 'Der musikalische Quacksalber,' 1700; reprint by Curt Benndorf, 1900.
[3] Stadtarchiv Erfurt, Ratsprotokolle of December 1, 1716.
[4] Stadtarchiv Erfurt, Ratsprotokolle, 1682.

These so-called *Accidentien* were especially important as the Council itself, owing to the tribulations of war, was often unable to pay its employees for years at a time, during which only the small fees collected from private persons kept the musicians going. In theory the regulations forbidding other than the town musicians to perform were very strict; in practice methods to bypass the law were found, and the feuds with the so-called 'beer fiddlers' (musicians not holding any permanent appointment) were constantly recurring vexations in the town musicians' existence.

Besides 'blowing' from the tower and performing at public functions and private festivities, the town musicians were required to play in the church orchestra and were supposed to master both stringed and wind instruments. In the case of Johann Bach, his duties at church were strictly regulated, as he had been since 1636[1] organist of Erfurt's *Predigerkirche*, a beautiful Gothic church of the 13th century. It speaks for the high esteem in which the organist was held that he succeeded in having the church's old organ rebuilt by the renowned master, Ludwig Compenius, an undertaking for which, in spite of the terrific shortage of money, the amount of 1461 fl. was raised within a short time. Though the organist knew how to solicit funds for an artistic purpose, he was unfortunately less able to look after his own needs. In 1669 Johann found it necessary to complain that within twenty-two years he had no more than once received the yearly supply of a *Malter* (some 250 lbs.) of grain, which constituted his only fixed honorarium as an organist at the daily service held at 9 a.m.

A document like that poignantly illustrates Johann's economic status. He had indeed to display a maximum of resourcefulness and frugality in order to steer his household through those precarious times. Nevertheless he showed the hospitality and deep sense of responsibility to the entire family which we meet again and again among the Bachs. When he came to Erfurt, his brother Heinrich (6) stayed with him until being called to Arnstadt in 1641, while two brothers-in-law, Johann Christoph and Zacharias H. Hoffmann, studied with him for many years.

When his first wife died giving birth to a still-born child, Johann, with his house full of relatives, had quickly to marry again. He chose Hedwig Lämmerhirt, a member of the family which was to produce, to its lasting glory, the mother of Sebastian Bach.

The story of the Lämmerhirts bears a significant resemblance to that of the Bachs. Though they were apparently of Thuringian origin—their name occurs as early as 1419 in a village near Gotha—they lived for

---

[1] Spitta gives the year 1647 for Johann Bach's appointment. Johann himself, however, mentions the year 1636 in a tax declaration he filed. Cf. Rollert, *l.c.*

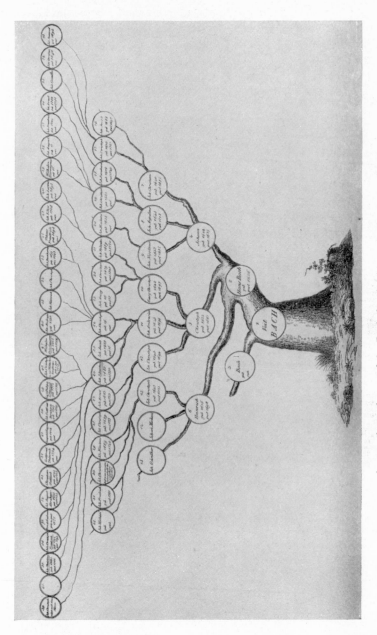

II. A genealogical tree of the Bach family drawn in the 19th century

III. A genealogical tree of the Bach family beginning with the year 1530

several generations in Lower Silesia in Eastern Germany. Persecution of their faith forced them to leave this district just as it had driven Veit out of Hungary, and around 1620 they took up their residence in Erfurt, where the family, which followed the trade of furriers, quickly gained a good social standing and a modest fortune. They owned several houses and one of their members, Valentin Lämmerhirt, was three times, in the years 1648, 1658, 1663, the representative of the furriers' guild in the City Council. He must have given his daughter, Hedwig, a good dowry, for she was able to buy in later years, at a price of 120 fl., the house 'The Three Roses' from her widowed stepmother.

Although the Lämmerhirts did not produce any professional musicians, it is noteworthy that several musicians married into the family. The example of Johann Bach was imitated by his nephew, Ambrosius Bach, and by a later successor to Johann Bach's position in the *Predigerkirche*, the organist Johann Heinrich Buttstädt. Another Lämmerhirt girl was the mother of the distinguished composer and music scholar, Johann Gottfried Walther. But if the Lämmerhirts' musical gifts are only conjectural, the family's strong religious feeling seems certain. A deeply mystical strain is revealed in the family's faithful attendance at the 'Christian music' meetings conducted by Esajas Stiefel,[1] an eccentric heretic who was influenced by the tenets of the Anabaptists. He believed that every Christian should strive for direct contact with the Divine Spirit, and in his meetings music, composed partly by himself, was the principal means of attaining the ecstasy leading to union with God. Between the orthodox Church and Stiefel there was a continual feud, his ideas on the social reforms destined to establish the Kingdom of Heaven on Earth being particularly unpopular with the authorities. But the Lämmerhirts held firmly to their beliefs, just as the Bachs would have done in a like situation; and when Stiefel was sentenced to imprisonment, he was able to point in his written defence to three men of the highly respected Lämmerhirt family as his friends. A son of the heretic married a Lämmerhirt girl and was godfather to Johann Christian Bach (7), the eldest surviving son of Johann and Hedwig. Undoubtedly the Lämmerhirts brought a new element into the Bach clan: a certain mysticism, a passionate striving for the inner vision of God, which was to be one of the wellsprings that fed Sebastian Bach's artistic personality. Whether the children of Johann and Hedwig showed similar traits cannot be ascertained to-day, but we know that they were fine musicians who upheld the tradi-

[1] Cf. P. Meder, 'Der Schwärmer, Esajas Stiefel,' in 'Jahresbericht des Erfurter Geschichts- und Altertum-Vereins,' 1898.

B

tions started by their father. The eldest son, Johann Christian (7), born in 1640, held the post of director of the Erfurt town band. When he died in 1682 from the plague, his younger brother, Johann Egidius (8), born in 1645, succeeded him. These two brothers not only did similar work, but had as wives two sisters, daughters of the town piper Schmidt from Eisenach. Egidius seems to have been more versatile than Christian, for he held, like his father, positions both as organist and member of the town band. Another son, Johann Nikolaus (9), born 1653, a city musician like his brothers, was an excellent player of the viola da gamba, but fell in early years victim to the plague that also took Johann Christian. If these Bachs composed any music at all, it has not been preserved. Great creative gifts can be proved only in the following generation, in the person of Johann's grandson, Johann Bernhard (18).

TWO BACHS AT ARNSTADT
(CHRISTOPH AND HEINRICH BACH)

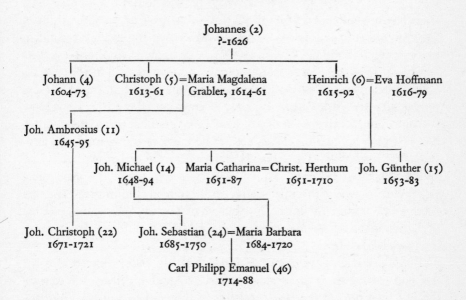

Johannes (2)
?-1626

Johann (4)
1604-73

Christoph (5)=Maria Magdalena
1613-61 | Grabler, 1614-61

Heinrich (6)=Eva Hoffmann
1615-92 | 1616-79

Joh. Ambrosius (11)
1645-95

Joh. Michael (14) Maria Catharina=Christ. Herthum Joh. Günther (15)
1648-94 1651-87 1651-1710 1653-83

Joh. Christoph (22) Joh. Sebastian (24)=Maria Barbara
1671-1721 1685-1750 | 1684-1720

Carl Philipp Emanuel (46)
1714-88

LITTLE is known about the life of Johann's brother, *Christoph*, and no composition of his has been preserved. He was born at Wechmar in 1613 and received musical instruction from his father. If we may accept the information given by his grandson in the Genealogy, Christoph was interested only in instrumental music. His first employment was as a 'court servant' to the Duke of Weimar. This probably meant that, in addition to the duties of a valet or footman, he had to play in the sovereign's band, a combination of work frequently to be found in this period. About 1640 he married Maria Magdalena Grabler, a farmer's daughter of Prettin, Saxony, and moved to Erfurt to work with his brother as town musician. Here six children were born to him, among them three highly musical sons, one of whom was to become the father of Sebastian. In 1654 Christoph was called to Arnstadt as head of the town musicians, probably on the recommendation of his younger brother, Heinrich, who had been living there since 1641. Christoph's position corresponded in various respects to that of his kinsman and predecessor, Caspar Bach, but he was no longer required to do watch duty and to live in the tower. According to the contract signed by the Count of Schwarzburg-Arnstadt,[1] he was expected to 'serve with his assistants faithfully, proficiently and dutifully, both at church and at court, performing on viols and wind instruments.' His yearly salary amounted to only 35 fl.,[2] from which he had also to defray his rent. For this pitifully inadequate cash allowance he was somewhat compensated by the allotment of 10 *Mass* (about one ton) of grain and the right to brew about 1100 quarts of ale taxfree. Moreover the exclusive right of performing at weddings and funerals was guaranteed to him. Nevertheless it was hard for a large family to make ends meet, and in 1661 we see Christoph applying for a position in the city of Naumburg. But before this matter was settled he died, and only twenty-four days later his widow followed him. Christoph seems to have been less interesting and creative an artist than his two brothers. Yet the heritage he transmitted was anything but negligible. Through his marriage to the girl from Saxony he added important features to the Bach character. There is considerable divergence between the imaginative, full-blooded Thuringians and the more energetic and intellectual inhabitants of Saxony, and the descendants of Christoph and Magdalena were bound to be different from other branches of the clan.

Johannes Bach's third son, *Heinrich*, born in 1615, showed as a lad tremendous interest in the organ, and since his native village of Wechmar did not then possess any such instrument, he used to walk on Sundays for miles, just to hear an organ played in some other town. He studied music with his father and his eldest brother, Johann, and for six years worked under the latter in Erfurt, until in 1641 he was appointed organist in Arnstadt, an office which he held for more than fifty years. Now he was ready to set up a household of his own. He chose Eva Hoffmann, a sister of Johann's first wife, Barbara. That two brothers should marry two sisters was by no means unusual among the Bachs. Indeed, two sons of Johann as well as two sons of Heinrich imitated their father's example in this respect. The union of Heinrich and Eva was, in the words of the preacher J. G. Olearius, a 'peaceful, blessed and loving' one, which lasted through thirty-seven years. Eva was the daughter of the town musician of Suhl (cf. p. 13), and the mixture of the heritages from two musicians' families seems to have produced particularly favourable results, for the

---

[1] The complete document is reproduced in German by Wiegand, *l.c.*

[2] To give an idea of the value of a fl., we might mention that in 1653 1 lb. of beef cost 20 pf., 2 lbs. of bread 1 gr., a pair of soles for men's shoes 12 gr. Cf. Rollberg in *BJ*, 1927.

couple had three sons of outstanding musical talent. The father was their teacher and must have thoroughly enjoyed such pupils. But while life in all human aspects was satisfactory enough, the economic conditions presented grave problems. The lot of organists in Germany had never been a good one, and even in 1619, before the war had critically affected the whole economy, Michael Praetorius had to complain:[1] 'It is regrettable how very small are the salaries paid even in some illustrious cities to their masterly organists. These men can make but a wretched living and sometimes even curse their noble art and wish they had learned how to be a cowherd or some humble artisan instead of an organist.' At the time when Heinrich settled down in Arnstadt, the small principality was destitute through war taxations and other tribulations, and neither the Count of Schwarzburg nor the city fathers were in a position to pay their servants regularly. Heinrich was entitled to a salary of 52 fl.[2] a year plus 5 fl. for rent; yet three years after his appointment he was forced to complain to the Count that he had not received any remuneration for a whole year, and before that had 'to beg for it almost with tears.' The treasurer, when ordered by the sovereign immediately to satisfy the organist, merely promised he would endeavour to do so, hinting that the disastrous state of finances made continual payments quite impossible. However, Heinrich somehow managed to keep his family from starvation, probably mainly thanks to his own piece of land; and it bears testimony to their resilience and vitality that of his six children five reached maturity, a feat rare in those times. Heinrich himself took all hardships with fortitude and even cheerfulness, and he was, like his great-grandson, Philipp Emanuel, always ready for a joke. His never-failing friendliness made him beloved by everybody. When he had to test a very mediocre musician for the work of organist in Rockhausen, he reported to the Consistory that the man was 'able enough for the salary allowed,' thus getting the applicant the position and at the same time enjoying a gentle reproach to the authorities for their miserable salaries. His modesty is revealed by the fact that only after serving for thirty-one years in Arnstadt did it occur to him to ask for the yearly allotment of grain which his predecessor used to receive. While this request was granted, his superiors were less accommodating in other respects. When Heinrich's two elder sons found positions in cities nearby, their father often felt tempted to visit them. Although he left a substitute to take care of his duties, he was reprimanded for repeated absences and urged not to leave the town without special permission.

[1] 'Syntagma Musicum,' II/89.
[2] Subsequently he received another 20 fl. from a trust fund.

Here we meet for the first time with a particular difficulty under which all the Bachs laboured. According to the custom of the time, both court and town musicians were greatly restricted in their movements, and the Bachs, who all possessed a strong sense of independence, deeply resented this state of affairs and transgressed again and again. From Heinrich, through Sebastian, to Friedemann Bach, conflicts with the authorities arose from such causes.

At the age of 67 Heinrich petitioned the Consistory to appoint his youngest son, Johann Günther (born 1653), his deputy. The authorities complied, and presently young Günther married the daughter of a former mayor of the town. Their joy was not to last long, however, for only five months later Günther died suddenly at the age of 30.[1] As Heinrich was now left quite alone, his wife having died in 1679, he went to live with his daughter, Maria Catharina, and her husband, Christoph Herthum, who was both organist and kitchen-clerk to the Count of Arnstadt. Herthum gradually took over Heinrich's duties, as the old man was less and less able to move around, and was assisted in 1689-90 by Sebastian Bach's eldest brother, Johann Christoph (22). In the end Heinrich was blind and bedridden, but he did not lose the composure that had upheld him through all the hardships of his long life. A great joy were his grand- and great-grandchildren (altogether twenty-eight in number), who read his favourite religious works to him. When he felt his end near, he wrote to the Count on January 14, 1692:

'Through God's graciousness I have for more than fifty years been organist here, but for some time I have been laid up and I am now expecting a blissful ending from God. During my illness my son-in-law has done my work to the satisfaction of your Lordship, the ministers, and the whole community. After my death the service will have to be entrusted to a suitable person, and as I am daily expecting my blissful passing, I have wanted to present my humble request on my deathbed . . . that your Highness shall be pleased to favour your kitchen-clerk with this position, on account of his well-known perfection and outstanding art, and make him my successor before I depart. Such graciousness will give me particular joy and consolation in my miserable condition, and I will not fail, while I am still alive, most humbly to implore the Highest day and

[1] His widow, Barbara Margaretha, married one year later an Arnstadt clergyman, whom she lost after four years. She let six years elapse and then married another Bach, Ambrosius, the father of Sebastian. Again misfortune struck and she lost her third husband two months after the wedding.

night that He shall bless your Lordship and keep your Lordship and his gracious spouse in good health and long life.'

The matter-of-fact way in which Heinrich refers here to his forthcoming death is highly characteristic of this deeply religious man, and of the period in which he lived. His intense preoccupation with death (which we shall find again in his grand-nephew, Sebastian) is also revealed by the fact that as long as Heinrich could move about he attended every funeral, even that of the poorest person. The last wish of the old organist was fulfilled and Herthum was appointed his substitute *cum spe succedendi*. A few months later Heinrich was 'gently and blissfully called from this temporary abode' (Olearius). Hardly ever had a funeral in the little town been so well attended as that of the beloved musician.

Artistically, Heinrich's interest centred round keyboard instruments. It is probable that he performed on the clavier when he was called to Court, but his main occupation was that of playing the organ in Arnstadt's two big churches, the *Oberkirche* and *Liebfrauenkirche*, and he enjoyed a very great reputation as an outstanding virtuoso. The work of an organist in those times was highly responsible. He had not only to accompany, but frequently to conduct the chorus. He was expected to be thoroughly familiar with the old traditional music, and at the same time to master the new forms introduced from Italy, and elsewhere. Great skill in improvising fugues and chorale variations was required of him, and a candidate had to prove his craftsmanship and superior knowledge in this respect before he was appointed to a more important position.[1] All this Heinrich Bach did to perfection and he was not only a master of improvisation, but, as Emanuel Bach, his great-grandson, proudly proclaimed, 'a good composer.'

MUSICAL TRENDS IN THE 17TH CENTURY— THE COMPOSITIONS OF JOHANN AND HEINRICH BACH

The Baroque period, covering the phase from the end of the 16th to the middle of the 18th century, showed in the field of music numerous features distinguishing it from the preceding Renaissance.

The compositions displayed a new quality of excitement and strong emotionalism. Sharp dissonances never before used to such an extent

[1] Cf. Arno Werner in *SIMG*, IX, 310 and foll.

were now employed, and the halftone progressions of chromaticism began
to play an important part in the melodic language. Contrary to the calm
evenness of the Renaissance music, the Baroque period tended towards
dramatic changes in tempo and dynamics. The pleasure taken in rhythmic
and colouristic variety led to a predilection for the variation-form, which
at the same time satisfied an urge for structural unity. Once more composers discovered the unlimited potentialities of the solo human voice,
both for dramatic expression and for producing beautifully sounding
tunes. The highest part, the melody, became a dominating factor in every
composition; but it had to share the limelight with the sustaining bass,
the *basso continuo*, the performers of which were also entrusted with the
improvisation of the filling middle parts.

Strong contrasts were used throughout the works of art. Baroque
music might be sweet and tender, and then again powerful and monumental. The bowed string instruments, and in particular the violin, which
matched the human voice in mellowness and expressiveness of tone,
became the favourites of the period; at the same time the musical palette
was enriched by the construction of the mighty double bassoon and the
contrabass trombone. The *stile concertato* with its vigorously competing
sound groups played a prominent part both in instrumental and vocal
music, in secular as well as in sacred compositions.

Protestant church music, on which the first masters of the Bach
family concentrated, was bound to show the main features of Baroque
art. It is true that the novel ideas emanating from Italy reached Germany,
and especially its smaller cities, only several decades later; nevertheless
the cantors and organists of little Thuringia were as eager to keep up
with the progressive trends in music as their colleagues in larger centres.

The core of the Lutheran service was formed by the German hymns,
called *chorales*, as they were sung in unison or *choraliter* by the congregation. The finest of these texts and tunes originated in the 16th century,
but all through the Baroque period additions were made, with new tunes
frequently derived from secular sources. In particular the sacred *aria*, a
hymn assuming a more personal and subjective character, was cultivated
by 17th-century composers.

The *motet* in which each voice could be sung, although the reinforcement by instruments was favoured, also went back to Renaissance sources.
Nevertheless the frequent use of two competing choruses, and the
dramatic combination of Bible-word and hymn texts were dictated by the
spirit of the Baroque. Most exciting were those motets in which one
voice presented in long-extended notes a chorale melody with its words,

while at the same time a text from the Gospel was interpreted by the rest of the singers.

The connection with the past was less noticeable in those vocal compositions which also prescribed independent instrumental parts. The *sacred concerto* sometimes made use of traditional chorale melodies, and at others it was freely invented. The treatment of the human voices was more brilliant than in the motets, with ample opportunities for the display of technical skill and an individual interpretation of the text. The instruments were no longer confined to mere accompaniment. They alternated with the voices, and a purely instrumental introduction to a *concerto* was not unusual. In its numerous forms—for a single voice, as a dialogue, or as a composition for three and more solo voices, mostly with chorus—it paved the way for the great church cantatas of the 18th century.

In their compositions of pure instrumental music, the Bachs confined themselves to works for the keyboard, intended mainly for the church. It had been an old habit of the Lutheran service that not all the countless verses of a hymn were sung by the congregation. Some of them were performed by the chorus, others by the organist, in a more or less polyphonic setting. For such purposes the great masters of the 17th century wrote whole sets of *chorale-variations* to be played on the organ, as well as individual *chorale-preludes*, resembling a single one of these variations.

It is noteworthy that such chorale preludes often display the same construction as the chorale-motet, just as the instrumental fugues of the time resemble their vocal counterparts. Variations on a chorale, to be played in church on an organ, use a technique similar to that of variations on a dance-tune meant for secular purposes and employing a stringed clavier. As organ music of the 17th century usually has no separate pedal parts, modern research students often find it quite difficult to determine whether a composition was meant for the 'king of instruments' or for a clavier equipped with strings.

Altogether the ambiguousness and interchangeability of musical idioms which is still noticeable in the works of Sebastian Bach constitute one of the most intriguing aspects of this music.

Three compositions by Johann Bach have been preserved in the *Alt-Bachisches Archiv*, a collection of Bach works started by Ambrosius Bach and continued by his son, Sebastian. The invaluable documents were passed on to Philipp Emanuel Bach and after his death came into the possession of one Georg Pölchau and Goethe's friend, Carl Friedrich Zelter. These two men authorized in 1821 a first publication of nine of these pieces through Johann Friedrich Naue, music director of the Halle

University. His edition is unfortunately marred by numerous omissions, arbitrary additions, and even changes of the names of the composers. Nevertheless, for almost a century it was the main source for knowledge of the music of the older Bachs, since the original manuscripts were transferred to the Berlin Singakademie, whence they mysteriously disappeared. They were rediscovered at the end of the First World War through the efforts of Max Schneider. His publication of numerous scores in *EDM* 1 and 2 (1935) offers a solid basis for the research on Sebastian's ancestors.

Simplest in character is Johann Bach's *aria* for four voices *Weint nicht um meinen Tod* (Don't mourn my death). The brief melody used for each of the nine verses of the text is harmonized in a completely homophonic four-part style. Obviously it can also be performed as a piece for soprano solo with organ accompaniment. The unassuming composition with its attractive, partly modal chord sequences, displays both simple dignity and beauty. The constant changes of its free rhythms provide the melody with inner life and unfettered pulsation (*Ex* 1).

Ex.1

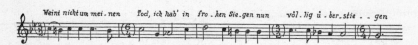

The flexible declamation in this *aria* contrasts favourably with the monotonous isometric chorales of a later generation, which give to each note the same length.

Johann's eight-part motet for two choruses *Sei nun wieder zufrieden* (Be contented again; *Schn.*[1] 30) was published by Naue, in the early 19th century, as a composition by Johann Michael Bach, although the original parts clearly indicate the authorship of the older composer. Besides, the simple and austere style of the composition distinguishes it from the smoother and more elaborate writings of Johann Michael. The composer uses a purely homophonic technique, similar to that of the *aria*, but there are no strophic repetitions of the tune. As soon as the whole text has been dealt with, the motet abruptly reaches its end. The composition derives its effect mainly from the contrast in tone-colour produced by the employment of two choruses of four voices each. One is a higher-pitched group of two sopranos, one alto and one tenor; the other a lower-pitched group of an alto, two tenors and a bass. Each part of the higher chorus is re-

[1] The works of the older Bachs are quoted according to Schneider's catalogue in *BJ*, 1907 (see list of Abbreviations). *Weint nicht um meinen Tod* is missing in this catalogue.

inforced by an instrument, presumably stringed, while there is no re-inforcement of the lower chorus.[1] This work is of solid craftsmanship, although the absence of a clear formal construction somewhat weakens its effectiveness.

On quite a different level is the third composition of Johann Bach, the chorale motet *Unser Leben ist ein Schatten* (Our life is but a shadow; *Schn.* 31), a work of weird grandeur. This piece too was wrongly edited by Naue as a work of Johann Michael Bach, although the original score is unmistakably initialed with 'J. B.' and the starkly monumental character of the music should have warned the editor that it is the product of an earlier generation. Following the general tendency of the time, Johann effectively combines Bible texts and church hymns. The whole motet is constructed in a sort of rondo form, with three chorales separating the hymn quotations from the Scriptures. The contrast between two strongly differentiated choruses is again employed. The main group of singers consists of six parts, two sopranos, one alto, two tenors and one bass, while the second chorus employs only one alto, tenor and bass voice each. A most unusual feature of this motet is the composer's own designation of the small choral group as *chorus latens* (hidden chorus). The six-part chorus begins with a description of the frailty and uncertainty of human life,

offering a weirdly realistic picture of quickly moving and vanishing shadows (*Ex.* 2). This sinister picture is interrupted by the hidden

---

[1] Max Schneider, who edited the motet in *EDM*, assumed that all the voices were to be doubled by instruments. This does not seem correct, since the catalogue of the *Alt-Bachisches Archiv*, printed in the list of Philipp Emanuel's estate, clearly indicates that the composition was written 'for 8 vocal parts and 4 instruments.' The old parts which are our source for knowledge of the composition, contain 2 instrumental parts for the sopranos. As the 4 voices of each chorus always appear as a compact unit and are never separated, it seems obvious that the remaining 2 instruments were used to reinforce alto and tenor in the first chorus. Our assumption that strings were employed is based on the Bachs' apparent preference for this type of instrument.

chorus, intoning, like a congregation in a distant church, the comforting message: 'In the darkness of the grave Jesus is my shining light' (fourth and fifth stanzas of the chorale *Ach was soll ich Sünder machen*). The group of dejected men seem to derive consolation from this heavenly message, and in complete rapture they repeat the last words of the prophecy. The terror of the beginning is replaced by quiet confidence when the main chorus sings 'I am the resurrection and the life.' A hymn of the hidden chorus follows, again intensified by certain repetitions through the main body. With the words 'I depart' the vision of the distant congregation disappears and once more earth seems drab and full of menace. From here to the end the hopeless mood of the beginning dominates the work. The last words of the composition seem to have come out of the very heart of a man who had witnessed the horrors of unending war:

> O Lord teach us to know that we are mortal,
> That we cannot stay on this earth,
> And must all go;
> The learned, the rich, the beautiful,
> They must all go, all go.

Striking, like the whole of this dramatic and unconventional composition, is also its ultimate measure. After all the other voices have ceased, the two sopranos repeat the words 'all go' (*davon*) like a last sigh (*Ex. 3*).

Ex.3

With a feeling of envy and frustration the music lover reads in the funeral sermon by Olearius of the different chorales, motets, concertos, preludes and fugues produced by Heinrich Bach. Of all the numerous compositions which the Arnstadt organist is bound to have accumulated during a long and laborious existence devoted to music, only a single one has been preserved.[1] This, however, is a powerful work, worthy in every respect of the high reputation enjoyed by its composer. *Ich danke dir, Gott* (I thank Thee, God; *Schn.* 1) is an excellent specimen of the *stile concertato*.

---

[1] The lament *Ach dass ich Wassers gnug hätte*, listed in 1907 by Schneider as a work of Heinrich Bach, has in the meantime been recognized as a composition of his son, Johann Christoph (cf. p. 52). The two chorale preludes, *Christ lag in Todesbanden* and *Erbarm dich mein*, edited by Ritter and others as works by Heinrich Bach, are by a composer with the initials J. H. B. (possibly Johann Heinrich Buttstädt), but not by Heinrich Bach.

There is a harmonious contest, a permanent rivalry between different sound groups. Under the influence of sacred concertos by Scheidt, Schütz, and others, older forms of church composition are here gradually assuming features of the 18th-century cantata. The human voices do not dominate the composition as they did in the *aria* and motets by Johann Bach; four instruments, two violins and two viols, are assigned important parts. The vocal body is subdivided into a small group of solo singers or *favoriti* and a larger chorus of accompanying *ripieni*, each consisting of five parts, viz. two sopranos, an alto, a tenor and a bass. Most of the musical development is entrusted to the instruments and to the *favoriti*, while the *ripieni* are employed only as an occasional reinforcement. A spirited competition between upper and lower voices may already be observed in the bright and gay instrumental *Sinfonia* serving as an introduction to the work. The following vocal section introduces a powerful homophonic setting of the words 'I thank Thee, God,' in which the whole body of sound is employed. Then the *favoriti* take over, using a transparent style, rich in sparkling coloraturas and not unlike the performance of instrumental soloists in a contemporary concerto grosso (*Ex.* 4). At key

points of the composition, especially whenever the name of the Lord is mentioned, and at the end of the cantata, the full assembly of singers and players is united in vigorous plain chords. Heinrich's unusual technical skill, but more still the emotional fervour and unshakable trust in God expressed in this composition, make it one of the most significant works of the older Bach generation.

HEINRICH'S TWO GREAT SONS
(JOHANN CHRISTOPH (13) AND JOHANN MICHAEL BACH)

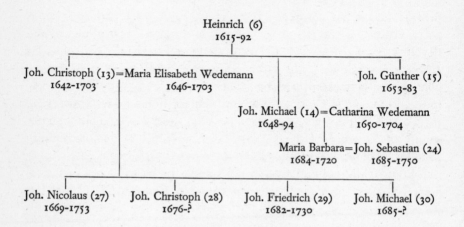

Heinrich (6)
1615-92

Joh. Christoph (13)=Maria Elisabeth Wedemann
1642-1703   1646-1703

Joh. Günther (15)
1653-83

Joh. Michael (14)=Catharina Wedemann
1648-94   1650-1704

Maria Barbara=Joh. Sebastian (24)
1684-1720   1685-1750

Joh. Nicolaus (27)   Joh. Christoph (28)   Joh. Friedrich (29)   Joh. Michael (30)
1669-1753   1676-?   1682-1730   1685-?

THE scene now shifts to the little town of Eisenach, beautifully situated at the north-west end of the Thuringian forest, and dominated by the imposing medieval castle of the Wartburg.[1] Eisenach was from 1662 to 1741 the capital of a miniature duchy which had come into existence through the partition of the estate of the Prince of Weimar, and its rulers did their best to act like great sovereigns and patrons of the arts. This was not easy, as the pocket-size territory did not admit the raising of heavy taxes, and the private means of the ducal family were very limited. Thus it came about that many interesting personages were invited to Eisenach, who after a short stay decided to move to another place which offered more scope for their talents and better financial opportunities. At four different times[2] the Dukes secured the service of the violinist, Daniel Eberlin, a gifted man with a most unusual career that included, besides musical activities, a captainship of papal troops fighting the Turks, and work as a banker in Hamburg. At Eisenach Eberlin held the posts of private ducal secretary and conductor, and at one time even that of director of the ducal mint. In 1677 Johann Pachelbel, the great organist

[1] For a poetical description of Eisenach and the Wartburg, cf. W. G. Whittaker, 'The Bachs and Eisenach,' in 'Collected Essays,' London, 1940. (See also Ill. V.)

[2] Cf. Wilhelm Greiner, 'Die Musik im Lande Bachs,' Eisenach, 1935.

and composer, joined the court orchestra as 'Musicus,' but moved as early as 1678 to Erfurt. Later the ruler succeeded in engaging as conductor Pantaleon Hebenstreit, a renowned dancing master and inventor of the 'Pantaleon,' a kind of dulcimer, which created a sensation at the court of Louis XIV. Hebenstreit put up with Eisenach from 1706 to 1709, and was followed by no less a master than Georg Telemann, who remained in the little Residenz for four years.

The Eisenach authorities in their search for musical talent did not, of course, overlook the Bach family. Heinrich's reputation as a masterly organist had travelled far beyond Arnstadt, and when in 1665 the death of the city organist created an opening, Heinrich's eldest son, 23-year-old *Johann Christoph* (13), who worked as court organist in Arnstadt, was invited for the customary trial performance. The young musician passed the test with flying colours, but had to get permission from his patron, the Count of Schwarzburg-Arnstadt, before accepting the new position. He submitted therefore a petition[1] in which he explained that the Eisenach appointment had come about without any special effort on his part and therefore might be regarded as an act of divine providence. For his successor he suggested his younger brother, Johann Michael, an arrangement acceptable to the Count, who liked to see a member of the Bach family in this position and conferred it on Heinrich Bach's son-in-law, Christoph Herthum, when Michael moved to Gehren in 1673. Thus Johann Christoph was duly appointed Eisenach's city organist, which meant that he had to play in the three churches of the town, in particular in the *Georgenkirche*. The city fathers must have been well pleased indeed. Here was a young and extremely able musician, who had been brought up and trained by a man generally beloved for his great art and his gentle, modest nature as well. They were in for some surprises, however. Artistically everything was satisfactory, of course; the organist was not merely capable, he was brilliant. On the other hand, young Bach showed a disappointing unwillingness to put up with the hardships of an organist's position in an impecunious little town. On October 10, 1670, he complained to the superintendent in no uncertain words:[2]

'As is well known to your Honour, the complete salaries of the church employees are payable at the end of the year only. . . . I was therefore

---

[1] The document (Thüringisches Staatsarchiv, Rudolstadt, Sign. 679) was only recently unearthed and kindly supplied to me by Mr. Fritz Wiegand, Stadtarchivar, Erfurt.

[2] Superint. Archiv Eisenach: B 25 B 1, Bl. 4, where all the documents referring to Johann Christoph, unless otherwise mentioned, are preserved.

instructed by the Honoured Council to collect 10 fl. in quarterly instalments from the Hospital-Bursar, Joseph Herman, to defray the bare necessities of life until the entire salary became due at Michaelmas day. With sadness I have to report, however, that this sum can be obtained only very slowly from the Hospital-Bursar. Either he sends me to another place, or he holds out hopes for the future, and he is so dilatory with his payment that one loses one's credit with honest people. . . . As it is very hard for me to subsist with my family, having no income whatever beside my salary, I cannot help informing your Honour of these facts. . . . So far, whenever an instalment has been due, I have been obliged to send for this money so often that I felt ashamed. I hope your Honour will help to redress this as I have had to report it out of urgent need.'

We don't know whether Johann Christoph's request was granted, but judging from subsequent documents in Eisenach's archives, it seems that the authorities did not care for their organist's far too outspoken approach. From the year 1679 another lengthy complaint to the Consistory is preserved. This time the organist deplored his inability to collect the *Accidentien*, viz. the fees to which he was entitled for playing at funerals, weddings, or christenings. Only too often, he claimed, the bereaved one, the bridegroom, or the happy father found some way of slipping out of his obligation, forgetting to remunerate the organist at all, or paying him only part of the amount prescribed. Johann Christoph claimed that no less than 46 fl. 20 gr. (almost half as much as his basic yearly salary) was outstanding from such sources. But he was not satisfied just to complain; he felt he ought to advise his superiors how to remedy the abuse. Why could not the written confirmation of published banns be handed to the prospective couple only after they had paid the fee for the organist? The Consistory, however, apparently did not like to receive advice from Mr. Bach. So matters went on as before and petitions survive from a later date to show that Johann Christoph was again airing his grievances about unpaid wedding fees. On this occasion he pointed out that whenever needy persons were concerned he would gladly waive his fee, provided the other church employees were willing to do the same.

Numerous other documents reveal the organist's eternal problem of finding suitable living quarters. While the house in Arnstadt known as that of Heinrich Bach was occupied by him throughout the greater part of his long life, Johann Christoph changed his domicile again and again. Excerpts from a long petition he wrote on February 15, 1692, to the

IV. Hans Bach. Engraving, 1617

v. Eisenach, where Johann Sebastian Bach was born and members of the family served from 1665 to 1797. In the background on top of the hill the Wartburg, the scene of the famous singers' competition of Wagner's 'Tannhäuser'. Engraving by Merian, 1650

Burgomaster and City Council will illustrate the wretched position of the organist:

'It is well known to your Honour that while being in your Honour's service for the past twenty-seven years, I have often besought your Honour for a free lodging. I was, however, unfortunate in not achieving my aim, and have, to my gravest detriment and misery, been forced to move from one place to another. After living in ten different rented houses, I felt no longer able to bear such unsettled conditions and decided to buy a place of my own. As I had no means available to pay the deposit, until an inheritance from my hometown of Arnstadt came my way [this matter-of-fact reference to the impending death of his father is quite in accordance with the general attitude of the time!], I had to borrow the capital at interest. Afterwards I had to pay for indispensable repairs to the house, and as my creditors insist on payment, while the expected remittance [from Arnstadt] has not arrived, I am again cast out of this house, with what despair, your Honour, knowing my domestic circumstances, can well imagine. . . . I am aware, of course, that I was favoured only recently with an increase in salary. On the other hand your Honour knows that from 1677 onward more work has been given me on Wednesdays and Thursdays [at prayer hours and confession service], which I had to undertake for several years without receiving further benefit, and I therefore cannot assume that this [recent increase] will now be held against me. . . .'

And then, in the typical Johann Christoph Bach manner, which was so irritating to his superiors, he suggested that the house occupied by a certain teacher of a German school[1] should be vacated and given to him; he was even undiplomatic enough to mention the necessity of making some important repairs and adding a cellar.

The City Council failed to be impressed by the organist's plea, although the Ducal Consistory and even the Duke himself intervened in his favour. The Council felt that Bach had a salary on which he could 'honestly subsist in an orderly life and household,' while the city funds were depleted and the house in question could not possibly be vacated. Nevertheless Johann Christoph tenaciously fought on, and even after he had wrenched a contribution of 10 th. toward his rent from the tight-fisted Council, the correspondence between the city and the Duke on his behalf continued. At last the city fathers cut off any further discussion

[1] The leading school was Eisenach's Latin school, besides which there existed some German schools.

c

by observing spitefully: 'Perhaps the alleged afflictions are due to a disorderly household. It would be good if Bach had administered the alms more satisfactorily and not employed them *ad proprios usus* [for his private good],' a remark implying that the organist had at some time treated the charitable gifts he collected for the church as an advance on his outstanding salary.

The Duke, however, did not take this accusation seriously. He was far more aware of the organist's artistic importance than the city fathers, and was therefore intent on helping him. Since 1690 he had paid Johann Christoph a separate salary for service in the ducal band. When in 1694 the organist's family was stricken by serious illness,[1] he sent them food and firewood, continuing such contributions at regular intervals throughout the following year. Finally he found a way to satisfy the artist's great wish. The ducal mint building had been vacated in 1694, when the sovereign decided not to have money minted there, after various supervisors had been found guilty of dishonesty.[2] In this house seven rooms, attic, and stables were in 1796 put at the disposal of the overjoyed Johann Christoph, who believed that his troubles were now over. However, Duke Johann Georg II died two years later and his successor, Johann Wilhelm, decided to restore the mint building to its former use, with the result that in 1700 the unlucky organist again had to start househunting. To soften the blow, the new ruler conferred on Johann Christoph the title of ducal chamber musician and allowed him a yearly salary of 24 th., plus a single payment of 12 th. for a uniform, and certain supplies of firewood, rye, and barley.[3] Moreover he urged the City Council to grant the organist a loan of 300 th. for the purpose of buying a certain house Johann Christoph wished to acquire. The Council, unco-operative as ever, refused, but suggested three other houses mortgaged to the Duke, each of which could be purchased very cheaply if the Duke waived his claims. These, however, did not suit the stubborn organist, and so the struggle with the equally stubborn Councillors went on, until in 1702 a compromise was reached and Johann Christoph again had a house of his

[1] Johann Christoph complained in a letter to the Duke that his house looked like a hospital, and the church entries reveal that in October 1694 six persons in the organist's household were given private communion. It is also significant that Johann Christoph's third son was 234 times absent during the school-year 1693-94, while the youngest did not attend school at all in 1695. Cf. Helmbold in *BJ*, 1930.

[2] Cf. Friedrich Schäfer, 'Der Organist Johann Christoph Bach und die Eisenacher Münze,' Luginsland, 1929.

[3] In the decree mention is made of the organist's 'wretched condition.' Cf. No. 471 in Weimarer Archiv, Eisenacher Dienersachen.

own. But he was not to enjoy it for long; one year afterwards the artist died at the age of 61. The funeral sermon was preached on the text by Paul Gerhardt: 'The head, the feet, and the hands are glad that now the end of toiling has come.' The choice seems appropriate, for Johann Christoph must have been worn out from continuous petty worries.

It is not a pretty story, this life of an artist who may be considered the greatest Bach before Sebastian. The numerous documents preserved[1] paint a tragic picture of ever-recurring financial troubles and desperate attempts to solve them, attempts which entangled the artist more and more. At the time he died, he had, for instance, received his salary for three years in advance, probably in order to pay for his house. It seems as though the artist had never led anything but a harassed existence. Yet his salary was not bad, as salaries went in those days. He had 116 fl. a year from the city, plus the customary *Accidentien* and the salary from the Duke. This was by no means a starvation income and his father had subsisted on much less. But Johann Christoph, conscious of his artistic mastery, felt himself entitled to a better way of life. When he was established in Eisenach and thus able to marry, he chose as his bride Maria Elisabeth Wedemann, who came from a family of higher social standing. His father-in-law was town clerk and syndic of Arnstadt, and a brother-in-law was to be mayor of the town. An invitation to the wedding has been preserved and it seems that a rather elaborate feast took place in honour of the occasion. Moreover in Eisenach the couple aimed at a standard of living superior to that of their colleagues. For instance the house Johann Christoph owned in 1679 was so large that he had to pay four times as much tax on it as was assessed on his cousin Ambrosius' property.[2] In the schooling of his children too Johann Christoph did not conform to custom. While most musicians took their sons out of the Latin school at the age of 14 or 15 in order to apprentice them with a member of their profession, two sons of the organist stayed there up to the age of 21 and 20 respectively, and the eldest even went to the University of Jena, an enterprise on which no other Bach of his generation had ventured. All this must have seemed somewhat presumptuous to the Eisenach Council and it served to aggravate still further the city fathers' feelings against their difficult employee. He was certainly anything but popular with the city authorities; yet they did not allow him to take another post. Johann Christoph once had a chance to leave the stifling

---

[1] The basic research was made by Schumm and Rollberg. Cf. Bibliography.

[2] Cf. Tax registers for 1679. The organist paid 1 fl. 6 gr. 6 pf., while Ambrosius paid 6 gr.

atmosphere of Eisenach, being offered in 1686 the position of town organist in the city of Schweinfurt. He accepted joyfully, but had to write a few weeks later that neither the Council nor the Duke of Eisenach was willing to grant him permission to leave.[1]

Only in one respect was a satisfactory intercourse maintained between the Council and the organist. The authorities could not help being impressed by Johann Christoph's continuous endeavours on behalf of the organ entrusted to his care. The instrument of St. George's built in 1576 was proving more and more inadequate. In the first decades of his service, the organist merely succeeded in having the worst defects repaired, but ultimately he convinced the Council that a thorough rebuilding of the instrument was imperative. His own draft of the contract with the organ builder, Georg Christoph Stertzing, dated March 19, 1696, is preserved.[2] It comprises ten pages and offers an interesting insight into Johann Christoph's mastery of the subject. But even when the draft was accepted, the organist did not feel quite satisfied. He continued pondering the problem of how to get a really first-rate instrument, and in the following months he presented so many additional suggestions, that the Council eventually voted on ordering a new instrument from Stertzing, using only some material from the old organ. Johann Christoph not only worked out all the specifications,[3] but tried to obtain better performing conditions for the church musicians. He urged the 'building of a so-called half-moon (in front of the organ), such as was found in other high-class churches' and the addition of 'two little choir-lofts on both sides of the half-moon. This would provide in the nicest manner for the performance of two-chorus motets, a convenience never yet enjoyed in Eisenach.' When he submitted his last project for improvement on October 30, 1697, he made the following, very characteristic remarks: 'There is no profit for myself in this, but I have the interests of the church, the town, and the organ at heart, and I take care of the instrument as though I were to play it in all eternity. . . . As we have now come so near to having an exquisite organ, it would be a shame not to afford the little that is still necessary. After all, the money for this is not needed right away; there is still time to obtain it. Thus we shall, with God's help, get a very fine instrument, which will bring us fame and honour far and wide, especially

---

[1] Three letters on this matter are preserved in copies in the Bach Museum of Eisenach, according to kind information by the Curator, Dr. Conrad Freyse.

[2] Cf. Werner Wolffheim, 'Die alte Orgel zu St. Georg in Eisenach,' Eisenacher Tagespost, 1911, and Hans Löffler, 'Nachrichten über die St. Georgenkirche in Eisenach,' in 'Zeitschrift für evangelische Kirchenmusik,' IV, V.

[3] They were reproduced in Adlung's 'Musica mechanica organoedi,' 1768.

with organ and music experts, while other towns in the neighbourhood won't be pleased about it. As for myself, I will . . . gladly do my share and advise the builder regarding this or that stop, so that each is accurately measured, correctly pitched, and all the notes within each stop are of equal tone, and well-sounding. For whenever you find a well planned fine organ, good organists flock to it. Indeed, an instrument of such a kind makes good organists. How greatly would it have helped me in my work and profession, had I had since 1665 such an organ under my hands!'

Johann Christoph's characteristic *insouciance* in money matters for once proved justified; for when in 1698 a general collection was started for St. George's new organ, an amount of 3047 th. was obtained, which by far exceeded the actual costs. Thus the organist's plans could be executed in full. No one was happier about that than their instigator; but he was not spared to witness the completion of the large project. On February 23, 1703, he was still writing to the Council regarding some details of the construction; on March 31 he breathed his last, four years before the work on his organ was finished.

Johann Christoph was in many respects a forerunner of his second cousin, Sebastian, with whom he has more traits in common than Sebastian's own father. In profundity and creative originality he among all the older members of the clan came nearest to the culminating genius of the family; even their handwriting reveals a certain similarity. Moreover Johann Christoph's fighting spirit, stubbornness, and lack of diplomacy in his dealings with his superiors, clearly recur in Sebastian. But there was one tragic difference. Sebastian had the driving power to start a new life when he felt this to be beneficial to his development and career. Fighting against heavy odds, including imprisonment, he wrenched himself free and changed his appointments. Johann Christoph, tied by the conceptions of his family and his generation, gave in when a supreme effort was imperative. Thus he stayed for 38 years in Eisenach, where his art found little recognition and even his performances suffered from an inadequate instrument; and these uncongenial surroundings made him dissatisfied and unsuccessful in his dealings with the outside world.

About Johann Christoph's sons little is known, but the little seems significant. All four were musicians. Two appear to have inherited the father's restlessness and desire for change, while each of the other two held one and the same position throughout his life. Johann Christoph the younger (28) was in Northern Germany when his father died. He applied for the position in Eisenach, but the Council decided on another Bach, Johann Bernhard (18), who had made a name for himself in the city of

Magdeburg. It may be doubted whether young Johann Christoph was really unhappy about this slight, for according to the Genealogy he 'found his greatest pleasure in travelling.' He did not even stay in Germany, but went to Holland and eventually settled down as a clavier teacher in England. His youngest brother, Johann Michael (30), a trained organ builder, was also not content to live in Thuringia. He went to Northern Europe and was not heard of again. About the careers of the two steady sons of the great organist, more will be said in Part II.

The great Johann Christoph's brother, *Johann Michael* (14), born 1648, seems to have been of a less problematical nature, and to have fitted well into the established Bach pattern. He also received his training from his father, Heinrich, and was employed in Arnstadt as court organist until 1673. In that year his uncle, Johann Bach, the head of the Erfurt branch, died and the organist's position at the *Predigerkirche* became vacant. The Erfurt town fathers chose Johann Effler, who had so far held the position of organist to the parish of Gehren near Arnstadt. This created an opening in Gehren, and Michael Bach, then 25 years old, was invited for a trial performance in this city. Afterwards a city Councillor wrote[1] to Michael's patron, the Count of Arnstadt, who seems to have recommended the young man for the post: 'The minister as well as the Council declared that Johann Michael's person and art left nothing to be desired, and that they owe humble thanks to your gracious Lordship for having presented to the community and church a discreet and well-behaved applicant who was experienced in his art. Therefore the Council undertook to grant the new organist, in addition to the regular salary provided for this position, the additional 10 fl. allowed to the former organist for his industry and merits, which payment the new organist will receive not only for service in church but for work as town clerk as well.'

Michael must have made a good impression to be granted the privileges acquired by his older and more renowned predecessor. His salary was a comparatively good one—certainly higher than his father's—for in addition to a yearly amount of 73 fl. he got firewood, the use of half an acre of land, and various contributions of food as well as free lodging. Moreover he must have received payment from his former ducal patron as well, since he was frequently commanded to play at the Arnstadt court. Another source of income was opened for this versatile artist through the construction of instruments for the music lovers of Arnstadt and its vicinity. While many Bach musicians had a most thorough knowledge of organ building (which enabled them to make precise suggestions for the

[1] Letter dated October 13, 1673. Cf. Bitter, 'J. S. Bach,' 2nd ed., Berlin, 1881.

repair of their instruments), Michael was an expert in clavichords and violins; a seal of his preserved in the Manfred Gorke collection proudly displays two bows and two violin scrolls. This craft was mastered also by his younger brother, Johann Günther, whom the Genealogy praises as 'a skilful builder of various newly invented instruments,' and by his nephews, Johann Nicolaus (27) and Johann Michael (30), who were probably trained by him. In his private life, Michael was following closely the model of his older brother, Johann Christoph. He married Catharina Wedemann, a sister of his brother's wife, and the wedding took place in 1675, two years after Michael's appointment to the Gehren position, just as the elder son of Heinrich had set up his own household two years after getting the post in Eisenach. Here, however, the similarity between the lives of the two brothers ends. No son of Michael survived to carry on the father's work and Michael himself passed away at the age of 46, leaving five unmarried daughters[1] behind, the youngest of whom, Maria Barbara, was only 10 years old. Michael's wife survived him by ten years, dying on October 19, 1704. Some of the orphaned girls moved to Arnstadt, and Maria Barbara stayed with her uncle and godfather, Martin Feldhaus, the mayor of Arnstadt, in his house inscribed 'The Golden Crown.' Here it was that she met her cousin and future husband, Johann Sebastian Bach.

THE MUSIC OF JOHANN MICHAEL BACH

The compositions of Johann Michael and Johann Christoph are to each other as promise and fulfilment. The two brothers worked along similar lines, but in every field of composition—with possibly the single exception of the organ prelude—Christoph was the more successful. Where the short-lived younger brother tried and experimented, the elder achieved success. Therefore, in the discussion of their works, the logical rather than the historical order will be used, so that the analysis of Michael's compositions will precede that of his brother's works.

There are eleven motets and five cantatas by Michael at present known, and they give a good idea of this interesting composer's versatility. Although most motets are based in the traditional manner on Biblical texts and chorales, they display in their treatment a surprising variety. Only a single work, the New Year's motet *Sei lieber Tag willkommen* (Welcome, beloved day; *Schn.* 27) makes no use of any church hymn.

[1] Their names are given by Wiegand, *l.c.*

The composition is written for two sopranos, one alto, two tenors and one bass, a combination not to be found in any other of the composer's motets. Similarly the light and transparent polyphonic setting of the piece with its interplay of higher and lower voices compares favourably with the homophonic style prevailing in Michael's motets. Near the end, at the word 'death,' Michael as a true composer of the Baroque period, indicates an impressive sudden piano.

Completely different is the motet *Nun hab' ich überwunden* (Now I have overcome; *Schn.* 32) which dispenses with any Biblical text. The third stanza of Melchior Vulpius' familiar hymn, *Christus, der ist mein Leben* (For Christ my Saviour live I), is used as a text for this composition, written for two mixed choruses in four parts each. The beginning, with its eleven repetitions of the word *nun* (now) alternately uttered by the two choruses, did not present to a 17th-century audience the slightly humorous touch which it has for the modern listener. Such restatements of brief words by way of an introduction to a vocal composition were intended to heighten the suspense of the audience and were still used by Sebastian Bach (cf. p. 212). Michael's motet consists of two main sections. In the first the text of the chorale is divided into brief phrases, which are presented in the form of a dialogue with concertizing elements. The ardent fervour and devout strength of Michael's style is here displayed to the very best advantage. The second half of the motet, in which the two choruses join forces, employs the more familiar *cantus firmus* technique; the chorale melody is presented in long notes in the soprano part, while the other voices introduce counter-melodies partly derived from the hymn tune itself (*Ex.* 5). This technique is used in like manner in contemporary chorale preludes for the organ.

Ex.5

In each of the remaining nine motets Biblical text and church hymn are combined. Particularly impressive are the shorter and more condensed compositions such as *Unser Leben währet siebenzig Jahr* (Our life lasts seventy years; *Schn.* 23) with the chorale *Ach Herr, lass deine liebe Engelein* (Lord Jesus, Thy dear angels send) as a *cantus firmus* in the soprano. The contrast between the two text elements, which is at first hardly noticeable, increases all through the motet until the last twelve measures represent two strictly separated worlds of heaven and earth. Weird scurrying and rushing takes place in the lower sphere, inspired by the words 'for life quickly passes, as though we were flying away.' In the upper realm a serene calm reigns, the soprano, in high, long extended notes, praising the Lord Jesus Christ. This contrast between the subjective suffering of mankind and the objective bliss of divinity is emphasized by the bold use of a striking dissonance between soprano and alto (*Ex. 6*).

Somewhat similar in character, although not of equal dramatic power, is the five-part motet *Das Blut Jesu Christi* (The blood of Jesus Christ; *Schn.* 20) introducing one stanza from Johann Heermann's song *Wo soll ich fliehen hin* (Whither shall I flee). Here for once the composer prescribes the use of wind instruments as a reinforcement to the chorus. He calls for a *Zink* (a descant horn with finger holes) to play in unison with the top voice, and for four trombones of different sizes to support the lower parts. The first seventeen measures are restricted to the Biblical text. Here the soprano is treated like any of the other parts, and participates vigorously in the interpretation of the Gospel. After a short rest its function changes, however, and henceforth it utters the hymn tune. At the end of the composition fourteen measures are literally repeated, causing an anticlimax, of which Michael's elder brother would hardly have been guilty.

Michael's familiarity with the emotional subjectivity of 17th-century Italian music is apparent in the five-part motet *Ich weiss, dass mein Erlöser lebt* (I know that my Redeemer liveth; *Schn.* 22), based on the passage from the book of Job that Handel uses in his 'Messiah.' The chorale *Christus, der ist mein Leben* (For Christ my Saviour live I) is added to the Scriptural text. Like the great Heinrich Schütz, Michael allows himself to be inspired by the rhythm of the text and, as a result, achieves an emphatic and agitated style of strong expressive power. The irregular three-measure phrases often repeated lend an urgency and emotional appeal to the work found only in the best German choral compositions of the period.

More conventional is the Christmas motet *Fürchtet euch nicht* (Be not afraid; *Schn.* 34), a work of solid craftsmanship, scored for double chorus. At first the two groups develop the words of the angel in a simple homophonic dialogue of the kind to be found in the works of Hans Leo Hassler and Michael Praetorius. Then they join forces, and while the soprano introduces the chorale *Gelobet seist du, Jesu Christ* (Praise be to Thee, Jesus Christ), the lower parts present contrapuntal counter-melodies.

The five-part chorale motet *Herr, wenn ich nur dich habe* (Lord, if I have but Thee; *Schn.* 21) follows a course which is the exact opposite. From an initial contrast between Biblical text and chorale it gradually works up towards a complete unification. Michael uses five stanzas of the hymn *Ach Gott, wie manches Herzeleid* (Ah God, how sad and sick at heart), which is introduced in the traditional way by the soprano, while the lower parts present the Biblical text. Particularly impressive is the section preceding the third verse of the chorale, when the four deeper voices anticipate the melody of the hymn in the manner of a chorale prelude and develop it in polyphonic style. In the last stanza words from the Scripture are eliminated and all five voices join in a powerful harmonization of the chorale. Of peculiar charm is the quickening of the tempo, which the composer prescribes with the unexpected indication *Presto*. In spite of the exultant jubilation of this ending, the composer has the very last four measures of the motet sung piano. One cannot help being reminded of another Protestant master who, some two hundred years later, used the same effect to end the second movement of his 'German Requiem.'

A striking similarity in form may be noticed between the three motets for eight-part double chorus *Herr, du lässest mich erfahren* (Lord, Thou lettest me know; *Schn.* 35), *Dem Menschen ist gesetzt einmal zu sterben* (It is the law that man must die; *Schn.* 36), and *Halt, was du hast* (Hold what thou hast; *Schn.* 33), all of which are also in the same key of e. After a short introduction by the second chorus, which is entrusted with the Biblical text, the first chorus enters with the chorale. Alternately the two groups present lines from their respective texts, as if vying with each other, until the church hymn triumphs. Near the end of each motet, the two choruses join forces in singing the last sentences of the hymn. The continual shifting of interest from one chorus to the other, the alternation of very short sections, and the countless echo effects, particularly in the last chorale verses, give these motets a quality of restlessness.

In *Herr, ich warte auf dein Heil* (Lord, I wait for Thy salvation; *Schn.*

37) Michael was led by a longing for death to write one of his most stirring compositions, solving the problem of the chorale motet in yet another manner. It is written for eight-part double chorus; and the text of the Scripture is at first, in the traditional way, entrusted to the second chorus, while the first chorus presents the church hymn, *Ach wie sehnlich wart ich* (Oh, how anxiously do I await). After a mere four lines of the chorale, the pent-up emotions become so strong that the hymn tune is altogether swept away. Instead of the usual ending with the glorified chorale, the second half of the composition calls on all the voices to join in the fervent supplication 'Lord, I wait for Thy salvation; oh come and take me.' The motet reveals Michael's gift of harmonizing melodies in a straightforward and convincing way, and at the same time his naïve pleasure in pictorial characterizations such as the long melisma on 'I wait' (*Ex.* 7). It displays a simplicity and directness which cannot fail to move the listener.

Ex.7.

Five vocal compositions, which have been discovered in the past few decades, contribute towards completing the picture of Michael Bach's artistic personality. In each of these a five-part string group is employed, besides the organ, to accompany the singers and to supply brilliant instrumental preludes and interludes. In this respect the five strongly differentiated works foreshadow 18th-century cantatas.

The simplest form is displayed in the two arias, for soprano and alto respectively, based on Michael's favourite *Ach wie sehnlich wart ich* (Oh, how anxiously do I await; *Schn.* 18) and on the hymn *Auf! lasst uns den Herrn loben* (Let us praise the Lord; *Schn.* 17). The accompanying string body consists of a violin exhibiting a certain amount of virtuosity and four unnamed instruments, probably three viole da gamba and a double bass. Each aria starts with a 'Sinfonia,' which, after a few calm measures of introduction, assumes a freely flowing toccata-like character. The hymns themselves are treated as strophic songs, and the composer avoids monotony by prescribing changes for the last line of each verse. In *Ach wie sehnlich* he indicates *lente*, while in *Auf! lasst uns* the triple time of the beginning is transformed into common time. These are pieces of simple and noble beauty meant for singers of modest technical skill such as the little parish of Gehren could muster.

More intricate is the solo cantata *Es ist ein grosser Gewinn* (It is of great advantage; *Schn.* 16). Each of its three sections starts with a vocal solo, accompanied by the continuo instrument only, in which the soprano exhibits a certain amount of *gorgia* (the Italian coloratura singing of the period). Then the strings and voice take up this melody in a gay concerted dialogue. The instruments used in this composition are, besides organ, two violins, a *violino piccolo* and a *quart violino non di grosso grande*. It is not quite clear what Michael had in mind when he referred to the *quart violino* 'not of the large size,' but probably it was, like the *violino piccolo*, a small violin tuned a fourth higher than the standard type. We may assume that the unusual way of describing the instrument is due to the fact that Michael built it himself in an unorthodox manner.

Liebster Jesu, hör mein Flehen (Dearest Jesus, hear my prayer; not in Schneider's catalogue), written for the second Sunday in Lent, has the character of a dramatic dialogue between Christ (bass), the Canaanitish woman (soprano), and three disciples (alto and two tenors). The accompanying string instruments are specifically allotted to the different characters: the two violins to Christ, the two violas to the Canaanitish woman, and the double bass to the disciples. Only in the chorale which concludes the dialogue are all the voices and instruments united. Latin headings in the score help to clarify the content of the work. After a very short *Symphonia*, the Canaanitish woman implores the Lord to save her daughter, who is possessed of the Devil. The three disciples intercede for her, and after some hesitation the Master orders Satan to relinquish his prey. We might well expect the stricken child's recovery of health to be represented in the ensuing instrumental interlude, but the alternation of plain chords and rests that we find there does not do justice to the situation. The form of the epic dialogue in which Hammerschmidt, Ahle, and other 17th-century composers excelled, apparently did not appeal to Michael. The only composition of this type which has been preserved shows a stiff formalism not to be found in his other works.

The most ambitious of Michael's cantatas is *Ach bleib bei uns, Herr Jesu Christ* (Abide with us, Lord Jesus Christ; *Schn.* 42) for two violins, three violas, bassoon, organ, and four-part mixed chorus, employing the familiar chorale text without its original tune. Bach sets each line of the hymn separately, as in a 16th-century motet, exploring the pictorial possibilities of every phrase, and paying special attention to dynamic shading. While such a technique is not conducive to structural unity

within the whole cantata, it is productive of many attractive details. In
the introductory *Sonata*,[1] the two violins and first viola develop spirited
competition in which the vocal ensemble joins with vigour and gusto
during the main part of the cantata. When the text refers to the 'heavenly
word, the bright light,' Michael boldly leads the first violin up to giddy
heights (*Ex.* 8). In spite of occasional awkward progressions in the

voice and string parts, this cantata gives us a good example of the high
standard of his technical skill, proving that he was fully conversant with
both German polyphony and the Italian *stile concertato*.

Ernst Ludwig Gerber states in his *Neues Lexikon der Tonkünstler* of
1812-14 that he owned a manuscript with 72 chorale preludes by
Johann Michael, some of them followed by as many as eight or ten
variations. He claims further that 'there is great . . . variety among these
preludes, and none of them is quite unworthy of the name of Bach.' This
manuscript has unfortunately disappeared; and all we know to-day are
eight preludes, which give only a narrowly restricted insight into this
part of Michael's activity.[2] They show him as an organist of sound judgment and technical skill, but of limited imagination and originality. The

---

[1] The terms *Sonata, Sinfonia,* and *Symphonia* were used at that time indis-
criminately for instrumental preludes. In *Liebster Jesu* Michael calls the introduction
Symphonia, but writes after the first entreaty of the Canaanitish woman: *Sonata
repetatur.*

[2] An 'Aria with 15 Variations' is known only in a corrupted arrangement for
Harmonium by L. A. Zellner from the second half of the 19th century. Since we are
ignorant of the source of this arrangement, we cannot be sure what its original was like
and even whether it was actually by Michael. Wilhelm Martini claims in 'Johann Sebastian
Bach in Thüringen' that a composition by Michael is to be found in tablature in the
archives of the parish of Elleben at Osthausen, but I have been unable to get further
information about it.

simplest form of Michael's chorale prelude is exemplified by his arrangement of *Von Gott will ich nicht lassen* (From God I'll not be parted; *Schn.*
47). It is a three-part composition in which the soprano has the hymn
tune, accompanied by rapidly moving counter-melodies in the two lower
voices. An introduction of one and a half measures and a brief interlude
are the only deviations from a plain and unassuming presentation of the
chorale. A more personal note can be found in such arrangements as *In
dich hab' ich gehoffet, Herr* (Oh Lord, as I have trusted Thee; *Schn.* 50) and
Nun freut euch, lieben Christen G'mein (Now dance and sing, ye Christian
throng; *Schn.* 52), in which the entrance of the *cantus firmus* in the
soprano is preceded by a fugato of the two lower parts, using as a subject
the first line of the chorale melody. The technique of Pachelbel, with
whom the Bach family was on terms of personal friendship, is unmistakable in this arrangement. Particularly impressive, in *In dich hab' ich
gehoffet, Herr,* is the gradual increase from three parts in the first half of
the composition to four and ultimately five voices, corresponding to the
emotional content of the hymn text. In *Dies sind die heil'gen zehn Gebot*
(These are the holy ten commandments; *Schn.* 49) and *Allein Gott in der
Höh'* (To God on high alone be praise; *Schn.* 51) an attempt is made to
use a more polyphonic style for the preludes and interludes, contrasting
with a predominantly harmonic setting in the *cantus firmus* sections.
Possibly the finest work in this group is *Wenn mein Stündlein vorhanden
ist* (When finally my hour comes; *Schn.* 46), in which Michael allots the
cantus firmus alternately to soprano and bass, thus creating a lively
dialogue between highest and lowest parts. The composer's contrapuntal
skill reveals itself in a stretto with partial diminution of the first chorale
line inserted in the middle of the composition (*Ex.* 9).

Different from the rest is *Wenn wir in höchsten Nöten sein* (When we
are troubled through and through; *Schn.* 48), a set of chorale variations in
the style of Samuel Scheidt. In the first verse the melody is partly broken
up into coloraturas and given to the soprano. The second verse restores
the simple metrical construction of the tune and entrusts it to the middle
voice, above a harmonic bass and beneath a cantabile soprano part. The

third verse brings the composition to its climax. Running sixteenth notes dominate its two voices, almost completely obscuring the chorale melody. This last verse displays a light and emotional quality, suggesting that at times Michael Bach aimed at a subjectivity of expression that is almost romantic.

In conclusion it may be stated that Michael was a composer of great, but uneven talent. He was fully conversant with the art of his time and used both German and Italian models with considerable success. The composer was technically well trained, his music abounding in interesting details and expressive power. Nevertheless, his compositions were too often lacking in the compelling qualities of a real work of genius. While some of them are stirring and exhilarating, others hardly rise above the level of respectable mediocrity. As a rule his harmonic language is impressive; but there are few attempts at introducing a more polyphonic texture, and perfect construction is only rarely achieved. Michael may have been better as an instrumental than as a vocal composer; but since so little of his instrumental work survives, we are not able fully to judge its merits. It is possible that some of his finest compositions are lost; but it is just as probable that his untimely death prevented him from reaching the zenith of his artistic development.

THE MUSIC OF JOHANN CHRISTOPH BACH

Among the older members of the Bach family Johann Christoph (13) is undoubtedly the leader. Even the few works preserved show the wide range of his creative output. He wrote clavier and organ compositions, cantatas and motets, works for a single voice and for a ten-part double chorus. Serene confidence and trust, sadness rising to agonized despair, and on occasion a fine sense of humour, can be detected in his compositions. Johann Christoph creates beautiful and poignant melodies; he cleverly mingles the old church modes with the modern major and minor, thus achieving a striking harmonic variety; he indulges in bold successions of chords and sudden modulations of great intensity. Above all, his works display a clear and logical construction, the outcome of his strong sense of form. Sebastian praised Johann Christoph's work as 'profound,' while Philipp Emanuel characterized its curiously romantic character by describing Johann Christoph in the Genealogy as 'the great and expressive composer.' Forkel in his book on J. S. Bach refers to the admiration which Emanuel had for his ancestor. 'It is still quite fresh in my memory,' the historian writes, 'how good-naturedly the old man smiled at me at the most remarkable and hazardous passages when once in Hamburg he gave me the pleasure of hearing some of these old pieces.'

Among Johann Christoph's simplest vocal compositions are his arias *Es ist nun aus* (It is now past; *Schn.* 59) and *Mit Weinen hebt sich's an* (With weeping there begins; *Schn.* 60). These are plain four-part songs in which a purely harmonic support is given to an unadorned melody. As in similar arias of a hymnlike character, a solo soprano accompanied by the organ may take the place of the full chorus. In spite of their unpretentious character, these two pieces are deeply stirring. The former is a funeral song, or *Sterb-Aria*, with the refrain 'Farewell, O World' on a bold downward leap of a ninth in the soprano (*Ex.* 10). The little piece gives

moving expression to the general longing of the time for repose, and it is not surprising that Sebastian took a special interest in it. Apparently he had it performed, since he supplemented the text in the old parts and made several corrections in the music. According to a note in the manuscript, the aria *Mit Weinen hebt sich's an* was written in 1691. The free rhythms of this composition are remarkable, and they arise from Johann Christoph's practice of lengthening the notes at the beginning and end of each line of text, thus constantly interrupting the basic trochaic metre and producing a feeling of restlessness, which realistically depicts the sorrows and pain man suffers on earth.

More elaborate are the two five-part motets *Sei getreu bis an den Tod* (Be thou faithful unto death; *Schn.* 63) and *Der Mensch vom Weibe geboren* (Man born of woman; *Schn.* 62). These brief compositions display a combination of the motet and aria form. The first half of each work is based on the Bible (Revelation ii, 10, and Job xiv, 1, respectively) and exhibits a loosely knitted, somewhat polyphonic texture; the second half is an aria, using a hymn text and the traditional homophonic style. Neither the quietly confident *Sei getreu* nor the dark and restless *Der Mensch* (which is influenced by Johann Bach's *Unser Leben ist ein Schatten*) is a particularly impressive composition. Their settings are somewhat conventional and hardly reflect the wilful subjectivity so often noticeable in

VI. Autograph of the first page of the Cantata for the 16th or 24th Sunday after Trinity by C. Philipp Emanuel Bach. It uses as a first chorus Johann Christoph Bach's Motet 'Der Gerechte'

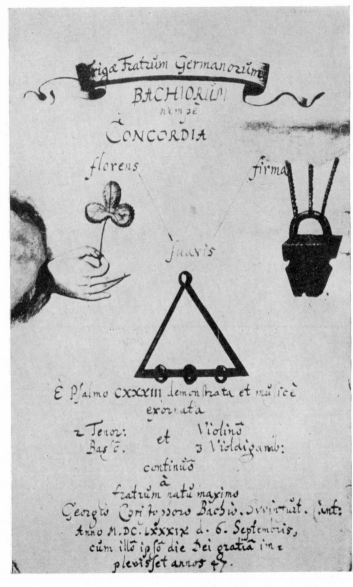

VII. Title-page of the Birthday Cantata by Georg Christoph Bach

Johann Christoph's compositions. It is noteworthy that these two works were not considered sufficiently valuable to be included in the *Alt-Bachisches Archiv*. Our only sources for their musical text are reliable, but very late copies made in the second half of the 19th century.

On quite a different level are two other five-part motets *Fürchte dich nicht* (Be not afraid; *Schn.* 61) and *Der Gerechte* (The righteous; *Schn.* 64) which belong to the composer's most significant works. In *Fürchte dich nicht* the church song, presented like a *cantus firmus* in long notes in the soprano, alternates with the Bible text in the four lower parts. For the main body of his motet Johann Christoph chose the words of Isaiah xliii, 1, 'Fear not, for I have redeemed thee. I have called thee by thy name, thou art Mine,' and follows up with Luke xxiii, 43, 'Verily I say unto thee, To-day shalt thou be with Me in Paradise.' Old and New Testament are here associated to give to mankind the Lord's message of salvation. To this the tormented soul (soprano) adds the last stanza of the song 'O woe and grief':

> O Jesu! Thou my hope and rest,
> With tears I kneel before Thee,
> Help, that in life and death
> I ever may adore Thee.

The motet begins quietly in the four lower voices; gradually the motion increases and a lively fugato appears, leading to a monumental dialogue between the voices of God and man. The beseeching words 'With tears I kneel before Thee' are answered with the solace 'Fear not, for I have redeemed thee'; and the repeated anguished cry 'Help, help' with the prophecy 'To-day shalt thou be with Me in Paradise.' The postlude of alto, tenor, and bass resumes the mood of the beginning. The work is beautifully proportioned, rising slowly to a climax in its middle section and returning gradually to the initial atmosphere. It is not surprising that Sebastian, who must surely have known his cousin's composition, was inspired to write a motet[1] based on the same text and using the identical conception of a dialogue between Christ and humanity.[2]

The motet *Der Gerechte* was a favourite composition of Philipp Emanuel Bach, who added strings and organ to the five voice parts of the original and employed this arrangement as the first chorus in one of his own cantatas (cf. p. 373). Emanuel informs us also that this motet of his great-uncle's was written in 1676, when the composer was 34 years old. Its text is taken from the Apocryphal 'Wisdom of Solomon,' ch. iv,

---

[1] Motet No. IV.
[2] Cf. also Sebastian's early cantatas, especially No. 106 *Gottes Zeit* (see p. 209).

D

'Though the righteous die before his time, yet shall he come to heaven.'
The pictorial element is here particularly strongly developed. At the
beginning, the death of the righteous is expressed by descending melodic
lines, and the pleasure which God takes in him by an ascending melody.
At the words 'quickly he is taken,' a motive in dotted rhythm shows
the suddenness of the event; and the 'evil, evil, evil life' is described
by significant chords (*Ex.* 11). Winterfeld points out that Johann

Christoph was influenced in this composition by Giovanni Gabrieli's
motet *Sancta Maria, succurre miseris.* The two compositions undoubtedly
resemble each other in many details; but more important still is the sense
of balance and form which the Thuringian composer acquired in his study
of the Italian master's work. The first section of *Der Gerechte* is majestic
and slow; then follow two parts inscribed as 'Presto' and 'Adagio'
respectively, and a gay dance in triple time marks the end. Clearly there
are four sections in this piece, the tempi of which are slow–fast–slow–fast,
corresponding to the four movements of the *Sonata da chiesa* which at
approximately the same time was assuming a definite pattern in Italy.

There survive four eight-part motets by Johann Christoph Bach, each
of which uses two antiphonal four-part groups of mixed voices. *Ich lasse
dich nicht, du segnest mich denn* (I will not let Thee go, except Thou
bless me; *Schn.* 68) is based on Genesis xxxii, 26, to which later is added
the third stanza of the beautiful song 'Why art thou troubled' by the 16th-
century German poet and shoemaker, Hans Sachs. In the initial section
the Bible text alone is employed. The two choruses alternate in a simple
and purely harmonic style. Gradually the tension grows; instead of
following each other, they overlap and finally they sing together. The
force of this prayer is heightened by the outcry of a single soprano voice
'My saviour,' which is quickly lost in the general excitement. In the second
section Bible text and chorale are combined. The melody of the church
hymn is used as a *cantus firmus* in the soprano, while the three lower
voices introduce rapidly moving counter-melodies. In spite of the fact
that the initial eight parts are here condensed into four parts, the motet
reaches its culmination in what is possibly the best piece of polyphonic
writing in any of Johann Christoph's vocal compositions. There are two
main subjects among the counterpoints of this section: a stubborn, defiant

one to the words 'I'll not let Thee go,' and an imploring one illustrating the ardent supplication 'I pray Thou bless me.' Each of these strongly contrasting ideas is skilfully developed, not only in simple imitation but also in stretti and inversions. The fact that this motet was for some time considered to be a composition of Sebastian's is mainly due to this powerful and highly passionate polyphonic setting. The last part of the composition again approaches the homophonic style of the beginning. It introduces a simple harmonization of the chorale in plain four-part chords. The dramatic excitement of the middle section is here replaced by a mood of quiet happiness and confidence. This motet, which is also harmonically bold and unconventional, is one of the finest works produced by the older Bach generation.

The remaining three motets are in eight parts throughout. *Herr, nun lässest du deinen Diener in Frieden fahren* (Lord, now lettest Thou Thy servant depart in peace; *Schn.* 65) is based on the words of Luke ii, 29-32, which Johann Christoph employs without the addition of a church hymn. Sudden changes between two keys, a whole tone or a semitone apart, and bold mixtures of major and minor, of medieval modes and modern tonality, give this composition an iridescent life which makes up for the simplicity of its homophonic structure. By repeating the first line of the text at the end of the composition, Johann Christoph rounds off his motet to a ternary form. The mighty invocation 'Lord, Lord,' which begins the work, also comes at its close. Even the third section taken by itself is in a kind of tripartite form, since the composer quotes in its middle a phrase from the second part, thus linking also these two sections of the motet.

Lieber Herr Gott (Gracious Lord; *Schn.* 66), which, according to the manuscript, was composed in December 1672, uses as a text a hymn or prayer of the period. Bach may have found the words among the compositions of Heinrich Schütz, whose *Geistliche Chormusik* No. XIII, from 1648, is based on the same poem. An additional similarity between the two works is to be found in their change from common to triple time in the middle and their return to common time at the end. Johann Christoph's composition is clearly divided into two sections: a more homophonic first one, and a glorious fugue on the words 'Through our Saviour, Thy beloved son.' Here the composer uses the trick of always introducing subject and answer stretto-like in quick succession, thus increasing the intensity of the musical language. At first four voices only are employed, but gradually the remaining parts fill in the polyphonic texture. An even balance is maintained between the two choruses, which are linked by skilful imitations. Johann Christoph's study of Italian models is manifest in the natural flow of his parts. The mixture of tonalities, in which now G, then e, and again the Mixolydian mode, seems to be prevalent, contributes to the feeling of unrest and excitement pervading this dramatic composition.

Equally moving is the motet for two choruses *Unseres Herzens Freude* (The joy of our heart; *Schn.* 67) based on words from the Lamentations of Jeremiah v, 15, 16. Quite justly, Spitta said about this remarkable composition: 'For variety, energy, and appealing fervour of expression, for the development of sound into bold and striking imagery, for the highest perfection of form as affecting the whole work, it can find no equal except among the very best examples of its kind.' With simple dignity the words of the lamentation are set to music: 'The joy of our heart is ceased; our dance is turned into mourning.' In a second section the eight voices unite to the heartrending outcry: 'Woe unto us that we have sinned!' Bach's only means of expression here are bold chromatic progressions, such as the juxtaposition of the chords of A flat and G. The first section is now repeated in a most poetical combination with the second one. Again and again the words of the lamentation are interrupted by the cry of distress, until nothing remains but the voice of despair. It is not surprising that Sebastian copied part of this motet with his own hand; its musical expression and its architecture point far into the future.

Different from the motets are the five compositions of Johann Christoph which employ not only the organ but also stringed instruments for the accompaniment of the voices. Two of these pieces are laments for a single voice, using the dramatic declamation which Heinrich Schütz had introduced into German Protestant music. *Ach, dass ich Wassers gnug hätte* (Oh, had I only enough water; *Schn.* 5 and 57), written for contralto, violin, three viole da gamba, and bass, was formerly considered a composition of Heinrich Bach. However, the list of the property left by Philipp Emanuel mentions among Johann Christoph's compositions a work of this name; moreover the emotional intensity of the lament and its bold harmonic language indicate the authorship of Heinrich's son. This solo cantata written in da capo form is unusually concise. There is a brief instrumental introduction, after which the voice enters, dominating henceforth the musical structure, which is supported and enriched by the strings. The style of this lament is a kind of dramatic recitation, closely following the rhythm and melody of German speech, and adorned with tonal pictures inspired by the text.

On a much larger scale is the second lament written for bass solo accompanied by five stringed instruments, *Wie bist du denn, o Gott, im*

Zorn auf mich entbrannt (How art Thou, God, enraged in fury against me; *Schn.* 58), which is based on a 17th-century version of the penitential psalms. This too was originally attributed to another composer, Johann Philipp Krieger (1649-1725), and has only recently been recognized as the work of Johann Christoph Bach.[1] It is a powerful composition in five extensive sections. In contrast to the preceding work the stringed instruments, particularly the violin, which is treated with the greatest brilliance, play an important part in its development.[2] A dignified introduction in the main key of e prepares for the entrance of the voice. Each of the following three sections starts quietly, accompanied by the continuo only. After a few measures the strings enter and gradually the expression becomes more passionate, building up towards a climax. The most dramatic section is the third, in which the agitated figures of the violin depict the merciless treatment that the sufferer is accorded by God. In the last part the tormented soul tells of its anguish and fear. The rhythm changes from common to triple time; the prayer becomes more ardent until the words are reached: 'My God, no longer be inflamed in wrath against me, let Thine anger be transformed into goodness.' Hope gradually replaces despair and the final measure of the lament by its melodic inversion (*Ex.* 12) expresses most graphically that the harassed spirit is looking

forward to a reversal of its fate. Although this cantata makes excessive demands on the vocal range of the singer (almost two octaves), its sincerity, poignancy, and fire amply repay the artist.

The wedding cantata *Meine Freundin, du bist schön* (My love, thou art fair; *Schn.* 71) for four solo voices, chorus, violin, three violas, and basso continuo, based mainly on words from the Song of Solomon, holds

---

[1] Cf. *EDM*, I, p. viii; *BJ*, 1907, p. 132; and *SIMG*, I, 1899/1900, p. 214.

[2] Max Seiffert, the editor of the work (in *DDT*, zweite Folge, VI, 1, p. 125) suggests the use of a bassoon for the fourth part in the score. This is hardly appropriate, since in a list of music left by F. E. Praetorius (1655-95) the work is catalogued as written for 'B. solo, 1 Violine, 3 Violen con B. cont.'

a unique position among the works of Johann Christoph. It displays a robust sense of humour one is hardly led to expect from a composer of such lofty works as *Ich lasse dich nicht* or *Der Gerechte*. To treat the venerated Song of Solomon, which was usually interpreted in a purely symbolic fashion, in so realistic a manner for a wedding celebration was highly unorthodox, and bound to create hilarity among the listeners. Moreover, Johann Christoph added a running commentary to be recited before or during the performance, which brings into relief the inherent humour of the composition, intensifying it by facetious observations. The 'Wedding Cantata' was a great favourite among the Bachs. Ambrosius copied the parts and the commentary—indeed, it is not at all unlikely that he co-operated with his cousin in preparing it for a special occasion. Sebastian, on the other hand, took the trouble to make a new cover for the parts his father had copied.

As an example of the Bachs' earthy sense of humour, most of this commentary is reproduced here.

'A lover saunters along, all by himself, as the bass illustrates. Unexpectedly he comes across his sweetheart, whom he addresses flatteringly: *My love, thou art fair*. Moreover he gives her food for thought by saying: *Turn away thine eyes from me, for they overcome me*. Possibly he is afraid that people might read his inmost thoughts in his eyes.

'His sweetheart, acting like a true German [in a straightforward way] and also longing for a suitable and convenient place wherein to express her pure love without being disturbed, answers: *O that thou wert really my brother, that I might find thee in the street, kiss thee, and no one despise me*. But presently she offers him a chance saying: *Let my beloved come into his garden*. The lover, who did not expect so bold a suggestion, but is anxious not to make her suspect from his long silence that he might refuse or be timid and irresolute, declares himself quickly: *I come to my garden, my sister, my bride*. After they have thus agreed to meet . . . they part, this time quickly, without any long-winded Finale. . . .

'The girl takes a *chackan*[1] [heavy stick] in her hand and walks to the garden. On the way she is in a cheerful mood and constantly talks to herself, showing herself gay and merry in different ways, which the violin illustrates [in a *ciaccona*] with many variations. She also imagines in natural colours the one or other thing which is going to happen in the garden (quite likely it is not her first visit either!). Therefore she delights

---

[1] The author employs here the unusual Slavonic expression *chackan*, as the composition turns at this point into a *ciaccona* (chaconne).

herself with these words: *My beloved is mine and I am his; he feedeth among the lilies and his desire is toward me; his left hand is under my head and his right hand doth embrace me.* . . . Mostly, however, she utters these words in between: *My beloved is mine, and I am his*, words of which undoubtedly her heart must have been full.

'When she is not far from the garden, a couple of men suddenly appear crossing the field; and as they have probably often seen this girl wandering to the garden, or perhaps have heard gossip about the affair, they do not inquire in the usual fashion, asking "Where from? Whither? Why alone?", but act as though they knew already whom she was looking for, and therefore inquire: *Whither is thy beloved gone?*, flattering her at the same time by saying: *Oh, thou fairest among women.*

'She, who does not keep it secret any more and probably does not mind being teased about it, admits: *My beloved is gone down into his garden to the beds of spices, to feed in the garden and to gather lilies.*

'Thereupon both out of politeness offer to accompany her: *That we may seek him with thee.*

'After that the two men walk up and down in the garden. The basso continuo runs round continuously and searches; the other instruments also move occasionally, then again they stop and look around, until finally, when they perceive the lover in the garden, they all unite and pay their respects in a piano and adagio passage.

'He, the lover, while certainly expecting his sweetheart alone and not with such a retinue, appreciates that these men have joined her only to serve her; moreover they are not strangers but a couple of good friends, so he greets them telling them what he did in the garden: *I have gathered my myrrh with my spice.* . . .

'And after he has led them all into the little pavilion and set refreshments and food on the table, he as well as his sweetheart, who has somewhat assumed the role of hostess, exclaim . . . *Eat, O friends; drink, O beloved, and become drunk.*[1]

'When the feast is over, one hears the guests call to the musicians: *The gratias*, thus letting them know that they should intone a song of thanks; whereupon the musicians play the chorale, while all those present join in singing, and the instruments keep active as well.

'Finally, as everyone shows the effects of the entertainment, it is decided to break up the party. Thus one hears everywhere: *Good night! Sleep well! Many thanks! Good luck! For you too!*'

---

[1] The Luther translation used by the composer has here the words *und werdet trunken* (and become drunk), while the King James version reads 'drink abundantly.'

The music of the cantata reaches its climax in a *ciaccona* with 66 variations for voice and strings, based on the theme in *Ex.* 13. It serves the

Ex. 13

bride to express her deep love for the groom, and the composer seems to have chosen this particular form to demonstrate that every utterance of an infatuated person appears like a new variation on the same theme. Johann Christoph's fine sense of balance and proportion leads him to establish in this number, with the help of harmonic changes, a kind of rondo form within the larger framework of the *ciaccona*.[1] When the scene turns into a feast, a big ensemble develops in which, for the first time, the chorus joins with brief exclamations. The composer takes special delight in the invitation of the text to get drunk, which the voices present with a sort of hiccough (*Ex.* 14). The end of the composition, how-

Ex. 14

ever, reverts to the serious character sanctioned by tradition. In a dignified hymn solo voices and chorus join to express thanks to God for His gifts. The very last note (G) of all the singers is held for ten measures and gradually dies away, while the violin alone keeps up the motion, thus describing the reluctant departure of the guests.

Another cantata of a pseudo-dramatic character is *Die Furcht des Herren* (The fear of the Lord; not enumerated in *Schn.*) for five solo voices, mixed chorus, strings and organ. In the score, written by Johann Christoph himself, most of the singers, and even the instrumental basso continuo, are identified with one or other of the functionaries of a city, thus suggesting a performance in honour of a newly elected city council. The bass, for instance, is called 'the senior mayor,' the chorus 'the whole city council,' and the basso continuo (organ) 'the city clerk.' In the main section of this composition, each line of a prayer is started by the senior

[1] Var. 1-17 are in the tonic, 18-22 in the dominant, 33-51 again in the tonic, 52-59 in the subdominant, and 60-66 back in the tonic.

city chamberlain (tenor), and after a measure or two the rest of the singers and players join him. Particularly moving is the middle part, a secular version of the traditional combination between church hymn and Bible text. 'Wisdom' (soprano), boasting of its great merits, is implored by the city functionaries to impart to them something of its blessing. The single soprano voice is confronted by solo quartet and full chorus, and the loose polyphonic texture realistically describes with its successive entrances and imitations the uncertainty and confusion of men pining for enlightenment. When 'Wisdom' proudly announces 'Kings are ruling through me,' both the melody of the voice and the accompaniment of strings imitate trumpet fanfares. Johann Sebastian wrote various works on a much larger scale for similar occasions. Yet the less pretentious composition of his kinsman by no means suffers by comparison with them.

The St. Michael's Day cantata *Es erhub sich ein Streit* (And there was war in heaven; *Schn.* 69) is the biggest and, as far as orchestration goes, the most ambitious work that Johann Christoph created. Philipp Emanuel wrote about it in a letter to Forkel:[1] 'This composition in 22 parts is a masterpiece. My blessed father performed it once in a church at Leipzig and everybody was surprised by the effect it made. I have not enough singers here [in Hamburg], or else I would produce it sometime.' The cantata is based on Revelation xii, 7-12, and modelled on the lines of a composition using the same text by Andreas Hammerschmidt,[2] whose works were well known to the older Bachs. Its subject, the war of Michael and his angels against 'that old serpent called the Devil and Satan,' is a monumental one and very well suited to the belligerent personality of its composer. The treatment of the Scripture words is epic and oratorio-like; majestic power and restrained dramatic fire give to this outsized composition a character of its own. The 22 parts to which Emanuel refers in his letter are formed by two five-part choirs, two violins, four violas, continuo [bassoon and organ] and—a most uncommon feature in the works of the earlier Bachs—four trumpets and timpani. The cantata begins with a two-part *Sonata*, in character somewhat reminiscent of a French Overture. An imitative recitative by two basses leads to the first climax: the description of the struggle between the powers of light and of darkness. This gigantic tone picture, in which the trumpets hold a prominent place, is for more than 50 measures exclusively based on the single triad of C. A brilliant instrumental section, describing the triumph of the angels, concludes this part. Johann Sebastian, who set the same scene to

[1] Dated Hamburg, September 20, 1775. See Bitter, 'C.P.E. . . . Bach,' I, 343.
[2] 'Andern Theil geistlicher Gespräche über die Evangelia,' Dresden, 1656, No. 26.

music, was obviously influenced by the work of his cousin. However, he
not only used a great variety of forms (recitative, aria, chorale, and polyphonic chorus), but he also divided the words of the Scripture between
two independent cantatas (Nos. 19 and 50). Johann Christoph unites both
sections into a single mighty work.[1] He comes to a second culmination
when the words 'Now is come salvation, and strength' are pronounced,
and a third one to describe at the end the general rejoicing. However, in
some respects the composer strives at more economy than seems
advantageous to his work. There are no solo voices, polyphonic devices
are sparingly employed, and the harmonies are of the utmost simplicity
and limited diversity. This is a work full of interesting orchestral effects;
it made the greatest contribution towards the fame of its author, but it
may be doubted whether it is actually his strongest and most inspired
creation.

Philip Spitta called the organ works of Johann Christoph Bach 'imperfect' and 'disappointing to anybody who knows the master's vocal
output.' This severe verdict was obviously caused by an insufficient insight into the meaning and purpose of this part of the composer's music.
The 44 *Choräle welche bey wärenden Gottes Dienst zum präambulieren
gebraucht werden können* (chorales to be used as preludes during the
service; *Schn.* 82) are mere improvisations on the organ which Johann
Christoph committed to paper, possibly for the benefit of his pupils. The
collection consists of short and easy pieces intended to prepare the
congregation for the following hymn, and presenting no particular
technical difficulty even to an organist of mediocre executive ability. This
is music for practical purposes, designed to save the player the trouble of
improvising a chorale prelude on the spur of the moment, and at the same
time of such simple texture as not to lead the audience to suspect its
previous composition. In accordance with Mattheson's recommendations
for organ improvisations,[2] none of the preludes exceeds two minutes.
No early print of the collection has yet been unearthed, but the title of
the existing manuscripts with the remark 'composed and edited by
Johann Christoph Bach' implies that the author intended his work for
publication.

Like the preludes of Pachelbel, each of the 44 chorales begins with a
brief fugato. In contrast to this polyphonic section, the second half of the

---

[1] Johann Christoph Friedrich (the 'Bückeburg') Bach, who dealt with the same
subject in his cantata *Michaels Sieg* (cf. p. 401), was influenced by his father's work;
yet, like the former Johann Christoph, he used both sections of the text in his composition.

[2] 'Grosse Generalbasslehre,' 1725-27.

prelude introduces as a rule a more homophonic texture, employing a pedal point which serves as a kind of extended cadence, and gives stability to this part of the composition. In about half his preludes Johann Christoph follows the style of older masters, such as Scheidt and Ahle. He uses the entire chorale melody, entrusting the fugato with the first line of the hymn and the pedal point section with the remainder. In more than 20 of his preludes, however, Johann Christoph works with selected lines of the hymn tune only, even occasionally confining himself to the single line of the beginning. The composer's contrapuntal treatment is of the simplest kind. Parallel thirds and sixths are frequently employed, and while rarely more than three parts are played simultaneously, a sort of mock polyphony is used which makes the listener imagine the presence of four or even five real voices.[1] No. 13, *Nun lasst uns Gott den Herren loben* (Now let us praise God the Lord), for instance, is a three-part composition, introducing five entrances of the fugue theme, each on a different level and with not less than three octaves between the highest and lowest statement. Stretti, although not very frequent, are occasionally to be found in this collection (cf. Nos. 3, 11, 13).

There are many attractive pieces in this set of preludes. No. 9, *Wir glauben all an einen Gott* (We believe all in one God) with its interesting combination of different motives belongs to the most highly developed pieces of the collection. No. 41, *Aus meines Herzens Grunde* (From out my heart I praise the Lord) in the unusual 3/8 time has a gay and light character which matches the joyous content of the text extremely well (*Ex.* 15). Perhaps the finest number of the set is the last one, *Warum*

Ex. 15

betrübst du dich mein Herz? (Why art thou troubled, oh my heart?). This is one of the very few preludes of the 17th century which does not merely attempt to follow the mood of the chorale text in a general way. It interprets the *changing* emotions of the text in much the same way as Sebastian was to do in the chorale preludes of his *Orgelbüchlein*. The text begins with the words: 'Why art thou troubled, oh my heart? So sore, distressed and sad thou art, why mourn earth's transient joys?' Accordingly the com-

---

[1] The remark in the Obituary for J. S. Bach published in Mizler's 'Musikalische Bibliothek,' that Johann Christoph never used less than five real parts in his organ playing, might be explained in this way.

position introduces chromatically descending passages which, since the times of Monteverdi and Scheidt, have been the generally accepted medium of expressing sorrow and grief. In the last two lines, however, the mood changes completely. Here the text reads: 'Put thou thy trust in God the Lord, Creator, He by all adored.' As soon as the composer reaches these lines the wailing halftone progressions disappear; the music, supported by the powerful pedal point, expresses serene confidence and trust in God. This prelude is so far ahead of its time, that the composer himself seems to have felt he overshot the mark, and desisted from any further attempt in this field.

What Johann Christoph was able to achieve in strict instrumental style is demonstrated by his *Praeludium und Fuge ex Dis* (E flat; *Schn.* 81). This is a Toccata with runs and passages displaying the brilliant Italian writing introduced into Germany by the Austrian court organist, Johann Jacob Froberger. In the middle of this fine fantasy stands a four-part fugue on a chromatic descending bass theme. It comprises 45 measures and its construction is as intricate as that of the chorale preludes is loose. Johann Christoph uses four real parts, without any attempt at giving the illusion of a greater number of voices. There is a strong rhythmic motion, the interesting chromatic theme is effectively harmonized, and the modulations are logically planned. It is not surprising that the powerful composition was long considered as a work of the young Johann Sebastian and was published as such by the editors of the *BG* (Jhrg. xxxvi, 12).

Johann Christoph was also active in the field of clavier music, as is shown by his *Sarabande. Duodecies variat.* (*Schn.* 76), a set of twelve variations on a saraband-like theme. This composition, which to judge by the echo effects it employs was probably meant for a harpsichord with two manuals, is based on a theme of the simplest kind, the formal construction of which is preserved in each of the variations. Nevertheless the effect of the composition is far from monotonous. Johann Christoph gives it greater life by employing a slightly unorthodox pattern of repetition. The first eight measures of the theme and of each variation are played twice in the ordinary way; the second eight measures are subdivided, and the performer repeats each phrase of four measures separately. Thus an illusion of slight asymmetry is created. The sixth, and still more the twelfth variation skilfully employs chromatic effects of great expressive power. The architecture of the whole work is clear and logical. The motion increases, reaching a climax in variations 5 and 7, and then decreases again. Independently of the rest, variations Nos. 3, 6, 9, and 12 provide pauses in the natural flow of the whole set, by reverting to the more meditative character of the slow saraband theme. It can hardly be doubted that Sebastian remembered Johann Christoph's composition while working on his own 'Aria with 30 Variations' (cf. p. 277). The fact that the later composition is likewise in G, that its theme is in 3/4 time and of saraband character, and, most of all, that here too a clear connection between every third variation can be detected, are proof enough. Obviously this is another of the many instances when Sebastian was stimulated and inspired by the artistic heritage of his ancestors.

Closely related to the variations on a saraband is Johann Christoph's *Aria Eberliniana pro dormiente Camillo, variata (Schn. 77)*, a set of fifteen variations on an air by Eberlin written, according to the original, in March 1690. The theme is the work of the Eisenach court composer, Daniel Eberlin (cf. p. 30), who, in spite of his rather varied interests, was an outstanding musician according to the testimony of his son-in-law, Georg Philipp Telemann. Nothing is known about the origin of his aria 'for the sleeping Camillo,' but it must have been a rather well-known piece, since as late as 1713 Johann Heinrich Buttstädt used part of it as a theme for a set of variations.[1] Johann Christoph preserves the very simple and rather charming melody in almost half his variations, furnishing it in each successive piece with new counterpoints. Variations 9 and 11, which do not fit into the overall pattern of a gradually intensified and subsequently slowed-up rhythmic motion, are perhaps the most attractive pieces of the set. No. 9 is a chromatic variation with progressions of rare boldness and expressive power (*Ex.* 16), while the 11th places the melody of the

Ex. 16

air into the tenor, surrounding it, as in a medieval motet, with highly significant counter-melodies. If the set in G was primarily intended for the harpsichord, the almost romantic feeling of the 'Aria Eberliniana' would call for the use of a clavichord, the only keyboard instrument of the period on which a modulation of tone was possible. While the 'Variations on a Saraband' influenced Sebastian, this work with its stronger emotional life points the way towards the clavichord composer Philipp

---

[1] In 'Musicalische Klavier-Kunst und Vorraths-Kammer.' Cf. Conrad Freyse in publications of *Neue Bach Gesellschaft*, XXXIX/2.

Emanuel. However, Sebastian also knew the composition, as the 10th variation of the 'Aria Eberliniana' seems to have been the model for the younger master's organ chorale *Wer nur den lieben Gott lässt walten* from the *Orgelbüchlein*. Not only the gay and energetic rhythm, but the whole treatment of the *cantus firmus* and even the lengths of the pieces are similar.

No other works of Johann Christoph are accessible in our time.[1] Those that have survived prove that the Eisenach organist's compositions were not only important as an inspiration and model for the works of later members of the Bach family, particularly Sebastian; they are masterpieces in their own right, written by a man who undoubtedly belongs to the most remarkable composers of his period.

[1] A set of clavier variations in a, the manuscript of which Philipp Spitta owned, seems to be lost to-day. Cf. *Schn.* 78.

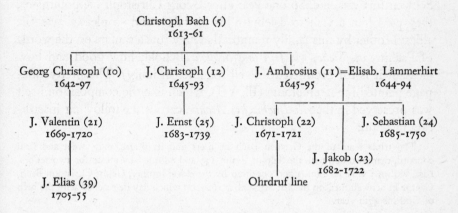

Christoph Bach (5)
1613-61

Georg Christoph (10)   J. Christoph (12)   J. Ambrosius (11)=Elisab. Lämmerhirt
1642-97   1645-93   1645-95   1644-94

J. Valentin (21)   J. Ernst (25)   J. Christoph (22)   J. Sebastian (24)
1669-1720   1683-1739   1671-1721   1685-1750

                                                 J. Jakob (23)
                                                 1682-1722
J. Elias (39)   Ohrdruf line
1705-55

WHEN Christoph Bach (5), the brother of Johann and Heinrich, died in Arnstadt at the age of 48, he left behind three sons and a half-witted daughter (cf. p. 65).[1] The eldest, *Georg Christoph* (10), born on September 6, 1642, was best able to fend for himself. Probably with the help of his relatives in Suhl, the Hoffmann family (cf. p. 13), he obtained a post as assistant to the teacher in a nearby school, and while thus supporting himself, he continued his studies with such success that in 1668 he was appointed Cantor of the town of Themar. This meant an important step upwards on the social ladder. Not only was the Cantor director of the church music, and thus the superior of the organist and the town musicians who played in church, but he also had to instruct the young people in the Latin school. In filling such positions preference was given to men who had studied at a University, and it is a well-known fact that the Leipzig authorities hesitated to appoint Sebastian Bach because of his lack of a University degree. The Council of the little town of Themar was, of course, less exacting, but nevertheless Georg Christoph must have been an educated man to get the appointment. Apparently he did well in this position; for he stayed twenty years at Themar, after which he

[1] The Erfurt register mentions two more children of Christoph: Johann Jakob, born 1647, and Maria Barbara, born 1651, but nothing could be found out about their fate.

was called in the same capacity to the more important city of Schweinfurt in Franconia.[1] This town had tried two years earlier to secure the services of the Eisenach organist, Johann Christoph Bach, but his employers refused their permission to accept the call. Thus Georg Christoph was the first Bach to settle down in Schweinfurt, and he became the founder of a long line of Franconian Bach musicians. His two brothers, Johann Christoph and Ambrosius, were naturally anxious to see what life in Schweinfurt was like. So one year after Georg Christoph's appointment, they paid him a visit to celebrate his birthday, and so pleased was the eldest brother by this family reunion that he wrote a cantata on the words of Psalm 133, *Siehe, wie fein und lieblich* (Behold, how good and how pleasant it is for brethren to dwell together in unity). The pretty title-page painted in watercolours (Ill. VII), which like the composition itself was preserved in the *Alt-Bachisches Archiv*, carries the following inscription in Latin:

The triple team of the German Bach brothers and its flourishing, sweet and firm concord, demonstrated with the help of Psalm 133 and adorned by music for two tenors, bass, violin, 3 viole da gamba and continuo by the eldest brother, Georg Christoph Bach, Cantor in Schweinfurt, on the 6th September 1689, on which day he reached with the help of God his 47th year.

Everything in this work is intended to express the complete concord of the three brothers. The illustrations on the title-page show under the word 'flourishing' a hand holding a *three*-leaf clover, under 'sweet' a triangle with *three* rings, and under 'firm' a lock with *three* chains. In the same way the composition is written for *three* solo voices (two tenors and one bass); it uses *three* viole da gamba among the accompanying instruments; there are usually *three* entrances of every subject; and the instrumental intro-duction develops *three* successive themes. In spite of the rather humorous persistency with which the triad is emphasized all through this composition, the work is artistically significant proving that Georg Christoph was both talented and well trained. The instrumental *Praeludium* consists of one section in common and one in triple time. This arrangement is adhered to in the vocal section, where, moreover, the composer, near the end, repeats the text and music of the beginning, thus creating a kind of ternary construction. The instrumental interludes develop themes which are subsequently taken up by the voices, and altogether an uncommonly compact and strongly unified form is thus

[1] This was stated by Spitta, *l.c.* Recently Oskar Stapf pointed out (in 'Johann Sebastian Bach in Thüringen') that Georg Christoph's name does not appear in the Themar church or school registers after 1683, which makes it seem possible that the move to Schweinfurt took place as early as 1684.

I. The Bach cities on the map of Germany

created. The composition is energetic, fiery, and brilliant; it contains interesting parts both for voices and instruments, which more than compensate for the obvious weaknesses in the contrapuntal treatment caused partly by the programme-like character of the cantata.

Georg Christoph seems to have been something of a poet too. In a collection of 20,000 funeral sermons assembled by the Dukes of Stolberg,[1] there are four poems which the learned Cantor wrote, two of them even in Latin.

Georg Christoph was not fated to enjoy his new position for long. He died nine years after his appointment, at the age of 55. Three years before his death, he had the satisfaction of seeing his eldest son, *Johann Valentin* (b. 1669), engaged as town musician of Schweinfurt. Valentin's sons followed in the family tradition. The second one, *Johann Elias* (b. 1705), Cantor in Schweinfurt like his grandfather, interests us the most as we owe to him the preservation of valuable biographical material about Sebastian Bach and the Thomas Cantor's family.

Georg Christoph's two younger brothers, *Johann Christoph* (12) and Johann Ambrosius, with whom he felt so closely united, were twins, born February 22, 1645. Sebastian merely mentions this fact in the Genealogy, but his son, Philipp Emanuel, added the following details, which he must have heard again and again in the family circle: 'These twins are perhaps the only ones of their kind known [in our family]. They loved each other tenderly, and looked so much alike that even their own wives could not distinguish them. They were a subject of astonishment to noblemen and everyone who saw them. Their speech, their way of thinking—everything was alike. As musicians, too, they were not to be told apart: they played similarly and planned their performances in the same way.' The twins were only 16 when they lost their father and mother, and in a letter describing their desperate financial situation they asked their father's employer to allow them Christoph Bach's salary for the current quarter. This the Count granted, but it did not help much, and the family had to come to the rescue, especially as there was also a girl to provide for, who, according to the petition of her brothers, was 'of an imbecile mind and misshapen figure.' The twins both went to Erfurt to join their uncle Johann, and before long they were both appointed members of the town band to which their father had belonged.[2] *Johann Christoph* (12), however,

---

[1] Cf. 'Mitteilungsblatt des Bach'schen Familienverbandes,' 1939, No. 2.

[2] Cf. Otto Rollert, *l.c.*—Wiegand, *l.c.*, did not agree with this assumption, but has, according to personal information to this author, changed his attitude after a thorough study of the Erfurt archives, and now accepts Rollert's theory.

E

felt drawn towards Arnstadt and he tried whenever possible to play there on special occasions. Apparently he made a good impression, for in 1671 he was appointed court musician by Count Ludwig Günther of Schwarz-burg-Arnstadt. The violin seems to have been his main instrument, as the contract specifically mentions that he was expected 'further to work on the elegance and grace of his fiddling.'[1] Apart from his performances at court he had to play regularly at the church services, in the musical improvement of which the Count was particularly interested. As his yearly salary was even smaller than that of his father (cf. p. 20), amounting only to 30 fl. plus a certain quantity of wood, and $5\frac{1}{2}$ *Mass* of grain, he needed an additional source of income. The town musician, Heinrich Gräser, was therefore instructed by the Count, whenever music was to be played at special functions, to invite first of all Johann Christoph Bach and give him preference over the town musician's assistants. It can well be imagined that such vague instructions were bound to lead to disputes among the musicians, who all needed these *Accidentien* so desperately. In fact, the Arnstadt archives hold quite a number of petitions on the matter from Gräser as well as Bach. In particular, Gräser, an elderly and rather embittered man, complained in the most aggressive way about his young colleague. He could not help being jealous of the latter's popularity at court and once exclaimed: 'If my name were Bach, I would find help everywhere!' It was also a blow to his pride when the burgomaster's son, anxious to have a really first-class entertainment at his wedding, asked young Johann Christoph to provide the music together with his twin brother and a cousin, all of whom had to travel from Erfurt to Arnstadt for this purpose.[2] Gräser therefore fought against Johann Christoph with all the weapons at his disposal; he ridiculed the court musician's violin playing as 'the brushing of flies' wings' (*Fliegen-gewedel*); he complained about the young man's 'guzzling of tobacco,' arrogance, and so forth. When he eventually began to utter grave calumnies against the whole Bach clan, he had to be stopped. In 1677 a joint petition was made by the Arnstadt Bachs, headed by old Heinrich, together with their Erfurt cousins, that Gräser should be made to apolo-gize in public. A compromise was finally reached, but as controversies continued to occur, the Count dismissed both Gräser and Johann Christoph Bach in 1681. Hard times followed; however, a year later, when

[1] Cf. H. Albrecht and A. Bach (see Bibliography), and Wiegand, *l.c.*

[2] Formally Gräser's claim was justified, as Johann Christoph was at that time not yet officially appointed in Arnstadt, but it may be assumed that the burgomaster paid Gräser the compensation customary in such a case.

the old sovereign had died, Johann Christoph was appointed by young Count Anton Günther both as court and town musician, with the exclusive privileges his father had enjoyed,[1] while Gräser was left without an official post. The new ruler, influenced by his music-loving wife, the Countess Auguste Dorothea,[2] made great efforts to improve Arnstadt's musical life. In 1683 he engaged as conductor Adam Drese, an excellent viola da gamba player, who raised the court orchestra to 21 members, among whom the Bachs were represented by Johann Christoph, his uncle Heinrich (so long as he was physically able), his cousin, Johann Michael (14), and Heinrich's son-in-law, Christoph Herthum.

Economic difficulties were not the only ones Johann Christoph had to surmount. In his private life there were problems as well. While most of the Bachs married with clockwork regularity as soon as they had reached a settled position,[3] Johann Christoph was 34 when he entered holy matrimony with Martha Elisabeth Eisentraut, daughter of a school assistant at Ohrdruf. Six years before, he had passed through a disturbing experience which made him reluctant to get involved with the fair sex. He had been courting a girl at Arnstadt, and had even given her a ring, at her request, but he eventually came to the conclusion that she would not be the right wife for him, whereupon the ring was returned. The church Consistory of Arnstadt had found out about the matter, and subjected both the girl and the young man to repeated and most unpleasant interrogatories which dragged on for almost two years. As no real offence could be proved, the Consistory tried by persuasion to make the two young people decide on marriage. The girl indeed was willing. The young man, however, showed himself most obstinate. The more pressure the Consistory exercised, the more determined he became to preserve his freedom. Although his livelihood depended to a great extent on the very people he had to fight in this matter, Johann Christoph recklessly decided to appeal to the higher court, the Consistory of Weimar, in order to obtain his rights. There he pleaded his case with such vigour that he was absolved of any responsibility towards the girl. The incident is indeed

---

[1] They were even extended to the nearby districts of Keula and Schermberg, where no one but Johann Christoph Bach and his assistants was allowed to play. The resulting increase in *Accidentien* caused the Count to reduce Bach's salary at court to 20 fl.

[2] She was the daughter of Duke Anton Ulrich of Wolfenbüttel, who was a great patron of music and dramatic art. A sister and an aunt of hers achieved similar improvements to the theatres at the courts of Coburg and Meiningen. Cf. Gresky, 'Die Arnstädter Musikverhältnisse zur Zeit der Bache,' in 'Arnstädter Anzeiger,' 1935.

[3] His cousins, Johann Christoph (13) and Johann Michael (14), were 25 and 27 respectively, his twin brother, Ambrosius, only 23, when they married.

significant. To appreciate Johann Christoph's action, we should bear in mind that in those times, and in that social sphere, the choice of a wife was far from being a matter of love. It was dictated mainly, if not exclusively, by economic considerations. Men married to succeed in the father-in-law's profession, to set up homes of their own, to beget children who would help with their work. Love played a most insignificant part in these decisions. It would have been quite in keeping with the attitude then prevalent if the young man, after being gently prodded by his spiritual advisers, had married the girl. But Johann Christoph just did not like to be prodded in any way. Instead of being curbed by the pressure brought to bear upon him, he mustered up courage to defy his superiors and public opinion as well. Maybe young Sebastian remembered his stubborn uncle's attitude, when he refused to be talked into marrying the daughter of Buxtehude, in order to succeed to the great master's position in Lübeck.

This outburst of resistance was eventually forgiven, and Johann Christoph enjoyed great esteem and popularity in Arnstadt. For although he had the innate stubbornness of all the Bachs, he was quite skilful in handling people, certainly more skilful than his great cousin and name-sake, Johann Christoph, the organist of Eisenach. It is interesting to note how he became the proprietor of a house in which Bach musicians were to live for many years to come. A contract between Johann Christoph Bach and an aged wealthy baker's widow dated September 12, 1687, has been preserved. She undertook to leave him her house with its entire furnishings, a garden, and six acres of land,[1] provided he would lodge her, take care of her, and supply her with warm food and two quarts of beer daily. Johann Christoph undoubtedly came out very well under this agreement; for the widow died only a few months later, and he acquired a good house and other property. His income, too, thanks to various *Accidentien*, grew, and he managed to save quite a sizable amount of money. But again, like his father and his brothers, he was not fated to enjoy this more prosperous state of affairs for long; he reached exactly the same age as Christoph Bach, dying when 48 years old. He left three children, among them Johann Ernst (25), who was to be Sebastian's successor at the 'New Church' of Arnstadt.

Among the music of the *Alt-Bachisches Archiv* is an unidentified composition which may with some probability be ascribed to Johann

---

[1] The house was at Kohlgasse No. 357, now No. 7, which still stands to-day; the garden at Borngasse; 4 acres on Rabenhold, 2 acres on Eulenberg. Cf. Albrecht-Bach, *l.c.*, and Wiegand, *l.c.*

Christoph. The manuscript does not bear any name or initials, and the hand of the writer is also unknown. However, at the end of the score the date 'Arnstadt, 6 July, 1686' is to be found. At that time Heinrich and Johann Christoph Bach lived in Arnstadt, but as Heinrich was a man of 71 and hardly able to write this vigorous piece, it seems likely that we have here the only preserved composition by Johann Christoph Bach (12). *Nun ist alles überwunden* (Now everything is overcome) is a four-part funeral aria similar in character to Johann Bach's *Weint nicht um meinen Tod* (cf. p. 26). The piece is in common time without any rhythmic complications. It has a simple, heart-rending melody and an expressive harmonization effectively alternating between the keys of e and G. Each of the six verses ends with the same words, 'Now farewell and good night.' Sebastian, who wrote the text of five of these stanzas on a separate piece of paper, crossed out the word 'now' and replaced it by 'world.' Thus the ending of the verses was changed to 'World, farewell and good night,' and assumed a new significance and beauty.

Philipp Emanuel Bach owned an oil-portrait[1] of his grandfather, *Johann Ambrosius*, the twin, who bore so striking a likeness to Johann Christoph. This portrait (Ill. VIII), which later became the property of the Berlin library, shows Ambrosius without the customary wig or the elaborate costume which appears in most portraits of the time. His camisole is open at the neck, and a coat is carelessly wrapped around his figure. His attitude is not stiff and ceremonious, but easy and natural, so as to give the impression that he has just made music in his workroom, through the window of which the Eisenach Wartburg is to be seen. The strong throat, the massive chin, and the bold fleshy nose, features his son Sebastian was to inherit, seem to proclaim the stubborn tenacity of the Bach clan. His shrewd eyes and dark hair complete the picture of a full-blooded, vigorous and somewhat earthy personality. It may well be imagined that the appearance of two such striking men who were absolutely alike was a 'subject of astonishment to everyone.'

Ambrosius started his musical career in the Erfurt musical band, taking over the work formerly done by his cousin, Johann Christian (7), who had gone to Eisenach to assist the town musician, Christoffel Schmidt. In 1667 Ambrosius was officially appointed, and now his thoughts turned

---

[1] It is likely that it was painted by an employee of the Eisenach court, perhaps by Johann David Herlicius, who made twelve engravings to a 'Neues vollständiges Gesangbuch' printed in 1673. Cf. Conrad Freyse, 'Eisenacher Dokumente um Sebastian Bach,' publications of *Neue Bach Gesellschaft*, 1933, and Fritz Rollberg, 'Johann Ambrosius Bach,' *BJ*, 1927.

to marriage. In the house of his uncle, Johann (4), he met Elisabeth
Lämmerhirt, who was a much younger half-sister of Johann's wife,
Hedwig.[1] She lived at 'The Three Roses' on Junkersand, a street in Erfurt
where all the Bachs were domiciled, and so Ambrosius and Elisabeth had
plenty of opportunity of seeing each other. Hardly a year after
Ambrosius' definite appointment, the wedding took place, and the
couple moved into a neighbouring house on Junkersand. The bridegroom
was 23, the bride one year older. Elisabeth probably could not bring
more than a modest dowry to Ambrosius, for her father was dead and in
the seven years of his illness most of the little fortune he had accumulated
had been spent.[2] But the Lämmerhirts still enjoyed a good social
standing—the Genealogy proudly describes Elisabeth as daughter of
Valentin, 'member of A Noble Council in Erfurt'—and other members
of the family were still well off. This is apparent from the legacies which
Elisabeth's brother, Tobias, subsequently bequeathed to his sister's
children.[3]

Young Ambrosius was not over-anxious to stay on in Erfurt, as his
cousin, Johann Christian (7), had returned from Eisenach bent on resuming his place in the Erfurt band. A chance to move away presented itself
when the Eisenach town musician, Christoffel Schmidt, died. Had
Christian not left Eisenach, he would probably have succeeded Schmidt,
who was his father-in-law. But as he had returned to Erfurt, the eyes of
the Eisenach authorities turned to another Bach. They invited Ambrosius
to give a trial performance at the *Georgenkirche*, where his cousin, the
great Johann Christoph (13), had been organist for the past six years.
Ambrosius appeared there on October 12, 1671,[4] and gave so excellent

---

[1] Hugo Lämmerhirt, *BJ*, 1925, sees in Elisabeth a niece of Hedwig. Ziller in 'J. H.
Buttstädt' contends that Elisabeth was a half-sister of Hedwig, an assumption upheld also
by Rollert, *l.c.*

[2] Cf. Walter Dieck, 'Die Beziehungen der Familie Bach zu Erfurt,' in 'Thür. Allg.
Ztg.,' 1935.

[3] The testament granting these legacies gives us some idea of the spiritual atmosphere
in which Elisabeth had grown up. This document, as the notary points out, was dictated
by Tobias, the uncle of Sebastian, in 'clearly audible words,' which makes it obvious that
the following powerful introduction is the old man's own: 'Both husband and wife commend their souls, when according to God's gracious will they shall be separated from their
mortal bodies, into the hands of God, their dearest heavenly Father, as the all-powerful
Creator of heaven and earth, and into those of His son, Jesus Christ, as their only
Redeemer and Giver of bliss, and into those of the Holy Ghost which in holy baptism hath
sanctified them unto eternal life; but their bodies they commend to the cool earth, which
is the mother of us all, to be buried in it according to Christian custom.'

[4] Emanuel Bach's contention in the Genealogy that the twins led similar lives is
confirmed by the fact that Johann Christoph (12) was also officially appointed in 1671.

an account of himself that even from the outset he was granted better terms than his predecessor. While Schmidt's yearly salary from the town had been only 28 fl., to which, of course, the *Accidentien* were added as the main source of income, Ambrosius got a yearly payment of 40 fl. 4 gr. 8 pf., plus free lodging for the first three years of his stay.[1] His duties were to play 'twice a day, at 10 in the morning, and 5 in the evening, with his four men on the tower of the town hall, and to perform at church on all holidays and Sundays before and after the morning and afternoon sermons, according to the Cantor's instructions.'

The new town musician certainly knew how to satisfy his superiors. A relationship developed that was utterly different from that under which his cousin, Johann Christoph, was suffering. A few months after his appointment Ambrosius petitioned Prince Johann Georg I of Eisenach, who had taken over the government soon after the new town musician started his work, to be allowed to brew a certain amount of ale tax free. When the Prince asked for the Council's opinion, the city fathers urged him to grant Ambrosius a privilege which his predecessor had also enjoyed, adding: 'The new *Hausmann* (town musician)[2] is not only conducting himself in a quiet and Christian way agreeable to everybody, but in addition he shows such outstanding qualifications in his profession that he can perform both *vocaliter* and *instrumentaliter* in church and in honourable gatherings in a manner we cannot remember ever to have witnessed in this place before.' This was of course sufficient for Ambrosius to get the requested permission. Shortly afterwards the Council suggested to the Prince that during periods of public mourning after the death of a member of the princely house, when instrumental music was forbidden at weddings, etc., the town musician should be compensated for the resulting loss of *Accidentien* by payment of one florin for each wedding. Again the argument ran like this: 'Such a compensation was granted to the former *Hausmann*; how much more is it deserved by the present most competent town musician!' The Prince agreed, and from a statement of account for 1672-73 we learn that Ambrosius was paid 20 fl. under this title. To be granted such a premium after only eighteen months' service was something unheard-of in the impecunious little *Residenz*. There is no doubt that Ambrosius was highly thought of by

---

[1] Cf. Stadtarchiv Eisenach B, XXV, CI, where the documents referring to Ambrosius, unless specifically mentioned, are to be found.

[2] Rollberg in 'Von den Eisenacher Stadtpfeifern,' Jena, 1932, claims that the expression *Hausmann* frequently used for the town musician points to his duties in the city house, i.e. the town hall. He was sometimes also called *Haustaube*, house-pigeon, because of his domicile in the city tower.

the very Council which had not a single word of appreciation for Johann Christoph Bach's outstanding contribution to Eisenach's musical life. In this the city fathers only echoed what the whole population felt. Two other contemporary appreciations relating to Ambrosius have been preserved. One is by a certain Georg Dressel, a carpenter, who wrote a chronicle of important events in the years 1648-73.[1] Dressel describes a festal Easter service, in which the Cantor, Schmidt, and the organist, Johann Christoph Bach, took part together with the town musician and his assistants. The chronicler's entire attention, however, is centred on brilliant Ambrosius, and he records: '1672 at Easter, when Prince Johann Georg and his spouse made their entry, the new *Hausmann* performed with organs, violins, singers, trumpets and kettledrums, as no Cantor or *Hausmann* has done as long as Eisenach stood.' A more indirect description of Ambrosius' achievements is supplied by a petition which his subsequent colleague, the Cantor Andreas Christian Dedekind, made after the town musician's premature death. He recommended a kinsman of Ambrosius, the town piper Christoph Hoffman of Suhl, for the position and remarked: 'Hoffmann has so assiduously worked on his music, that in addition to good violin playing, he has mastered the *cornetto*, *trombone*, *violone*, and especially the *trombetta*, and eventually may hope almost to equal Mr. Bach.'

It is obviously easier to fall under the spell of a gifted performer than to understand the new creations of a very original and profound composer. We therefore cannot be too surprised at the Council's preference for Ambrosius over his cousin, Johann Christoph, who, on the performing side, was badly handicapped by the defective instrument of St. George's which he generally used. Moreover artistic reasons were not the only ones urged in Ambrosius' favour; what weighed still more was his 'quiet and Christian' conduct. We hear nothing of debts, advances, or frequent changes of domicile. For the three years when the city paid the rent, Ambrosius lived in a house, which still stands to-day (Ill. IX), with the chief forester, Balthasar Schneider, who was godfather to the first of his tenant's children to be born in Eisenach.[2] Afterwards Ambrosius bought

---

[1] Cf. H. Helmbold, 'Bilder aus Eisenachs Vergangenheit,' II, Eisenach, 1928.

[2] This house (to-day Rittergasse 11, situated at the back of the present Bach-Museum) offers with its beautiful wood-carved façade a fine example of 17th-century architecture. It is the only house in Eisenach which can definitely be proved to have been the domicile of Ambrosius Bach, while the old tradition, claiming the house on 'Frauenplan 21,' housing the Bach-Museum, as Sebastian's birthplace, is not upheld by the thorough researches of Rollberg, Helmbold, and Kühn (the latter a Bach descendant himself). These experts ascertained through the study of tax assessments and other

2. Signatures of various Bach musicians (Caspar, Christoph, Heinrich, J. Christoph (13), J. Egidius, J. Nicolaus (9), J. Günther (15), J. Ambrosius, J. Christoph (12), J. Sebastian)

his own house, paying his tax regularly. It required a thrifty disposition to run a household as large as that of the town musician. Ambrosius' duties involved keeping at least two apprentices and two assistants; his mother-in-law and the half-witted sister stayed with him until they died;[1] and, finally, eight children grew up in the Bach household. Among them were Johann Christoph (22), christened in Erfurt on June 18, 1671; Johann Jakob (23), christened in Eisenach on February 11, 1682; and finally Johann Sebastian christened in Eisenach on March 23, 1685.[2] It is also probable that yet another Johann Christoph Bach (17), son of Johann Christian in Erfurt, who attended the Eisenach Latin school in 1683-84, stayed with the hospitable Ambrosius (cf. p. 97). To provide for all these called for excellent management, and apparently both Ambrosius and Elisabeth were much better qualified to cope with such problems than their cousins in Eisenach, the great Johann Christoph and his spouse, Elisabeth. It is significant that while Johann Christoph Bach the organist kept going only with the help of loans and advances, Ambrosius Bach the town musician was well enough off to give up the income derived from some of the extra-musical duties of the *Hausmann*. According to an account preserved, more than a quarter of Ambrosius' salary was withheld by the city fathers, as a deputy had to perform the following parts of the town musician's work: ringing the bell in the bell-tower as a time signal; ringing a certain bell intended to remind the people

contemporary documents that the house was owned at the time of Sebastian's birth by Heinrich Borstelmann, rector of the Latin school, while it was in nearby Lutherstrasse 35 that Ambrosius and his family lived in 1685. A heated controversy raged between these scholars on the one side and their opponents, H. A. Winkler and C. Freyse, curator of the Bach-Museum; a controversy which was ultimately stopped by the German Government, which was anxious to preserve the attraction of the Bach-Museum to tourists. But even if the claims as to the authenticity of the house on 'Frauenplan 21' as Sebastian's birthplace cannot be upheld, the Museum deserves our attention. The beautiful house is located in a part of Eisenach where Ambrosius actually lived, and as it dates from the right period, it gives a good idea of what Sebastian's birthplace may have looked like. On the other hand, the house on Lutherstrasse is of no interest, as nothing of the old structure has been preserved. In the last war the Bach-Museum was badly damaged through air attacks, but thanks to the help of American troops, the house was quickly restored with material taken from other contemporary buildings, and the work has been done so skilfully that even old friends of the Museum did not notice any change in it when they visited it after the war. Cf. the report of the Curator Conrad Freyse in *BJ*, 1940-48.

[1] Eva Barbara Lämmerhirt was buried in Eisenach in 1673; Dorothea Maria Bach in 1679.

[2] The other five children were Johann Balthasar (1673-91), Johann Jonas (1675-85), Maria Salome (b. 1677), Johanna Juditha (1680-86), Johann Nicolaus (b. 1683). The last one is not mentioned in the Eisenach church register, but Helmbold found his name in the school register and places him between Johann Jakob and Johann Sebastian.

that taxes were due on that day; and the yearly safety inspection of fire-places. Evidently Ambrosius was so much in demand for musical work that he could afford to lose this not inconsiderable amount. At times he even played at weddings in other towns; Cantor Dedekind reports, for instance, that he once performed at such an occasion at Ohrdruf together with Johann Pachelbel and with his kinsman, Christoph Hoffmann.[1] From 1677 onward Ambrosius also formed part of the newly established small band of Prince Johann Georg I, and got a yearly honorarium of 19 fl., 9 pf., plus a generous New Year's gift, which in 1679, for example, amounted to half the salary paid by the Prince.[2]

Taking all this into account, Ambrosius earned not more, perhaps even less, than his cousin. But not only was he a clever manager—a gift he was to pass on to his youngest son—he was more frugal in his ambitions. For instance, he did not burden himself with a costly schooling for his children, but thought rather of their musical training. The two sons, who reached maturity while their father was alive, were both apprenticed to musicians after they had finished with the third class of the Latin school. It will be remembered that Ambrosius' cousin, Johann Christoph, thought differently in this matter. The divergences in their outlook and in their financial status may have prevented the two families from becoming really friendly. It is significant that neither of the two Bachs appeared as godfather to the other's sons.[3] Ambrosius certainly had a high regard for his cousin's creative work, whereas Johann Christoph may have looked down on the town musician as merely a performer. For it seems that Ambrosius' composing, if he undertook any at all, was of no great importance. None of his descendants ever mentioned him as a creative artist, and not a line of music by him has been preserved. As he started a collection of compositions by other Bachs—an enterprise eagerly continued by Sebastian—it seems unlikely that he would have omitted his own works had there been any.

Altogether Ambrosius spent twenty-four years in Eisenach. When he had served there for a dozen years, he seriously considered a change. In Erfurt Johann Christian (7) and Johann Nikolaus Bach (9) died in 1682

---

[1] It may be that the three musicians gathered to celebrate the wedding of Ambrosius' eldest son, Johann Christoph, to Dorothea von Hof, which took place in Ohrdruf in October 1694. Pachelbel may have attended the wedding, as he was the bridegroom's teacher.

[2] Cf. Weimarer Archiv, Eisenacher Dienersachen No. 49, and Wartburg-Archiv (Rechnungen des fürstlichen Hauses).

[3] Johann Christoph once acted as a substitute at the christening of a daughter of Ambrosius, since the godfather, Johann Pachelbel, was detained in Erfurt.

from the plague, and while their brother, Johann Egidius (8) took over as director of the band, the positions of the two other Bachs had to be filled. The authorities remembered Ambrosius and invited him to return to Erfurt.[1] Ambrosius felt very much like accepting; he was ready for a change, and his wife may have urged him too, as she had many relatives living in Erfurt. First, however, his resignation had to be accepted by his Eisenach superiors. In April 1684 he addressed a lengthy petition to them in which he brought forth all the matters giving cause for complaint, mainly his bad financial status due to numerous periods of public mourning, the unwillingness of many citizens to pay the prescribed rates for wedding music, and the ever-recurring difficulties with the 'beer fiddlers' (cf. p. 16) which made him 'quite impatient and vexed.' Another reason for dissatisfaction, which Ambrosius did not see fit to mention in his petition, was a cut in the salary he received for his services at court. When after nineteen days no answer came, he urged a decision in a second petition, emphasizing his troubles with the 'beer fiddlers' who, according to regulation, were supposed to perform at weddings only with the special permission of, and on payment to, the town musician: 'I always have arguments with them, as they never care to accept my arrangements if it so happens that several weddings occur at the same time; one runs hither, the other thither, to get the preference, and I have nothing but trouble.' But poor Ambrosius had no luck. The Eisenach city fathers were too satisfied with their *Hausmann* to grant him the requested permission. Instead they wrote to the Erfurt authorities informing them of their determination to keep Ambrosius in their service and asking them to desist from further offers. Ambrosius had to stay on in Eisenach. It does not seem likely, however, that he took his defeat too hardly, once his first anger had cooled off. Somehow his complaints in the two petitions do not ring as true as the repeated desperate appeals of his organist cousin. Of course he would have liked to better his position, but after all he was not so badly off in Eisenach; for one thing, it had the great advantage of having been left untouched by the plague that had ravaged Erfurt in past years. Moreover his work at court became more interesting when in 1685 the versatile Daniel Eberlin again appeared in Eisenach and became conductor of the princely band. The size of the orchestra was increased and performances took place more frequently. Thus the town musician found a greater amount of employment at court, and Prince Johann Georg II, who took over the government in 1686, decided to cancel

---

[1] It is quite possible that the directorship was offered to Ambrosius, and only given to Egidius when Ambrosius was unable to accept, but this point cannot be decided as yet.

the cut in salary which his predecessor had seen fit to impose on Ambrosius.

There followed a pleasant time in the life of the town piper. His eldest son, Johann Christoph, who had studied in Erfurt with the great Johann Pachelbel and subsequently assisted his aged kinsman, Heinrich Bach, in Arnstadt, was appointed organist in the city of Ohrdruf,[1] a position he was to hold throughout his life. Besides experiencing the satisfaction of seeing the youth well established, the father had the joy of discovering the unusual talent of his youngest child. Ambrosius taught little Sebastian the violin and could not fail to be gladdened by the boy's response to his teaching.

Unfortunately this happy family life did not last long. In August 1693 Ambrosius suffered a grave loss, when his beloved twin brother, his second self, died in Arnstadt. Only a few months later yet another tragic event occurred with the sudden death of his dear wife, Elisabeth. While still reeling from the impact of these two shocks, the harassed widower had to keep the household going for his young sons, his apprentices and assistants. As his only daughter was just leaving home to marry an Erfurt citizen, and since for people of his social standing the engagement of a paid housekeeper was out of the question, there was only one solution open to Ambrosius: he had to marry again as speedily as possible. He chose an Arnstadt woman well known to the Bach family, Barbara Margarethe Keul, twice widowed, who had been married to his cousin, Johann Günther (cf. p. 22). The wedding took place in November 1694, half a year after Elisabeth's death. But though Ambrosius valiantly strove to continue his normal way of life, the two losses he had suffered undermined his health. Two months after the wedding he fell ill; on January 31, 1695, he received Holy Communion at home, and on February 24 he was buried. The happenings of the last months had necessitated much expenditure and there was little money left over for the widow and orphaned children. Barbara Margarethe endeavoured to make the best of a difficult situation. She wrote a spirited petition to the Council in which she cited the case of Ambrosius' twin brother in Arnstadt, whose position had been handled by the widow with the help of the assistants and apprentices for eighteen months, and asked for the same privilege. In this lengthy

---

[1] The appointment may have been secured through the recommendation of his Arnstadt uncle, Johann Christoph (12), whose wife came from Ohrdruf. Incidentally the young organist was not the first of the name to reside in Ohrdruf. The name of Bach is found among the Ohrdruf citizens as early as 1472. In 1564 and 1565 two girls by the name of Bach from Wechmar were married in Ohrdruf; they may well have been sisters or aunts of Veit Bach.

document she claimed that the Count of Schwarzburg-Arnstadt was most anxious to employ a Bach again, but 'as the good Lord had apparently dried up the whole clan of Bach musicians within a few years,[1] the best he could do was to engage the widow of a Bach.' Naturally Sebastian's stepmother could not foresee that what seemed to her the end was in fact the beginning of the most glorious phase in the history of the Bach family. Her pleadings to the Council were of no avail, however. The Eisenach city fathers, quickly forgetting their appreciation of Ambrosius' services, paid the widow only what was strictly and legally due to her, viz. the salary for one-and-a-half quarters. They engaged Johann Heinrich Halle from Göttingen as town musician, and Ambrosius' family had to leave. The widow returned to Arnstadt; the elder son, Johann Jakob, was to be apprenticed with the new *Hausmann*, and the younger one, Johann Sebastian, remained in the care of his eldest brother, Johann Christoph, organist at Ohrdruf.

[1] Actually the Count of Schwarzburg-Arnstadt had lost in 1692 the organist, Heinrich Bach; in 1693 the town musician, Johann Christoph Bach (12); in 1694 the organist of Gehren, Johann Michael Bach (14).

EPILOGUE

LOOKING back on the lives of the Bach musicians in the first hundred years of their professional service, we find a definite pattern established. Certain Bach centres were formed where the sons followed the father in office, and simultaneously various kinsmen were attracted as reinforcements. The largest group was assembled in Erfurt, where all three sons of Johannes Bach found work at certain times, and where many of their children were born. Arnstadt was hardly less important; it witnessed the activities of Heinrich and Christoph Bach, and of several sons. In Schweinfurt and Ohrdruf too, Bach musicians settled down, establishing a tradition to be upheld through several generations. Most significant of all, however, was Eisenach. Here lived the greatest Bach composer of the 17th century side by side with the man whose son was to bestow immortality on the clan.

After the Bachs had grown roots in certain towns and become an integral part of each town's musical life, a social rise took place. Instead of living as 'house-pigeons' in the city tower, they became house-owners. They took their wives from higher social ranks. While the wife of Johannes Bach was an innkeeper's daughter, and her sons, Johann and Heinrich, stayed strictly within their own sphere by marrying two daughters of Johann's master, the town piper of Suhl, Heinrich's sons were more ambitious. Two of them married daughters of an Arnstadt syndic, the third the daughter of the town's former mayor. Their cousin, Ambrosius, did just as well by choosing the daughter of an Erfurt Council member. It is also significant that many of the younger Bachs attended all the classes of the Latin school, and some aspired to the position of a learned Cantor.

To achieve all this during one of the hardest periods in German history required outstanding vitality and driving power. These the Bachs certainly possessed, and in addition they were endowed with a deep loyalty to the family which made them give each other unstinted help in critical situations. But even if there was no practical purpose involved, they loved getting together. At that time the family gatherings were instituted which Forkel, on information supplied by Emanuel Bach, described as follows:

'As it was impossible for them all to live in one place, they resolved at least to see each other once a year and fixed a certain day upon which they had all to appear at an appointed place. Even after the family had become much more numerous and first one and then another of the members had been obliged to settle outside Thuringia . . . they continued their annual meetings, which generally took place at Erfurt, Eisenach, or Arnstadt. Their amusements during the time of their meeting were entirely musical. As the company consisted wholly of cantors, organists, and town musicians who had all to do with the Church, the first thing they did . . . was to sing a chorale. From this pious commencement they proceeded to drolleries which often made a very great contrast with it. For now they sang popular songs, the contents of which were partly comic and partly naughty, all together and extempore, but in such a manner that the several parts thus extemporized made a kind of harmony together, the words, however, in every part being different. They called this . . . a quodlibet, and not only laughed heartily at it themselves, but excited an equally hearty and irresistible laughter in everyone that heard them.'

As artists the first Bachs worked almost exclusively for the Protestant Church. The substantial number of motets they produced shows their faithful adherence to the great traditions of the past. Judging from the works preserved, the realm of secular music was hardly discovered by these early masters. Their most daring advances into this unexplored territory consisted of occasional semi-sacred cantatas or a set of clavier variations on a dance theme. Real versatility was still lacking in the family.

The Bachs produced in this period a number of great talents. Johann, Heinrich, Georg Christoph, and particularly Johann Michael were all composers fully conversant with the style and technical innovations of the church music in their time. On a much higher level stood the work of Johann Christoph (13), who might be considered the first genius of the family. His artistic independence, his emotional fervour, and his genuine sense of humour secure him a unique position among the composers of his period. It is by no means accidental that works by Johann Christoph and by his father, Heinrich Bach, were to be found in a collection of choral music established in Lüneburg some 200 miles north of Thuringia.

Johann Sebastian, a true Bach in every respect, faithfully and proudly collected the works of his forebears. He studied and performed them and, as a matter of course, he followed in his own compositions the path the older Bachs had shown him.

VIII. Johann Ambrosius Bach, father of Sebastian

IX. The house, 11, Rittergasse (centre of picture), in which J. Ambrosius Bach lived during the first three years of his stay in Eisenach

PART II

EXPANSION
AND
CULMINATION
(1700-1750)

F

INTRODUCTION:
PARTICULARISM AND UNIVERSALISM IN GERMANY

A s a result of the Thirty Years War in Germany, the central government had practically ceased to exist. The ruling family of the Hapsburgs was far more concerned with increasing its private possessions than with the common good of the *Reich*; Swedish and French influences were strong within Germany; and no attempt was made to pursue a unified national policy.

Instead of a central government, more than three hundred independent princes reigned in Germany. Although the domain of some of them measured no more than a few square miles, they considered themselves little short of Caesars. They were absolute rulers within the borders of their states, aping the characteristic maxim of their great model, Louis XIV, *l'état, c'est moi*. Each of them wished to build his own Versailles and to organize festivities that would emulate in magnificence and splendour those of the *roi soleil*. This attitude of absolutism finds perfect expression in the monument to the Great Elector of Brandenburg erected in the first decade of the 18th century by Andreas Schlüter and his pupils. In lonely grandeur, like a Roman Emperor, with majestically extended arm, the Prince sits on his passive horse, while at his feet four slaves are shown writhing in their chains. For the Baroque observer, the figures of these slaves were essential as symbols of the sovereign's unlimited power.

The funds for the traditional displays of lavishness were raised mainly by excessive taxation of the peasants, who formed more than two-thirds of the population and who were kept in a condition little short of slavery. Sometimes even worse methods were employed to fill the empty treasuries. The landgrave of Hesse and other German princes made millions of thalers by selling their subjects to the British and Dutch who needed soldiers for their foreign wars. In America, too, German mercenaries were employed in an attempt to suppress the United Colonies' movement towards independence. The princes considered themselves particularly fortunate if these men were killed in action, since an extra premium was paid for those who failed to return.

Not only the sovereign but the common man, too, was desirous of being seen in oversized dimensions. The successful merchant and burgher tried to compete in lavishness with the Prince. In Munich, two artists—

the brothers Cosmas and Egid Asam—built a church next to their residence almost entirely at their own expense; it was small in dimensions, but as resplendent as a cathedral in its display of magnificent pictures and gilded statues. The rich decorated the walls of their houses with paintings simulating vistas of wide colonnades and formal gardens; while clouds painted on the ceilings of ballrooms and even vestibules seemed to lead the glance right into heaven. The formal, full-bottomed wig with curls which men were pleased to wear, and the pompous crinoline of the women were intended to add dignity to the wearers.

Particularism flourished in the Christian Church too. Besides being subjected to merciless attacks from the ranks of freethinkers, the Church was also divided within itself. Catholicism, tenaciously struggling to regain the territory it lost during the Reformation, was confronted by a divided force of Lutherans and Calvinists, whose members attacked each other with the same bitterness as they displayed in their fight against the Pope. A deep cleavage of opinion separated even the members of the Lutheran faith. While the Orthodox group adhered with stubborn and narrow-minded bigotry to the letter of the Word, and refused to admit the slightest deviation from petrified traditions, the 'Pietists' claimed the rights of the heart and the necessity for an individual approach to the faith. As in other doctrinal feuds, the strife between the two factions was conducted with the utmost violence and no mercy from either side was asked or granted.

It cannot surprise us that the detrimental effects and dangers of such excessive particularism were keenly felt, and that everywhere the best thinkers were striving to counteract it. In the field of religion, attempts were made to reconcile the Calvinistic and Lutheran Churches, and to unite them in a new 'Evangelical-Apostolic' creed. Some wise men even tried to regard Catholics and Protestants not as enemies engaged in a deadly struggle, but rather as brothers able to reconcile their disagreements. Karl Ludwig, the Calvinist Elector of the Palatinate, built in Mannheim the famous 'Peace Church,' to be used by all three creeds, Catholics, Lutherans, and Calvinists alike. Although none of these endeavours met with any tangible success, they were nevertheless of vital significance, since they paved the way for the idea of religious tolerance which was to become of fundamental importance in the second half of the century. Whereas in the 16th century each religious party had attempted to force its ideas on the others, towards the end of the 17th it was gradually realized that each faction would have to make concessions in order to reach a reconciliation of the different points of view. When agreement seemed to be impossible, even on this basis, the best minds of the 18th century came to the conclusion that it was the duty of the different denominations to preserve their idiosyncrasies, while respecting and tolerating those of other religious sects.

The existence of similar urges towards unification may be detected in the fields of political and philosophical thought. Leibniz, the greatest German thinker at the close of the 17th century, dreamed of a sign language, on an algebraic basis, which would enable all nations to understand each other. This utopian idea took a practical turn in the founding of academies in Berlin, and later also in St. Petersburg, with the object of promoting the study and knowledge of science, and with it a mutual understanding between nations. The new academies were based on the conviction that human society can be better served by co-operation and mutual help than by individual efforts.

Leibniz's philosophy, which was of the greatest importance to the spiritual life of the 18th century, was a monumental attempt to view the universe as a harmonious structure, governed in all its aspects by identical laws. According to his ideas, 'monads' are the constituent elements of all things. They are not dead objects, but living forces, imbued with a tendency to act. Every 'monad' is a microcosm, reflecting in 'pre-established harmony' the ideas of the universe, although with immensely varying degrees of perfection. The lowest monads, such as those contained in metals and stones, have only dim and vague notions, while the most exalted monad, God, is endowed with completely distinct and lucid perceptions. Man stands somewhere in the middle of this ladder; his imperfect senses place him among the lower monads, but his reasoning mind advances him towards the highest one. Thus Leibniz succeeded in creating a cosmology into which every element, even the least significant, fits harmoniously.

In the fine arts a certain co-ordination of styles was also achieved, although not by conscious effort. It was rather the consequence of conditions altogether hostile to the arts. As a result of the Thirty Years War there existed a kind of artistic vacuum in Germany, until the need for new forms and ideas was satisfied by the neighbouring countries. The Catholic South of Germany, and in particular Austria, was stimulated by Italian architecture and painting; and in the North the strict Dutch style influenced sculpture and architecture. Finally, during the 18th century, French forms, penetrating the whole of Central Europe from the West, invaded every type of art. Thus Germany became a meeting-ground for the artistic products of different nations.

In the field of music a movement towards unification was as much in evidence as it was in any other branch of spiritual life. In distinction to the fine arts, the bond connecting the 16th and 17th centuries had never been completely severed. The German Renaissance tradition of a sturdy poly-phonic texture was carried over into the Baroque period, and the develop-ment of an interesting harmonic basis added substance and solidity to the contrapuntal structure. To these specifically Central European character-istics there were added numerous other features, which had been imported both from the South and West. Italy contributed the sensual charm and dramatic power of its melodies, the great art of *bel canto* and of singing on stringed instruments, and the *stile concertato* with its competitive employ-ment of choruses of diverse character. It also gave German music the concerto, with one or more solo instruments, and the 'trio sonata' for two melody instruments and figured bass. France furnished the technique of training and equipping an orchestra, as well as the form of the 'over-ture,' consisting of a slow introduction, a substantial fast fugue, and a deliberate epilogue. She also provided impressive achievements in the field of harpsichord composition, the form of the dance suite, and the idea of programme music. There were composers in Germany, such as Christoph Graupner, who followed Italian models; others, like J. K. Ferdinand Fischer, came under the influence of French forms; a third group headed by the great organist, Johann Pachelbel, tried to achieve artistic unity within Germany itself by introducing the South-German virtuosity into the Northern part of the *Reich*. Of even greater significance was the contribution of those men who felt the need for a fusion of Western, Southern, and Central European music. The Austrian Georg Muffat, for instance, studied first in Paris with Lully and later in Rome with Corelli. The results of this diversified instruction can easily be detected in Muffat's orchestra suites, his *concerti grossi* and trio sonatas. Other composers too, like Johann Friedrich Fasch and the versatile Georg Philipp Telemann, were equally at home in the national styles of the West and the South. However, it must be strongly emphasized that these men never imitated their models mechanically. By a slow process of assi-milation, and always conscious of their own polyphonic and harmonic heritage, German composers gradually evolved the strongly unified style that is characteristic of the 'late Baroque' era (1700-1750) in their country.

The Bach family, whose home lay in the very heart of Germany, played an important part in this movement. Its central offspring, Johann Sebastian, became the greatest force in this struggle to achieve musical unification.

THE JENA AND THE MÜHLHAUSEN BACH
(JOHANN NICOLAUS AND JOHANN FRIEDRICH BACH)

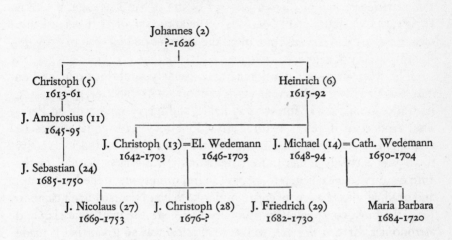

Johannes (2)
?-1626

Christoph (5)
1613-61

Heinrich (6)
1615-92

J. Ambrosius (11)
1645-95

J. Christoph (13)=El. Wedemann
1642-1703   1646-1703

J. Michael (14)=Cath. Wedemann
1648-94   1650-1704

J. Sebastian (24)
1685-1750

J. Nicolaus (27)
1669-1753

J. Christoph (28)
1676-?

J. Friedrich (29)
1682-1730

Maria Barbara
1684-1720

IT will be remembered that the sons of the great Johann Christoph (13) were given a good education, and that the eldest, Johann Nicolaus (27),[1] christened October 17, 1669, even had the opportunity of attending the University of Jena after leaving the Eisenach Latin school in 1689. This was a luxury which Johann Christoph, constantly harassed by financial worries, could ill afford, but somehow he managed it. Possibly some help was given by the Jena organist, Johann Magnus Knüpfer,[2] who had been Johann Christoph's pupil and may have been glad to have young Nicolaus to help him in the discharge of his duties. Although poverty must have excluded the youth from most of the students' favourite pastimes, it was still a wise move for him to go to Jena. The talented and versatile musician quickly made friends, and he was so well thought of that in 1695 he was given the position of town organist and music teacher at the University.

By the time Nicolaus, at the age of 26, received his permanent appoint-

[1] He acquired the name of Nicolaus, rather infrequently chosen among the Bachs, from his godfather, the court organist, Nicolaus Kerner, of Gotha. Another godfather was his kinsman, Johann Christoph Hoffmann from Suhl (cf. p. 64).

[2] Knüpfer was the son of Sebastian Knüpfer, Thomas Cantor at Leipzig from 1657 to 1676. The fact that the Thomas Cantor sent his son to Eisenach for his musical training proves the high esteem enjoyed by Johann Christoph Bach. Cf. H. A. Winkler, 'Neues über den Jenaer Bach,' in 'Jenaische Zeitung,' 1933.

ment, he had seen much more of the world than his father had. An opportunity rare indeed among the Bachs had come his way when a young friend, Georg v. Bertuch (incidentally, a student of Daniel Eberlin, the former Eisenach conductor), had invited him to travel to Italy. Bertuch had been forced to give up his plan just when they arrived at the Italian border, but Nicolaus had continued. Many benefits were derived from this experience, one of them a mastery of the Italian language, which is apparent in an album-leaf [1] Nicolaus wrote at the age of 75 in remarkably clear handwriting. Yet, in spite of all the beauties he had seen in Italy, he found Jena a good place to live in.

The town's site was considered an extremely salubrious one, and an enthusiastic visitor had gone so far as to compare its 'fresh air, good water, high mountains, shady forests, gay fields, and merry vineyards' to Paradise. And even if Jena's natural attractions may with equal justice be attributed to lovely Eisenach, the mental atmosphere in the University town was certainly much more stimulating. In the later decades of the 17th century science began to assume an important role in the University, and gradually to change its entire outlook. When Nicolaus Bach came to Jena, the most conspicuous personality there was the mathematician and astronomer, Erhard Weigel, whose reputation was so great that it made young Leibniz move from Leipzig to Jena for his studies. The house that Weigel built was a source of incredulous astonishment to every visitor to Jena. Nicolaus Bach, who was himself tremendously interested in technical inventions, must have loved being carried upstairs by block-and-tackle, seeing water pumped up by a hydraulic engine to all the storeys of the unusually high building (something like a 17th-century skyscraper), and most of all, watching the Professor's ingenious 'Cellar-maid' at work. By this device, when water was poured into a funnel in the living-room and a nearby faucet was opened, real wine came tumbling out, brought right up from the cool cellar. Not only in science, but also in various other domains of knowledge there was much activity to be observed in Jena; and it is significant that the tiny town boasted no less than nine printing firms and eight book-stores. The exceeding roughness of the students' manners was probably accepted as a matter of course by the organist. Being a Bach, for whom belligerency was something like a clan-attribute, he may even have enjoyed the ever-recurring fights and duels between students. Rowdiness also prevailed in the 'Collegium Musicum,' a students' organization for the performance of music which flourished in Jena from the time of the 16th century. On one occasion tempers rose so

[1] Preserved in the Manfred Gorke Collection, now in Leipzig.

high that a horn and a viol were broken on the body of the director.[1] If this incident occurred during the conductorship of Nicolaus Bach, he probably gave back as much as he received. It is also unlikely that he minded the general heavy drinking, a custom sanctioned even by the medicos, who pronounced that 'the city's dry air made imperative a constant humectation of the throat.'

A few years after receiving his appointment, Nicolaus had the chance of a change in his work. Both his father and his mother died in 1703 and Nicolaus, as the eldest son, was anxious to help his younger brothers, especially Johann Christoph (28). His father had wanted the latter to succeed him as Eisenach's city organist, but as Johann Christoph was then in Lübeck, probably to hear Buxtehude, just as his cousin Sebastian was to do two years later, Nicolaus made the application on his brother's behalf. He informed the authorities that Johann Christoph was hastening back to Eisenach to give a trial performance, and stressed the importance of having the work on the organ of St. George's Church, in which his father had been so deeply concerned (cf. p. 36), concluded under the supervision of a member of the family. If the city fathers found young Johann Christoph too inexperienced, he, Nicolaus, would be glad to work for the time being until the authorities considered the young man ready to assume the duties of the appointment.[2] In a second petition Nicolaus mentioned that Prince Johann Wilhelm of Eisenach was favourable to this suggestion. But it was all to no avail. The City Council was definitely not interested in the former organist's young namesake, and offered the position to Nicolaus himself, who had proved his ability at Jena and, incidentally, given an excellent trial performance in Eisenach. Nicolaus declined, however, feeling averse to leaving the University town, especially as he was just trying to induce the city authorities to build a new organ. In this he followed closely in his father's footsteps. Not only did he recommend the organ builder, Georg Christoph Stertzing, who had been employed for Eisenach's *Georgenkirche*, but he also urged the Council, in spite of low funds in the treasury, to plan a first-rate instrument. He felt sure the citizens would welcome the ambitious project as a means of expressing their gratitude for the privilege of living in Jena. 'It is hardly conceivable,' he wrote, 'that infectious diseases may spread in

---

[1] Cf. Fritz Stein in 'Die Musik,' 1912.

[2] The application is somewhat vague at this point, probably on purpose. Rollberg in 'Jenaische Zeitung,' 1933, assumes from it that Nicolaus was willing to resign in Jena. It seems more likely, however, that he planned to engage a substitute in Jena who would do his work until he could entrust the work in Eisenach to his brother.

this city; one knows of no real war trouble here; good food, easily obtainable, is not lacking; and who could enumerate all the benefits which God hath granted this town above others.' Nicolaus was as persuasive as his father had been for a similar purpose. An outstanding organ of 44 voices with 3 manuals and pedal was erected which was to serve Jena up to the 20th century, and Nicolaus could proudly claim in 1708 that 'many organists came to Jena merely for the organ's sake, and left the town quite contented and with amazement.'

The city organist's consummate skill in everything pertaining to the organ made the University authorities invite him subsequently to take charge of their own *Kollegienkirche* too. The instruction of the University, dated December 12, 1719, is preserved, and we see that Nicolaus was to play the organ on Sundays and holidays in the mornings and afternoons, as well as at *actibus academicis*; that he was expected to produce 'fine music' on high feast-days and other occasions of thanksgiving, and to tune his instrument and attend to minor repairs.

Nicolaus carried out all these duties in both churches up to the age of 80, when, after an illness, he was forced to look for a substitute. Unfortunately he was not destined to see one of his sons take over his work. In decided contrast to his own robust health, his offspring showed a sad lack of vitality and resiliency. Of the six children from his first marriage, contracted in 1697, only a single daughter survived early infancy, and she too died unmarried a few years before her father. The four children which a second wife bore him were healthier; but there was only one son among them and he died at the age of 21 as a student of philosophy. Nor was Nicolaus granted the joy of seeing one of his grandchildren grow into a musician likely to continue the family tradition. None of his daughters married young, and the only wedding in the family that he witnessed took place three weeks before his death. So Nicolaus chose as his substitute a certain Johann Heinrich Möller, a student of theology, who helped him for five years and, on the organist's death in 1754, became Bach's successor; whereupon he conformed to tradition by marrying in 1757 his predecessor's youngest daughter. But this couple, too, was not destined to carry on the Bach heritage. Their first son died as an infant; the mother passed on while giving birth to a second son; and the latter was run over and fatally injured by a carriage at the age of six. Another of Nicolaus' daughters became a widow after five weeks of married life, and the third had only one daughter, who died unwedded at the age of 32. Thus there was no progeny to inherit the vigour and versatility of the 'Jena Bach.'

If Nicolaus' private life was full of sorrow and disappointment, he found an antidote in ceaseless industry in the most variegated fields. Apart from his work in the two Jena churches and his participation in the 'Collegium Musicum,' Nicolaus devoted much time to teaching, for which, like his cousin Sebastian, he seems to have had a definite bent. Many young musicians came to Jena to study with him, among them the writer and organist, Jakob Adlung, and the lutanist, Ernst Gottlieb Baron. Bach was also most successful as a craftsman. Like his uncle, Johann Michael (14), by whom he had probably been trained, he was greatly interested and very proficient in the construction of musical instruments, delighting in planning various improvements. The harpsichords which he constructed were equipped with a special device invented by him. This enabled the player to select and combine the various registers by simply sliding the keyboard forwards or backwards, instead of using the traditional stop-buttons. Adlung seemed to think very highly of this invention, since he described it in great detail in his 'Musica Mechanica Organoedi.'[1] Nicolaus Bach was also famous for his *Lautenwerk*, which was meant to revive the diminishing interest in the lute by providing the instrument with a keyboard. The result was a kind of harpsichord using gut-strings of a length equal to those found on a lute. Nicolaus also added a lower register, so that his *Lautenwerk* included the compasses of the larger theorbo. When the inventor played this instrument, he 'deceived,' according to Adlung, 'the best lutanist; and as long as this man did not see the *Lautenwerk*, he would have taken his oath that it was an ordinary lute.'[2] The scholar further states that Nicolaus' *Lautenwerk* and his harpsichords were both easy to play . . . and accordingly, quite substantial amounts of money were paid for them. 'Herr Bach was given 60 Reichsthalers for one with three manuals (a terrific amount considering the prices which are paid to-day!).' When in 1706 the new organ was built in the *Stadtkirche*, Nicolaus supervised the construction 'down to the minutest detail.'[3] He also invented little gadgets such as a counterweight filled with sand to facilitate the action of the organ bellows. In order to improve the tone of organs he developed a stopped pipe ending in a long cylinder that could be inserted more or less deeply into the pipe, thus changing its pitch. By marking on this cylinder the intervals of the tempered scale, Nicolaus hoped to have designed a reliable tool for the tuning of organs. However, he did not carry his theoretical speculations too far. When Johann Georg Neidhardt, the champion of the 'well-

[1] Berlin, 1768, II, pp. 108-9.
[2] 'Musica Mechanica Organoedi,' II, p. 137.
[3] Adlung, *ibid.*, I, pp. 244-5.

tempered' system, offered to tune a register of stopped organ pipes with the help of a monochord (an acoustical instrument with a single string), Nicolaus challenged this method by tuning on the same organ a set of stopped pipes solely by ear. He was very pleased indeed when the result of his work sounded much better than that of the learned scholar.[1]

Nicolaus' brother, *Johann Friedrich* (29), was 21 when his parents died. He thereupon left the Latin school; he had been attending the first class, apparently with fine success, as the school authorities praised his *ingenium bonum* (good intellect). It seems likely that Nicolaus took care of him, having him attend the University of Jena and giving him musical instruction, and in return Friedrich helped the elder brother in his various duties. Anyway it was as a *studiosus* that Friedrich was described to the City Council of Mühlhausen, when Johann Sebastian Bach suggested that his cousin should succeed him in the position of organist at St. Blasius, which he was giving up in order to move to Weimar. Sebastian's recommendation had great influence with the city fathers. Moreover, Friedrich Bach was on his mother's side related with Councillor Bellstedt,[2] who had also been instrumental in securing Sebastian Bach's services. Thus *studiosus* Bach received the appointment, although at a lower salary than his cousin, and for twenty-two years, up to his death in 1730, he remained at his post in St. Blasius. Very little is known about his activities there; we only have a report that he, like his brother and his father, took a great interest in the reconstruction of an organ which was carried out under his direction. We may assume that he got on well with his superiors, for we find in the contemporary files no mention of any differences, such as those the Eisenach archives preserve in great numbers with regard to Friedrich's father. The lack of any evidence in the matter seems to disprove the report perpetuated in Gerber's Dictionary that Johann Friedrich Bach wasted his great talent through his predilection for drinking, which eventually made him unable to discharge his duties in a sober state. Johann Nikolaus Gerber claims to have heard this tale from his father, who as a youth had attended the Latin school at Mühlhausen and met Friedrich Bach there, learning much about the organ from him. Probably the older Gerber's memory was not quite reliable on this point; for we cannot imagine that the Mühlhausen Council, which

[1] Adlung, 'Anleitung zur Musikalischen Gelehrsamkeit,' Erfurt, 1758, p. 311.

[2] A brother of Councillor Bellstedt was city clerk in Arnstadt and married to a Wedemann girl. Friedrich's mother was also born a Wedemann, and so was Maria Barbara Bach's mother. Thus Friedrich Bach was both on his father's and his mother's side a cousin of Maria Barbara Bach.

always showed itself to be most exacting, should have tolerated a drunken church employee for twenty-two years, and that not a single reprimand of the organist should be recorded in the city archives.[1]

Friedrich married late in life, at the age of 40. When his wife died four years later, he concluded a second union; but neither marriage produced any offspring. Thus, not through this son either was the heritage from the great Johann Christoph destined to be handed on to the later generations.

That he was a composer worthy of the name of Bach seems to be revealed by an organ fugue in g, which Max Seiffert found in a manuscript of organ fugues by various masters handed down by the Leipzig organist, Johann Andreas Drobs.[2] Seiffert characterizes Friedrich's fugue as one of the best pieces written by any Bach before Sebastian. The author has failed to trace this composition, or any other work by the Mühlhausen organist, and was thus unable to pierce the darkness surrounding the creative work of Johann Friedrich Bach.

THE MUSIC OF JOHANN NICOLAUS BACH

Friedrich's brother, Nicolaus, was no less versatile as a composer than he was as a craftsman. Although only a few of his works have been preserved, they reveal an artistic personality worthy of his great father. There is but little that can be said about his activities as an instrumental composer. Adlung mentions that he wrote 'several suites,' but none of them has so far come to light. A brief *bicinium* (two-part composition) for the organ on *Nun freut euch, lieben Christen G'mein* (Now rejoice, dear Christian community) is influenced by similar works by Johann Pachelbel. Greater importance, however, attaches to a *Kyrie* and *Gloria*, a short Mass as it may be called, which was probably written in 1716,[3] for two violins,

[1] Cf. Georg Thiele, 'Die Familie Bach in Mühlhausen,' Mühlhausen, 1921.

[2] Cf. *BJ*, 1907.

[3] A manuscript of the work (which was in 1939 in the possession of Breitkopf & Härtel, Leipzig) is dated 'Meiningen, September 16, 1716.' Neither Spitta's theory (*l.c.*, I, p. 130) that it may have been written by Johann Ludwig Bach, nor the assumption of the catalogue of the archives of Breitkopf & Härtel (Leipzig, 1925, p. 2, No. 8) that it is a manuscript by Sebastian Bach, can be upheld. The handwriting shows strong similarities to that of Nicolaus' Italian album-leaf (cf. p. 88) and it seems likely, therefore, that it represents an autograph by the Jena composer (cf. Winkler, *l.c.*). Perhaps Nicolaus had come to Meiningen to deliver an instrument of his construction and gave the score of the Mass to his kinsman, Johann Ludwig Bach, on this occasion. A second manuscript of the Mass has the date 1734; apparently the copy was written in this year.

two violas, mixed chorus, basses, and continuo. This composition clearly reveals the influence that the trip to Italy had exercised on Nicolaus. The treatment of the voices and instruments, the melodic lines, particularly in the *Christe eleison*, the brief fugue of the second *Kyrie* leading after a short development to a completely homophonic section: these can easily be traced to North Italian melodies and particularly to sacred music by Caldara and Lotti. Nevertheless Nicolaus' work, using as its text two sections from the Ordinary of the Latin Mass, fits perfectly into the spirit and the liturgy of the German Lutheran Church. The composer deals with the *Gloria* as though it were a chorale motet, employing as a *cantus firmus* in long notes the melody of the hymn *Allein Gott in der Höh'* (To God alone on High be praise), which in the Protestant liturgy replaces the *Gloria* of the Mass. Thus he combines in a single composition both the Protestant and Catholic versions of the same text. Such a procedure was not unusual in the Bach family. Sebastian himself in his short Mass in F employs the hymn *Christe, du Lamm Gottes* (Christ, Thou Lamb of God) as a *cantus firmus*; and his pupil Johann Ernst Bach (34) writes a *Kyrie* and *Gloria*, introducing the chorale *Es woll uns Gott gnädig sein* (God have mercy on us). Similar instances may be detected even in the works of Sebastian's Leipzig predecessor, Kuhnau, and in compositions by Zachau and Telemann.

The brief *Kyrie* of Nicolaus' Mass, consisting of the traditional three sections, makes an effective preparation for the more elaborate *Gloria*. In the latter, each of its four sections employs one verse of the chorale as a *cantus firmus*, sung by a mezzo-soprano, thus providing the fifth vocal part of the composition. The dramatic contrast between the quiet long notes of the hymn tune and the fast-moving, agitated setting of the Mass text is strengthened by the simultaneous use of two languages: German for the chorale, Latin for the Ordinary. No doubt the introduction of their native tongue into the Latin original made the Lutheran congregation fully aware that the Popish text had completely become their property.[1] To avoid the inevitable monotony resulting from four statements of the

---

[1] Spitta's idea (*l.c.*) that the *cantus firmus* was originally meant for instruments and not for voices does not seem justified, since he subconsciously applies Johann Sebastian's attitude to the work of Nicolaus. For the Jena composer, Italian and German, Catholic and Protestant, were two excitingly opposed spheres which he tried to combine to the best of his ability; for the Leipzig master they formed an organic unit, the elements of which did not present any disturbing contradictions. The slight difficulty that the range of the soprano voice in the mixed quartet is usually higher than that in the *cantus firmus* may be easily overcome by giving the hymn tune to a larger group of singers, so as to make it always clearly audible.

same *cantus firmus* melody, Nicolaus changes its rhythm from the common to triple time in the first section, *Gloria in excelsis Deo*, and the fourth section, *Quoniam tu solus Sanctus*. This fourth section also substitutes four violas for the ordinary combination of two violins and two violas. The return of the violins in the coda provides the impressive free double fugue of the *Cum Sancto Spiritu* with an element of additional brilliance.

There is (through the absence of the *cantus firmus*) a stylistic relation between introduction and coda, a rhythmic relation between the first and fourth sections, and a melodic link between the introduction and the second section. Only the third section, *Domine, fili unigenite*, modulating effectively from the predominant key of G to b at the words *miserere nobis*, preserves the independence of a somewhat contrasting middle part. It is deeply regrettable that this vigorous and exciting piece is the only product of Nicolaus' church music that has so far come to light.

The Jena composer's second large work is as different from this Mass as two compositions by the same man can possibly be. It is a burlesque cantata of the kind known to us from Sebastian's 'Peasant Cantata,' a work that might equally well be performed on the stage as in the concert hall. *Der Jenaische Wein- und Bierrufer* (The Jena wine and beer crier) dramatizes a little farce taken from student life in Jena. Two timid young 'foxes' (the nickname for inexperienced freshmen), Monsieur Peter and Monsieur Clemon, come from their little home-town to Jena, where they put up at the inn of their fellow countryman, Monsieur Caspar. The publican is advising them in a rather patronizing way how to behave, when their conversation is interrupted by the appearance of the wine and beer crier, Johannes, who announces the opening of a fresh cask in a neighbouring tavern. Urged on by the innkeeper, the two boys begin to tease the old man, who without the slightest hesitation repays them in kind. The students employ quite a few foul names, and at last an abusive term so enrages their victim that he threatens to complain to the President of the University. This intimidates the youths and they leave, singing a final aria in praise of Jena, in which the publican joins.[1] The work, which was probably written for the 'Collegium Musicum,' makes ample use of the student jargon with which Nicolaus was naturally fully conversant; and it reveals the composer as not averse from the occasional use of gross and vulgar jokes, a tendency he possessed in common with other members

[1] The new edition of the work by Fritz Stein calls for Johannes, also, to sing in the final number. This is both dramatically and musically wrong. The crier is far too angry to fall in with the students' song, and the composer did not provide any part for him.

of his clan. The wine and beer crier, Johannes, is by no means a character invented by Bach. As early as 1681 the 'wine and beer crier who is also used as a nightwatchman and lives in the Johannisturm' is mentioned in a description of Jena.[1] This functionary held yet a third job; on Sundays and festival days he operated the bellows for the organist. Nicolaus therefore had a good chance of studying his eccentricities at close range, especially since the same individual, whose real name was Hans Michael Vater, occupied the position from 1724 to 1743. It seems probable that the organist's humorous satire was aimed at Vater and was written during the latter's term of office.

The music to this burlesque is of the simplest kind, very similar to the plain *Singspiele* of the contemporary Hamburg opera. The minute orchestra of two violins and basso continuo, which enlivens the musical texture by gay little accompanying figures (*Ex.* 17), the plain folksong-

Ex. 17

like melodies, the absence of any overture or complicated vocal forms, the use of singers who for most of the time are heard only in *secco* recitatives or in simple arias: all this shows that some of the spirit of the new comic opera had found its way into Bach's work. There are only two ensemble numbers in this score: a gay duet at the beginning, and the charming trio at the end. The main attraction of the remaining numbers is furnished by the composer's art of humorous characterization. There are the students, alternately timid and insolent; the pompous crier, who one moment praises his wares in a majestic manner and then in the same breath addresses his opponents with the most vulgar invective; and finally, the innkeeper who pretends to be very superior but is at the bottom of the whole mischief. Here we see the dramatic talent revealed in the compositions of Johann Christoph Bach coming to full blossom in the work of his son.

[1] Cf. Adr. Beier, 'Architectus Jenaensis,' 1681

x. Johann Ludwig Bach. Pastel by Gottlieb Friedrich Bach

XI. J. Ludwig Bach's Cantata 'Gott ist unser Zuversicht' in the hand of J. Sebastian Bach. In order to make best use of the expensive paper Sebastian starts the following aria on the bottom of the page although the first chorus is not yet finished

THE DESCENDANTS OF JOHANN BACH
(JOHANN CHRISTOPH (17) AND JOHANN BERNHARD BACH)

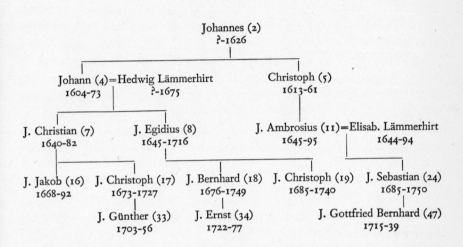

THE Genealogy mentions four grandsons of the Erfurt town musician, Johann Bach. One of them, Johann Jakob, was assistant to Ambrosius Bach, in whose house he died at Eisenach aged 24. Jakob's younger brother, *Johann Christoph* (17), born in 1673, also seems to have stayed with the hospitable Ambrosius for a short time after his father's death, for the register of the Eisenach Latin school mentions him as a pupil in 1683-1684. How he obtained his further education is not known; but he must have been ambitious and very able, since the orphaned youth, besides receiving the musical training traditional in the family, managed to study Theology. Thanks to these double qualifications he found a position as Cantor in a village near Erfurt, exchanging it in 1698 for a similar one in Gehren, where an uncle, the late Johann Michael (cf. p. 38), had been very successful as an organist and town clerk. Unfortunately Johann Christoph's life in the little community was very different from that of his kinsman. Poor and very irregular payments together with attacks from a hostile superior (who accused the Cantor, for instance, of using dance motives in his church music[1]) made up the tenor of his existence.

[1] Cf. Wiegand, 'Die Arnstädter Bache,' in 'J. S. Bach und seine Verwandten in Arnstadt,' 1950.

Since the stubbornness and belligerence of the Bachs were very strongly developed in the Gehren Cantor, he fought back violently, with the result that his existence was a very unhappy one. Yet he stayed on at Gehren for twenty-nine years, until 1727 when he was felled by a sudden illness. His three sons, however, were anxious to leave the uncongenial town. Two served as musicians in Sondershausen, where they died at an early age; the third, Johann Günther (33), whom Sebastian praised as a good tenor, became a schoolmaster in Erfurt, working at the same time with the town musicians.

Much more satisfactory were the careers of two other grandsons of Johann, children of Johann Egidius. The younger one, another Johann Christoph (19), born in the same year as Sebastian, followed his father as director of the Erfurt town musicians, and held the position up to his death in 1740. The elder one, *Johann Bernhard* (18), born 1676, must have been an eminent organist; for after he had served at Erfurt's *Kaufmanns-kirche* his reputation was so high that he was called away from Thuringia to the city of Magdeburg. However, he returned to his native state when, on the death of the great Johann Christoph Bach, the position as Eisenach's organist was offered him. Working at the fine organ, re-modelled according to his predecessor's instructions, must have proved satisfactory to Johann Bernhard; for, following the old-established Bach pattern, he remained at Eisenach until he died in 1749. For the greater part of this period he seems to have lived in the same house; thus being spared the problems from which Johann Christoph had suffered so much. Shortly after his arrival in Eisenach, the general musical activities in the town were greatly improved by the efforts of two outstanding conductors who served there in succession, the eminent virtuoso, Pantaleon Hebenstreit, and the energetic and highly productive Philipp Telemann. A contemporary writer, Johann Limberg, described the local musical conditions as follows:[1] 'On this [new] organ every Sunday graceful music is performed in the honour of the Lord, often with kettledrums and trumpets. The Council has engaged for this purpose Mr. J. Konrad Geisthirte as Cantor, Mr. J. Bernhard Bach as organist and Mr. J. Heinrich Halle [the successor of J. Ambrosius Bach] as *musicus instrumentalis*. All three are renowned and well experienced in their art. Recently the church music has been really perfected, as the newly appointed court musicians, who are all outstanding, have been commanded to the organ loft so as to be heard for the honour of God and the edification of the congregation. This whole body of musicians is under the direction of Mr. Telemann, a man of pro-

---

[1] Cf. 'Das im Jahre 1708 lebende und schwebende Eisenach,' 1709.

found knowledge and eminent invention.' Telemann stayed for four years only, and after his departure the music-loving Duke Johann Wilhelm may have appreciated all the more the talent of his organist, who also supplied him with delightful orchestral suites. Bernhard's salary was eventually almost doubled and remained undiminished even when, in 1741, Eisenach became part of the principality of Weimar and its ducal band was dismissed.

There was a great friendship between Bernhard and Sebastian, who were related both on their fathers' and on their mothers' sides.[1] Bernhard was the godfather of Sebastian's third son, Johann Gottfried Bernhard, while Sebastian acted in the same capacity for the Eisenach organist's eldest son, Johann Ernst, whose teacher he subsequently became. But above all Sebastian thought very highly of Bernhard's creative work.

THE MUSIC OF JOHANN BERNHARD BACH

Not many of Bernhard's compositions have survived. They consist exclusively of smaller works for the keyboard instruments and suites for string orchestra. Their preservation is mainly due to two great kinsmen of his: the organ chorales were copied by Bernhard's pupil, the outstanding organist and lexicographer, Johann Gottfried Walther (whose mother was a Lämmerhirt too), while the orchestral suites were apparently performed by the Thomas Cantor, who personally wrote out parts for them.

It is significant that Luther's powerful and yet so simple chorale *Wir glauben all' an einen Gott* (We believe all in but one God) particularly appealed to Bernhard Bach. He used it in three different organ preludes which all express the same deep and unquestioning faith. Straightforwardness and simplicity mingled with richly flowing imagination are also apparent in his organ works.[2]

There are various types of chorale prelude in his output. The simplest kind is to be found in two-part arrangements (*bicinia*), in which one quickly moving part accompanies the chorale melody presented in long notes. But even in this unpretentious form Bernhard attempts to portray the mood of the text in the counter-melody. Moreover he occasionally alternates the *cantus firmus* between the soprano and bass parts, and the

---

[1] Bernhard's grandmother, Hedwig Lämmerhirt, was a half-sister of Sebastian's mother, Elisabeth Lämmerhirt.

[2] They are equally revealed in his very characteristic handwriting. Cf. H. Kühn, 'Vier Organisten Eisenachs aus Bachischem Geschlecht,' in 'Aus Luthers lieber Stadt,' 1935.

individual sections start with melodic references to the following chorale line. Among his three-part preludes, *Vom Himmel hoch* (From heaven above to earth I come) is particularly interesting. Here the *cantus firmus* is given to a middle part, while the highest voice offers delightful free passages expressing Christmas cheer and portraying the fluttering of angels' wings.[1]

Bernhard also cultivated the Chorale Partita, a form of composition based on a chorale tune, which is stated at the beginning in simple harmonization, and then followed by a number of variations or 'Partitas' corresponding to the number of verses in the chorale text. Bernhard's four variations on the hymn *Du Friedefürst, Herr Jesu Christ* (Thou Prince of Peace) surround the melody with expressive ornamentations, thus achieving a warm sonority and appealing emotional fervour.

The composer's skill in handling the variation form is equally displayed in his organ[2] Chaconne in B flat. The 20 variations on a vigorous 8-measure subject present the forceful harmonic sequence in patterns of quickly changing rhythm and melody. Within the narrow limitations of this form the composer succeeds in exhibiting a series of highly engaging vistas.

Among his best works for keyboard instruments are two fugues in D and F, into which Bernhard, stimulated by the unlimited possibilities of the well-tempered system, introduced chromatic progressions and sequences of unusual boldness (*Ex.* 18). It is moreover interesting to note

Ex 18

that the composer, like his cousin Sebastian, favoured the concertante principle in the episodes connecting the thematic developments of his

---

[1] Cf. Frotscher, *l.c.*, I, p. 586.

[2] The great distance between the three parts in variation VII, which makes a performance without pedals impossible, shows that the composition usually referred to as a work for the clavier was probably meant for the organ.

fugues. This is by no means the only point of contact between the keyboard works of the two kinsmen. In particular, Sebastian's early Partitas show the influence of Bernhard's style.[1]

Even more conspicuous is the artistic affinity between the two composers' orchestral suites. Each of them wrote four suites, of which Bernhard's in g for solo violin and strings and Sebastian's in b for solo flute and strings are closely related. The Overtures in both works use the concerto fugue, and not only their themes,[2] but even the figurations show a certain resemblance. Each suite has among its dances a vigorous movement entitled *Rondeau*, a heading not too frequently found in orchestral suites of this period. But apart from this comparison Bernhard's suite is, in its own right, a work of fine craftsmanship and vivid inspiration. In addition to the two movements mentioned, it includes a lofty Air, in which the orchestra supports a gentle cantilena of the solo violin, a fascinating *Fantaisie* in da capo form, and a witty *Passepied*.

His other three works of this kind, although not quite on the same level as the Suite in g, contain many delightful movements. These compositions are for strings only without any solo instrument. The solidly constructed Overtures are always most remarkable; but the amusing *Tempête* (a naïve description of a storm) concluding the Suite in G, the sparkling *Les Plaisirs*[3] in the Suite in e, the pompous *Marche* and the charming 3 *Caprices* with their attractive imitations (*Ex.* 19) in that in

E x 19

D, would also justify a revival of the works they adorn. Not many composers of the time wrote orchestral suites of equal significance and technical mastery.

[1] The bass in the first variation of *Sei gegrüsset Jesu gütig*, for instance, is surprisingly similar to that in Bernhard's *bicinium, Jesus, Jesus, nichts als Jesus*.

[2] The theme in Bernhard's Overture must have impressed Sebastian particularly, since he quoted it almost literally in the Andante of his first Sonata for flute and harpsichord.

[3] The title *Les Plaisirs* for a Bourrée was also used by Telemann in his Suite in a. Telemann's work contains moreover a *Réjouissance*, a title employed by Sebastian in his Suite in D.

THE MEININGEN BACHS
(JOHANN LUDWIG AND NIKOLAUS EPHRAIM BACH)

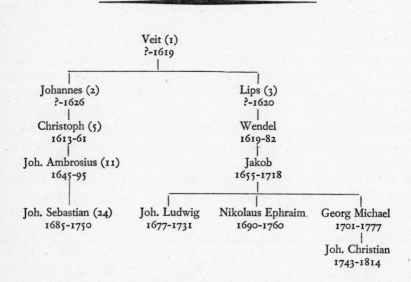

Veit (1)
?-1619

Johannes (2)
?-1626

Christoph (5)
1613-61

Joh. Ambrosius (11)
1645-95

Joh. Sebastian (24)
1685-1750

Lips (3)
?-1620

Wendel
1619-82

Jakob
1655-1718

Joh. Ludwig
1677-1731

Nikolaus Ephraim
1690-1760

Georg Michael
1701-1777

Joh. Christian
1743-1814

THE 18th century witnessed the formation of an important Bach centre at the court of Meiningen. According to family tradition, the branch was descended from Lips Bach, a brother of Johannes, the *Spielmann* (cf. p. 11), but the further development of this branch is shrouded in darkness and family legends. We reach firm ground only in the later part of the 17th century with the person of *Jakob Bach*, born in 1655,[1] in the Thuringian village of Wolfsbehringen. Our knowledge of this founder of a line of eminent artists—a line, incidentally, which has continued up to the present day—is comparatively large, for by a lucky chance a *curriculum vitae* which Jakob had to write for a school Superintendent has been preserved.[2] Jakob's father, Wendel (1619-82), seems to have been a simple farmer[3] with very little money but with much ambition for his son. In 1669, at the age of 14, Jakob was sent to the Eisenach Latin school, an institution

[1] Jakob Bach himself mentions 1654 as the year of his birth; Spitta and Terry give it as 1655, which seems to be the correct date according to the entry in the register of deaths.

[2] It is to be found in the archives of the *Landeskirchenrat der Thüringer evangelischen Kirche* at Eisenach.

[3] That is how Rollberg interprets the description 'Innwohner,' which Jakob Bach uses. Cf. his article in 'Thüringer Fähnlein,' H. 8, 1933.

which was to be attended later by many of his kinsmen. Eisenach, however, did not prove to be a good choice. At that time the hospitable Johann Ambrosius Bach had not yet come to the city, and Johann Christoph, the great organist, was just trying to get established and to provide for his young wife and first son. Probably Jakob could not get much support from him and was unable to make ends meet; whatever the cause, the school register reports that Jakob left school in 1671 after being found guilty of a theft. He transferred to a similar school in Gotha, where he apparently received good musical instruction[1] and found conditions so much to his liking that many years later he sent his own son, Johann Ludwig, to the same institute. Whilst in Gotha, he fell in love with Anna Martha Schmidt, daughter of a hatmaker. Neither of the young people was more than 18 years old when they ran away from Gotha and married. After a short period of bliss, they found they had nothing to live on. So young Martha returned to her parents, while Jakob attempted to conclude his studies in the city of Mühlhausen (thus being the first Bach to stay in this town, which was to harbour three other kinsmen, among them the greatest of them all). Unfortunately the free lodging on which he was counting did not materialize, and after a stay of six months Jakob's financial worries became so acute that he decided to become a musketeer in the army of the Prince of Eisenach, which was just taking part in the Emperor's war against France. But army life did not suit Jakob either, and after a year he managed to buy himself out; he then tried to become a schoolmaster. At last luck was with him. When a position in the Thuringian village of Thal became vacant, the youth of 21 applied for it, and passed the examination by the Consistory, as well as the test in organ playing and singing before the community, with such good results that he was appointed. Now his beloved wife could join him at last. The product of their blissful reunion was Jakob's first son, the handsome and highly gifted Johann Ludwig. Henceforth Jakob's life was spent as a teacher and Cantor, and his inherent restlessness manifested itself merely in a not infrequent change of positions which took him subsequently to the cities of Steinbach, Wasungen, and Ruhla. That he was everywhere considered a most respectable member of the community is apparent in the highly placed godparents whom he was able to provide for his numerous children. His married life was not lacking in variety. He buried not only his beloved Martha, but two other wives. At the age of 61 he

[1] That the Gotha school provided satisfactory training in music is proved by the case of Georg Böhm, who attended it a few years later. As organist at Lüneburg, Böhm was to exercise a deep influence on young Sebastian Bach.

entered matrimony for the fourth time, and still had two offspring before
he died in 1718. The musical talent he handed on must have been considerable, for each of his first two marriages produced a highly gifted
musician.[1]

Jakob's eldest son, *Johann Ludwig*, was born on February 4, 1677, at
Thal, and received a good education. He attended the Gotha *Gymnasium*
from 1688 to 1693 and subsequently studied Theology.[2] His first position
was, like that of his father's, a double one; he worked, as he described it
himself, in the 'school and church' of Salzungen. When he was 22 he
was called to Meiningen, the capital of a newly established little Principality of Saxe-Meiningen, which arose from the division of the estate of
Prince Ernst ('the Pious') of Gotha among his seven sons. The third son,
Bernhard, was allotted Meiningen with a number of neighbouring towns
and villages; he took possession in 1680. Prince Bernhard I was the
typical pocket-size sovereign of the time, both in his good and bad aspects.
He was anxious to promote the material and spiritual welfare of his
subjects. Under his rule agriculture, fruit-growing, and mining were improved, an orphanage was built, attempts were made to provide for the
poor of the district, an excellent Latin school was established, and new
churches were built. A very religious sovereign, he wrote down from
memory all the sermons he heard—and sermons at that time lasted much
longer than in our days!—leaving behind 14 folios of transcripts. He had
a Communion service printed, the prayers for which he collected himself.
On the other hand, he believed firmly in witchcraft, and he spent huge
sums on alchemistic experiments in the hope that the gold so produced
would solve his increasing financial embarrassments once and for all.
When the gold failed to materialize, he chose the easier expedient of
trading his subjects to the Doge of Venice to serve in the fight against the
Turks, receiving 36 thalers for each soldier. This, of course, brought only
temporary relief. Indeed, the state finances were at so low a level that the
sovereign's own son and heir, Ernst Ludwig, published anonymously a
pamphlet advising the Prince how to save Meiningen from bankruptcy.

But whatever may have been Bernhard I's faults, he certainly showed
wisdom in securing young Bach for his court. Perhaps he was first
attracted by Johann Ludwig's unusual good looks, but it did not take him
long to see that he had acquired an extremely capable servant. In 1703

[1] Georg Michael Bach (1703-71), an offspring of Jakob's third marriage, was also a
musician, and worked as Cantor at St. Ulrich, Halle. His son, Christian (1743-1814), later
known as the 'Clavier-Bach,' was Wilhelm Friedemann Bach's pupil.

[2] He mentions this fact in a petition he made in 1725. Cf. Mühlfeld, 'Die herzogliche
Hofkapelle in Meiningen,' Meiningen, 1910.

Johann Ludwig was entrusted with two different spheres of work, being appointed court Cantor and master of the ducal pages. His duties were manifold indeed: holding prayer meetings with the pages and certain court servants every morning and evening; keeping careful check on attendances at these meetings according to lists given him, and notifying the court marshal or chaplain of any absentees; teaching the young noblemen first of all the catechism, then, in addition, other far less important subjects such as writing, arithmetic, and history; working out the pages' schedule for lessons and sports; watching his charges day and night; keeping the church books; and, finally, the occupation which really mattered to him, supervising the church music.[1] The position certainly had both advantages and drawbacks. The remuneration was fairly satisfactory, since it provided free board and lodging at court as well as a sizable stipend in cash.[2] On the other hand, Ludwig had almost as little freedom as his young charges; he could not absent himself even for an evening without permission from the court marshal. Moreover his various duties did not leave sufficient scope for the development of his musical gifts. Perhaps these were the reasons why he attempted a change. On October 26, 1706,[3] his father wrote a petition on his behalf to Eisenach to secure the position of Cantor which had become vacant through the death of Ambrosius Bach's friend, Andreas Christian Dedekind. It is significant that the applicant stressed his son's interest in all musical duties, adding, however, that the teaching work might better be entrusted to a substitute to be paid by Johann Ludwig. Jakob's attempt failed, but fortunately conditions changed in Meiningen itself. Prince Bernhard I died in April 1706, and his successor, Prince Ernst Ludwig, on recognizing the Cantor's special gifts, relieved him in 1711 of all his previous duties, entrusting him instead with the direction of the enlarged court orchestra, which in past years had been conducted by Georg Kaspar Schürmann, a very prolific opera composer. About that time Johann Ludwig married a daughter of the architect, Samuel Rust,[4] and as his presence at the castle for the supervision of the pages was no longer required, he was allowed to set up a household of his own. In lieu of board and lodging he was granted a contribution of 16 thalers to the rent, and a certain yearly

---

[1] The instructions published in full by Mühlfeld, l.c., only mention that 'he has to sing the chorale at the service on Sundays and during the week,' but as the document addressed Bach as court Cantor, it may be assumed that he had to undertake all the musical duties of a Cantor.

[2] A yearly amount of 99 fl. 12 gr.

[3] Cf. Superint. Archiv Eisenach: B 25, B 2, p. 20.

[4] Rust built Meiningen's new castle, the Elisabethenburg.

amount of rye, wheat, barley, carp, game, and candles. Apart from instruction in painting which he gave to the Princes,[1] his time was now devoted
to music and he produced a great number of compositions, in addition to
being kept busy as a performer. His orchestra paid regular visits to neighbouring courts, thus starting a tradition which was in the 19th century to
come to glorious life again in the famous Meiningen orchestra tours under
von Bülow and Brahms. Even when the musicians were at home, performances took place once, and sometimes twice, a day. Johann Ludwig
used to accompany on the harpsichord the visiting artists who often
appeared on these occasions; or he performed himself on the violin. What
part music played in celebrations at the Meiningen court is apparent in
the instructions issued for the birthday of a Prince, which read as follows:

> Monday at 4 a.m. (!). Intrada with trumpets and kettledrums.
> Monday at 7 a.m. The usual morning music by the whole band.
> Monday at 9.30 a.m. Church service, Te Deum with trumpets and kettledrums, 3
> salutes by cannon.
> At dinner-music improper tuning to be avoided, an Overture to be played first; the
> text of the Cantata to be handed to Serenissimo; after the Cantata kettledrums and
> trumpets. At the supper-table strong instrumental music with trumpets and kettle-
> drums. Large orchestra for the following ball.

Posterity does not view Prince Ernst Ludwig in too pleasant a light.
Apparently it did not occur to the new sovereign that the sound economic
advice he had given his father should be applied to his own way of life.
He was just as extravagant, spending excessively large sums on the
building of new castles and churches. The luxuries enjoyed at his court
would have been appropriate for a much more important sovereign, and
this was especially true when he brought to Meiningen as his second wife
a daughter of the 'Great Elector' of Brandenburg; on that occasion one
large-scale festivity followed another. The Prince was not only a prodigal
spender, he was ruthless in his dealings with other members of the family
who had claims on the estate, and he continually waged war against the
neighbouring small principalities, with the object of increasing his possessions. But all this probably did not seriously concern his music director,
for to Johann Ludwig the fact that his Prince was a passionate lover of the
Muses was the most important thing. The sovereign wrote poetry himself, mostly of a religious nature, and occasionally set it to music; as for
instance, when he composed the funeral music for his own brother. His
music director could always count on the Prince's support and understanding, and thus Johann Ludwig was able fully to develop his great
creative gifts. When the Prince died in 1724, mainly from the shock he

---

[1] Cf. H. Löffler, 'Bache bei Sebastian Bach,' *BJ*, 1949-50.

suffered on the sudden death of his beloved eldest son, Johann Ludwig Bach mourned him deeply. He composed a funeral cantata based on verses the Prince had written long before for a similar occasion.[1] This cantata once more expressed the close artistic relations that had existed between the Prince and his music director.

In the following years confusion reigned in Meiningen. As the surviving sons of the deceased potentate were too young, two uncles who were on the worst possible terms with each other ruled as guardians. So much energy was expended in the pursuit of their quarrels that the Muses were neglected. It seems, however, that one of the guardians, Prince Anton Ulrich, showed some sympathy for the composer. At all events, Johann Ludwig mustered up enough courage to write a petition to the Prince entreating him to have the emoluments of which he had been deprived for many years paid to him again. It may be assumed that the Prince granted the musician's wish; for in 1728, when Anton Ulrich returned from a long visit to Vienna, Johann Ludwig celebrated this event in a special Festival Cantata. Three years later the composer died, and he was buried on May 1, 1731.[2]

Before discussing Johann Ludwig's contributions to the music of his time, mention should be made of his younger brother, who also served the princely family of Saxe-Meiningen throughout his life. *Nikolaus Ephraim Bach* was born on November 26, 1690, at Wasungen. At the time when he was ready for musical training, Johann Ludwig was settled at the Meiningen court, and it seems likely that Ephraim stayed there with him as his pupil. The Prince's half-sister, Elisabeth Ernestine Antoinette, interested herself in the promising youth, who shared her love for music and painting; and when she was called as Abbess to the important Protestant convent of Gandersheim,[3] she took Nikolaus Ephraim, then 18 years old, with her. The young musician certainly had quite an unusual patroness to work under. The Princess was famous all over Europe for her beauty and wit, and two of the greatest monarchs, the German Emperor Charles VI, and the French King Louis XIV, had asked for her

[1] It is typical of the time that Prince Ernst Ludwig quite early in his life selected a special Psalm and wrote a poem for his own funeral; he also prepared a funeral sermon for himself, which was found in his desk after his death.

[2] This date was recently ascertained by the Meiningen church authorities from their registers of deaths. The year 1741 given by Spitta and Terry for Ludwig's death is therefore wrong.

[3] This Nunnery, founded in the 9th century by the Princes of Saxony, had become Lutheran in 1586 and was used now as a place of retreat and contemplation for high-born Protestant spinsters. It retained its political independence, being under the jurisdiction of the Emperor only, had its own vote in assemblies, and possessed considerable property.

hand, the former for his son, the latter for his grandson. The paramount condition of both offers was that she should enter the Catholic Church; this the deeply religious Princess was unwilling to do, so, in order not to give offence to such important suitors, she vowed never to marry but to devote her life to Christ; whereupon the Emperor appointed her Abbess of Gandersheim, a position she was to hold for fifty-three years. It was by no means an easy-going mistress that Ephraim had to serve throughout his life. She quickly found out that young Bach was extremely capable in many ways, and she gave him ample opportunities for using his various gifts. Several documents preserved in the Brunswick Archives of Wolfen-büttel give us some conception of the wide range of his appointments. Not only was he court musician and organist, providing compositions of his own when needed, he was also in charge of the Abbess's large art collection and had moreover to instruct the court employees in painting. As he was also most efficient in practical matters, he became master of the princely cellars, as well as auditor of the Abbess's accounts, rising even-tually to the position of intendant in charge of his mistress's entire house-hold.[1] How highly Nikolaus Ephraim was esteemed is revealed by the im-posing array of princes and princesses, including the Abbess, who stood godfather and godmother to his two children, the offspring of a second marriage which the robust court intendant, following the example of his father, contracted at the age of 65.[2] In spite of all the work piled on him, Nikolaus Ephraim's life seems to have been easier than that of his elder brother. From his 18th year to his death at the age of 70 he worked under the same patroness, enjoying her full trust and appreciation. No composition by Ephraim has come to light so far, and we are therefore unable to form an idea of his musical abilities. What attracts our interest apart from his versatility is his apparent leaning towards the fine arts which was to assume large proportions in Ephraim's nephew and grand-nephew, the descendants of Johann Ludwig Bach.

THE MUSIC OF JOHANN LUDWIG BACH

If the number of scores that Johann Sebastian copied from the works of any composer can be considered as an indication of the esteem in which he held him, Ludwig Bach ranked particularly high in his kinsman's

---

[1] When the wide range of his duties forced him to give up some of his musical work, another kinsman became Cantor in 1717. This was Tobias Friedrich, son of Sebastian's eldest brother and teacher, Johann Christoph, of Ohrdruf.

[2] No descendants from the first marriage are known.

favour. The Thomas Cantor made careful copies of 18 German church cantatas by his Meiningen cousin, producing a full score and set of parts for each of them.[1] These copies offer a good example of the kind of score the Leipzig music director prepared for his own practical use. The music, although apparently written in great haste, is clearly legible, whereas the text is often so much abbreviated that deciphering proves difficult. Sebastian observed the greatest economy in his handling of the expensive music paper, and used every available bit of space to the utmost.[2] It was in Leipzig that he performed these 'concertos' (he gave them the name then in general use which he employed for his own cantatas); for the parts contain a figured bass transposed a whole tone down, a sure sign that it was intended for the organ of St. Thomas' or St. Nicholas' (cf. p. 207). The composer's appreciation of this music was shared by his son, Philipp Emanuel, who praised it to an unknown correspondent in these words: 'The elaboration is diligent throughout, the counterpoint especially is flawless; the choruses are exceptional.'

Ludwig's cantatas well deserved his kinsmen's interest, and it is to be regretted that none of them has so far been printed. It is vigorous music, full of strength and inspiration, rich in variety, and imbued with a sensuous pleasure in tonal beauty. The treatment of the voices, particularly in the solo numbers, reveals a composer who has studied Italian models (for which the performances at the Meiningen court offered ample opportunities). The texts are based on the Bible, which is sometimes literally quoted, but more often, according to prevailing fashion, freely paraphrased. Prince Ernst Ludwig of Meiningen may have been responsible for at least part of these 'madrigalian sections.' Each of the cantatas is destined for a special event of the church year, but their texts are of a general character; which, as Emanuel points out, permits their use at almost any time.

[1] This information was given by Philipp Emanuel Bach to a prospective buyer in a letter preserved in the Berlin Library. 17 of these cantatas are listed in *BG*, 41, Appendix. The 18th was obviously the *Trauermusik* for Prince Ernst Ludwig of Meiningen. Not all of these autographs of Sebastian's are available to-day. 12 cantatas exist in full score, others in parts only. The score we have of the *Trauermusik* is not in Sebastian's hand, nor does it seem to be the one Emanuel had in his possession. The MSS. of Johann Ludwig's music are to-day to be found in the libraries of Berlin, Marburg, and Tübingen, which kindly supplied the author of this book with photographic reproductions.

[2] In the cantata *Gott ist unser Zuversicht* Sebastian fills about three-quarters of each of the first three pages of the manuscript with the opening chorus. The remaining quarter of each page would have been too small to accommodate the 8 lines of this chorus; accordingly he filled it with the 5 lines of an aria, which is actually the third number of the composition, being separated from the chorus by a *secco* recitative (cf. Ill. XI).

The majority of the cantatas are scored only for the traditional string and organ accompaniment, also used by the older members of the Bach family. In some cases oboes are added; in one cantata there are flutes as well as oboes, in another two *corni di silva* (a literal translation of the German term *Waldhorn*=French horn) and an oboe; while the whole of the resources at his disposal are employed only in his Funeral Music (cf. p. 107). With his small instrumental body the composer achieves surprising effects of colour; in particular he gives his favourite, the violin, ample opportunities for brilliant display. How successfully he blends vocal and instrumental timbres is shown by a beautiful duet between violin and soprano in the cantata *Ich aber ging* (Though I went). Of equal charm is an aria in *Ich will meinen Geist* (I shall relinquish my spirit), where a solo soprano alternates with the tone of horns, oboe, and strings. It is interesting to note (whether this be the work of the composer or the 'copyist') that both score and parts contain many indications regarding changes of tempo and expression as well as the directions 'solo' and 'tutti.'

The longer cantatas (which are occasionally divided into two sections) begin with a brief full chorus displaying a rich polyphonic texture; others have as their initial number a duet or a simple arioso by one of the solo voices. A real introductory number for instruments only is nowhere to be found, although a few measures by the orchestra usually precede the entrance of the voices. Ludwig was particularly addicted to the repetition of these instrumental measures as an introduction or postlude to the last piece, thus giving firmer cohesion to his works. The first number is followed by a free succession of *secco* recitatives, arias (mostly in da capo form), and duets. Each cantata is concluded by a large chorus, usually consisting of three sections: a short and powerful harmonic opening, a polyphonic middle part, and the final chorale which is intoned by the singers in plain chords, while the briskly moving instruments of the orchestra provide a vigorous accompaniment.

The emotional content of the text is vividly reflected in the music. In the cantata *Ja, mir hastu Arbeit gemacht* (Ye caused Me pain), Christ's suffering is poignantly represented in the sigh motives which dominate both the introductory arioso and the final chorus. On the other hand, in *Wie lieblich sind auf den Bergen* (How beautiful upon the mountains), the atmosphere of bliss and remoteness from human strife is charmingly expressed in a sort of round dance. The composer never misses an opportunity for dramatic changes. In *Ich aber ging* (Though I went) ponderous chromatic sequences, inspired by the words 'lying in thy blood,' are interrupted by vigorous and joyful coloraturas describing the text 'thou shalt live.' In the magnificent *Mache dich auff, werde Licht* (Arise and let there

be light), an introduction of Handelian vigour (*Ex.* 20) and brilliant melismata of the solo voice are suddenly replaced by an adagio at the

words 'for, lo, darkness covers the earth' (*Ex.* 21). The effective change in tempo is enhanced by the simultaneous harmonic descent from a to g.

The cantata *Gott ist unser Zuversicht* (In God is our trust) is built entirely on the contrast between the uproar of the elements, symbolizing human sin, and the Lord's victory over the storm's fury. It reaches its climax in a sort of operatic scene; the violins express the violent motion of the waves, until Jesus (bass) exhorts the dispirited people to muster courage and silences the wind and sea (*Ex. 22*). Little imagination is needed to see a connection between this dramatic episode and features of Sebastian's Passions.[1] (Cf. also Ill. XI.)

Occasionally the composer's tendency to create dramatic changes is detrimental to the proper development of the musical ideas, and creates an atmosphere of unrest. In *Die mit Thränen säen* (Those who sow in tears shall reap in joy), a text well known from Brahms' 'Requiem,' only 4 measures are allotted to the description of the tears; then the time signature changes, the composer prescribes allegro, and gay music illustrates the reaping in joy. After 5 measures this second choral section is succeeded by a contrasting duet of soprano and tenor on 'they go out and weep.' The movement concludes with a repetition of the two initial choral pieces, with the result that this comparatively short number consists of no less than 5 distinct sections. However, such deficiencies are rare; in most cases the changes in style and mood are not so numerous, and have the effect of enhancing the work's dramatic vigour and vitality.

The most attractive features of Ludwig's cantatas are a beautiful melodic invention of an Italian nature and his engaging colouristic effects. His style is predominantly homophonic; he is more concerned with variety than with monumental grandeur, and this gives his cantatas a patchwork character far exceeding that in Sebastian's earlier works (cf. p. 209). The individual numbers are usually short, and there is often no clear demarcation between arioso and aria. The difference between Sebastian and his Meiningen cousin is particularly obvious in the recitatives, which are calm and gentle in Ludwig's cantatas, lacking the vehemence and poignancy of those of his kinsman. Everything Ludwig writes, however, sounds well and makes the most efficient use of the human voice. To achieve full clarity, the solo voices in arias and duets usually take turns with individual instruments, while the full orchestra accompanies only the chorus.

A link between Ludwig's cantatas and motets is established by his

---

[1] It might be mentioned in this connection that in *Ja, mir hastu Arbeit gemacht*, the bass arioso No. 4 depicts the flagellation of Christ with the dotted rhythm used for the description of the same situation in the contralto arioso 'O gracious God' of the St. Matthew Passion. Likewise in the cantata *Und ich will ihnen einen einigen Hirten erwecken* (Lo, I will raise up a shepherd) the tenor arioso No. 4 uses this rhythm to illustrate the killing of the sheep by the wolf.

Funeral Music composed in 1724 on the death of Duke Ernst Ludwig. The text is based on Psalm 116, verses 16-19, partly literally quoted, partly freely paraphrased. As the composer mentions on the title-page, the second part contains verses by the Duke himself. This is the only cantata by Ludwig written, like his motets, for two choruses. Each of the four-part mixed choruses is accompanied by an individual orchestra. That of chorus I consists of strings and harpsichord only; while chorus II uses, in the first section, woodwinds, strings, and harpsichord, and in the second, woodwinds and harpsichord, to which are added, in the third section, three muted trumpets, and timpani. In writing this composition, Ludwig exerted himself to the utmost to offer a fitting memorial for his dear patron. The composition is not only much longer than any of his other cantatas; it exhibits greater dignity and even stronger expressive power. Very moving, for instance, is the alternation of a tenor solo with the full chorus voicing the longing for the heavenly Jerusalem (*Ex.* 23). When

the tired soul finally arrives in Paradise, it is greeted by a Hallelujah, the jubilant spirit of which one would hardly expect in a funeral cantata.

Although this cantata is not preserved in Sebastian's own handwriting, it may be presumed to have been among his collection.[1] The double chorus in 12/8 time, *Meine Bande sind zerrissen* (My bonds are broken), concluding the first section of the *Funeral Music*, may have been in Sebastian's mind when he wrote the first chorus of his St. Matthew Passion.

---

[1] Emanuel Bach refers in the aforementioned letter to a cantata using 3 trumpets.

While Ludwig's cantatas consist of many short and vividly contrasting sections, the motets[1] are designed on a large scale. Most of them are long and substantial works of a dignified, solemn, and festive character. The subjective, almost nervous, style of the cantatas is here replaced by epic grandeur.[2]

In all his motets Johann Ludwig displays the feeling for clear and well-disposed musical forms that might be expected from a student of Italian art. The da capo form is frequently used for large sections or for complete motets. *Gott sey uns gnädig* (God be gracious unto us) is even given such spacious dimensions that the composer is unable to manage with ternary form. He doubles it, thus producing a kind of rondo form with three statements of the main idea.

The Meiningen master's motets are anything but easy to perform. He expects from his singers tremendous coloraturas, a big range, and the faculty of hitting difficult intervals.[3] Combined with this is a purity and nobility of melodic line usually encountered only in Italian vocal music. Two choruses, each consisting of the same mixed quartet of soprano, alto, tenor, and bass, are Ludwig's favourite means of expression. Even in the three motets which are written for six, nine, and ten voices respectively,[4] the classical combination of four voices always provides the foundation for the tonal structure.

These motets are predominantly homophonic. Ludwig has an insatiable urge for exploring the possibilities of tone-colour. His two choruses, which were apparently posted at a distance from each other, toss the musical material over to each other. Sometimes they alternate, then again they overlap; echo effects are frequently used, and the scores are filled with dynamic signs. Johann Ludwig likes to have groups of high-pitched voices interchanging with low-pitched ones, large bodies of singers with small ones. In *Die richtig für sich gewandelt haben* (Those who

---

[1] Like the cantatas, most of the motets remained in manuscript. They are preserved mainly in the Berlin Library. Only a single one, *Uns ist ein Kind geboren* (Unto us a child is born) is available in a modern score. The editor, Rudolf Moser, by adding a third chorus to the two choruses of Ludwig Bach, introduced a contrast between solo and tutti voices which is alien to the original.

[2] An exception is provided by *Die richtig für sich gewandelt haben* (Those who walked in righteousness) which prescribes no less than 10 changes of time signature, thus creating an atmosphere of restlessness.

[3] The motet *Gedenke meiner, mein Gott* (Remember me, O my God) repeatedly prescribes a descending seventh interval in the soprano, and in the bass a descending octave immediately followed by an additional descending fifth.

[4] They are *Unser Trübsal* (Our light affliction), *Gott sey uns gnädig*, and *Die richtig für sich gewandelt haben*.

walked in righteousness), a third chorus of two voices only is prescribed merely to achieve a contrast of timbre, since of the ten voices in the score never more than eight are used at the same time, and frequently as few as two or four.

Even in the comparatively infrequent polyphonic sections, such as the eight-part fugue in *Uns ist ein Kind geboren* (Unto us a child is born), harmonic beauty is not neglected. There is a luxuriant richness of tone in this music which reminds us of the Catholic Church compositions of a Durante or Caldara.

Johann Ludwig did not follow the custom of the time in using the chorale as a *cantus firmus* in his motets. The interweaving of Biblical text and Protestant hymn by which Johann Christoph, Johann Michael, and most of all Johann Sebastian, obtained such powerful effects is foreign to his style. His motets are based mainly on the Scriptures and it is only near the end that he introduces a simply harmonized hymn, often of considerable length and with many stanzas. Only in exceptional cases does he approach the *cantus firmus* technique. In the magnificent *Gott sey uns gnädig*, a bass voice, moving in majestically extended long notes, utters the ascending and descending scales of B flat supporting the agitated dialogue of the two choruses. The strong effect of this scale, which is reiterated twice in the course of the motet, is enhanced by the unbending rigidity of a pedal point on the note F, introduced between the two entrances of the scale. The text of the motet includes these words: 'The Lord make His face shine upon us.' It seems likely that the rows of ascending and descending notes symbolize the permanent interrelation between heaven and earth as expressed in the story of Jacob's ladder:

> And he dreamed, and behold a ladder set up on the earth, and the top of it reached to heaven: and behold the angels of God ascending and descending on it (Genesis xxviii, 12).

In the motet *Uns ist ein Kind geboren*, based on Isaiah ix, 6, at the words 'And the government shall be upon His shoulder' the basses and tenors of both choruses introduce in long extended notes a melody (*Ex.* 24) which is strongly reminiscent of the Gregorian chant of the Magnificat

Ex. 24

(*tertii toni*). Later, at the words 'And His name shall be called wonderful, counsellor,' a similar tune is sustained by the soprano as if angels' voices were intoning it.

As in his cantatas, so in his motets Ludwig Bach reveals himself as a master of expressive power, imbued with dramatic tension. *Gedenke meiner, mein Gott* (Remember me, O my God), begins quietly in g with full chords. Gradually the motion increases and with it the excitement, until an outcry is heard at the words: 'My God!' (*Ex. 25*). The third

inversion of the dominant seventh chord which the composer uses here was not common at that time. Of equal audacity is the motet *Sei nun wieder zufrieden* (Return unto thy rest). At the words: 'For Thou hast delivered my soul from death, my eyes from tears,' the prevalent key of G changes suddenly to g to illustrate the word 'death.' Chromatic progressions represent the tears, and eventually the section comes to a tired, almost exhausted ending on the chord of F sharp.

The motets deal with happiness and bliss more frequently than with pain and suffering; and to describe the former emotions Ludwig Bach uses the same type of joyful coloraturas that most composers of his time, including Johann Sebastian, employ. He likes to emphasize their effect by giving the quickly moving melismata to one group of voices while others accompany with massive chords (*Ex. 26*). Particularly impressive is a

(„Das ist meine Freude", Motet)

passage in *Ich will auf den Herren schauen* (I will look unto the Lord) where, after fast-moving coloratura passages, the soprano and alto suddenly stop and with a shout declaim the word 'hear' for six measures, while the remainder of the voices with grim energy repeat 'me, me, me' (*Ex.* 27); the realistic vigour of this effect is hard to surpass.

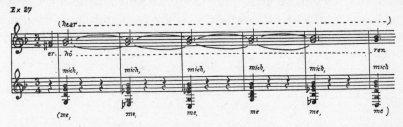

There is no inferior work among the motets of the Meiningen Bach, and many, like *Gott sey uns gnädig, Ich will auf den Herren schauen, Uns ist ein Kind geboren, Wir wissen* (We know), belong to the best that the period produced in this field. The author of this book hopes to present in modern editions a selection from Johann Ludwig's church compositions,[1] a venture that has long been overdue.

Only a single instrumental composition of Johann Ludwig Bach has come to light: an overture, with a following suite of dances, dated 1715. It is written for stringed instruments and continuo, to which a solo oboe is occasionally added. The impressive slow section of the overture is followed by a gay and energetic fugue based on the theme (*Ex.* 28). Like

other compositions by Ludwig Bach it shows in its vigorous, melodious and straightforward nature an almost Handelian character. Among the dance movements following the overture two 'Airs' are most interesting. The first exhibits a kind of trill motive running through the parts from the solo oboe to the basses. The second, a gay dance in 6/4 time (for which Johann Ludwig had a predilection), is based on the contrast between the questioning of a single instrument and the answer of the full chorus.

---

[1] A Passion from the year 1713 (cf. Spitta, *l.c.*, I, p. 572) and numerous other works by the master have probably been lost. On the other hand, there is little reason to assume that the three Masses which were tentatively attributed to Ludwig Bach are really his work. The Mass in c (*BWV*, Anh. 26) is of inferior quality, not in keeping with that of Ludwig's other works. The Mass for double chorus in G (*BWV*, Anh. 167) published in 1805 as the work of J. Sebastian, seems to be by an Italian composer, perhaps Antonio Lotti, as Spitta suggests (*l.c.*, II, p. 509). The Mass in e (*BWV*, Anh. 166) is by Nicolaus Bach (cf. p. 93, footnote 3).

A merry game develops in which not only the oboe and the violins, but also the viola and the basses are entrusted with the sprightly solo. A graceful minuet, a stately *Gavotte*, and a brisk *Bourrée* form the rest of the movements; they make us deeply regret that we know no other instrumental compositions by this master, who was apparently as competent in the treatment of stringed instruments as he was outstanding in his vocal works.

I

APPRENTICESHIP

(1685-1703)

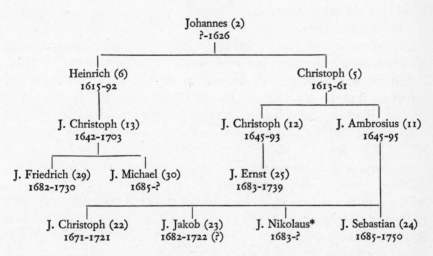

Johannes (2)
?-1626

Heinrich (6)
1615-92

Christoph (5)
1613-61

J. Christoph (13)
1642-1703

J. Christoph (12)
1645-93

J. Ambrosius (11)
1645-95

J. Friedrich (29)
1682-1730

J. Michael (30)
1685-?

J. Ernst (25)
1683-1739

J. Christoph (22)
1671-1721

J. Jakob (23)
1682-1722 (?)

J. Nikolaus*
1683-?

J. Sebastian (24)
1685-1750

* J. Nikolaus has no number in the Genealogy, as he died at an early age.

IN the northern side-aisle of the *Georgenkirche* in Eisenach there stands a baptismal font erected in the year 1503. This venerable relic, which is still intact to-day,[1] has witnessed many significant events through the centuries, but none more so than the ceremony on March 23, 1685, to which the pastor still refers to-day whenever a baby is christened there. On that day the town musician Johann Ambrosius Bach had a son baptized under the name of Johann Sebastian. Of the two godfathers, one, the town musician Sebastian Nagel, came all the way from the city of Gotha; the

---

[1] It remained intact in spite of the fact that the church itself suffered various injuries both outside and inside from air-pressure during bombing raids. According to information kindly supplied by Eisenach residents, all the repairs needed to make the beautiful building fit for use again were completed by 1951.

other, Johann Georg Koch, was a ducal forester in Eisenach.[1] It seems
deeply symbolical that Sebastian Bach was made a member of the Christian community in a church steeped in German tradition and legend. At
St. George's the saintly Elisabeth was wedded to the Landgrave Louis IV
of Thuringia, originator of the Tournament of Song in the Wartburg.
From St. George's pulpit Luther, on May 3, 1521, thundered his sermon
of defiance after returning from the fateful *Reichstag* at Worms. But even
apart from such historical considerations, the church meant much to the
Eisenach Bachs as the centre of their musical activities. Now, in the
building in which the greatest of the older Bach generation had been
serving for the past twenty years, the member of the family who was to
excel him was being baptized.

No definite facts are known about Sebastian's early youth, but it
seems safe to assume that he was taught to play stringed instruments by
his father, while his uncle, Johann Christoph, started him on the organ.
When he was 8 years old, he entered the Eisenach Latin school,[2]
attending it at the same time as two of his brothers, Johann Jakob and
Johann Nikolaus, and two of his cousins, Johann Friedrich (29) (later his
successor at Mühlhausen) and Johann Michael (30). The pupils usually
started at the age of 7, and remained in each successive class for two or
three years, until they were ready for promotion. Sebastian advanced very
quickly, always holding a place slightly higher than his brother Jakob,
who was three years the elder. He achieved this excellent progress in spite
of frequent absences, amounting to 59 school hours in 1694 and 103 hours
in 1695. It was probably not so much illness as musical activities in the
school choirs that were responsible for his poor attendance. Educational
and musical periods often conflicted in the schools at that time, and Sebastian, in spite of his keen interest in scholastic subjects, was naturally
among those pupils for whom the school choirs were of paramount importance; he advanced rapidly from the '*Kurrende*' choir, which sang one-
part hymns, to the *Chorus Symphoniacus* performing motets and cantatas.
Fortunate was the congregation of St. George's to be able to enjoy the
Sunday music provided by the Bachs, with Johann Christoph releasing
magnificent sounds on the organ, Ambrosius performing in a masterly

[1] Freyse in 'Eisenacher Dokumente um J. S. Bach' thinks it probable that Ambrosius
Bach, who also lodged for several years with a forester, was a member of the *Schützengilde*
(shooting-association), founded in the 13th century, which had St. Sebastian as their
patron saint. If the assumption is correct, it would prove Ambrosius Bach's high social
standing in the community.

[2] From 1544 the school was housed in a former Dominican monastery built in 1232.
In 1707 the institute was raised to the rank of a *Gymnasium*.

manner on a stringed instrument, and little Sebastian singing in a lovely, pure soprano voice,[1] joined by other relatives, who were all intensely musical. And fortunate were the Bach children, who grew up in this atmosphere of deep-rooted and natural musicianship!

It was only for a brief space of time that Sebastian was granted the happiness of so sheltered an existence. He lost his mother when he was 9 years old, and his father less than a year later. Now the family had to help. Both Sebastian and his brother Jakob were admitted to the home of their eldest brother, Johann Christoph (22), organist at the little town of Ohrdruf situated half-way between Arnstadt and Eisenach. In accepting them Johann Christoph followed the Bach tradition of mutual assistance. We can imagine, however, that the offer of such hospitality was not easy for him. The ties of blood had never been strengthened by a home life enjoyed in common, for shortly after the birth of Sebastian, Johann Christoph had left his parents in order to study with Pachelbel; so his young brothers were really strangers to him. Besides, he had married only a few months previously, a child was on the way, and the stipend paid by the Ohrdruf Council was an extremely meagre one.[2] It is therefore understandable that the elder of Johann Christoph's two charges, Jakob, after attending Ohrdruf's Latin school for a year, left his brother in order to be apprenticed to the Eisenach town musician who had succeeded Ambrosius Bach. Sebastian, however, stayed on in Ohrdruf for five years. During this time he contributed to the household expenses by earning a not inconsiderable amount as a singer;[3] but once again such work did not prevent the precocious youth from a brilliant career at Ohrdruf's highly renowned Latin school. His promotions followed one another very rapidly, and Sebastian was usually the youngest in his class as well as one of the highest-placed pupils. He became a senior at 14, the average age of his classmates being 17.7 years. In this school, which he attended at the same time as his cousin, Johann Ernst (25),[4] he received a thorough training in Latin and, what was important for his subsequent religious attitude, in Lutheran orthodoxy. His keen mind permitted him to enjoy the intellec-

[1] Sebastian's 'fine, penetrating voice of great range and high singing culture' is mentioned by Forkel, who derived his information from Emanuel Bach.

[2] He received 45 fl. a year plus allowances in rye and wood. In 1696 he was granted an increase of 10 fl. after he had refused an offer from Gotha.

[3] The prefect of the chorus was Johann Avenarius, whose cousin, J. Georg Schübler, became Sebastian's pupil and publisher. Cf. Günther Kraft in 'Johann Sebastian Bach in Thüringen,' 1950.

[4] This was the eldest son of Johann Christoph (12) of Arnstadt, twin brother of Ambrosius. After the death of Johann Christoph in 1693 the widow sent young Johann Ernst to Ohrdruf, where she had relatives.

tual gymnastics of theological dialectics. This predilection was to develop
later into a hobby probably unique among composers, that of collecting
theological books and pamphlets and reading them by way of relaxation
from creative work.

Nevertheless, school work could touch no more than the outer fringes
of his wide-awake mind. What really mattered to Sebastian was the
thrilling voyage of exploration into the immense domain of music. He
had the opportunity for storing away a great deal of practical knowledge
by observing the construction of a new organ at his brother's church. In
this as in all musical matters Johann Christoph was his mentor, a guide of
high quality, trained by his father, Ambrosius Bach, and by the great
organist and composer, Johann Pachelbel. It may be assumed that he was
artistically on the same high level as so many other Bachs, a conjecture
borne out by two entries made by his superior, Superintendent Kromeyer.
When Johann Christoph married, Kromeyer noted in the church register:
'young, but artistic,' and when the organist died he described him in the
death-register as 'an artist of the first rank.'[1] According to Forkel, Johann
Christoph taught Sebastian the clavier; but we can safely assume that he
also instructed him in other instruments, as well as in the elements of composition. Young Sebastian absorbed all instruction as readily as a sponge
does water. His thirst for new information was unquenchable, and continued so throughout his life. There is the touching story, first reported in
Mizler's *Necrolog*,[2] of how Sebastian stole a volume of music by leading
clavier composers that his brother had denied him as being too advanced;
how, lacking candles, he copied it painstakingly by the light of the moon,
thus seriously injuring his sight; and how he suffered the worst possible
blow when, after months of toil, he was found out and deprived of the
copy he had made. If the story in this form is true, it would make Sebastian's eldest brother appear a singularly unpleasant person. But it may be
that he normally treated his brother quite decently, and that it was only
exasperation with the young genius's unceasing battery of questions and a
sudden jealous awareness of Sebastian's superior gifts that provoked this
spiteful outburst. That Sebastian was, on the whole, not treated too
harshly in Ohrdruf is apparent from his subsequent attitude towards his
relatives there. He dedicated one of his early clavier works to Johann
Christoph (cf. p. 261), and repaid his elder brother by giving two of the

---

[1] Cf. Ferdinand Reinhold, 'Die Musik-Bache in Ohrdruf,' 'Ohrdruf Festschrift,' 1950.
[2] The article, which appeared in Mizler's 'Musikalische Bibliothek,' was written by
Philipp Emanuel Bach and Sebastian's pupil, Johann Friedrich Agricola, and is one of
our main sources for the details of Sebastian's life.

latter's sons musical training in his own house. Yet it seemed out of the question for him to remain much longer at Ohrdruf. Johann Christoph's home was becoming more and more crowded owing to additions to his family; while the school on the other hand, unlike other institutions of its kind, did not place impecunious students in the houses of rich citizens. Nor could Sebastian have recourse to the expedient of joining any other member of the family for further training, as had been the practice in previous generations. The number of Bach musicians had been sadly reduced during the preceding decades; a decline that had provoked Sebastian's stepmother to declare that the family was dying out. Not only did Ambrosius die in the prime of life; the same fate befell his two brothers and his cousin, Johann Michael. So Sebastian, by necessity, had to break away from family ties. He probably did not mind this overmuch. A zest for travelling had suddenly broken out among the young Bachs, whose fathers had so steadfastly worked within the narrow confines of Thuringia. Around the turn of the century J. Nicolaus (27) went to Italy, J. Christoph (28), and J. Ernst (25) to Northern Germany, and Sebastian's own brother, J. Jakob (23), was, before long, to travel as far as Turkey. It is not surprising, therefore, that young Sebastian himself began to search eagerly for an opportunity to study in a distant part of Germany.[1]

Luck, or fate, would have it that a new Cantor by the name of Elias Herda had recently joined the Ohrdruf school Faculty. Although a Thuringian himself, Herda had as a student held a scholarship at St. Michael's in the city of Lüneburg in Northern Germany. He knew that good singers were in great demand for the church's exquisite *Mettenchor*, which consisted of 12-15 musicians who took over the solos or led the choir of the *Ritterakademie*, a school for young noblemen attached to St. Michael's whose schedule did not include musical training. The choir members, according to the statutes, had to be the 'offspring of poor people, with nothing to live on, but possessing good voices'; in addition to free board and tuition they were entitled to a small income.

As Herda taught music at the Ohrdruf school, Sebastian could not fail to hear of his teacher's experiences in Lüneburg. The boy, once he learned of such a fine opportunity, was most eager to grasp it. The great difficulties involved in travelling 200 miles without adequate funds did not scare him in the least. He felt quite ready to exert his feet to the utmost,

---

[1] The files of the Ohrdruf school mention concerning Sebastian 'Luneburgum ob defectum hospitiorum se contulit die 15 Martii 1700.'

and to limit his appetite to the scantiest rations, if this could bring him to
an institution which for long had been a revered centre of choral singing.
Fortunately, a schoolmate of his, Georg Erdmann, was interested in the
same project; being a friend, maybe even a relative, of Herda's, from
whose native village he came, he succeeded in obtaining the Cantor's full
assistance for himself and Sebastian. Herda wrote to Lüneburg, and his
report on Sebastian must have been enthusiastic indeed; for the answer
was positive, despite the fact that as a rule St. Michael's only accepted
younger boys able to serve for a longer period, or youths of 17 or 18,
whose voices were full-grown. Thus, early in March 1700, two eager
youths, Bach, not quite 15, and Erdmann, aged 18, set·out on the arduous
trek to Lüneburg. They left Ohrdruf just in time, for we see from the
church registers that soon afterwards a terrible epidemic struck the little
town.[1]

In April the list of the Lüneburg *Mettenchor* mentions Bach among
the sopranos as a recipient of a monthly payment of 12 groschen. This
seems very little, but fortunately it did not constitute his whole income;
for he was entitled to a share in all the monies earned for singing in the
streets, performances at weddings, funerals, etc. As, moreover, his domicile and board as well as a supply of firewood and candles were provided,
his financial position was certainly not worse than it had been in Ohrdruf.
As to the educational opportunities, they were ideal for a youth with so
ravenous a musical appetite. Performing at Lüneburg differed in many
ways from what Sebastian had been used to in Ohrdruf. The church of
St. Michael itself was of breathtaking loftiness, and the famous High
altar with its centrepiece of pure gold interspersed with lovely enamels,
near which the choir had its position, must have impressed young Sebastian as deeply as it did many of his contemporaries. The music offered was
worthy of so exquisite a setting, and in its great variety most helpful in
providing a young musician with a thorough knowledge of contemporary
and older choral literature. Ever since the first Protestant Cantor had established an imposing music library at St. Michael's in 1555, the tradition had
been faithfully continued by his successors. The Thuringian Cantor,
Friedrich Emanuel Praetorius (1623-95), in particular, had done a great
deal in this respect, with the result that the collection included, besides a
huge amount of printed music, some 1100 manuscript compositions by
175 composers, among them even two members of Sebastian's family,
Heinrich Bach and the great Johann Christoph. Thus the church had huge
resources on which to draw, and the programmes accordingly included a

---

[1] Cf. Günther Kraft, *l.c.*

wealth of fine music unknown to Sebastian, but with which he became familiar through performing it.[1] Not long after his arrival he lost his fine soprano voice. This did not mean dismissal, however, as young Joseph Haydn was to experience in a similar position at St. Stephen's in Vienna. In Lüneburg it was the custom to let the scholarship boys continue as best they could as tenors and basses. In Sebastian's case, moreover, his various excellent qualifications made him extremely valuable in other respects. It is significant that just in the year 1700 the church employed only 3 instrumentalists (against 6 in 1660, and 10 in 1710), and 15-year-old Sebastian was probably from the outset admitted because of his usefulness as a violinist in the orchestra and as an organist.

Added to a very heavy schedule of musical duties was the curriculum imposed by the *Michaelisschule*, a Latin school for non-aristocratic youths, where Sebastian studied religion, rhetoric, logic, Latin, and Greek, mainly under Rector Johann Büsche. Since the teacher was an orthodox Lutheran, the religious foundations initiated in Ohrdruf were greatly strengthened and were to remain of vital importance to Sebastian throughout his life.

While the scholarship boys had to attend the *Michaelisschule*, they roomed and boarded in the old convent, where the *Ritterakademie* was housed. In some ways this was not too pleasant an arrangement; for the young noblemen were apt to treat the poor singers scornfully, and to require many a menial service from them. Sebastian, however, who had not been exactly spoiled in his brother's house, cannot have minded this overmuch; and he was, on the other hand, fully aware of the tremendous advantages he derived from living close to these aristocrats. The Academy was a centre of French culture. French conversation, indispensable at that time to any high-born German, was obligatory between the students; and Sebastian with his quick mind became familiar with this language which he had no chance to study in his own schools. He attended French plays, and, what was more important, he learned a great deal about French music. At the academy a pupil of Lully, Thomas de la Selle, taught dancing to French tunes, thus introducing the fascinated Sebastian into a new world of music. When de la Selle noticed the youth's enthusi-

---

[1] Gustav Fock in his valuable study 'Der junge Bach in Lüneburg,' Hamburg, 1950, considers Spitta's and Terry's assumption that Sebastian copied many of the works in this collection to be erroneous. He contends that the music was partly the private property of the Cantor, who had bought it from the estate of Praetorius, and that it was probably housed in its entirety in the Cantor's rooms, to which a pupil of the school would hardly have had admission.

astic response he decided to take Bach to the city of Celle, to which he was attached as court musician.[1]

Celle, residence of the Dukes of Brunswick-Lüneburg, was at that time ruled by Duke Georg Wilhelm, who, like so many German sovereigns with small domains and large ambitions, did everything conceivable to create a miniature Versailles at his court. His French wife fully shared his enthusiasm and between them they achieved a veritable centre of Gallic culture in Celle. French Huguenots who had fled from their country were sure of hospitality there and enjoyed the French musicians and singers, who produced an unending series of performances. The Duke could certainly expect a high artistic standard, as he spent huge sums (for instance, some 14,000 thalers in 1690) on his music and theatre. It is significant that one of the greatest oboists of the time, Johann Ernst Galliard,[2] was trained at the Celle court; the Duke paid his teacher, Maréchal, 100 thalers a year for instructing the promising youth.

We can well imagine what the visits to Celle must have meant to an artist with a mind so wide open to all new experiences. There Sebastian became familiar with the idiom and style of Couperin and other keyboard masters; he heard French instrumental music and listened to French organ compositions in the castle's exquisite Renaissance chapel with its jewel of a small organ. Various copies made by him[3] testify to the eagerness with which he applied himself to these studies.

It was a stroke of luck that Sebastian happened to go to Celle at that particular time; a few years later, the artistic Duke Georg Wilhelm died, the orchestra was dismissed, and the little court ceased to be a centre of French music.

In Lüneburg, besides de la Selle there were other interesting persons living in the convent which housed the Academy. In 1701 the excellent organ builder, Johann Balthasar Held, stayed there in order to undertake repairs to St. Michael's organ. With what interest must Sebastian have watched him, and listened to the reports about the outstanding instru-

---

[1] Fock, *l.c.*, has succeeded in establishing in the person of de la Selle, employed both in the *Ritterakademie* and at Celle, the person most likely to have been responsible for Sebastian's admission to the court of Celle, about which the *Necrolog* reports. None of the previous theories sounded very convincing. Pirro assumed that Bach was introduced by the court physician, Scott, son-in-law of Lüneburg's mayor, Reinbeck; Spitta saw the link in the Celle town organist, Brinckhorst, with whom Bach had contact after 1703, while Wolffheim pointed to the trumpeter, Jan Pack, in the Duke's service, who might have been a kinsman.

[2] Galliard was subsequently court conductor in London, and Handel's predecessor.

[3] E.g. the suites by Nicolas de Grigny and Charles Dieupart, and the former's 'Livre d'orgue.'

ments in Lübeck and Hamburg, on which Held had worked! Young Bach was thus able to add further to his store of knowledge regarding the construction of organs—a field in which he was later to become the greatest authority.

Perhaps even more important than all these contacts was the one established with Georg Böhm,[1] organist of Lüneburg's *Johanneskirche*. It seems indeed a very friendly gesture of Providence that this distinguished Thuringian should have settled down in Lüneburg in 1698, thus being available to young Sebastian when he arrived in the northern town two years later. Böhm, born in 1661 in a village near Ohrdruf, naturally had various links with the Bachs. He probably attended the very school at Ohrdruf that Sebastian had just left; later he went to the Gotha Latin school with a kinsman of Sebastian, and he attended the University of Jena together with three men, who subsequently became Sebastian's teachers at Ohrdruf. Thus it was not difficult for the youth to gain access to the great organist and composer. The connection proved most fruitful, and Sebastian's early organ works especially clearly show him under the spell of his compatriot and teacher.[2] Before he came to Lüneburg, Böhm had stayed for years in Hamburg, and Sebastian, hearing his reports about the great organist, J. A. Reinken, felt irresistibly drawn to this city, in order to hear the outstanding artist, then 77 years old. The 30 miles' distance and lack of funds were negligible matters once Sebastian's artistic curiosity was aroused. He walked over to Hamburg during the summer vacation of 1701, and so great was the wealth of impressions he received from the aged organ virtuoso, and from another master of the Northern style, Vincenz Lübeck, so fascinating was Hamburg's teeming musical life, with the great Reinhard Keiser at the opera house, that he repeated the trip more than once. How he managed in Hamburg without starving, we do not know. Perhaps he received shelter and a little help from cousin Johann Ernst (25), his former classmate at Ohrdruf, who had also gone to Hamburg to improve his musical knowledge.

Thus a variety of circumstances combined to give the young genius an abundance of different musical experiences. With passionate eagerness he absorbed them all—Reinken's and Lübeck's virtuosity; the Hamburg

---

[1] The connection with another Lüneburg organist, Johann Jakob Löw(e), conjectured by Spitta and Terry, seems of minor importance only. Löw was not really a Thuringian, but a Viennese, who called himself 'von Eisenach' because this was his father's native town. When Sebastian came to Lüneburg, Löw was 72 and probably not interested in a young singer.

[2] Fock, *l.c.*, contends that almost all the organ and clavier works by Böhm which have been preserved may be traced back to copies made by Sebastian.

opera; the French elegant *manières*, Böhm's individual language; the old choral music—until they all became an integral part of his own personality. Lüneburg, with its peculiar location near two important, and so very different, musical centres, was indeed an ideal place for Sebastian's musical training. At the same time nobody could have displayed a fiercer determination to get hold of, and to exhaust to the uttermost limit, all the golden opportunities that were within his grasp.

II

YEARS OF GROWTH

(1703-1708)

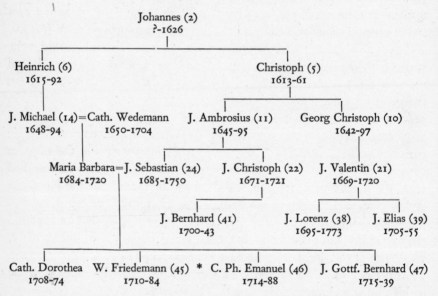

* The twins who died in the year of their birth are not specifically mentioned here.

By Easter 1702[1] Sebastian had finished his studies at the *Michaelisschule* and was ready for a University. Attending any such institution with-

---

[1] The assumption of former biographers that Sebastian stayed at the Latin school in Lüneburg for three years seems unfounded, cf. Fock, *l.c.* Sebastian had already started work on the last class of the Latin school in Ohrdruf, and in view of his former scholastic progress it cannot be assumed that it took him more than three years altogether to master the curriculum of the senior year. What he did until he found a position in 1703, and where he lived, is not known.

XII. Corridor in the Eisenach 'Bach House.' Oil-painting by Paul Bach

XIII. First page of J. Sebastian Bach's Cantata 'Es erhub sich ein Streit'

out funds would have presented a big but not insoluble problem to so
energetic and resourceful a youth. But Sebastian did not seriously consider studying at a University; he was most eager to start musical work in
earnest and felt ready for any position that might come his way. In later
years he may have regretted this decision, as in 18th-century Germany
attendance at a University made a tremendous difference to a musician's
standing both socially and economically. For this reason, when it came to
his own sons, he was anxious to give them a University education, although there was no doubt in his mind that they would eventually choose
musical professions. But as a youth of 17 Sebastian was not far-sighted
enough to adopt such a policy, and there was nobody close enough to him
to advise him. Where to look for suitable employment was the question
that now arose. Significantly enough, he did not consider staying in
Northern Germany, where he had established numerous contacts, any one
of which might have led to an appointment. For purposes of study and
artistic improvement this part of Germany had been excellently suited.
But when it came to settling down, he decided to travel all the 200 miles
back to Thuringia, where his forebears had tended the musical soil for
almost two centuries. This he did out of a deeply rooted allegiance to the
family tradition, and out of longing for contacts with his kinsfolk, a
longing particularly strong in one who, since the age of 10, had missed
normal family ties. Apart from this consideration, there were also practical
reasons in favour of Thuringia. There the very name of Bach was
honoured and would be enough to secure the beginner a position. The
family was also sure to lend all the help it could, just as Sebastian was to
do again and again for other musicians of the clan, and its members were
often in possession of the necessary inside information regarding a vacancy
which sometimes spelt the difference between success and failure.

In 1703, three different organist's posts were due to be filled in
Thuringia. One was at the *Jakobikirche* at Sangerhausen, the organist of
which had died in July 1702. That Sebastian applied is revealed in a letter
he himself wrote some thirty years later to a Sangerhausen Council
member. From it we learn that after all the votes had been cast in his
favour, and the post promised to him, the Lord of the town, a Duke of
Saxe-Weissenfels, had interceded, as he wanted the position to be filled
by a more mature musician, Joh. Augustin Kobelius. Naturally the Duke's
protégé was appointed, and Sebastian had to content himself with a
promise of subsequent favours (a promise he was to redeem successfully
for one of his sons).

At Eisenach, also, the town organist's position became vacant through

I

the death of Johann Christoph Bach on March 31, 1703. Sebastian must have been greatly attracted by this opening in the city of his birth. Whether he applied for the position or not, we do not know. At all events the post was given to an older and more renowned member of the family, Johann Bernhard Bach. A more promising opportunity, however, seemed to be materializing in another Bach centre, Arnstadt. There the old church of St. Boniface, which in 1581 had been devastated by fire, had been rebuilt some hundred years later and was now once more in use under the name of the *Neue Kirche*.[1] At first it had no organ at all, but eventually enough money was collected to start building an instrument, for which an organist would be needed before long. Early in 1703 the work was nearly completed, and Sebastian's relatives began to exert themselves on his behalf. Naturally such endeavours could not be rushed, and in the meantime Sebastian had to earn his daily bread. He therefore took the first position that presented itself, entering as a 'lackey and violinist' the small chamber orchestra[2] of Johann Ernst, a younger and very artistic brother of the reigning Duke of Weimar. It looked as though Sebastian were following the tradition established by his father and grandfather (the latter had also begun his career at Weimar in the double capacity of servant and instrumentalist), but he was really only marking time until an organist's post, on which he had set his heart, was offered to him. Meanwhile he tried to play the organ as much as possible, acting as deputy for the aged court organist, Johann Effler.[3] This was not only a valuable experience for young Sebastian, it was also helpful for the negotiations in Arnstadt. Martin Feldhaus, mayor of the town and kinsman to the Bachs as son-in-law of the town clerk Wedemann (cf. p. 35), did not fail to make good use of this fact. Indeed, when he succeeded in having the 18-year-old Sebastian Bach invited to test the new organ, the receipt he drew up on payment of Sebastian's expenses gives the youth the exaggerated title of 'Princely Saxonian Court Organist at Weimar,' which was by no means in accordance with the facts.

Testing and playing the new organ, young Sebastian had a chance of revealing his stupendous mastery to the Arnstadt citizens, and there is no doubt that he swept them off their feet. The usual procedure of inviting several candidates for trial performances was dispensed with, and hardly

---

[1] In 1935 its name was changed to *Bach Kirche*.

[2] Sebastian probably received the position through the intervention of a member of this orchestra, his distant kinsman, David Hoffmann, who was a grandson of the Suhl town musician, Christoph Hoffmann (cf. p. 74).

[3] Effler had preceded Michael Bach at Gehren (cf. p. 38) and succeeded Johann Bach at Erfurt.

a month after his appearance, Sebastian received a contract granting him a yearly salary of 50 fl., plus 34 fl. for board and lodging.[1] This income was, as organists' remunerations went in those days, an excellent one. Heinrich Bach, in his 50 years of service, had never received so much, nor was Sebastian's eldest brother in Ohrdruf ever to earn what his pupil was granted from the outset. It is significant that Sebastian, although anxious to work in the same capacity and in the same place as his kinsmen, was, even as a youth of 18, determined to build up his life on more favourable material conditions. Like his great relative, Johann Christoph of Eisenach, he felt that the service he rendered entitled him to a fair subsistence and, in contrast to Johann Christoph, he had enough self-assurance and driving power to convince his superiors of the rightness of his claims.

On August 14, 1703, the new organist entered upon his duties. These were not extensive; he was to play every Sunday from 8-10 a.m., every Monday at an intercessory service, and every Thursday from 7-9 a.m. Since his church had not engaged a Cantor, he was supposed, although his contract did not specifically mention it, to train a small choir formed of pupils from the Latin school for performances during the Sunday service. It seemed to be an ideal position for a young musician who needed plenty of time for his own improvement and creative work. Arnstadt, a city of 3800 inhabitants, was also a pleasant place to live in. Its many linden trees had earned it the name of the 'Linden-town'; the gardens surrounding its castle, with their flower-beds arranged in patterns of beautiful tapestries, their grottoes and fountains, were considered outstanding in Germany, while the Romanesque *Liebfrauenkirche* and the Renaissance Town Hall belonged to the gems of Thuringian architecture. In the reign of Anton Günther II,[2] various prominent men were assembled at the small court; among them, in charge of the numismatic collection, was the learned Andreas Morelli, who had formerly been attached to the Paris court.[3] The court orchestra was directed by Paul Gleitsmann, and as it did not consist of court employees only, the conductor would certainly have secured the services of so eminent and versatile a musician as Sebastian.

In addition to the advantages of a good position, there was the pleasure of renewing contact with members of his own family. Of the

---

[1] Sebastian was paid 25 fl. out of the beer taxes, 25 fl. out of the church treasury, while the additional 34 fl. were granted by the Hospital 'on command of the Princely Consistory.'

[2] He was elevated to the rank of Prince in 1697, but only used the title as late as 1707.

[3] From 1689 to 1697 the poet, Salomo Franck, was active there as 'government-secretary.' Sebastian was to meet him subsequently in Weimar and set various cantatas of Franck's to music.

older generation there was only Heinrich Bach's son-in-law and successor, Christoph Herthum, and the widow of Ambrosius' twin brother, Johann Christoph. But of Sebastian's own age group there were the widow's three children, among them Johann Ernst, with whom he shared unforgettable artistic experiences in Hamburg; and there was Maria Barbara, youngest daughter of the late organist of Gehren, Johann Michael Bach. Both the girl's parents were dead by 1704, and she lived with her uncle, Martin Feldhaus, and an aunt, Regina Wedemann, in the house of 'The Golden Crown,' where, according to documents preserved, Sebastian also boarded for several years. Sebastian and Barbara were of approximately the same age; both had been reared in homes where music was considered of paramount importance; and both were orphans drifting along without strong personal ties. Each could lighten the other's solitude and provide in each other's lives the anchorage they both needed. No wonder the two young people were drawn irresistibly towards each other, and 'The Golden Crown' witnessed the growth of an idyllic love affair. The blood relationship was considered too remote to present an obstacle, since they were second cousins, their grandfathers having been brothers. Sebastian and Barbara planned to get married as soon as his position was secure enough to enable them to set up a home of their own. Several years were to pass, however, before this plan could materialize, years which were not too easy for either of them.

There were certain difficulties involved in Sebastian's work, which in course of time assumed larger and larger proportions. The choir he was supposed to train was small and of very poor quality. As the 'New Church' was the least important in Arnstadt, it was inevitably allotted the worst material, while the good singers were employed in the other two churches of the town. Not only were Sebastian's charges mediocre musicians, they were also an unruly lot, behaving (as the City Council complained to the Consistory) in 'a scandalous manner.' To achieve good results with such an unco-operative group, a mature man of high authority was needed; a musician like Sebastian, who was younger than some of the singers, had a difficult position indeed. These complications were further aggravated by the young genius' lack of patience with incompetent musicians, and by his temper, which, when provoked, could assume violent proportions. Thus his intercourse with the recalcitrant group was by no means characterized by the dignified behaviour to be expected of a servant of the church. After two years of unpleasantness, things came to a head in a street brawl which occurred between the organist and a particularily offensive rowdy by the name of Geyersbach. The latter, by three years Sebastian's senior, happened to meet Bach on a dark night and attacked him with a stick, calling him a 'dirty dog' because the organist had made fun of him as a 'nanny-goat bassoonist.' Sebastian drew his sword, a fight began, and blood would have been shed had not the spectators intervened after sundry holes had been pierced in Geyersbach's camisole. The incident made Sebastian even more disgusted with the choir, and gradually he stopped working with it. Various unpleasant cross-examinations by the Consistory followed (of which the files have been preserved). Again and again his superiors urged him to accept the 'imperfect conditions,' which they readily admitted, and work with the choir, but he stubbornly persisted in his point of view that the contract did not provide for this work, and that it should be entrusted to a choir master.[1]

Maria Barbara must have worried a good deal over this conflict between her beloved and the authorities, but she could not learn too early the hard lesson that there was no pliability in Sebastian's nature. When he considered his claim justified, he would fight for it to the bitter end, even at the risk of endangering his own position. Indeed, the choir was not the only point of difference between the youthful organist and his superiors. Soon after the Geyersbach affair, Sebastian, anxious to forget his personal problems in a great musical experience, asked for four weeks' leave to visit the famous organist, Dietrich Buxtehude,[2] in Lübeck, and suggested that his cousin, Johann Ernst, should act as his substitute at the 'New Church.' The Consistory well understood their gifted young organist's desire to improve his art and gave him their permission to make the trip. So Sebastian turned again towards the North, this time travelling a distance of 230 miles.[3] His plan was to attend the famous 'Evening musics' which Buxtehude conducted at St. Mary's on five Sundays around Advent.[4] He arrived in Lübeck just in time for these events and found that the reality actually exceeded his highest expectations. Performances on such a scale (with 40 instruments taking part in addition to the choir) and of such perfection Sebastian had never previously witnessed. He even had a chance of attending the stirring 'Evening music' held in memory of the

[1] It seems that when Sebastian refused to co-operate, the training of the choir was done by Herthum's son-in-law, Andreas Börner.

[2] He had probably heard much about Buxtehude from Böhm, whose work was greatly influenced by the Lübeck organist.

[3] The *Necrolog* states that he made the trip on foot, but this seems unlikely because of the short time available.

[4] They took place on the last two Sundays after Trinity and the second, third, and fourth Sunday in Advent.

deceased Emperor Leopold I, as well as the celebration of the new Emperor's accession. Sebastian was held spellbound in Lübeck, and the idea of returning to his post at the end of the four weeks' leave did not enter his mind. He did not even trouble to write his superiors an apology for his greatly delayed return. The only thing that mattered was to absorb all the intricacies of Buxtehude's art. These were indeed glorious days for Bach, who was forever making new and exciting discoveries which were to be most fruitful in his own creative work. For Barbara, however, far away at Arnstadt, worrying over the reaction of Sebastian's superiors, they may have been hard to bear. It seems not unlikely that her beloved was so engrossed by his tremendous artistic experiences that he did not even write to her. But he did remain faithful; for when it was hinted to him that he might become Buxtehude's successor, providing he married, according to custom, the master's daughter, Anna Margreta, then 30 years old, he declined, although the position at St. Mary's must have seemed most attractive to the organist of the smallest church in Arnstadt.[1]

It was after an absence of four months instead of four weeks that Sebastian reappeared in Arnstadt. Soon the congregation noticed a change in their organist's playing. Encouraged by what he had heard in Lübeck and overflowing with new ideas, Sebastian became rather unconventional in his accompaniments of the hymns, and his improvisations between the verses seemed never to come to an end. The congregation was amazed, bewildered, outraged and at times unable to stumble through the chorales. Finally the organist was again called before the Superintendent, Olearius, who, after reproaching him for his unauthorized long absence, took him to account for the 'many curious variations' he was inserting into the accompaniment. Strict orders were given him 'if he used a *tonus peregrinus*' (a strange key) 'to hold it out and not quickly to pass on to something else or even, as he liked to do, to use a *tonus contrarius*' (a key conflicting with the former one).

Though furious at these instructions, Sebastian had no alternative but to obey them, and all the joy went out of his work. If the good burghers wanted a dull organist, no doubt he could satisfy them, he thought. Hence, where he had previously done too much, he now did too little; and this time he was criticized because his preludes were too short. So it went on through the year 1706: complaints from the choral prefect, cross-examinations by his superiors, and ultimata issued to the organist, who promised

---

[1] Buxtehude had also tried unsuccessfully to win first Mattheson, and later Handel, as successor and son-in-law, but he eventually achieved his aim with J. Christian Schiefferdecker, who was of Bach's age and accordingly ten years younger than the bride.

to answer in writing and never did. This Arnstadt position certainly did not offer a suitable basis for matrimony, poor Barbara felt; and finally she herself was the cause of another disagreement with the Consistory. Sebastian asked her to come to the organ gallery when the church was empty, and sing to his accompaniment. This she did, and their music-making must have delighted them both and further strengthened the bond between them. But the aftermath was not so pleasant. In Arnstadt nothing remained a secret for long. Someone had heard Barbara singing, tongues were set wagging, and Sebastian was again summoned by the Consistory to explain the presence of a 'strange maiden' in the organ gallery.

By that time the organist was aware that he would have to look for another position. Fortunately a good opportunity presented itself before long. In the Free Imperial City of Mühlhausen, the highly renowned composer and organist of St. Blasius', Johann Georg Ahle, had died in December 1706. Once more the family got busy to secure the position for Sebastian. Maria Barbara was related on her mother's side to the Mühlhausen Councillor, Johann Hermann Bellstedt,[1] and it was he who carried on the negotiations with young Bach. His recommendation was probably supported by the Mühlhausen organ builder, J. F. Wender, who had built Arnstadt's new instrument, which Sebastian had tested and approved in 1703. Thus it came about that young Bach was invited to give his trial performance at Easter 1707. Again he overwhelmed the congregation with his superb playing, and the pattern established at Arnstadt repeated itself.

The authorities were truly anxious to secure his services and were even prepared for financial sacrifices. Asked to state his terms, Sebastian requested the salary he got at Arnstadt; and although Ahle, in spite of the esteem he had enjoyed, had received only 66 fl. 14 gr. yearly, the new organist was granted a yearly income of 85 fl. plus the amounts of grain, wood, and fish allowed to Ahle. The Council also undertook to send a waggon to Arnstadt for the transport of the organist's belongings.

In June Bach again appeared before the Arnstadt Consistory, but with very different emotions! No recriminations were uttered this time, no evasive answers were necessary on his part; he merely notified the authorities of his appointment at Mühlhausen and asked for permission to hand back the keys of the organ. Everything went off smoothly; none of the two parties expressed their relief at this fortunate solution of an awkward problem, and young Sebastian in voicing his thanks displayed for once all

[1] Susanna Barbara Wedemann, aunt and godmother of Maria Barbara Bach, had married in 1680 Johann Gottfried Bellstedt, a kinsman of the Mühlhausen Councillor.

the courtesy that custom demanded. This was most necessary, for the Consistory had, in effect, the power to annul his appointment by not accepting his resignation; and he knew that it was for such reasons that both his father, Ambrosius, and his uncle, Johann Christoph Bach, had been compelled to refuse outside offers and stay on in Eisenach. However, nothing of this kind happened, and the Consistory felt friendly enough disposed towards the Bach clan to appoint as Sebastian's successor his cousin, Johann Ernst, though with one significant stipulation: Johann Ernst's salary was to be only 40 fl., less than half Sebastian's stipend.[1]

Sebastian was now 22 years old and anxious to end his bachelor existence. Having exchanged a good position for another equally good, he felt able to take care of a wife and children. If he still had any fears about the extra expenses he would incur over the wedding and the furnishing of a modest home (responsibilities which he might have to shoulder alone, as his fiancée was an orphan without means), such fears were dispelled by a small legacy that came his way just at that time through the death of his uncle, Tobias Lämmerhirt.[2] At first Sebastian went to Mühlhausen alone, to start his work and to find suitable accommodation; but it was not long before he returned to Arnstadt for his bride. On October 17, 1707, the little church of Dornheim, a village near Arnstadt, witnessed the simple wedding ceremony of Sebastian and Barbara Bach. The choice of this church was due to the family's friendship with its pastor, Lorenz Stauber, who himself was to marry Barbara's aunt, Regina Wedemann, a few months later.[3]

So Sebastian Bach assumed the responsibilities of a married man at a

---

[1] Johann Ernst (25) retained this position up to 1728, when, after the death of his kinsman, Andreas Börner, he became organist of Arnstadt's other two churches and received a salary of 77 fl. He died, almost blind, in 1739, and as his only son was but 2 years old at the time the organist's position which had been held by the Bach clan ever since 1641 (by first Heinrich Bach, then his son-in-law Herthum, the latter's son-in-law Börner, and finally Johann Ernst Bach) was lost to the family. A daughter of Johann Ernst lived on at Arnstadt up to her death in 1792, the last member of the family to be traced in this town.

[2] By a curious coincidence another legacy reached him fourteen years later, when he was about to conclude a second marriage. This time it came from the widow of Tobias Lämmerhirt.

[3] Stauber's first wife was a Hoffmann, probably a kinswoman of the Bachs. The wedding of Stauber and Regina Wedemann occurred on June 5, 1708, and was attended by the young Bach couple. It is probable that Sebastian's wedding cantata, Der Herr denket an uns, was written for this occasion. The friendship between the Staubers and Bach was maintained even after the latter's removal to Leipzig. When Regina died in 1731, her last will provided a legacy for the Thomas Cantor and his second wife.

very young age. This was entirely in keeping with the family tradition, although it seems early to us who are used to consider freedom from personal ties and responsibilities as one of the requirements for the development of a young genius. But such freedom was not what Sebastian needed. To him, who at the age of 10 had been deprived of his parents, nothing seemed so desirable as a peaceful home where he really belonged. If ever a genius was suited to the state of matrimony, it was Sebastian Bach. He chose his partner with deep wisdom (such as neither Haydn nor Mozart possessed), and made of each of his two marriages a tremendous success. Home meant for him not only material comforts, but the sharing of his most profound interests. His spouse had to be more than a good housekeeper; she had to be a musician, able fully to appreciate her husband's work. Sebastian's second wife was a professional singer. Although no evidence has come down to us about Maria Barbara's musicianship (apart from her singing in the Arnstadt church) we can reasonably assume that someone who was descended from a line of outstanding artists, and who became the mother of two of Sebastian's most talented sons, was also a real helpmate to her husband in musical matters.

The newly-wed pair spent a few days with their kinsfolk in Erfurt, and then travelled to Mühlhausen, where Sebastian threw himself vigorously into his new duties.

The position at St. Blasius' conferred greater distinction than that at Arnstadt's least important church. The city of Mühlhausen had harboured a number of eminent musicians, and during the past fifty years St. Blasius' in particular had possessed quite outstanding organists in Johann Rudolph Ahle and his son, Johann Georg. Sebastian could not fail to be stimulated by the standard set by such renowned predecessors. All his aspirations for the improvement of church music, which had lain dormant in the uncongenial Arnstadt atmosphere, now manifested themselves with elemental force. The way he shouldered his new responsibilities would have amazed his former employers. Once more the contract merely stipulated that he should play the organ at all the services held at St. Blasius'. This time, however, such work was by no means sufficient for Sebastian. He felt responsible for the entire music offered in his church, and, furthermore, he even took a lively interest in the musical progress of the neighbouring villages. At St. Blasius' he found the repertory somewhat old-fashioned, as the Ahles had mainly favoured the simple chorale-like sacred aria with instrumental ritornelli, neglecting the type of cantata developed by Buxtehude and other North German masters. This had of course to be changed, and so Sebastian, together with his pupil, Johann

Martin Schubart, diligently set about copying suitable works for the church library. He sometimes found performances more to his taste in the villages, and in his undiplomatic manner did not hesitate to say so, which was not exactly pleasing to the Mühlhausen citizens. He rejoiced in helping the village musicians and even provided some of his own compositions for their services, as he also did for the requirements of Mühlhausen. For the solemn inauguration in February 1708 of the new burgomasters and members of the Council, he wrote the 'congratulatory motet' *Gott ist mein König*, making splendid use of what he had learned from Buxtehude. The congregation could not help being thrilled by this solemn music, and his employers were so pleased that they had the work printed.[1] The Councillors' appreciation of their new organist was further heightened when he handed them soon afterwards a careful survey of the deficiencies of his organ with advice on how to repair the instrument. So convincing was the craftsmanship and intrinsic knowledge revealed in each of his suggestions that they were accepted without demur, and an organ builder was entrusted with their execution. Sebastian's specifications have been preserved, and from them we may reconstruct the young organist's idea of a good instrument. He liked the Baroque arrangement of the organ stops in groups, the members of which are closely interrelated in construction and tone-quality, while each group is sharply contrasted from the remainder in sonority and timbre. As he wished to increase the possibilities of such contrasts in dynamic power and tone-colour, he wanted the addition of a third manual to the two manuals and pedal of the Mühlhausen organ, as well as an increase in the number of bellows.[2] Moreover, 'as a novel inclusion' he urged the building of a set of chimes operated from the pedal, which he had devised himself. It is interesting to note that the organ he suggested for Mühlhausen had much in common with the remodelled instrument of the Eisenach *Georgenkirche*, which Johann Christoph Bach had planned with so much care (cf. p. 36). Although the reconstruction

[1] Although such 'congratulatory motets' were often published, this was by no means the rule. In the years 1710 to 1713, for instance, in Mühlhausen, the text but not the music was printed.

[2] Though this is generally done, it does not seem justified to deduce from a document which Bach drafted at the age of 23 the *mature* master's conception of the ideal organ. It appears that the Leipzig Bach tried to avoid strong contrasts in the timbre of the stops and aimed rather at mixing and combining them. He worked towards their arrangement in two groups: the clear and bold open diapasons and the softer, less distinct accompanying stops suited for the execution of the continuo. In this way the solo and tutti arrangement of the concerto (a form which was of paramount importance for Bach's later organ works) also found expression in his conception of the ideal organ. Cf. W. Gurlitt, 'J. S. Bach,' 3rd ed., 1949.

work at Eisenach was not begun until a year after Sebastian left, he doubtless had heard all the details of it from his relatives, and had perhaps even examined the instrument itself on its completion in 1707. That he let Johann Christoph's plan influence him so strongly in rebuilding his own organ shows again how firm were the artistic ties that bound him to his great forebears.

Although his advice regarding the organ was fully heeded in Mühlhausen, troubles for the young organist arose in other respects. Sebastian's pastor, Superintendent Frohne, had decided leanings towards Pietism, that new trend towards a more subjective faith that had been born out of a healthy reaction against the increasing petrifaction and narrow-mindedness of the Lutheran doctrine as preached in the orthodox churches. The conflict was somewhat akin to that which had once existed between early Protestantism and the Catholic Church. Pietism stressed the importance of the Christian *life* against that of the mechanical adoption of dogma. In their striving for a religious revival, the Pietists shunned much that played an important role in the Protestant service. Some declared the Bible word preached in church to be 'dead,' unless its meaning found a deep response in the listener's soul; music, too, could become dangerous if it had too strong an effect on the senses. Thus many Pietistic theologians fought energetically against the inclusion of concerted music in the service,[1] decrying it as 'sirensongs disturbing meditation, mixing the world's vanity with the sacred, and corrupting the gold of divine truth.'[2] It was an anti-artistic attitude very much like that of the Puritans. Pastor Frohne may have been responsible for the musical austerity prevalent at St. Blasius' before Sebastian arrived, and when he found his organist eagerly bent on remedying such shortcomings, he must have hesitated to support him. Nor can we assume that the congregation followed the newcomer's lead too readily. Reforms are nowhere accepted by the majority without demurring, and Mühlhausen certainly was no exception to the rule. What they had been accustomed to hear in the 33 years' service of Johann Georg Ahle (who, after all, was a native of Mühlhausen, and not just an outsider like this young Bach) was good enough for them, they felt. So quite a few rejected the organist's innovations as 'too worldly' and 'carnal.' Neverthe-

---

[1] This was not true of all the Pietists. Some sects, as for example the *Herrenhuter*, were in favour of elaborate church music; on the other hand, there were also orthodox pastors who condemned the concertizing organ style. Cf. Besch, 'J. S. Bach. Frömmigkeit und Glaube,' Kassel, 1950.

[2] These remarks are quoted by Bach's predecessor, J. G. Ahle, in a new edition of his father's 'Kurze und deutliche Anleitung zu der lieblich und löblichen Singekunst' of 1704.

less, such difficulties might eventually have been smoothed out and a compromise agreed upon with pastor Frohne, who was not a fanatic and was likely to have appreciated his organist's true faith. Unfortunately, Sebastian could not help taking sides in a feud between Frohne and the pastor of St. Mary's, Georg Christian Eilmar, on matters of dogma. The latter, a passionate upholder of Orthodoxy, had started violent attacks against Frohne's Pietism as early as 1699. At that time the Council intervened and interdicted any further dispute of the kind. Now, however, the old conflict was again brought into the open and the fight conducted in anything but a Christian spirit. Eilmar was the more aggressive, and his rigid insistence on the letter of the dogma does not make him appear in too pleasant a light. But he had one point in his favour: he allowed music an important part in the service. He wrote libretti for some of Sebastian's cantatas,[1] and apparently thought much of the organist's talent. To receive encouragement both in his general aims and in his creative efforts from so important a man must have meant a good deal to the young composer, and it naturally drew him towards Eilmar. He closed his eyes to Eilmar's narrow-mindedness and reactionary formalism and became sufficiently friendly with the pastor to suggest his being godfather to the first child which his young wife was expecting. Eilmar accepted, and when the girl was born in December 1708 he went to Weimar, whither the Bachs had moved, to attend the christening ceremony. The friendly connection continued, and for Sebastian's first son, Friedemann, Eilmar's daughter, Anna Dorothea Hagedorn, stood godmother.

Looking at Sebastian's attitude from the viewpoint of his artistic personality, we are faced with a paradox. How could one who expressed with such eloquence the yearning for a mystic union with Christ, whose music was imbued with a longing to be relieved from the fetters of the mortal flesh, how could such an artist fight these very same emotions in the Pietistic doctrine? The clue to this riddle may perhaps be found in Sebastian's background and in his youth. He had been brought up in Lutheran Orthodoxy, and a man so deeply conscious of his family ties naturally felt bound to adhere to the type of religion his forebears had believed in. At the age of 23, overflowing with creative impulses, and eager to try out all kinds of artistic experiments, Sebastian had little time for introspection. He did not probe into the depths of his own faith, but

---

[1] This is certain for *Gott ist mein König* and probable for *Aus der Tiefe rufe ich* which bears at the end the note 'at the request of Mr. Georg Chr. Eilmar set to music by J. S. Bach, organist of Mühlhausen.' He may also have provided libretti for other cantatas of this period.

simply followed the way which both his artistic interests and the tradition of the Bach clan (though not that of his mother's family!) clearly indicated. The Pietists, with their rejection of elaborate church music, were his enemies; the Orthodox, who saw in beautiful music a means of glorifying the Lord, his friends. Beyond that he did not venture. This does not mean, however, that he maintained so intransigent an attitude throughout his life. There is no definite proof that he remained intolerant in his adherence to Orthodoxy;[1] certainly the texts he used for some of his cantatas show him to have been anything but inimical to the spirit of Pietism.

But whatever his subsequent attitude may have been, in Mühlhausen Sebastian could not see eye to eye with his Pietistic pastor, and consequently, less than a year after taking over the position, he was anxious to give it up. Luck was with him. In Weimar a court organist was needed to replace the aged and infirm Johann Effler, and Sebastian presented himself in June 1708, gave his trial performance, and was naturally accepted. Thereupon he wrote the following letter to the Mühlhausen Council:

'*Magnificenz*, High and very Noble, High and
        respected Gentlemen,
  Most Gracious Patrons and Gentlemen,

   'This is to express to your *Magnificenz*, and to my highly esteemed Patrons who of your grace bestowed on me, your humble servant, the office, vacant a year ago, of Organist to the church of St. Blasius, and granted me the enjoyment of a better subsistence, that at all times I desire to recognize your favours with obedient gratitude. I have always kept one end in view, namely, with all good will to conduct a well regulated church music to the honour of God, in agreement with your desires, and besides to assist, so far as possible to my humble ability, the church music that has grown up in almost all the neighbouring parishes, which is often better than the harmony produced here. To that end I have obtained from far and wide, and not without expense, a good collection of the choicest pieces of church music.

   'Furthermore I have laid before you the report of the defects in the

---

   [1] The tendency of many Bach biographers to conclude from Sebastian's attitude in Mühlhausen that his strict adherence to Orthodoxy and his animosity towards Pietism lasted throughout his life does not seem justified. This would mean a lack of spiritual growth not in keeping with the nature of genius. As a further proof of Bach's Orthodoxy his library is usually referred to, which contained some 80 theological works, most of which were by leaders of Lutheran Orthodoxy. This certainly reveals the composer's strong interest in these problems, but we cannot deduce from it that he completely shared the several authors' views.

organ needing repair, and at all times and places have with pleasure fulfilled the duties of my office. Yet this has not been done without opposition, and at present there is not the slightest appearance that things will be
altered, though in time, no doubt, our congregation will be brought to
approve. Moreover I have humbly to represent that, modest as is my way
of life, with the payment of house-rent and the purchase of indispensable
articles of consumption, I can only with difficulty carry on a fitting
establishment.

'Now God has so ordered it that a change has unexpectedly been
presented to me, in which I foresee the attainment of a more sufficient
subsistence and the more effective pursuit of my aims in the due ordering
of church music without interference from others, since His Royal and
Serene Highness of Saxe-Weimar has graciously offered me the *entrée* to
His Court Capelle and Chamber Music.

'In consequence of this privilege I hereby, with obedience and respect,
represent it to my Most Gracious Patrons, and at the same time would ask
them to take my small services to the church up to this time into favourable consideration, and to grant me the benefit of providing me with a
gracious dismissal. If I can in any way further contribute to the service of
your church I will prove myself better in deed than in word, as long as life
shall endure.

'I am, Most Honourable Gentlemen, Most Gracious Patrons,
                    Your Most Humble Servant,
                                    Joh. Seb. Bach.

Mühlhausen, June 25, anno 1708.'

The concluding remark evidently refers to the organ repairs started at
his instigation. The authorities, while regretfully consenting to the
organist's departure, asked him to continue to supervise the work; he
promised gladly. Indeed, so friendly remained his relations with the Mühlhausen Councillors that he was again commissioned, in 1709, to write the
'congratulatory motet' for the inauguration of the new Council.[1]

Before leaving, Sebastian was able once more to suggest a cousin as
his successor. The Council agreed, but insisted (again in the pattern of
Arnstadt) that the new organist should receive a much lower salary. Thus
Sebastian was replaced by Johann Friedrich, son of the great Johann
Christoph of Eisenach, who, in the good old family tradition, retained

---

[1] Although this cantata was printed too, no copy has been traced so far, and we do
not even know its title. Yet the Mühlhausen files prove irrefutably that Bach wrote such
a work. Cf. 'Mühlhäuser Geschichtsblätter,' 1932.

the position up to his death in 1730. But such stability was as yet impossible for Sebastian, and so we see him in July 1708 joyfully starting a new life at Weimar.

III

THE GREAT ORGANIST
(1708-1717)

The geographical distance between Mühlhausen and Weimar is not more than 40 miles. Socially and economically, however, Sebastian travelled a long way when he exchanged his position in the Free Imperial City for one at the ducal court. From the outset his new salary was almost twice what he received in Mühlhausen, and it was destined to grow steadily throughout his stay at Weimar. And although succeeding the Ahles, father and son, at St. Blasius' had been a privilege indeed, yet, in the eyes of the world, a good position at a ducal court bestowed still more prestige. Added to the material advantages there were other considerations which meant much to the organist. His new patron was a fervent and deeply religious Lutheran, who valued music as an important means of glorifying the Lord. Here Sebastian found encouragement for carrying out his schemes for 'a well regulated church music,' and no opposition was to be anticipated from other religious sects, as the Duke, who ruled his land with an iron hand, would not tolerate anything but orthodox Lutheranism.

Later in the century, the small court of Weimar was to become the Athens of Germany, witnessing the golden age of literature dominated by the gigantic figures of Goethe and Schiller. Then, like a magnet, Weimar was to attract men eminent in all the realms of culture, men who were to find in the small residence of the enlightened Duke Carl August a most congenial atmosphere. In Bach's time there was as yet hardly a breath of that invigorating cultural climate, but even then Weimar was clearly different from the average small German court. Here religion was the axis around which everything revolved. The serious-minded Duke Wilhelm Ernst, in the 45 years of his rule, struck this note, and the court followed his lead. All ducal servants had to attend daily devotions and take turns in reading the Bible aloud. To let the attention wander during a sermon was highly dangerous, for the Duke had the unpleasant habit of questioning his servants personally on every detail of the chaplain's discourse. It was also the Serenissimus himself who worked out the order in which his

employees were to appear at the altar for Communion. Not only was the
Duke engrossed in matters of religious dogma; he also attempted to lead
a truly Christian life. Hence there arose at Weimar an atmosphere of
austerity which was in strong contrast to the frivolity and extravagance
prevalent at other German courts. Not a glimmer of light was visible
about the castle after 8 p.m. in the winter and 9 p.m. in the summer.
Festivities were rare, and even the troupe of actors[1] which the Duke
had employed for some years was dismissed before Sebastian's arrival.
Wilhelm Ernst's tastes were frugal but he insisted on a supply of fresh
flowers every day; to meet his needs he had the castle's bearpit, where his
predecessors had kept wild beasts, transformed into a beautiful garden.
Whilst allowing only a small budget for entertainment, the Duke spent
considerable sums on welfare and cultural institutions; showing himself
in all such enterprises an important precursor of that type of enlightened
ruler which Germany and Austria were to produce some 50 years later.
Yet, on the other hand, he was convinced of his absolute power, and
accepted as a matter of course the idea, characteristic of the epoch, that an
unbridgeable gulf existed between his august self and his subjects. He was, in
short, a despot, though a well-meaning one. In the field of music, however,
the new organist's ideas seemed to move along the same lines as those of
the patron, and there was every prospect of a harmonious relationship
between Duke Wilhelm Ernst and Sebastian Bach. The Prince came to
value his organist's gifts very highly, and to trust his judgment in musical
matters implicitly. Although the organ of the *Schlosskirche* had been
reconstructed as recently as 1708, Bach succeeded in inducing his patron
to spend further substantial sums on it. First he had a set of chimes installed similar to those he had prescribed for the Mühlhausen church, and
before long he suggested a complete reconstruction, which the organ
builder, Heinrich Trebs, executed between 1712 and 1714.[2] The Duke's
co-operative attitude was all the young musician needed to unfold his
genius. It was at Weimar that Bach the organist climbed to the loftiest
heights. As his patron allowed him frequent absences, during which his
competent pupil, J. M. Schubart, deputized, Sebastian often played at
other courts and cities too, and his fame as an organ virtuoso spread all
over Germany. Legends began to circulate; how all unknown he had
visited a village church and coaxed such magnificent sounds out of a
wretched instrument that the village organist whispered: 'This can only

---

[1] In 1696 the theatre was inaugurated with a work bearing the characteristic title
'Of virtuous Love as opposed to sinful Desire.'

[2] Cf. Jauernig in 'Johann Sebastian Bach in Thüringen,' 1950.

be the devil or Bach himself!' But the awe and admiration of his contemporaries for Sebastian's stupendous virtuosity are also laid down in authentic reports. Constantin Bellermann, a rector of Minden, describes Bach's performance on the pedals at the court of Cassel thus: 'His feet flew over the pedal-board as though they had wings, and powerful sounds roared like thunder through the church. This filled Frederick, the Crown Prince, with such astonishment and admiration that he drew from his finger a ring set with precious stones and gave it to Bach as soon as the sound had died away. If the skill of his feet alone earned him such a gift, what might the Prince have given him had he used his hands as well.' To which we may add: and what would have been the just reward to the composer of the works that the performer interpreted so miraculously? For simultaneously with the organ virtuoso the organ composer Bach also climbed to the peak of his creative mastery, and the majority of his important organ works were written or at least started in Weimar. Kindled by the prevailing religious atmosphere they achieved a 'disembodied spirituality' (Forkel) which has perhaps been best characterized by the Weimar genius who heard them a century later. Goethe, listening to Bach's organ works, wrote: 'It is as though eternal harmony were conversing with itself, as it may have happened in God's bosom shortly before He created the world.'

Such insight was not given to Sebastian's contemporaries. Though learned musicians could not fail to be impressed by Bach's profound knowledge and superb craftsmanship, to most listeners his dazzling exploits as a performer necessarily obscured his creative achievements. Sebastian's own attitude in this matter will never be known. His was not an age of self-expression and introspection. What he is reported to have said about his own work is therefore quite unrevealing. Complimented on his great organ playing, he answered deprecatingly: 'There is nothing to it. You only have to hit the right notes at the right time and the instrument plays itself.' And Forkel reports: 'When he was asked how he had contrived to master the art to such a high degree, he generally answered: "I was obliged to work hard; whoever is equally industrious, will succeed just as well."' It seems doubtful whether Bach was as modest as these utterances suggest. They were dictated rather by innate reserve and a natural contempt for people who asked questions that defied a real answer.

There is yet a third aspect of Sebastian's activities in connection with the organ. He gradually attained the position of a highly skilled expert on the construction of the instrument, and in this capacity he constantly received invitations to test newly completed or repaired organs. 'He was,' as Forkel reports, on the basis of information from Philipp Emanuel Bach, 'very severe, but always just, in his trials of organs. As he was perfectly acquainted with the construction of the instrument, he could not be in any case deceived. The first thing he did in trying out an organ was to draw out all the stops and play with the full organ. He used to say in jest that he must know whether the instrument had good lungs. After the examination was over, he generally amused himself and those present by showing his skill as a performer. . . . He would choose some subject and execute it in all the various forms of organ composition, never changing his theme, even though he might play, without intermission, for two hours or more. First he used it for a prelude and a fugue, with the full organ. Then he showed his art of using the stops for a trio, a quartet, etc. Afterwards there followed a chorale, the melody of which was playfully surrounded in the most diversified manner by the original subject, in three or four parts. Finally, the conclusion was made by a fugue, with full organ, in which either another treatment of the first subject predominated, or one or two other subjects were mixed with it.'

Success won outside Weimar naturally had some bearing on his standing there; this was particularly true in the case of Halle. Five years after his arrival in Weimar, Sebastian visited this town and was greatly impressed by the plans for a rebuilding of the huge *Liebfrauenkirche* organ. To work on such an outstanding instrument (with 65 stops!) was tempting indeed; and as the organist's position, held up to 1712 by Handel's teacher, Friedrich Wilhelm Zachau, was still vacant, Sebastian applied for it. The Halle authorities showed themselves very interested, and at their urgent request Sebastian not only gave the customary performance on the organ but also produced a cantata of his own composition. The electors were naturally much struck by his mastery, and hardly had Sebastian returned to Weimar when he received a contract from Halle for signature.[1] The conditions, however, were not too attractive. The yearly salary paid in Halle was 196 fl. (to which some *accidentien* for weddings, etc. could be added) whereas in Weimar he received 225 fl. He therefore wrote back noncommittally and tried to obtain better conditions. Halle remained firm, however, and while Sebastian was weighing

---

[1] Paragraph 4 of this contract stipulated that the organist should accompany the hymns 'quietly on 4 or 5 stops with the Principal, so as not to distract the congregation . . . eschewing the use of Quintatons, reeds, syncopations, and suspensions, allowing the organ to support and harmonize with the congregation's singing.' This shows that Arnstadt's earlier complaints against young Sebastian's too elaborate accompaniment were quite in keeping with the prevailing opinion.

its artistic attractions against the financial loss involved, his Duke considerably improved the Weimar contract, with the result that Sebastian now definitely declined the Halle position. The electors were mortified and hinted that the organist had used them simply as a means of securing better conditions at Weimar. Such insinuations he contested in an energetic letter, and his arguments must have been persuasive enough to calm the Halle authorities; for, two years later, when the great organ was completed, it was Sebastian who, together with the organ experts, Johann Kuhnau and Christian Friedrich Rolle, was invited to test it. Bach, delighted with the Halle electors' change of mind, accepted with alacrity and had a very good time indeed. Not only was it fascinating to try out the new organ, but he also enjoyed co-operating with the Thomas Cantor, Kuhnau, little foreseeing that he would succeed the great musician 7 years later. Halle, on the other hand, outdid itself in courtesies to the three organists. Servants, coaches, and refreshments were more than plentiful. The menu of the concluding banquet is certainly impressive and deserves to be quoted in full:

> Bœuf à la mode.
> Pike with Anchovy Butter Sauce.
> Smoked Ham.
> Sausages and Spinach.
> Roast Mutton.
> Roast Veal.
> Peas. Potatoes. Boiled Pumpkin. Asparagus. Lettuce. Radishes.
> Fritters.
> Candied Lemon Peel. Preserved Cherries.
> Fresh Butter.

The wine is not mentioned especially, but there is every reason to believe that the guests of honour sampled no small amount of it.[1]

From now on work in Weimar was even more absorbing. At the beginning of his employment, Sebastian had been engaged as court organist and chamber musician, the latter title meaning that he also played the violin in the ducal band. A contemporary chronicler reports: 'The Duke's ears frequently enjoyed the playing of 16 well-disciplined musicians clad in Hungarian haiduk uniforms,' and on these occasions Sebastian probably had to appear in this fanciful attire. Nominally the conductor of the band was Johann Samuel Drese, but infirmity and old age made him unable to officiate. For a considerable time his place had been filled

---

[1] In Sebastian's expense bills the item for wine was quite a considerable one. For instance, when he went to Gera in 1724 to examine a new organ, he received 30 fl. as a fee, 10 fl. for transportation, 17 fl. 8 gr. 8 pf. for food, and 7 fl. 8 gr. for wine.

by deputies, the last being Drese's own son, Johann Wilhelm, who had been trained at the Duke's expense in Italy and now held the rank of vice-conductor. The Duke, although supporting the Dreses out of loyalty to an old servant, could not help realizing that it would be a wise move to entrust part of the conductor's duties to his admirable organist. So, when Sebastian received the invitation from Halle, he created for his organist the new post of Concertmaster with a salary of 240 fl., and the obligation of composing and performing a new cantata every month; leaving to the younger Drese the duty of supplying the court with new secular music.[1]

The result was that Sebastian now had an opportunity of working with both singers and instrumentalists, and was able to lay the foundations of his mastery as a conductor. The rehearsals, like the performances, took place in the court chapel, a Baroque monstrosity in the worst taste,[2] which, however, bore a name most appropriate to the music resounding in it, being called the 'Castle of Heaven.'[3] This time the conductor, who led the group with his violin, had no trouble with the singers. There were 12 well-trained vocalists at his disposal, among them the excellent altist, Christian Gerhard Bernhardi, himself a composer, for whom Bach wrote some very intricate parts.[4] The widening of his musical duties brought much joy to the new Concertmaster, and several great cantatas using texts by the eminent Salomo Franck, Secretary of the Consistory, first saw the light in Weimar.

In other respects, too, life was satisfactory at the small Court. Sebastian's home was a happy one. Children arrived regularly, among them three sons—Wilhelm Friedemann, Carl Philipp Emanuel, and Johann Gottfried Bernhard—destined to display outstanding musical talent.

Godparents for the Bachs' offspring were not chosen locally, and it is interesting to note that among 15 persons who acted in this capacity, 13 came from other places. It would seem that Bach, deeply absorbed in creative work, had not too much time for establishing new contacts in Weimar. Yet there was one fellow musician with whom he struck up an important friendship: the town organist, Johann Gottfried Walther, also born in 1685, a pupil of Sebastian's cousin, Johann Bernhard Bach, and, moreover, a kinsman on the Lämmerhirt side (cf. p. 17) who had spent his childhood in the house 'The Three Roses,' where Sebastian's mother was

[1] Cf. Jauernig, l.c.

[2] The chapel was destroyed by fire in 1774 together with the castle, and new buildings were erected according to Goethe's plans.

[3] It was originally called 'Path to the Castle of Heaven' on account of a small pyramid which rose from the altar to the ceiling carrying little cherubs towards Heaven.

[4] Cf. Cantatas 132, 161, 185.

born.[1] The two Weimar organists were both newly married, and when Walther's first son was born, Bach stood godfather. In Walther, an eminent organist and a composer of outstanding chorale preludes, Sebastian found a congenial spirit; in his zeal for self-improvement he discovered that much could be learned from his colleague. In particular, their common interest in Italian music formed a strong bond, and there was a friendly competition between them in the arrangement of Italian concertos for keyboard instruments. According to Walther, Bach presented him with no less than 200 compositions, partly his own and partly Böhm's and Buxtehude's. Friendly relations were also established with Johann Mathias Gesner,[2] vice-principal of the Weimar *Gymnasium*, who became one of Sebastian's staunch admirers. Of course there was also frequent intercourse with kinsmen and with musicians in nearby places. In Eisenach there was Johann Bernhard Bach, and from 1708 to 1712 the celebrated and prolific Georg Philipp Telemann, who, after moving to Frankfurt, stood godfather to Sebastian's second son. The city of Jena, which formed part of the Duke of Weimar's territory, was within reach, and visits to Johann Nicolaus Bach could easily be arranged.

Gifted pupils provided a further enrichment of his life. Among them were the excellent organists, Schubart and Vogler, and also Johann Tobias Krebs, a Cantor himself, who walked regularly for seven years from the village of Buttelstädt to Weimar, in order to receive instruction from Walther and Bach. Continuing the old family tradition, Sebastian undertook the training of two young kinsmen, Johann Lorenz (38), grandson of Georg Christoph (10) from Schweinfurt, and Johann Bernhard (41), son of Sebastian's own teacher and eldest brother, Johann Christoph (22) of Ohrdruf.[3] With four children, various pupils, and one of his wife's sisters who lived with them, Sebastian's home was just as full of life as his hospitable father's had been.

He also had sundry pupils of a more exalted rank. The princely patron whom he had served when first working in Weimar for a few months in 1703 (cf. p. 130) died in 1707, but he left two sons in whom Sebastian was greatly interested. The younger, Johann Ernst, had a really outstanding

[1] The house belonged to Valentin Lämmerhirt, from whose widow it was bought by Hedwig Bach, the wife of Johann. It remained in the family until 1688, when J. Egidius Bach sold it to J. Stefan Walther, the father of the organist.

[2] Gesner had studied at the University of Jena and probably made friends with J. Nicolaus Bach.

[3] J. Lorenz stayed at Weimar from 1713 to 1717, whereupon he was appointed Cantor in Lahm, Franconia. J. Bernhard moved with Sebastian to Cöthen, staying until 1719. In 1721 he succeeded his late father in office.

musical talent, and three of his violin concertos were transcribed by Bach
for keyboard instruments; these works written in the Italian style were
even granted the honour of being mistaken for compositions by Vivaldi.
Johann Ernst's real teacher was Walther; but there was undoubtedly much
artistic intercourse between the court organist and the young Prince, and
Sebastian must have grieved indeed when a tragic fate carried off the
talented youth in 1715 at the age of 19.

But there was an elder brother, Prince Ernst August, who was also
interested in music, and he studied the clavier with Bach. Ernst August
was not what one would call a lovable character; contemporary reports
make him appear a highly eccentric man, whose actions sometimes
bordered on insanity. His ideas about government were decidedly old-
fashioned; for when he succeeded his uncle, Wilhelm Ernst, as a ruler of
Weimar, he issued an edict threatening any subject proved to have
'reasoned,' i.e. criticized conditions in his land, with six months' imprisonment. At the time of Sebastian's work at Weimar, the Prince's views had
not yet assumed so excessive a character. Bach spent a good deal of time
in Ernst August's castle, taking part in its very active musical life,[1] and
the Prince, according to a statement from Emanuel Bach to Forkel, 'particularly loved him and rewarded him appropriately.'[2] This was destined
to be fatal to Sebastian's position in Weimar. The relations between
Wilhelm Ernst, the reigning sovereign, and his nephew and heir, Ernst
August, were very strained indeed. According to the charter of the Duchy
of Saxe-Weimar, all executive power was centred in the eldest Duke, his
younger relatives having a purely consultative role in the government.
So vague a provision naturally opened the door to family quarrels of all
kinds; during Sebastian's stay at Weimar these assumed inordinate proportions. Duke Wilhelm Ernst definitely had a mind of his own and did
not relish any advice from his nephew. Ernst August, on the other hand,
insisted on voicing his opinions and there was constant friction and
antagonism. These were difficult times for the court employees, who
needed a good deal of tact not to become involved in the feud between the
two Princes. The court musicians in particular found themselves in a sad
predicament when Duke Wilhelm Ernst, on pain of a 10 thalers fine,
forbade them to play in his nephew's castle. This was most unfair, as the

---

[1] Jauernig, *l.c.*, points to items in the *Particulier Cammerrechnungen der Fürstl.
Sächs. Jüngeren Linie* revealing considerable expenses for copying music, and buying
instruments. One of these was a *Lautenwerk* acquired for the price of 41 fl. 3 gr. from the
Jena Bach.

[2] Cf. letter to Forkel of January 13, 1775.

musicians counted among the 'joint servants' and were remunerated from the joint treasury. Bach's sense of justice and his independent spirit made him pay no heed to so unreasonable an order. Indeed, on Duke Ernst August's birthday he performed a cantata with musicians from the nearby court of Weissenfels,[1] and handed the Duke a birthday poem bound in green taffeta, for which he was handsomely rewarded. Naturally the elder Duke's ire was roused and he soon found a way to punish his concert-master.

In December 1716 old Drese, the Kapellmeister, died, and by all rights the position should have been conferred on Sebastian Bach, who in the past two years had assumed most of its duties. This was what Sebastian himself expected as a matter of course. The Duke, however, first tried to secure Telemann, and when this proved impossible he conferred the position on the former vice-conductor, Johann Wilhelm Drese. Sebastian's disappointment and humiliation at having been passed over for the sake of a nonentity like young Drese were intense, and the work at Weimar lost its attraction for him. It is significant that after old Drese's death no trace of any cantatas written by the Concertmaster is to be found. Even at the Bicentenary of the Reformation, celebrated in grand style, the fervent admirer of Luther remained silent. It is possible that the Duke, when conferring the conductorship on young Drese, expected him henceforth to supply all the new cantatas required. Bearing in mind Sebastian's behaviour in Arnstadt, however, it seems just as likely that the headstrong Concertmaster simply stopped composing for his patron in order to express his grievance.

The sequence of events bears an interesting resemblance to that in Mühlhausen. Again Sebastian was drawn into a conflict that did not really concern him; just as he had supported Eilmar against his own superior in Mühlhausen, so in Weimar he revealed his attachment to the younger Duke, and infuriated his actual patron. In each case a less straightforward nature could have avoided entanglement in such feuds. Sebastian, however, was anything but a tactician. Indeed, there was a definitely pugnacious streak in his disposition; far from trying to avoid difficulties, he acted rather to provoke them, and then used all his energy and resource-fulness to overcome the resulting trouble.

Accordingly, after nine years of service at Weimar, Sebastian began to consider moving again. Those friendly relations with the younger

---

[1] Jauernig claims that this was Bach's *Jagdkantate* (cf. p. 226). Spitta's assumption that the performance of this work in Weimar took place after 1728 (the year in which Duke Wilhelm Ernst died) seems less probable.

Duke that had spoiled his promotion now helped him to reach his goal. Duke Ernst August had married in 1716 a sister of Prince Leopold of Anhalt-Cöthen, the young ruler of a tiny principality that had come into existence through the partition of the little Duchy of Anhalt. Bach was on excellent terms with the Duchess, and it did not take long for her brother to discover what a prize he could acquire for his own court. He therefore decided to reorganize his music staff; his conductor was to retire in August 1717, and the Prince offered the position to Sebastian on highly favourable terms. The character of the work was the diametrical opposite of that in Weimar. No organ playing and no composition of church music was expected from the conductor; for the Cöthen court had adopted as early as 1596 the Reformed (Calvinistic) Church, which meant that except for certain feast days only the simplest kind of unadorned psalmody was permitted in the service. On the other hand, the Prince was deeply interested in instrumental music, and in this field the conductor was expected to be constantly at work. Acceptance of the Cöthen position therefore meant breaking with almost everything that Sebastian had hitherto aimed at and accomplished. As a musician, and with his consuming zest for experimenting, he could not fail to be fascinated by the very novelty of his prospective artistic duties. So, although Sebastian did not uphold the religious doctrine of the Cöthen court, he accepted the offer; and from August 1, 1717, he was on the princely pay-roll, despite the fact that he had not yet received his leave from Weimar. At the same time the generous Prince Leopold paid him an additional amount of 50 thalers to defray the expenses of his removal, and it appears that Sebastian settled his large family in Cöthen before matters were straightened out in Weimar. From Cöthen he travelled to Dresden, where at that moment a French organist and clavier player, Louis Marchand, was making a tremendous impression. Sebastian, who had known and admired Marchand's compositions for some time, naturally could not miss so good an opportunity to hear the great man perform and possibly to meet him. Little did he suspect that instead of his honouring the French master, the honours would be bestowed on him. For as soon as his presence became known in Dresden, an influential courtier (possibly Count Flemming) suggested holding a competition on the clavier between the French and the German master. The challenge was accepted on both sides, but when Sebastian presented himself before the exalted audience which was to witness the contest, his opponent was not there. After a prolonged wait, a messenger sent to Marchand brought word that the Frenchman had secretly left Dresden that very morning, thus admitting the superiority of his German rival. Any disappointment the guests may have felt at missing so thrilling a spectacle was quickly dispersed by the inimitable art of Bach, who now entertained them on the clavier.

With the enthusiastic acclaim of the Dresden nobility still ringing in his ears, Sebastian returned to Weimar to settle the little formality of getting official release from his duties. In his former appointments this had never presented any difficulty, and apparently Sebastian did not anticipate any trouble in Weimar. His pupil, Johann Martin Schubart, who had deputized for him on the organ, would be well qualified to succeed him. The post of Kapellmeister, with all pertaining duties, was held by the younger Drese, and a Concertmaster was no longer needed. With Duke Wilhelm Ernst, however, such reasonable arguments counted as little as the fact that Bach was offered a substantially higher stipend at Cöthen. Changes in his personnel were always annoying to him; he even retained old servants who were of no use. Moreover, although he was angry with Bach, his renowned organist was an asset to the court which he did not like to surrender. Finally, it would be most vexing to let Bach go to the Prince of Cöthen, who, as the brother-in-law of Prince Ernst August, naturally belonged to the enemy's camp. He therefore decided to refuse Bach's release, and thought that the organist, though upset at first, would eventually calm down. In this assumption he was mistaken, however, for Bach did not submit to the decision of his patron. Indeed, so outspoken was his insistence that (according to the court secretary's report) 'he was put under arrest for too obstinately requesting his dismissal.' From November 6 to December 2 Sebastian remained in jail, making the best use of his enforced leisure by working on his *Orgelbüchlein*; but as he showed no inclination whatever to give in, and as the Duke on the other hand did not care for an open wrangle with the Cöthen court, the recalcitrant organist was at last released 'with notice of his unfavourable discharge.' As was to be expected, Schubart was appointed his successor and retained this position until his early death in 1721, when he was replaced by another Bach pupil, Johann Caspar Vogler; thus the Bach tradition of organ playing was kept alive in Weimar until Vogler's passing in 1765. This does not mean, however, that Sebastian Bach was kindly remembered in Weimar's official circles. Two facts clearly illuminate this unrelenting attitude. Walther treated Bach in his *Musiklexikon* in a strangely superficial manner; he did not even list those works which he himself had received from Sebastian. This was not due to an estrangement, for we know from other sources[1] that Walther continued to feel the greatest

[1] Cf. Schünemann in *BJ*, 1933.

esteem for this 'cousin and godfather,' but as an employee of the city of Weimar he apparently had to pay heed to the dictates of the local censor. The same official exercised his veto when, five years later, Wette published a history of Weimar; in it, among the names of the Weimar court organists, the one who had conferred lasting glory on the town was simply left out.[1]

Sebastian Bach's determined defiance of his patron's wishes constitutes an important, though as yet isolated, landmark in the artists' fight for social freedom. At this point of his career he certainly broke with the family tradition. Ambrosius Bach and Johann Christoph had both been forced to stay on in Eisenach against their will; Sebastian refused to be cowed by similar restrictions. How gleefully would his forebears have applauded had they been privileged to hear his 'stiff-necked protestations,' which finally opened the jail doors for him!

IV

COURT CONDUCTOR AND PRINCELY FRIEND

(1717-1723)

When Barbara's seventh child was born, an august group of godparents assembled at Cöthen for the christening; three members of the princely family joined forces with a Court Councillor and the wife of a Court Minister, both members of the aristocracy.[2] This fact clearly reveals Sebastian's position at Cöthen. At Weimar such exalted godparents had not been available for any of the six Bach children born there. The Cöthen Court Conductor, however, was a person of high standing. His salary of 400 thalers equalled that of the Court Marshal, the second highest official, and his princely patron treated him as a revered and cherished friend. Prince Leopold, 23 years old, and thus nine years his conductor's junior, was a true lover of the Muses. From a trip to Italy he brought home valuable objects of art, and he greatly enlarged the court library. As regards music, he was much more than a mere enthusiast. He played with professional skill the violin, viola da gamba, and clavier; moreover he was a competent singer who had a pleasant baritone voice. Sebastian bestowed on him the highest praise in claiming that the Prince 'not only loved but

---

[1] Significant is the remark on the title-page of Wette's book: 'Unter hoher Censur und Bewilligung des Hochfürstl. Ober-Consistorii ans Licht gestellet.'

[2] The child received with such pomp died after ten months.

knew music.' The profundity of Leopold's understanding is indeed revealed by the works which the new conductor wrote for his master. Compositions such as the sonatas for violin solo and the suites for violoncello solo can be truly appreciated only by someone with the deepest musical insight.

Under the rule of Prince Leopold's widowed mother the small court of Cöthen had been run on strictly economical lines; music had hardly any place in it, and only three musicians had been employed in the princely service. As soon as Leopold came of age, decisive changes were made. An orchestra of 17 players was established, and the Prince was fortunate in securing some eminent players in Berlin, where the anti-musical King Friedrich Wilhelm I had dissolved his own band in 1713. When Bach took over he found a well-trained instrumental body.[1] Gradually fine instruments were purchased too, such as a harpsichord, for the acquisition of which Bach was sent to Berlin, and two Stainer violins. Inspired by the new possibilities thus opening to him, and by his patron's passionate interest and delighted approval, Bach now created a profusion of works. The accounts of the bookbinders who bound the parts copied from Bach's scores attest the new conductor's frenzy of productivity;[2] on the other hand, the sums spent on the acquisition of music from outside were negligible. A great part of Bach's output in these years is lost; but what has been preserved—works like the suites for orchestra and the Brandenburg Concertos—reflect the exuberance of an artist discovering new means of expression, and the peace of mind of the composer who had found real understanding and appreciation in his new patron.[3] Peaceful indeed were these first years at Cöthen, and this, significantly enough, in spite of the fact that the little residence itself was by no means free from the religious dissensions prevalent in Bach's time. The Prince's parents had belonged to different

[1] There were 8 soloists, designated as 'chamber musicians,' mentioned in the accounts; they received higher salaries than the ripienists. The soloists took care of the following instruments: 2 violins, 1 'cello, 1 viola da gamba, 1 oboe, 1 bassoon, 2 flutes. The lack of a chamber musician for the viola is explained by Bach's predilection for the instrument, a predilection which Emanuel reported to Forkel. Among the players, Christian Ferdinand Abel should be mentioned; he was the father of Carl Friedrich Abel, whom we shall later meet in London as the partner of Johann Christian Bach. Sebastian's violoncello suites were probably written for the elder Abel.

[2] Smend, who carefully went through the accounts in the *Landesarchiv* Sachsen-Anhalt at Oranienbaum, estimates that in 1719-20 at least 50 works of ensemble music must have been bound. Cf. his 'Bach in Köthen,' Berlin, 1951.

[3] Smend has proved that Bach also composed a number of cantatas in Cöthen, some for the Prince's birthday, some for New Year's Day and similar occasions. In some cases this music was later used for church cantatas of the Leipzig period (cf. Nos. 32, 66, 120, 134, 173, 184), while the music of others is lost.

denominations. His father had fallen in love and married Gisela Agnes v. Rath, although this was socially and religiously a *mésalliance*; for his bride came from the ranks of the lesser nobility and was a Lutheran, while he himself, like the majority of the Duchy's population, belonged to the Reformed Calvinistic Church. Neither of the two partners changed his or her religious adherence, and Gisela Agnes did her best to obtain privileges for her fellow Lutherans. Yielding to her persuasion, the happy husband allowed a Lutheran church and school to be built in Cöthen, thus provoking the wrath of his own Consistory. Heated feuds raged over the allotment of church taxes, the use of the Calvinistic church bells, etc., and finally appeals to revoke the Prince's decisions were made even to the Emperor. When the young Prince Leopold assumed the government, he confirmed his father's policy, claiming that the 'greatest happiness of his subjects depended on their freedom of conscience being safeguarded.' A very enlightened point of view, to be sure, but unfortunately one that was not shared by the majority of the citizens. Thus at the time when Bach came to Cöthen religious quarrels and disputes had by no means abated. The Sebastian of Mühlhausen would have felt in duty bound to take up the cudgels and fight for his own denomination. Not so the Cöthen court conductor. For the time being he was much more interested in musical than in religious problems. From the outset he had been aware that he would find a religiously uncongenial atmosphere at the Cöthen court, and he had decided to take this in his stride. Naturally he never conceived the idea of adopting his patron's religion. On the other hand, he did not intercede in favour of his fellow Lutherans. He contented himself with attending the Lutheran church and sending his children to the Lutheran school. Beyond that he let things alone, and was very happy indeed in his artistic work and in the economic and social prestige he had achieved.

A new source of satisfaction was opening to him in his children. By now it had become clear that the eldest son, Wilhelm Friedemann, possessed great talent, and the father decided to train him in earnest. On January 22, 1720, when Friedemann was nine and a half, Sebastian started a 'clavier book' for him, which was subsequently to be used for all the Bach children, and for other pupils as well. It is a most interesting document on Sebastian Bach the teacher, revealing his methodical mind and revolutionary fingering (cf. p. 265). This *Clavierbüchlein* belonged to the series of books of instructive keyboard music already started in Weimar, a series which comprised such masterworks as the *Orgelbüchlein*, the Inventions, and the Well-Tempered Clavier. The master apparently enjoyed creative work which served educational purposes, occupying in this respect a unique position among the great composers. The planning of a systematic course of instruction satisfied his keen and logical mind. His creative fire was always kindled by self-imposed restrictions, and the challenge afforded him by the solution of certain problems of teaching inspired him to real works of art. Forkel, relying on the testimony of Philip Emanuel Bach, described Sebastian's method as clavier instructor as follows:

'The first thing he did was to teach his pupils his peculiar mode of touching the keyboard. For this purpose he made them practise for months nothing but isolated exercises for all the fingers of both hands, with constant regard to the production of a clean, clear tone. Over a period of some months no pupil was excused from these exercises, and, according to his firm opinion, they should be continued for six to twelve months at least. But if he found that anyone, after some months of practice, began to lose patience, he was so considerate as to write little connecting pieces, in which these exercises were linked together. To this type belong the six little Preludes for beginners, and still more the fifteen two-part Inventions. He wrote down both during the hours of teaching, and, in so doing, attended to the immediate requirement of the pupil; afterwards he transformed these pieces into beautiful and expressive little works of art. With the finger training was combined the practice of all the ornaments in both hands. After this he set his pupils to the task of studying his own greater compositions, which, as he well knew, would give them the best means of exercising their powers. In order to lessen the difficulties, he made use of an excellent method; this was to play to them the whole piece which they were to study first, saying: "This is how it must sound."'

That some pupils lost patience during these first hard months seems understandable. That the teacher did not strikes one as amazing. Did Bach not feel that he could use his time better than by watching beginners struggling with their first exercises? Apparently he did not. To a great extent he regarded music as a craft, and in instructing his 'apprentices' he acted as generations of Bach musicians had done before him. However, he exhibited such patience only with gifted pupils. Lack of talent and a lukewarm attitude towards his craft made his temper boil over. He was the perfect teacher for talented youths, but he was unable to put up with mediocrity.

There was, to be sure, no musical mediocrity in Sebastian's children;

they were, as he proudly wrote, 'all born musicians,' and their instruction was a delight to their father. To the student of hereditary problems Sebastian's sons are a strange and puzzling phenomenon indeed. They seem to disprove the theory of Wilhelm Ostwald that a genius uses up all the latent creative and spiritual forces inherited from ancestors, and is thus unable to produce a genius himself. Perhaps this exception to the general rule is explained by the enormous musical inheritance piled up in the Bach family, an inheritance which even Sebastian could not entirely exhaust; and, moreover, by the fact that the musical inheritance of his two wives was only latent, and they were thus able to hand it on in full strength to their own great sons.

In July 1720, when Friedemann had reached his tenth year, an event occurred that tragically broke up the Bach idyllic existence in Cöthen. While Sebastian was at the Bohemian spa of Carlsbad, accompanying his patron, who did not want to forgo the enjoyment of chamber music while taking the waters, Barbara Bach was suddenly prostrated by illness. There was not even enough time to summon her husband; when he returned in high spirits, a scene of desolation greeted him, and he had to be told that his beloved wife had died and been buried. The children, aged 12, 10, 6, and 5, had lost their mother, and Sebastian was without the devoted companion who had shared courageously the vicissitudes of his early struggles. This was indeed a cruel fall from security and gaiety to loneliness and grief, and to bear it he needed all the spiritual resources which his faith provided. To Sebastian Bach death had always seemed as a release fervently to be longed for, which in destroying the body would simultaneously relieve the soul of its sins. Death was for him not the end, but the culmination of spiritual life. Possibly during the first joyful years spent at Cöthen he had to some extent put aside such thoughts. Now, however, he turned to them again, and religious experiences assumed their old significance for him. He began to realize that for all the pleasure he derived from the association with his beloved patron, there was something lacking in his existence at Cöthen, and he was again filled with a longing to express his innermost faith through church music. Just at that time the organist of Hamburg's *Jakobikirche* died, and 8 musicians, among them Sebastian Bach, were invited to compete for the position. To Sebastian Hamburg was still hallowed by the youthful impressions he received there, and eagerly he travelled to the Northern city to find out more about the vacancy. He learned that the trial performances were to take place on November 28, and that three Hamburg organists, among them venerable Reinken, had been named adjudicators. The date did not suit Bach, who had to return earlier to Cöthen for the celebration of his patron's birthday, but he arranged to play before that day on Reinken's organ in the *Catharinenkirche*. Out of courtesy to the veteran master he chose as subject for his improvisations the very same chorale *An Wasserflüssen Babylons* which in Reinken's dazzling treatment had held young Sebastian spellbound some twenty years previously. For a long time he played, piling one gigantic structure on the other and revealing his stupendous mastery. Finally Reinken, who as a rule did not indulge in praise of other musicians, exclaimed: 'I thought this art was dead, but I see it still lives in you.' Whether the *Necrolog* (cf. p. 122) is right in reporting that Bach played 'before the Magistrate and many other distinguished persons of the town, to their general astonishment,' or whether the master performed only to the three musical experts, is not known. Anyway there is no doubt that the Hamburg Council favoured his appointment. But there was one serious drawback. Sebastian was informed during his visit that it was customary at Hamburg to sell certain offices to the highest bidder; even in the churches a newly appointed employee was expected to make a handsome payment. A passage in the minutes of the meeting determining the policy regarding the election of the new organist for the *Jakobikirche* reads thus: 'The capacity of the candidate should be considered more than the payment, but if the chosen candidate of his own free will desires to make a contribution as a token of his gratitude, it will be accepted for the benefit of the church.' In spite of such cautious language it was clear to everybody concerned that such 'voluntary' payment could not be dispensed with. This must have displeased Sebastian greatly. He probably did not have the money available, but even if he had, it would have been a matter of pride for him not to pay for a position in which he would make an outstanding contribution to the religious life of Hamburg. He left the town promising to write to the Council; and the decisive board meeting was postponed for a whole week until the arrival of Bach's letter. The contents cannot have been encouraging, for after reading the letter the committee decided to appoint a certain Johann Joachim Heitmann, who acknowledged his gratitude by paying the tidy little sum of 4000 Marks. The pastor of the church, Erdmann Neumeister (famous for his outstanding cantata texts, several of which Bach had set to music) was disgusted indeed with the affair. As this happened shortly before Christmas, he found a chance of airing his grievance in the festival sermon. Speaking eloquently of the angelic music at the birth of Christ, he remarked acidly that if one of those angels came down from Heaven wishing to become an organist at his church and played divinely, but had no cash, he might just as well fly away again, for they would not accept him in Hamburg.

On his return from Hamburg, Bach set to work on a meticulous copy of six orchestral concertos which he sent in March 1721, with a courteous French dedication, to Christian Ludwig, Margrave of Brandenburg, whom he had probably met on one of his visits to Carlsbad. The works had been written for, and performed by, the excellent Cöthen orchestra, as is proved by many details of orchestration (cf. p. 286). Margrave Christian Ludwig, however, had no musical resources of the kind available, and it is not surprising that Bach's score was never used at his court.[1]

At this time the composer was also deeply engrossed in his work on the first set of the Well-Tempered Clavier. Such creative activities helped to heal the wound inflicted by Barbara's death and made Bach ready to face the necessity for establishing a new home. Remarrying after a very short lapse of time was the general custom in his family (and indeed in his time), and it proves Bach's deep attachment to Barbara that he waited from June 1720 to December 1721 before entering holy matrimony again. His bride, Anna Magdalena Wilcken, the daughter of a court trumpeter, then 20 years old, was descended from musicians on both paternal and maternal sides; and in her own right she was an excellent soprano singer, who since the autumn of 1720 had been employed by the Cöthen court, where she had appeared as a guest as early as 1716. The young singer retained her position after she married the court conductor, and earned half as much as her husband. The disparity in age between the girl of 20 and the man of 36 was balanced on the other hand by their common profession. Magdalena may well have been more interested in operatic music than her husband (it was her youngest son who was the only one of Sebastian's children to become a successful opera composer), but she was certainly able to appreciate Sebastian's greatness, and young enough to adopt his own artistic creed. When she started her married life, Magdalena must have been afraid of her new responsibilities, which included looking after four stepchildren, the eldest of whom was a girl only seven years her junior. We don't know how her young charges acted towards her. In the case of the eldest boy, Friedemann, then 11 years old, the possibility cannot be excluded that he resented seeing his mother supplanted by a stranger, and that this experience contributed to the shaping of his very problematical personality. But while we are in the dark as to her stepchildren's attitude, we do know that for her husband Magdalena succeeded

[1] When the Margrave died in 1734, the autograph of the six Brandenburg Concertos was valued at 24 gr., a little less than a dollar.

in creating a cheerful, comfortable home. Visiting musicians and an end-less stream of kinsfolk were received cordially, and felt happy with the Sebastian Bachs. Magdalena knew the secret of enjoying the simplest pleasures with all her heart. Once when she received a present of six carnation plants, she 'treasured them more highly than children do their Christmas presents and tended them with the care usually bestowed on babies.'[1] This disposition helped her a great deal in a life that was filled to the brim with the duties of running a large household most thriftily, a life in which she had to go through the ordeal of child-bearing thirteen times, and seven times saw a child of hers carried to the grave. How Sebastian on such occasions tried to instil courage into her suffering heart is revealed in Magdalena's music book, which he presented to her in 1725. Three times he wrote into it a different version of his aria based on Paul Gerhardt's hymn 'Fret not, my soul, on God rely,' meant to lift her out of the day's turmoil with simple and deeply felt music. The little book also contains a song which Sebastian clearly intended for his wife:

> If thou be near, I go rejoicing
> To peace and rest beyond the skies,
> Nor will I fear what may befall me,
> For I will hear thy sweet voice call me,
> Thy gentle hand will close my eyes.

The sincerity and warmth of the composer's feelings are evident to any-one listening to the heartfelt tune. Most likely the poem too was by Sebas-tian, who found it quite natural to link an expression of love to the idea of death.

Whether Magdalena was able to follow him in such thoughts we do not know. Maybe she was too young and too firmly rooted in the material world to understand her husband's intense preoccupation with death. Yet she could not help delighting in the deep love expressed in such personal messages. This love, together with her genuine admiration of Sebastian's creative work, helped her through the many professional crises that Sebas-tian's stubbornness and pugnaciousness created for them through their 29 years of married life.

We know nothing of Magdalena's appearance. Her husband had her painted by Cristofori—at that time quite an unusual distinction for a woman of her social standing—but the portrait, which was listed in Emanuel's collection, has been lost. So we must content ourselves with the mental picture of a hard-working, warm-hearted, and highly musical

---

[1] Cf. the letters of Johann Elias Bach reproduced by Pottgiesser in 'Die Musik,' 1912-13.

L

woman; a true helpmeet to her husband, glorying in his artistic achievements, painstakingly copying his music in a handwriting which gradually assumed the features of Sebastian's own hand, and sharing with fortitude the burdens which life imposed on them.

Shortly after they were married, the outward conditions of Bach's existence underwent a decisive change. Up to that time, as he stated in a letter to his old friend, Erdmann (cf. p. 180), he had intended to spend the rest of his life in the service of Prince Leopold. Now, however, the Prince gave up his bachelor existence and married a Princess of Anhalt-Bernburg. Even before the ceremony, the happy bridegroom had been so occupied with redecorating his quarters, creating a new 'princely guard,' whose exercises and parades he attended, and preparing for the festivities which were to last through five weeks, that he was unable to give much thought to music. And when things finally calmed down at Cöthen, life assumed a different aspect. The young Princess was, according to Bach's verdict, an 'amusa,' a person without love for music or art. Not only was she in her disposition quite unsuited to share her husband's greatest predilections, she was even unwilling to try. She was probably somewhat jealous of the court conductor's influence on the Prince, and anxious to break up this close relationship. Gradually music was removed from the centre of the Prince's activities and Bach felt neglected and somewhat superfluous. As months went by and Leopold maintained his 'somewhat lukewarm' attitude, his conductor began to ask himself whether under such conditions it was worth while to stay at the little court. Would not a position with wider responsibilities, in particular one where he could again serve the Lord in a church, and through the power of his music lead a large congregation towards Christ, give him deeper satisfaction? He had also to consider his boys; he was determined that they should enjoy the benefits of the University education of which he himself had been deprived. Thus he gradually began to familiarize himself with the idea that the secluded and secure existence in Cöthen had only been a happy interlude ultimately to be exchanged for the weightier duties and inevitable struggles of a position in a more important musical centre.

V

THOMAS CANTOR AND DIRECTOR MUSICES AT LEIPZIG
(1723-1750)

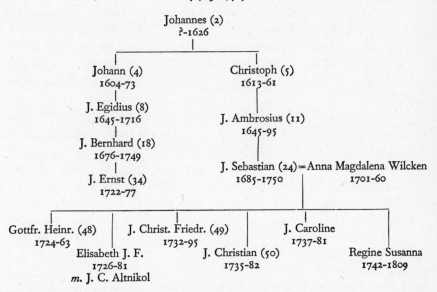

The manner in which Sebastian Bach received his appointment in Leipzig supplies a *leitmotiv* for the 27 years he was destined to spend there. He offered his services reluctantly, and was accepted reluctantly, with Councillor Platz's comment, memorable for its very incongruity: 'Since we cannot get the best man, we shall have to be satisfied with a mediocre one.'

When the great Johann Kuhnau died on June 5, 1722, the question of his successor in the post of the Leipzig Thomas Cantor occupied the minds of musicians all over the country. In Protestant Germany the position, combined as it was with the musical directorship of Leipzig's churches, enjoyed a very high prestige; for Leipzig at that time was a bastion of Protestantism, a city where religion was a living, driving force.[1] Ever

---

[1] The abundance of services offered in Leipzig was characteristic of the time. On Sunday, worship at St. Thomas' and St. Nicholas' occupied the greater part of the day. It started with early Matins, followed by the main service lasting from 7 to 11 a.m. Half an hour later the noon service took place, and at 1.30 p.m. vespers followed, which took up about 2 hours. On every weekday there was a service at 6.45 a.m. in one of the main churches and an hour of prayer in the afternoon. On Saturday at 2 p.m. a very important service was held in preparation for the communicants of the following Sunday. To discharge these extensive duties, no less than five ministers were officiating at St. Thomas' as well as at St. Nicholas'. The other churches, too, engaged a comparatively large amount of clergy to satisfy the spiritual needs of this city of 30,000 people.

since its foundation in 1212 the Alumnate (choir-school) of St. Thomas' had supplied singers for the church services, and the venerable institution could look back with pride on a line of great Cantors (among them the illustrious Johann Hermann Schein), whose creative work had greatly contributed to the growth of German music. The opening in Leipzig seemed to offer all that Bach had been missing in Cöthen. Nevertheless it took Sebastian six months to make up his mind about the desirability of the position, and he was first mentioned as an applicant in December 1722. The reasons for his long pondering were manifold.

From a previous visit to Leipzig in 1717, and from his intercourse with Kuhnau, Bach was fully aware that the Thomas Cantor's position was altogether different from his present one. While the Cöthen *Kapellmeister* had to comply with the wishes of a single patron, the Thomas Cantor had something like two dozen superiors. In his educational work he had to conform to the ruling of the rector of the school. But the running of the institute was in the hands of the City Council, consisting of three burgomasters, two deputy burgomasters, and ten assessors; and it was this body of fifteen which engaged the Thomas Cantor and kept a check on all his activities. Finally, there was the ecclesiastical authority of the Consistorium, which was responsible for the services in the churches, and became therefore the chief arbiter in all matters concerning the music to be offered by the Thomas Cantor in his capacity as church music director. To be dependent on these different governing bodies, which, as might be imagined, would not always live in perfect harmony, did not seem too pleasant a prospect for any man, least of all for one who had so little of the diplomat in his character. There was also the matter of social rank, to which Sebastian was by no means insensitive. According to the general view, a court conductor was on a higher social level than a Cantor, and Sebastian found it somewhat strange (as he admitted to his old friend, Erdmann) to climb down the ladder. As to financial considerations, he did hope to earn more in Leipzig than in Cöthen, but the former pleasant feeling of security would be lacking. The basic salary in Leipzig was low, not more than 100 fl. a year, less than one-fourth of what Prince Leopold paid his conductor. To it were added the *Accidentien*, a certain percentage of the statutory fee for funerals, weddings, etc., and one-fourth of the weekly tuition fee of six pennies which the boarders had to pay, and which, when lacking funds, they collected every week from charitable families. The Cantor's income might grow out of pennies and farthings to the sum of 700 thalers, but there was no certainty about it; and when 'a healthy wind was blowing'[1] and the death-rate went down, the receipts showed a sad decline.

Anna Magdalena Bach may have felt even more reluctant than her husband to go to Leipzig. At Cöthen she held a good position as court singer, which brought her a yearly salary of 200 thalers. In Leipzig she would be deprived of an artistic career and an income of her own. The wife of the Thomas Cantor would have to lead a very secluded and unobtrusive existence. She might enjoy singing Sebastian's music in the privacy of their own home, but it would be utterly out of the question for her to undertake a solo in a church, in which women were not allowed to perform. Thus to the young singer the removal to Leipzig would mean the renunciation of any professional activity of her own.

And yet, in spite of such various misgivings, Sebastian was drawn towards the new position. At St. Thomas', and subsequently at the renowned University of Leipzig, his gifted sons would be given the right kind of education, which provincial Cöthen was unable to offer. He himself would be in entire charge of the church music of an important city, and would thus be able to make his ideas for its improvement become reality. Tremendous forces within him urgently sought release in the composition of sacred music, forces which burst forth triumphantly in the 'Passion according to St. John' which he was writing for Leipzig. After months of wavering, the voices of caution were silenced, and Bach, driven by his daemon, decided on the Leipzig position in order to fulfil his artistic destiny.

In the six months since Kuhnau's passing, the Leipzig Council had been singularly unsuccessful in their attempts to secure a suitable Thomas Cantor. At first matters had seemed to shape just perfectly. Among the six applicants was Georg Philipp Telemann, newly appointed Music Director and Cantor of Hamburg; from his former activities as organist of Leipzig's New Church, as a composer of, and singer in, popular operas, and as an extremely successful conductor of a Collegium Musicum, he was very dear to the Leipzig citizens. The Council was delighted to acquire so spectacular a musician and, the day after he had conducted a cantata of his own composition in Leipzig,[2] voted unanimously for his appointment. Telemann, noticing Leipzig's eagerness, managed to obtain important concessions. He caused the city fathers to waive

---

[1] Cf. Bach's letter to Erdmann of 1730, in which he complained about this, for him, unfavourable wind.

[2] The Council even printed the libretto of this cantata for the use of the congregation.

one part of the Thomas Cantor's statutory duties, viz. the teaching of Latin in certain classes, and he secured the musical directorship of the University Church. Armed thus with all the requirements necessary for a satisfactory position in Leipzig, he returned to Hamburg to press for a higher salary. His policy proved successful, and the badly disappointed Leipzig Council had to continue their search. Yet when Sebastian Bach made his application in December 1722 he was not considered the most desirable of the candidates. There was Christoph Graupner, who, as a former pupil of St. Thomas' and the highly renowned conductor of the Prince of Hesse's orchestra in Darmstadt, seemed much better qualified. Graupner was invited to direct the Christmas music (including a *Magnificat* of his own), and some weeks later to conduct a cantata, all of which he did with so much success that the position was offered him. But Leipzig had bad luck again, for this desirable candidate was also unable to accept. The Prince of Hesse firmly refused to let his conductor go, and as he added very strong arguments in the form of a rise of salary and a munificent gift, Graupner was not too reluctant to stay in Darmstadt. He explained the situation to the Leipzig Council and warmly recommended Bach as a musician as competent on the organ as he was in directing church and orchestra music. By the time the letter arrived, it was outdated by the recent events. Bach was no longer a stranger to the Leipzig community. He had performed the required 'trial cantata' of his own, probably singing the bass solo himself,[1] and he had, moreover, presented his St. John Passion on Good Friday. The Council was now determined to engage Bach in the event of Graupner's refusal.

Their initial lack of enthusiasm for the Cöthen candidate is not hard to understand. Bach's tremendous fame as an organist did not count for much, as the Thomas Cantor was not supposed to play this instrument. Of Bach's creative work the Council could know nothing, for no composition of his except the two Mühlhausen cantatas had ever been printed. In the eyes of the Leipzig authorities, a candidate's present position was of paramount importance, and it cannot be denied that the conductor of the tiny court of Cöthen enjoyed less prestige than the Hamburg or Darmstadt music directors. Finally, Bach seemed inferior to the majority of former Thomas Cantors by his lack of a University education. Kuhnau, for instance, had been a successful lawyer before being appointed to St. Thomas', and had published masterly translations from the Greek and

---

[1] It was the Cantata No. 22, *Jesus nahm zu sich die Zwölfe*, in which the bass solos are unusually high, in accordance with the composer's own voice. Cf. Schering, 'J. S. Bach und das Musikleben Leipzigs im 18. Jahrhundert,' Leipzig, 1941.

Hebrew. Compared with him, Sebastian Bach could hardly be called erudite. On the other hand, the Council was thoroughly tired of the unsettled conditions that had prevailed since Kuhnau's death, in which the church music had suffered, and so it was willing to engage Bach. This time, however, they wanted to take precautions against another failure, and Bach was requested to supply a letter of dismissal from his patron before the final election took place. Prince Leopold, though grieved at his conductor's decision, was certainly not going to put any obstacles in his way, and wrote a very gracious testimonial for the 'respectable and learned J. S. Bach.' Another point of contention between the various candidates and the Council was removed by Sebastian's pledge either to instruct the pupils in Latin or to remunerate another teacher undertaking the work in his stead. When all difficulties were thus overcome, the formal election took place on April 22, 1723. The minutes of the meeting are significant. Burgomaster Dr. Lange, who had conducted the negotiations, did his best to make the appointment palatable, mentioning Bach's excellence on the clavier, and even venturing to declare that 'If Bach were chosen, Telemann, in view of his conduct, might be forgotten.' The other Councillors followed his lead, but they stressed, as the main point in the candidate's favour, his willingness to teach Latin and to study the Latin catechism with the pupils. It was characteristic that although the city fathers had naturally all attended Bach's trial performances, only one referred to him as a composer, and this with the sole object of emphasizing that his church music (the dramatic expressiveness of which the St. John Passion had clearly demonstrated) should not be 'too theatrical,' a stipulation which was promptly included in the contract.

Bach, determined now to get the position, signed whatever was requested of him; he also promised meekly not to leave town without the permission of the Burgomaster (with the mental reservation that he would break such a pledge whenever necessary). He then passed the requisite theological examination, and was declared fit for the office of Thomas Cantor.

Before these irrevocable steps were taken, fate seemed to give Bach a last chance of staying on in idyllic Cöthen. The Princess, whose lack of love for music Bach had so deplored, died on April 3, and the conductor could have expected to see the old state of affairs revived. But his was a nature not easily turned off a path once chosen. It had been a long and arduous struggle to make up his mind; now, however, he was ready for a new adventure, and ten days after the Princess's death, on April 13, 1723, the bereaved husband signed the letter of dismissal for his conductor.

Nevertheless, their close friendship persisted, and in spite of his many new duties, Bach found time to visit Cöthen regularly for some fine music-making, especially that in celebration of Leopold's birthday on December 10. He had the joy of seeing his Prince united two years later to a music-loving wife; for her birthday he wrote the cantata *Steigt freudig in die Luft*, which he performed with his Leipzig singers, while Prince Leopold took over the important bass solo in the tradition of their former delightful days. When the Prince's son was born in 1726, Bach dedicated to the infant his first clavier partita, and even coaxed his Muse into writing a dedicatory poem for the baby. These pleasant ties were tragically severed by Leopold's sudden death in November 1728. Bach came to Cöthen for the last time to perform an imposing funeral music on the night of March 23, 1729, when the body was interred, and another cantata on the following day, when the funeral sermon was preached.[1] Under Leopold's successor the orchestra declined steadily, until even its last five members were dismissed. Clearly Bach had done the right thing when he decided not to tie his fate to the little principality.

On June 1, 1723, the new Cantor was formally installed at St. Thomas'. Various addresses were given, music was sung by the pupils, and the new official responded in a dignified speech promising to serve a 'Noble and Most Wise Council' to the best of his abilities. There was, however, a slightly discordant note in the ceremonies, typical of the state of affairs in Leipzig. The Consistorium had requested the pastor of St. Thomas' to welcome the new Cantor in the name of the church authorities. This act of courtesy did not please the town officials, who considered the installation of the Cantor their prerogative and claimed that never before had a church official been designated for such a ceremony. A discussion ensued that was subsequently continued in a lengthy correspondence. The new Cantor may have been somewhat perplexed by this incident; however, he could not learn too quickly that henceforth he would have to deal with a host of officials, all of whom, minor as well as major, insisted on the full recognition of their vested rights. To find a path through the maze of prerogatives and conventions determining the work of the various city and church employees, and to learn how to observe the countless un-written rules, seemed almost a full-time occupation, and there was so much else for the new Cantor to do! He found the school in a shocking

---

[1] Cf. Smend, 'Bach in Köthen,' Berlin, 1951. The connection with the Cöthen court was not severed even after Sebastian's death. When Friedemann's daughter, Friederica Sophia, was christened on February 15, 1757, two members of the princely house of Anhalt-Cöthen were among the godparents.

state of disorganization. Rector Johann Heinrich Ernesti, a weak and tired man of 71, had for years been unable to control either pupils or teachers, and the standard of the institute had steadily declined. The students consisted of a number of paying day scholars and some fifty-two foundation scholars, mostly sons of poor parents who on account of their musical talent were admitted as boarders for a nominal payment. Many of these boys had not received a good upbringing at home, and a firm hand was needed to keep them in decent discipline. This unfortunately the rector did not possess. Furthermore, it was almost impossible to obtain good order in a building that had hardly been altered since its erection in 1554, and was now completely outdated and overcrowded. There was not even a separate bed available for each boarder, and one classroom had to accommodate three classes at the same time, besides serving as a dining-room. The pupils' schedule was bound to fill Bach with even greater concern. The few capable musicians were sadly overworked and unable to keep their voices in good condition. The pupils had to accompany every funeral (except those of the very poor) singing hymns—rain, storm, or snow making no difference; and who could suggest a change in these conditions, when the fee for funerals meant so much to pupils and teachers? From New Year's Day to the middle of January all the Thomasians sang daily in the streets, naturally often in bad weather, in order to attract charitable contributions; and again nobody dared raise his voice against this lucrative old custom. Fatigued, poorly fed, and badly housed, these pupils easily succumbed to illness, and contagious diseases spread rapidly in the unsanitary, overcrowded school building.

Between the teachers relations were not too harmonious. Indeed it was a turbulent and rather frightening world for which Sebastian Bach had surrendered the idyllic seclusion of the Cöthen court.

He had to live in the very midst of it. His quarters, occupying the left wing of the school building,[1] had a separate entrance; yet his sanctum, the *Componierstube*, traditionally reserved for the Cantor's creative work, was separated from the classroom of the sixth form by only a plaster wall. How much concentration must it have required not to hear the loud voices of his young neighbours! Yet even such little privacy as this was not granted him continuously. Every fourth week, for the 7 full days, the Cantor had to serve as inspector, maintaining discipline from 4 or 5 a.m., according to the season, when the boarders rose, through prayers,

---

[1] It was inevitable that Sebastian should bring disease germs from the school into his own quarters, and this was probably the main cause of the death of so many of Anna Magdalena's babies.

meals, and lessons, up to 8 p.m., when it was his duty to check all the lights after the boys had retired. These thirteen weeks a year (sometimes even more if one of the other high-ranking teachers was not available) meant work of the most uncongenial kind. They unsettled Sebastian's creative activity and called for a special expenditure of nervous energy, inasmuch as the maintenance of discipline did not come easily to a man of his quick temper. Fortunately the other extramusical work was negligible. As Bach's Latin classes were taken over by a colleague, for a sum of 50 thalers paid by the Cantor, he had only to teach Luther's Latin catechism once a week, which could not have been a burden to one so fully conversant with and interested in the Protestant dogma.

The bulk of his duties were of an artistic nature and were covered by the title 'Director musices,' which Bach always used with his signature, thus stressing that it was the one he held to be important. He was responsible for the musical programme in all the municipal churches, two of which, St. Thomas' and St. Nicholas', had very elaborate music on Sundays, especially during the main service, which lasted for four hours.[1] The main musical work was the cantata, performed alternately at St. Thomas' and St. Nicholas' by the best singers of the school (the so-called 'first Cantorei') and conducted by the Cantor himself, while the performance of the preceding motet and the direction of music in the other three churches was entrusted to senior students appointed as assistant conductors. Of the two churches, Bach preferred St. Thomas'. The organ had recently been repaired, and the building itself remodelled, and the church was considered, according to a chronicler of the time, 'one of the most elaborate and beautiful places of worship in existence . . . adorned with an exquisite and costly altar.' The music director was particularly pleased with the very convenient wooden galleries placed on the left and right of the organ. While the choir stood in front of the instrument, the galleries accommodated the instrumentalists and were admirably suited for double choirs, inspiring Bach to use them, for instance, in the St. Matthew Passion. In

---

[1] Bach noted the order of Divine Service on the title-page of his Cantata No. 61. His aide-mémoire reads as follows:

'1. [Organ] prelude; 2. Motet; 3. Prelude on the Kyrie, which is [afterwards] performed throughout in concerted music; 4. Intoning before the altar; 5. Reading of the Epistle; 6. Singing of the Litany; 7. Prelude on the chorale [and singing of it]; 8. Reading of the Gospel; 9. Prelude on [and performance of] the main music work; 10. Singing of the Credo; 11. The Sermon; 12. Singing of several verses of a hymn; 13. Words of Institution [of the Sacrament]; 14. Prelude on [and performance of] the composition [2nd part of the cantata]. Afterwards alternate preluding and singing of chorales to the end of the Communion, and so on.'

addition to the large organ, there was a small instrument placed high up on the altar wall, which seemed to Bach to symbolize heavenly tunes. He liked to use it for special effects, such as the insertion of German Christmas chorales into the Latin *Magnificat* performed at Christmas, or the playing of the *cantus firmus* in the first chorus of the St. Matthew Passion. The church of St. Nicholas' had no such advantages and the choir-loft was smaller. Bach therefore avoided it for more elaborate works. When his St. John Passion had to be produced there in 1724, he insisted energetically on some repairs being carried out so as to have more space available for his performers. On the other hand, the organ at St. Nicholas' was more powerful, and Bach preferred to use it for works in which the organ is treated as a solo. Either at St. Thomas' or at St. Nicholas' a new cantata adapted to the special liturgical requirements of the day had to be offered on every Sunday and all the feast-days of the ecclesiastical year. The only exceptions were the last three Sundays of Advent and the five Sundays of Lent; but these provided no real rest-period for conductor and performers, since particularly ambitious and extensive programmes had to be prepared for Christmas and Easter (two performances each on December 24, 25, 26, as well as on Good Friday, Easter Sunday and Monday). As to the works performed, the majority were composed by the music director himself. Bach threw himself into this part of his duties with breath-taking vigour. Of cantatas alone he supplied, according to Forkel's statement, five complete sets for the entire ecclesiastical year, 295 different works in all. Even if we grant that a few of these were older compositions or rearrangements of secular music, we may still accept as a fact that Bach composed an average of one cantata per month up to 1744. And besides cantatas he had to provide Passions for Good Friday, motets for important funerals,[1] and festive compositions for the yearly inauguration of the new City Council, as well as for other special events, such as visits from royalty, etc. The first Christmas at Leipzig gives a good idea of the creative fury that possessed Bach. On each of the three feast-days he offered a new cantata,[2] while in the vesper service his new *Magnificat* was performed; in spite of this he had another composition ready for New Year's Day.

The other civic churches, using the inferior singers of the school,

---

[1] For instance, shortly after his arrival in Leipzig, he was called on to compose music for the commemoration service held for the wife of a high official. It is likely that the motet *Jesu, meine Freude* was written for this occasion.

[2] Schering, *l.c.*, conjectures that the third cantata (No. 64) may have been the arrangement of another composer's work, although the final chorus is certainly by Bach.

called for little work by the music director, except in the allotment of the performers to the different groups, which were continually fluctuating in numbers or competence owing to illnesses or other causes.[1]

In addition to the directorship in the four civic churches, it was important for Bach to have charge of the music at St. Paul's as well. This was the University church, which in former times had offered services only on the high feast-days and the quarterly solemn orations, on which occasions the Thomas Cantor had been responsible for the music. But from 1710 onwards the University, in addition to this 'Old Service,' inaugurated a 'New Service' for every Sunday, and Kuhnau had had some difficulties in securing the musical directorship of this, as the University wanted to be as independent as possible of town officials. It was only by undertaking to do the additional work without further payment that Kuhnau eventually achieved his aim. After his death, J. G. Görner, a former organist of St. Paul's, filled the position temporarily, and he had been far-sighted enough to refrain from asking for a remuneration. This impressed the University officials so favourably that they graciously acceded to his subsequent application and, a few weeks before Bach's appointment, they conferred on him the Directorship of the 'New Service,' while reserving the 'Old Service' for the Thomas Cantor. Bach was anything but pleased about this turn of events. The University appointment was not only important because of financial considerations; it was also useful for establishing contacts with University students performing at St. Paul's, who might be willing to help the music director on other occasions. Bach, convinced that the position ought to be his by precedent, valiantly strove to regain it. On his settlement in Leipzig he immediately started work at St. Paul's by providing beautiful music for Whitsunday, May 10, which happened to occur even before he was formally installed in his new office. He continued in this way through the following three years, offering his services for as many as eleven festive occasions. The University was not displeased with this state of affairs, but when it came to paying, Bach was unable to obtain the statutory stipend. After many discussions he was given half of what constituted the former salary due to the Cantor from the University, while the rest went to Görner. Some 14 thalers were withheld, but this seemed important enough to Bach to justify direct appeals to the highest authority, Augustus

---

[1] They were the church of St. Peter and the 'New Church.' In the latter more elaborate music was performed on holy days and during the Leipzig Fair. For this the church organist was responsible (on Bach's arrival, G. B. Schott, and after 1729, J. G. Gerlach) and he had the help of University students and professional musicians.

'the Strong,' Elector of Saxony. If it appears rather surprising to us that the master should have bothered his monarch with such petty details, we must not forget that the Cantor's income was made up of small items, careful attention to which provided the difference between an adequate and an insufficient sustenance. Moreover, it was not in Bach's nature to put up with what he felt to be unjust. So he dispatched three petitions to the Elector in the last months of 1725; the third, a masterwork of logical presentation and clarity of diction, amounted to some 3000 words. He asked for the restitution of the legal emoluments and for the directorship of both the Old and the New Service. The monarch acceded to the first request, but gave the University freedom to settle the 'New Service' in whatever way they wanted. Bach got the outstanding money, but as it had become apparent that the University would not let him have the directorship of both services, he lost interest in St. Paul's and henceforth had the music for the 'Old Service' conducted by his prefects. On the other hand, his energetic action had not exactly endeared him to the academic authorities; from the outset they had looked down on the new Cantor's lack of academic training (a shocking state of matters that had not occurred in Leipzig during the past century!), and they now did their best to bypass Bach whenever a special composition was required for a festive occasion, thus depriving him of not insignificant fees.

Their hostile attitude is best illustrated by an incident that happened two years later. In September 1727 there occurred the death of Christiane Eberhardine, wife of the Elector of Saxony, who was dearly beloved in Lutheran Leipzig because she had remained faithful to the Protestant religion when her husband adopted Catholicism in order to gain the Polish throne. To express the prevailing emotion, an aristocratic University student, Hans Carl von Kirchbach, volunteered to hold a commemorative service in the University church at his own expense, in which he was to deliver the funeral oration. When he was given permission for this act of loyalty, he commissioned the poet, Johann Christoph Gottsched, to write a funeral Ode, and Bach to compose it. He could certainly not have made a wiser choice—although this was by no means the opinion of the learned professors. Their colleague, Gottsched, a great reformer of the German language, was eminently suitable, but his Ode, they contended, should be set to music by Görner. When Kirchbach refused this suggestion, claiming that Bach had already done the work, he was informed that the composer would not be allowed to perform the music, as this was Görner's duty. In high irritation, the young nobleman threatened to give up the whole project, whereupon a compromise was reached. Görner was to receive a present of 12 thalers from the student, and Bach was to sign a pledge that he would never again make an agreement concerning music at St. Paul's without previously obtaining the consent of the University. The first part of this arrangement worked out satisfactorily: Görner received his money and was content. But as to the pledge, the University official dispatched to Bach's lodgings to obtain the signature of the document had no success; the Cantor refused in no uncertain words to sign it.

There was one brighter aspect to this unpleasant episode: young Kirchbach's insistence on Bach's composition. While to the erudite professors the work of a third-rate musician like Görner (who, as Bach once shouted in a fit of fury, 'would have done better as a cobbler'[1]) seemed in no way inferior to that of Bach, the young people fell under the spell of the great man at St. Thomas'. They were anxious to secure his cooperation, when they prepared musical entertainment for some special occasion, and several of Bach's secular cantatas owe their existence to such commissions.[2] What was even more important, gifted University students were attracted by his genius and took part in the church music directed by him. We know, for instance, from a testimonial Bach wrote for C. G. Wecker, subsequently Cantor at Schweidnitz, that this student of law gave him 'creditable assistance' both as a singer and instrumentalist. Young J. G. Gerlach, who had graduated from the Thomas School in 1723, was also a valuable helper, whom Bach rewarded by recommending him successfully for the position of organist and music director at Leipzig's 'New Church.'[3]

Thanks to such talented and enthusiastic aides, not forgetting Bach's own three sons, who were gradually developing into first-class musicians in their own right, the master was able to carry out one of the most ambitious projects of his whole career. On Good Friday, 1729, his St. Matthew Passion had its first performance at St. Thomas'. The body of executants must have seemed quite enormous compared to those usually employed in Leipzig's churches. The parts used in a subsequent performance under Bach's direction have been preserved, and they show that 17 players were employed for each orchestra, 12 singers for either of the two choruses, and a third group of 12 vocalists for the chorale in the first

---

[1] Cf. C. L. Hilgenfeldt, 'J. S. Bach's Leben, Wirken und Werke,' 1850. Bach had plenty of opportunity of seeing Görner at work, as the latter was his subordinate as organist of St. Nicholas', a position which Görner gave up in 1729 for a similar one at St. Thomas.'

[2] Cf. Friedrich Smend in *AfMf*, 1942.

[3] Bach took Gerlach as soloist to Weissenfels in 1729, to take part in the celebration of Duke Christian's birthday, which certainly brought the young singer a handsome fee.

number. In 1729 the number of singers was smaller, as the *cantus firmus* was not sung, but played on the little organ over the altar; nevertheless the groups of executants must have seemed unusually large to the Leipzig congregation. In spite of its considerable length (well over three hours), the Passion was performed within the framework of the traditional Good Friday services, for which the following schedule was laid down: (1) 1.15 p.m. ringing of all bells; (2) the Hymn *Da Jesu an dem Kreuze stund* sung by the choir; (3) Passion Music, first part; (4) Versicle, *Herr Jesu Christ, dich zu uns wend*; (5) Sermon; (6) Passion Music, second part; (7) Motet, *Ecce quomodo moritur* (Jacobus Gallus); Intonation of Passion Versicle, Collection; Hymn, *Nun danket alle Gott*.

It is hard for us to-day to estimate Leipzig's response to the sublime work. Bearing in mind the pledge Bach had signed not to write operatic church music, it is to be feared that a good many listeners may have been confused, if not actually shocked, by the poignancy of this music.[1]

But whatever the response of the congregation may have been, it must be reported that neither the work itself, nor the tremendous achievement in presenting it in spite of countless obstacles, helped to impress Bach's superiors favourably. Their attitude is clearly reflected in an incident that happened in the very same year. Every spring new pupils were admitted to the Thomas school to replace those graduating. In May 1729, a few weeks after the performance of the St. Matthew Passion, Bach handed the Council a detailed list of the candidates he had examined, naming those he found suitable and unsuitable respectively, and the Rector seconded his recommendations. The wise city fathers, however, had their own opinions: they admitted four candidates the Cantor had warned against, one he had not even tested, and only five he had recommended. Apparently they were more interested in defying the Cantor than in obtaining good musicians for their church music. Nor was this an isolated episode. At a Council meeting a year later, the shortcomings of a certain Magister Petzoldt, Bach's deputy for the Latin classes, were under discussion, and this led to complaints about the Cantor himself. 'He has not conducted himself as he should,' criticized one of the members; 'he is doing nothing,' complained another; while a third described him as 'incorrigible.' Not a single voice was raised in Bach's defence; nobody even

---

[1] Bitter, Terry, and David-Mendel assume that the St. Matthew Passion is referred to in Gerber's story about the elderly lady who on hearing the Passion threw up her hands in horror, exclaiming: 'God help us. 'Tis surely an Opera-comedy.' Smend in 'Bach in Köthen' gives the entire quotation from Christian (not Heinrich Nikolaus) Gerber's 'Geschichte der Kirchen-Ceremonien in Sachsen,' 1732. The present author agrees with Smend that the passage read in its entirety seems to point to Dresden rather than Leipzig

mentioned the St. Matthew Passion or the brilliant festival Bach had arranged in June of that year for the bicentenary of the Augsburg Confession. Finally, it was decided to punish the Cantor for his many deficiencies by reducing his income. A change in the contractual salary or the statutory allotment of *Accidentien* was impossible, but the Council could, and did, restrict the offender's share in unexpected revenues.[1]

The city fathers' feeling of animosity towards Bach was heartily reciprocated by the Cantor. In August 1730, Sebastian, probably still unaware of the punitive action planned against him, submitted a memorandum in which he pointed out that the admittance of unsuitable pupils and the lack of adequate funds were jeopardizing his efforts to maintain the church music at a high level. The very title of the document, and the condescending manner with which all the details of an organization well known to the officials were explained in it, must have been irritating to the recipients:

> '*A short, but indispensable sketch of what constitutes a well-appointed church music, with a few impartial reflections on its present state of decline*

'For a well-appointed church music, vocalists and instrumentalists are necessary. In this town the vocalists are provided by the foundation pupils of St. Thomas', and these are of four classes: trebles, altos, tenors, and basses.

'If the choirs are to perform church music properly . . . the vocalists must again be divided into two classes: concertists [for the solos] and ripienists [for the chorus]. There are usually four concertists, but sometimes up to eight if it is desired to perform music for two choirs. There must be at least eight ripienists, two to each part. . . .

'The number of the resident pupils of St. Thomas' is fifty-five; these are divided into four choirs, for the four churches in which they partly perform concerted music, partly sing motets, and partly chorales. In three of the churches, i.e. St. Thomas', St. Nicholas', and the New Church, all the pupils must be musically trained . . . those who can only sing a chorale at need go to St. Peter's.

---

[1] The following instance reveals their policy. After the death of the old Rector in October 1729, and until a new official was installed, Bach had to conduct the school inspection every third, instead of every fourth, week. Later, when it came to allotting the Rector's very considerable share of *Accidentien*, the two other teachers who had taken over extra duties received sizable shares of this money, while Bach was left out and got nothing at all.

'To each choir there must belong, at least, three trebles, three alti, three tenors, and as many basses, so that if one person is unable to sing (which often happens, and particularly at this time of year, as can be proved by the prescriptions of the *medicus* sent to the dispensary), a motet can still be sung with at least two voices to each part. (*N.B.* How much better would it be, if it were so arranged as to have four singers available for each part, each choir thus consisting of sixteen persons!). Consequently, the number of those who must understand music is thirty-six persons.

'The instrumental music consists of the following performers:

two or even three	violino I
two or three	violino II
two each	viola I, II, violoncello
one	double bass
two or three, according to need	oboes
one or two	bassoons
three	trumpets
one	drum

In all, eighteen persons at least, for the instruments.

'*N.B.* Since church music is often composed with flutes . . . at least two persons are needed for them; altogether, then, twenty instrumentalists. The number of players engaged [by the city] for church music is eight, viz. four town pipers, three professional violinists, and one apprentice. Discretion forbids my speaking at all truthfully of their competence and musical knowledge; however, it ought to be considered that they are partly *emeriti* and partly not in such good practice as they should be. This is the list of them . . . [viz. 2 trumpets, 2 violins, 2 oboes, and 1 bassoon]. Thus the following important instrumentalists . . . are lacking: two players each of first and second violin, viola, violoncello, and flute: one player of double bass.

'The deficiency here shown has hitherto had to be made good partly by the University students, but chiefly by the Thomas pupils. The [University] students used to be very willing to do this, in the hope that in time they might . . . receive . . . an honorarium. But as the small payments which fell to them have been altogether withdrawn, the readiness of the students has likewise disappeared, for who will give his service for nothing? In the absence of more efficient performers, the second violin has been at most times, and the viola, violoncello, and double bass have been at all times played by the [Thomas] pupils, and it is easy to judge what has thus been lost to the vocal choir. So far only the Sunday music has been mentioned [which takes place alternately in St. Thomas' and St.

M

Nicholas']. But if I come to speak of the holy days, when music must be provided for both the principal churches at the same time, the lack of the necessary players is even more serious, since then I have to give up . . . such pupils as can play one instrument or another, and thus am obliged to do without their assistance [as singers] altogether.

'Furthermore, I cannot omit mentioning that through the admissions hitherto granted to so many boys unskilled and ignorant of music, the performances have necessarily . . . fallen into decline. A boy who knows nothing about music, who cannot even sing a second . . . can never be of any use in music. And even those who bring with them some elementary knowledge, do not become useful as quickly as is desirable. . . . However, no time is allowed for their training . . . but as soon as they are admitted, they are placed in the choirs. . . . It is well known that my predecessors, Schelle and Kuhnau, were obliged to have recourse to the assistance of the [University] students when they desired to perform complete and well-sounding music, which they were so far warranted in doing that several vocalists, a bass, a tenor, and an alto, as well as instrumentalists . . . were favoured with salaries by a Most Noble and Wise Council, and thereby were induced to strengthen the church music. Now, however, when the present state of music has greatly changed—the art being much advanced and the taste definitely altered, so that the old-fashioned kind of music no longer sounds well in our ears—when, therefore, performers ought to be selected who are able to satisfy the present musical taste and undertake the new kinds of music, and at the same time are qualified to give satisfaction to the composer by their rendering of his work, now the few perquisites have been altogether withheld from the choir, though they ought to be increased rather than diminished. It is, anyhow, astonishing that German musicians should be expected to perform *ex tempore* any kind of music, whether Italian or French, English, or Polish, like some of those *virtuosi* who have studied it long beforehand, even know it almost by heart, and who besides have such high salaries that their pains and diligence are well rewarded. This is not duly taken into consideration, and our German musicians are left to take care of themselves, so that under the necessity of working for their bread many can never think of attaining proficiency, much less of distinguishing themselves. To give one instance of this statement, we need only go to Dresden and see how the musicians there are paid by his Majesty; since all care as to maintenance is taken from them, they are relieved of anxiety, and as, moreover, each has to play but one instrument, it is evident that something admirable and delightful can be heard. The conclusion is easy to arrive at: that in ceasing to receive the perquisites I am deprived of the power of getting the music into a better shape.

'Finally, I will list the present foundation pupils, stating in each case the extent of his musical skill, and leave it to further consideration whether concerted music can be properly performed under such conditions or whether a further decline is to be feared . . . [There follows a list of names under the headings 'those who are efficient,' 'those needing further training before they can take part in concerted music,' and 'those who are not musical at all']. Summa: 17 serviceable, 20 not yet serviceable, 17 useless.   Joh. Seb. Bach,

                                              Director Musices.'

Leipzig, August 23, 1730.

This is, indeed, a highly significant document. Not only does it offer valuable glimpses into the performing practice of the time; it reveals, too, the inflexible nature of its author and his lack of the graces of diplomacy which would have made life so much easier for him. Bach was angry with his superiors, and when he penned his report he did not try to hide his feelings under the flowery phrases of respect and submission which the exalted city officials deemed their rightful due. That he did master all the intricacies of polite letter-writing, and could use them if he so wished, is shown by other petitions to the Council.[1] This time, however, he went straight to the point with a bluntness that could only turn against him. It was also a tactical error to praise conditions at Dresden at the expense of Leipzig. Such a comparison was not quite fair, since Dresden, as the residence of the Elector, naturally enjoyed privileges denied to other towns. It merely had the result of increasing the animosity of his superiors.

Anyway, the Burgomaster, to whom he handed the report, was not at all impressed by it. He did not even mention it at the following meeting, and merely remarked that the Cantor 'showed little inclination to work.' No vote was taken regarding the payment to University students, for which Bach had pleaded so strongly. This must have angered him all the more as he was well aware that the Council was not as tight-fisted in dealing with another music director. Young Gerlach, who, at Bach's recommendation, had been appointed to the New Church, was granted in this same year a 100 per cent increase in his salary, and allowed 30 thalers for the purchase of new instruments. It really looked as though the

---

[1] Cf. his letter dated September 20, 1728, in which he, for once, requested the City's help against a member of the Consistory, who had infringed Bach's right to choose the church hymns.

Council were anxious to develop the musical service in this insignificant church at the expense of venerable St. Thomas' and St. Nicholas', which were under Bach's direction.

All this caused Sebastian to investigate the possibilities of finding another position, and on October 28, 1730, he wrote to his old school-mate, Georg Erdmann, now settled as Imperial Russian 'resident' (ambassador) in Danzig, asking him whether he knew of any good opening there. He gave the following reasons for his wish to leave Leipzig: 'Since I find (1) that this appointment is by no means as advantageous as it was described to me, (2) that many fees incidental to it are now stopped, (3) that the town is a very expensive place to live in, (4) that the authorities are very strange people, with small love of music, so that I live under almost constant vexation, jealousy and persecution, I feel compelled to seek, with God's assistance, my fortune elsewhere.'[1]

Reading this outburst, and bearing in mind the sublime masterpieces which Bach, alleged to 'have done nothing,' was pouring out over Leipzig, one cannot help feeling outraged by the Council's attitude. However, it must not be overlooked that one of the main sources of Sebastian's feud with the authorities lay in the double aspect of his position. He was engaged as teacher (Cantor) and music director. To Bach only the music directorship mattered, while to the Council the duties of the Cantor seemed of paramount importance. The city fathers heard of lack of discipline at the school, of outbursts of fury on the part of the irascible Cantor, and of lengthy visits to various courts, for which he did not ask permission, and they knew that his prefects often took over the singing classes which he was supposed to hold. Other Cantors before him had taken similar liberties, but these had known how to ingratiate themselves by submissive and deferential behaviour, whereas this 'incorrigible' Bach acted with maddening presumptuousness. Altogether, it was one of those human relationships which defy a satisfactory solution; for the engagement of a composer at the peak of his creative productivity as school official and disciplinarian in a badly organized institute is a contradiction in itself. Bach would certainly have been better off at the court of an important sovereign, who would have expected nothing from him but musical compositions. As no such opening presented itself, he was forced to remain in Leipzig.

Fortunately the following years saw a slackening of the tension

---

[1] We do not know whether Erdmann, in answer to this appeal, did anything to find a congenial position for his old school-mate. Any plans he may have entertained for bringing Sebastian to Danzig were cut short by Erdmann's death in 1736.

between him and his official superiors. Johann Mathias Gesner, a good friend from Sebastian's Weimar days, for whom the Thomas Cantor had only recently written a cantata,[1] became Rector of the school, and with tact and discretion he calmed the waves of mutual indignation. Gesner is recognized to-day as one of the pioneers in the field of classical philology. Before him German scholars had been pedantically investigating trifles of antiquarian or grammatical interest; Gesner grasped the very spirit of antique culture and in his lectures and commentaries opened up new vistas to the German mind. This outstanding philologist was at the same time a born teacher, genuinely interested in young people, whose devotion he won by the power of his own humanity and enthusiasm. Thus he was perfectly suited for carrying out the long-needed reforms at the Thomas school. As soon as he started on his duties, he prevailed on the Council to make definite plans for a building programme. Before long two new storeys were added to the school, and though this entailed a good deal of inconvenience—all the teachers, including Bach, having to find temporary quarters outside the school—the result was well worth the trouble. The Rector also issued new regulations for the school, in which music was allotted an important place. He explained to the pupils that their praising the Lord through music linked them with the heavenly choirs and that he expected them to be proud of this privilege and even to sacrifice leisure hours for the sake of good performances. More effectively than by such general advice and the listing of fines to be imposed on those neglecting their musical work, the Rector succeeded in improving the pupils' attitude by changing the general atmosphere in the school. It was a much happier group that now worked together at St. Thomas', and naturally in all fields better results were obtained. As for the Cantor, Gesner endeavoured to smooth out his differences with the Council. At the Rector's suggestion Bach was freed from any teaching assignments outside music and in their place was put in charge of the daily visits to the morning service, at which 8 choristers alternately provided the music at either St. Thomas' or St. Nicholas'. Gesner also induced the authorities to let the Cantor henceforth have his full share of all accruing moneys. Bach, on the other hand, could not but enjoy working with this outstanding Rector who really valued his musical work. This attitude of Gesner's is proved by a delightful description he offered of Bach's art both as virtuoso and conductor, sufficient in itself to endear the scholar to every music historian. Some years after leaving Leipzig he wrote a Latin com-

[1] It is the Italian Cantata No. 209 composed in celebration of Gesner's return to his native city. Cf. Luigi Ansbacher in 'Bach Gedenkschrift,' 1950.

mentary to an edition of Quintilian's *Institutio Oratoria* and used the
mention of a cithara-player's versatility to plunge into this panegyric:

'All these [outstanding achievements], my Fabius, you would deem
very trivial could you but rise from the dead and see our Bach . . . how
he with both hands and using all his fingers, plays on a clavier which seems
to consist of many citharas in one, or runs over the keys of the instrument
of instruments, whose innumerable pipes are made to sound by means of
bellows; and how he, going one way with his hands, and another way, at
the utmost speed, with his feet, conjures by his unaided skill . . . hosts of
harmonious sounds; I say, could you but see him, how he achieves what
a number of your cithara players and 600 performers on reed instruments[1] could never achieve, not merely . . . singing and playing at the
same time his own parts, but presiding over thirty or forty musicians all
at once, controlling this one with a nod, another by a stamp of the foot,
a third with a warning finger, keeping time and tune, giving a high note
to one, a low to another, and notes in between to some. This one man,
standing alone in the midst of the loud sounds, having the hardest task of
all, can discern at every moment if anyone goes astray, and can keep all
the musicians in order, restore any waverer to certainty and prevent him
from going wrong. Rhythm is in his every limb, he takes in all the harmonies by his subtle ear and utters all the different parts through the
medium of his own mouth. Great admirer as I am of antiquity in other
respects, I yet deem this Bach of mine to comprise in himself many
Orpheuses and twenty Arions.'

Such genuine admiration from a man of Gesner's intellectual stature
must have warmed Bach's heart. Their intercourse may also have stimulated the master in other ways. In 1731 appeared Gesner's outstanding
Chrestomathia Graeca, and we can well imagine Bach discussing certain
pieces with his learned friend and receiving much food for thought from
the Rector's vision of antique glory. Gesner, incidentally, was not the only
one in Leipzig who was responsible for new trends in the conception of
the past. There was, for instance, Johann Friedrich Christ, Professor at
the University, who opened the students' eyes to the all but forgotten
beauties of antique sculpture and paintings. Bach may have heard about
these lectures from his young University friends, and on his frequent visits
to Dresden he had a chance to test the truth of Professor Christ's asser-

---

[1] The Latin expression Gesner uses is *tibia*, a Roman instrument somewhat in the
character of an oboe.

tions by visiting the exquisite collections of antiques, which since 1728 were being assembled there.

By a fortunate coincidence the years of pleasant co-operation with Gesner also brought other improvements in Bach's position. He now had some excellent vocalists in his chorus, among them his favourite pupil, Johann Ludwig Krebs,[1] his first sopranist, Christoph Nichelmann, the gifted Christian Friedrich Schemelli, and several others. Moreover he was able to consolidate his connection with the University students by taking over, on the departure of G. B. Schott in 1729, a Collegium Musicum, founded in 1702 by Telemann for regular weekly performances of music in Zimmermann's Coffee-house. Leipzig had two associations of this kind, each numbering fifteen to twenty members, and as they were independent of the University authorities, there was nobody to prevent Bach from assuming the directorship. These Collegia Musica served a dual purpose: they kept musicians among the students in good training, and they helped them to obtain recognition and eventually a position. Visitors from out-side, especially during the Leipzig fair, thronged the two Coffee-houses to hear the young musicians display their virtuosity, and valuable contacts were established in this way. The direct financial returns for the players must have been insignificant, if we are to believe the remarks of the poetess Marianne von Ziegler:[2] 'Most of the listeners seem to think that these sons of the Muses just extemporize the music; the reward they get is very poor indeed, and often they have to be content with a bare bone to pick for all the hours of preparation they have put in.' This may have been true for the students, but certainly not for Bach, who would not have directed the group for over ten years without receiving adequate financial com-pensation. Zimmermann, the owner of the establishment, would have paid him a considerable honorarium, which the astute business-man amply recovered by the afflux of guests, who consumed great quantities of his coffee, cake, or beer, while enjoying such artistic treats. In the summer the Collegium performed in Zimmermann's open-air restaurant outside the city, where works for a larger group, such as Bach's cantata 'Phoebus and Pan,' could be played. The work with the Collegium Musicum in-spired Bach to compose a number of delightful secular cantatas, but he did not by any means limit himself to the performance of vocal music. The Brandenburg Concertos, many other chamber music works, and new compositions for keyboard instruments resounded at Zimmermann's

---

[1] He was a son of Johann Tobias Krebs, Bach's student in Weimar. The older Krebs admired Bach so greatly that altogether he sent three of his offspring to St. Thomas.'

[2] This outstanding woman supplied 9 texts for Bach's Cantatas.

together with compositions by other masters. And if Bach was in a good humour, he could be induced to improvise on the clavier, to the delight of the assembled guests.

Many performances of the Collegium Musicum took place as an act of homage to the ruling monarch. In particular, the year 1733, when the Elector Augustus III succeeded his father, was distinguished by a series of such festive acts. Bach exerted himself by producing no less than four different cantatas during the period from August to December of that year in order to celebrate the name-day and birthday respectively of the new ruler as well as the birthdays of the Crown Prince and the Electress; and he continued with hardly diminished efforts in 1734. Yet all these contributions sink into insignificance when compared to the one monumental work he wrote for Augustus III. The new ruler's first visit to Leipzig, to accept the oath of allegiance, was celebrated with great pomp, and the City Council commissioned their Director Musices to write a *Kyrie* and *Gloria* to be performed on April 21, 1733, at St. Nicholas' before and after the festive sermon.[1] Bach, knowing that on this special occasion much of the usual liturgy in the service would be omitted and that, on the other hand, he would have more singers than usual at his disposal, supplied a *Kyrie* and *Gloria* surpassing the customary sacred music in every respect. The *Kyrie* was meant as mourning music for the deceased Elector, Augustus 'the Strong,' while the triumphant strains of the *Gloria* following the sermon celebrated the ascension to the throne of his heir. The Elector, as a Catholic, was, significantly enough, deprived of the joy of hearing this glorious music performed in his honour. However, Bach seems to have been encouraged by friends in Dresden to hope that a whole Mass of his composition might be played for the Coronation ceremony of Augustus III as King of Poland.[2] Thus he set about completing the gigantic composition, for which task he had ample leisure, as the mourning period for the deceased Elector made the performance of 'figural' music in the Leipzig churches impossible. The *Mass in b* was handed to the Elector, but the composer's hope was not fulfilled. This meant a disappointment for Bach, but it may, on the other hand, have saved him a good deal of unpleasantness. For although at that time individual movements from the Mass, especially the Latin *Kyrie* and *Gloria*, still figured in the Protestant ritual, the composition of the complete Ordinary of the

---

[1] Cf. Schering, *l.c.*, p. 217 and foll. Smend in 'J. S. Bachs Kirchenkantaten,' VI, assumes that the *Credo* from the Mass in b was performed as early as June 5, 1732, for the inauguration of the remodelled Thomas school.

[2] Cf. Schering in *BJ*, 1936.

Mass was tantamount to an invasion of Catholic territory. Bach himself apparently felt no scruples in this respect. His employers in Leipzig, however, might have resented seeing their music director connected in so conspicuous a manner with the Coronation service in a Catholic church.

Bach had good reasons for making continual efforts to prove his loyalty to the new ruler. He felt increasingly in need of the Elector's support as the situation in Leipzig was changing again. Rector Gesner had always cherished the wish to lecture at a University too, and as this apparently proved impossible in Leipzig, he accepted a call to the newly founded University of Göttingen, where he was to serve with the greatest distinction. He was succeeded in November 1734 by the former vice-principal of the school, Johann August Ernesti, a man only 27 years of age, who deservedly enjoyed a fine reputation as a classical scholar. In some respects he continued his predecessor's policy by raising the scholastic standard; but in his ambition to create an outstanding institute of learning, the young Rector saw in the students' musical duties nothing but an obstacle to the fulfilment of his plans. His attitude was not wholly unjustified. The type of school capable of serving both scholastic and musical purposes had become definitely outdated. The range of subjects to be studied was greatly widened in the 18th century, and with natural science playing an increasingly important part, it gradually became impossible for the young people to cope with both their scholastic and musical tasks. The Rector wanted to modernize his institute and hated to see his charges waste so much time by singing in the streets, attending funerals or weddings, and rehearsing for performances. His problem was further aggravated by the kind of music the Cantor expected the choir to sing; it often necessitated serious studying and additional rehearsals. All this displeased the Rector exceedingly. He did not, like Gesner, compare the Thomasians to the angelic choirs. Instead, when he came across a boy practising his music, he would remark sneeringly: 'So it's a pothouse fiddler you want to become,' and thus make the performance of music seem an inferior kind of occupation. To work in harmony with so intolerant and ambitious a superior would have been hard for any musician; it was utterly impossible for Bach. Thus there was tension, more and more of it, until it burst out in a controversy which assumed terrific proportions and lasted through more than two years (during which time the two deadly enemies had to live next door to each other!). The incident provoking it was petty, and the details need not concern us to-day. It had to do with the appointment of musical prefects, those senior pupils who took over much of the Cantor's duties and whose satisfactory work was

of vital importance to a smoothly running musical organization. Bach's
top prefect provoked the Rector by punishing a recalcitrant young pupil
too severely, whereupon Ernesti, against Bach's wish, forced him to
leave the school. The Rector then promoted another prefect to the first
place, a youth whom the Cantor declared unfit for so responsible a position. Clearly the right was on Bach's side, as no one but he was supposed
to judge a pupil's qualifications for the musical prefectship. Unfortunately,
however, the hot-blooded Cantor damaged his own unassailable position
by letting his temper run away with him. Shocking scenes occurred
during the church services when Bach, seeing the hated prefect at work,
chased him away with 'great shouting and noise,' whereupon Ernesti sent
the youth back, threatening the whole choir with penalties if they sang
under anybody else. Thus utter confusion reigned at St. Thomas', and the
discipline built up with so much difficulty was carried off as in a whirl-
wind. Bach, however, did not care for anything but the restitution of his
rights, 'cost it what it might.' A stream of reports and appeals began to
flow from both adversaries to the authorities. Bach's were a model of
clearness dealing merely with the problem in question. Ernesti, on the
other hand, not only blamed the Cantor for shirking his duties in various
ways, but even contended that Bach was venal and accepted unsuitable
candidates whose fathers were willing to make him a payment. Such a
remark about Sebastian Bach, whose unshakable fairness and justice in
the examination of organs had become a byword over all the country,
shows best with what type of superior the Cantor had to deal. The Council
and the Consistory, both of whom had received various appeals, found
themselves in a most unpleasant situation—they did not care to offend
Ernesti, of whom they thought highly, but on the other hand they could
not help admitting the justice of the Cantor's complaints. Therefore they
chose the old expedient of doing nothing, hoping that with the gradua-
tion of the offensive prefect the storm would pass over. Ultimately Bach
appealed to the highest authority, the Elector, who in 1736 had conferred
on him the title of Royal Polish and Electoral Saxon Court composer[1]
in gratitude for Bach's many musical homages, not forgetting the B minor
Mass. It seems that the monarch, on a visit to Leipzig at which festive
music by Bach was performed with the greatest pomp, personally inter-

---

[1] The title, which Bach had already solicited in 1733 when handing in the first 2
movements of the Mass in b, was only conferred on him on November 19, 1736, after he
had lost the minor title of conductor to the court of Weissenfels through the death of
Duke Christian. Apparently Augustus III had waited so long because he did not care to
be associated with a lower ranking ruler in the titles he awarded.

vened in favour of the composer, for thenceforth the feud at St. Thomas' is not mentioned in any official document. This does not mean, however, that either of the two parties forgot or forgave. Ernesti persevered in his anti-musical policy, and Bach grew less and less concerned with the duties of his office. Not only did he neglect his teaching assignments, but he did so to such an extent that in 1740 it became necessary to appoint a master for musical theory to the school. Even the stream of new compositions for his choir diminished considerably at that time, and old works were performed in their stead. Bach was still deeply interested in the training of gifted musicians, but, significantly enough, such outstanding pupils as J. F. Agricola, J. F. Doles, J. P. Kirnberger, and J. C. Altnikol came to him as University students. Of talented pupils of the Thomas school practically nothing is known during these years: either there were none in the Alumnate, or Bach, knowing Ernesti's attitude, was not disposed to spend much of his time and energy on them.

However, neglecting St. Thomas' did not mean a life of leisure for him; he continued to be an indefatigable worker, but one whose energies were directed towards different goals. As a composer he became less concerned with sacred music, perhaps because the spiritual climate of Leipzig was changing under the growing impact of 'Enlightenment.' Now he concentrated on instrumental composition; and he also paid more attention to the problems of publishing his music. His zest for travelling and meeting fellow musicians found satisfaction through frequent and well-paid invitations to test organs in various cities. He also spent a good deal of time at Dresden, appearing at court, giving organ recitals, and making music with the prominent court musicians, who also came to Leipzig to play at his home.[1]

A unique experience was granted him in a meeting with King Friedrich 'the Great' of Prussia. Since his second son, Emanuel, had been appointed in 1740 court accompanist to the enlightened and highly musical ruler, Bach was greatly interested in the Northern capital. It is probably his own opinion that is reflected in the remark of his secretary, J. Elias Bach,[2] that 'at Berlin the golden age of music seemed to be inaugurated.' Sebastian may even have entertained hopes of finding in Berlin the kind of position he was longing for. It is noteworthy, anyway, that as early as 1741 he visited his son there. The time was not well chosen, for the King was involved in the first 'Silesian war' against Austria; besides,

---

[1] Cf. letter of Elias Bach to Cantor Koch, dated August 11, 1739, in 'Die Musik,' 1912-13.

[2] Cf. letter of Elias to J. Ernst Bach, dated January 9, 1742, l.c.

Sebastian's sojourn had to be broken off because of a serious illness of Anna Magdalena; as a result, no appearance at court took place. The following years saw the monarch still mainly engaged in martial exploits, which even interfered with Bach's own life. In 1745 the Prussian armies laid siege to Leipzig, ruthlessly burning and ransacking the lovely countryside around it; and great was the distress of the Leipzig population. To raise their morale, Bach wrote, to the accompaniment of rumbling cannons, his powerful cantata *Du Friedefürst*, in which some inaccuracies in the continuo part and a score difficult to read in some places[1] testify to the peculiar conditions prevailing at the time of its composition. But Sebastian, a true son of the period, was not really concerned with the quarrels of the rulers, and once the danger was over and peace restored, he again planned an appearance at the Prussian court. This time conditions were much more propitious, since a distinguished friend of the Bachs had come to Berlin in 1746 as Russian ambassador. This was the *Reichsgraf* Hermann von Keyserlingk,[2] who had been stationed in Dresden from 1733 to 1746, and had received from Sebastian the 'Goldberg Variations' for which he sent the composer a golden goblet filled with a hundred Louis d'or. The ambassador's enthusiastic praise of the Leipzig master naturally excited the Prussian king's curiosity, and so an invitation was extended through Emanuel. In the spring of 1747 Sebastian complied and came to Berlin, where he also had the joy of seeing his first grandson, Johann August,[3] born on November 30, 1745. 'Old Bach,' as the King spoke of him, was received most graciously. He had to try out all the fine forte-pianos built by Silbermann that were in the palace, and on each he displayed his incredible mastery of improvisation. Finally he asked the King, who was a composer himself, to give him a subject of his own for a fugue. This Friedrich did, and Bach was so intrigued by the possibilities of the royal theme that on his return to Leipzig he wrote a truly royal set of polyphonic compositions in the strictest style based on this subject; he had them engraved under the title *Das musikalische Opfer* (Musical Offering) and dedicated them to the King. Having intercourse with, and

---

[1] Cf. preface to *BG* 24, pp. 26 and foll.

[2] Keyserlingk was also mainly responsible for the awarding to Sebastian of the title of Saxon court composer. In 1748 he was godfather to Emanuel's youngest son, Johann Sebastian. Friedemann dedicated a Sonata in E flat major to him in 1763.

[3] It is likely that the 'Capellmeister Bach' mentioned as one of the child's god-fathers was Sebastian, but this does not necessarily imply that he attended the christening ceremony. Perhaps he was represented by someone else. The same applies to Anna Magdalena Bach, who is mentioned as godmother of Emanuel's second child, Anna Carolina Philippina, christened on September 12, 1747. Cf. Miesner in *BJ*, 1932.

being so warmly applauded by, the great monarch gave intense satisfaction to Sebastian, and in this particular case he may not even have
minded that no financial benefits were derived from the visit or the
subsequent dedication. (Friedrich's account books, at least, make no
mention of any payment to the guest from Leipzig.)

The Berlin visit was the last great artistic success granted to Bach.
Not long afterwards an old affliction of his began to assume threatening
proportions. His eyesight had been poor for many years, and the constant
strain of writing small music notes by candlelight finally exacted its toll—
as it did with his kinsmen, Johann Gottfried Walther and Johann Ernst
Bach (25). In 1749 Bach was nearly blind, and rumour had it that his
health was badly impaired as well. Whether this was correct, whether he
had had a stroke, as some historians conjecture, can no longer be verified;
the *Necrolog* written by his own son, Emanuel, and his pupil, Agricola,
certainly stressed that, apart from his eye-trouble, Bach had been physically quite fit. But, whatever was the truth behind the rumours, they
caused the writing of a letter to Leipzig's Burgomaster, in which the
Dresden conductor, Johann Gottlob Harrer, was recommended for the
vacancy expected to occur through Bach's death; and it was suggested
that Harrer should prove his skill by giving a trial performance immediately. As the author of the letter was the all-powerful Saxonian
minister, Count Brühl, his suggestion amounted to an order. The good
city fathers complied—whether or not with a feeling of guilt at this
flagrant lack of reverence we don't know—and so it came about that
in the inn of the 'Three Swans,' where secular concerts used to take place,
Harrer on June 8, 1749, gave a public performance of a church cantata
he had brought with him, as a test piece for the 'future position of
Thomas Cantor, if the director musices, Sebastian Bach, should pass away.'
Thus a chronicler[1] records nonchalantly. Bach could not help hearing of
the shameful incident. His fighting spirit was roused; he would prove to
them that he was still in the possession of his strength. Tenaciously he
continued the struggle for more than a year, and Harrer, dismayed and
disappointed, had to go back to Dresden. At that time news of a visiting
English oculist, who had performed amazing operations, spread through
Germany. This Chevalier John Taylor happened to pass through Leipzig,
and Bach resolved to entrust himself to the renowned surgeon. Taylor
performed two operations on him, but they were both failures; moreover
the various drugs administered shattered the master's whole system and
he grew steadily weaker. On July 18, sight was suddenly restored to him,

---

[1] Johann Salomon Riemer, 'Chronik Leipzigs,' 1714-71, Ratsarchiv, Leipzig.

but a few hours later a stroke occurred followed by a raging fever, to which he succumbed on July 28, 1750. Musicians and music lovers in Leipzig deeply mourned the loss. The City Council, however, in its next meeting, did not waste much time in eulogies on the departed composer. Some remarks were uttered such as 'the school needs a Cantor, not a conductor,' or 'Bach was certainly a great musician, but no school teacher,' and Harrer's appointment was formally decided on. Furthermore, when Bach's widow applied for the customary payment of the Cantor's honorarium through the following half-year, the city accountant was smart enough to remember that Bach, when entering office 27 years previously, had received full payment for the first quarter, although he started work only in February; so the Council had the satisfaction of deducting 21 th. 21 gr. from the relief-sum due to the widow. The intractable Cantor was replaced by a man whose 'very quiet and accommodating nature' Count Brühl had emphasized, and the Council looked forward to a peaceful era at St. Thomas'.

VI

SEBASTIAN AND HIS FAMILY

Our conception of Sebastian's appearance during his service at Leipzig was, until recently, based mainly on the portrait painted towards the end of his life by Elias Gottlieb Haussmann.[1] It shows a man of tremendous power and stubborn energy, whose face reveals the suffering, the disappointments, and the bitter fights which formed so decisive a part of his life as Thomas Cantor. This is the Bach with whom the Leipzig authorities had to deal; clearly a formidable man who made the good burghers feel uncomfortable and only too often definitely hostile. There is, however, another portrait of the master of the Leipzig years (Frontispiece). For more than 200 years it had been hidden in private collections and was only made

---

[1] It was painted for the *Societät der musikalischen Wissenschaften*, an association of learned musicians founded by Lorenz Christoph Mizler, of which Bach became a member in 1747. Haussmann seems to have made several copies of it. That of 1747 is reproduced in C. S. Terry's 'Bach,' London, 1928. There is also a Haussmann portrait of 1748, in a much better state of preservation, which is owned by an English collector and was published in 1950 (cf. Hans Raupach, 'Das wahre Bildnis J. S. Bachs'). The authenticity of a Bach portrait claimed to have been painted by Haussmann in 1723 and preserved in an American collection (cf. Herz in *MQ*, 1943) is doubtful, and so are the paintings by Ihle, as well as the so-called Volbach portrait. The Bach painting by Liszewski was only done after the composer's death. The Haussmann portrait of 1748 was acquired in 1953 by William H. Scheide, Princeton, N.J., U.S.A.

available to the present writer in 1950.[1] It was executed in pastel in the 1730's during a visit to Leipzig by a young member of the family, Gottlieb Friedrich, eldest son of Johann Ludwig Bach, the Meiningen conductor, with whom Sebastian had been in close artistic contact (cf. p. 108). In this beautiful pastel, Sebastian's characteristic features—the lofty brow, fleshy face, prominent nose, stubborn mouth—are of course the same, but the expression is a very different one. It is easy to find physical reasons for Sebastian's more relaxed attitude in this pastel. Gottlieb Friedrich's sitter was a man ten or twelve years younger, whose eyes did not yet reveal the strain that a subsequent disease was to produce. But the difference between Haussmann's and young Gottlieb's portraits reaches far deeper. The kinsman painted the master as he saw him when visiting Sebastian's home, which, as Emanuel later wrote to Forkel, 'was like a beehive, and just as teeming with life.' Here, as the centre of his own private world, Sebastian was by no means the man whom the Leipzig Council resented and feared. He was generous, courteous, and helpful; he rejoiced in his children and kinsmen, training them in his art and assisting them in every conceivable way. The man whom young Bach portrayed was not harassed by 'jealousy and persecution' (cf. p. 180). There is strength and determination combined with joy and pride in his face, pride in his position as the father and mentor of the many gifted musicians who sat at his feet and drew inspiration from his supreme mastery and powerful personality.

The picture we have drawn of Sebastian at Leipzig would therefore be incomplete were we not to follow him into the privacy of his home and watch the destinies of the younger generation take shape under his guidance.

When Bach moved to Leipzig, in 1723, four children accompanied him and his young wife.[2] The eldest, Catharina Dorothea, was 15 and thus capable of being a valuable help in the household. The three boys, Wilhelm Friedemann, Philipp Emanuel, and Gottfried Bernhard, aged 13, 9, and 8 respectively, were enrolled in the Thomas school and did well there. Some of Friedemann's exercise books have been discovered and

---

[1] The pastel belongs to Mr. Paul Bach, a great-grandson of the painter. Cf. for the following statements Karl Geiringer, 'The Lost Bach Portrait,' Oxford University Press, New York, 1950.

[2] It is characteristic of Sebastian's loyalty to the family that shortly after his appointment he had a nephew from Ohrdruf join the school. This was *Johann Heinrich* (born 1707), fourth son of Sebastian's eldest brother and teacher, Johann Christoph, who had died not long before. This youth stayed at the Thomas school for 4 years receiving ample musical instruction from his uncle; he subsequently became Cantor in Oehringen.

they reveal him as a very bright boy, well versed in Latin and Greek, and one who, on the other hand, knew how to enliven boring lessons by drawing caricatures and scribbling jokes into his books. Sebastian, who was determined that his sons should enjoy the academic training denied to himself, was pleased to note their scholastic aptitude. As a symbolic gesture, in the very year of their arrival in Leipzig, he had Friedemann's name entered at the University for ultimate matriculation, and at Christmas he presented the boy with the certificate of registration. Hand in hand with school work went a most thorough musical education, which must have kept the three Bach boys very busy indeed. They were naturally important members of Sebastian's choir; they studied organ and clavier with him, and they were gradually introduced into musical theory and the science of composition. But Sebastian was still not satisfied as far as his beloved 'Friede' (the family name of the eldest boy) was concerned. Studying with an eminent violinist seemed to him an essential part of musical training, and therefore, in 1726, he sent Friede to Merseburg, to work for almost a year with the excellent Johann Gottlieb Graun, a pupil of Tartini, and subsequently a colleague of Emanuel Bach in Berlin. The result of the Merseburg studies was probably quite satisfactory; nevertheless Friede's interest remained centred in the keyboard instruments which his father had taught him. As regards the younger sons, musical instruction outside the home did not seem so important to Sebastian. In any case, since Emanuel was left-handed he was not well qualified for playing stringed instruments. The father therefore trained him to become an outstanding clavier player, and he had the satisfaction of seeing Emanuel, at the age of 17, engrave a clavier minuet of his own, which was published almost simultaneously with Sebastian's opus I, the *Clavier Übung*. Yet it was always Friede in whom Sebastian was most interested. He loved doing things in company with his eldest boy, and their trips to Dresden, to attend opera performances and visit the local musicians, were great treats for both of them. The father's sympathy and care, so unstintingly given at all times, at first made life easier for Friedemann, but proved ultimately a fatal gift. Sebastian's genius could not but overwhelm one who was so close to him. Friedemann naturally adopted his father's artistic tastes and opinions, and was unable fully to follow the trends of his own generation. He was also keenly conscious of the great expectations the father cherished for him and felt alternately inspired and heavily burdened by them. Emanuel, on the other hand, never achieved Friede's intimacy with his father; he admired Sebastian tremendously, but did not try to imitate him and thus his own individual style was able to develop more freely.

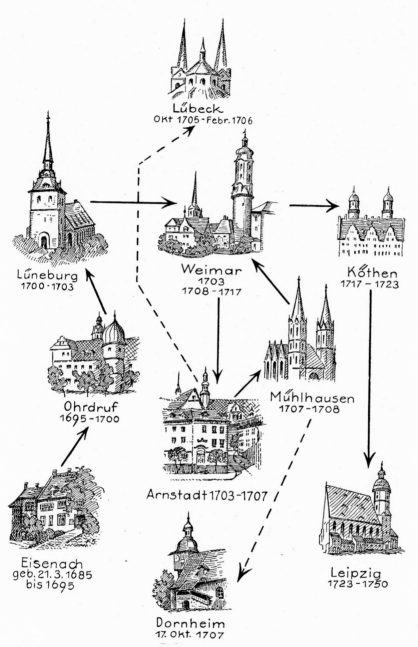

Lübeck
Okt 1705 - Febr. 1706

Lüneburg
1700 · 1703

Weimar
1703
1708 - 1717

Köthen
1717 - 1723

Ohrdruf
1695 - 1700

Mühlhausen
1707 - 1708

Arnstadt 1703 - 1707

Eisenach
geb. 21. 3. 1685
bis 1695

Dornheim
17. Okt. 1707

Leipzig
1723 - 1750

3. Places significant in Johann Sebastian Bach's life

On his return from Merseburg, Friedemann continued at the Thomas school and in 1729 he graduated, offering a public valediction. He then began his studies at Leipzig University, where he remained for four years, taking courses in law, philosophy, and mathematics. Emanuel closely followed his brother's example; he entered the University two years later, at the age of 17, and remained as a student at this institute until 1735. Both brothers would, of course, have been perfectly able to find positions as musicians after graduating from the Thomas school, but their father was by no means anxious for them to do so. He did not mind supporting them for a few more years so as to give them the benefits of a scholarly education. The musical performances that he arranged with their help in his home were among his greatest joys. Proudly he wrote to Erdmann in 1730: 'All my children are born musicians and from my own family, I assure you, I can arrange a concert *vocaliter* and *instrumentaliter*.' Besides, the sons were real helpers, copying music for him, taking over the instruction of some of his pupils,[1] and rehearsing for performances; they thus cleared the path for Sebastian's creative work. It is no mere accident that the St. Matthew Passion was composed and first performed in the years when Friedemann and Emanuel lived with their father, assuming many of Sebastian's responsibilities. In 1733, however, the post of organist at Dresden's *Sophienkirche* fell vacant, and this seemed a highly suitable opportunity for Friedemann to start on his musical career. Sebastian Bach was of course well known and highly appreciated in Dresden since his notable success in the projected contest with Marchand (cf. p. 152), and he enjoyed most cordial relations with the eminent court musicians there. On the exquisite little organ built by Silbermann, the control of which Friedemann was now seeking, his father had given a recital two years earlier that had enraptured the Dresden courtiers and music lovers. Friedemann could thus count on a friendly consideration of his application, and all the more so since the decisive voice regarding the appointment belonged to the famous Pantaleon Hebenstreit, who as a former conductor at Eisenach (cf. p. 31) was well acquainted with the Bach family. But help of such kind was hardly necessary, for young Friedemann was an inspired virtuoso who profoundly affected his listeners. On the day after the trial performance the official document of appointment was executed, and Sebastian's eldest son settled down in Dresden. The father was pleased indeed. The position was not a lucrative one, but as it did not involve much work, the young musician would have plenty of time for

---

[1] Friedemann instructed Christoph Nichelmann, who later became, as second accompanist at the Prussian court, Emanuel's colleague.

N

further study and creative activity. Besides, Dresden was not far from Leipzig, and it would be easy for father and son to visit each other, thus enabling Sebastian to watch his Friede's artistic growth.[1]

Emanuel was only 21, two years younger than Friedemann, when he left his father's home. He went to Frankfurt-on-the-Oder to continue his law studies at the University, supporting himself mainly with what he earned as a clavier teacher, for at that time he was already a masterly pianist. Three years later he found a position he was to hold for 27 years, being appointed accompanist to Friedrich 'the Great' of Prussia.

By 1735 Sebastian had thus lost the two most important helpers in his family. Although the gap left by these two was further widened by the departure of some of his best pupils, such as J. Ludwig Krebs and Chr. F. Schemelli the younger, Sebastian yet saw fit to find a position for his third son, *Johann Gottfried Bernhard* (47). There was a vacancy at the organ of St. Mary's in Mühlhausen, and as Sebastian had, in the 27 years since his own service in this city, maintained friendly relations with some influential citizens, he now applied on behalf of his son. There was some opposition from members of the Council favouring a local organist, but the weight of Sebastian Bach's name, coupled with Bernhard's excellent trial performance, was too strong, and young Bach was appointed. Sebastian had apparently forgotten how difficult he himself had found conditions in Mühlhausen. His life at this moment was dominated by the vicious dispute raging between him and Rector Ernesti, and any other place may have seemed to him preferable to the thunderous atmosphere in Leipzig. Besides, he could not yet be sure of the outcome of his feud, and it therefore seemed advisable to make young Bernhard financially independent. This was to prove a fatal decision. Bernhard, 20 years old, was not more mature, perhaps even less so, than his brothers had been at that age. Sebastian's wise policy of allowing his children to develop slowly would have been particularly beneficial for this unstable son. But instead of receiving a full University education he was sent away to Mühlhausen, where difficulties started right away. The minutes of the Council meetings have been preserved[2] and they clearly reveal the animosity of some members towards the new organist. Their remarks sound like echoes of the complaints raised against 20-year-old Sebastian in Arnstadt (cf. p.

[1] We hear of one such visit in 1739 in a letter of Elias Bach. Friedemann spent a month's vacation with his father and brought the famous Dresden lutanists, Sylvanus Weiss and Johann Kropfgans, with him for glorious music-making.

[2] Cf. Georg Thiele, 'Die Familie Bach in Mühlhausen,' 'Mühlhäuser Geschichtsblätter,' 1921.

134). One Councillor argued: 'Bach has preluded far too much and too long, and thus unduly shortened the time meant for the service and devotion. Besides, he often only confuses the congregation with his playing.' Another, taking offence at the young artist's powerful playing, exclaimed: 'If Bach continues to play in this way, the organ will be ruined in two years, or most of the congregation will be deaf.' (Young Bernhard had apparently adopted Sebastian's unconventional method of drawing all the stops at the same time, which, according to Emanuel, at first struck terror in the hearts of the organ builders or organists present.) The Mayor, who from the outset had been on Bach's side, tried to stem the tide of complaints. His remarks confirm Bernhard's fine musicianship: 'We should thank God that we have acquired an artistic and learned organist, and should neither order him to shorten his preludes nor forbid him to play his instrument in so masterly a manner. Had we wanted to appoint a bungler, we needn't have invited an artist from out of town.' Various Councillors were not dissuaded, however, and persevered in describing Bach's preludes as 'unnecessary and troublesome.' The young organist could not help noticing their inimical attitude. While his father in the same situation had felt angry, but never shaken in his self-confidence, Bernhard was by no means so resilient and consequently suffered more. It grieved him also that he was not asked to co-operate in consultations regarding the new organ which was being erected in his church. All this made work at Mühlhausen hateful to him and he besought his father to find him another position. Sebastian thereupon succeeded in having his son appointed to the *Jakobikirche* of Sangerhausen, a position for which he himself had applied in 1703 (cf. p. 129). Bernhard gave notice, and the local organist who had from the outset been favoured by some of the Councillors got the position. When in March 1737, eighteen months after his arrival, Bernhard left Mühlhausen, he might have rejoiced at leaving this uncongenial place had he not at the very end been treated with wounding suspicion. Those Council members who had objected to his vigorous playing insisted that before his departure another organist should check whether Bernhard had left the organ in good condition. It was a humiliating and, as it proved, quite unnecessary action to take against a son of *the* organ expert, who infused into his pupils a profound knowledge of, and veneration for, the king of instruments. We can imagine Sebastian's anger at this affront. Nor were Bernhard's personal affairs less unpleasant. For the young man, shaken by his artistic failure, had not adhered to the strict standards of economy and honesty instilled into him at home, and had incurred debts. What happened subsequently in Sangerhausen can only be guessed. Apparently Bernhard could not settle down there or rid himself of the habit of spending more than he earned. (A certain carelessness with money may have been inherited from the great Johann Christoph of Eisenach, to whom he was related on both sides.) After less than a year he suddenly disappeared from Sangerhausen, leaving various debts behind him. The father, informed thereof, wrote as follows to a certain Mr. Klemm, who had been responsible for Bernhard's appointment:[1]

'So loving and tender a father as yourself will understand the grief and sorrow with which I write this letter. I have not seen my, alas, undutiful boy since last year, when I enjoyed so many kindnesses at your hands. Your Honour will remember that I then paid what he owed for his board at Mühlhausen, discharged the bonds . . . and left a sum of money to meet his other debts, hoping that for the future he would reform his *genus vitae*. You will therefore understand how pained and surprised I am to learn that he has again been borrowing money on all sides . . . and has absconded without giving me, so far, the slightest indication of his whereabouts. What can I do or say more, my warnings having failed, and my loving care and help having proved unavailing? I can only bear my cross in patience and commend my undutiful boy to God's mercy, never doubting that He will hear my sorrow-stricken prayer and in His good time bring my son to understand that the path of conversion leads to Him.

'I have opened my heart to your Honour, and beg you not to associate me with my son's misconduct, but to accept my assurance that I have done all that a true father, whose children lie very close to his heart, is bound to do to advance their welfare. I recommended him to Sangerhausen when the vacancy occurred, trusting that its more cultured society and distinguished patrons would incite him to better behaviour. As the author of his promotion, I must once again thank your Honour, confident that you will not allow the *vacance* to be filled until we have discovered his whereabouts (God, who sees all things, is my witness that since last year I have not set eyes upon him) and learn his future intentions, whether he resolves to change his course, or intends to seek his fortune elsewhere. . . .'

In the meantime Bernhard had gone to the University of Jena to study law, probably receiving shelter from his kinsman, Johann Nicolaus Bach (cf. p. 87). It seems likely that the youth was disappointed at having been deprived of the scholastic training which his two elder brothers had received, and now wanted to make up for it. The choice of Jena was a

---

[1] Translation by Ch. S. Terry, *l.c.*, reproduced by kind permission of Oxford University Press, London.

wise one. Nicolaus Bach's only son had died a few months earlier, and the aged organist must have gladly welcomed his gifted kinsman, who could relieve him of part of his duties and eventually become his successor. But whatever Bernhard's plans were, they came to nothing; for only four months after his matriculation, this third son of Sebastian died suddenly of 'fever' at the age of 24.

While the sons from Sebastian's first marriage were pursuing their own careers, a new generation was growing up in the Thomas Cantor's house. The cradle never stood empty. In the first decade of their Leipzig stay ten children were born to the couple; three more followed at wider intervals up to the year 1742. But for Anna Magdalena the joy of motherhood was inextricably mixed with tragedy, for death was far too frequent a guest in this house. Of the six children surviving out of thirteen, the eldest, Gottfried Heinrich, caused the parents much grief and heartache. In the Genealogy the note referring to this son reads: 'Gottfried Heinrich, likewise inclined towards music, especially clavier playing. His was a great talent, which, however, remained undeveloped.' These words veil the tragic fact that this son was feeble-minded.[1] Among the remaining offspring there were three girls, and two sons, Johann Christoph Friedrich, born in 1732, and Johann Christian, three years younger, both highly gifted. How to educate them was rather a problem, for Sebastian did not care to have them attend the Thomas school, with whose rector he had quarrelled so violently. Fortunately a satisfactory solution was offered by the visit of a cousin from Schweinfurt, *Johann Elias Bach* (39), a grandson of Ambrosius' brother, Georg Christoph (10), who in 1738, at the age of 33, came to Leipzig to study Theology on a scholarship granted by the council of his native town and by a rich benefactor.[2] Sebastian, who had also trained Elias' brother (cf. p. 149), suggested that Elias should stay at his home, and in return for board and lodging teach the three sons and do some secretarial work. A contract was concluded, and before long most cordial relations developed between the Schweinfurt cousin and the Thomas Cantor's family. Various drafts of Elias' letters have been preserved, and they reveal the writer as a lovable person who participated with faithful devotion in all that happened in the Bach household. He took his teaching duties very seriously, especially when he was preparing his charges for Communion. In 1741 another position was offered him,

---

[1] A case of this kind had occurred in an earlier Bach generation, a sister of Ambrosius Bach having been half-witted.

[2] Elias had started his University studies many years earlier at Jena, but had been forced through lack of funds to return home before finishing the courses.

but he refused it stating that the relatives under his care, especially the eldest, were 'in the greatest need of a solid and faithful instruction.' Elias wrote about his eminent cousin's new works to other musicians; he tried to brighten Magdalena's hard life by obtaining plants and singing birds for her; and he urged his sister to send Sebastian a supply of her excellent home-made cider. Once, when the master was in Berlin, Elias, knowing his cousin's tendency unduly to extend absences from Leipzig, reminded Sebastian of the imminent Council election, for which a new composition by the Director Musices was expected. So Elias was a great help in many respects and always eager to serve his relatives. On the other hand, he would not have exerted himself so much had he not, as he wrote, 'received so much kindness' from Sebastian and the family. We learn, for instance, that the Thomas Cantor lent Elias his huge furlined boots and raincoat, both particularly dear to him as the indispensable paraphernalia of those trips out-of-town which he enjoyed so much. Sebastian also took his secretary with him on journeys to Dresden and introduced Elias to as high-ranking a music lover as Count Keyserlingk (cf. p. 188). Besides, the concerts at the Thomas Cantor's home, frequently attended by outstanding visiting musicians, must have been experiences never to be forgotten by the kinsman from Schweinfurt. Indeed, so greatly indebted to his Leipzig cousin did Elias feel that years after his departure he sent to Leipzig a cask of his home-made wine. Sebastian's answer[1] shall follow here, as a good example of the composer's outspokenness and careful consideration of even a minor financial matter:

'Worthy and respected cousin:

Your letter, received yesterday, brings me the good news that you and your dear wife are well. For the delectable cask of wine that came with it accept my best thanks. Unfortunately the cask suffered a jar, or some other accident, on the journey, for on examination here it was found to be one-third empty and contains, the *Visitator* declares, only six quarts. It is regrettable that the smallest drop of so noble a gift of God should be wasted, but I am none the less heartily obliged by my worthy cousin's kind present. *Pro nunc* I am not *réellement* in a position to reciprocate; still *quod differtur non auffertur* [what is postponed, is not relinquished], and I hope to find an opportunity to discharge my obligation.

'It is unfortunate that we live so far apart, for otherwise I should give myself the pleasure of inviting my cousin to my daughter Liesgen's wedding, which takes place in January 1749, to the new Naumburg

[1] Translation by Ch. S. Terry, *l.c.*, reproduced by kind permission of Oxford University Press, London.

organist, Herr Altnikol. However, though for that reason, and because of the inconvenient season, he cannot be present, I will ask him to assist them with his good wishes, and with the same I commend myself to my good cousin's remembrance. With warmest greetings to you from all here, I remain,

Your Honour's devoted cousin and faithful
servant to command
Joh. Seb. Bach.

P.S. Though my good cousin offers to send me more of the same *liqueur*, I must decline on account of the heavy charges at this end. The carriage was 16 gr., delivery 2 gr., *Visitator* 2 gr., provincial excise 5 gr. 3 pfg., general excise 3 gr. So my cousin may calculate that the wine cost me nearly 5 gr. a measure, too expensive a present!'

By the time this letter was written, Elias was well settled in his home-town as Cantor and inspector of the Alumneum. When, in 1743, he had secured 'a permanent place and an assured small sustenance for his life-time,' he had seen to it that 'an honest engagement which he had entered into after careful consideration with a young lady in Leipzig, should now receive the minister's blessing.'[1] However, the happiness of the newly-wed did not last long; Elias' wife died two years later, and in 1746 we see him entering holy matrimony again.[2] When his second wife wanted to acquire citizenship of Schweinfurt, Elias applied to the Council to grant her this privilege free of charge, and offered in return a set of cantatas of his composition for the whole church year. He frequently wrote works of this kind,[3] but he had been too close to the genius of the family to think highly of his own achievements.[4]

[1] Letter dated May 27, 1743 to Herr v. Pflug, 'Die Musik,' *l.c.*

[2] One of the children, *Johann Michael*, born in 1754, or 1753, seems to have been the first, and probably only, Bach musician to travel to the United States. After returning to Europe, he eventually gave up music in favour of the practice of law, and settled down as lawyer at Güstrow, Mecklenburg, far from his native Franconia. He is probably the author of the 'Kurze und systematische Anleitung zum Generalbass und der Tonkunst' published at Cassel in 1780. The whimsical introduction is dated 'Göttingen, 3 July 1780.' This short manual of 47 pages consists of 8 chapters dealing with consonances, dissonances, changing notes, passing modulations, pedal points and figured bass. The last chapter offers numerous examples. The same Michael Bach may be the composer of an extensive *Friedenskantate* for solos, 4-part chorus, flute, bassoons, trumpets, timpani, horns and strings, which was formerly the property of the Berlin Library (p. 399). According to its style, the work belongs approximately to the same period as the 'Anleitung.'

[3] In 1743 he received 20 thalers from the Council for two sets of church cantatas.

[4] While in Leipzig he wrote to his benefactor, Herr v. Segnitz, that he was anxious to obtain a position as teacher, 'music being by no means my main occupation, as one might think.'

While Elias was in Leipzig, he became much attached to a young kinsman, who was working with Sebastian. This was the master's godson, *Johann Ernst Bach* (34), b. 1722, a son of the Eisenach organist, Johann Bernhard (18), who, on the other hand, had been godfather to Sebastian's unlucky third son. At the Thomas school young Ernst was not very successful. Apparently he too possessed the Bach predilection for exceeding a leave of absence that so often caused trouble with the authorities. In Ernst's case it resulted in his dismissal from the alumnate. However he stayed on in Leipzig, probably boarding with his godfather, and eventually he matriculated at the University as a law student. But he was not permitted to finish his studies, for by the end of 1741 his father requested him to return to Eisenach. This was a hard blow for the ambitious youth. There was a great difference between the stimulating atmosphere in Sebastian's home, with its stream of visiting artists and enthusiastic disciples, and life in provincial Eisenach; a difference all the more noticeable since the court orchestra, on which Ernst had apparently counted, was disbanded in 1741 owing to the fusion of the little principality of Eisenach with that of Weimar. Ernst wrote about 'annoying conditions' and his kinsman, Elias, probably prompted by Sebastian, had to admonish him as follows:[1] 'It seems to me necessary and advisable for you to bear for some time with the solitude there, in order to assist your honest old Papa, for, as the *Herr Kapellmeister* [Sebastian] assured me, the post of organist in Eisenach carries an income that can support an honest man.' Ernst followed the advice, assisting his father competently, and when Bernhard died in 1749, the position was, as a matter of course, conferred on the son. Thus Sebastian had the pleasure of seeing yet another highly gifted student of his well settled.

Similar satisfaction was granted him through the achievements of his own children in his last years. In 1746 he saw Friede moving from Dresden into an important position at Halle, which he himself had once considered (cf. p. 146). Emanuel was gaining fame with his compositions and was happily married. Liesgen, the eldest daughter from his second marriage, was as we have heard, wedded to Sebastian's excellent pupil, Johann Christoph Altnikol, after he had, with the Thomas Cantor's help, secured a position in Naumburg. It was the only wedding ever celebrated in Sebastian's home, and therefore an occasion of much rejoicing. Even his 18-year-old son, Johann Christoph Friedrich, was appointed, early in 1750, *Kammermusikus* to Count Wilhelm of Schaumburg-Lippe in Bückeburg. A very small family-group was with Sebastian while darkness

---

[1] Letter dated January 9, 1742.

closed around him. There was his eldest daughter, a spinster of 42; half-witted Gottfried Heinrich; two young girls, aged 13 and 8; and Johann Christian, aged 15. Of these the last-mentioned meant most to Sebastian, who took great delight in the brilliant musical talent of his youngest son and expressed it by presenting Christian, shortly before his death, with three of his claviers. Finally there was Anna Magdalena, ready as ever faithfully to share with her husband whatever life was bringing them, and by her very presence lightening his burden. The wish he had long ago expressed in his poem to his beloved wife (cf. p. 161), was now fulfilled; she was near him in the hour of final struggle.

THE MUSIC OF JOHANN SEBASTIAN BACH

If an attempt were made to characterize the art of the greatest member of the Bach family in a single word, it would have to be the word 'unification.' The most heterogeneous elements were welded together by him into a new entity, completely coherent in character.

Sebastian Bach is the greatest force in the unification of various regional and national styles. The sources of his art can be found in Central, Northern, and Southern Germany alike. Of equal importance in the development of his style were the impulses his music received from the works of Italian and French composers. And Bach was almost as much indebted to Catholic composers as he was to the masters of his own faith. Out of a soil nurtured by the most diversified elements grew the gigantic structure of Sebastian's personal style.

Bach acted as a typically Baroque composer in recognizing no fundamental difference between sacred and secular music, nor even between vocal and instrumental composition. Nothing gave him greater joy than experimenting in the various media. He applied devices of the keyboard style to music for strings alone, and the technique of the violin to clavier compositions. Elements of the Italian concerto may be found in almost every form of his music, including the cantata. Bach constantly arranged and improved compositions by others or by himself, transforming orchestral works into clavier compositions, instrumental into vocal music, secular into sacred, and German into Latin church works (cf. p. 240). He retained something of the medieval conception in which music was undivided, and a tune could be sung or played, used for a dance round the village tree or for the praise of the Lord in church.

Bach's inexhaustible imagination created an immense variety of architectural forms. No two of his inventions, fugues or cantatas show exactly the same construction. Nevertheless, there is a basic feature that recurs again and again in both his vocal and instrumental compositions. Bach was deeply concerned with the 'chiastic' form, built round a centre with corresponding sections on each side. In its simplest version it is the da capo form a b a, so often used by Bach; but also more complicated arrangements a b c b a or a b c d c b a are not unusual. The deeply religious composer may have found satisfaction in the thought that works in chiastic form have their visual equivalents in the structure of a cross, with two corresponding sidearms emerging from a middle beam, or in that of a church with side transepts flanking a central nave. Such correlations seemed quite natural to Baroque artists and Bach was in this respect a true son of his time.

This accounts also for the tremendous importance which pictorialism assumed in Bach's vocabulary, as it did in that of his contemporaries. High and low, long and short, bright and dark, were given in his music expressions typical of this era. From pictorialism Bach proceeded to symbolism, in which intellectual conceptions take the place of sensory impressions. In the Cantata No. 12 *Weinen, Klagen,* for instance, the bass sings 'I follow Jesus Christ.' The *imitatio Christi* is expressed through strict imitation of the vocal melody in the string parts. Moreover, this tune is derived from the chorale melody 'What God does, is with reason done.' Thus Bach uses symbolism here in two different ways within the narrow space of two measures. The symbolic employment of chorale melodies so frequent in Bach's vocal works will be discussed later.

Of particular importance is the figure symbolism, such as the use of an unlucky number in the 13 variations of the *Crucifixus* in the Mass in b. Moreover, substituting figures for the letters of the alphabet was a common practice of the time, and one from which Bach derived great satisfaction. Fourteen, for instance, is the figure symbolizing Bach, since b is the second letter of the alphabet, a the first, c the third, h the eighth, the sum of which is 14. Inverted, 14 turns into 41, which stands for J. S. Bach, as J is the ninth, S the eighteenth letter and 9 plus 18 plus 14 makes 41. In Bach's very last composition, 'Before Thy throne, my God, I stand,' the first line contains 14 notes, the whole melody 41 notes, as though the dying composer wanted to announce that he, Bach, J. S. Bach, was entering the eternal choir.[1]

The composer's profound intellectualism made him adopt polyphony as his favourite means of expression, and in this respect his work marks the summit of a magnificent development through several centuries. But while Bach, in his contrapuntal style, was firmly linked to the past, the harmonic idiom he employed was of a most progressive nature, opening up new realms of musical expression, to which even 19th-century harmony did not find much to add. No other composer succeeded in bringing polyphony and harmony to so complete a fusion. Bach's most intricate contrapuntal creations are always conceived on a strictly harmonic basis, while

---

[1] The amazing forms which figure symbolism assumed in the canon Bach wrote for his admission to Mizler's Societät are analyzed in Friedrich Smend's 'J. S. Bach bei seinem Namen gerufen,' Cassel, 1950.

even in his plain harmonizations of the chorale, the linear progression of the individual voices is superb. Vertical and horizontal elaboration are completely balanced and equally breathtaking.

The development of J. S. Bach's art resembles that of other great men. It shows features which we find again in the spiritual growth of such widely differing composers as Schütz, Haydn, Beethoven, Brahms, Verdi, and Stravinsky. As happens so often, changes in the composer's style coincide with alterations in his surroundings and occupation.

Bach's first creative phase, the period of youth, lasted up to the year 1708. It was the time of his apprenticeship, terminated by engagements in Arnstadt and Mühlhausen. Bach eagerly absorbed the music of his contemporaries and predecessors by playing it, listening to it and, above all, copying it. The number of works he acquired by writing them down faithfully is substantial indeed. It comprises compositions by members of his own clan, works by North Germans and South Germans, Protestants and Catholics, and Italian and French masters. Like the young Mozart he found himself by imitating others. In this first period the contents of a work seemed of greater interest and importance to the composer than the form in which it was cast. The works are rich in ideas, imbued with ardent fervour, and tender subjectivity; they are colourful, and their emotional expression is often of elemental strength. At the same time their technical immaturity is obvious. They are overlong, vague in their formal construction, uncertain in their harmonic and polyphonic texture. It was a period of experimentation, in which young Sebastian tried his hand on various types of composition such as sonatas, toccatas, capriccios, preludes and fugues, chorale preludes and cantatas.

Bach's second creative period, the transition from youth to maturity, was spent in Weimar (1708-1717). It was still a phase of extensive studies, but Sebastian did not merely make copies of works that interested him; he rearranged them, imbuing them with his own personality. He adapted concertos by Italian and German musicians for clavier and organ, and occasionally used Italian themes as subjects for his own fugues. The study of the Southern masters developed Bach's feeling for poignant melodies, solid harmonies, and well-rounded forms. 'Through a singing polyphony he achieved a heretofore unknown warmth, vividness and intensity.' (Besseler.) In Weimar Bach wisely concentrated on a single type of music, church composition, systematically exploring all its possibilities. The Bach of the second period was the great virtuoso on the 'king of instruments.' Youthful exuberance and fantastic imagination are still apparent in some of the organ works of this period, while others reveal the newly acquired mastery of contrapuntal form and well-balanced architecture. Similar in character is Bach's vocal music. The Weimar cantatas, combining elements of the chorale motet, the sacred concerto, and the Italian opera, present formal aspects later to be found in Bach's mature cantatas. However, their lyric ardour and subjective expression point to their affinity with earlier works.

In 1717, at the age of 32, Bach became conductor in charge of all chamber music at the court of Cöthen. This appointment marked the beginning of his period of maturity, lasting until 1740, in which he created the greatest number of supreme masterpieces. During these years Bach's career reached its culminating point. After working as Kapellmeister to a princely court, he was entrusted in 1723 with an even more important position, that of Thomas Cantor and *director musices* in Leipzig, thus assuming a central post within the Lutheran faith. In this period Bach no longer concentrated on a single type of music, as he had more or less done in the transitional phase. He was active in practically every field of music cultivated in his time, with the sole exception of opera proper, although he made ample use of its style and forms both in his secular and sacred vocal music. The unification of leading national styles culminated during this period, and in the field of religion, too, Bach approached the conception of a more universal Christianity. Though he had been brought up as an orthodox Lutheran, the mystical fervour of many of his Weimar and Leipzig church cantatas reveals a leaning towards the same pietistic ideas that he had so fiercely denounced in his youth, as an organist in Mühlhausen. Without any compunction the mature Bach worked for many years at the reformed court of Cöthen, and wrote Masses for the Catholic Elector of Saxony and for Count Sporck, who was famous for his attempts 'to unify all Christian denominations into a single great community of a tolerant and active Christianity.'[1]

It is significant that Bach, the great organ virtuoso, first reached the climax of his creative output in the field of instrumental music, and only afterwards in vocal music. Cöthen saw the creation of such works as the two- and three-part Inventions, the French and English Suites, the first part of the Well-Tempered Clavier, the orchestral Overtures, and the Brandenburg Concertos. Among the compositions created in Leipzig, however, were the majority of the church cantatas, the *Magnificat*, Christmas Oratorio and St. Matthew Passion as well as the B minor Mass.

Bach's creative ability in this period was so powerful that he felt a

[1] Cf. H. Benedikt's biography of Sporck, 1923, p. 160.

strong urge to teach others the great art of music. The majority of his clavier works are meant for educational purposes. Bach was possibly the only great composer who, far from resenting the necessity of teaching others, wrote instructive works on the highest level of perfection.

Bach's fourth period comprises the ultimate decade of his life (1740-1750). Like other masters nearing the conclusion of their existence, Bach felt closer to the distant past than to the near present. At the same time future trends are significantly foreshadowed in his compositions. Though the amount of music written during this last period gradually decreased, it included works imbued with the deepest meaning, such as the Canonic Variations on *Vom Himmel hoch, da komm ich her*, the Musical Offering, and the Art of the Fugue. Each of them is monumental in its scope, and archaic in its form and character. The Canonic Variations lead us back to the organ chorales of Scheidt, almost a hundred years before Bach; while in the fugues and canons of the Art of the Fugue the composer presents an abstract course in the most exalted contrapuntal forms of earlier centuries. These works might be considered as the artistic testament of the greatest genius in the field of contrapuntal writing. In this same period, however, we occasionally find, in form, harmony, and melody, traits which it seems that only a composer young and progressive in spirit could have produced. A strict chorale cantata contains so simple and naïve a number as the duet 'We hasten' (cf. p. 222), and the potpourri of folksongs in the Peasant Cantata precedes the Canonic Variations only by a few years. It is of symbolic significance that the Musical Offering contains a *Ricercar*, one of the earliest forms of fugal writing, conceived for the pianoforte, the keyboard instrument of the future.

Whether archaic or progressive elements predominate, the supreme strength, the variety and vitality of Bach's music made it an inexhaustible source of inspiration to later generations. Indeed, his influence on the 19th and 20th centuries has probably not been exceeded by that of any other composer.

WORKS FOR VOICES AND INSTRUMENTS

Bach's vocal works form an inseparable unit. The interrelations are even stronger here than among the instrumental compositions. It is the church cantata that forms the core of his vocal output; motet, oratorio, and passion, as well as the secular cantatas, are all closely connected with it, and it therefore seems advisable, in discussing the various aspects of Bach's music for voices, to begin with the *Church Cantatas*.[1]

Only very few of these cantatas bear a date in the composer's hand. Scholars have nevertheless succeeded in most cases in ascertaining at least the approximate time of composition. Changes in Bach's handwriting, certain watermarks in the paper, and the date of publication of the libretto, have offered valuable clues. Of particular significance was Bach's peculiar way of transposing the parts of wind instruments and organ respectively. In Weimar the organ he used seems to have been tuned in the so-called *hoher Chorton* (high choir pitch), a minor third above the *Kammerton* (chamber pitch) of the other instruments. The inexperienced composer used the following rather complicated device to cope with this difficulty. He wrote for organ and strings in the same key, expecting the string players to tune their instruments a third higher, according to the pitch of the organ. Since most wind instruments could not change their pitch, these parts were written in the key in which they were to sound, viz. a third higher than the strings.[2] Any manuscripts written in this way clearly belong to Bach's Weimar period.[3] In Leipzig the organs of St. Thomas' and St. Nicholas' were tuned in the ordinary *Chorton*, one whole tone above the other instruments. Here Bach used a much simpler notation; he merely transposed the figured bass part meant for the organ one whole tone down, while all the other instruments were written in the key in which they sounded. The transposed organ part is therefore characteristic of the music written in Leipzig.

The widespread conception that Bach himself played the organ in the Leipzig performances of his vocal works cannot be upheld. It would have

[1] The great number of sacred and secular *Songs for Solo Voice and Instrumental Bass* formerly attributed to Bach has shrunk considerably in view of recent research. To-day only a few of the songs in Anna Magdalena's Notebook, such as the heartfelt *Bist du bei mir* (*BWV* 508) and the three different settings of *Gib dich zufrieden* (*BWV* 510-12, cf. p. 161), are considered as Bach's own works. For Schemelli's *Gesangbuch* (*BWV* 439-507) of 1736 Bach provided the figuring of the basses, but again only three of the songs, viz. *Dir, dir Jehova will ich singen* (*BWV* 452), *Komm süsser Tod* (*BWV* 478) and *Vergiss mein nicht* (*BWV* 505) may be claimed to be authentic Bach compositions.

[2] Smend, 'Bachs Kirchenkantaten,' VI, rightly maintains that cantatas without wind instruments known to have been composed in Weimar, such as Nos. 152, 161, 162, ought to be performed in a key one third higher, since it is obvious that during Bach's time they were heard at this higher pitch.

[3] It was recently pointed out that the Weimar organ with the 'high choir pitch' described by G. A. Wette in 1737 was an instrument fundamentally reconstructed in 1719-1720, i.e. after Bach's departure from Weimar. Cf. Jauernig, *l.c.* Yet the peculiar notation of cantatas that we know were performed in Weimar, offers ample evidence that the composer's instrument was tuned in the same way as that described by Wette.

been beneath the dignity of the *director musices* to accompany on this instrument. He conducted with the help of music rolls in both hands, standing next to the organ, the way the conductor acts in a picture to be found in J. G. Walther's 'Music Lexicon.' Another misconception, that a harpsichord was used for the accompaniment of solos, and the organ for that of the chorus, was conclusively proved to be wrong by Arnold Schering. In both solo numbers and choral sections, Bach had the figured bass executed only by the organ, and not by the harpsichord.[1] This latter instrument was employed exclusively to accompany Bach's motets, since the composer, as a true son of his time, never considered using voices without instruments.

Bach's cantatas were performed by very small groups. On ordinary Sundays the composer had approximately 25 musicians at his disposal: 12 singers and 13 instrumentalists (cf. his report to the Council, p. 177). For certain occasions the number might be increased to 40, and for the St. Matthew Passion, with its special demands, he even managed to get 60 musicians together. The soloists were also utilized in the chorus, and all vocalists were either boys or men. It seems that the breaking of a boy's voice at that time occurred later in life than it does to-day, so that Bach was not forced to rely only on very young boys for his soprano and alto parts. Besides, University students who had mastered the falsetto technique helped out occasionally. In all these performances the number of instrumentalists slightly exceeded that of the vocalists, a fact present-day conductors might well bear in mind.

According to Forkel, Bach wrote five sets of church cantatas for all the Sundays and holy days of the ecclesiastical year. If this statement is correct, he must have produced almost 300 cantatas, of which, however, less than 200 have been preserved. These compositions were written over a period of 41 years, the first in 1704, the last in 1745.

Bach's early works in this field, up to about 1712, are strongly dependent on models provided by the North and Central German cantata of his time. They are basically similar to those by older members of the Bach family, or those of Pachelbel, Böhm, and Buxtehude. Their texts are based on the Bible and on church hymns; the music often consists of comparatively short sections contrasting in tempo and time signature and in the number of voices employed. The *concertato* principle rules the choruses, in which vocal groups of varying sizes compete with instrumental bodies. As a basis for the arias, ostinatos are frequently employed, repeating a

---

[1] Nevertheless, some modern conductors feel that in a concert performance of Bach's oratorios the harpsichord should alternate with the organ for the sake of variety.

bass-phrase (often with modulations to other keys), while the melodic line changes. Of great importance in these early cantatas is the 'arioso,' a kind of recitative, accompanied by instruments which interrupt the vocal part with independent *ritornelli*. The freely declamatory recitative, accompanied by a figured bass only, is not yet to be found in the early forms of Bach's church cantata. Instrumental introductions, if used at all, are usually short.

Bach's first cantata, *Denn du wirst meine Seele* ('Suffer not Thou my soul';[1] No. 15 in *BG* and *BWV*[2]), written at the age of 19, conforms on the whole to this pattern, although the work was obviously revised by the composer at a later date. The foundation of its text is provided by 7 verses from a church hymn. There is ample evidence that this is the work of a very young composer, for the declamation is frequently awkward, the expression exaggerated and the texture predominantly homophonic. Nevertheless, even at this very early stage, genius manifested itself in Bach's masterly combination of two melodies inspired by completely opposite moods (*Ex.* 29); and although the cantata consists of about a

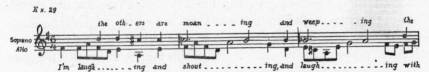

dozen sections, its rambling construction is held together by the simple and powerful scheme of the main modulations: C–a–C–G–C.

The number of cantatas written in Mühlhausen is not certain. Among them are: No. 131, *Aus der Tiefe* ('From the deep, Lord') composed, as the autograph indicates, for Bach's friend, the Reverend Eilmar (cf. p. 140); No. 71, *Gott ist mein König* ('God is my Sov'reign'), performed on February 4, 1708, in honour of the newly elected city council; and perhaps No. 106, *Gottes Zeit* ('God's own time'), which may have been written for the commemorative service held for Bach's uncle, Tobias Lämmerhirt, or for a funeral in 1711.[3]

These cantatas are similar in construction. Each introduces three

---

[1] The English titles and quotations are as a rule given in the translation by Henry S. Drinker. Cf. 'Text of the Choral Works of J. S. Bach,' vols. 1-3.

[2] The numbering of the church cantatas used in *BG* which is generally adopted in quoting these works was also accepted by *BWV*. Hence each cantata number is also the number of the *BWV*.

[3] Jauernig, *l.c.*, assumes that it was written for the funeral of Bach's predecessor in Weimar, Johann Effler, who was buried on April 7, 1711. Bach had worked with Effler when he first came to Weimar in 1703 (cf. p. 130).

choruses, of which the second forms the centre of the composition. The text of *Aus der Tiefe* is based on Psalm 130 and two stanzas from a chorale. Remarkable in this early composition is the instrumental character of Bach's vocal style. Coloraturas to be sung on a single syllable are frequently interspersed with rests, a mannerism by no means unusual in vocal works of the time, but as a rule avoided by Bach in his later works. The final vocal fugue is so strongly instrumental in its design that it even slipped in with the master's organ works in an arrangement by one of Bach's pupils (*BWV* 131a).

Gott ist mein König is the only cantata by Bach to be printed during his lifetime that has been preserved;[1] its printing was due not so much to the qualities of the composition as to the significance which the population of Mühlhausen attributed to the political event it celebrated. In this *Motetto*, as Bach himself calls it, the technique of the *concertato* reaches a climax. One brass choir, two woodwind groups, and one string choir compete with one larger and one smaller vocal group in a manner recalling the splendour of Venetian art as reflected in the cantatas of Buxtehude. The duet No. 2, 'Full fourscore years I am,' entrusts an ornamented chorale tune to the contralto, while the tenor voice and an organ obbligato introduce counter melodies. The result is a vocal form surprisingly similar to an organ prelude. Yet the final chorus of this cantata shows that the composer had begun to free himself from an excessively instrumental conception. The concluding fugue employs voices and orchestra as equal partners and does not require them to double each other in the usual way; they rather take turns and enhance one another's lines.

The finest and most important among Bach's early cantatas is *Gottes Zeit*, known as the *Actus tragicus*. Its text, taken from the Bible and from church hymns, was probably assembled by Bach himself, possibly with the assistance of the Reverend Eilmar. The basic idea of this 'German Requiem'[2] is that Death's curse and punishment implied in the Old Testament was transformed through the intervention of Christ into promise and bliss; the threat of the old covenant was changed into hope. The cantata begins with an instrumental introduction for flutes, viole da gamba, and continuo, whose content Schweitzer justly describes with the words of the Revelation: 'And God shall wipe away all tears from their

---

[1] Regarding Bach's cantata printed in 1709 cf. p. 142.

[2] The similarity both in content and architecture to Brahms' 'German Requiem' is quite striking (cf. Geiringer, 'Brahms,' New York, 1947, p. 311). Brahms certainly knew Bach's cantata, which was first published in 1830 and was a favourite of his friend, Julius Stockhausen.

eyes; and there shall be no more death, neither sorrow, nor crying, neither shall there be any more pain.' The first chorus starts with a surprisingly folksong-like melody such as Bach used only in his early works. Magnificent short arias by tenor and bass lead to the heart of the drama, the great middle chorus. In a ponderous fugue, symbolizing the strictness of the law, the 3 lower voices present the words of Ecclesiastes 'For the covenant from the beginning is, Thou shalt die.' In dramatic contrast the light voices of boy sopranos interrupt with the words 'O come, Lord Jesus, come.' This invocation gains in intensity, and at the end the dark menace is completely vanquished, while the sopranos sing the last notes without any instrumental accompaniment. To emphasize the preponderance of the Christian spirit, Bach had the flutes intone at the same time the tune of the chorale 'My cause is God's, and I am still, let Him do with me as He will.' The words of the hymn were not needed to convey this message to a congregation familiar with Protestant church songs. The musical architecture of this cantata is as simple and powerful as its meaning. Its modulatory basis displays a chiastic arrangement (cf. p. 202) $E\flat - c - f - b\flat - A\flat$ (f) - c - $E\flat$

With their vigorous language, their highly subjective idiom, and their richly flowing imagination, these early cantatas present a picture of lofty achievement rarely equalled by so young a composer.

During the years Bach spent in Weimar he wrote about 20 church cantatas, most of them basically different from his earlier works in this field. In the years 1712-14 he had turned towards a new type of cantata the texts of which were introduced by Pastor Erdmann Neumeister (cf. p. 159). The main feature of this reformed cantata was, as the librettist himself expressed it, that 'it looked hardly different from a section of an opera.' It used paraphrases of the Bible text or of Protestant hymns (known as 'madrigalian' texts) for secco recitatives and da capo arias which formed the core of the cantatas. The former arioso was but rarely used, and the choruses and hymns, whose place was now mainly at the beginning and the end of the work, were greatly reduced in number. Even cantatas without any chorus were not infrequent. Neumeister's texts were similar in content to his sermons which they preceded in the service. If the cantata was in two parts, the first was performed before and the second after the sermon.

Bach wrote five of his Weimar cantatas (Nos. 18, 59, 61, 142, 160) to texts by Neumeister, but he preferred librettos by Salomo Franck, secretary of the Protestant Consistory in Weimar. There was much in these texts that recommended them to the young composer. Franck was more conservative than Neumeister, a tendency which suited Bach, who was, in this phase of transition, by no means willing to make a clean break with the past, and rather liked to intermingle old and new elements in his music. What attracted him particularly, however, was the deep mystic feeling prevailing in Franck's texts which satisfied a craving in Bach's own soul.

The Cantata No. 21, *Ich hatte viel Bekümmernis* ('My heart and soul were sore distressed'), composed in 1714[1] to words by Salomo Franck, belongs to the comparatively few compositions by Bach in which his art meets with that of his greatest contemporary in the realm of music. It has been observed that certain melodic details prove that the Weimar *Concertmeister* knew Handel's opera 'Almira.' Moreover, the final chorus 'The Lamb that was sacrificed,' with its brilliant trumpets, exhibits the simple al-fresco technique of Handel. On the other hand, it should be noted that the beginning of 'Worthy is the Lamb' in the 'Messiah' reveals a certain kinship with this chorus. On the whole the cantata shows the typical aspects of the Weimar works. The *Sinfonia* to its first part, with its holds on dissonant chords and the oboe's outcry in the penultimate measure, is among the most passionate instrumental numbers Bach ever conceived, and it creates the right atmosphere for the feeling of desolation which predominates at the start of the opening chorus. The three ejaculations 'I, I, I' at the beginning of this number have often been commented on.[2] The repetition of the first word at the start of a composition is typical of 17th-century music, and in this particular case Bach may have reverted to it to stress the work's subjective character. Even more old-fashioned is the next chorus with its quick emotional contrasts and the sudden changes between solo and tutti, fast and slow, forte and piano. On the other hand the solo numbers show how much the composer had learned from contemporary opera. The dialogue between the soul and Jesus, for instance, is a love duet of sensuous beauty which might well have shocked some members of the congregation. Pieces like these were responsible for the clause in Bach's Leipzig contract that his compositions 'should not make an operatic impression.'

The composer's tendency in the Weimar years towards investigating

---

[1] Jauernig's assumption, *l.c.*, that the work was written and performed in this year to celebrate the completion of the new organ in Weimar is convincing.

[2] Mattheson, 'Critica Musica,' II, p. 368, derides it in a rather unfair manner.

new artistic possibilities without sacrificing the familiar manifests itself in a curious experiment he made in his Cantata No. 61, *Nun komm der Heiden Heiland* ('Come Thou, of man the Saviour'), composed in 1714 to words by Neumeister. The first chorus is a chorale fantasy in the form of a French overture. The movement begins with the traditional slow tempo and dotted rhythms of Lully's introductions, to which the voices intone the first two lines of the chorale 'Come Thou, of man the Saviour, Thou child of a Virgin born.' The time signature then changes and Bach prescribes *Gai* as tempo. A fast and merry fugue on the third chorale line 'Mortals over all the earth' now forms the middle section, which leads to the slow conclusion using the last line 'Marvel at Thy holy birth.' A magnificent tour de force which the mature artist never attempted to duplicate.

The years at Weimar witnessed the creation of some of Bach's most subjective works in the field of church music. The Arnstadt and Mühlhausen cantatas had already revealed a strongly individualistic touch. Now the *Jesusminne* (love of Jesus), the all-consuming yearning for release from earthly fetters, the welcoming of death as the gate to heavenly bliss, assumed proportions unparalleled in the music of the time. While the new form of the cantata had been devised by orthodox ministers vigorously opposed to the ideas of Pietism, a mystic undercurrent in many of the texts chosen by the composer, tremendously strengthened by Bach's intense music, brought these works perilously close to the hated doctrine. Yet Bach probably never admitted that to himself, for he was wont to fight Pietism for its inimical attitude towards concerted music, and to brush aside the fact that his own leaning towards mysticism was not so very different from that of the Pietists.

A characteristic example is supplied by the Easter cantata *Der Himmel lacht, die Erde jubilieret*[1] (No. 31, 'The heavens laugh, the earth exults in gladness') based on words by Franck. The cantata begins in a mood of rejoicing and jubilation, which soon turns to thoughts of death and suffering. For Franck and Bach the idea of resurrection was inextricably bound up with that of decay and annihilation, and they saw in death not a menace, but a goal eagerly to be sought by the Christian. Therefore it is not the pompous introductory *Sonata* in concerto form, nor the first jubilant chorus that constitutes the climax of the work; it is the last aria 'Hour of parting, come to me.' Here a soprano, assisted by oboe and bass, performs a trio in dance rhythm of irresistible sweetness, to which violins and violas add, in the manner of the *Actus tragicus*, the immortal chorale

---

[1] The work was composed in 1715 but revised by Bach in 1731.

tune 'When finally my hour comes.' This chorale is then taken up by the full chorus and orchestra, with the trumpets reaching the highest clarino registers, thus proclaiming the glory and bliss of death leading to the soul's reunion with Christ.

Even more transcendental is the character of No. 161, *Komm du süsse Todesstunde* ('Come sweet death, thou blessed healer') composed in 1715 to words by Franck. Here the death-chorale 'My heart is ever yearning for blessed death's release' (which was to play so important a part as Passion chorale in the St. Matthew Passion) constitutes the framework for the whole composition. In the first aria, for contralto, in which the dis-embodied tune of the flutes (recorders) seems to extend a promise of eternal life, the organ intones this chorale, and it is taken up again at the end by the full chorus in a vision of trance-like bliss. Among the other numbers is a recitative accompanied by full orchestra which provides a deeply stirring illustration of sleep and awakening. In the singer's part the yearning for deliverance from earthly fetters reaches its ecstatic climax, while the flutes, with quickly repeated high notes, the strings with sombre *pizzicati*, and the basses with majestic octave leaps, sound a weird chorus of tolling death bells (*Ex.* 30).

The last composition in this period of transition is in all likelihood the powerful cantata No. 4, *Christ lag in Todesbanden* ('Christ lay by death enshrouded'). It was probably written in Weimar, although Bach revised it for a Leipzig performance in 1724. Rarely did he compose a work looking so decidedly into the past and at the same time showing features of so progressive a nature. Like the cantatas of the first period, it has no 18th-century elements in the text, but simply uses Luther's power-ful hymn as a libretto. Nevertheless distinctly separated choruses, arias, and duets are used in a manner revealing the influence of the reforms initiated by Neumeister and Franck. The music is based on a 12th-century melody, and a cantata by Kuhnau on the same tune might be considered as its godfather. The harsh modal harmonies and the doubled middle parts of the violas contribute to the very archaic character of the composition, which appears like a series of vocal interpretations of organ chorales in the manner of Böhm and Pachelbel. But the dominating position which the hymn assumes throughout the work also points to the chorale cantatas written by Bach in the later Leipzig years. *Christ lag in Todesbanden* consists of seven vocal movements, each presenting a variation on the same hymn tune and using one stanza of Luther's chorale as a text. The form is compact

chorus	duet	aria	chorus	aria	duet	chorus;
1	2	3	4	5	6	7

even the introductory instrumental *Sinfonia* in the style of Buxtehude makes use of the basic tune. The combination of contrapuntal art with expressive power and Baroque symbolism is overwhelming. Only one detail can be mentioned here, a detail that is usually lost to English audiences owing to a free translation. Luther's stark 16th-century language proclaims that after the fight between life and death 'one death devoured the other.' Bach symbolizes it by a kind of canon in which the parts seem to be entangled in a mortal struggle until one after the other disappears.

Both in quantity and in artistic significance the church cantatas written in Leipzig form an entity unique in the history of music. Bach aims at a fusion and complete unification of the most diversified aspects of his art. The wide range of the texts staggers the imagination; it encompasses all transitions from the strictest Lutheran orthodoxy to the most tender and emotional pietism, from the plastic diction of the Reformation period to the effeminate mannerisms of the 18th century. In the music, too, old and new trends are brought into a perfect integration. The intensity of the polyphonic thinking is now completely balanced by the abundance of harmonic inspiration. The cumulative effect of Bach's technical brilliance, graphic pictorialism, profound symbolism, and emotional intensity is overwhelming.

In most cases we do not know who were the authors of Bach's texts. It seems by no means impossible that he himself wrote some of them. If it was a question of changing the words of a previously written composition or quickly making up a libretto for some special occasion, Bach relied on the services of his friend, Friedrich Henrici (1700-64), better known under his pen-name, Picander. It was this writer who was probably responsible for the paraphrasing of many of the hymn texts used in Bach's chorale cantatas of the later years. In addition, such widely contrasting texts as the librettos to the Coffee Cantata and the St. Matthew Passion were produced by this able and musically gifted writer.

To the cantatas whose librettists are unknown belongs the magnificent No. 46, *Schauet doch und sehet* ('Look ye then and see'), written in the first Leipzig years for the tenth Sunday after Trinity. The work deals with a favourite religious idea of the Baroque era; it first threatens the sinner, and subsequently comforts him with promises of the Lord's forgiveness. The powerful initial chorus uses flutes, *oboi da caccia* (English horns), trumpet, and strings. The emotional content of its slow first section can best be deduced from the fact that Bach used it later for the *Qui tollis* of his B minor Mass. Perfect declamation and poignant feeling are combined with a polyphonic texture of supreme artistry. The intensity of grief is expressed both with the help of harsh dissonances and with mighty strettos. The recitative which follows recalls Neumeister's plea that a cantata ought to resemble a sermon, for here a fanatic preacher seems to threaten the cowed congregation. The sinister mood reaches a climax in the ensuing aria. Its violent trembling of the strings and the weird trumpet-fanfares draw a strikingly realistic picture of the annihilating thunderstorm in which the last judgment takes place and the sinner must face 'God's wrath unceasing.' And then, with typically Baroque suddenness, the picture changes; the threat of damnation is replaced by the promise of salvation. A contralto solo combined with two flutes and two *oboi da caccia* playing in unison creates an atmosphere of celestial sweetness. To avoid all earthly heaviness Bach even does away with the traditional basso continuo. The concluding chorale, with an instrumentation similar to that of the first chorus, seems to condense the significance of the whole work: 'Through Jesus' intercession, forgive Thou our transgression.'

The delightful cantata, No. 65, *Sie werden aus Saba alle kommen* ('From Sheba shall many men be coming') was written for the Epiphany of 1724 or 1725 to words which Bach himself may have compiled. The famous first chorus is a lofty piece of concerted music in which four groups of instruments—horns, flutes, oboi da caccia, and strings—compete with human voices to create a richly glowing picture of the stately procession leading camels and dromedaries laden with gold and incense as offerings to the Lord. Inexhaustible inspiration, unerring judgment in the combination of musical colours, and a highly emphatic declamation join forces to give the most powerful utterance to the prophecy of Isaiah.

The tremendous range of Bach's descriptive power can be shown by a third cantata from this period, No. 19, *Es erhub sich ein Streit* ('See how fiercely they fight'), written for St. Michael's Day, 1726. Again the composer himself may have written the words, using as his model an earlier libretto by Picander. The text based on Revelation describes the war in Heaven, with Michael and his angels battling 'the great dragon called Satan'; a subject that had been set to music in a masterly composition by Johann Christoph Bach (cf. p. 57), which was well known to Sebastian. Without any introduction the basses intone the powerful melody of the battle (*Ex.* 31) which works its way upward through the voices. Presently

trumpets and timpani set in, leading the hearer right into the heart of the furious fight. The combat reaches its climax at the beginning of the passionate middle part, when the powers of darkness make a supreme effort to conquer Heaven. But Michael foils the foe; victory is won, and the unison of 3 trumpets confirms the doom of the horrible dragon. A composer who had a dramatic effect primarily in mind would have ended his movement here, and this is what Johann Christoph Bach did. To Sebastian, however, it seems essential to round off the chorus, and give it a perfect musical form. He therefore retraces his steps and starts once more: 'See how fiercely they fight.' Then he relinquishes the description from Revelation (to which his kinsman had adhered throughout his work, in the manner of the older cantatas) and proceeds to describe in a partly lyric, partly epic manner the results of the victory. There is a tender da capo aria for the soprano with two oboi d'amore (oboes tuned a minor third lower and equipped with pear-shaped bells) and a *recitativo accompagnato* referring to the loving kindness of the Saviour, to which the full string body in a manner later used in the St. Matthew Passion contributes a kind of halo. In a moving tenor aria the soul prays 'Bide ye angels, bide with me,' and to enhance the power of the supplication, the trumpet intones 'Lord, let Thy blessed angels come' from the hymn *Herzlich lieb*

('I love Thee, Lord, with all my heart'). In the last chorale the angels are implored to assist mankind in the hour of final need. The orchestration here is the same as in the first movement, thus implying that Michael's victory prepared the way for the soul's eternal triumph.

It should be mentioned that the first page of the autograph bears the following title in Bach's hand: *J. J. Festo Michaelis Concerto a* 14. The first two letters stand for *Jesu Juva* (Jesus help), an abbreviation often employed by the composer at the beginning of his works. The 14 voices are 3 trumpets, 3 oboes, 3 stringed parts, the vocal quartet, and continuo (as usual, the composer does not count the timpani). The author's name is not on the manuscript, although there would have been room enough to insert it, and as a rule Bach does write it on his scores. In explaining this Friedrich Smend[1] alleges that for those initiated in figure symbolism the number 14 stood for Bach (cf. p. 203), and that the composer considered it unnecessary to write his name a second time in letters (cf. Ill. XIII).

In the years following 1730 Bach gradually widens the scope of his cantatas, taking a strong interest in both the solo and the chorale cantata. One of the most beautiful of his compositions for a single voice, in which the vocal virtuosity is markedly increased, is No. 56, *Ich will den Kreuzstab gerne tragen* ('I will my cross-staff gladly carry'), a work of intimate chamber character, originally written for Anna Magdalena's soprano, later, however, transcribed for contralto, and eventually for bass. In its final form (completed probably in 1731 or 1732) the heartfelt work has delighted not only church congregations, but innumerable concert audiences. The cantata has no introduction and starts with a broadly conceived da capo aria. In its middle part the solo voice suddenly sings in triplets, while the instruments keep up the former movement in eighth notes. The resulting combination of different rhythms expresses the passionate yearning in the words 'There will I entomb all my sorrows and sighs, my Saviour will wipe all the tears from my eyes.' In the following beautiful arioso, inspired by the words 'My journey through the world is like a ship at sea,' Bach depicts the movement of the waves through a rocking motive given out by the 'cello. This accompaniment is suddenly discontinued when the weary traveller reaches heaven and leaves the ship. Of equal beauty is a recitative near the end of the cantata expressing the soul's readiness to receive its eternal reward from the hands of the Lord. Here the composer makes use of the sustained notes of the strings which he also uses in the recitatives of the St. Matthew Passion to symbolize the appearance of Christ. In its second half the recitative very poetically

[1] 'Bachs Kirchenkantaten,' III/41.

turns into a quotation of the middle section of the first aria, thus creating a firm link between the initial and concluding solo numbers of the cantata. Even in a work so little suited to the inclusion of a hymn, Bach is loath to omit it, and he finishes his cantata with a four-part chorale, probably sung by the congregation.

For his larger church compositions Bach showed an increasing interest in the chorale cantata in which a hymn constitutes the basis of both text and music. In its pure form the chorale cantata could be found in *Christ lag in Todesbanden*. Bach now prefers the freer form in which only the first and last stanzas of the hymn text are preserved in their original version, while the stanzas in between are transformed and paraphrased according to 18th-century taste into texts suitable for recitatives, arias and duets. Even complete movements that are only indirectly connected with the basic poem are occasionally inserted. For the first chorus a polyphonic treatment of the hymn tune is generally used, for the last a simple four-part harmonization. The variety of form in these chorale cantatas, which Bach seems to have conceived in connection with Picander, is truly staggering. Hymn tunes are woven into the fabric of instrumental introductions, and are used in big chorale fantasias, chorale passacaglias, and in movements of a motet-like character. Bach employs them in recitatives, arias and duets, and he presents them in permanently renewed harmonic splendour at the end of the cantatas. More and more the chorale becomes the life-blood of the composer's sacred music.[1]

The cantata No. 80, *Ein' feste Burg* ('A mighty fortress'), was probably first performed in 1730 at the Reformation Festival. It consists of six movements written as early as 1716 on a libretto by Franck, based on Luther's famous hymn but later completely revised, and two movements composed for the ultimate version. A second revision seems to have been made by Friedemann Bach, who inserted trumpets and kettle-drums into the choruses Nos. 1 and 5; an addition which so greatly enhances the effect that it has been generally adopted. The first chorus is a magnificent chorale fugue framed by a canon presenting the hymn tune in long notes in the highest and lowest instrumental parts. The ultimate degree of contrapuntal artistry is used here to symbolize the rule of the divine law

---

[1] Bach seems to have written many chorale harmonizations not contained in his cantatas. Between 1784-7 Philipp Emanuel Bach and J. Ph. Kirnberger published 4 volumes of 'Joh. Seb. Bachs vierstimmige Choralgesänge' comprising 371 numbers, of which 162 can be traced back to cantatas, oratorios, Passions, etc. Of the remaining pieces (*BWV* 253-438) some may have been taken from choral works lost to-day. Even at a time when the work of Sebastian Bach was very little known, these exquisite arrangements were greatly admired.

throughout the Universe. Completely different is the second chorus in which all 4 voices for once present the hymn tune in powerful unison. Around them roars the wildly turbulent orchestra, the 'fiends ready to devour' of the hymn. Whoever hears this grandiose piece will realize that for the composer just as for Luther, the author of the hymn text, the devil was somebody quite real.

Very different is the mood in No. 140, the chorale cantata *Wachet auf* ('Sleepers, wake') probably written in 1731.[1] Nicolai's beautiful hymn on which it is based deals with the parable of the wise and foolish virgins, and turns later to a description of heavenly Zion. In the first movement the chorale melody is presented in long notes by the soprano, under which the lower voices weave a vivid contrapuntal texture inspired by the words rather than by the melody of the church song. The orchestra adds a completely independent accompaniment picturing the approach of the heavenly bridegroom (*a*) and the eager anticipation of the maidens (*b*) (*Ex.* 32). Out of these various strata grows a sound picture of over-

whelming sensuous beauty. In the second chorale fantasia the hymn tune intoned by the tenors is joined by a completely different violin melody of a caressing sweetness rarely to be found in Bach's cantatas; this depicts the graceful procession of the maidens going out to meet the heavenly bridegroom (cf. p. 258). In the two duets following this number the objective chorale is silent, and the pledges which Christ and the soul exchange sound not very different from those of earthly lovers. The second duet in particular, with its similarity of motives in both voices, points far into the future, to the duets between husband and wife in Haydn's 'Creation' and Beethoven's 'Fidelio.'

During his final period of cantata production—the last work that can be dated with certainty is No. 116, *Du Friedefürst* ('Thou, Prince of Peace'), performed November 22, 1745—Bach cultivated the chorale cantata in its strict form, based in all its parts on a specific well-known Protestant hymn text and omitting any numbers not dependent on this church song. Good examples of the style of these last 25 odd cantatas are furnished by Nos. 92 and 78, both composed around 1740.

---

[1] The date 1742, suggested by Rust for this cantata, seems less likely.

Cantata No. 92, *Ich hab in Gottes Herz und Sinn* ('To God I give my heart and soul'), consists of 9 numbers, 3 of which use the words of Paul Gerhardt's poem unchanged, while in the remaining sections the hymn text is either interspersed with words by an unknown 18th-century poet or altogether paraphrased. Bach uses the old French tune to which Gerhardt's poem is usually sung in more than half the numbers of the cantata, whenever he employs the original text.[1] The introductory chorus is a powerful chorale fantasia with the melody in the soprano, while the lower voices and the orchestra contribute to the interpretation. In No. 2, *Recitativo e Corale*, we find most striking contrasts between the chorale lines, accompanied by a kind of ostinato bass, and the very dramatic recitatives inserted in between. The rapid succession of short and basically different sections, declamation alternating with singing, results in a strangely disturbing piece, typically Baroque in its expression. The following aria for tenor, which describes the breaking down and the destruction of everything not sustained by God, brings the wild excitement to a climax. Both the singer (whose part presents almost insurmountable difficulties) and the orchestra create a mood of fierce exultation. No. 4, in which chorale text and melody are presented by the contralto, is again more objective in character. It resembles in its construction the tenor aria of the cantata *Wachet auf.* Here Bach inserts the individual lines of the hymn tune into a trio for two oboi d'amore and continuo, a beautiful musical composition complete in itself. The last aria in 3/8 for soprano, with its oboe d'amore solo and strings pizzicati sounding almost like a serenade, presents a picture of the paradisian joy experienced by a soul resting in Jesus. In the narrow confines of a cantata forming but one section of the service, Bach has been able to conjure up the whole wide world of Baroque Protestantism. His congregation had to pass through the horrors of the powers of darkness before the glory of salvation rose dazzlingly before them.

In cantata No. 78, *Jesu, der du meine Seele* ('Jesus, by Thy Cross and Passion'), the first movement is one of the loftiest exhibitions of contrapuntal art, outstanding even among Bach's works. It is a passacaglia on

---

[1] The relation of Bach's composition to the poem by Paul Gerhardt is shown in the following table, in which [ ] surrounding a figure indicate that the respective stanza is presented with 18th-century additions, while ( ) indicate that it is used as the basis of a paraphrase:

B:	Chorale Fantasia	Chor. & Recit.	Aria	Chor. & Aria	Recit.	Aria	Chor. & Recit.	Aria	Chorale harmon.
G:	I	[II]	(III-IV)	V	(VI-VIII)	(IX)	[X]	(XI)	XII

a chromatically descending bass (*Ex.* 33) such as Baroque masters liked
to use in their 'Lamentos,' and such as Sebastian himself employed in the

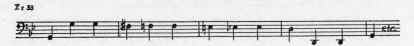

Crucifixus of his great Mass. In the course of the 27 variations, this woeful
figure is raised to the upper voices, and it appears in transposition and in
contrary motion. Into this highly artificial shell Bach builds without any
apparent effort a complete chorale fantasia. The result is an awe-inspiring
description of the Lord's suffering. After this overwhelming chorus,
scored for a large orchestra, there follows a delicate duet for soprano and
contralto ('We hasten with feeble yet diligent footsteps') accompanied
only by 'cello, organ, and a stringed bass 'staccato e pizzicato.' In its
ingratiating melody, strong dance rhythm with accent on first and third
beats, uncomplicated harmonies and frequent progressions in parallel
thirds and sixths (*Ex.* 34) we discover a Bach with leanings towards folk-

song-like simplicity.[1] While the ageing master was mainly concerned
with revealing the glory of a vanishing age to a younger generation, he
could, if he chose to do so, always beat them with their own weapons. A
joyful tenor aria and a dramatic bass aria are each preceded by recitatives
which introduce not only literal quotations from the text of the hymn,
but also allusions to its melodic material. Particularly moving is the second
one accompanied by strings. After sudden and repeated changes, a fervent
arioso ensues for which Bach even prescribes 'con ardore.' The final
chorale expresses the confidence of the faithful that they will be united
with Jesus all through 'sweet eternity.' Bach gives the whole cantata a
kind of rondo-like character by using the hymn tune not only in the first

---

[1] It is curious to note that the piece bears a certain resemblance to the delightful
duet 'Hark, hark' in Purcell's Masque to 'Timon of Athens.' The possibility that Bach
knew the score cannot be completely discarded.

and seventh movements, but also, to a lesser extent, in Nos. 3 and 5. A relationship to the Vivaldi concerto form, which was of so basic an importance for Bach, is not difficult to detect.

Bach composed no Latin *Motets*, since he was not obliged to by his duties and he considered the genre old-fashioned. He did, however, write six German motets for special occasions. One of them, *Lobet den Herrn* ('Praise ye the Lord'; *BWV* 230), was probably completed before he came to Leipzig. Four motets for funeral services, *Jesu, meine Freude* ('Jesus, dearest Master'; *BWV* 227, comp. 1723); *Fürchte dich nicht* ('Be not dismayed'; *BWV* 228, comp. probably 1726); *Der Geist hilft unsrer Schwachheit auf* ('The Spirit also helpeth us'; *BWV* 226; comp. 1729); and *Komm, Jesu, komm* ('Come, Jesus, come'; *BWV* 229), originated in the first half of his service as Thomas Cantor, while the sixth, *Singet dem Herrn* ('Sing to the Lord'; *BWV* 225), was composed for New Year 1746, to celebrate the end of the second Silesian war.

In these motets Bach uses the same kind of texts as in his early cantatas. The sources of his words are chorales and the Bible. His familiarity with the material, unusual even in that time of most thorough Bible-knowledge, helped him to compile deeply stirring and poetical texts.

The retrospective character of the motet form makes it understandable why Bach established in these works a certain connection with the productions of older members of the family. Johann Christoph Bach, too, wrote a motet *Fürchte dich nicht*, in which Bible words are combined with a chorale text, and Dietrich Buxtehude composed a cantata *Jesu, meine Freude*, which is in E minor like Sebastian's work of the same title. Nevertheless, Sebastian's main sources for these compositions were not the older German motets, but his own cantatas. Both the melodic and the harmonic treatment of the voices, the rich polyphonic texture, and, most of all, the basic importance of the chorale melodies, are the same as in the cantatas. It is true that there are no arias, duets or similar forms in the motets and they do not contain any independent instrumental parts. Nevertheless they were not performed by voices only. For the motet *Der Geist hilft unsrer Schwachheit auf*, a full autograph set of orchestral parts doubling the voices, as well as a figured bass, has been preserved. For *Lobet den Herrn*, too, Bach's continuo part exists. Real a capella music was at that time not heard in Germany, and it seems certain that an organ or harpsichord (preferably the latter) was used for every performance of these motets.

Four of them (*BWV* 225-26, 228-29) are written for 8-part double chorus. Unlike former composers, Bach does not use a higher and a lower chorus, but prescribes two evenly balanced mixed vocal groups. At the performances he usually had only one singer for each voice.

In *Fürchte dich nicht* Bach sets to music 2 verses from Isaiah. The brisk alternation of the two choirs ends at the words 'I am He who has redeemed thee,' and a fugue by the 3 lower voices ensues, in which the composer symbolizes Jesus' sacrifice with the help of a chromatically descending theme (*Ex.* 35) while the sopranos intone the chorale 'Lord, my Shepherd,

Ex 35

I am He who has - re _ _ deemed _____ (thee)

Fount of Gladness.' The result is a work that despite its more traditional form surpassed in emotional intensity anything yet written in this field.

The 5-part motet *Jesu, meine Freude* resembles in its construction the earlier forms of Bach's chorale cantatas. In its 11 numbers, 6 stanzas from Johann Franck's hymn alternate with 5 verses from the 8th chapter of the Epistle to the Romans. The first and sixth stanzas are presented in almost identical four-part harmonizations, while each of the stanzas in between is treated in a different manner: as a five-part harmonization, as a kind of fantasia, or, in stanza 3, as a strange mixture of homophonic and polyphonic elements only loosely connected with the main tune. Interpretation and exegesis are offered after each verse by the appropriate quotation from the Bible. To achieve formal symmetry, Bach uses practically the same music for the first and fifth insertion, while both the second and the fourth are the only pieces in the motet written for 3 parts. Once more the two gigantic pillars of Protestantism, gospel and church song, are joined, through the power of Bach's spirit, in an edifice of rock-like strength.

This work, like all the other motets, can only be mastered by performers of the highest musicianship endowed with a tremendous voice range and a capacity for interpreting the countless shades of Bach's emotional palette. Such difficulties have not discouraged performers; in fact, the motets were almost the only vocal compositions by Bach never wholly forgotten. Mozart heard *Singet dem Herrn* in 1789 in Leipzig, and 'his whole soul seemed to be in his ears' (Rochlitz). As early as 1803 five of these works were made available in a printed edition.[1] This was not due only to the superb musical qualities of the motets; the deep abiding faith radiating from them brought to later generations a spiritual sustenance badly needed in periods of religious decline.

Among Bach's vocal compositions the *Secular Cantatas* play an important part. The composer wrote them for special occasions, such as weddings, birthdays, and name-days of members of the ruling house, or for events at the Leipzig University. Many of them were first played by his Collegium Musicum and show clearly in their instrumentation whether they were meant for winter performances at the coffee house, or for an open-air concert in summer. The dramatic power of Bach's art, an earthy sense of humour, and love of nature are strongly in evidence in the secular cantatas.

The exact number of these compositions is not known. The thrifty composer did not cherish the idea of having some of his finest music performed once only. He used it over and over again, sometimes for other secular compositions, but frequently also for sacred works. The Christmas Oratorio, for instance, to mention only a single example, contains music from several secular cantatas. In most cases the new text was, in its emotional content, akin to the original words. The 'affections' remained the same, even though Divinity might replace a human being in the libretto. Bach's time had no qualms in this respect. For a Baroque composer, as for an artist of the Renaissance, there was no fundamental difference between profane and sacred works. Anything that stood artistically on a high level was suitable as a part of worship. Bach had clearly shown this attitude by introducing operatic and concerto elements into his church cantatas. A good 'contrafactum,' in which a secular work was raised to a higher spiritual level, without changing the prevailing mood, has at times been effective in producing some of Bach's finest compositions. And in the process of adapting earlier compositions to new texts, Bach often made considerable changes, modifying the instrumentation, adjusting the melodic line, or inventing new counterpoints and modulations in order to achieve a better co-ordination of word and sound. Nevertheless it is true that occasionally a new composition had to be written so quickly that neither composer nor librettist could give proper care to the

---

[1] The only one missing was *Lobet den Herrn*. Printed in its place was Johann Christoph Bach's *Ich lasse dich nicht*, then considered to be a work by Sebastian.

P

adaptation, in which case a regrettable discrepancy between the libretto and its musical setting was the result. Such instances, are however, not numerous.

To the Weimar period belongs cantata No. 208, *Was mir behagt, ist nur die muntre Jagd* ('The merry chase, the hunt is my delight'), written in 1716 for the birthday of the Duke of Weissenfels, to words by Salomo Franck. Its charming da capo aria for 2 recorders and soprano solo 'Sheep may safely graze' belongs to the most intimate and delightful pastorales Bach ever wrote. The composer used the fresh and attractive music of the cantata with more or less changed words at least three times for similar purposes. Besides, two of its arias[1] were later enlarged and rewritten for the Whitsuntide Cantata No. 68, and the final chorus became the first number in Cantata No. 149.

A product of the Cöthen years is the lovely cantata No. 202, *Weichet nur, betrübte Schatten* ('Vanish now, ye winter shadows') for soprano solo, oboe, strings, and continuo, which was performed during the wedding feast of an unknown couple. Bach offers here a singularly beautiful picture of youth and spring. The arpeggios at the beginning, describing the gently lifting wintry fog, would hardly seem amiss in the score of Haydn's 'Seasons' (*Ex.* 36). The aria next to the last number resembles a

passepied, and the place of the traditional final chorale of the church cantata is taken here by a gay gavotte, in which all the instruments join the soprano to wish the best of luck to the newly married couple.

The number of secular cantatas written in Cöthen seems to be larger than is usually assumed. Smend recently listed[2] ten compositions either known in their original form or through movements later incorporated into church cantatas. The words to three more cantatas have been preserved, though their music has not yet been found.

Various secular cantatas were written in Leipzig. On August 3, 1725, No. 205, the 'Dramma per musica' *Der zufriedengestellte Aeolus* ('The pacified Aeolus'), was performed to celebrate the name-day of Dr.

---

[1] The 'cello theme of one of these arias (*BWV* 68/2) was also used in an instrumental movement for violin, flute, and continuo (*BWV* 1040).

[2] Cf. 'Bach in Köthen,' p. 68.

Augustus Müller, member of the faculty of Leipzig University. The libretto, based partly on Virgil, tells how Aeolus, the God of the winds, is planning to release the autumn gales. Zephyrus, the mild west wind, and Pomona, the fruit goddess, implore him in vain to wait; but when Pallas Athene approaches him and tells him that she is preparing a festivity in honour of Dr. Müller, this impresses the God so strongly that he recalls his subjects. Bach's very striking music is unusually richly scored, with trumpets, horns, flutes, various oboes and strings, as the work was meant for an outdoor performance. The first chorus and the ensuing recitative present some of the wildest descriptions of turbulent elements that the composer has ever written. Similar in expression is the last aria of Aeolus (bass) accompanied by trumpets, timpani and horns, without any wood-wind or strings. A most effective contrast is achieved by the aria of Zephyrus, whose gentle nature Bach portrays with the help of the silvery viola da gamba and the tender viola d'amore. Nine years later the composer used the same music in honour of another man by the name of Augustus, when he celebrated the coronation of the Saxonian Elector, Augustus III, as King of Poland. The new text, possibly written by Bach himself, substitutes Valour for Aeolus and Justice for Zephyrus. It cannot be denied that this substitution is not altogether successful. The text of the aria of Justice, for instance, with its shallow praise of the ruler, is not in accordance with the peculiarly delicate instrumentation taken over from the original.

Der Streit zwischen Phoebus und Pan (No. 201, 'The contest between Phoebus and Pan'), probably performed in 1731 by the Collegium Musicum, is a satiric burlesque by Picander, based on Ovid's 'Metamorphoses,' in which Bach ridicules the new trends in music. Phoebus, representing tradition, has a singing competition with Pan, the representative of new-fangled notions. Among the judges, Tmolus is in favour of Phoebus, while Midas prefers Pan's foolish song, and in punishment for his faulty judgment is given long donkey's ears. In this Bach had a chance to vent his contempt for the aesthetic views held by a younger generation, views that were to find before long an eloquent advocate in Johann Adolf Scheibe. The ill-advised Midas in praising Pan's song,[1] which he could grasp and remember after a single hearing, and in criticizing Phoebus' art as too complex, only echoed what Bach had to hear time and again from younger musicians. The music to this satire is quite delightful. Phoebus' prize-song, prescribing muted strings, oboe d'amore, and flute

---

[1] This song (No. 7) was also used by Bach with changed words in his 'Peasant Cantata,' No. 212.

for the accompaniment, exhibits great artistry in its intricate rhythmic
differentiation and dynamic shading. Pan's aria is simple and rather crude
and is written in the form of a rustic dance; while in the ensuing aria of
Tmolus there are remarkable dynamic signs. In its first measure the composer clearly asks for a crescendo, which according to general belief was
never used by Bach (*Ex.* 37). When Midas defends his opinion, Bach

indicates in the music that this was the judgment of a donkey, deserving
to be punished by the growth of asinine ears. These the singer describes,
while the violins imitate the braying in a manner similar to Mendelssohn's
'Midsummer Night's Dream' Overture (*Ex.* 38).

Of more general interest and appeal is another humorous work, the
Coffee Cantata (No. 211), first performed in 1732 by the Collegium Musicum. To judge by its small orchestra (strings and one flute only), it was
meant for an indoor performance in winter. Again two generations confront each other, but this time the younger one is victorious. Father
Schlendrian (whose name Henry S. Drinker aptly translates as 'Old Stick-
in-the-Mud') is worried because his daughter Liesgen has fallen victim to
the new craze for coffee drinking. All his attempts to lure her away from
so detestable a habit by promise or threats are of no avail, until he offers
her a husband as a bribe. This she enthusiastically accepts, and the father
rushes off to secure one. Picander's little poem ends at this point. Bach,
however, had learned only too well from his own family-life that it is not
so easy to influence the young. He therefore adds a recitative, in which
Liesgen's plans are revealed; any man who wishes to wed her must consent
to a clause in the marriage contract entitling her to drink coffee whenever
she pleases. Finally, there is a short *coro* of the 3 singers accepting the
coffee-craze as something inevitable. This amusing libretto is treated by
Bach in the manner of an oratorio. A 'Historicus' imitating the style of the
Evangelist in the Passions, explains the plot at the beginning and again

near the end. In between there are arias and recitatives, and with the help
of masterly little touches a kind of comic opera is created that makes a
charming effect both in the concert hall and on the stage. The composer
succeeds in building up two characters who are very human indeed: a
grumbling boorish father and an obstinate, wily daughter. The caricature
of the father is drawn with particular gusto. When the 'Historicus' first
mentions him, heavy dotted rhythms appear in the bass, with the prescription *con pompa*, while in the first aria the violins growl to indicate his
vicious temper. When he later threatens to deprive Liesgen of the fashionable crinoline, Bach indicates its terrific width by the skip of a ninth (*Ex.*
39). Liesgen's aria in praise of coffee is a little conventional in its musical

diction, as though the composer wanted to hint that the girl had adopted
coffee drinking merely to follow the fashion. In the second aria, however,
her enthusiasm for a prospective husband is not simulated. The joy she
expresses in this folksong-like tune in dance rhythm is quite infectious and
carries the listener away. The composer's earthy nature is manifest in the
middle section of the aria. During a rather immodest allusion by Liesgen[1]
(meas. 81-89) the higher instruments are omitted from the accompaniment to ensure that the audience hears every word of it. This aria must
have sounded particularly funny to the coffee-house audience, when,
owing to the exclusion of women from such places, a male student, singing
falsetto, proclaimed his ardent desire for a 'husky hero.'

There is less artistry and a more popular trend in the *Peasant Cantata*
(No. 212) which Bach wrote in 1742 for a rustic celebration held in honour
of Karl Heinrich v. Dieskau, new lord of the manor of two villages near
Leipzig. The text of this *Cantate en burlesque*, as Bach called it, is by
Picander; it is in Saxon dialect and Bach has given each of the numbers
the character of a then fashionable dance, such as bourrée, mazurka and

polonaise, while the overture is a medley of fragments from various folk-
dances. Three actual folksongs such as *Ex.* 40 are even inserted in the

---

[1] This detail is omitted in any English translation of the work known to the author.

arias,[1] and Bach aims at similar results with his own tunes. The orchestra, in true peasant manner, consists in most of the numbers of only one violin, one viola and a double bass (continuo). Equally economical is the vocal apparatus: one soprano and one bass. The humorous plot, the very limited number of performers, and the unassuming, catchy musical idiom clearly indicate that Bach was adopting the language of the new generation. Once more he showed that although his main interest belonged to older forms he was quite willing at times to forsake his aloofness, and to write music so simple and appealing that even his youngest critic could not find fault with it.

Three of Bach's church compositions, written in the middle of the thirties, were designated by the composer himself as *Oratorios*. They are the Christmas Oratorio (*BWV* 248), which, according to the printed libretto, was performed in 1734;[2] the oratorio for Ascension Day, generally known as cantata No. 11, from approximately the same period; and the Easter Oratorio (*BWV* 249) of 1736. It has been known for a long time that parts of the Christmas Oratorio are 'contrafacta' of secular cantatas.[3] Friedrich Smend proved the same to be true of the two other works of this group.[4] The Easter Oratorio occupies an isolated position among Bach's vocal compositions, since it is his only work for the church whose entire text consists of a dialogue in rhymes. The Ascension Day Oratorio, on the other hand, is not very different from Bach's cantatas.

The most important and, at the same time, the most extensive of these three works is the *Christmas Oratorio*. Although it is a series of six cantatas, which were performed on the three Christmas days, New Year's day, the following Sunday, and Epiphany, it yet shows unity in its construction. As in the Passions, sections from the New Testament are narrated by an evangelist, while the utterances of individual persons are entrusted to soloists, and those of a group to the chorus. Bach interrupts the Biblical story again and again with lyrical episodes such as chorales

---

[1] Bach also did not hesitate to include a melody by Anton Seemann, conductor of Count Sporck, in Aria No. 16.

[2] Schering's contention in 'Musikgeschichte Leipzigs,' III, p. 223, that the work was performed one year later, has not been sufficiently proved.

[3] Nos. 4, 19, 29, 30, 39, 41 are taken from Cantata No. 213; Nos. 1, 8, 15, 24 from Cantata No. 214; No. 47 from Cantata No. 215; No. 45 from the St. Mark Passion.

[4] Cf. *AfMf*, VII (1942), and 'Bach Gedenkschrift,' 1952.

and arias. Thus he creates pure music for the church, serving the purpose of edifying and uplifting the congregation. The sequence of keys and the orchestration give a kind of rondo-like character to the work. Cantatas No. I, III, VI are in the main key of D, and are scored for a big orchestra (with trumpets, timpani, woodwind, strings). Nos. II, IV, V, which are in the related keys of G, F, and A, do not use trumpets.

The Christmas Oratorio offers us a chance to study the technique employed by Bach in his 'contrafacta.' As model for one of its numbers he uses an aria which, in the secular cantata *Hercules auf dem Scheidewege* (No. 213, 'Hercules at the crossroads'), Sensuality sings to young Hercules. It begins with the words 'Sleep, my beloved, enjoy thou thy rest,' and accordingly the composer set it as a lullaby. Without compunction he could use it for another lullaby in the Christmas Oratorio, starting with the words 'Sleep, my beloved, and rest thee a while.' But in the case of the aria 'Prepare thyself, Zion' of the Christmas Oratorio it is rather different, as a comparison with the original text from 'Hercules' will show.

Hercules	*Christmas Oratorio*
I will not regard thee	Prepare thyself, Zion,
but wholly discard thee,	with tender emotion
Contemptible pleasure,	The Fairest, the Dearest
I value thee not.	to welcome to thee.
Like the serpent	With what yearning
who attacked me in my cradle	must thy heart to-day be burning,
Thee will I strangle	Welcome thy dear one
thou serpent, destroy thee.	with loving devotion.

To overcome the emotional disparity between the two texts, Bach changed both the scoring and phrasing. The original was for violins I and II in unison and continuo. In the oratorio he omitted violin II and replaced it by the tender oboe d'amore. At the same time the bassoon was added to the bass. The threatening 'unisono e staccato' in the secular

cantata was, with the help of slurs and appogiaturas, transformed into a caressing tune (*Ex.* 41). The winding line in the bass used in 'Hercules' to portray the snake was not conspicuous enough to call for a change. Thus Bach achieved a successful adaptation with a minimum of effort.

It is hard to single out individual numbers of this masterpiece. Among the highlights is the *Sinfonia* at the beginning of the second part; a Siciliano of singular beauty, akin in character to the *Sinfonia Pastorale* in Handel's 'Messiah,' but deviating from it significantly in its more intricate orchestration and texture. The treatment of the chorales is also outstanding. At the end of the second cantata the chorus sings the tune of 'From heaven above to earth I come,' while the orchestra again intones the enraptured Pastorale of the beginning. Although the general mood of the oratorio is one of exultation, the thought of Christ's sacrifice also plays an important role. The Passion-hymn 'Oh sacred head now wounded' appears both as the first and as the ultimate chorale of the whole oratorio; thus emphasizing that only through the death of Jesus did the birth of the heavenly child result in the salvation of mankind.

In its original form the *Magnificat* (*BWV* 243) was also meant for a performance at Christmas. In this version, written in 1723, the Bible text (Luke i, 46-55) was repeatedly interrupted by chorales, Christmas songs, etc. Around the year 1730 Bach revised the composition, changing its key from E♭ to D, altering the instrumentation, and eliminating the insertions; thus making the work suitable for performance on other occasions. In its definitive form the *Magnificat*, except for the concluding *Gloria*, contains nothing but Mary's Hymn, from the Vulgate. It is one of the most compact compositions by Bach, imbued with joy and exultation, and radiating the same happy optimism which had found so irresistible an expression in the Brandenburg Concertos. The brief movements (lasting an average of 3 minutes) are clearly united in three groups, each starting with an aria and ending with a full chorus. The individual sections are framed by the mighty initial *Magnificat* chorus and the concluding *Gloria*, which, at the words *Sicut erat in principio* ('As it was in the beginning'), quotes the music of the first number.[1] Each individual piece, in spite of its brevity, has its own clearly defined emotional character. The first *Magnificat*, scored for full orchestra (trumpets, timpani, woodwind, strings, organ) and five-part chorus, carries us away with its brilliance and exuberance. An overwhelming effect is produced later, in the aria for alto solo, *Quia respexit*

---

[1] In the motet, *Jesu, meine Freude*, also written in 1723, we find the same device. Here too the beginning and end of the composition are musically alike.

('For he hath regarded the low estate of his handmaiden'), when at the words *omnes generationes* ('all generations shall call me blessed') the full chorus suddenly cuts the solo voice short. Of transcendent beauty is the trio for 2 sopranos and alto *Suscepit Israel* ('He hath holpen his servant Israel') to which the 2 oboes intone in unison, like a *cantus firmus*, the venerable *Magnificat* tune. Only Sebastian Bach could write a composition so strict in form and yet so tender and ethereal. To the following *Sicut locutus est* ('As he spake to our fathers') the composer gives an old-fashioned motet character by writing a vocal fugue, unaccompanied by the orchestra, to stress the connection with the past. After this austere piece, the re-entrance of the orchestra in the ensuing *Gloria* is all the more dazzling. Twice the voices rise in a mighty arc to glorify the Father and the Son. At the words *et Spiritui sancto* the melodic line is inverted to symbolize the descent of the Holy Ghost. Here the entrance of the trumpets leads to the climax of the work, triumphantly proclaiming in its music 'My soul doth magnify the Lord.'

According to the *Necrolog*, Bach wrote five Passions, but only two of them have actually been preserved: the Passions according to St. John and according to St. Matthew. The earlier of these is the *St. John Passion* (*BWV* 245), which the composer wrote while still in Cöthen in order to present it on Good Friday, 1723, at Leipzig. For four subsequent performances under Bach's direction, the composer made various alterations. Basically the work already shows the construction to be found in the later Passion and in the Christmas Oratorio (cf. p. 230). The main part of the text is supplied by the Bible, in this case taken from St. John xviii-xix (with short insertions from St. Matthew). The narration is done in recitative form by a tenor, the Evangelist; individual characters, including Christ, are sung by soloists; and utterances of the crowds by the chorus. Arias inserted in between express the reaction of the individual to the events described, and chorales that of the whole congregation. The work is in two sections, to be performed before and after the sermon. It seems that Bach himself was responsible for the selection of the chorales, and that he also provided the texts for the arias. In these he often followed the model of a text by the Hamburg Councillor, Barthold Heinrich Brockes, *Der für die Sünde der Welt gemarterte und sterbende Jesus* ('Jesus tortured and dying for the sin of the world'), which had been set to music by Handel,[1]

---

[1] Bach owned a copy of Handel's work.

Telemann, Mattheson, Keiser and others. But even in these pieces Bach never copied Brockes literally, and, in particular, he did not adopt the poet's rhymed paraphrases of the Bible text. Moreover, he included some words from J. G. Postel's 'St. John Passion,' which Handel had set to music at the age of 19. Bach apparently knew this score, as there are a few slight analogies between the two works.[1]

An interesting peculiarity of Bach's score is the repeated use of the same music for various short choruses of the crowds. Some pieces are employed twice, one (No. 3, 'Jesus of Nazareth') with little variations as often as five times (also in Nos. 5, 29, 46, and in the accompaniment of No. 25). It has been suggested that lack of time in preparing the score for the first performance caused Bach to adopt this method. Had this been the case, the composer could easily have remedied this deficiency when he subsequently revised the work. Actually, these repetitions are indispensable for the architectural plan of the whole work as Bach had conceived it. In order to achieve the 'chiastic' arrangement which was one of Bach's favourite forms throughout his life (cf. p. 202), the composer distributed related choruses in widely separated sections of his score. To take, for instance, the 'heart-piece'[2] of the second part: the chorus No. 29, the solos Nos. 31/32, and the chorus No. 34 form a unit that recurs with similar music in Nos. 46, 48, 50.[3] The chorus No. 36 corresponds to No. 44, and No. 38 is practically identical with No. 42. In the centre of the section is a chorale (No. 40), just as chorales (Nos. 27 and 52) frame the whole 'heart-piece.' The overall arrangement is therefore this:

A	B	C	D	E	D	C	B	A
27	29, 31/2, 34	36	38	40	42	44	46, 48, 50	52

The perfect symmetry of form is matched by inexhaustible harmonic imagination in the chorales and a tremendous power of expression. It is hard to decide what to admire more in this score: the pithy, exciting choruses, creating a weird picture of the turgid crowds, or the intensely dramatic, at times almost violent recitatives. How stirring, for instance, is the recitative depicting the tears of Peter after his denial of the Lord, which is followed by the aria in f sharp minor expressing man's confusion and desolation! This first large work by the new music director must have

---

[1] Handel's Passion is available in a Swiss recording conducted by B. Henking.

[2] Cf. Smend in *BJ*, 1926.

[3] The numbers in between, not mentioned here, are those of the connecting recitatives.

sounded strange indeed to the ears of the Leipzig congregation, accustomed as they were to Kuhnau's gentle tunes.

In later years Bach felt it was necessary to improve this youthful composition. The final visionary chorale was added, and the soulful introductory chorale fantasia 'O man, thy grievous sins bemoan'[1] was replaced by a powerful da capo chorus. On the other hand, the beautiful aria and chorale which originally followed No. 15 were altogether omitted in the interests of structural cohesion. The aria 'Do not writhe, tormented souls,' with its somewhat exaggerated pictorialism, was supplanted by a poignant arioso with following aria (Nos. 31/32) to which the accompaniment of 2 viole d'amore and lute added mellowness. In making this change Bach achieved an overwhelming contrast between the crude picture of tortured Jesus and the unearthly bliss derived from His sacrifice. This arioso reveals, with an intensity only rarely equalled in Bach's works, the composer's innermost faith.

Bach performed his *St. Matthew Passion* (*BWV* 244) for the first time on Good Friday, 1729.[2] We do not know how long he was engaged in the tremendous task of its composition, but while still working on the Passion news reached him that on November 19, 1728, his beloved friend, Prince Leopold of Anhalt-Cöthen, had suddenly died, and that he was expected to supply and perform a funeral music at the memorial service in the following spring. Nothing seemed more appropriate than to use parts of his sublime new work for this purpose, and so Picander, the librettist of the St. Matthew Passion, was requested to paraphrase the text of nine pieces[3] from it. The funeral cantata *Klagt, Kinder* ('Lament, O children'; *BWV* 244a[4]) was played on March 24, 1729 at Cöthen. Shortly afterwards the mighty Passion itself resounded at St. Thomas'.

The St. Matthew Passion represents the climax of Bach's music for

[1] It was instead inserted into the St. Matthew Passion as the concluding number of the first part.

[2] Schering's theory that the performance of the St. Matthew Passion did not take place until 1731 and that the St. Mark Passion was played in 1729 (cf. *BJ*, 1939) can no longer be upheld, in spite of the many psychological reasons which seem to corroborate the later date. Smend pointed out in *BJ*, 1940-48 that Zelter, in the programme notes to the first Berlin performance of the St. Matthew Passion in 1829, referred to the 'old church text,' evidently the church programme of the Passion, in his possession, which was clearly dated 1729.

[3] They are Nos. 10, 47, 58, 66, 29, 26, 75, 19, 78.

[4] Smend, *l.c.*, proved from the Cöthen account books that not one but two funeral cantatas were performed on this occasion, one on March 23 at night, the other on March 24. Of the first no trace has been found yet, but it is evidently the work to which Forkel alludes in his Bach Biography, praising its 'double choruses of uncommon magnificence.' The score which Forkel owned has been missing since 1818.

the Protestant Church. It uses the largest performing apparatus and is in scope one of the composer's most extensive works. Bach's own conception of its importance is clearly revealed in the exquisite score he made of it after 1740, one which is unique even among his many beautiful manuscripts. He worked on it with ruler and compass, and he used red ink for the Bible words to distinguish the divine message from the rest of the text. The composer wanted this Passion to be of general appeal, and indeed there is in this work a simplicity and directness not often to be found in Bach's larger compositions. The motto which Beethoven placed in front of his Missa Solemnis—'It comes from the heart—may it go to the heart'—can well be applied to this work also.

Although the basic elements are once more the same, the 'Passion according to St. John' and that 'according to St. Matthew' are highly different in character. In the later composition vehemence and violence no longer dominate. The work radiates tenderness and love; harsh contrasts are toned down, and a heart-stirring blend of bliss and grief such as only Bach could create, prevails throughout the composition. According to the Gospel, the Christ of the St. John Passion was endowed with sublime calm and remoteness. The gospel of St. Matthew, however, allowed Bach to express his own fervent *Jesusminne*. Here there is no unbridgeable gap between the human and the divine; the Lord approaches mankind in His suffering, and mankind suffers with Him. While in the earlier Passion the utterances of Christ are in recitatives accompanied by the organ only, the St. Matthew Passion, following the example of Schütz and Telemann, uses a string quartet to surround the personality of the Lord with a kind of halo.[1] Only once is this recitative transformed into an arioso: when at the last supper Jesus explains the mystic significance of bread and wine. And only once are the accompanying strings silenced: when Christ in agony cries out 'My God, why hast Thou forsaken me?' the halo is extinguished.

In accordance with the great store Bach set by the work, he had recourse to a wealth of executants far exceeding that in the St. John Passion, indeed hardly used in any of his other compositions. In its definitive form the St. Matthew Passion employs 2 mixed choruses, 2 orchestras, and another group of boy-singers for the *cantus firmus* of the first chorus. The use of the two choirs is scrupulously indicated in the score. If there are no independent parts for each of the 8 voices, Bach prescribes which choir should perform an individual number, or whether

---

[1] This very apt comparison was coined a century ago by Winterfeld in his 'Evangelischer Kirchengesang.'

they should join forces. The composer's zest for experimenting and for mingling stylistic elements found ample satisfaction in this work. The recitatives of the Evangelist, accompanied by basses and organ only, speak an exciting tonal language, such as had hardly been conceived before. For certain occasions, as the crying of Peter, the recitative changes to a melisma of deep intensity. At times the bass accompaniment matches the highly dramatic narration; for instance, in the famous description of the rending of the Temple veil and the earthquake after the death of Christ. Among the gems of the score are the accompanied recitatives preceding the arias. These brief ariosos contain some of the most exquisite music Bach ever wrote, such as No. 74, 'At even, sweet, cool hour of rest,' which, quite in the romantic manner, links the stillness of evening with the peace achieved through Jesus' death. In two cases recitatives are combined with choral numbers. In No. 25, 'Ah woe, how trembles His tormented heart,' an accompanied recitative alternates with verses from a chorale, a technique Bach was to employ in his late chorale cantatas. Similarly in No. 77, 'And now the Lord is laid to rest,' each of the four soloists in a brief arioso says a tender farewell to the Master, and in between the chorus sings a deeply moving refrain.

The arias are often arranged as duets between a singer and an instrument of approximately the same range. No. 58, for instance, 'For love, oh my Saviour,' is scored for soprano voice and solo flute, and, to enhance its poignant character, the accompaniment is provided by 2 oboi da caccia (English horns) without any strings or organ. In the aria No. 26 for tenor solo and chorus, Bach's feeling for pictorialism makes a characteristic excursion into the realm of numbers. The tenor, representing Peter, sings 'Yea, I will watch with Jesus gladly.' The chorus adds the refrain, 'So all our sins have gone to sleep' ten times, once for each of the remaining disciples (except the absent Judas) who are gradually succumbing to sleep. Similarly the duet with chorus (No. 33) after Christ's capture can be interpreted as the expression of grief by two distressed disciples, who are being interrupted by nine (three times three) brief ejaculations of the chorus 'Loose Him—Halt ye—Bind Him not,' one for each of the remaining followers of the Lord. This leads us finally to the well-known chorus 'Lord, not I?' after Jesus has said that one of His disciples will betray Him. The same question is asked eleven times, and Bach thus implies that each of the disciples, except Judas, raises his voice.

In the St. Matthew Passion the composer avoids the repetition of music in the crowd scenes that played so important a part in the structure of the St. John Passion. The variety in these choruses is quite overwhelming. Stupid slander could hardly have been better portrayed than in the canon (No. 39), in which one false witness slavishly repeats every word of the other witness's accusation. How stunning are the 3 powerful chords used at the word 'Barrabas'; the senseless fury of the crowd in 'Let Him be crucified,' ending abruptly in an unexpected key; and the increasing vigour in the 8-part chorus (No. 67) 'Saviour was He of others,' in which the 2 choruses at first respond to each other, then join forces, and end in a weird unison, accusing Jesus of blasphemy for having said 'I am God's own son' (*Ex.* 42).

Ex. 42

This man has said: „I am God's own son."

The chorale tunes, on the other hand, are repeated in this work even more frequently than in the earlier Passion. Bach's favourite, 'Oh sacred Head now wounded' appears no less than five times in different places, with words and harmonization superbly matching the mood of the moment. In the selection of the venerable tunes and texts, and in the choice of their appropriate position within the score, Bach shows a poetical power and insight given only to one who was the product of many generations of Protestant church musicians.[1]

In the initial number of the St. Matthew Passion Bach introduced a chorale melody as a *cantus firmus*. It was played by the organ in the first performances, but was later taken over by a separate boys' choir. This is the most elaborate piece of the whole composition. Two wildly excited groups confront each other with terse questions and sorrowful answers, against a background of floods of tears, suggested by the heaving and milling orchestra. Above the passionate grief of humanity thus depicted rises the crystal-clear, serene church tune, thus setting the stage for this work on mortal frailty and divine strength.

Of the St. Mark Passion (*BWV* 247), first performed on Good Friday 1731, only Picander's libretto has been preserved. A small part of the composition has survived, however, in other sacred works. Two choruses and three arias originated with the *Trauer-Ode* (Cantata 198,

---

[1] Picander omits the chorales in his edition of the libretto, thus indicating that they were not chosen by him.

written in 1727 in memory of the Electress Christiane Eberhardine (cf. p. 173); one aria is to be found in Cantata 54; and one chorus in the Christmas Oratorio. About the two other Passions nothing definite is known. The St. Luke Passion (*BWV* 246) printed by *BG* is in all likelihood not by Bach.

Around the year 1737 the composer wrote 4 short Masses (*BWV* 233-36) consisting of *Kyrie* and *Gloria* only. Most of their numbers are only adaptations from earlier church cantatas. The Mass in G, for instance, is based on choruses, arias, and a duet from Cantatas 17, 79, 138, and 179. The *Kyrie* of the Mass in F, one of the few movements which is not a 'contrafactum,' gives the ancient melody of the Litany to the bass voices, while at the same time horns and oboes intone, as an additional *cantus firmus*, the chorale tune *Christe, du Lamm Gottes* ('Christ, Thou Lamb of God'); a remarkable attempt to bring elements of the Protestant and Catholic services into an artistic whole.[1]

A similar venture of far greater significance had been made by Bach in an earlier work. In 1733 he composed a *Kyrie* to mourn the death of Augustus 'the Strong' and a *Gloria* to celebrate the ascension to the throne of Augustus III (cf. p. 184). Subsequently he expanded the work into a complete setting of the Latin Ordinary of the Mass, the only one of its kind he has left us. It seems that Bach, the protagonist of Protestant music, did not see anything inappropriate in this action. He knew that Luther had never entirely removed the Latin Mass from the Protestant service, and that sections from it were still used in his own time. Above all, he wanted to write a work that spoke to the whole of Christianity. The composition known as the *Mass in B minor* (*BWV* 232) is a monumental work of lofty grandeur abounding in forms of intricate technical mastery, such as a superb passacaglia, highly artistic fugues with stretti, augmentations, and other devices of the strict contrapuntal style. There is an awe-inspiring remoteness in this work, and only when the text refers to Jesus does the musical idiom assume a more personal and intimate character. Thus the duet *Christe eleison* ('Christ have mercy on us') radiates ethereal bliss and ecstatic longing, in marked contrast to the first and the second *Kyrie eleison* which address God the Father and God the Holy Ghost in a spirit of sadness, guilt, and despair. Similarly the two choruses *Qui tollis*

[1] The 5 'Sancti' which are preserved in Bach's own hand (*BWV* 237-41) are believed to be mainly arrangements of works by other composers.

peccata mundi ('Which taketh away the sins of the world') and *Et incarnatus est* ('And was made man') are both simple, heart-stirring compositions, fervently expressing Bach's *Jesusminne*.

The composer did not hesitate to include in the Mass numerous 'contrafacta' of movements from his church cantatas, and at least 9 of the 24 numbers of the score are remodelled from earlier works closely related in content. Not one of these adaptations is mechanically done; indeed, each of them shows a higher degree of perfection than its model. The *Expecto resurrectionem mortuorum* ('I look for the resurrection of the dead') is taken from Cantata 120, *Gott man lobet*, using the second movement 'Shout ye, all ye joyful voices.' While the orginal contains a 4-part chorus only, with supreme mastery Bach adds a fifth obbligato part, which in a completely natural way enriches the polyphonic texture. The *Crucifixus* is a famous example; it is based on a passacaglia from cantata 12, *Weinen, Klagen*, and was given its exquisite ending, modulating from minor to major, only in the Mass. In making this addition, Bach not only prepares for the glory of the immediately following *Et resurrexit* ('And rose again'); but he thus has 13 variations instead of the original 12 and so symbolizes the tragedy by that ill-fated number.[1]

As Bach in this work went back to a time when the Christian Church was as yet undivided, he felt the inclusion of venerable forms of the past to be appropriate. The *Credo*, for instance, in its first and last sections uses the melodies of the Gregorian chant in grandiose fugues of a definitely antiquated motet character. Moreover, the frequent 5-part choruses and the old-fashioned *alla breve* rhythms (4/2) in several sections enhance the retrospective aspect of this music.

On the other hand there is no lack of contemporary forms either. The Mass contains arias equipped with the coloraturas of the Italian opera, and superb duets in the style of Agostino Steffani. These numbers, too, afford a deep insight into Bach's mentality. In the duet *Et in unum Dominum Jesum Christum filium Dei unigenitum* ('And in one Lord, Jesus Christ, the only-begotten Son of God'), the mystic unity of the Father and His Son Jesus Christ is symbolized by an imitation in unison which presently turns into a canon at the fourth. The gentle duet of the oboi d'amore in the aria No. 18 for bass, with its reference to *unam sanctam Catholicam et apostolicam Ecclesiam* ('One Holy Catholic and Apostolic Church'), is particularly beautiful. Since this forms part of the Creed

[1] Smend points out that with the help of the figure alphabet (cf. p. 203) the word 'Credo' can be expressed as 43. It is significant that in the Credo movement of Bach's Mass the word 'Credo' appears 43 times.

accepted by all Christian denominations, it might well be that the peaceful dialogue of the two 'love oboes' is intended to signify harmony and understanding between Catholics and Protestants.

In spite of heterogeneous stylistic elements in this Mass, Bach succeeds in giving it unity and cohesion. It is true that the original score consists of four sections. The composer inscribed as *Missa* the *Kyrie* and *Gloria* which he handed to Augustus III, Elector of Saxony. The *Credo* bears in the autograph the title *Symbolum Nicenum*. The third section is the *Sanctus*, and the fourth comprises the remaining movements, *Osanna*, *Benedictus*, *Agnus Dei*, *Dona nobis pacem*. Each of the first three sections shows a well-balanced structure. In the *Symbolum Nicenum*, for instance, the *Crucifixus* is the 'heart-piece.' It is preceded and followed by a chorus (*Et incarnatus est*, *Et resurrexit*). These 3 numbers are flanked by solo pieces; a duet and an aria respectively. At the beginning of the *Symbolum*, and at the end, are the mighty double pillars of connected choruses, in each of which Gregorian chants form the melodies of the first half.

Looking at the work as a whole, we find that the name of Mass in B minor, which is generally used in modern times, is not justified. The composition comprises 12 movements in D and only 5 in b. D is the key of the jubilant, resplendent *Gloria* and of the majestic *Credo* (here intermingled with the mixolydian mode). In D also is the dazzling Easterpiece of the *Resurrexit* and the awe-inspiring *Sanctus*, in which Heaven and Earth seem to resound with the praise of the Lord. (The six parts of this chorus may have been inspired by the six wings of the Seraphims in Isaiah vi.) Each section of the whole work ends in D and all, except the first, start in it. The predominance of this brilliant key holds the individual sections firmly together. To this should be added the fact that the last number, *Dona nobis pacem* ('Grant us peace'), uses the same music as the chorus *Gratias agimus tibi* ('We give Thee thanks'), which stands in the very centre of the Mass. This connection is of more than musical significance. Bach felt that he did not have to implore his maker for peace, and instead thanked Him for granting it to the true believer. In this way the composer also concluded his Mass with the expression of gratitude traditional in the Lutheran service.

Owing to its colossal dimensions this work fits into neither the Protestant nor the Catholic church service. Yet it is one of the greatest manifestations of the religious spirit and belongs, together with Beethoven's *Missa Solemnis*, to the immortal documents of man's quest for the eternal truths.

Q

II

WORKS FOR THE ORGAN SOLO

Organ music accompanied Bach throughout his whole life. Among his earliest compositions were works for the 'king of instruments' and his last, which the master, nearly blind, dictated to his son-in-law, Altnikol, was an organ chorale. Since the principal aim of Bach's art was to magnify the Lord, the organ offered him the most direct way by which to pursue his goal, without the co-operation of other musicians. Almost every one of the more than 200 works he wrote for the organ was designed for liturgical purposes.

The master's contemporaries held him in awe as one of the greatest virtuosi on the organ. They eagerly sought his advice on the building of new and the remodelling of old instruments. Our time sees in Bach the unmatched master of organ composition. In these works, 16th- and 17th-century music reaches its climax, while later generations feebly attempted to regain and reproduce parts of its lost grandeur.

As in other fields of Bach's creative output, it is impossible to determine the exact date of composition of most of his organ works. Nevertheless, the stylistic features of these compositions enable us to establish certain significant patterns for each of his creative periods. The situation is somewhat complicated by the fact that Bach often revised and rewrote organ compositions many years after their first conception. If such works reflect the features of the period in which they received their final form, they will be discussed with the compositions of that phase.

The works of the *First Creative Period* are typical of a young composer who is trying to find himself and to master the intricacies of his craft. Bach was always eager to learn from others, but naturally this tendency was never as apparent and predominant as in the works of his youth. The incipient organist studied the works of his own clan, among them especially the compositions of Johann Christoph (13) and Johann Bernhard (18). Next to his relatives, the great masters of keyboard music in Italy and Southern, Central and, most of all, Northern Germany were his models. He copied and imitated their music, sometimes barely reaching their level, and only rarely surpassing it. His musical language is often voluble, his harmonic and polyphonic technique immature, a sense of balance and form as yet undeveloped. It is typical of the uneven character of Bach's early organ works that, while some of them contain very difficult and brilliant pedal parts, others dispense with the pedals altogether.

Nevertheless these works of the young Bach are anything but unattractive. They are highly emotional, exuberant and, in their subjective expressiveness, typical products of a growing young genius. Bach's first period shows a definite resemblance to that of Brahms, whose early compositions compensate for their lack of formal perfection by their stirring and passionate content.

There are two main groups of organ works by Bach: those which are freely invented, and those which are based on some chorale. The former group consists of a number of *Preludes or Toccatas with Following Fugues*. The free preludes and toccatas frequently reflect the brilliant Venetian style of Merulo and the Gabrielis, which was passed on to Bach through the fantastic art of the Lübeck master, Dietrich Buxtehude, and his follower, Georg Böhm. North German influence may also be detected in the loose and rhapsodic construction of the fugues. Good examples of Bach's Lüneburg period (1700-1703) are furnished by the *Preludes and Fugues in a and c* (*P.* III/84 and IV/36, *BWV* 551, 549). The work in a for instance is a kind of toccata, a show-piece, containing in its middle part two fugal sections. The brief first fugue, consisting of 17 bars only, uses a gaily rambling theme of the Buxtehude type (*Ex.* 43), without any

attempt at serious elaboration. The second fugue seems to employ a new theme, but this subject is accompanied by a running counter-melody which, as the piece proceeds, gains in importance and at the same time increasingly resembles the theme of the first fugue. Even in this very primitive composition, Bach's attempt to unify the different sections of his composition is apparent.

An effective thematic interrelation between three successive movements is achieved in the *Fantasy in G* (*P.* IX/25, *BWV* 571).[1] The last movement culminates in an 'ostinato' figure consisting of 5 stepwise descending notes, which appear not only in the bass but also in the soprano

[1] The authenticity of the Fantasy has been doubted, but the present writer feels inclined to consider it as a work of young Bach. Altogether the composer's organ music still presents unsolved problems in this respect. Some of the works that the 19th century considered as compositions by Johann Sebastian are recognized to-day as the works of others, while in several cases the question is yet unsettled. The organ chorales *P.* VI/3 and 62 (*BWV* 693, 748), for instance, might be by J. G. Walther. The chorale partita *BWV* 771, which Hull considered one of the finest works by the young Bach, is in all likelihood by A. N. Vetter, while *P.* IX/38 (*BWV* 585) and *P.* VIII/48 (*BWV* 553-60) are probably by J. L. Krebs. Cf. Keller in *BJ*, 1937.

and alto parts. This is the earliest example of Bach's use of a technique that was to reach its magnificent climax in the great Passacaglia in c.

The *Toccata and Fugue in d* (*P*. IV/27, *BWV* 565) is the most striking work of the Arnstadt period.[1] Bach's dependence on models is as easily traceable here as in any other composition of his first period. The toccata sections at the beginning and end of the work are strongly rhapsodic. The freely flowing fugue in the centre is loosely constructed with runs and broken chord episodes separating the different entrances of the theme. Obviously Bach wishes to maintain the predominant character of brilliant improvisation even in the middle section. The theme seems to be inspired by a technique adopted from the violin, that of playing simultaneously on two neighbouring strings, a procedure Bach was often to employ in his music for keyboard instruments. The Toccata's torrents of sound and dazzling fireworks have made Pirro see the work as a piece of programme music describing the fury of the elements in a thunderstorm, yet there is a masterly craftsmanship underlying all this outpouring of the emotions. The work was written by an organist who had so deep an insight into the possibilities of his instrument that he was able to produce the most powerful effects without unduly taxing the technical abilities of the player. In its intensity and exuberance this is clearly a product of Bach's 'Storm and Stress' period, but there is no youthful groping and uncertainty in it.

Among the *Organ Chorales* of the first period three main types may be discerned: (*a*) the chorale fughetta (short fugue); (*b*) the chorale-fantasy; (*c*) the chorale partita (chorale variations). Some of the *Chorale Fughettas* closely follow earlier models. For instance, *Herr Jesu Christ, dich zu uns wend'* ('Lord Jesus Christ, I turn to Thee'; *BWV* 749),[2] which treats the hymn tune partly as a fugal subject and partly as a basis for free imitations, is fashioned after the arrangement of the same chorale by Johann Christoph Bach. Other chorale fughettas introduce, in addition, a counter-subject that is preserved throughout the whole prelude, thus firmly linking together the different sections of the work. In *Vom Himmel hoch* ('From Heaven above'; *P*. VII/54, *BWV* 701), for instance, the chorale melody is accompanied by a running counter-subject (*Ex*. 44) which is maintained all through the composition, possibly to express the fluttering of the angels' wings in this Christmas prelude.[3]

[1] It seems more likely that the work was written in Arnstadt rather than in Weimar, as some scholars have assumed.

[2] Cf. also *BWV* 750 and 756.

[3] Somewhat similar in construction are the Fughettas *P*. V/7, 18, 20, 23, 39, 43 (*BWV* 696-99, 703, 704).

In his chorale fughettas, as in various organ works of his youth, Bach omits the pedal altogether; and a very modest use of the pedal may also

Ex 44

be observed in the only *Chorale Fantasy* he ever wrote, based on *Christ lag in Todesbanden* ('Christ lay in Death's dark prison'; *P. VI/15, BWV* 718). This type of composition, which deals with the complete melody of the chosen hymn, treating each verse in a different manner, was a favourite with North German masters, whereas Johann Christoph Bach and Pachelbel ignored it. The direct model for Sebastian's chorale fantasy was one composed by Georg Böhm on the same melody;[1] however, it is also easy to detect references to the style of two masters from Lübeck. Sebastian starts with a richly ornamented treatment of the first two lines of the chorale; the third line he develops as a brief fugato, the fourth as a kind of gigue in 12/8 time in imitation of similar movements by Buxtehude, and in the fifth line he uses the mystical echo-like effects so dear to Buxtehude's father-in-law, Franz Tunder.

On a much larger scale than the chorale fughettas and the fantasy are the highly imaginative and exuberant *Partite Diverse*, for which Johann Bernhard Bach's (cf. p. 100) and Georg Böhm's Partite seem to have been the direct models. Sebastian's variations on *Christ, der du bist der helle Tag* ('O Christ who art the Light of Day'; *P. V/60, BWV* 766) and *O Gott, du frommer Gott* ('O God, Thou Holy God'; *P. V/68, BWV* 767) bear all the traces of an early origin. The pedal is only rarely used and then *ad libitum*, and the harmonization of the chorale melody is at its beginning rather clumsy, with frequent repetitions of tonic and dominant and heavy 5- and 6-part chords on the weak beat (*Ex.* 45). *Sei gegrüsset, Jesu gütig*

Ex 45   O Gott, du frommer Gott

('Thee I greet, Thy love I treasure'; *P. V/76, BWV* 768) which may have originated in the same period, clearly shows traces of a later revision;

---

[1] Sämtliche Werke, Leipzig, Breitkopf & Härtel, 1927, vol. II, p. 98.

it displays the youthful fervour of the other sets, but is not marred by their weaknesses.

During the nine years the composer spent in Weimar (1708-17), he was primarily an organist, and the majority of his organ compositions were written or at least conceived there. This *Second Creative Period* was a typical phase of transition. Bach's output comprised a substantial number of studies and transcriptions, which served him as a means of widening his artistic horizon and of becoming fully conversant with new types of musical expression. But towards the end of this period the composer gained such stylistic perfection that it is often difficult to draw the line, and to determine whether a given organ composition belongs to this phase or to the following period of full maturity.

In Weimar Bach was at first a student of the Italians. In Lüneburg and Arnstadt their works had reached him only in versions transformed and remodelled by German composers. In Weimar he had the chance of making a direct study of their compositions. The effect on Bach was somewhat similar to that which Italian art had exercised on the foremost German painter, Albrecht Dürer. The serene and well-balanced works of the Adriatic peninsula helped the two masters to find themselves. They discarded the excessive harshness and angularity of the North, and replaced it by a plastic clarity and a simple structure. Eventually Bach completely assimilated Italian music, and, by fusing it with his own contrapuntal heritage and the Northern idiom, he created what we now regard as the typical Bach style.

The transcriptions and studies of the Weimar period begin with a number of *Arrangements of Violin Concertos* both for the clavier and for the organ. Apparently Bach was encouraged to do this work by studying similar arrangements which his friend and relative, the organist J. Georg Walther, made at about that time in Weimar. Bach transcribed for the organ one concerto and a separate movement (*P.* VIII/2, 44; *BWV* 592, 595) written by the talented Prince Johann Ernst of Weimar, himself a faithful disciple of the Italians, as well as three concerti by Vivaldi (*P.* VIII/10, 22; the third arrangement is usually printed under the name of Friedemann Bach; *BWV* 593, 594, 596).[1] As a rule Sebastian adheres faithfully to the

[1] Friedemann wrote on the title-page of Sebastian's autograph: 'di W. F. Bach, manu mei patris descript.' (by W. F. Bach, copied by my father). The actual facts were clarified by Max Schneider in *BJ*, 1911.

text of the original composition. He was strongly impressed by the natural grace of the Italian style and fascinated by the results that could be achieved by using Vivaldi's Concerto form in a work for organ solo. These transcriptions also confirmed his conviction that the violin idiom could be employed to good advantage in keyboard compositions. At the same time it is obvious that Bach had no intention of mechanically transferring into his works every note of his model. His new versions strengthen the harmony and introduce—particularly in the middle parts and bass— small rhythmical and contrapuntal details which lend significance to the composition (*Ex.* 46). In the C major Concerto Bach went even further;

Ex 46

The large notes represent Vivaldi's original, the small ones Bach's additions.
In the first measure Bach replaced the ('large) eighth notes of Vivaldi by (small) sixteenth notes.

he made considerable changes in the cadenzas of the first and third movements, and replaced the middle movement by a kind of German toccata.

Another type of work following Italian models may be found in the *Allabreve* (*P.* VIII/72, *BWV* 589) and particularly in the *Canzona* in d (*P.* IV/58, *BWV* 588). These are works reflecting the influence of the great Italian organ master Frescobaldi whose *Fiori Musicali* Bach copied in 1714. Both the principle of thematic variation employed in the *Canzona* and the quiet, dignified and solemn mood of the *Allabreve* are obviously inspired by the Roman composer. The first movement of the well-known *Pastorale* in F (*P.* I/88, *BWV* 590) also belongs to the same category. This piece (probably unfinished, since it begins in F and ends in a), with its long pedal points, its gentle and lyric character, and the 12/8 *Siciliano* rhythm, reflects the spirit that can be found in countless Italian musical descriptions of the Nativity.

In both clavier and organ compositions of this period Bach occasionally used Italian themes. A *Fugue in c* (*P.* IV/40, *BWV* 574) has the title 'Thema Legrenzianum elaboratum ... per J. S. Bach' while his *Fugue in b* (*P.* IV/50, *BWV* 579) makes use of a theme by Corelli.[1] Bach's com-

---

[1] The source of the theme by Legrenzi (1626-1690) has not yet been found; the Corelli arrangement is based on the second movement of the composer's op. III/4.

position is almost three times as long as Corelli's and employs four parts
instead of the three in his model. Nevertheless it is easily understandable
that the simple and plastic theme of the Roman master (*Ex.* 47) fascinated

Ex 47

the young composer. Preoccupation with such music helped Bach to
develop the expressive architecture of his later fugue themes.

As to works which are neither transcriptions nor based on a specific
model, the first results of Bach's study of Italian music may be detected in
a number of compositions which contain Southern and Northern elements
in rather primitive juxtaposition. The *Toccata and Fugue in C* (*P.* III/72,
BWV 564) belongs to this group as it combines the style of the German
toccata with that of the Italian concerto. The middle movement, which
follows the bravura passages of the toccata, contains one of the sweetest
and most poignant cantilenas Bach ever wrote. In this piece the master
obviously had in mind a long-drawn-out violin solo of the kind to be
found as second movement in a concerto.

A number of preludes and toccatas written during the later part of the
Weimar period reveal the process of simplification resulting from Bach's
study of Italian models. The *Dorian Toccata*[1] (*P.* III/30, *BWV* 538), for
instance, no longer shows the abundant contrasts of the North German
type. The whole powerful piece grows out of a simple motive which is
stated in the first half-measure, and elements of which may be found in
almost every one of its measures. The well-planned modulations and Bach's
art of melodic evolution protect the work from any danger of monotony.
Like the preludes, the fugues of this phase are less brilliant but more
solidly built, discarding more and more the running motion of the North
German toccata fugue. Bach likes to augment the variety in these fugues
by introducing into the middle sections new ideas to which he attaches
varying degrees of importance. The energetic *Fugue in c* (*P.* III/55, *BWV*
537), for instance, brings into its development section a chromatically
ascending counter-melody which for a time even displaces the main subject, and only in the final climax does it give way to the original theme.
Similar ternary constructions were used by the mature Bach in the remodelling of many of the Weimar works.[2]

[1] The designation is due to the fact that this composition in d has, according to the
Dorian church mode, no flat in its signature.

[2] Owing to Bach's tendency to rearrange his Weimar works, the autographs, generally
supposed to reflect a composer's intentions in their purest form, have at times to be

Probably the best known of the organ works of the second period is the *Passacaglia in c* (*P. I/76, BWV* 582).[1] Bach found the first half of the theme for this work in the *Trio en Passacaille* by the French organ master, André Raison (1650-1720), and the formal model in similar works by Buxtehude. The idea of using mathematical patterns as a basis for musical construction was also familiar to the Baroque period. In spite of such easily traceable relationships, Bach's work is unique. Its theme, comprising eight measures instead of the traditional four, shows a dignity, strength, and intensity which make it well suited for further treatment. The twenty variations of the set are divided into two groups of ten. Each of these shows in its turn a clear separation into subgroups of five. Even within those subgroups a further organization may be observed. As a rule the first two of the five variations are rhythmically connected, forming a pair, and the same is true of the last two, while the third variation stands alone. Only the fourth subgroup (var. 16-20) presents a slightly different aspect. It appears like a condensed recapitulation of the first ten variations,[2] with the result that the passacaglia as a whole displays the same tripartite construction that can be found within each subgroup. With the majestic ending of No. 20, Bach exhausted all possibilities of the variation form, but instead of concluding, he decided to carry on in a different manner. In the fugue following the passacaglia he employed only the first four measures of the theme, but he adorned Raison's melody with a counterpoint that remains all through the fugue as the subject's faithful companion. As always, Bach drew the strongest possible inspiration from the apparently barren soil of self-imposed restrictions and limitations. What in the hands of a smaller mind might have developed into a sterile mathematical tour de force, was transformed by him into an immortal creation; the technical mastery is as nothing compared to the power and magnificence of Bach's inspiration.

In the field of the organ chorale, Bach's main work of the second period was the so-called *Orgelbüchlein* (Little organ book; *P. V, BWV* 599-644). It seems that he was engaged on this extensive composition

subordinated to a source of less importance, such as a copy made by someone else. In the case of Bach the version that counts most is the one which, according to our knowledge of the master's style, represents the composer's intentions in their most mature form.

[1] The common conception that this work was originally written for a clavier equipped with pedal can no longer be upheld. Cf. Kinsky, 'Pedalklavier oder Orgel bei Bach,' Acta Musicologica, 1936.

[2] No. 16, in its partly harmonic character, is reminiscent of No. 1, while 18 is rhythmically related to 4; the contrasting No. 17 helps to reproduce the three-sectional organization of the first subgroup. Nos. 19, 20 are rhythmically related to the variations of the second subgroup.

during the last years he spent in Weimar, penning it in two versions that differ in parts; but he did not complete it after he had moved to Cöthen.[1] Bach had originally planned this work on a very large scale. It was to comprise 164 chorales, the names of which the composer wrote at the top of the empty pages, arranging them in the order in which they were to be employed during the liturgical year. However, more than two thirds of the sheets remained unused, since Bach discontinued his work after completing 46 arrangements (4 for Advent, 13 for Christmas and New Year, 13 for Holy Week and Easter, and 16 for other events of the church year).

According to the autograph title-page the *Orgelbüchlein* was designed for the 'incipient organist,' who should learn how 'to develop a chorale in sundry ways and at the same time perfect himself in the use of the pedal which is treated here as an obbligato. To the glory of God in the heights, to the instruction of the fellow-man.' At about that time Bach had several gifted pupils, and he was becoming more and more interested in the problem of how to pass on his craft to others. The *Orgelbüchlein* is the earliest in a long row of important educational compositions.

This work is typical of Bach's period of transition. The chorales are presented in a simple and concise way; introductions or interludes are dispensed with; and, as a rule, the soprano offers an unadorned version of the chorale melody, which is supported by the three lower voices with consummate contrapuntal mastery. The same rhythmical pattern is maintained throughout each arrangement; thus Bach obtains a form resembling an individual variation in a chorale partita. This leaning towards the chorale variation is, as we saw, a feature of Bach's early organ works. Another youthful characteristic is the subjectivism in the interpretation of the chorale melodies. Bach often expresses in the three lower parts a fervour and intensity of feeling, of which only the young are capable. On the other hand, the extreme economy of the musical language, so widely different from the inexperienced organist's volubility that perplexed his Arnstadt congregation, and the superb craftsmanship displayed in the strictly polyphonic treatment of the lower voices, show the composer to be close to his period of maturity. With supreme craftsmanship he succeeds within the extremely limited space available, both in presenting the chorale melody and in interpreting the emotional content inherent in the text.

Johann Gotthelf Ziegler, who studied with Bach in Weimar, has re-

---

[1] Rust's theory (*BG*, XXV/2), recently upheld by Gurlitt and Bukofzer, that the *Orgelbüchlein* was mainly a product of the Cöthen period, does not seem convincing to the present writer.

corded a very significant piece of advice given by his master on the performance of chorales: the pupil should not merely concentrate on the melody, but should also express the 'affections' (the emotional content) of the text. The *Orgelbüchlein* clearly illustrates what Bach had in mind. In *O Lamm Gottes* ('O Lamb of God') the succession of 'sighs' (descending appoggiaturas) in the accompanying parts, and the wailing chromatic progressions in *Das alte Jahr vergangen ist* ('The old year is past') both create an atmosphere of poignant sadness, while the running triplets in *In dulci jubilo* and the skipping rhythm in *Mit Fried' und Freud' ich fahr' dahin* ('In peace and joy I go my way') express happy confidence. Perhaps the most deeply stirring of these chorales is *O Mensch, bewein' dein' Sünde gross* ('O man, thy grievous sin bemoan') in which Bach, near the end, inspired by the final words of the text 'In sacrifice miraculous He shed His precious blood for us, upon the cross suspended,' unfolds both the drama of Golgotha and its message of redemption. Particularly striking is a chorale in which at first sight Bach seems to have misinterpreted the text. In *Alle Menschen müssen sterben* ('Every mortal must perish') the dance-like rhythm of the bass produces a serene atmosphere only to be explained by the vision of eternal life evoked near the end of the text: 'There the faithful souls will see God's transcendent majesty.' Following a general trend of his time, Bach sometimes evolves motives out of pictorial references in the text. In *Durch Adam's Fall* ('Old Adam's fall'), the interval of a descending diminished seventh in the bass describes the sinful fall, while an undulating alto voice symbolizes the snake in paradise (*Ex.* 48). Nine of the finest arrangements are treated canonically,

Ex. 48

(*Tenor voice omitted*)

among them five at the interval of an octave and four at that of a fifth. There is a certain symbolism in this technique, most clearly apparent in *In dulci jubilo*, where the canon is inspired by the words 'Trahe me post te' ('Draw me after Thee') in the second verse. Similarly in the chorale *Hilf, Gott, dass mir's geling'* ('Lord, help me to succeed') the imitation of Christ is symbolized through a canon of the fifth. *Dies sind die heil'gen zehn Gebot'* ('These are the holy ten Commandments') belongs to the few chorales in the *Orgelbüchlein* in which the counterpoint to the hymn tune is not freely

invented, but, following the earlier organ chorale tradition, is derived
from the melody of the *cantus firmus*. It is characteristic of the pleasure
Bach takes in numerical symbolization that the motive of the counterpoint appears exactly ten times in its original version.[1]

In his subsequent chorale arrangements Bach no longer used the
method employed in the *Orgelbüchlein*. The subjective song-like treatment of the sacred tune, which is presented in unaugmented notes in the
soprano, may later have seemed too intimate to him. Possibly this was
one of the reasons why he left the work unfinished. His way of giving a
uniform accompaniment to the simple melodies was to be taken up, however, in the romantic *Lied* of the following century.

Of the organ works of Bach's *Third Creative Period* only very few
were written in Cöthen (1717-23). Possibly the best known product of
these years is the *Fantasy and Fugue in g* (*P. II/26, BWV* 542) written
for the visit to Hamburg in 1720. In its whole conception the piece was
well suited to impress old Reinken, one of the chief adjudicators for the
position in which Bach was interested. The Fantasy is a chromatic toccata
somewhat reminiscent of the rhapsodic North German style. The fugue
has a long-drawn-out and gay theme closely related to an old Dutch folksong and at the same time to a piece by Reinken himself (*Hortus Musicus*,
Sonata V). In spite of its great dimensions the work is well organized and
clearly proportioned. In its happy and powerful character it voices the
feelings of the genius in his early manhood. Old Reinken may have
blinked when confronted with the cascades of pedal passages, or the
sequence of more than 30 chords in inversion, presented in a tornado of
sixteenth notes. Another composition which Bach may have written or
revised for his Hamburg visit is his five-part arrangement with double
pedal of *An Wasserflüssen Babylons* ('By the waters of Babylon'; *P. VI/
12a, BWV* 653b). Its rich colouristic treatment and the brilliant double-
pedal technique show Bach as a follower of North German masters,
particularly Buxtehude. The same hymn tune was used by Bach for his
famous improvisation which impressed Reinken so deeply.

[1] Schweitzer is mistaken when he points out (*l.c.*, 453) that the first section of the
melody occurs 10 times in the pedal. Actually it appears there only 3 times. However,
this melody-fragment is used 10 times (on tonic, subdominant, and dominant) in the 3
lower voices accompanying the chorale melody. In each repetition the intervals of the
first statement are carefully preserved. Only the very last statement in the pedal bass is
slightly changed so as to produce the final cadence.

A third product of this period is the *Fugue in d* (*P*. III/42, *BWV* 539) based on the master's own fugue in g for solo violin.[1] Although the style of the model is completely idiomatic and displays the deepest insight into the possibilities of the violin, Bach preserved the bulk of the original composition, making only such additions as were necessary to transform the work into an organ fugue. To this end, the harmonic and polyphonic texture is intensified (*Ex.* 49), there are new entrances of the theme, a bass

The large notes in the upper line are also to be found in the violin version (there they are a fourth higher,
The small notes in the lower line are additions of the organ arrangement.

part is supplemented, and mock imitations of the original are replaced by real imitations. The result is a piece written almost as well for the organ as the model was for the violin.

These few works conceived in Cöthen already give a good idea of the artistic goal that Bach was to pursue in the great organ works written (or finished) in Leipzig. He aimed at cohesion and unification within each work, even though its dimensions were increased; he strove for greater technical proficiency, particularly in the use of polyphonic devices; and he tried to enrich the organ's idiom by the introduction of elements from other fields of music. Each of these features can occasionally be found in Bach's earlier works. What is new, however, is the intensity and the prodigious success with which the composer applied them in his Leipzig years.

Such tendencies are clearly revealed in the *Toccata in F* (*P*. III/16, *BWV* 540) which precedes an earlier fugue in the same key. In this composition the fantastic and improvisatory character of former toccatas is completely discarded. There is an introductory section over an organ point followed by a long-drawn-out pedal solo; the whole section is then restated, and transposed to the dominant, thus bringing the exposition to an end. The following section, a sort of development, clearly consists of four corresponding subdivisions. A third part, resembling a restatement of the first section, leads to another pedal point supporting a figuration in which the ascending motive of the beginning is inverted. In spite of its gigantic dimensions—the piece has more than 400 measures—the disposition of the material is unusually lucid. The work is a miracle of logical and well-balanced construction.

[1] The fugue also exists in a version for lute (*BWV* 1000).

How important it was at that time for Bach to round off his musical forms can be shown by the *Prelude in C* (*P.* II/2, *BWV* 545) which also exists in an earlier version. In the final arrangement Bach added a little introduction of 3 measures which he repeated at the end of the work, thus producing a ternary form.

Three-part construction is also to be found in the fugues of the Leipzig period, and this to an even greater extent by far than in the Weimar works. One of the best known compositions of the Thomas Cantor is the *Fugue in e* (*P.* II/64, *BWV* 548), named in the English-speaking countries 'the wedge,' since its theme, containing one ascending and one descending line, gradually widens from the interval of a third to an octave. This composition, conceived on a very large scale, exhibits in the middle a free toccata section of more than 100 measures, after which the first part is restated without modification.

The influence of other forms is often noticeable in the Leipzig organ works. In the stirring *Prelude in b* (*P.* II/78, *BWV* 544) the melodic lead is given to the upper part, while middle voices and bass all participate in the imitations. This prelude shows melodic features of an aria in which elements of the main tune are taken up in a fugue-like manner by the lower parts. The introduction of foreign elements into organ music is particularly obvious in the 6 *Sonatas or Trios* (*P.* I, *BWV* 525-30) which Bach wrote after 1727 (or possibly after 1723) mainly for the instruction of his son Friedemann. It is not quite certain whether he had the organ or a pedal clavier with 2 manuals primarily in mind for these compositions, since the title 'for two claviers and pedal' is ambiguous. These sonatas undoubtedly make excellent exercises for developing the complete independence of the organist's hands and feet. At the same time the lack of a truly idiomatic organ style can hardly be overlooked. The thematic elaboration is that of the trio sonata for one or two solo instruments with basso continuo; the three parts of the trio sonata are never augmented or reduced, and the model of the concerto plays a large part in the formal construction. Bach himself used the adagio of the third sonata as a slow movement for his Concerto in a for flute, violin, and harpsichord, and the first movement of the fourth sonata can be found scored for oboe d'amore, viola da gamba, and continuo in his Cantata No. 76. In either case the composer employed two melody instruments and continuo for the interpretation of his ideas. More recently, the trios have been edited by R. Todt in a version for violin, viola, and clavier,[1] and it is debatable

---

[1] Naumann and David arranged them for violin and piano, thus imitating Bach's procedure in his trios for violin and clavier or viola da gamba and clavier.

whether such arrangements are not better suited to revealing the intricate beauties of these superb works than Bach's own setting for the organ.

Bach's earliest organ work to appear in print was published in 1739 under the title 'Third part of the *Clavier Übung* (keyboard exercise), consisting of sundry preludes on the catechism and other hymns for the organ written for the enjoyment of amateurs and in particular for the connoisseurs of such work.' The collection begins with a *Prelude in E flat* (P. III/2; *BWV* 552) which is obviously connected with the so-called *St. Anne* or *Trinity Fugue* printed in the same volume as its last number. Although twenty-one organ chorales separate the two movements, they are linked together by the symbolic emphasis on the number three, employed as a reference to the Holy Trinity. Both the prelude and the fugue require *three* flats, and each consists of *three* main sections and uses *three* themes.[1] In between the two powerful tuttis of the beginning and the end, the prelude introduces two different subjects which are presented alternately with the main idea. In the fugue, one of the most dazzling works of the kind Bach ever wrote, thematic variation plays a big role. Each of the three sections in this movement has a subject of its own, but the second and third sections employ in addition a rhythmic alteration of the first theme in contrapuntal combination with their own ideas. Perhaps the clearest expression of the symbolic meaning in the 'Trinity fugue' can be found in the three versions of the same main theme used here.

The collection of chorale preludes contained in the *Clavier Übung* (P. III, V-VII; *BWV* 669-89) supplements, in a way, the earlier one of the *Orgelbüchlein*. Whereas the Weimar preludes deal only with chorales for the different holy days of the church year, the *Clavier Übung* contains arrangements of German hymns corresponding to sections of the *Ordinarium Missae*. The hymns are presented in an order similar to that of the Lutheran catechism, and as Luther compiled two versions of the catechism for adults and children respectively, so Bach wrote every chorale in a more elaborate form for 'connoisseurs' and in a simplified version without pedal for 'amateurs.' There are preludes on the German *Kyrie*, *Gloria*, *Credo*, and *Pater noster*, followed by the hymns for Baptism, the Confession of Sins, and Communion. In most of the smaller and simpler arrangements without pedal, Bach's starting point is the traditional form of a fughetta, based on the beginning of the chorale melody in its original

[1] Although Forkel, Griepenkerl, Spitta and others sensed a relation between the two movements, the similarity in construction is often overlooked. Grace (*l.c.*, p. 226) even flatly denies 'any alliance in spirit or form.'

or in an ornamented form. Several organ preludes are also built on the complete hymn tune used as a *cantus firmus* and accompanied by counter-melodies. These long-established patterns are employed, however, in a manner clearly revealing Bach's full maturity. There is a significance in these preludes, a conception on a large scale, an art of welding the different sections into a homogeneous unity, and a supreme mastery of the contra-puntal style, that marks them as products of his third period. Again the composer is constantly attempting to incorporate seemingly unrelated stylistic elements into the body of his organ music, thus creating new artistic conceptions. The ornamentation of the tune in the fughetta *Wir glauben all'* ('We believe all'; *P.* VII/81, *BWV* 681), for instance, gives it the character of a French overture. The most significant among the *cantus firmus* arrangements for the manual only is *Allein Gott in der Höh'* ('To God on high alone'; *P.* VI/10, *BWV* 675), in which a kind of two-part invention surrounds the chorale melody (*Ex.* 50). In the great arrange-

Ex 50

ment with pedal of *Vater unser im Himmelreich* ('Our Father in Heaven'; *P.* VII/52, *BWV* 682), the hymn tune is introduced as a canon between soprano and alto. A complete trio sonata, with its typical bass and imita-tions between the upper parts, is added to this strict form, thus producing a five-part composition. The work presents almost insurmountable diffi-culties to the organist who attempts to keep the two basic elements of the piece distinctly audible, since he has to play one part of the trio sonata as well as one part of the *cantus firmus* with each hand. At the same time it makes the widest possible use of all the colouristic resources of the instru-ment. In the version with pedal of *Dies sind die heil'gen zehn Gebot'* ('These are the holy ten Commandments'; *P.* VI/50, *BWV* 678) Bach simplifies the technical problem by entrusting to the organist's right hand the upper parts of the trio sonata and to his left the strict canon of the *cantus firmus* voices. The symbolic exegesis in this prelude is not confined to the sub-division of the trio sonata into ten sections; the prelude has a definite two-part form by way of reference to the two tablets on which the commandments were inscribed. Moreover, the use of the canon form in this as well as in the preceding prelude may be intended to symbolize the observation of God's law. The highly intricate six-part arrangement of

Aus tiefer Not ('In my despair'; *P*. VI/36, *BWV* 686) is inspired by the models of Scheidt and of early North German composers. The style of the work is strictly polyphonic, introducing different types of diminution and strettos; at the same time the gradual increase in rhythmic motion gives the prelude a magnificently urgent character. The rigid contrapuntal laws supply, as they so often did, the best foundation for Bach to express intense emotion.[1]

The organ works of Bach's *Last Period* are particularly characteristic of the old master's state of mind. More and more his thoughts dwelt on bygone eras and on the future, while the links with his own time became loosened. The *Eighteen Chorales of various types to be performed on an organ with two manuals and pedal* were written down between 1747 and 1750. The composer probably meant to publish them, but was prevented by death from doing so. The majority of these preludes are works of the Weimar period which Bach revised in Leipzig, and only a few were conceived during the last years of the composer's life. The 'Eighteen Chorales' are characterized by a predilection for melodic ornamentation and the absence of canonic forms. In contrast to the two earlier collections, no liturgical plan can be detected in the selection of the chorales. Bach's intentions seem to have been primarily of an educational and artistic character. Particularly striking is *Jesus Christus unser Heiland* ('Jesus Christ our Saviour'; *P*. VI/87, *BWV* 665), where the various counterpoints to the individual lines of the chorale are fused together by the employment of the same gently flowing Allemande rhythm. *Schmücke dich, o liebe Seele* ('Deck thyself, bright soul'; *P*. VII/50, *BWV* 654) uses, as a companion to the *cantus firmus*, a poignant Sarabande melody developed from the first two lines of the hymn tune. The 'state of bliss' expressed in this chorale deeply moved such romantic artists as Mendelssohn and Schumann.

In all these arrangements, the use of dance and variation forms points

---

[1] Four duets (*BWV* 802-5) which appear near the end of the third part of the *Clavier Übung* have greatly puzzled research students. Owing to their invention-like character and the absence of a pedal part, Spitta and Schweitzer considered them to be clavier music which had been inserted by mistake, and in 1952 Ralph Kirkpatrick recorded them as harpsichord pieces. It seems far more likely, however, that these are organ compositions too. Neither the style of the music nor the absence of pedal parts furnishes conclusive evidence that Bach erroneously included them into a collection of organ music. In support of this, Klaus Ehricht recently proved (*BJ*, 1949-50) that there is a thematic relation between the duets and some of the smaller chorale arrangements without pedal.

to the artistic inspiration Bach received in his youth from the works of Buxtehude and Böhm. This is equally true of the 'Canonic Variations on the Christmas hymn *Vom Himmel hoch da komm' ich her*' (*P*. V/92, *BWV* 769) which were written on the occasion of Bach's joining the Mizler Sozietät, and were printed around 1748. Here he once more adopts the partita form, this time to display his superb skill in the solution of contrapuntal problems. Throughout the work the polyphonic texture grows more and more intricate. Bach begins with a canon at the octave, followed by a canon at the fifth and the seventh. The fourth variation introduces a canon of the augmentation, the fifth, and last, canons of the inversion, successively at the intervals of the sixth, third, second and ninth. The final stretto actually presents all four lines of the melody simultaneously. In spite of this forbidding display of consummate learning, the canonic variations are basically a piece of lyric music impregnated with the spirit of Christmas. The same attitude can be found in Bach's very last composition, the short organ chorale *Vor deinen Thron tret' ich hiemit* ('Before Thy throne I step, O Lord'; *P*. VII/74, *BWV* 668) to the tune *Wenn wir in höchsten Nöten seyn*, printed, together with the Art of the Fugue, soon after the master's death. Here Bach uses a succession of expositions, in each case skilfully combining the melodies with their own inversions. He had also dealt with this same chorale in a richly ornamented arrangement in his *Orgelbüchlein*. Now, however, the artist, preparing himself to face his Maker, does away with all unnecessary melismata and presents the unadorned melody, surrounded only by the products of his polyphonic fantasy.

It is remarkable that the ageing Bach showed following generations the way to write organ music on a purely homophonic basis too. Between 1747 and 1750 he had a collection of 6 chorales published by his pupil, Georg Schübler. The tendency of the mature composer to introduce stylistic elements from other fields of music reached its peak in this collection. With a single exception (the model of which may have been lost) all the organ chorales are literally transcribed from movements in Bach's cantatas.[1] Polyphonic treatment is almost completely abandoned here. The *cantus firmus* is escorted by broadly flowing melodies of a songlike character which have but a loose melodic connection with the chorale tune. In the famous *Wachet auf, ruft uns die Stimme* ('Wake ye maids, hark, strikes the hour'; *P*. VII/72, *BWV* 645), Bach writes a heartfelt, purely lyric and monodic tune (expressing the procession of the maidens

[1] The 6 Schübler Chorales are printed as *P*. VII/72, 84, 76, 33; VI/4; VII/16 (*BWV* 645-50). Their models are to be found in cantatas No. 140, ?, 93, 10, 6, 137.

to meet the heavenly groom) that has little melodic relation to the tune of Nicolai's hymn with which it is interwoven. The 'Schübler Chorales' were widely imitated by Bach's pupils and became models for organ chorale composition in the second half of the century. Thus the old composer not only brought the ancient craft of polyphony to a climax, but at the same time heralded future developments of his art.

III
WORKS FOR THE CLAVIER SOLO

The term 'clavier' (from Latin *clavis*, a key) was used in Bach's time to indicate any instrument with a keyboard. The first, second, and fourth parts of Bach's *Clavier Übung* (keyboard exercise) for instance, contain works for stringed keyboard instruments, while the third part is for organ. Similarly, works for the organ are often inscribed as compositions for 'two claviers and a pedal.'

However, the employment of the term in this wider sense was not very common. As a rule, 'clavier' denotes one of three main types of stringed keyboard instruments known to musicians in the Baroque period:

(1) a harpsichord (Italian, *cembalo*; French, *clavecin*) furnished with one or two manuals, different register stops and several sets of strings, plucked by pieces of quill or leather;

(2) a spinet or virginal, with a single manual, no register stops and one set of strings, plucked by pieces of quill or leather;

(3) a clavichord, with a single manual, no register stops, and only one set of strings, struck by thin metal tangents.

The pianoforte, although in existence before the middle of the century and known to Bach, was probably used only in his 'Musical Offering.'

In a few isolated cases such as the 'Goldberg Variations' or the 'Italian Concerto,' Bach expressed a wish that a harpsichord should be used. But as a rule he did not indicate any preference, and only from an analysis of each particular composition can it be conjectured whether the harpsichord, with its crisp tone and its capacity for undergoing sudden changes in colour and strength, the spinet, with its brilliant, yet unbending sound, or the clavichord, with its more flexible, though extremely soft tone, is best suited. Pieces without rests, for example, would not allow a harpsichord player to change his register stops, which in Bach's time were always operated by hand. On the other hand, the need for dynamic changes, particularly in compositions in concerto form, with its contrasts between solo and tutti, could be satisfied only on this instrument; while melodic lines of a singing character would be best interpreted on a clavichord.

In the second half of the 18th century the meaning of 'clavier' was gradually narrowed down to clavichord. This accounts for the faulty translation of *Das wohltemperierte Clavier* widely used in the English-speaking countries. The English title of 'Well-Tempered Clavichord' would imply that Bach had only a single instrument in mind for his work, whereas the composer did not in fact indicate any such preference.[1]

In the absence of more specific evidence it must be assumed that during Bach's lifetime the term 'clavier' could mean any stringed keyboard instrument, and it is in this general sense that the expression will be used in the present chapter.

The majority of Bach's works for the clavier were products of his period of maturity. Bach himself must have thought highly of them, since among the few compositions he had printed, clavier works took up the greatest space. To the generations that followed him, he was primarily a master of clavier composition, while the great vocal works and the chamber and orchestral music were only rediscovered during the 19th century.

The clavier works from Bach's *First Period of Composition* were primarily dependent on models provided by masters from Central and Southern Germany. North German influences, which were of such importance for Bach as an organ composer, are far less in evidence here. A *Fugue in e* (*BWV* 945), obviously one of the composer's earliest works, attempts to imitate Pachelbel. It is an awkward composition, completely lacking in modulations, and written against the clavier rather than for it. A *Sonata in D* (*BWV* 963) is still under the influence of the great Johann Kuhnau, who was the first to write sonatas in several movements for the clavier. The last movement has the heading *Thema all' Imitatio Gallina Cucca*. Translated from the faulty wording of the old manuscript[2] the title reads: 'Theme imitating hen and cuckoo,' and these two birds can in fact be heard merrily raising their voices all through the movement (*Ex.* 51). The Austrian Poglietti's *Henner- und Hannergeschrey*

---

[1] Forkel's statement that Bach liked best to play upon the clavichord need not be taken literally. Forkel received much information from Emanuel Bach, the foremost exponent of clavichord playing. It is not impossible that the Hamburg composer attributed to his father an attitude which was basically his own. Equally unconvincing is the attempt of Hans Brandts-Buys to prove that the Well-Tempered Clavier was written for the organ.

[2] The composer probably meant: *Tema all'imitazione della gallina e del cuculo.*

(cries of hens and roosters) and the notes of the cuckoo in works by the Bavarian Kerll may have acted as godfathers to this gay composition.

Ex 51

Also pointing to South German sources is the name *Capriccio* which Bach gave to a kind of toccata-fugue in E (*BWV* 993) with the interesting inscription: *In honorem Joh. Christoph Bachii, Ohrdruf.* While the work dedicated to Sebastian's eldest brother and teacher is rather insignificant, inspiration flowed much more freely when the young composer wrote a clavier piece for another member of the family. It is the humorous *Capriccio sopra la lontananza del suo fratello dilettissimo* ('Capriccio on the departure of his most beloved brother'; *BWV* 992) written in 1704, when Johann Jakob Bach decided to join the army of Charles XII, King of Sweden. This delightful work is a jocose interpretation of devices introduced four years before by Kuhnau in his 'Biblical Sonatas.' The technique which the earlier master had applied to the description of incidents from the Old Testament was employed by young Sebastian to depict some tender and amusing domestic scenes. Each of the six movements has a 'programmatic' heading, partly in German, partly in Italian: '(1) Arioso. Adagio, represents the coaxing of the friends to prevent his journey. (2) [Andante], outlines various accidents that may happen to him in foreign lands. (3) Adagissimo, is a general lament of friends. (4) Here the friends, seeing that it cannot be otherwise, come to take leave. (5) Aria of the postilion. Adagio poco. (6) Fugue, imitating the sound of the posthorn.' The most variegated devices are used to convey the different emotions. The 'coaxing' of the friends is described with the help of a wide array of cajoling French ornaments. For the description of the dangers that might befall the traveller in foreign lands, modulations into distant keys are selected. The 'general lament' introduces the chromatically descending bass figure which for Baroque composers is the typical vehicle for the expression of supreme grief. (Purcell uses it in the death song of Dido, and Bach himself does likewise in the *Crucifixus* of the B minor Mass.) Here the composer temporarily relinquishes the clavier style proper; the 'lament' appears like a solo for a melody instrument and figured bass, to which the performer has to add filling parts not contained in the manu-

script. The 'Aria of the postilion' uses the gay octave jump which was
produced by the tiny posthorns of the 18th century. This simple motive
and a second more elaborate horn-call return in the double fugue of the
finale with the beginning (*Ex.* 52). In its lively mood, its effortless flow

of ideas and clever utilization of sound effects characteristic of the clavier,
this is one of the most attractive compositions of the young Bach. The
charming spirit of light merriment present in the whole 'Capriccio' was
but rarely recaptured in Bach's later clavier works.

In Bach's *Second Period* we notice a more systematic application to
the solution of specific clavieristic problems. The arranging of violin
concertos now became the focal point of his efforts both for the organ
and the clavier. The acquaintance with such works, in particular those
of young Vivaldi, proved an experience that was to shape decisively
his whole creative output (cf. p. 246).

The exact number of Bach's arrangements of Vivaldi's violin concertos is not yet known. The 42nd volume of the Bach Gesellschaft, issued
in 1894, contains '16 concertos after Vivaldi' (*BWV* 972-87). It has
been proved, primarily by Arnold Schering, that of these works three
(Nos. 11, 13,[1] and 16) were based on concertos by Duke Johann Ernst of
Weimar, one (No. 14) on a violin concerto by Telemann, and one (No. 3)
on the oboe concerto by Marcello.[2] Of the remainder, six (Nos. 1, 2, 4, 5, 7,
9) have been ascertained to be works by Vivaldi. The sources for the other
concertos have not yet been found, but it seems likely that there are some
more compositions by Vivaldi, Marcello and Telemann among them.[3]

Bach did not mechanically transfer the string parts to the keyboard
instrument. Wherever it seemed necessary, he gave greater flexibility to
the bass line, filled the middle parts, enriched the polyphonic texture, and

---

[1] The first movement of the Concerto No. 13 was also arranged by Bach for the organ.
[2] This concerto, too, is occasionally attributed to Vivaldi.
[3] Cf. Szabolcsi Bence, 'Europai virradat,' Budapest, 1949.

ornamented the melodic lines, in order to adapt the sustained tone of strings to the transient sound of the clavier (*Ex.* 53). These arrangements

Ex 53

were primarily made by Bach for his own artistic development. They satisfied his zest for experimenting, but they also served the purpose of supplying good clavier music for his own performances.[1]

Bach's own compositions reveal the strong interest which he took during his Weimar years in music of the Apennine peninsula. One result of his preoccupation with that country's string music is the *Aria variata alla maniera italiana* (*BWV* 989). It appears like a duet between violin and 'cello, and occasionally direct allusions to Bach's concerto arrangements can be noticed. The variation technique, too, is of the Italian type, ornamenting and transforming the melodic line of the tuneful air in a rather superficial manner, contrary to that of Bach's later variations which was much more intricate.[2] The magnificent *Prelude and Fugue in a* (*BWV* 894) are constructed like the first movement and finale of a concerto. These two movements show such perfection that it becomes understandable why Bach at a later date reversed his ordinary procedure and

---

[1] In addition, Bach made clavier adaptations of two sonatas and a fugue for two violins, viola da gamba and bass taken from Johann Adams Reinken's 'Hortus Musicus' (*BWV* 965-66), and of an organ fugue of the Freiberg organist J. C. Erselius (*BWV* 955). In these cases he gave more to his sources than he received, since he transformed and enriched the original compositions considerably.

[2] In the same category belongs the so-called *Toccata in G* (*BWV* 916) in the form of an Italian *sinfonia*. Its first movement sounds like one of Bach's clavier arrangements of a Vivaldi concerto. It consists mainly of a tutti which is repeated several times in various keys, with modulating solo episodes connecting the different entrances. The fugal finale which follows after a slow middle section also displays the bright and cheerful mood of a concerto. Four other *Toccatas* (*BWV* 912-15) are somewhat similar in character.

orchestrated the clavier work, transforming it with consummate skill into a real concerto for flute, violin, clavier and strings (*BWV* 1044). At the same time the composer added a middle movement which he borrowed from the third of his organ sonatas. Two *Fugues in A and b* (*BWV* 950-951) based on trio sonatas for two violins, 'cello and keyboard instrument by Tommaso Albinoni (1674-1745) would seem to belong to the master's arrangements. Actually Bach changed so much and preserved so little that it appears justifiable to consider them as independent works inspired by Italian models. Bach was particularly impressed by the plastic themes of the Italian composer,[1] but their elaboration could not satisfy him. As a matter of fact, the fugue in b exists in two versions: one fairly close to the Italian work, and another from a later period which is almost three times as long; it exhausts the contrapuntal possibilities of the theme to an extent of which its original composer had never been aware, and it imbues the fugue with an intensity of feeling quite different from the calm serenity of Albinoni's music.

In certain clavier compositions written during the last Weimar years (or possibly at Cöthen) a complete sublimation of the Italian influence is in evidence. These superbly proportioned pieces, beautifully worked out in every detail, could not possibly have been written if Sebastian had not gone through a period of the most intense study of Southern art; but there is no direct reference to Italian sources and it almost seems as if Bach were retracing his steps. In the *Toccatas in f sharp and c* (*BWV* 910-11) the different sections no longer show the separation into four movements of the Italian church sonata. They follow each other without interruption and, to make the connection even closer, in the Toccata in f sharp Bach evolves the subject of the end fugue out of the theme of the slow section (*Ex.* 54). The composer returns here to the traditional one-piece toccata

Ex 54

of Georg Muffat and the variation technique of Froberger, imbuing them with his own striving towards unity and cohesion of parts.—A work that in its rhapsodic spirit belongs to an earlier phase, although it probably

----

[1] Compare the use of themes by Legrenzi and Corelli in Bach's organ works of the period (p. 247).

received its final form in Cöthen, is the *Chromatic Fantasy and Fugue* (*BWV* 903). In spite of its emotional intensity the Fantasy has a logical construction, being clearly divided into three sections. The fugue, with a theme based on chromatic progressions, is mainly responsible for the epithet given to the whole work. It starts in strict contrapuntal style but gradually loosens up as the composition progresses. The majestic ending, with its organ-point and the powerful harmonization of the theme, confirms the character of grandeur which prevails in this dramatic composition. One would like to think that it was with a work of this type that Bach won his laurels when he regaled the spellbound Dresden audience after Marchand had evaded the contest with his German rival.[1]

The mature Bach was by inclination and vocation a teacher. Unlike the majority of great composers, he considered instructing others not a tedious chore but a stimulating experience. Keyboard instruments were particularly well suited for teaching purposes, and Bach wrote a great number of works that are primarily intended as technical studies, but which developed under the hands of the master into creations of supreme beauty as well as craftsmanship. They are by no means études written for his personal pupils only, but collections devised on the largest possible scale and intended for all students and music-lovers alike.

The title-page of the *Orgelbüchlein* (cf. p. 250) by its reference to the 'beginning organist' and the 'instruction of the fellow musician' clearly reveals its pedagogical purpose. This purpose is just as obvious in a document of a different nature started in 1720 for Sebastian's eldest son, Friedemann, then 9½ years old. This *Clavierbüchlein*[2] ('Little clavier book'), partly written by Bach and partly under his supervision, contains a progressive manual, starting with an explanation of clefs and ornaments, and leading the pupil from the simplest to the more advanced pieces. In an *Applicatio* (*BWV* 994) at the beginning of the *Clavierbüchlein*, a short composition is completely fingered by the composer himself, showing Sebastian's bold innovation in the use of the thumb (which had hitherto hardly been employed on the clavier), but also his liking for the old-

---

[1] The first notes of the fugue theme are, according to the German designation, A-B-H-C. These letters make up the name of the composer, although in a different order. It is well known that Bach intended to use the letters of his name in the unfinished fugue of his Art of the Fugue.

[2] The original manuscript is the property of Yale University, New Haven, Conn.

fashioned method of passing the third over the fourth finger (*Ex.* 55).
Other compositions likewise fingered by the master (*BG*, 36/126 and 224,

Ex. 55

225) reveal a similar attitude. Bach systematically combined traditional
and new devices, relinquishing little that came to him from the past, but
lifting it nearer to perfection.

The *Clavierbüchlein* contains nine easy preludes (*BWV* 924-32),
which were not meant as introductions to fugues but as independent
musical vignettes, valuable both as preparatory studies and for the enjoyment they provided for the young pupil.[1] Of greater importance are the
fifteen *Praeambula* and fourteen *Fantasias* in the manual, which we now
know as the 'Two-part Inventions' and the 'Sinfonie' (Three-part inventions; *BWV* 772-801). Bach must have used these compositions a great
deal, since they also exist in two other autographs, the later of which
bears the following interesting inscription:

> Honest guide, by which lovers of the clavier, and particularly those desirous of learning,
> are shown a plain way not only to play neatly in two parts, but also, as they progress, to
> treat three obbligato parts correctly and well, and at the same time to acquire good ideas
> and properly to elaborate them, and most of all to learn a singing style of playing, and
> simultaneously to obtain a strong foretaste of composition. Executed by Joh. Seb. Bach,
> capellmeister of the Prince of Anhalt-Cöthen, Anno Christi, 1723.

The title once more announces the educational purpose. These works
are meant as studies for the performer and for the budding composer as
well. The reference to the singing style of playing seems to indicate that
for the execution of these studies Bach intended the clavichord to be
used, on which modulations of the tone-quality are possible. The manuscript begins with a revised version of the *Praeambula* (now called inventions) and presents them in order of ascending keys—C, c, D, d, E flat, E, e,
F, f, G, g, A, a, B flat, b—omitting only the less common ones. Next follow
the *Fantasias* in their definite form. There are now fifteen of them in the
same keys and presented in the same order as the inventions. Their new
name is *Sinfonie*. It is easy to trace the models which Bach followed in

---

[1] A collection of Bach's 6 preludes of a similar nature is inscribed in an old manuscript *A l'usage des commençants*.

writing these compositions. The two-part inventions are fashioned after preludes by Johann Kuhnau and J. Kaspar Ferdinand Fischer. Bach found the unusual name in Bonporti's *Invenzioni* for violin and bass, compositions which interested him so much that he copied four of them (*BWV*, Anh. 173-76). The *Sinfonie* (now usually referred to as three-part inventions) are based on Kuhnau's attempt to transplant the Italian trio sonata to the clavier, but what Bach creates out of these elements is nevertheless entirely new. No other composer had ever considered imbuing clavier compositions of such small dimensions with a content of similar significance. There are studies in independent part writing using all the devices of fugue and canon, double and triple counterpoint, but without strict adherence to any of them. Bach offers fantasias in the realm of polyphony, freely blending all known techniques, and creating forms which are held together by the logic, and the iron consistency, of his musical thought. An analysis of the very first of the two-part inventions for instance shows that the simple initial idea (*Ex.* 56a) together with its inversion (*Ex.* 56b) dominate the whole composition. Apart from the

cadences, there is not one measure that does not contain either or both of them. The invention is divided into five sections (b. 1-6, 7-10, 11-14, 15-18, 19-22) which are of approximately the same length, and there is a marked relationship between the first and last section, as well as between the second and fourth.

Similar instances of perfect musical architecture may be found in many of these 30 microcosms. As always in Bach's work, technical perfection is combined with the strongest emotional intensity. In the three-part invention in f, for instance, the intricate polyphonic interpretation of the three subjects and the magnificent formal construction are employed in an atmosphere of sinister pathos, the dramatic power of which Bach himself has hardly ever surpassed. Like some of the short clavier compositions of the Romantic period, the two- and three-part inventions could be presented in groups. The second autograph of the work shows each two-part invention followed by a three-part invention in the same key. There is a definite inner relation between the members of the resulting pairs (particularly obvious in the two- and three-part inventions in C, E, and A respectively); yet the performance of the work in the order of the last autograph is equally successful.

Eleven preludes from the *Clavierbüchlein* written for Friedemann Bach were used in revised and enlarged form for a third and particularly significant composition. This work, finished in 1722, has the title:

The Well-Tempered Clavier, or preludes and fugues in all the tones and semitones, both with the major third or 'Ut, Re, Mi' and with the minor third or 'Re, Mi, Fa.' For the use and profit of young musicians who are anxious to learn, as well as for the amusement of those who are already expert in the art.

The 24 preludes and fugues of the *Well-Tempered Clavier* (*BWV* 846-869), one for each major and minor key, were so successful that in Leipzig Bach compiled a second collection of 'Twenty-four New Preludes and Fugues'[1] (*BWV* 870-93) which was completed between 1740 and 1744. These forty-eight pairs have since become the basic material of the literature for keyboard instruments, and it is on them that Bach's fame as the greatest master of fugue composition largely rests.

The unusual name that he chose for the first collection was inspired by a most important innovation made at the end of the 17th century. Andreas Werckmeister, a German organist, published in 1691 a treatise entitled 'Musical Temperament or . . . mathematical instruction how to produce . . . a well-tempered intonation on the clavier.' In this work the author demands the use of 'equal temperament' for all keyboard instruments. The 'pure' or mathematical intonation which was the basis of the older systems had the disadvantage that it contained half-tones of different sizes. The possibilities of modulation were therefore very limited, and keys with many sharps or flats could not be used. In Werckmeister's 'equal temperament,' on the other hand, the octave was artificially divided into twelve half-tones which were exactly alike. Each of them could therefore take the place of the tonic and there was no limitation to the use of modulations. German musicians were quick to explore the potentialities of the new system. J. P. Treiber published, in 1702 and 1704, two compositions which, according to his claim, employ 'all the keys and chords.' Of great importance for Bach's work was Fischer's *Ariadne Musica . . . per XX Praeludia, totidem Fugas* (1710?) in which the composer, with the aid of the 'Ariadne thread' of modulation, leads his hearers through the labyrinth of the keys. In 1719 Mattheson presented in his *Organistenprobe* '24 easy and as many somewhat more difficult examples in all the keys,' and in 1722, the year of the Well-Tempered Clavier, Friedrich Suppig, an

---

[1] This title is quoted by Marpurg. The autograph in the British Museum does not have a title. Its designation as second part of the Well-Tempered Clavier apparently originated after the composer's death.

organist in Dresden, wrote *Labyrinthus Musicus*, a 'fantasy through all the keys, 12 major and 12 minor.'[1]

Sebastian's work in this field is not only greater than that of any of his predecessors, but it explores all the possibilities of the 'well-tempered' system with a thoroughness that none of the other composers had attempted. Bach realized that in 'equal temperament' lay the seeds of a revolution in the traditional clavier fugue. It was no longer necessary permanently to introduce new subjects or counter-subjects, or to employ variations of the fugal theme. These earlier features, which tended to give the fugue a certain patchwork character, could be dispensed with if modulation were systematically employed. Loosely built fugues with a certain amount of modulation had often been used in both chamber and orchestral music. In Bach's work they are transferred to the clavier, and take on the greater solidity of texture peculiar to keyboard music. Entries of the main theme solidly establish each key, while the connecting episodes provide the necessary modulations. Since the material of the episodes is derived from the main theme or the counterpoint which escorts it, the uniformity of the musical substance is complete within each fugue. As a rule full cadences or general rests are avoided; the different sections are carefully interlinked in order to increase the feeling of absolute oneness which the hearer receives from these works.

The prevailing tendency towards unification by no means prevents the existence of tremendous differences between the individual compositions. No two preludes or fugues resemble each other in mood; each of them represents a particular frame of mind. There is a similar variety in the formal construction and the technical devices used in this work. We find fugues not only with three and four voices, but also with two and five. Next to fugues of the highest polyphonic intricacy, like No. 8, the Well-Tempered Clavier contains fugues as loosely constructed as No. 10, the two parts of which are carried on for several measures in simple parallel octaves. Old-fashioned fugues of Froberger's *ricercar* type (No. 4) alternate with highly progressive fugues introducing chromatic and modulating themes (Nos. 12 and 24). And, of course, all kinds of transitional forms can be detected between such extremes. Even greater contrasts can be found in the different types of preludes. There are preludes imitating lute improvisations (No. 1), those of the étude type (No. 5), some resembling two-part and three-part inventions (Nos. 11 and 19) and

---

[1] Bernhard Christian Weber's Well-Tempered Clavier with the forged date 1689 was not a model for Bach's work, but merely a later imitation of it, probably written around 1750.

preludes imitating the slow movement of a church sonata (Nos. 8 and 22).
Bach's tendency to enrich his compositions through the transfer of forms
originating in other types of music is particularly noticeable here. The
relation between preludes and fugues also shows a great amount of variety.
In general the first volume of the Well-Tempered Clavier displays a
firm coherence between the two members of each group, and the preludes
effectively prepare for the following more strictly polyphonic composition. In rare cases there is even a real thematic bond, as the beginning of
No. 1 can show, where the top notes of the arpeggios in the first 7
measures anticipate the main notes of the fugal subject (*Ex.* 57).

The '24 New Preludes and Fugues,' usually referred to as the second
part of the Well-Tempered Clavier, were written at a time when Bach's
older sons were beginning to make their contribution to the development
of musical forms. Accordingly the preludes are frequently in two-part
dance form (Nos. 8 and 18), and even take on a sonata form with complete
recapitulation, although still lacking any subsidiary theme (No. 5). Instead of a coda, one prelude has a kind of fughetta (No. 3) and another
resembles a three-part fugue (No. 22). In these two cases Bach para-
doxically uses fugues as introductions to fugues. The progressive as well
as the clearly unorthodox character of these preludes is also to be found
in the fugues. The fantastic and unconventional beginning of No. 20
could hardly have received its final shaping before 1740. While the fugues
of the older volume display the highest degree of polyphonic virtuosity,
the later set is more restrained in its parade of contrapuntal devices. There
is notably a marked decrease in the number of strettos, and the second
book contains no counterpart to the intricate chromatic fugues of the first
collection, its whole character being more diatonic and even modal. In
No. 9 for instance with its plainsong theme, something like a spirit of

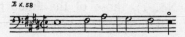

austere early vocal polyphony manifests itself (*Ex.* 58). Thus the second
book does not achieve Baroque monumentality to the same extent as the

first. It is a loose collection of individual numbers, emphasizing a more homophonic style and displaying modernistic tendencies coupled with retrospective features.

After the *Clavierbüchlein* for Friedemann, two other works of a similar nature were begun by Sebastian. The first, written in 1722 and probably meant as technical exercise and entertainment for members of his household, is predominantly in the hand of the master himself. It contains the first five French suites (*BWV* 812-16) as well as some fragments and insignificant little pieces. The binding of this *Notenbüchlein* deteriorated through the centuries and some sheets are missing altogether, yet it still gives a good idea of the kind of music Bach liked to have performed in his own home. In much better condition is the big *Notenbüchlein* for Anna Magdalena Bach, which her husband presented to her in 1725. He personally inserted Nos. III and VI of his Partitas (*BWV* 827 and 830), but the rest of the pages were given to his wife to do with as she pleased. The book contains a number of little dance pieces (minuets, polonaises, marches, a musette) which were not composed by Sebastian and may not even reflect the taste of Magdalena who entered them in the book. These agreeable and technically very simple representatives of the *style galant* were probably meant for the little hands of Emanuel, aged 11, and for the younger children. They were also particularly well suited for use in the dancing lessons which, according to the custom of the time, every growing boy and girl had to take. Bach's authorship may also well be doubted in such anonymous works as the philistine aria 'Elevating Thoughts of a Tobacco Smoker' (*BWV* 515) and the not very refined wedding poem. A little love song *Willst du dein Herz mir schenken* by Giovannini, a Rondeau by Couperin, and a Minuet by Böhm also slipped into the collection. The composer Sebastian is not represented in this family music book as often as one would expect. Besides the 2 Partitas, it again contains 2 French Suites (*BWV* 812, 813: the second one incomplete), the first prelude from the Well-Tempered Clavier, and a handful of chorales and arias, among them the tender *Bist du bei mir* ('Are you with me'; *BWV* 508). Altogether the *Notenbüchlein* presents a rather amusing medley with entries not only by father and mother Bach, but occasionally also by their children, with Sebastian's attempts to correct mistakes and even to provide for his sons a systematic course in the realization of a figured bass. After the 15th rule, however the master gave up, with the excuse that 'the rest could be better explained orally.'

The two *Notenbüchlein* introduce a new form of composition, hardly cultivated by Bach during his first period, but becoming of the utmost importance in his maturity: the suite of dances. The so-called 'French Suites' included in the two little note books are not however, the earliest works that Bach wrote in this field. They are preceded by another set, known to-day as *English Suites*. All attempts to find a valid reason for this name have so far proved unsuccessful. The designation, though not originating with Bach himself, was probably coined at an early date. On a copy of the set, in the handwriting of Sebastian's youngest son, Johann Christian, there is written: '*Fait pour les Anglois*,' and Forkel states in his Bach biography that the work was composed for a distinguished Englishman. Another and more probable theory is that the study of the suites by Dieupart, who lived in London as a teacher and composer, induced Bach to write this collection. Actually Sebastian made a copy of Dieupart's clavier suite in f and used this composer's gigue in A as a model for the prelude to his own English suite in the same key.[1] Apart from this, hardly any English features can be detected in the six suites of the set. Bach followed the tradition of the German suite which during the second half of the 17th century had imported from France the four dances, Allemande, Courante, Sarabande and Gigue, inserting some optional *Galanterien* (dances or dance-like movements different in character from the main numbers) between Sarabande and Gigue, and placing an introductory number at the head of each suite.

The first number of the English Suites (*BWV* 806-11) always bears the same, rather nondescript title of *Prélude*. Actually, the first *Prélude*, which introduces near its beginning an arpeggio of specifically harpsichord character (*Ex.* 59), is a kind of fantasy based on the Gigue form.

Ex. 59

The remaining five introductions display interesting combinations of fugue, concerto, and da capo forms, resembling clavier reductions of movements in a concerto grosso.[2] In each suite Bach uses only a single pair of *Galanterien*, consisting of two dances of the same type, the first in the original key of the suite, the second like a trio in the parallel key. The

---

[1] Cf. E. Dannreuther, 'Musical Ornamentation' (1893-95), I/138.

[2] Following a suggestion by the author of this book, the introductions to the suites Nos. 3 and 4 were arranged by students of Boston University for three solo instruments (violin, oboe, and bassoon) accompanied by strings and harpsichord; these new versions were extremely effective.

number of voices remains constant throughout each piece, and a definite dance character is in evidence.

The exact year of composition of the English Suites is not known, but it seems probable that Bach was engaged in their composition for many years, starting at an early date and ultimately finishing the work in Cöthen. The English Suites contain direct references to music by other composers of the kind to be found in Bach's first two creative periods. Apart from the aforementioned relation of the *Prélude* to No. 1 to the Gigue by Dieupart, there is a resemblance between the theme starting the *Prélude* to No. 2 and the fugue subject of Corelli's op. III/4;[1] while the Gigue of No. 6 seems to be fashioned after an organ composition by Buxtehude.[2] Moreover, in some of the turbulent Gigues of this set the spirit of Bach's earlier years is revived, and even an occasional youthful volubility is noticeable in the Allemandes. On the other hand, the didactic thoroughness with which the composer elaborates on the execution of the *agréments* in Suites 2 and 3, writing out every detail and taking no chance with the possible incompetence of his performers, reflects the pedagogue Bach of the Cöthen period. The descending order of keys used for the English Suites appears like a counterpart to the procedure employed in the Inventions, while the Sarabande in No. 3, with its extensive modulations and the use of even an enharmonic change (*Ex.* 60), might have

been written at the same time as the Well-Tempered Clavier. Altogether the English Suites show a rather confusing combination of earlier and later features which makes it seem possible that they were begun before, and concluded after, the French Suites.

The six *French Suites* (*BWV* 812-17) are shorter, simpler, and easier to play than the 'English' set. They use the same four basic dances, as well as a number of *Galanterien*, but they have no introductory movements, and each suite begins with an Allemande. The French names of all the movements (while the Italian-type *Préludes* are no longer in evidence) may have been responsible for the designation of the whole set as French

---

[1] The same theme was also used by Bach as a basis for an organ fugue (cf. p. 247).
[2] Collected Organ Works, I/94.

S

Suites. But the Italian influence has not really disappeared; it only shifts from the introduction to the main numbers. In four suites (Nos. 2, 4-6) the Courantes are not of the slow and deliberate French type, but show the vivacious character of the fast moving Italian Corrente in 3/4 time. Of still greater importance are the graceful and supple Italianized melodies which Bach uses here, cleverly combining the styles of the two nations. In spite of their apparent facility, these suites are more intricate and show greater variety than the earlier set. Bach now develops his themes, and the second parts of the dances often begin with the main subject transferred to the bass, a technique he used again later in the Partitas. There are not only different types of Courantes but also several kinds of Gigues, varying in rhythm and character. Particularly interesting is the Gigue in No. 1, a stately composition, resembling the introduction of a French overture, and quite unlike the usual gay and carefree finale of the suite. Similar diversities may be noticed in the *Galanterien*. The first suite introduces a pair of dances of the same type, the second two different dances, the third one pair and one separate dance, the fourth and fifth three different dances, and the sixth four different ones. Moreover the mood of the set is by no means uniform. The first three suites are more serious, while the second half of the work displays a serene and even joyful character. These are the most compact, the most unified, and in a way the most perfect suites Bach has written. With the following series the disintegration of the suite form sets in.

Bach's third collection of suites (*BWV* 825-30) was published (and possibly also engraved) by the composer himself. Sebastian was 41 when the first suite appeared in 1726, and each subsequent year saw the publication of a fresh suite until in 1731 the whole set of 6 was available and designated as his op. I. He called this collection *Clavier Übung* (keyboard exercise) and each individual suite *Partita*. Both these titles had been employed by Kuhnau, and in using them Bach once more professed himself an admirer and follower of his great predecessor at St. Thomas'. In the traditional sequence of the four main dances interspersed with optional movements and preceded by an introduction Bach reverts to the form of the English Suites. On the other hand, there is no lack of progressive features pointing towards the gradual absorption of the Suite into the 18th-century Sonata. The customary order of the movements is not uniformly maintained. In Nos. 4 and 6 there are *Galanterien* not only between Sarabande and Gigue, but also between Courante and Sarabande. Besides, the main dances do not always preserve their typical character. The quietly flowing Allemande of the earlier sets is superseded in No. 6

by a dramatic composition with dotted rhythms. In addition to the French Courante (Nos. 2 and 4) the Italian Corrente type (Nos. 1, 3, 5, 6) is also used, while the Sarabandes in Nos. 3, 5 and 6 have discarded their original stately character. Under the influence of Italian music the Gigue in No. 1 is transformed into a completely homophonic virtuoso piece making continuous use of Scarlatti's favourite device—crossing the hands.[1] The composer fully realized that his dances did not always conform to the customary pattern, and he accordingly stressed in his headings that he had observed the traditional tempo only (cf. *Tempo di Gavotta* in No. 6, *Tempo di Minuetto* in No. 5). To make his progressive intentions perfectly clear, Bach occasionally avoids both the traditional names and types of dances altogether. The *Burlesca* in No. 3 might be considered as a kind of minuet, while the *Scherzo* in the same suite somewhat resembles a Gavotte. In No. 2 the Gigue is replaced by a *Capriccio* which only in its general construction approaches the character of the original movement. In this set Bach increasingly employs simple phrases and periods of 4, 8, 12 and 16 measures. The forms used in the dances are as unorthodox as those employed in the second part of the Well-Tempered Clavier. The Sarabande in No. 4, for instance, contains important elements of a condensed sonata form: exposition with initial and concluding subject, richly modulating development and complete recapitulation. Although each section is on the smallest possible scale and the themes are not yet clearly separated from each other, the germs of future forms are clearly noticeable. The introductory numbers to each *Partita* reveal the tremendous versatility of the master. The *Fantasia* heading No. 3 is a kind of two-part invention, the *Praeludium* in No. 1 a three-part invention. No. 6 is introduced by a *Toccata* with a fugue in the middle, while the *Praeambulum*[2] in No. 5 is a toccata with features of the concerto. No. 4 is preceded by a French *Ouverture* and No. 2 by a *Sinfonia*. In the latter the fusion of styles, so characteristic of the mature Bach, is in full evidence. While the Andante of the middle section and the fast finale conform to the usual idea of an Italian *Sinfonia*, the *Grave* of the first section belongs to a

---

[1] How strongly a younger generation felt the progressive character of this music is shown by the fact that the aria *Je t'implore* in Gluck's *Iphigénie en Tauride* is to some extent fashioned after this movement.

[2] In the Partitas Bach uses not only French headings for his dances and introductory movements but also Italian and even Latin names. It is regrettable that several later editions corrected the master by changing every title into French. Even the *BG* and, following it, the *BWV* suppressed the distinction between *Courante* and *Corrente* which the composer himself made, and in Nos. 1, 3, 5, 6 changed the Italian form of the original title into the conventional French form.

French overture. Out of the conventional forms of the two nations Bach created a new type which is entirely his own.

The single *Partita* (or *Ouverture* as it is called after its introductory movement) in b (*BWV* 831) which Bach included in the second part of the *Clavier Übung*, published in 1735, is similar in character to the earlier set, but the dissolution of the suite has (partly under the influence of the orchestra suite) progressed even further. There is no Allemande in this *Partita*, and *Galanterien* are inserted both before and after the Sarabande, and even after the Gigue. The last movement of the suite is a delightful *Echo* meant to display the dynamic contrasts available on a harpsichord with two manuals. Since the suite was expressly designed for this instrument, it may be assumed that the first 6 *Partitas* were also intended primarily as harpsichord music.

The *Partita* is preceded in the original edition by a *Concerto in the Italian taste* ('Italian Concerto'; *BWV* 971), a work in which Bach reverts to his Weimar arrangements of violin concertos. Unlike the preludes to some of the English Suites, which are based on the idea of adapting a concerto grosso with several solo instruments to the keyboard, this 'Concerto' represents the clavier arrangement of an orchestral work with a single soloist, the exact model of which exists in the composer's imagination only. Vivaldi's concerto form is clearly recognizable in the brilliant first movement,[1] in which a massive *tutti* section in the tonic serves both as introduction and conclusion. Fragments of this basic idea appear at regular intervals but transposed to related keys and they are connected by thematically contrasting and modulating solo passages. The lofty middle movement sounds like a broadly extended violin solo accompanied by strings. Particularly clever is Bach's method of suggesting in the accompaniment a pedal point of the string basses (*Ex.* 61). In the dashing

last movement, which has a form similar to that of the initial movement, some of the phrases in the main *tutti* seem to result from the adaptation of one-part string passages.

In spite of this mock realism which keeps up the pretence that the composition is an arrangement, the work is extremely well suited to the

---

[1] The beginning displays a striking resemblance to the theme of a *Sinfonia* in Georg Muffat's 'Florilegium Primum' (1695).

clavier. Indeed, not only from a musical but even from a technical point of view it rates among Bach's finest keyboard compositions. The Italian Concerto displays the accomplished master's serenity and joy in supreme craftsmanship; with its perfect equilibrium between emotional content and musical form it seems ideally suited to introduce the non-expert into the art of the Thomas Cantor.

In this volume of the *Clavier Übung* Bach gives directions for the use of the register stops of the harpsichord with two manuals. He prescribes frequent changes between *forte* and *piano* and even likes to indicate *forte* in one hand and *piano* in the other simultaneously. He apparently wanted a different volume of tone on each manual; probably two strings in unison or octaves on the *forte* manual, and single strings on the *piano* clavier. As a rule the *tutti* sections are to be played by both hands in *forte*, while in the solos the melody is *forte* and the accompaniment *piano*. But there are very attractive deviations from this rule showing that Bach was, on occasion, not averse to a dynamically diversified style.

The third part of the *Clavier Übung* consists of organ works only. The fourth part, published in 1742, is again written for a harpsichord with two manuals, according to the indication on the title. It contains a single work, an 'Aria with 30 Variations' in G (*BWV* 988). This composition was written for Bach's pupil, Goldberg, and is usually referred to as the *Goldberg Variations*. Bach wrote no other clavier composition of similar length and compactness. It demonstrates the consummate technical skill of the mature master combined with a soaring fantasy, pointing, particularly in the treatment of the instrument, far beyond Bach's own time.[1]

The Sarabande in the French style, which forms the theme, is probably not by the master himself. It dates from a somewhat earlier period, and already appears in the *Notenbüchlein* for Anna Magdalena of 1725. Bach may have chosen this Aria for its lucidity of form—two parts consisting of sixteen measures each—and for its plain, yet powerful harmonic construction. Here the composer no longer uses the simple technique of his early variations in the Italian manner. The element that joins the Sarabande and its variations is the bass line of the theme with the harmonic progressions dependent on it. This bass foundation recurs in each of the 30 variations, although it does not always appear in the lowest voice (cf. var. 25). Bach's technique is inspired by passacaglia and chaconne, but

---

[1] In most variations Bach indicated whether they are to be performed on a single manual or on two. Those for two manuals call for an even more advanced technique of clavier-playing.

differs from them in the unusual length and character of his theme. The problem of incorporating the same bassline into 30 effectively contrasting variations did not seem big enough to Bach. Without deviating from the variation form he presents in his set 9 different kinds of canon, one in every third variation. There is a canon at the unison, one at the second, the third, etc. Each time the interval of imitation is augmented by one tone until var. 27 ends up with the canon at the ninth. Besides, the canon at the fifth (var. 15) is not in straight imitation, but in inversion. There is also a *Fughetta* among the variations (No. 10), a stately French *Ouverture* with a following fugue (No. 16), and in the finale a roguish *Quodlibet*, which fits melodic phrases taken from two comic folksongs[1] into the frame-work of the variations. This little joke probably amused the master particularly, because it alluded to the humorous habit of singing several folksongs simultaneously, which was a favourite pastime at the family gatherings of the Bach clan. In between these contrapuntally elaborate variations are a number of highly diversified character pieces; the gay and vigorous var. 4, the gracefully skipping var. 7, the brilliant var. 14, the light var. 20 in the manner of Scarlatti, the deeply moving chromatic var. 25 (like Nos. 15 and 21 in the parallel key), and the magnificent Nos. 28 and 29, containing passages which vigorously contradict the traditional conception of the conservative Bach (*Ex.* 62). The mixture of the strictest logic with

Ex. 62

imaginative freedom of expression that manifests itself in this work finds its closest analogy in similar works by Beethoven and Brahms, for the 18th century produced little or nothing in this field that could stand comparison with Bach's gigantic work.[2] Yet even this, his supreme achievement in the field of clavier music, is linked to the past, and it is extremely significant that a connection can be established between the Goldberg Variations and a work of Sebastian's greatest forebear, Johann Christoph (cf. p. 61).

---

[1] They are: *Ich bin so lang' nicht bei dir gewest* ('I long have been away from you') and *Kraut und Rüben* ('Cabbage and turnips').

[2] Bach's two last works, the Musical Offering and the Art of the Fugue, which have a certain connection with the clavier, will be discussed in the next section.

IV

WORKS FOR STRING AND WIND INSTRUMENTS, CONCERTOS

Bach's superb craftsmanship, exquisite in the most minute details, lent itself especially to the filigree style of instrumental chamber music. Some of his works in this field belong to the most inspired compositions he ever wrote. The majority owe their conception to Bach's activity in Cöthen, which helped him to develop his instrumental style to supreme mastery.

Significantly enough, it was not the *Sonata for a solo instrument and figured bass*, so widely used in his time, that really interested him. This traditional form was not too well suited for the rich polyphonic and harmonic texture of Bach's musical language. His 3 Sonatas and the Fugue for violin and figured bass (*BWV* 1021, 1023-24, 1026) as well as the 3 Sonatas for flute and figured bass (*BWV* 1033-35), probably products of his early years in Cöthen, clearly reveal a certain indifference towards this type of music.[1] Bach felt that it offered both too much and too little, and there is a certain groping for new musical forms in these works. In the Fugue in g the violin part is frequently treated in a very polyphonic manner, while the bass contains one rest of 15 and a half measures, subsequently followed by 20 measures on the same note d. A similar pedal point, lasting through 29 measures, is to be found at the beginning of the Sonata in e. Clearly this prepares for the violin compositions *senza Basso*. On the other hand, the Violin Sonata in G also exists as a Trio for flute, violin, and figured bass[2] (*BWV* 1038), a type which appealed far more to the composer.

In 1720 Bach wrote 3 *Sonatas and 3 Partitas for violin solo* (*BWV* 1001-6) and at about the same time 6 *Suites for violoncello solo* (*BWV* 1007-12), which count among the most powerful creations of his genius. Although the polyphonic treatment of the violin had been used in Italy, and particularly in Germany, before Bach's time, no other composer had written works of similar grandeur and magnificence for this instrument. Here violin and 'cello are used not so much as singing melody-instruments but as carriers of harmonic and polyphonic expression. Bach, the great fighter, sets himself the almost impossible task of writing 4-part fugues

---

[1] The 4 Violin Inventions published in *BG*, 45 (*BWV*, Anh. 173-76) were recognized as works by Bonporti. (Cf. p. 267.)

[2] Even if F. Blume's assumption (*BJ*, 1928) is correct and this arrangement is not by Bach, it must have satisfied him, as it was preserved in his own handwriting. This autograph which Wilhelm Rust used for his edition of the Trio in *BG*, 9/221 is lost to-day.

and complicated harmonic successions for a single and unaccompanied stringed instrument, with all its technical limitations. This he achieves by making the utmost demands on the ability of the player, and at the same time taxing the imagination and perception of the listener to the very limit. While the performer can never present more than two notes simultaneously,[1] Bach expects the arpeggios of 3 and 4 notes and even successions of notes to be understood as harmonic unities.

The composer's joy in experimenting and adapting certain stylistic devices to changed conditions had previously caused him to use features of violin technique in his keyboard compositions. Here the process is reversed, and he adopts basic designs of keyboard technique in his music for a stringed solo instrument. The organistic character of the Fugue in C of the third Sonata is particularly noticeable; in a completely unprecedented manner it employs as theme a chorale melody (*Komm, heiliger Geist*). The implied polyphony and the rich harmonic texture in these compositions have their counterpart in the painted architecture of the period, with its simulated collonades and vistas.

It is characteristic that many movements from these Sonatas were subsequently transcribed for keyboard instruments.[2] In all these cases the implied contrapuntal writing of the original was changed with the greatest of ease into real polyphony.

As to form, the 3 Violin Sonatas all use the 4 movements of the Church Sonata (slow-fast-slow-fast) with a fugue in the second place, and the slow inner movement as the only piece in a different key. On the other hand, the 3 *Partitas*, which in the autograph alternate with the Sonatas, show a great variety of dance forms. The first consists of 4 dances, each followed by a variation ('Double'); the third omits most of the standard movements and replaces them by free intermezzi in the manner of an orchestral suite.

---

[1] The theory expressed by Schering (*BJ*, 1904) and Schweitzer that the German players of Bach's time could produce full chords with loosely strung bows without resorting to arpeggios was refuted by Gustav Beckmann ('Das Violinspiel in Deutschland vor 1700,' 1918) and Andreas Moser (*BJ*, 1920). Nevertheless attempts were made to build curved bows for the performance of Bach's music for violin solo (cf. 'Bach Gedenkschrift,' 1950, p. 75 and foll.). Occasionally (Sarabandes of the Partitas in b and d) Bach prescribes chords which can only be played as slow arpeggios, since the same finger is required on the lowest and highest string.

[2] The fugue of the Sonata in g was transcribed for the organ (*BWV* 539), and the whole Sonata in a and the first movement of that in C were transcribed for the clavier (*BWV* 964 and 968). The prelude to the 3rd Partita was equipped by the composer with an orchestral accompaniment and in this form used as introduction to Cantatas Nos. 120a and 29. There is also a version for lute (*BWV* 1000) of the fugue from the Sonata in g.

The second attaches, at the end of the series of dances, the famous Chaconne, which is longer than all the 4 preceding movements together and overshadows them in importance. It is an imposing set of variations on several, closely interrelated 8-measure themes, moulded into a powerful 3-part form and imbued with dramatic power; possibly the most stirring example of the 'triumph of spirit over substance' (Spitta) Bach achieved in these works.

The 6 'Cello Suites do not present so great a variety of forms. They all start with a prelude, followed by Allemande, Courante, Sarabande, 2 *Galanterien* and a Gigue. The similarity of their structure to that of the English Suites makes it appear likely that these two works were written at about the same time. The fifth Suite is composed for a 'cello, of which the top string is tuned to G instead of A; while the sixth Suite requires an instrument with five strings.[1] Although the technical limitations in the unwieldy 'cello were even greater than in the violin, thus making the inclusion of real fugues impossible, Bach succeeded in creating works of consummate mastery, equal, if not superior, to his music for violin solo. In the Prelude to the fourth Suite, for instance, he achieves, with the simplest means, the illusion of an organ pedal point used as a foundation for slowly gliding harmonies.

While the master reached in his solo sonatas a lonely peak of grandeur to which for a long time nobody dared follow him, his *Trios* are imbued with stylistic trends which were to prove highly important for the future. Again Bach did not care too much for the favourite Baroque type, the Sonata for 2 melody instruments supported by figured bass. His output in this field is confined to 2 Sonatas in G (*BWV* 1038[2] and *BWV* 1039), one of which was later transcribed into a Sonata for cembalo obbligato and viola da gamba (*BWV* 1027). The procedure which the composer adopted here is as simple as it is ingenious. He gave one melodic line to the viola da gamba, and the other to the right hand of the harpsichord player, while the bass part was assigned to the left hand of the clavierist. Such 'trios,' in which the keyboard instrument executed two parts and a string or wind instrument one, were used at least a century

---

[1] Such a *violoncello a cinque corde*, in which a top E string was added to the ordinary four strings of the 'cello, was used occasionally in Bach's time. It was certainly not the *viola pomposa*, as Schweitzer assumes, and most likely not the *violoncello piccolo* either. Cf. C. Sachs ('Musical Instruments,' New York, 1940), who also rightly questions the old myth that Bach was the 'inventor' of the *viola pomposa*.

[2] Regarding the Sonata for flute, violin and continuo in G (*BWV* 1038), cf. p. 279. A sonata for 2 violins in C (*BWV* 1037) often attributed to Bach is probably the work of one of his pupils.

before Bach,[1] but no other composer employed them as successfully and systematically. They became his favourite form of chamber music and include some exquisite pieces like the 6 *Sonatas for harpsichord and violin* (*BWV* 1014-19), 3 *Sonatas for harpsichord and viola da gamba* (*BWV* 1027-29), and 3 *Sonatas for harpsichord and flute* (*BWV* 1030-32).

Bach's zest for experimenting made him break with the traditional aspect of the Trio Sonata in many other ways as well. Hitherto this had been a polyphonic composition in which the two upper parts had equal shares in the melodic material. The composer now fused it with elements of the Concerto, using da capo and rondo forms, and inserting long solo sections. He did not hesitate at times to employ the harpsichord as a mere accompanying instrument, or its upper part as a unison reinforcement of the melody. Altogether there is no uniformity in these Sonatas. Bach by no means confined himself to writing the conventional three parts; he occasionally used four and even five or six voices. There are movements in canonic or passacaglia forms, others of a prelude-like character. Their number also varies; three movements are employed in the flute Sonatas, four in the majority of the violin and viola da gamba Sonatas, and five in the last violin Sonata (in G). The variety of forms is matched by an abundance of different emotions. There are pieces happy and gay, energetic, stubborn, tender, sad, melancholy, or tragic in character. To emphasize the wide emotional range of this music, individual movements are given such descriptive headings as 'Andante un poco,' 'Adagio ma non tanto,' that are not too common in Bach's music.

In ascribing the Sonatas for violin and harpsichord to the Cöthen period, Forkel is apparently right, at least as far as their first draft is concerned. It seems most likely that the viola da gamba Sonatas also originated in this period, as Prince Leopold was very fond of this instrument. On the other hand, the flute Sonatas appear to be products of a later period. The Sonata in E flat shows a progressive character that is to be found in Bach's music at the time when the artistic personalities of his eldest sons were beginning to unfold. Its 'Siciliano' has a tender sweetness that seems to belong to the period of *Empfindsamkeit* (sensibility). These works may have been written for the eminent Dresden flutist, P. G. Buffardin, with whom Bach was in close contact. In this same period he also revised his earlier violin Sonatas. There is a manuscript written by his son-in-law, Altnikol, that shows significant changes in the original works. The Adagio of the fifth Sonata increases the motion of the accom-

---

[1] Cf. Arnold Schering, 'Zur Geschichte der Solosonate in the 1. Hälfte des 17. Jahrhunderts,' in 'Riemann-Festschrift,' 1909.

panying harpsichord from sixteenth to thirty-second notes, thus creating a prelude-like composition of an almost impressionistic character. An earlier version of the sixth Sonata starts with a movement in da capo form, which is repeated again after three slow movements. In later years Bach found this too monotonous; he retained the first two movements and added three new ones, thus creating an unorthodox but well-proportioned form: fast-slow-fast-slow-fast, with a movement for harpsichord solo in the centre.

These different Sonatas show Bach again and again exploring all the possibilities to be derived from the transformation of the old trio into a workable duo for a melody instrument and clavier obbligato. Thus he planted new seeds for the growth of chamber music; his own sons in particular were strongly stimulated by their father's output in this field.

Bach's *Concertos* stand at the very centre of his creative output. The composer's interest in the concertante principle and the concerto form had already manifested itself in his early works. But before he came to Cöthen he had no opportunity to write real concertos. There were two different paths open to him: he could follow the model of Corelli's concerti grossi, which consisted of a number of brief movements contrasting in character and aiming at monumental simplicity; or he could adopt the type which had been given its definite form through Vivaldi, works in only three movements (fast-slow-fast), emphasizing the concertante principle, and using a rondo-like construction for the fast sections. Bach, while not overlooking the possibilities of the Corelli type, showed a decided preference for Vivaldi's concertos, as their compact and symmetrical architecture appealed to him. He made his first thorough study of them while engaged in arrangements for keyboard instruments in Weimar (cf. p. 149). However, when he started writing concertos of his own, he by no means copied Vivaldi's style, but imbued it with new ideas. He both clarified and simplified the Italian composer's rondo-form, presenting a straightforward eight-bar ritornel of all the players in the main key at the beginning and end of the movement, while fragments from it, transposed to related keys, appeared within the movement at strategic points. Between the massive pillars of these *tutti* passages are the graceful garlands of the solo episodes, providing modulating connections and mostly introducing new thematic material. Bach often reinforced the architectural solidity by using the da capo form of the Italian aria, or a chiastic construction (cf. p. 202), in which not only the first and last parts correspond, but a firm connection is also established between the second section and the one next to the last. He liked to combine the concerto form with that of the fugue, and even in homophonic movements, figurations of the solo instrument are accompanied by thematic ideas derived from the main ritornel (*Ex.* 63) in a way we would look for in vain in a Vivaldi concerto.

It seems strange that only two *Concertos for violin solo and orchestra* and one *for two violins and orchestra* (*BWV* 1041-43; all three were probably written in Cöthen) should be preserved, while there are more than twice as many transcriptions of such works for solo harpsichord and strings in existence (cf. pp. 288-89). Did Bach discard some of the original compositions as soon as the arrangements were completed; did these models only exist in his imagination and were never put to paper; or were some violin concertos lost after his death? These questions will probably never be answered; anyway, judging from the transcriptions, we may safely say that the three works preserved must have been among the very best Bach wrote in this field.

The first movement of the Violin Concerto in E, written in da capo form, is typical of the supreme mastery with which solo instrument and accompanying orchestra confront each other and at other times join forces. In the Concerto in a, on the other hand, the initial movement anticipates features of the Sonata form in a manner which was to be

adopted before long by Friedemann and Emanuel Bach. The slow movements in these two concertos exhibit a kind of ostinato bass, the serious
character of which contrasts most effectively with the poignant sweetness
of the solo violin. Of equal beauty is the slow movement of the Double
Concerto, one of the most intimate and subjective cantilenas Bach ever
wrote. While the orchestra is used here merely to support the soloists, the
finale presents remarkable instances of the inversion of the traditional
relationship between soloists and orchestra. The solo violins are entrusted
with broad organistic chords, while the melody is supplied in vigorous
unison by the orchestra[1] (*Ex.* 64).

The six so-called *Brandenburg Concertos* (*BWV* 1046-51), which
Bach dedicated in the spring of 1721 to Christian Ludwig, Margrave of
Brandenburg (cf. p. 160), are not concertos for a single solo instrument,
but examples of older forms of concerted music, showing, in the German
fashion, a preference for wind instruments. In three of them (Nos. 1, 3, 6)
the orchestra is composed of evenly balanced instrumental choirs, which
toss the themes to and fro among themselves in charming conversation,
only occasionally surrendering the lead to a single instrument out of their
midst. Such compositions, based upon the old Venetian *canzone* with its
contrasting instrumental choirs, are known as 'concerto symphonies.'
There are also 3 concerti grossi in the set (Nos. 2, 4, 5) in which an
accompanying orchestra, the *ripieni*, is confronted by the *concertino*
consisting of three or four solo instruments.

Even the Bach student, who expects the utmost variety in every work
of the master, is amazed at the abundance of changing scenes in these six
works conjured up by the composer's inexhaustible imagination. No. 2,
which in its perfect structural proportion seems like the very prototype

---

[1] The first movement of this Concerto is influenced by Torelli's Violin Concerto
No. 8, known to Bach from an organ arrangement by his friend, J. G. Walther. Cf. Schering,
'Geschichte des Instrumentalkonzerts,' Leipzig, 1905.

of the concerto grosso, employs a *concertino* of trumpet, recorder, oboe, and violin. Of particular colouristic appeal is the use of the brass instrument in the high *clarino* register; indeed, the trumpet is treated in so brilliant a manner that the concerto grosso at times assumes the character of a solo concerto. The same is true of No. 4, with a *concertino* of 2 recorders and a violin, where far greater demands on the virtuosity of the violinists are made than in any of Bach's concertos for this instrument. Likewise in No. 5, written for a *concertino* of flute, violin, and harpsichord, the keyboard instrument predominates and even has an unaccompanied solo cadenza of 65 measures in the first movement. For the first time the humble harpsichord, whose role in ensembles had always been that of supporting other instruments, assumes the proud part of a leader. Unlike the majority of Bach's concertos for clavier solo and orchestra, this work was obviously intended for the clavier from the outset; it thus constitutes a milestone in the history of music as the first original clavier concerto ever written. Maybe Bach, who played the part himself, was inspired to compose it by the exquisite 'clavecyn' he had purchased in 1719 for his Prince in Berlin.[1] As in Concerto No. 2, the middle movement uses solo instruments and bass only, thus assuming the character of real chamber music. The symphonic Concerto No. 1 employs the tiny *violino piccolo* (a third above the ordinary violin and shriller in tone) together with 6 wind instruments, strings, and continuo. The traditional 3 movements are followed by a gay Minuet with 3 graceful trios meant to provoke applause, like the *licenza* at the end of a contemporary comic opera. The third Concerto introduces 3 powerful choirs of strings, each subdivided again into 3 parts. In order not to break up the gay mood, Bach omits the slow middle movement, inserting in its place a simple cadence, and he achieves the necessary contrast by using the two-part form of contemporary dances for the second fast movement. The most unusual scoring is to be found in No. 6 written for 2 viole, 2 viole da gamba, 'cello and continuo, while omitting wind instruments and even violins, and it seems to reflect the peculiar conditions at Cöthen.[2] The most striking feature is the canon at a distance of one eighth note in the ritornel of the first movement. Bach's pupil, J. P. Kirnberger, used this in his *Kunst des reinen Satzes* as an illustration for counterpoint in its strictest

[1] No less than 130 thalers were paid to Bach for this instrument, plus his travelling expenses.
[2] Cf. Smend, *l.c.* The Prince wanted a viola da gamba solo, which was therefore planned with not too great difficulties. Bach chose for his own part his favourite, the viola, and therefore entrusted it with an interesting task.

form. It is characteristic of the non-academic quality of Bach's music, however, that the hearer who does not realize the polyphonic intricacy will yet derive immense enjoyment from the gaiety and brilliance of this work. In all the Brandenburg Concertos the strong rhythmic life and the inspired colouristic garb contribute towards loosening up and dissolving the solidity of the polyphonic texture. These compositions seem to embody the splendour and effervescence of court life at Cöthen, and, moreover, they clearly reveal the composer's delight in writing for a group of highly trained instrumentalists. There is an exuberance and optimism in this music that only a genius aware of his newly achieved, full mastery could call forth. Craftsmanship and inspiration, iron logic and zest for experimenting, here counterpoise each other to an extent rarely equalled again even by Bach himself.

The two *Orchestral Suites*[1] in C and b (*BWV* 1066-67) also belong to the Cöthen period, while two other works of the same kind, both in D (*BWV* 1068-69), were probably written between 1727 and 1736.[2] To some extent these compositions show features linking them to Bach's concertos. The overture and some of the dances in the Suite in b for flute and strings use the woodwind instrument with such virtuosity that they appear like movements in a flute concerto. The Suite in C for 2 oboes, bassoon, and strings, on the other hand, occasionally employs a *concertino* of the 3 wind instruments, thus assuming the character of a concerto grosso. The second Suite in D, for 3 trumpets with timpani, 3 oboes with bassoon, and strings, makes the 3 choirs compete with each other in a manner not unlike a concerto symphony. The initial movement of all four Suites is a French Ouverture in which two slow movements are separated by a fast fugue frequently combined with the concerto form, the entrances of the theme in the full orchestral body being employed as ritornels, and the connecting and modulating episodes as solos. These overtures are followed in each case by a free succession of dances often arranged in pairs, and by little programmatic pieces, such as the high-spirited *Badinerie* (banter) in the Suite in b, the buoyant *Réjouissance* (rejoicing) in the second Suite in D, and the meditative *Air*[3] in the first Suite in D. In spite of the French titles and French forms, the orchestral Suites are true products of German soil, inspired as they are by the folklore of the country. This is joyful, radiant music, in which the composer does not

---

[1] Regarding the relation to J. Bernhard Bach's orchestral suites, cf. p. 101.

[2] The authenticity of a 5th Suite in g (*BWV* 1070) is very doubtful.

[3] This beautiful movement is best known in an arrangement for solo violin to be played on the G string.

overwhelm us with his stupendous mastery, but rather captivates our hearts with sparkling wit and serene charm.

An impressive array of concertos was, we might almost say, manufactured during the Leipzig years. At that time the need for 'clavieristic' material was pressing as Bach's sons needed effective compositions, especially for their appearances in the Collegium Musicum. Bach had recourse to the method he had used in his trios with harpsichord obbligato. He gave the solo part of a previously composed violin concerto to the right hand of the keyboard player, whose left hand reinforced the bass of the composition, and a *clavier concerto* with accompanying strings was produced. Such arrangements actually exist of the two violin concertos in E and a as well as of the fourth Brandenburg Concerto (*BWV* 1054, 1057-58). Three other clavier concertos (*BWV* 1052, 1055-56) evidently originated in the same way. The violin concertos on which they are based, however, have not survived. In such adaptations Bach transposed the pitch of the original composition one tone down, since the claviers of his time as a rule only went up to d''' and did not have e''', the traditional top note of his violin concertos.[1] Bach was naturally not satisfied mechanically to transfer the violin part to the right hand of the clavierist. He often wrote and rewrote the same arrangement several times, and in the course of this process his language became increasingly idiomatic. The bass part was enriched and middle voices were added, as the last movement of the Concerto in d (*BWV* 1052) exemplifies (*Ex.* [65]). This is a vigorous

Ex. 65

The larger notes are found in an early version; in a later arrangement Bach added the notes reproduced in smaller type.

composition, full of dramatic life which, if we may judge from its different versions, seems to have been a favourite with Sebastian. In the Concerto in f (*BWV* 1056) the original violinistic character is particularly noticeable, and it induced Gustav Schreck to attempt a reconstruction of the

[1] Cf. Howard Shanet in *MQ*, 1950. Contradictory theories regarding the originals which served Bach for his arrangements have been propounded by Spiro, Aber, Hirsch and others. Cf. 'Zeitschrift der Internationalen Musikgesellschaft,' XI, 100; *BJ*, 1913, 1929, 1930.

original violin concerto in the key of g.[1] A Concerto for harpsichord, flute and violin with strings (*BWV* 1044) uses the same combination of instruments as Brandenburg No. 5. It is an arrangement of a prelude and fugue for clavier from the Weimar period (cf. p. 263), which was particularly suited for transcription, as both its sections showed, from the outset, elements of the concerto form. Bach not only enlarged, but deepened the original, enhancing the power and dignity of the first version. Between the two fast movements he inserted a slow one from his organ trio in d, which he scored in the traditional manner for the solo instruments only, omitting the accompanying strings.

Similarly, of the six *Concertos for two, three and four claviers* respectively with string accompaniment, not one seems to represent the form in which it was originally written. That for four claviers (*BWV* 1065) is an arrangement of Vivaldi's Concerto for 4 violins op. 3/10, and it seems quite possible that the two Concertos for three claviers (*BWV* 1063-64) are also based on works by other composers. The two Concertos for two claviers in c (*BWV* 1060, 1062) are adaptations of his own works.[2] Somewhat different is the situation in the case of the Concerto for two claviers in C (*BWV* 1061). Here there is no trace of the violinistic character conspicuous in the other adaptations. It has the appearance of an original clavier composition, and as a matter of fact the two solo parts exist in autographs. However, as the accompanying voices, which are not preserved in Bach's own writing, are mainly reinforcing the parts of the keyboard instruments, it seems quite likely that the orchestration was a later addition, and that the work was originally written for two claviers only. It might be mentioned in this connection that there also exists in Sebastian's hand a *Concerto a duoi cembali concertati* without any accompaniment, which his son, Friedemann, composed at an early age (cf. p. 321), possibly under the influence of the Concerto in C.

In these concertos for two to four claviers Bach was confronted by the difficulty of having similar bass lines in the various solo parts. He tried to counteract the resulting monotony by using the claviers in turns as solo and as filling continuo instruments. In the Concerto in d for three claviers, the first harpsichord is given far more of the solo material than the other two. A better balance is reached in the solemn and brilliant Concerto in C for the same combination. Although these arrangements

---

[1] Peters Edition, No. 3069a. A different adaptation of this Concerto was made by J. B. Jackson for Oxford University Press.

[2] *BWV* 1062 is based on the concerto for 2 violins in d; stylistic reasons point to similar conditions for *BWV* 1060, although its model is not known.

T

show the hand of the artisan rather than that of the artist, they are highly attractive ensemble music, radiating joyous strength and vitality.

It is significant that clavier concertos formed the basis for further arrangements. With minor or major changes they made excellent introductions to cantatas, and at times the composer even adapted them into vocal numbers.[1] Once more, this furnishes evidence for Bach's conception of the unity of music.

In his last period of composition only two ensemble works were written, but they are among the greatest Bach ever created.

The *Musical Offering* (*BWV* 1079) belongs to the series of contrapuntal variations favoured by Bach during the latter part of his life (cf. p. 206). This time the basis of the variations is the 'truly royal theme' which King Friedrich of Prussia offered for elaboration during Bach's visit to the Palace at Potsdam[2] (*Ex.* 66). Bach felt that he had by no

Ex. 66

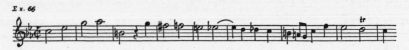

means exhausted all the possibilities of the theme in his improvisations before the King. He therefore worked on it after his return to Leipzig, and the result seemed so highly satisfying to him that he had the whole cycle engraved. Composition and production must have proceeded very rapidly, since the printed dedication to the King is dated July 7, 1747, the actual visit having taken place just two months earlier. Apparently the composer wanted to send his Offering at a time when the memory of his visit was still fresh in the mind of his host.

---

[1] The first movement of the Clavier Concerto in E was transposed to D, the solo given to the concertante organ, and 3 oboes were added, in which form it appeared as introduction to Cantata No. 169. The Siciliano of this Concerto was employed with an added vocal part for an aria in the same Cantata, while the last movement with added oboe d'amore made up the introductory *Sinfonia* in Cantata No. 49. All 3 movements of the Clavier Concerto in d were used as the introduction to Cantata No. 188, the solo being again taken over by the organ. Incidentally, the first movement of Brandenburg Concerto No. 1 was used unchanged as introduction to Cantata No. 52, and that of Brandenburg No. 3, with 2 obbligato horns and 3 oboes added, as introduction to Cantata No. 174.

[2] It seems unlikely that Bach changed the idea given to him by the King, as Hermann Keller suggests in 'Das königliche Thema,' 'Musica,' 1950. Such an action would have annoyed the King, who was a good enough musician to remember what theme he had given Bach.

The great speed of its production may have been partly responsible for the disconnected form of the original publication. The composer seems to have sent his manuscript in instalments, and the engraver[1] put it on copper whenever a batch arrived, at the same time taking good care to fill each of the costly plates as completely as possible by inserting short canons into spare places. Accordingly, the original edition presents the work in four separate sections printed partly on oblong paper, and partly in upright form. The confusing arrangement which resulted made it difficult for earlier students fully to comprehend the architecture of the work. Indeed, so outstanding an expert as Spitta describes the Musical Offering as 'a strange conglomerate of pieces, wanting not only internal connection but external uniformity.' Actually the work shows the perfect construction which we may expect of a composition written by Bach at the peak of his mastery.[2] At the beginning stands a three-part *Ricercar* (fugue),[3] at the end a six-part *Ricercar*; in the centre a Trio sonata containing two fugues. Between the first *Ricercar* and Trio are 5 two-part Canons, to which in a third voice the r.t. (royal theme) is added as a *cantus firmus*. The central Trio is again followed by 5 Canons, this time using the r.t. and its variations as subject for the actual canonic elaboration. It is characteristic of Bach's unerring feeling for form that the first of the Trio sonata's fugues, written in concerto style and da capo form, introduces the r.t. as a *cantus firmus* as the preceding 5 Canons had done. In the second fugue, on the other hand, a variation of the r.t. is employed as a subject, thereby anticipating the technique of the following 5 Canons. Thus the 13 numbers derived from the r.t. appear in the following, strictly chiastic order:

		TRIO SONATA			
Ricercar	5 *Canons*	1st *fugue*	2nd *fugue*	5 *Canons*	*Ricercar*
3-part fugue based on r.t.	using r.t. as *cantus firmus*	using r.t. as *cantus firmus*	using r.t. as fugue subject	subjecting r.t. to canonic elaboration	6-part fugue based on r.t.

The first and the last *Ricercar* are written for clavier.[4] They are directly connected with the visit to Potsdam, when Bach improvised on

[1] It was Bach's pupil, J. G. Schübler, who also engraved the composer's last organ chorales.

[2] Cf. H. T. David's edition of the work and accompanying booklet published by G. Schirmer, New York, 1945.

[3] Bach uses the expression *Ricercar* here to designate an instrumental fugue employing elements of the vocal style.

[4] The original edition prints the second *Ricercar* in open score, but it can be performed without difficulty by a single clavier player, and Bach's autograph presents it on 2 staves only.

one of the King's pianofortes a three-part fugue based on the r.t., bu
evaded the suggestion of employing the same subject in a six-part fugue.
The six-part composition which the master played in Potsdam was on a
theme of his own choice, and the elaboration of the r.t. was carried out
only after his return. Accordingly the two *Ricercars* are quite different in
character. The first (incidentally, Bach's only piece that we know to have
been written for the modern pianoforte) lacks the complete logic and
perfect balance of the last; it obviously represents Bach's improvisation
and may be taken as an example of his extemporizing in strict forms. The
six-part *Ricercar*, on the other hand, belongs to the most outstanding
fugues Bach ever wrote. It is a work of the largest proportions, whose
profundity of thought, magnificent poise, and loftiness of sound make it
one of the greatest monuments of polyphonic music.

While in these two works for the clavier the composer seems to stand
in the foreground, the remaining eleven numbers appear to be destined
for the exalted personage to whom the work is dedicated. These are
chamber music compositions, two of which (the Trio and one canon)
expressly prescribe the use of a flute for the top voice, while in the majority
of the others, although no instrumentation is indicated, the highest part
can be taken over by this favourite instrument of the King.[1] The ten
canons are predominantly retrospective in character; in the best traditions
of the past, canons in unison and octave, canons of the inversion and
augmentation, 'crab' canons as well as a canonic fugue[2] are introduced.
Bach's presentation of the canons tests the efficiency of the performer; as
a rule they are not printed in full score; in two cases not even a clue as to
the manner of imitation is given, and the composer provokingly remarks
'quaerendo invenietis' (if you seek, you will find). Here the 'puzzle
canons' of the late Middle Ages are being resurrected; and similarly Bach's
neglecting to indicate on what instrument most of his two-, three- and

---

[1] The copy which Bach sent to his royal patron contains several Latin inscriptions
to the King. On the first page is an acrostic, the first letters of which formed the word
'Ricercar': *Regis Iussu Cantio et Reliqua Canonica Arte resoluta* (According to the order of
the King the tune and the remainder are resolved with canonic art). To the Canon in
augmentation the composer wrote: *Notulis crescentibus crescat fortuna Regis* (May the
fortune of the King grow with the length of the notes), and similarly the spiral canon bears
the annotation: *Ascendenteque modulatione ascendat Gloria Regis* (And may the Glory of the
King rise with the rising modulation).

[2] In a canon of the inversion the imitating voice answers each step upward with a
similar step downward, and vice versa; in a canon in augmentation every note of the
imitating voice is longer (usually twice as long) than in the original; in a crab canon the
imitating voice proceeds backward, starting with the last note and ending with the first;
a canonic fugue combines features of canon and fugue.

four-part canons are to be performed re-creates the situation of earlier centuries, when the players used the instrument that happened to be available at the moment. However, the solid harmonic foundation of these contrapuntal masterpieces and the idea of a spiral canon belong to Bach's own time. This *Canon per tonos* (canon through the keys) modulates in its 8 measures one whole tone up; it has to be performed six times before all the parts once more reach the original key of c. Also a typical product of the 18th century is the Trio for flute, violin, and continuo, the heart of the whole work. It is a church sonata of great dignity and beauty, the most outstanding among Bach's trios.

Altogether the Musical Offering appears as the work of a master who is drawing conclusions not only from the experience of a lifetime, but from that of a whole era. It presents in a compact and monumental form a synthesis of the musical thought of three centuries.

The *Art of the Fugue* (*BWV* 1080) is Bach's last great composition. The master seems to have been engaged in this tremendous task after the completion of the Musical Offering, and in this case, too, he planned to have the work become generally known through print. He supervised part of the engraving, but before it was quite finished, and before he even had a chance of completing his manuscript, death overtook him. The Art of the Fugue remained a torso, and neither the autograph nor the original printing issued after Bach had gone, can give an exact idea of his intentions. There are doubts regarding the precise order in which the individual numbers were to be arranged; we do not know what end the composer had planned for his work, and it is possible that even the title, Art of the Fugue, was not conceived by Bach himself.

Yet, the sections which we have are of such awe-inspiring majesty that even in its fragmentary form the Art of the Fugue appears as one of the greatest products of the human mind.

The composition seems like a sequel to the Musical Offering. It too is a set of contrapuntal variations, all based on the same idea and all in the same key. There is even a melodic resemblance between the two works, for the subject of the Art of the Fugue appears like an ingenious condensation of the 'royal theme.' And again, in most of the variations, Bach omits any indication as to the instruments for which his composition is intended. It seems likely that the composer meant his swan song to be keyboard music primarily, but the Art of the Fugue sounds even more impressive when played by a string quartet or varying ensembles.[1] However, while in the former work the emphasis was on canonic elaboration,

---

[1] Cf. the editions by Roy Harris and Wolfgang Gräser.

here all the possibilities of fugal writing are explored. Even the four canons which are included are intended to illustrate aspects of fugal composition.

Despite, or perhaps because of, its deceptively plain and unobtrusive character, the short theme of the Art of the Fugue is well suited to serve as a foundation for the monumental edifice. It is completely regular and symmetrical in its construction; played in inverted form its main intervals remain practically unchanged. If it is introduced together with its inversion, the result is a satisfactory two-part composition.

While Bach presents this theme in ever-changing rhythmic and melodic variation (*Ex.* 67), he gradually unfolds a complete manual of

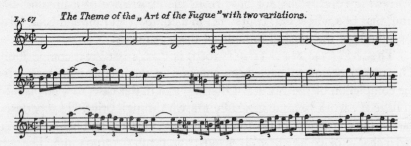

Ex. 67   The Theme of the „ Art of the Fugue"with two variations.

fugal composition. Each *Contrapunctus* (as he calls the individual variations to emphasize their learned character) gives a definite solution to a basic problem of fugal writing. The composition begins with a group of fugues which exhibit the theme partly in its original shape and partly inverted. Following this are counter-fugues and stretto-fugues,[1] presenting the theme not only in direct and contrary motion, but also in diminished and augmented form. Bach illustrates the possibilities of fugues with 2 and 3 themes, while the mighty quadruple fugue that was to form the climax of the work breaks off in its 239th measure. Just after the composer —like a medieval artist portraying himself in a corner of the picture—had inserted his own name B-A-C-H[2] into the work, this *Contrapunctus* abruptly stops, and later generations were faced with the fascinating, albeit dangerous, task of guessing at the master's intentions.[3] The most

[1] A counter-fugue uses the inversion of the subject as an answer. In a stretto two or more voices present a theme in such close succession that a new statement begins before the previous one is completed.

[2] The German name for the note b is H; for the note b flat it is B. Therefore the notes b flat-a-c-b natural signify in German B-A-C-H.

[3] Earlier historians like Moritz Hauptmann, Wilhelm Rust and Philipp Spitta assumed that the incomplete *Contrapunctus*, which did not contain the main subject of the whole cycle, did not really belong to the work. Gustav Nottebohm discovered, however, that the

stunning (though not necessarily the most complicated) *Contrapunctus* in the whole set is the four-part mirror fugue. Here Bach presents all the parts as *rectus* in their original form, and then again as *inversus* in inverted form. To make the mirror reflection doubly realistic, the soprano of the *rectus* becomes the bass of the *inversus*, the contralto changes into a tenor, the tenor into an alto, and the bass into a soprano, with the result that the whole composition now seems to stand on its head.

Such a playful and experimental character is not to be found in a second mirror fugue in 3 parts. This *Contrapunctus* is primarily intended for the clavier, but it can only be performed by two players, as the parts are too widely spaced to be executed by ten fingers. Since this is a 3-part composition, one of the four hands of the performers would remain idle, which seems a waste to the thrifty composer. He therefore inserts a filling fourth part which is completely independent of the highly artistic construction of the mirror fugue. Theoretically this foreign body, added merely for practical reasons, destroys the pure construction of the contrapuntal masterpiece, but it produces easily playable and attractive music, which seems to Bach of paramount importance.

This small detail offers a key to the understanding of the whole work. Like the Inventions and the Well-Tempered Clavier, the Art of the Fugue was intended as a didactic composition and as such it offers the quintessence of contrapuntal mastery. However, Bach was unable to write dry instructive precepts only. Under his hands the textbook changed into a poem imbued with the mystery of pure beauty. The solemn pathos which permeates each of these contrapuntal variations gives this farewell of a genius the transcendental character of art conceived on the threshold of eternity.

3 subjects of the fugue could be combined with the main theme of the Art of the Fugue, thus proving that Bach meant to write a quadruple fugue for his work. This shrewd conclusion inspired Riemann, Busoni (in his 'Fantasia Contrapunctica') and Tovey to attempt completions of the fugue. But nobody who has ever heard a performance of the work in which, without retard, the great fugue suddenly breaks off, would wish to exchange that deeply moving experience for a smooth and effective ending, however scholarly the execution.

EPILOGUE

LOOKING back on the activities of the Bach family as a whole during the first half of the 18th century, it may be said that simultaneously with the rise of an immortal genius out of their midst, the Bach musicians succeeded in greatly extending their spheres of influence beyond the original Bach centres. In Erfurt the descendants of Johann Bach were still active as organists and town musicians up to 1740, and as late as the 19th century Bachs of other lines were working there. In Eisenach Johann Bernhard (18) followed the great Johann Christoph (13) and was succeeded by a son, Johann Ernst (34). In Arnstadt another Johann Ernst (25), son of Ambrosius' twin brother, took over when Sebastian resigned as organist of the 'New Church,' and continued in this capacity up to his death in 1739. An important new Bach centre was established through Johann Ludwig in Meiningen. Here, after his death, his son and grandson served in the double capacity of court painter and court organist far beyond the period under discussion, in fact up to the year 1846. In the Franconian city of Schweinfurt three generations of Bachs worked either as cantor or organist, until Johann Elias (39) died in 1755. In Ohrdruf Sebastian's eldest brother, Johann Christoph (22), was succeeded by sons and grandsons serving up to 1814. In Jena Johann Nicolaus (27) held the post of University music director and organist for no less than 58 years. Mühlhausen, on the other hand, had three Bach organists in succession, among whom Johann Friedrich (29), a son of the great Johann Christoph, maintained the old tradition of stability in the 22 years of his service, while both Sebastian and his son, Johann Bernhard (47), stayed there for very short periods only. This list could be continued further, were we to include the Bach cantors or organists working in smaller communities of Thuringia. The locality of the Bach centres proclaims the family's deep-rooted loyalty to that part of Germany chosen by their forefathers. Yet there was an increasing number of Bach musicians who felt compelled to try their luck in new territories. The second son and namesake of the great Johann Christoph (13), after sojourning in Hamburg and Rotterdam, settled down as clavier teacher in England; one of his brothers travelled as organ builder to the North and was never heard of any more. Johann Jakob, too, (23), Sebastian's favourite brother, dreamed of adventures in foreign lands. He entered the Swedish army as a bandsman and his desire for travel found fulfilment, as he accompanied the army as far as Constantinople. Later he settled down as court musician in Stockholm, where he died in 1722. Sebastian himself, although passionately fond of travel, had no chance of undertaking such adventures. His creative urge dominated his life, and he went to those places where he hoped to find the best opportunities for congenial work. From 1717 onwards he lived away from Thuringia, and his sons, as will subsequently be shown, settled down in cities the family had never lived in before.

Sebastian held socially, economically, and artistically, a position of his own among his kinsmen. Not only did his income exceed by far that of any other member of the family, but he also enjoyed as Electoral and Royal Polish Court composer a social distinction not accorded to any other Bach of his time. And though his contemporaries could not grasp the importance of his achievements as a composer, he was considered the greatest German virtuoso on the organ and the most eminent expert on this instrument. However, in spite of his position high above all other Bach musicians, Sebastian was at one with them in his basic attitude towards his profession. Like most of his forefathers and relatives he considered it his main purpose to serve God in music. It was customary for him to start a new composition with the inscription J(esu)J(uva) and to end it with the letters s(olo) D(eo) G(loria). The Lutheran faith was the spiritual well-spring of his art, as it had been for the family in the past hundred years, and he was unaffected by the new trends of thought which threatened to undermine the mighty fortress of Protestantism. Being spiritually as well as artistically rooted in tradition was one of the sources of Sebastian's strength. On the other hand it was a decisive factor in determining the place he occupied in relation to contemporary music. By the time Bach had reached his zenith as a composer, a new generation had grown up which proclaimed a different artistic creed. They wanted music to be simple, natural and graceful and they criticized Sebastian Bach, as their spokesman, Johann Adolf Scheibe, put it, for 'his turgid and confused style . . . darkening beauty by an excess of art.' Here was a deep cleavage between old and new conceptions which Sebastian did not attempt to bridge. Although he occasionally showed that he was quite able to master the new language, he chose, with advancing years, to live in splendid isolation, concerned only with fulfilling his tremendous self-imposed tasks. The result was that the younger generation had little, if any, interest in a composer whom they considered hopelessly old-fashioned.

The era of J. S. Bach marked the peak of creative achievement in the family history. No longer was the output confined to a few forms of composition. In the first half of the 18th century the Bachs cultivated every type of music known in their time, with the significant exceptions of opera and Catholic church music. However, their widespread activities were not accompanied by commensurate recognition and fame. These were to come to the family in the following generation, whose contributions encompassed the entire realm of music.

PART III

THE LAST GREAT ACHIEVEMENTS
AND THE DECLINE OF
THE BACH FAMILY
(1750-   )

INTRODUCTION: ROCOCO AND CLASSICISM

IN the 18th century the triumphant rise of Natural Science brought about a complete change in man's general outlook and conception of the Universe. The former uncritical acceptance of doctrines handed down by the writers of antiquity had been replaced by empirical observation leading to the revolutionary discoveries of a Galileo, Newton, and Kepler. Before long scientific methods were not confined to the domain of Science. All manifestations of life were subordinated to Reason. Superstition and bigotry were relentlessly exposed, and in all realms of life antiquated prejudices were thrown overboard. The spirit of Enlightenment also gradually undermined the bastions of the Christian faith and even the Muses were expected to follow closely the dictates of Reason. A certain trend towards Naturalism may be observed in the Rococo style originating in the second quarter of the 18th century. Shepherds and shepherdesses became the fashion both in poetry and in painting; for they displayed the simplicity, charm and impudent gaiety which people of the Rococo era cherished. In music this spirit produced the *style galant*. The intricacies of Baroque contrapuntal art were forsworn as being contrary to reason, and a monodic style was the goal. 'The ear,' as Mattheson claimed, 'often derives more satisfaction from a single, well-ordered voice developing a clear-cut melody in all its natural freedom than from 24 parts which, in order to share in the melody, tear it to such an extent that it becomes incomprehensible.' As to the emotional content, the aim professed by the song-composer Valentin Görner is typical: 'to write engaging, charming, jocular, graceful, enamoured, and gay tunes.' It should not be overlooked that the new Rococo style in music grew at the very time when Baroque composition reached its climax in Sebastian Bach and Handel. On the other hand the *style galant* did not remain unchallenged even among the younger generation. The English philosopher, Edward Young, and the German, J. Georg Hamann, proved that the creations of genius are not based on reasoning and theoretical speculation, but on divine inspiration. In music the delicate and carefree artistic idiom which had conquered Southern and Western Europe was replaced, particularly in Northern Germany, by a more solid musical language in which emphasis was laid on expressive power and sensibility (*Empfindsamkeit*). 'It is the business of music,' declared Daniel Webb in his 'Observations on the Correspondence between Poetry and Music,' 'to express passions in the way they rise out of the soul.' And Philipp Emanuel Bach exhorted his followers with the axiom: 'A musician cannot move others unless he himself is moved.'

Even before the *Empfindsamkeit* reached its climax in the 'Storm and Stress' of the early seventies, to which most great spirits of the time made significant contributions, a fusion of the two main forms of Rococo music was envisioned. The *style galant* and the *Empfindsamkeit* were combined into a new idiom of early classicism that was gay and light, yet tender and deeply felt; an idiom which represented a fine balance of form and content, of the language of the heart and that of the intellect. Attempts towards reaching a union of these apparently incongruous elements were made as early as 1760, although the classical style did not reach its highest perfection until much later in the symphonies and quartets of a Haydn and Mozart.

This evolution may be observed in the most diverse artistic and spiritual manifestations of the time. There is a close affinity between musical classicism, the ideals of humanism and world brotherhood, and the noble simplicity and quiet grandeur manifested in contemporary literature and fine arts. The work of the Bachs was determined by these changing trends, and at the same time it contributed greatly towards shaping them.

THE HALLE BACH
(WILHELM FRIEDEMANN BACH)

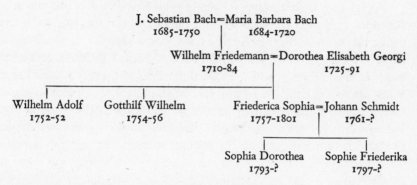

J. Sebastian Bach=Maria Barbara Bach
1685-1750   1684-1720

Wilhelm Friedemann=Dorothea Elisabeth Georgi
1710-84   1725-91

Wilhelm Adolf   Gotthilf Wilhelm   Friederica Sophia=Johann Schmidt
1752-52   1754-56   1757-1801   1761-?

Sophia Dorothea   Sophie Friederika
1793-?   1797-?

THE adolescence of Friedemann[1] was described in the story of Sebastian's life. We left the consideration of the career of this eldest son of the master when, in 1733, he started independently in Dresden. The fond hopes that accompanied him seemed fully justified. At the age of 23 Friedemann was an outstanding and inspired organ virtuoso whose improvisations approached those of his father in grandeur and imaginative power, while in the field of composition he also showed definite promise. The position he held at Dresden's *Sophienkirche* was not an important one, but it had the advantage of taking up but little of the organist's time. He was required to play every Monday at 8 a.m., and every Sunday and feast-day for a morning and an afternoon service; this gave Friedemann an opportunity for continuing his studies. Although music naturally occupied the centre of his activities, he still continued the mathematical work which had captivated his mind while he attended Leipzig University. In this respect Friedemann was the true son of his father, on whom the world of numbers and their symbolic use in music exercised a real fascination. Moreover, Friedemann did a great deal of teaching, and one of his pupils brought him much satisfaction and prestige. This was young Johann Theophilus Goldberg, whose name has survived in the history of music as the pianist who played Sebastian Bach's 'Aria with 30 Variations' at night to his protector, Count Keyserlingk, in order to help the Count forget the pains and insomnia caused by a serious illness. At times Goldberg

[1] Cf. Martin Falck, 'Wilhelm Friedemann Bach,' Leipzig, 1913.

was taken by the Count to Leipzig, to get instruction on certain problems from Sebastian Bach, but it was mainly Friedemann who taught the brilliant pianist; and though this virtuoso naturally held a unique position among the organist's pupils, it may be assumed that Friedemann at that time did not mind 'informing the youth' (as the 18th century described work of this kind) and was a capable teacher.

Social and artistic contacts were easily established. Friedemann had occasionally visited Dresden with his father and had met many musicians there. He knew the great Adolf Hasse, opera director at Dresden, and Hasse's wife, the renowned prima donna, Faustina Bordoni, and he saw much of the eminent flautist, P. G. Buffardin, who years ago had taught Sebastian's elder brother, Johann Jakob (cf. p. 297), when that adventure-loving musician came to Constantinople as oboist in the Swedish army. Friedemann also got on well with other court musicians and invited them to visit his father in Leipzig for communal music-making, an invitation which meant much to any good musician. After Sebastian was appointed in 1736 Royal Polish and Electoral Saxon Court composer (an honour for which the master expressed his gratitude by giving a most magnificent recital on the new Silbermann organ of Dresden's *Frauenkirche*), his son had no difficulty in making contacts with the music-loving aristocrats at the court. Thus in many ways the father extended from a distance a helping hand to his beloved 'Friede,' smoothing out difficulties which he himself, in his youth, had had to overcome unaided.

And yet, in spite of such manifest advantages, Dresden presented problems, and even dangers, to an unstable, highly impressionable young artist. How utterly different was life at the Saxon capital from that which Friedemann had experienced at the Thomas Cantor's home! There the strictest economy prevailed; every penny had to be accounted for and, for the sake of a few outstanding thalers, his father had spent hours and hours drafting lengthy petitions and complaints to his monarch. The Bachs' home contained just what was necessary for living; luxury in furniture, food or clothes would have been considered unseemly for a man in Sebastian's position. Those standards of economy, and even austerity, which were considered a matter of course by the Bach children, seemed strangely out of place in Dresden. At the court, operas, ballets, redoutes, sleigh-rides, and the most ingenious illuminations followed each other in a breath-taking succession, all presented with the most expensive settings and costumes. The monarch did not mind spending a sum of 40,000 thalers on one carnival season alone, besides a huge amount of money on the enormous entertainment programme for the rest of the year. It was a glittering fairyland into which Friedemann had moved, a land where a newly appointed ambassador was received by 30 state coaches, each drawn by 6 magnificent horses, and led over a bridge lit by some 3000 lamps. The musicians at the Dresden court lived in an atmosphere vastly different from that in Leipzig (a fact that Sebastian felt impelled to mention in a petition to his Leipzig superiors). Hasse drew for his 'pretty little tunes,' as Sebastian smilingly described them to his son, a salary quite beyond that of the Leipzig *director musices*. He and Faustina each received 6000 thalers a year, which was about eight times Sebastian's income, and were given besides a travel allowance of 500 thalers and the chance to earn a great deal through guest appearances.

All this was strangely disturbing and likely to upset a young man's set of values. Maybe Friedemann would have been able to throw over the family standard and to adopt wholeheartedly the outlook on life prevailing at the Dresden court; but this was impossible, for he did not belong to the luxurious, dazzling court world, and could only watch it with a fascination tinged with envy. A Protestant organist was of very little significance indeed in Dresden at that time. The Elector, following the example of his father, Augustus 'the Strong,' who had given up Protestantism in order to become King of Poland, was a devout Catholic; his wife was an Austrian princess with the traditional interest of the Hapsburgs in the Catholic Church, and during their reign Protestantism lost more and more ground in Dresden. It is significant that the Elector had a magnificent new Catholic church built; while the former Protestant court church in the castle was remodelled into living quarters for employees, and the Protestant court servants were ordered henceforth to worship at the *Sophienkirche*. Great indignation prevailed among the non-Catholics, and Friedemann especially had good reasons for being vexed. Not only was his work hampered by the alterations made in his church, into which equipment from the former court church was fitted, but he had to play on Sundays for two morning services (one extra for the court employees, who were unwilling to mix with the regular congregation), without receiving any additional remuneration.

Even in Dresden there were, it is true, better positions to be found for a Protestant musician. Working on the new organ of the *Frauenkirche*, for instance, carried greater distinction, and Friedemann must have had his eye on the vacancy which occurred there in 1742. It was filled, however, by another pupil of Sebastian's, Gottfried August Homilius, who gave such satisfaction that he was later appointed *Kreuzkantor* and musical director of Dresden's three main Protestant churches. Changing from one

U

organ to another within a town was by no means unusual—for example, Sebastian's rival at Leipzig, Johann Gottlieb Görner, had done so (cf. p. 174)—and the fact that Homilius was preferred to Friedemann Bach seems to point to young Bach's inability to establish cordial relations with his superiors. Nor did Friedemann make much headway as a composer of secular music. In Dresden the Italian taste reigned supreme, and the organist's language, although it adopted the Italian idiom in various details, seemed too complicated and too teutonic to please the capital's music lovers.

Gradually it became apparent that Friedemann would always remain an outsider in the glittering Saxon town, and that real success was not attainable there. He began to look for a chance to leave Dresden and find a position elsewhere with greater responsibilities and wider scope. When he was 36, a fine opportunity materialized, and it is significant that it took him to a place where his father was well known. It will be remembered that while working in Weimar, Sebastian, tempted by the outstanding merits of the organ built at that time in Halle's *Liebfrauenkirche*, had applied for the vacant organist's post and given his trial performance to everybody's delight. The negotiations had led to no result, much to the disappointment of the Halle electors, as Sebastian found the conditions offered less desirable than those granted him at Weimar. Eventually the master succeeded in conciliating the Halle authorities, and when work on the organ was finished, he was invited to test the instrument (cf. p. 147). Since then 30 years had passed, during which Gottfried Kirchhoff had served as organist at the *Liebfrauenkirche*. When on his death in January 1746 the position became vacant, the Bach family was naturally interested in securing this important appointment for one of its members. Sebastian probably got into touch with his former correspondent, August Becker, who was still a member of the church board. Friedemann himself must have been able to present recommendations of the highest order, for against all precedent he was given the position without passing the customary trial performance. There is some possibility that the decisive word in his favour was uttered by Friedrich II ('the Great') of Prussia. The King had just won a victory over Saxony in the 'second Silesian war' (1744-45) and in December 1745 occupied Dresden. During the nine days of his stay, this ardent friend of the muses enjoyed with the greatest zest all that the Dresden musicians had to offer; indeed, on the very day of his entry into the capital, he attended the première of a Hasse opera. As Philipp Emanuel Bach had for several years been in the King's service, it seems likely that Friedrich, interested in his accompanist's elder brother, heard him play while in Dresden. The city of Halle belonged to the state of Brandenburg which was united with Prussia, and although the appointment of an organist was a purely municipal matter, Friedrich could easily have hinted that the choice of Friedemann Bach would be agreeable to him. Anyway, on April 16, 1746, the contract was signed—it was identical with that sent to Sebastian in 1714—and on Whitsunday Friedemann assumed his new duties. It was a great step forward in every respect. The position formerly held by such eminent musicians as Samuel Scheidt and Friedrich Wilhelm Zachau, the teacher of Handel, carried much distinction. Friedemann's basic salary was more than twice his honorarium at Dresden,[1] and in addition he could hope for a larger income from *Accidentien*. The position gave him much greater responsibilities; for he served not only as organist, but as conductor of the concerted music played on high feast-days and every third Sunday at the *Liebfrauenkirche*, and as composer of many of the works to be performed. He held the title of *Director Musices*, as his father did at Leipzig, having at his disposal a large choir and a sizeable group of instrumentalists recruited from the town musicians and the *Collegium Musicum*.

If Friedemann, on leaving Dresden, had wanted a complete change of atmosphere, he certainly got it in Halle. Here was no glamorous court life, no display of luxury, no opera, and only isolated theatrical performances when King Friedrich overrode the objections of certain citizens. Halle had for the past fifty years been the centre of pietism, which, with its insistence on an ascetic life preparing for the hereafter, frowned on anything savouring of sensuous pleasure. Women were expected to be clad with nun-like simplicity; dancing and smoking were considered frivolities, and music was suffered only as a means of 'inspiring and refreshing the congregation in worship' (as it reads in Friedemann's contract). When the new *Director Musices* came to Halle, pietism had lost much of its original fervour and appeal. The leadership had passed from the great humanitarian, August Hermann Francke, unforgettable in Halle as the creator of large-scale charitable and educational institutions, which still exist to-day,[2] to his son, Gotthilf August, a domineering, narrow-

---

[1] The basic salary of 181 th. 12 gr. had not seemed adequate to his father in 1714, but Sebastian had to provide for wife and children at that time, while Friedemann was still a bachelor.

[2] Francke founded a school for poor children, an orphanage, a boarding school, and a Latin day school for paying students; later he added a mission institute for the East Indies. All these institutes, where girls also were taught, were united in a kind of school town with its own farm, clinic, book store, and dispensary. The production of certain medicines provided an important income for the various charitable institutions.

minded theologian whose outlook was typical of the gradual petrification taking place in the pietistic doctrines. It was bad luck for Friedemann that the younger Francke was archidiaconus of his church,[1] a superior lacking a real understanding of music. He and his colleagues were certainly not pleasant to work with. At Halle no musician could dare to behave with anything but exemplary propriety. Nothing was overlooked or ever forgotten by the church authorities. Even minor breaches of regulations were sharply reprimanded and a real offence brought instant dismissal.[2]

After living for 13 years in Dresden, it cannot have been easy for Friedemann to adapt himself to such diametrically opposed conditions. It is true that he had always been an outsider in the Saxon capital; but even as such he had absorbed enough of its easy-going, sensuous atmosphere to deviate from some of the strict standards on which he had been brought up. Now he was transplanted to a circle where the pleasures of life were regarded with suspicion, where a sober, austere mode of living was a matter of course. Had young Friedemann gone straight from Leipzig to Halle, he might have become a sincere pietist; but the man of 36, familiar with an entirely different philosophy of life, found such reorientation difficult indeed. Sometimes he may have come perilously near to sharing the opinion of his sovereign, Friedrich 'the Great,' who derided the Halle pietists as 'Protestant Jesuits and Pharisees.' Yet, a son of Sebastian Bach, so close to his father, must have possessed a great capacity for a genuine religious life, and Friedemann might eventually have achieved a real acceptance of the pietistic doctrine, had there not been a disturbing influence from another quarter.

On its foundation in 1693 the University of Halle, one of the most distinguished Protestant institutions of learning in Germany, mainly served the cause of pietism. However, its harmonious atmosphere was rudely shaken when the philosopher and mathematician, Christian Wolff, the foremost German exponent of the new trend of *Aufklärung* (enlightenment), started his lectures in 1707. In his system there was no place for the religious impulses and mystical experiences so dear to pietists, nor did he see in this world a vale of tears. Wolff based his philosophy on the sound working of human reason, and following his great model, Leibniz (cf. p. 85), he proved that the world we lived in was the best of all possible worlds. His system, with its emphasis on empirical methods of research, had dangerous implications for pietism, and indeed for all denominations, and was likely ultimately to lead to scepticism and atheism (though Wolff

---

[1] He died in 1769, one year before Friedemann left Halle.
[2] This happened to Friedemann's colleague, Cantor Mittag.

himself was a very religious man). He was therefore viciously attacked by the Church, and when he dared even to prove in a lecture on Confucius that morals were independent of theology, his enemies succeeded in enforcing in 1723 his expulsion from Halle. But they could not stop the triumphant progress of his doctrine, which was just what the young minds needed, and when Friedrich 'the Great' ascended the throne in 1740, one of his first acts was to recall Wolff to Halle. By the time Friedemann settled down in his new appointment, Wolff had gained an unassailable position, and his pupils were successfully applying the new rationalistic method in all fields of knowledge. Of particular importance for Halle was Johann Salomo Semler, who started the historical-critical interpretation of Biblical sources.

Naturally the new *Director Musices* (after being introduced into university circles by his friend, the publisher, J. J. Gebauer), could not overlook the two controversial trends which dominated Halle's intellectual and religious life. Tossed between the Scylla of rationalism and the Charybdis of pietism, Friedemann had not the strength to preserve the profound Christian faith in which he had been brought up. This is clearly revealed in his compositions written for the church, which are not on the same level as his instrumental music and lack real religious fervour. It was Friedemann's tragic fate that in Halle once again he did not become part of a leading faction, and yet, on the other hand, he was not strong enough to enjoy such splendid isolation. This may have been one of the reasons for his unhappiness there and his eventual breakdown.

The first years were quite pleasant, though; while Sebastian was alive, his very existence gave the son support. In the spring of 1747 the two travelled together to Berlin and Potsdam to pay a visit to the King; a great experience of which Friedemann loved to relate in later years. In 1750 he made the same trip again, but under what sad conditions! Sebastian had died, and Friedemann, after administering his father's affairs in Leipzig, took his half-brother, Johann Christian, to Emanuel, who had offered Christian a home. Shaken by the irreparable loss, Friedemann stayed in Berlin much longer than he had intended, and on his return to Halle he had to face public reprimand by the authorities. This was not his first trouble with the Board; for a few months earlier he had been threatened with dismissal for having, contrary to regulation, lent the church's drums to the Collegium Musicum. But Friedemann somehow managed to calm his superiors, and for several years no complaints are reported.

Doubly aware of his solitude now that visits to his father were no longer possible, Friedemann decided, at the age of 41, to marry the daughter of an excise official with whom he had resided since his arrival in Halle. The choice was a sensible one as the bride had some means of her own, and it looked as though the artist were now embarking on a life along traditional lines. Three children were born, for whom the father provided high-ranking godparents, such as the Dresden court-marshal, and the Princes of Anhalt-Cöthen. However, only one daughter, Friede-rica Sophia, born 1757, survived infancy, and in the long run marriage did not cure Friedemann of his restlessness and dissatisfaction. He tried several times to get a position elsewhere; in 1753 he applied for an organist's post at Zittau; in 1758 for similar work at Frankfurt, and his repeated absences, for which the Halle authorities reproached their music director, were probably connected with other unsuccessful attempts in this direction. Ten years after his arrival in Halle, the city became a most unpleasant place to live in. War broke out between Prussia, assisted by England and a few small North German states on the one side, and Austria Russia, France, Saxony and various other German states on the other; a struggle that was carried on through seven years. From the outset it was realized that Halle could not be defended, and so it was declared an open city. Again and again one of the various enemy armies quartered itself in the unfortunate town, using up all its resources and with threats of complete devastation through fire enforcing the payments of outrageous ransoms. All the citizens had to contribute to these payments, but even so it seems amazing how the population of 13,000 could manage to satisfy the various occupying troops, which in the year 1760, for instance, in-sisted on receiving 301,747 thalers and extensive deliveries in kind. This state of things went on for years with hardly any intermission. Work of every kind almost came to a standstill, the cattle succumbed to plagues, there was a scarcity of every foodstuff, and the inhabitants' nerves were strained to breaking point. Friedemann suffered like the rest, and although he was not a citizen he was taxed for contributions to the enemy because of the property belonging to his wife. This he felt to be unfair and he decided to appeal to the Church Board. It cannot be said that he chose a propitious moment for this step. On October 20, 1761, only a few days after the purely military danger seemed to be overcome for the moment through the arrival of Prussian troops in the vicinity, he wrote his peti-tion. Oblivious to the fact that the war was not yet over, that the city had in the last, worst year, lost literally all its resources, and that the church treasury was depleted, he not only asked for exemption from tax, claiming it had been granted to other church servants, but continued with this request: 'I venture at the same time submissively to ask your Honours for an increase in my salary. When I started work, the late chairman, Mr. Schäfer, assured me in the name of A Most Noble Church Council that he would see to such increase, should the conditions of the church improve. This assurance given me 15 years ago, and the present very hard times, with prices rising daily, induce me to appeal now to my Most Noble and Honoured patrons.' It was certainly true that Friedemann suffered from the catastrophic economic conditions prevailing in Halle, but it seems hardly credible that with the events of the past years in mind he could have ventured to request the increase which had been promised to him in the event of improved conditions. Indeed the letter reveals a degree of self-absorption and an inability to foresee the other person's reaction which clearly explains why the various attempts to secure a position, which Friedemann undertook after his father's death (and therefore without his support and advice), turned out to be failures. No wonder this letter did not produce the hoped-for result. The church elders, who had gone through such harassing times and as yet did not know how to save the town from bankruptcy, were outraged and did not hide their feelings. They curtly answered that the allotment to him of a share in the payments to the enemy was justified, as he was enjoying the protection resulting from such payments, and incidentally was taxed less than the meanest craftsman. As to the salary-increase, they did not see any reason whatsoever for it in view of 'his frequently improper behaviour and his lack of submission to the Church Board as, despite the reprimand given him *in pleno Collegii*, he had absented himself repeatedly without special permission.' Finally he was advised henceforth to show greater subordination so as not to force the Board to take further steps. It should be emphasized that Friedemann's 'improper behaviour' could certainly not have been anything of the kind implied by this expression in our time. Loose morals or dissolute habits would not have been tolerated by the Council for even a short period, and in 1761 Friedemann had been in office for 15 years! The Council had indeed to exert its memory to prove its point, for the reprimand referred to had been delivered eleven years before, when Friedemann had overstayed his leave after the death of his father!

The effect of this most outspoken letter on the organist, who felt he had given excellent service to Halle, can well be imagined. It must have been a true relief to him when one year later he got a most tempting offer. He was invited to succeed Christoph Graupner, at one time Sebastian's rival for the Thomas Cantorate (cf. p. 166), as conductor to the court of Darmstadt. The position was a highly important one carrying a salary of

900 fl. as well as contributions in kind; indeed, it was so good that Graupner had seen fit to decline the position at Leipzig for its sake. For Friedemann it must have seemed like the fulfilment of his greatest wishes; at Darmstadt he could start a new life, devote himself to instrumental music, and at last reap the rewards that he felt to be his due. Friedemann accepted and was urged to get started on the removal of his belongings, for which 100 fl. were offered to him. But the musician, 52 years old, did not like to be rushed. In the ensuing correspondence he insisted on receiving the official decree first, and with characteristic stubbornness he did not refrain from this request even when Darmstadt made it clear that the document would be handed to him on his arrival. What happened after that is rather obscure, as Friedemann's own letters have not been preserved; but it may be surmised that his hesitant manner of carrying on the negotiations and his lack of pliability made a bad impression. Anyway, he eventually got the coveted title, but not the position. The darkness veiling this chapter of Friedemann's history, which might have become a turning-point in his career, also shrouds the next fatal step he took. On May 12, 1764, he resigned his position at Halle, stopping work instantly, and not even appearing for the checking of the instruments entrusted to his care. No dispute has been recorded which might have provoked so sudden a decision; moreover Friedemann had no other position in prospect on which to fall back, though he may have hoped for a chance at Fulda. Apparently the resentment and disappointment engendered in Friedemann's mind for 18 years just had to find an outlet, and the artist felt irresistibly drawn to washing his hands of his ungracious and narrow-minded superiors, and to showing them that he did not depend on their favour. The satisfaction he derived from this act of defiance must have been great indeed, but so was the price he and his dependants had to pay for it.

Through six more years he stayed on in Halle, getting some help from his friend, the publisher Gebauer, and working as a music teacher. Some of his pupils in Halle were highly successful. Among them his kinsman, Johann Christian Bach (1743-1814), known as the 'Clavier-Bach,' should be mentioned. He was the son of Michael Bach, Cantor of St. Ulrich in Halle, and probably a nephew of the Meiningen court conductor, Johann Ludwig Bach. The relative received various gifts of manuscripts from his teacher, among them Sebastian's *Clavierbüchlein* written for young Friedemann. Another pupil was Friedrich Wilhelm Rust, whose grandson, Wilhelm Rust, was to become one of the foremost editors of the *Bach-Gesellschaft*, and to the elder Rust the generous teacher gave the autograph of Sebastian's French Suites. Johann Samuel Petri also proudly claims in his *Anleitung zur praktischen Musik* that he enjoyed 'the Halle Bach's friendship and instruction.'

In 1767 Friedemann tried to win the favour of Maria Antonia, Electress of Saxony, by dedicating to her his Clavier Concerto in e. In the accompanying letter he reminded the Princess that he had heard her singing in Dresden when he had brought his pupil, Goldberg, to perform for her.[1] We hope that the Electress rewarded him—a fact that cannot be checked, as the Princess' private accounts of this period have not been preserved— but nothing else resulted from this attempt, as Maria Antonia, a fertile composer herself, cared only for the Italian style in music.

In August 1770 Friedemann decided to leave Halle for good, and his wife's property was put up for auction. At the age of 60 he started a wandering life, following the chance of an appointment here or there, but never achieving tangible results. Wherever he appeared people were fascinated by his organ playing, and received him at first with enthusiasm and reverence; yet they did not desire to engage him. He was too old, too eccentric (for how else could one regard a man who had thrown away a perfectly satisfactory position without having secured another?), and too famous to fit into a regular routine job which a modest young man would fill so much more satisfactorily. Thus Friedemann failed in the city of Braunschweig—not the first Bach, incidentally, to live there, as a kinsman, Johann Stephan Bach, had served from 1689-1718 as a Dom-Cantor—and a visit to Göttingen, where his great admirer, Johann Nikolaus Forkel, worked as University organist, did not bring success either. The composer made a precarious living through organ recitals, teaching, writing works for special occasions, and, at times, selling manuscripts of his father's, always hoping that he would yet find a permanent position. In 1774 Berlin seemed to offer him such a chance, and in one of his sudden decisions—so characteristic of Friedemann in his old age—he rushed from Braunschweig without even taking time to provide in an orderly fashion for the most valuable property he owned, the bulk of the autographs of his father's works. He just left them with his friend, Professor Eschenburg, to be auctioned, and did not even bother to make a list of his possessions. Apparently the matter slipped his mind altogether,

---

[1] Maria Antonia, a Bavarian princess, entered Dresden as a bride in 1748, two years after Friedemann left the town. She may have come for a visit previously, and on that occasion received Goldberg and Bach; or else Friedemann may have visited Dresden from Halle. In the dedication he mentions Count Keyserlingk as Russian ambassador to Saxony, so the visit would have occurred between 1749 and 1752, when the Count was again attached to the Dresden court after leaving it in 1745.

and he only took it up again four years later, when his finances were running low.[1] Eschenburg's answer is not preserved and so we do not know what happened to Friedemann's priceless collection.

Berlin at first fell under the spell of the artist, and his superb organ recitals received enthusiastic praise. A reviewer in the *Berlinische Nachrichten* exclaimed: 'Everything that intoxicates the emotions, novelty of ideas, amazing development, dissonances dying away in a harmony like Graun's, force, delicacy, were united under the fingers of this master to convey joy and grief. Would it have been possible not to recognize the worthy son of a Sebastian?' Berlin's high-ranking music-lovers received him with open arms, especially as the King's sister, the artistic Princess Anna Amalia, who had appointed his brother, Emanuel, conductor to her court, and was besides a great admirer of Sebastian's style, showed him many favours. Friedemann, to express 'his most ardent feelings of gratitude,' dedicated 8 Fugues to her in 1778 and apparently cherished hopes of a court appointment. But, as so often in late years, he had been too sanguine, and before long the whole edifice of his plans crashed down on him. The Princess' conductor, Johann Philipp Kirnberger, a pupil of Sebastian Bach, had, out of reverent gratitude for Friedemann's father, greatly befriended the newcomer, and introduced him to influential people. Now Friedemann somehow deluded himself that the Princess might dismiss Kirnberger for his sake, and started an intrigue at court against his protector; but the result was that the weapon prepared against Kirnberger turned against himself, and he lost the patronage of the Princess as well as Kirnberger's support. Other distinguished supporters also were disappointed when they found the musician unwilling to exhibit his unique art of improvisation, for the sake of which they had invited him to their homes. If the atmosphere seemed uncongenial to him, he curtly refused to play, and thus earned the reputation of haughtiness and eccentricity. But when he met with genuine understanding, as in the case of the composer Carl Friedrich Zelter, the friend of Goethe, he would play for hours to his entranced audience. Teaching would still have procured him a modest income, had he not grown increasingly impatient with untalented pupils, and even refused to accept them, regardless of their wealth and position. Again he made exceptions in the case of genuine

[1] From this letter dated July 4, 1778, we also learn that Friedemann left at Braunschweig books that had belonged to his father, and of these also no trace has been discovered. This is the more regrettable, for Sebastian's library would have offered important clues as to his general interests. In the inventory of his estate only a rich supply of theological books is mentioned, which were listed for sale as apparently neither Friedemann nor Emanuel cared to take them.

musicianship, and he instructed, for instance, up to his death the highly gifted Sara Itzig, a great-aunt of Felix Mendelssohn,[1] who acquired an extensive collection of Friedemann's later compositions together with those of his brother, Emanuel. Some help came from the family of Count Keyserlingk,[2] thus continuing the tradition established through the writing of Sebastian's 'Goldberg Variations,' but such irregular support together with the small annuity Friedemann's wife still received from Halle[3] could bring only temporary relief. It was in such desperate straits that the old musician committed those acts of artistic dishonesty which posterity still holds against him: he claimed the authorship of an organ concerto which was really his father's arrangement of a Vivaldi violin concerto (cf. p. 246), a falsification to be cleared up only in 1911, although Zelter had already guessed the truth in his correspondence with Goethe. On the other hand, when it became clear to Friedemann that the market for Sebastian's music was better than for his own works, he erased the name on two of his compositions replacing it with that of his father.

For ten years Friedemann lived in Berlin, fighting a tragic struggle against poverty and increasing illness; again and again spoiling the few chances that still came his way by his fits of temper, his intransigence, and his increasing aversion from effort of any kind. Friedemann had not been born with any of his father's fighting spirit, and gradually he learned to substitute flights into the world of imagination for action. The constant failure of his hopes for an appointment and the lack of appreciation for his own compositions forced him more and more into a world of his own, and when he died in 1784 at the age of 74,[4] only one newspaper in Berlin reported the event, exclaiming that 'Germany had lost its foremost organ player, and the musical world a man whose loss was irreplaceable.'

The lot of Friedemann's widow was a sad one. At first she seems to have received some support from music friends, for it is known that part of the proceeds from a performance of Handel's 'Messiah' in 1785 were allotted to her. Gradually, however, her existence was forgotten, and when she died in 1791 she was given, like Anna Magdalena Bach, a pauper's funeral. Their only surviving daughter, Friederica Sophia, did not keep up the rigid moral standard to which the Bachs had for centuries adhered;

---

[1] Bitter, Falck and Miesner erroneously describe her as Felix Mendelssohn's grandmother.

[2] Cf. Miesner in *BJ*, 1934.

[3] Cf. Miesner in *BJ*, 1932.

[4] His long life best disproves Reichardt's reports about Friedemann's excessive drinking habits which, incidentally, are not referred to in any other contemporary source of information.

for when in 1793, at the age of 36, she married a musketeer in an infantry regiment, the ceremony took place five days after the birth of a daughter to the couple. The church-register also reports the birth of another daughter in 1797, but as the father had the very common name of Johann Schmidt, it proved impossible for research scholars to follow up the fate of these two great-granddaughters of Sebastian Bach.

The story of Friedemann, this truly gifted but tragically failing artist, has always exercised a fascination on writers of fiction. He was the hero of a highly romantic best-selling novel in the 19th century, and again more recently of a German film. Friedemann is certainly the most enigmatic of Sebastian's sons, and for some of his decisive actions it has—in the absence of clear evidence—been impossible to find a real clue. Yet the little we know about him is sufficient to show us a man so utterly absorbed in his own self that he was unable to estimate and gauge the reactions of other people. It is significant that the only two positions he obtained were won during his father's lifetime; when Sebastian's counsel and help were no longer at the son's disposal, Friedemann was singularly unsuccessful in whatever he attempted. He did not learn from his failures; they threw him into a deep depression which was suddenly succeeded by a bout of unfounded optimism[1] leading him to highly irresponsible actions. Looking back over Friedemann's life as a whole, we cannot help seeing in the great love and support which Sebastian unstintingly offered to his eldest son, a fatal gift. It atrophied Friedemann's initiative and it also reduced his artistic independence.

THE MUSIC OF WILHELM FRIEDEMANN BACH

Twenty-five years separated Friedemann from his father. He belonged to a younger generation which passionately desired to overcome the past and speak its own artistic language. Loyalty to Sebastian struggled in his heart against loyalty to his own time. As a result his music displayed a mixture of conservative and progressive elements. In his vocal compositions he used with equal success strict and free polyphony as well as completely homophonic forms. Nevertheless his attempts to develop

---

[1] My friend, Dr. Leo Hess, Boston, kindly pointed out that Friedemann's extremely beautiful, sensitive hands, shown on the well-known portrait in the City Museum of Halle, classify him as a personality disposed to emotional depressions and periodic fits of ecstasy.

further the language of Sebastian's church cantatas show little originality. Friedemann was far greater in his instrumental music. Here he adopted a style that was basically homophonic, though adorned with frequent imitations. He rarely used more than one subject in a movement, but like his brothers he was fond of changes in expression and sudden surprises. The static rigidity of mood in Baroque compositions was replaced in Friedemann's works by the sudden contrasts peculiar to the age of sensibility.

Yet so much of Sebastian's influence remained that the son's compositions were regarded by his contemporaries as old-fashioned and complex. The artist did not meet with the success which he felt he deserved. Frustration reduced the volume of his creative output and made him indulge more and more in a musical language that went far beyond the fashionable sensibility. The optimistic compositions of his early manhood already show a subjective and strongly emotional character; and as the composer grew older, this tendency increased. His later works display passion and grief, and then again, in some slow movements, a fervour and depth of feeling which few composers expressed in his time.

The inability of the ageing Friedemann to fit into any established pattern of life, his lack of social graces, his opposition to composing or even improvising 'on order,' and, on the other hand, the comparatively small number of works he wrote, among which compositions for the clavier play so important a part: all this could be better understood in an artist living sixty or even a hundred years later. Friedemann is the disappointed Romanticist among the sons of Sebastian, a man who seemed old-fashioned to his contemporaries, whereas in many respects he was far ahead of his time.

In spite of the impossibility of establishing exact dates of composition for most of Friedemann's works, the main periods of his artistic development are easily traceable. Only a few works from Friedemann's youth (1710-33) have been preserved. They are either in a superficial Rococo style which sounds strangely unsatisfactory when handled by Friedemann, or they follow closely the model of the greatest music teacher of the century. The period of maturity embraced the two long stays in Dresden and Halle (1733-70). At first Friedemann devoted all his energies to instrumental composition (Dresden, 1733-46), and only while living in Halle (1746-70) did he concentrate on a vocal output, which consisted almost exclusively of church cantatas. There is also a significant contrast in mood between the works of the Dresden and the Halle period. The compositions Friedemann wrote in his earlier years show a powerful, affirmative spirit and are predominantly in the major mode. For the organist in pietistic Halle and especially for the man who stayed afterwards in the same city without a job, life had lost much of this brightness and lustre. The compositions then created frequently display a passionate yearning and a tragic unrest, for which the minor mode is more often used than before. The last period (1771-84), which Friedemann spent in Braunschweig and Berlin without a permanent occupation, shows a marked decrease in the volume of his output, and not infrequently a decline in the quality of the works written. Both the retrospective and the romantic elements are now more strongly emphasized. The composer of 70 who so far had never had any connection with the stage, now worked on an opera,[1] but to the same period belong the fine little clavier fugues which he dedicated to Princess Amalia of Prussia.

The bonds linking Friedemann with the past are most evident in his *compositions for the organ*. Forkel writes in his biography of Johann Sebastian:[2] 'When I heard Wilhelm Friedemann . . . on the organ, I was seized with reverential awe . . . here all was great and solemn,' and Daniel Schubart[3] considered Friedemann's achievements as an organ virtuoso not only as equal but almost as superior to those of his father. Such enthusiastic reports are apt to arouse the highest anticipations for Friedemann's compositions for the king of instruments, but actually he seems to have improvised rather than written down. The number of his original compositions known to-day is pitifully small, even if we include the clavier fugues which might have been intended for the keyboard of the organ. There are seven *chorale preludes* (*F* 38/1) consisting mostly of a succession of brief fugatos on the individual chorale lines and ending with an extended pedal point, a form going back to Johann Christoph Bach and Pachelbel. Friedemann's arrangements to some extent combine the melodic material of the different hymn sections thus giving greater cohesion to the individual preludes. Nevertheless these little compositions are of minor significance and cannot stand comparison with the chorale preludes of Sebastian's maturity.

Of greater importance are two *fugues* with a pedal part, the solid yet old-fashioned Fugue in g (*F* 37), and the great triple Fugue in F (*F* 36). This latter work, which was written in Halle, is a well built and powerful composition; it cleverly manipulates its extended theme,

---

[1] Cf. C. M. Plümicke, 'Entwurf einer Theatergeschichte von Berlin,' Berlin, 1781, p. 338. Friedemann's music seems to be lost.

[2] *l.c.*, chapter IV.

[3] 'Ideen zu einer Aesthetik der Tonkunst,' Vienna, 1806, p. 89.

subdividing it and presenting the sections not only in succession but also simultaneously.[1]

The eight three-part fugues (*F* 31) which Friedemann composed in Berlin, and dedicated in February 1778 to the music-loving Princess Amalia of Prussia, may also be considered as works for organ, although they have no pedal part. These are short, pleasant and uncomplicated compositions of no great technical difficulty, but with numerous attractive features, such as the gay and rhythmically unconventional subject of No. 1 in C, or the merry gigue-like character of No. 5 in e. In this age of sensibility, which witnessed a general decline of contrapuntal forms, only a few composers were able to handle the fugue form with such complete ease. Friedemann's model for this little cycle was obviously a work of his father's. The prevalent systematic order of the fugues (No. 1 in C, No. 2 in c, No. 3 in D, No. 4 in d, etc.) is similar to that used in Sebastian's Three-part Inventions, and if any doubt should remain in this respect, it will be dissolved by a closer inspection of the subject in Friedemann's fugue in f (No. 8), which is obviously fashioned after the beginning of Sebastian's *sinfonia* in the same key (*Ex.* 68). Not only the

Ex. 68

J. S. Bach

W. Friedemann Bach

chromatically descending theme (a favourite with Baroque composers) but even the counterpoint accompanying it are those used by the father. The

[1] The Fugue in C (*F* 35) is an incomplete fragment, the Fugue in c with a pedal part (not contained in Falck, but printed in W. F. Bach's 'Complete Works for Organ,' edited by Power Biggs and George Weston, New York, 1947) of doubtful authenticity. It has also been attributed to Johann Christoph Friedrich, and even to Johann Christian Bach. It is interesting to note that this composition employs in rather thin disguise the same subject that Sebastian had borrowed from Corelli's Triosonata op. 3/4 for his own four-part organ Fugue in b. This Fugue in c may have been a study one of the Bach sons did under the watchful eye of the father (cf. Geiringer, 'Artistic Interrelations of the Bachs,' *MQ*, 1950).

separate Fugue in c (*F* 32) based on a theme resembling the *Fac ut portem*
from Pergolesi's *Stabat Mater*, is not quite on the same level as these
clever and inspired compositions. The Fugue in c is a vigorous work, but
formalistic in its polyphonic treatment and clearly showing a leaning
towards a more homophonic style.[1]

More than two dozen *compositions for clavier* (harpsichord, clavichord,
spinet or fortepiano) are known. To the composer's *First Period* of creative activity belongs a little characterpiece, in the style of Couperin, called
La Reveille (*F* 27), a brief *Gigue* in G (*F* 28), and a *Bourleska* (*F* 26),
which Friedemann's brother, Friedrich, named *L'Imitation de la Chasse*.
The latter is a gay and rather superficial composition in the style of Gottlieb Muffat, making ample use of the then fashionable device of crossing
hands. The most significant work from this period of preparation is the
little *Suite in g* (*F* 24). The choice of the form and the rather heavy polyphony of the Allemande point back to the Baroque period. Friedemann
also availed himself of features employed in his father's *Partitas*. The
partly French, partly Italian style of the Courante as well as the unconventional order of dances (a Bourrée and two trios after the Gigue)
point to this source. The spirit of a younger generation can be felt in the
Gigue with its sudden changes from major to minor and back to major,
and its droll rhythmic effects.

The *Concerto per il Cembalo solo* in G (*F* 40) is probably also a product
of Friedemann's youth. This work imitates a keyboard arrangement of
a concerto grosso and may possibly have been inspired by some of
the preludes to Sebastian's English Suites. The initial 'Allegro non

Ex. 69 Allegro non troppo

troppo' starts and also ends with a powerful tutti section, furnishing
material for the rest of the movement. Friedemann implies the use of an

---

[1] The clavier Fugue in B flat (*F* 34) is, as George B. Weston pointed out to the present
author, an arrangement of the fugue in Handel's overture to 'Esther.' The little clavier
Fugue in F (*F* 33) is an insignificant work dating from Friedemann's early youth.

xiv. Wilhelm Friedemann Bach. Drawing by P. Gülle

xv. First page of autograph of Wilhelm Friedemann Bach's unfinished Clavier Concerto in E flat

imaginary *concertino* of two violins and a 'cello by moving the bass into closer proximity to the upper parts (*Ex.* 69). The middle movement is given exclusively to this trio. It is an Andante in e of great simplicity and haunting beauty. Apparently it was a favourite of Friedemann's, who used it twice afterwards in compositions of his last years.[1] The finale is crisp and gay with amusing rhythmic effects.

Friedemann's artistic personality appears fully developed in the clavier compositions from his *second period*. To the beginning of the Dresden years belongs the *Concerto a duoi Cembali Concertati* (*F* 10; in modern editions called 'Sonata' for two claviers), a work which pleased father Bach so well that he personally copied it in parts. The result was that in the 19th century doubts arose as to its real author. The first man to recognize the truth was Johannes Brahms, who edited the 'Concerto' in 1864 at Rieder-Biedermann's as a composition of Friedemann; nevertheless it slipped thirty years later into the monumental edition of the *Bach Gesellschaft* as a 'hitherto unprinted' composition of Johann Sebastian.[2] The style of the composition as well as the appearance of the two manuscripts establishes beyond any doubt that in this case the father actually copied a work of the son, and that this is not a second case of an 'Organ Concerto by Friedemann Bach' (cf. p. 246). The expression 'Concerto' used by Friedemann for his work is only justified by the last movement. This brilliant and gay finale has the character of a solo concerto with orchestral accompaniment, arranged in the traditional way for two claviers. It has, basically, the same rondo-like alternation between tutti and solo episodes that Sebastian used in his Concerto in the Italian Taste. Quite different are the two preceding movements. The first is in almost fully developed sonata form, starting with the syncopated main theme that was a favourite of Friedemann's (*Ex.* 70), following up with a clearly differen-

tiated second subject, and introducing a substantial development. The recapitulation is incomplete; nevertheless this composition by young Friedemann is, from a formal point of view, as progressive as anything he has written. Similar in character, though shorter and simpler, is the slow middle movement. The entire 'Concerto' is predominantly homophonic

---

[1] In his wedding song *Herz, mein Herz* and in one of his fantasias in c of 1784.
[2] Vol. XLIII, pp. xv and 47.

and the regular imitations in the second clavier became accompanying figures imbued with thematic meaning.

Seven *Sonatas* for a single clavier belong in all likelihood to the Dresden period. In 1745 the composer made a bid for popular acclaim by publishing the Sonata in D (*F* 3) as the first of a planned series of 6 sonatas.[1] Unfortunately the author's expectations were not fulfilled. The Sonata had so little success that the series was discontinued. Only the Sonata in E flat (*F* 5) was published separately in 1748; the other four works of the set (in F, G, A and B flat; *F* 6-9) and a related Sonata in C (*F* 1), all of them probably written in or before 1744, remained in manuscript during the composer's lifetime.

Each of these seven sonatas is in three movements, with the traditional succession of tempi: slow-fast-slow. However, in the Sonata in C the middle movement is only ten measures long, and in the Sonata in F, which the composer revised twice, it eventually shrank to a mere four bars. Friedemann's liking for compact constructions is also expressed in the Sonata in D, in which the same concluding motive recurs at the end of each of the three movements, thus producing a kind of cyclic form. The composer does not show preference for any of the numerous formal varieties the time offers. There are movements in one-, two- and three-part constructions, the latter occasionally using two clearly separated subjects.

Similarly indecisive is Friedemann's attitude with regard to other stylistic idioms. There is no lack of retrospective features which show the composer's links with the art of the past. In the Largo of the Sonata in E flat with its homogeneous one-part construction, and in the Adagio of the Sonata in D with its polyphonic imitations, the spirit of the Thomas Cantor may be detected. Italian influences, which were particularly strong at the court of Dresden, manifest themselves in the chords accompanying the theme in the first and last movements of the Sonata in E flat, and in the brilliant passages divided between the two hands in the finale of the Sonata in B flat. At the same time these sonatas exhibit the vocabulary of the age of sensibility. Their language is often nervous, filled with sudden contrasts and surprising changes. In the first movement of the Sonata in G, and in the finale of the Sonata in B flat, repeated alterations in tempo occur, imbuing these movements with a highly subjective character. The dramatic, and often very humorous effects which the composer achieves through the use of rests can be shown by the finales of the Sonatas in E flat and G (*Ex.* 71). Great variety of mood is also to be found in the individual

---

[1] The title-page states that copies may be bought from the composer in Dresden, his father in Leipzig, and his brother (Emanuel) in Berlin.

movements. There is the serene first movement of the Sonata in C, and
the gay finale of the Sonata in A; but Friedemann seems even more in his

own element in the 'Lament' of the Sonata in G, or in the plaintive dirge
in the first movement of this work (*Ex.* 72).

Friedemann's *Fantasias*, written in Dresden, are different in character
from the dramatic scenes Emanuel offers under the same name. The works
of the elder brother rarely contain recitative-like passages, and it would be
difficult to imagine words or any kind of programme connected with
them. They are purely expressions of the composer's feeling, while
Emanuel, inspired by the opera of his time, prefers music that lends itself
to poetical and often quite rationalistic interpretation. Some of Friedemann's fantasias lean more in the direction of the toccata, with runs and
broken chords; others seem like an individual movement in a sonata, or
like a combination of different musical sections, contrasting in time and
tempo; but the majority have the logical and well-balanced construction
which is characteristic of the works of the mature Friedemann.

The Fantasia in D (*F* 17) is an effective piece of not inconsiderable
technical difficulty, based on swirling runs and broken chords, alternating

between the two hands. Eighteenth-century *Empfindsamkeit* assumes here
almost the character of 19th-century Romanticism (*Ex.* 73). Somewhat

similar, though more loosely constructed, is a Fantasia (F 18) starting in
d but ending in F. A second Fantasia in d (F 19)[1] is subdivided into three
sections, each of which is again in three-part form. Three musical ideas
(one of them a fugato) are used throughout the composition. The resulting
form A B A/B C B/A C A with its interweaving of sections might have
been studied by César Franck when he conceived his own 'Prélude,
Chorale and Fugue.'

Similar to a brief fantasia is the little *Preludio* in c (F 29), a delicate
character-piece of simple dignity and beauty. The short *March* in E flat
(F 30) ranks among the most attractive and least complicated compositions of Friedemann. It is characteristic of the composer's personality that
even here the serene character of the work is interrupted in its middle
section by a brief outbreak of anguish and fear.

The number of clavier compositions from the *Halle period* is not large,
but it embraces the exquisite 12 *Polonaises* (F 12) which, according to the
verdict of Julius Epstein, the distinguished Viennese pianist and friend of
Brahms, belong 'to the most beautiful clavier compositions of all times.'
The polonaise was a dance known in Germany since the 17th century.
Later, the political ties between Poland and Saxony increased the general
interest in this form, and after 1750 it became highly fashionable. As
Friedemann wanted to make a new bid for popularity, he announced in
1765[2] the composition of twelve of these works; but once again the public
remained indifferent, which greatly added to the composer's feeling of
frustration. The polonaises, which were not printed until thirty-five years
after the death of Friedemann Bach, are short compositions in two- or three-
part form which have mostly shed their original dance character. The
tempo is usually moderate or slow and the rhythmic picture is often quite
involved. If it were not for the 3/4 time maintained in all twelve pieces and
the frequent use of short notes at the beginning of the measures, their
name would have very little justification. Friedemann presents the
polonaises in an order of keys similar to that used in the fugues. The series
starts in C and ends in g, omitting the less familiar keys of C sharp and F
sharp (both major and minor). No two of these outstanding character-
pieces are alike. There is the resolute No. 1, the delicate and pensive No.
2, the youthful fiery No. 3, the tender lament of No. 4, the solemn No. 5
with its dramatic development, and the deeply felt and fervent No. 6.
More important, however, than the differences between the various

[1] Riemann's edition, published at Steingräber's, calls it *Capriccio*.
[2] George B. Weston, of Cambridge, Mass., owns a manuscript of the Polonaises
dated 1765.

polonaises are the contrasts within the individual numbers. No. 8 in e, for instance, starts with a yearning tune, using the big melodic skips which are frequent in Friedemann's compositions. After six measures a brisk and turbulent second theme sets in, displaying a mood almost diametrically opposed to that of the first subject. Despite the piece's shortness (only 24 measures) the work displays the basic features of the sonata form: an exposition with two contrasting subjects, a modulating development in which attempts are made to combine elements of the two themes, and a recapitulation only slightly modified. In their expressive power these tiny masterpieces point far into the future. They are, as Griepenkerl, their first editor put it, the 'truest expression of a noble, tender, and strongly agitated soul,' and it is not surprising that their importance was first realized in the romantic era.

A second Sonata in D (F 4) dedicated in 1778 or 1779 to Princess Amalia of Prussia may belong to the Halle period. The first movement of this work employs a musical idiom rather similar to that of the young Mozart. The following delicate and dreamy section entitled Grave displays a structure of classical simplicity. A playful and saucy Vivace concludes this work, which marks not only the end but also, in some respects, the culmination of Friedemann's sonata production.[1]

A comparison of Friedemann's two Fantasias in e may well serve to illustrate the stylistic differences between his second and *third periods of composition*. The first (F 20), composed in 1770 in Halle, is a noble composition, introducing two basic themes fitted into a solid, rondo-like construction. The second Fantasia (F 21) written in Braunschweig or Berlin shows an increase in nervous energy combined with a decrease in formal coherence. There are many stirring details such as the furious introduction, the lament in the recitative and the spirited cantilena, but the work is lacking in logic and suffers from a tendency to combine ideas which are not quite congenial in character. At the same time it is interesting to note that this fantasia seems to be intended not for the harpsichord, but rather for the modern pianoforte. Some of its accompanying passages will come to full effect only if played on an instrument with sustaining pedal.[2] The last two Fantasias, written in 1784, the year of Friedemann's death, are both in c (F 15 and 16). They incorporate sections from earlier works and show a decisive decline in the composer's abilities.

---

[1] A sonata in C from the same period (F 2) is not of equal importance and has remained in manuscript.

[2] Similar observations might be made regarding the Fantasias in C (F 14) and a (F 23), both products of Friedemann's third period of composition.

One of them is a potpourri of no less than 17 mostly unrelated little fragments.

A transition from Friedemann's clavier compositions to his ensemble music is provided by the *Concertos for Harpsichord and Orchestra*. They consist of four concertos for one cembalo and strings, and one concerto for two cembalos, brass instruments, timpani and strings, to which might be added one incomplete concerto of one and a half movements and one concerto of doubtful authenticity.[1]

The works are based on the concerto form of the late Baroque period with its rondo-like alternations between solo and tutti episodes. Friedemann progresses substantially beyond the style of his father; he enlarges both the tutti and the solo sections allowing them at the same time a greater amount of independence from each other. His tutti assume a more symphonic character and are built out of two, or even three and four contrasting ideas, often ending with a powerful unison. The figurations of the solo sections lose their mechanical character and are imbued with a more subjective emotional life. In Friedemann's concertos the two partners, solo instrument and orchestra, confront each other in a manner not unlike that of the great 19th-century concertos.

If the Concerto in g (*F*, top of p. 11) really is a composition by Friedemann Bach, it can only be the product of his period of apprenticeship. The conservative character of its first movement in which the same mood is rigidly preserved from beginning to end, and the inferior quality of the second and third movements make this appear most likely.

The Concertos in a,[2] D and F as well as the Concerto for two claviers

---

[1] A seventh concerto in c published under Friedemann's name by Schott, Mainz, is the work of Sebastian's pupil, Kirnberger. The Berlin Library owned the parts of two concertos (St. 270, 276) which were originally inscribed as W. F. Bach. This was changed by an old hand into J. F. C. Bach. Schünemann (*BJ*, 1914, pp. 127-8) believes that these are works by Friedemann. The parts were not available to the present author.

[2] There is strong disagreement regarding the possible date of composition of the Concerto in a. The handwriting of the autograph has a scribbled and rather uncertain character. This induced George B. Weston, according to information given to the present author, to consider the manuscript as a product of Friedemann's old age. Falck (pp. 87 and 96) on the other hand sees in it a work of the Leipzig period. The present writer feels inclined to place the work, for stylistic reasons, in the Dresden period. The composition shows great similarity to other concertos, sonatas and symphonies written at that time, and the handwriting resembles that of the Concerto in F for 2 claviers. The fact, mentioned by

in E flat (*F* 45, 41, 44, 46) probably belong to the Dresden period. They
are imaginative compositions, full of emotional life and expressive power.
Their style is basically homophonic, but canonic imitations are often used
to enrich the texture. As a rule five entrances of the main tutti ritornel
alternate with four solo episodes. The Concerto in a strikes a strange note
of sadness and even despair. Certain melodic features, transitions and
modulations in this work as well as in the middle movement in b of the
Concerto in D induce an atmosphere of *clair-obscure*, very rare in works
of this period.[1]

The Concerto in F is possibly the most advanced of these Dresden
compositions. It is interesting that a theme from the first movement (b.
31, 32) is again quoted in the last movement (b. 35, 37); once more the
composer sets out to interweave the individual movements of his composition.—Both the provision of two claviers and the use of brass instruments in the accompanying orchestra of the Concerto in E flat are unique
among Friedemann's works of this genre.[2] The reduction of the number
of tuttis from five to four points to the concertos of the Halle period, while
the old-fashioned unaccompanied trio style of the middle movement is
reminiscent of similar pieces by Sebastian.

More modern in character are the works written in Halle, the first
movement of the unfinished Concerto in E flat[3] (Ill. XV) and that in e
dedicated in 1767 to Maria Antonia, Electress of Saxony (*F* 42 and 43).
They show not only the aforementioned reduction in the number of
tuttis, but altogether a tendency towards greater concentration. Fewer
ideas are introduced in each movement and they are developed with
greater thoroughness. The style has lost the remnants of its polyphonic
character, and the use of parallel thirds and sixths in the solo parts seems
to indicate a growing interest in the possibilities of the modern pianoforte. It is deeply to be regretted that the second half of the charming
concerto in E flat is missing. Of the completed works, the tender, melan-

Falck, that the work was written on Leipzig paper also used by Sebastian, is not conclusive.
Friedemann could have used it while visiting his father on a vacation from Dresden or
taken the paper with him to Dresden.

[1] The same mood can be found a century later in the music of Johannes Brahms, who
was familiar with Friedemann's work.

[2] An older version in the Library in Königsberg is scored for strings and 2 horns. A
later version formerly in the State Library, Berlin, adds 2 trumpets and timpani to this
orchestration. It is reproduced in the score published by the New York Public Library.

[3] Friedemann transcribed it later into an ordinary orchestral composition by leaving
the ripieno sections more or less unchanged, while entrusting 2 oboes assisted by other
orchestral instruments with the clavier part. In this form he used the movement as an
introduction to his cantata *Ertönet, ihr seligen Völker* (*F* 88).

choly and romantic Concerto in e is the most mature composition; it is a
fine piece of exquisite craftsmanship.

Friedemann's *Chamber Music and Symphonic Works* are less progressive in character than his clavier compositions. They show his gift for
inventing poignant melodies, for equipping not only the treble but also
the middle parts and, in particular, the bass with rich thematic life. Some
of the development sections in the symphonies are among the best written
in Germany at that time, and the combinations of instruments occasionally
display a sensuous beauty of tone that is almost Italian. On the other hand
he is old-fashioned in his use of the brass, which he occasionally employs
as solo instruments in the highest register. His three-part forms lack a
contrasting second theme, and, unlike the progressive works of the
Viennese or Mannheim schools, none of his symphonies is supplied with a
minuet as a middle movement. To sum up, Friedemann's greatness is
revealed in his ensemble music almost as much as in his clavier compositions, but in the former he is far more indebted to the past.

To the period of maturity, and especially the Dresden years, there
belong four of the six sonatas for two flutes as well as all the trios. The
flute sonatas (in e, G, E flat and F; *F* 54, 59, 55, 57) are written for the
two wind instruments without bass. The style is strongly polyphonic with
a repeated crossing of parts. The two flutes are independent of each other
and equal in importance. Most of the sonatas consist of three movements
(fast-slow-fast); the Duo in G alone has a two-part fugue inserted between
a slow middle movement and the finale. Such little masterpieces as the
Cantabile of the Duo in G, the harmonically interesting first movement of
the Sonata in E flat, and the tragic *Lamentabile* in the Sonata in F with the
stirring beginning (*Ex.* 74) constitute a real enrichment of the scanty

Ex. 74

literature for flutes only. Rarely has music of equal significance been
written for two instruments so severely limited in their technical possibilities.

The two Trios for two flutes and continuo (*F* 47, 48) and the two
Trios for two violins and continuo (*F* 49, 50) are of a similar nature.

The playful imitative style which is so characteristic of the works of young Friedemann prevails in these compositions (*Ex.* 75). Particularly

Ex. 75   *Trio in D major (Bass omitted)* Vivace

attractive is the Trio in B flat, displaying a delightful mixture of manly energy and graceful charm.[1]

In his last period of composition Friedemann added two works (in f and E flat; *F* 58, 56) to his earlier flute duos and wrote the three duos for two violas (*F* 60-62). These five works, probably all composed in Berlin, are basically similar to the earlier flute duets, though an ever closer approach to strict forms may be detected. In the Duo in f for two flutes, both the first and last movements are fugal, and in the Duo in g for two violas, the *Amoroso* of the middle movement is a canon, and the finale a fugue. Even in the duos for stringed instruments the composer strictly maintains the two-part writing of the flute compositions, avoiding the temptation to insert double stops or chords. A gradual decline in creative power is unmistakable in these late compositions and in particular in the viola duets. The music occasionally has a stilted and laborious character, and the poetic names *Lamento, Amoroso, Scherzo,* which Friedemann chooses for his middle movements, cannot hide the fact that these sections, in which the composer's imagination formerly developed with utter freedom, are now sterile. Actually the *Scherzo* is a hardly disguised copy of the uninspired little *Amoroso*.

---

[1] Two 'trios' for one melody-instrument and harpsichord, following the style of Sebastian's sonatas for violin and harpsichord obbligato, are attributed to Friedemann. In either case the authenticity cannot be established beyond doubt. Both trios are more or less lacking in the quick little imitations and the repeated crossing of parts characteristic of Friedemann's music. The Sonata in B for violin and harpsichord with its mellow harmonic language sounds more like a composition by Emanuel than a work by Friedemann. The lovely sonata for viola and harpsichord in c (known from a manuscript in the Library of Congress, Washington, D.C., written by an unknown hand, and edited by Yella Pessl for Oxford University Press, London) is a strongly Italianized composition which seems to have been composed by a viola virtuoso familiar with all the secrets of the instrument. The wholly idiomatic style of the sonata with its many double and triple stops can hardly be found in any other string composition by Friedemann. In particular, his duos for viola bear no resemblance to this sonata for viola and harpsichord.

A single example of Friedemann's orchestral works, the Symphony in
d (*F* 65) for two flutes and strings, is in the old-fashioned form of the
French Ouverture. It begins with a slow introduction in which the two
wind instruments play a noble cantilena, accompanied by strangely hesi-
tating syncopated strings. The succeeding energetic four-part fugue
(without flute parts) shows how much Friedemann had learned in the
school of his father.[1] In spite of its rather conventional theme, this is a
spirited composition, which shows a clever use of the strings.

A retrospective character is also discernible in the Symphony in D
written in a single movement and used as an introduction to the cantata
Wo geht die Lebensreise hin (*F* 91/1). This brilliant work still makes
use of the Baroque *clarino* technique, taking the first trumpet up to
more than two octaves beyond middle c.

Seven symphonies (*F* 63, 64, 67-71) are in the Italian form, allegro-
andante-allegro, with two minuets attached at the end of the Symphony in
F. Three of these works are for strings only, one employs wind instruments *ad libitum*, while the remaining three compositions are for strings
and wind instruments. The use of a harpsichord to fill in the middle parts
is not always necessary. Occasionally the texture is so solid that a continuo
instrument would only coarsen the sound. All the movements are in two-
and three-part forms or in a primitive sonata form, introducing frequent
changes in mood, but hardly ever providing a clearly defined second
theme in the main section. On the other hand the developments show
the technique of interweaving parts, imbued with thematical life, in
a manner to be found in early Haydn works (*Ex.* 76). A youthful,

Ex.76 Allegro molto   Symphony C major

energetic and occasionally humorous spirit pervades these symphonies,
and it is to be regretted that of these attractive works which belong

---

[1] This symphony may have been used as an introduction to Friedemann's Cantata
O Himmel, schone ('O Heaven, spare'; *F* 90) written in 1758 in honour of the birthday of
King Friedrich 'the Great' of Prussia.

to Friedemann's most important compositions, only very little has been reprinted.[1]

Friedemann's *Vocal Music* shows less variety than his output in the field of instrumental composition. It consists almost exclusively of two dozen *church cantatas* written during the eighteen years Friedemann served in Halle as music director. Oratorio and secular cantata with their epic and humorous possibilities seem to have been of little interest to the composer. Although he is reported to have worked in his old age on an opera, its music is lost and almost nothing is known about this work.

Even among the church cantatas, one-third make use of 'contrafacta,' re-employing in some arias or choruses musical material from earlier cantatas. For instance in *Ihr Lichter jener schönen Höhn* ('Ye lights of yonder beautiful hills'; *F* 82) written for the second Sunday after Epiphany, the music to two arias is taken from the cantata *Wir sind Gottes Werke* ('We are God's workmanship'; *F* 74), and the music to one aria from the cantata *Der Herr wird mit Gerechtigkeit richten* ('The Lord shall judge with righteousness'; *F* 81). In *Verhängnis dein Wüten* ('Fate thy fury'; *F* 87) one chorus and one aria originate again in the aforementioned cantata, *F* 81, and two numbers in the cantata *Der Höchste erhöret* ('The Lord grants our prayer'; *F* 86). Only one number, a soprano recitative, is newly composed. In *Heraus, verblendeter Hochmut* ('Away with thee, blind pride'; *F* 96) three numbers are taken from the cantata *Ertönet, ihr seligen Völker* ('Sing, ye blessed people'; *F* 88), while only the two chorales are new additions.

While in the case of Sebastian, 'contrafacta' and 'paraphrases' usually meant lifting up the inspiration to a higher level, the opposite is true in the case of Friedemann. For him such an adaptation is, as a rule, just a means to save effort. The weakness of some of these cantatas is due to the fact that the arrangements are done in a superficial manner.[2] Only those sixteen cantatas which are original works are of real significance.

They show a remarkable variety in their emotional content. Joy and

[1] Modern editions have rendered accessible the Symphony in D (used as an introduction to the Cantata, *Dies ist der Tag*; *F* 85) with a simple and most attractive middle movement, and the tender *Siciliano* from the incomplete Symphony in A, belonging to those fine little character-pieces in slow tempo in which Friedemann excels.

[2] Bad declamation, resulting from a careless adaptation of new texts to precomposed melodies, is particularly noticeable in the contralto aria of the cantata *Ihr Lichter jener schönen Höhn* and in the tenor aria of the cantata, *Heraus, verblendeter Hochmut*.

jubilation find as true an expression as sadness and grief. In their technical aspects these cantatas fit into the overall picture of the Central and North German cantatas of the period. They are composed of a number of arias, recitatives and duets, usually concluded by a chorale. The beginning is made by a freely invented chorus or by a four-part chorale. Occasionally a *sinfonia* in one or three movements precedes the vocal section. As the *sinfonia* was often intended for a different purpose, it corresponded to the main part of the cantata only in its general festive character.

Sebastian gave greater significance and dignity to this form, extending the individual numbers and linking them firmly together. Friedemann followed his father in many details of melody, instrumentation and contrapuntal texture, and, in particular, in his arias and recitatives he was strongly dependent on Sebastian's model. The chorale, which was so often the germ-cell out of which a whole cantata of the Thomas Cantor grew, lost this function for the son, to whom, as to his contemporaries, the hymn sung by the full congregation no longer meant the very core of Protestant church music.

The choruses in these cantatas are obviously influenced by instrumental forms. Some of these numbers seem like free adaptations of the early sonata forms used in that period, while others resemble a prelude followed by a fugue in which the two sections (the introduction and the main part) are thematically firmly connected.[1] Even in his duets and arias Friedemann's instrumental way of thought is occasionally noticeable. The duet *Jesu, grosser Himmelskönig* from the Christmas Cantata *O Wunder* ('O miracle'; *F* 92), for instance, contains a canon for soprano and contralto which resembles in abbreviated form Friedemann's duos for two

flutes (*Ex.* 77). Similarly the 'Cavata' *Herz, mein Herz* ('Heart, my Heart'; *F* 97) results from the 'contrafactum' of an instrumental composition, the

---

[1] To the numbers resembling the early sonata form belong the first choruses in *Lasset uns ablegen, Der Herr wird mit Gerechtigkeit* and *Erzittert und fallet* (F 80, 81, 83). To the numbers in fugue form belong the first choruses in *Es ist eine Stimme, Gott fähret auf* and *Dienet dem Herrn* (F 89, 75, 84).

middle movement of the Concerto for cembalo solo in G, whose tender cantilena Friedemann used as a basis for this wedding song[1] (*Ex.* 78).

Ex. 78

Herz, mein Herz, sei ru.. hig, blei .. be ru.hig, still und har.re.

*) The ornament is omitted in the vocal version

Friedemann's first cantata *Wer mich liebet* ('If a man love Me'; *F* 72), written in 1746, soon after his arrival from Dresden, still shows traces of the Italianized style prevailing in the Saxon capital, where the composer had spent thirteen years. Languid melodies of a rather secular character, harmonies of little strength, long, extended and not too well organized forms are noticeable in this Whitsuntide music. It is characteristic of the greater independence Friedemann achieved in his instrumental music that hardly any of the works written in Dresden reveal the influence of the artistic atmosphere of that city as clearly as this first cantata. Such initial weaknesses were soon overcome and are no longer noticeable in later works. Two very attractive cantatas, *Gott fähret auf* ('God is gone up'; *F* 75) and *Lasset uns ablegen* ('Let us cast off the works of darkness'; *F* 80), were written during the following years; the latter in 1749, the former possibly somewhat earlier. *Gott fähret auf*, destined for the feast of the Ascension, was scored for trumpets, timpani, oboes, strings and 4 voices. It starts out with a magnificent fugue for chorus and includes a jubilant aria for bass.[2] The glory and majesty of the Lord find effective expression in this severe and powerful music. The Whitsuntide cantata *Lasset uns ablegen* describes in its first chorus, mainly with the help of harmonic changes, the contrast between the 'armour of light' and the 'darkness of sinful night.' The sudden descent from D to B flat, diminished seventh chords and modulations to minor keys depict the horrors of darkness, while the high-pitched notes of human voices and trumpets describe in brilliant major keys the blessings of those dwelling in brightness. The beautiful arias, recitatives, and chorales following this first chorus contri-

---

[1] It might be mentioned in this connection that in the aria *Zerbrecht, zerreisst* (*F* 94), one of the few vocal works by Friedemann available in a modern edition, which is scored for organ, horn, and soprano solo, the organ dominates and is treated with much greater care than the solo voices. Similar instances can also be found in other cantatas.

[2] This aria was used again later in the cantata written for the birthday of King Friedrich 'the Great.'

bute to ensure for this cantata an important place among the church music
of the period.

A second cantata written for Ascension Day, *Wo geht die Lebensreise hin*
('Where does life's journey lead to?'; *F* 91) has no initial chorus. The composer could dispense with this number, since the introductory symphony
in D with its oboes, trumpets, and timpani prepares in a general way for
the solemn mood of the work. In this cantata the emphasis is on the arias.
There is a brilliant number for tenor with trumpets and strings and, best
of all, a lovely aria for contralto and solo viola, *Der Himmel neigt sich zu
der Erde* ('Heaven leans down towards Earth'). This is a composition of
great fervour and melodic beauty in which solo voice and solo instrument
are combined to describe the mystery of Jesus' ascent to Heaven (*Ex.* 79)

in a manner reminiscent of Sebastian's style. Somewhat similar in
character is the Whitsuntide cantata *Dies ist der Tag* ('This is the day'; *F*
85) starting with a fine symphony in three movements. This carefree and
unproblematic instrumental piece is followed by four numbers for solo
voices and instruments, among which the forceful and heroic bass aria,
scored with bassoon, horns, and strings, excels.

To the most remarkable movements in these compositions belongs the
first chorus of the Easter cantata *Erzittert und fallet* ('Tremble and fall'; *F*
83). Its stirring description of Jesus' suffering at the words 'whom you
have beaten, sneered at and scorned' (*Ex.* 80) reveals the composer's
expressive power. Of equal significance is the initial chorus from the
cantata *Es ist eine Stimme* ('There is a voice'; *F* 89). This double fugue
shows Friedemann as one of the great writers of contrapuntal music in a
time that was more and more leaning towards a homophonic style. It is to
be regretted that the rest of this cantata is not on the same artistic level.
However, very few of Friedemann's vocal compositions attain musical perfection through all their numbers.

On the whole, Sebastian's eldest son was not so successful in his
cantatas as in his instrumental music. His solo numbers and the poly-

phonic choruses are dependent on his father's model, and only in the more homophonic choruses does he attempt to inject new blood into the body of Protestant church music.

THE BERLIN AND HAMBURG BACH
(CARL PHILIPP EMANUEL BACH)

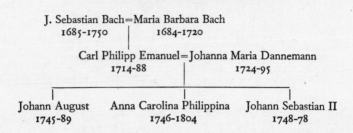

J. Sebastian Bach=Maria Barbara Bach
1685-1750 | 1684-1720

Carl Philipp Emanuel=Johanna Maria Dannemann
1714-88 | 1724-95

Johann August | Anna Carolina Philippina | Johann Sebastian II
1745-89 | 1746-1804 | 1748-78

EMANUEL, born on March 8, 1714, at Weimar, began to compose at an early age. It was typical of his enterprising nature that when he was 17 he engraved with his own hand his opus 1, a minuet for the clavier, and published it almost simultaneously with his father's opus I, the *Clavier Übung*. At that time he was already an outstanding clavier player. Sebastian, though certainly aware of this son's talent, was determined that, like Friedemann, he should enjoy the advantages of a good University training. Thus Emanuel studied law for three years at Leipzig, whereupon he moved to Frankfurt-on-the-Oder to continue his studies.[1] The family probably felt that enough had then been done for the education of the youth. Like Friedemann he had been allowed three years at Leipzig University; if he was anxious to continue on these lines, he ought to support himself by his musical abilities.[2] This was not easy in Leipzig, which, thanks to Sebastian's training, was stocked with many excellent young

[1] He was not the first Bach to be connected with this University. Veit Bach (1535-1610) lectured there as Professor of Theology before being appointed pastor to the court of the Elector Johann Georg in Berlin, and he returned to Frankfurt in his old age. The *Necrolog* stressed Veit Bach's 'powerful voice in intoning chorales and hymns.' He was born in Kronach, a little Franconian town near the Thuringian border, thus not far removed from other Bach centres. Yet Mr. Paul Bach, who unearthed material on the second Veit Bach, believes it to be unlikely that this outstanding preacher was related to the Bach musicians.

[2] The present author does not believe that Sebastian expected Emanuel to become a lawyer, a theory maintained, for instance, by A. E. Cherbuliez ('C. P. E. Bach,' Zurich, 1940). If Sebastian had had this aim he could have let his son continue studying at the highly renowned Leipzig University at less expense. Studying law was no rarity among prospective musicians, as the cases of Schütz, Kuhnau, Walther, Mattheson, and Handel prove. On the other hand, as early as 1733 Emanuel had applied, certainly with the approval and help of his father, for the organist's post at Naumburg.

musicians. In Frankfurt-on-the-Oder, however, there was as yet little musical activity, so that an ambitious talented youth could establish himself. And Emanuel did just that. According to the statement in the Genealogy, he gave clavier instruction; in addition, he 'directed a musical academy,' (as he related himself) and 'conducted and composed for public concerts and all the different festivities.'[1] Although the young Emanuel thus enjoyed at Frankfurt a position of uncontested leadership, he did not consider staying there permanently, for he felt the need of living in an artistic centre where he would meet other musicians and learn from them. In 1738 he was ready to leave the University and look for a good opening, but, unlike his brother Friedemann, he did not attempt to find work in one of the places where his father's reputation and influence would have been of great help. Pursuing the course of independent action that had taken him far away from Leipzig to Frankfurt, he decided to stay in Prussia and try his luck in Berlin, its capital. It may be that he was advised to do so by the two sons of the Prussian minister, von Happe, who attended the University simultaneously with him; for very cordial relations subsequently existed between the Bachs and Minister von Happe, who was godfather to one of Emanuel's and one of Friedemann's sons,[2] and may also have been instrumental in arranging Sebastian's visit to the Prussian King. Anyway, in 1738 Emanuel went to Berlin with the intention of settling down there. But soon afterwards he was invited to accompany a young nobleman on the customary continental tour and he accepted, eagerly anticipating the joys of foreign travel. All cravings of this kind were to remain unfulfilled for Emanuel throughout his life. Just when he was about to embark on his trip, he was called to Rheinsberg, where the Prussian Crown Prince, Friedrich, because of a feud with his father, resided in a sort of exile, planning gigantic reforms and cultural activities for the time when he would succeed to the throne, and enjoying meanwhile a feast of good music, which had to be kept secret from His Majesty, who was interested only in promoting military perfection. Yet the Crown Prince had a very distinguished little coterie at his disposal, with which, as an accomplished flutist, he played regularly. It is not known how Friedrich happened to become interested in Emanuel Bach. Maybe he had got hold of the various works for the flute which the young composer had written, or maybe the von Happe family praised Emanuel's out-

---

[1] Cf. his Autobiography, first published in the German edition of Burney's 'The Present State of Music in Germany.' An English translation is to be found in Lady G. M. Wallace's 'Letters of Distinguished Musicians,' London, 1857-59.

[2] Cf. Miesner in *BJ*, 1934. Friedemann dedicated his clavier sonata in E flat to von Happe.

Y

standing gifts to him. At all events he called Bach to Rheinsberg, and impressed by the young artist's superb clavier playing, engaged him as accompanist, although a formal appointment could not yet be made owing to Friedrich's peculiar position. Two years later he succeeded to the Prussian throne, and Emanuel, as he wrote in his autobiographical sketch, 'had the honour to accompany, alone at the harpsichord, the first flute solo that Friedrich played as a king.'

In spite of being, from the outset, engaged in the military campaigns which were to fill a large part of his reign, the monarch managed to carry out his ambitious artistic plans. Magnificent castles were erected in Charlottenburg and Potsdam, the latter by the name of *Sans-Souci*, his favourite residence and the scene of most of the King's musical activities; a beautiful opera house was built in Berlin and inaugurated in 1742 with a band of brilliant Italian singers and players which Burney praised as the 'most splendid in Europe.' During the carnival, opera performances took place twice a week and were free to all decently dressed citizens and visitors from outside. The King occupied a seat immediately behind the conductor, reading the score with him, and checking any slight inaccuracy or deviation, for which the musician responsible was severely reprimanded by His Majesty. The lavishness prevailing in the first years of the opera's existence is best illustrated by the fact that no less than 2771 thalers were spent on lighting for a single performance. In addition, the group of musicians who had served Friedrich so loyally at Rheinsberg was enlarged until it numbered some 40 artists assembling five times a week at Potsdam for evening concerts. Among them the outstanding flautist Johann Joachim Quantz enjoyed a unique position. He had been Friedrich's teacher off and on since 1727, and the pupil considered Quantz's style in playing and performing as the highest conceivable peak of mastery. Quantz wrote no less than 300 flute concertos in the Italian manner for his august disciple, and the King played them in rotation, performing six, or, with advancing years, four in every one of his *soirées musicales*, and in four decades of musical activity never grew tired of them. Quantz received a very high salary, 2000 thalers per annum, plus a generous honorarium for each new composition, and a hundred ducats for every new flute, which the skilful musician built himself. And not only was he well paid, he also enjoyed great power at court. He was the only musician privileged to interrupt the monarch's playing with a 'bravo,' which exclamation he very adroitly uttered whenever the King, after a difficult passage, was out of breath. The following joke, ascribed to Emanuel Bach, delighted all the court officials and made even the King laugh: 'Query: "What is the most frightening beast in the world?" Answer: "The lapdog of Mrs. Quantz. It is so terrifying that it scares Mrs. Quantz; Mr. Quantz is afraid of her, and he himself is feared by the greatest monarch on this earth."'

Second in influence at court were the two brothers Graun, Johann Gottlieb, outstanding violinist (cf. p. 192) and conductor of the royal orchestra, and Karl Heinrich, composer of the famous passion-oratorio 'Der Tod Jesu,' an excellent singer and director of the Berlin opera, for which he wrote within 14 years no less than 27 works in the Italian style. In addition, various members of the highly gifted Benda family from Czechoslovakia were serving at court, among them the composer, Georg Benda,[1] and the eminent violinist, Frantisek Benda, member of the original band in Rheinsberg, who on Gottlieb Graun's death in 1771 took over the latter's duties.

Compared with such luminaries as Quantz and the Grauns, Emanuel enjoyed only a very modest position. His initial salary amounted to 300 thalers and although it was raised to 500 in 1756 and was further increased later, when he received calls from outside and wanted to leave Berlin, it never approached the honoraria granted to the King's favourites. Emanuel unfortunately was not one of these. Although the position of accompanist entailed a close co-operation with the performer to be accompanied, there never developed between the two men a relationship of a more relaxed nature, such as had flourished between Sebastian and Prince Leopold of Cöthen. Emanuel, though much more worldly than his father and elder brother, still did not find it possible to recognize the King as the highest authority in artistic matters and to feign the enthusiasm which the monarch expected. There was a trait in his nature which made him singularly unfit for court service. As his former schoolmate, Johann Friedrich Doles,[2] put it: 'From his early youth, Emanuel suffered from a penchant frequently found in nimble-minded and agile-bodied youngsters, that of playing jokes on others.' (The word 'suffer' is not as unsuitable as it would seem at first sight, for Emanuel's jokes must have got him into a lot of trouble!) With advancing age this tendency became one for making caustic remarks. Even in the King's presence he could not at times restrain his tongue. When a guest once gushingly remarked to the august player: 'What rhythm,' Bach murmured audibly, 'What rhythms,' which certainly did not endear him to His Prussian Majesty. Nor did the King

---

[1] He had met Sebastian Bach and his sons as early as 1734 while visiting Leipzig.

[2] Doles, born in 1715, was a pupil of Sebastian Bach, and became Thomas Cantor in 1756, a position he held for 33 years.

care too much for the progressive trends in Emanuel's music. The monarch's taste was very clearly defined. He was capable of genuine enthusiasm for the style he loved; but, on the other hand, he absolutely ignored whatever lay outside the very narrow confines of his predilections. He fervently patronized Italian music, French literature, and the French Rococo style in architecture; asked, however, to listen to a German singer, he answered that he might just as well listen to the neighing of a horse.[1] The King's attitude eventually produced a certain petrification in Berlin's musical life, and it was this state of affairs which Burney described, to the fury of the local musicians, with the following words:[2] 'Of all the musicians who have been in the service of Prussia for more than 30 years, Carl P. E. Bach and Francis Benda have, perhaps, been the only two who dared to have a style of their own; the rest are imitators, even Quantz and Graun. . . . Of his Majesty's two favourites, the one is languid, and the other frequently common and insipid, and yet their names are *religion* at Berlin, and more sworn by than those of Luther and Calvin . . . for though a universal toleration prevails here as to different sects of Christians, yet, in music, whoever dares to possess any other tenets than those of Graun and Quantz is sure to be persecuted.'

Yet the accompanist stayed in the King's service for 28 years. Opportunities to accept other positions presented themselves, but Friedrich was loath to let him go, being aware of Emanuel's steadily rising fame which conferred distinction on the Prussian court. Emanuel, on the other hand, was in no position to force the issue, for though as a Saxon subject free to leave Berlin whenever he chose, he had to think of his wife[3] and three children who, as Prussian subjects, could be detained at the King's pleasure. Fortunately the routine work, bound to become increasingly boring, was lightened through the engagement of a second accompanist, alternating every four weeks with Emanuel. In 1754 Ch. Nichelmann, a former pupil of Friedemann and Emanuel, joined the band in this capacity, and was paid, to Emanuel's humiliation, twice as much as his former teacher. When he resigned after two years, Karl Friedrich Christian Fasch[4]

[1] It was the great Elisabeth Schmehling (married Mara), who, through Quantz's intervention, finally succeeded in getting an audition.

[2] 'The Present State of Music in Germany,' 1772, II, pp. 230 and foll.

[3] He had married in 1744 Johanna Maria Dannemann, daughter of a wine merchant.

[4] Fasch's father, Johann Friedrich Fasch, conductor to the Prince of Anhalt-Zerbst, was at first opposed to his son's going to Berlin, as he feared the youth would be contaminated by the irreligious spirit prevailing there. Emanuel thereupon offered to let his young colleague stay in his own home so as to watch over him carefully. Friedrich Fasch later became the founder of the Berlin Singakademie. Cf. the Biography of Fasch by C. Fr. Zelter, Berlin, 1801.

was engaged and, having a pliable nature, proved more acceptable to the royal flautist than Emanuel.

In spite of setbacks at court, these years in Berlin were by no means unhappy ones for Emanuel. He was an artist in living and knew how to derive enjoyment from almost anything; he found in Berlin much that gave him satisfaction. Not that the city was either beautiful or comfortable to live in. Emanuel may have heartily concurred with the contemporary visitor[1] from southern Germany who complained: 'On wet days high boots are as indispensable in this royal city as a spoon to eat soup with. In other towns streets are cleaned every week, not here. Whereas after a good rain one cannot manage unless one's feet are armoured and booted, in dry weather one yearns for armour to protect the eyes. Whole clouds of dust give to human beings strolling around the appearance of gods hiding their glory from mortal eyes in mist.' But such discomforts could be borne, for Berlin offered so much that was stimulating. Visiting the opera, for instance, was quite a novel experience for Emanuel, and it proved of decisive influence in the formation of his own style. Besides, there was a bracing intellectual climate in Berlin; eminent scholars and writers assembled here who vigorously cleared away old prejudices and probed into the cause of everything. To write treatises on musical and aesthetic matters became the fashion in Berlin; Marpurg, Quantz, Agricola, Kirnberger, Sulzer[2] and many others did important work in this field, and Emanuel himself was inspired to contribute in 1753 his epoch-making *Versuch über die wahre Art das Clavier zu spielen*. Six years later three young writers, the poet Gotthold Ephraim Lessing, the philosopher, Moses Mendelssohn (grandfather of Felix), and the publisher, Christian Friedrich Nicolai, started publishing their *Briefe die neueste Litteratur betreffend* (Letters regarding recent literature) which swept like a thunderstorm through Germany, destroying the prevailing influence of French literature, and paving the way for the glorious rebirth of German poetry in the classical era.

Life was indeed full of zest and excitement for a man like Emanuel Bach having wide interests and a keen intellect. Most of the capital's eminent writers and artistically-minded high officials were among the

---

[1] Josef Winkler, 'Hebe,' Nuremberg, 1782.

[2] Cf. Friedrich Wilhelm Marpurg, 'Der critische Musicus an der Spree,' 1749-50; J. J. Quantz, 'Versuch einer Anweisung die Flöte traversière zu spielen,' 1752; Chr. Gottfried Krause, 'Von der musicalischen Poesie,' 1752; J. Friedrich Agricola, 'Anleitung zur Singkunst,' 1757; J. G. Sulzer, 'Pensées sur l'origine et les différents emplois des sciences et des beaux-arts,' 1757; J. Philipp Kirnberger, 'Konstruktion der gleichschwebenden Temperatur,' 1760, and 'Die Kunst des reinen Satzes,' 1774-79.

friends he met at the Berlin Monday Club, at the Saturday concerts taking place at Agricola's house, and in his own hospitable home. He offered his friends many hours of delight by his improvisations on the clavichord, while to the wives he paid compliments in a unique way by writing charming musical portraits of them which appeared in various anthologies of the time. La Bergius, la Borchward, la Prinzette, la Buchholtz, la Stahl[1] were all wives of high officials whom he thus honoured. The gay atmosphere prevailing in Bach's circle is reflected in a letter which the poet Johann Ludwig Gleim wrote to a friend, Johann Peter Uz: 'Ramler,[2] Lessing, Sulzer, Agricola, Bach, Graun, in short all those belonging to the Muses and liberal arts, daily get together, either on land or on water. What a pleasure to glide in such company on the Spree [Berlin's river] competing with the swans! What a joy to lose one's way with this group in the *Thiergarten* among a thousand girls.'

It is interesting to note that Gleim's letter, dated August 16, 1758, was written at a time when Prussia had already been engaged for two years in the life-and-death struggle of the 'seven years war.' Apparently Bach and his gay friends possessed the talent of living for the moment. Shortly afterwards, however, Emanuel had to leave Berlin with his family, fearing a Russian occupation, and on his return he and Sulzer joined the citizens' guard. Although the long war did not bring Emanuel the hardships from which his brother, Friedemann, suffered in Halle, it involved him in great economic straits. All the court employees were paid their salaries in paper bills worth only a quarter of their former value, and had Emanuel not had a steady income from numerous private pupils, attracted by his reputation as the foremost clavier player in Germany, he would have been very badly off. When the war was won, the King, contrary to general expectations, did not compensate his musicians for the great losses they had sustained; Emanuel, like his father, was extremely touchy over financial matters, and he was 'very much upset about this and did not hide his feelings.'[3]

[1] Samuel Buchholtz, a historian, wrote, 'Versuch einer Geschichte der Churmark Brandenburg.' Frau von Printzen, wife of a *Kriegsrath*, was godmother to Emanuel's second son. Hofrat Dr. Georg Ernst Stahl was an old friend of the Bachs. Sebastian had probably stayed in his house on his visit to Berlin. Friedemann dedicated six sonatas to Stahl in 1744. Stahl was godfather to Emanuel's daughter, while his wife was godmother to the musician's first son.

[2] Cf. Carl Schüddekopf: 'Briefwechsel zwischen Gleim und Uz,' Tübingen, 1899. Joh. Ludwig Gleim (1719-1803) belonged with his friends, Joh. Peter Uz (1720-96) and Karl Wilhelm Ramler (1725-98), to the then fashionable 'Anacreontic school' of poetry, specializing in gay little poems in the style of the Greek poet. On the other hand, Ramler was the author of most successful cantata and oratorio texts.

[3] Cf. Zelter, *l.c.*

Moreover, the King, worn out from the strains of the long war, was now much less interested in music-making, so Emanuel felt the time to be ripe for leaving. His thoughts turned to Hamburg, where an opening was bound to occur before long. Emanuel's godfather, Georg Philipp Telemann, was well over 80 and had held the position of music director there for more than 40 years. Telemann thought very highly of Emanuel[1] and was quite likely to recommend him. Letters were exchanged regularly between them, and Telemann enlisted his godson's help in obtaining new Berlin compositions which he might perform in Hamburg. Emanuel eagerly complied, and one of his answers is quoted here as an example of his sense of humour. The letter was written on December 29, 1756, after the outbreak of the war, and Emanuel in his report felt tempted to ridicule the prevailing fashion for using military slang by describing his search for new music as the marauding action of the notorious Croatian 'pandours':[2]

'Most esteemed and honoured Director Telemann:

Nobody but Your Honour could have seduced me into adopting the profession of a pandour. Fortunately I am an honour-loving Saxon[3] who realized that not too much danger would be involved. My aide-de-camp, Mr. D. Roloff [a copyist] deserves much praise; he has reconnoitred according to instruction and his report is enclosed herewith. What do you think of this our first action? Do you think we might eventually amount to something? I think people like us ought to be engaged by you. For greater security I have put every parcel listed by Mr. Roloff once more in a paper valise, strapped tightly, and have pulled over all of them an oilcloth army blanket which is marked with the initials of Your Honour, our worthy chief. You will know better than I do, what part of it is winter, and what summer forage[4]. . . . The older Mr. Graun was to send me this very morning his [violin] concertos well wrapped, on pain of having to mail them himself, should he miss to-day's conveyance. As I have not seen them yet, I presume he has, of his own free will, submitted to said punishment. If need be, I await Your Honour's further orders. I am aware that I

---

[1] After Sebastian Bach's death Telemann wrote a sonnet at the end of which he expressed the belief that Sebastian's name was gaining special glory through his worthy son in Berlin. The sonnet was published in Marpurg's 'Kritische Beyträge,' 1754-55.

[2] Cf. Ernst Fritz Schmid: 'C. P. E. Bach und seine Kammermusik,' Cassel, 1931, p. 32.

[3] Saxony was among Prussia's enemies in this war, and the Saxons were derided as cowards.

[4] Forage being vegetable food for animals, Emanuel uses the expression 'winter and summer forage' to distinguish works suitable for different events of the church year.

am handling the jobs of gendarme and pandour with equal zeal, though, alas, not with similar efficiency. If my skill in plundering were only adequate, my good will could no longer be doubted. I almost forgot, in the rush, my New Year's wishes. May God keep you yet for many years healthy, lively, cheerful, for [Germany's] adornment, joy, and benefit. This is wished out of his most loyal heart by,

Your Honour's very own,

Bach.

P.S. Will Your Honour be good enough to convey my compliments to Mr. H. L. Schubuk, telling him I'll answer his last esteemed missive in the very near future. Not lack of a good conscience, but lack of time prevented me from doing so.'[1]

On June 25, 1767, Telemann died and applications for his position were made by four renowned musicians: Emanuel, his half-brother, Friedrich (cf. p. 381), his former colleague in the Prussian orchestra, Johann Heinrich Rolle,[2] and Hermann Friedrich Raupach, conductor of the Imperial Opera in Petersburg. The decision was taken five months later and Emanuel was chosen. The next step was to get King Friedrich's permission. Emanuel used all the persuasion of which he was capable, alleging that his bad state of health[3] necessitated less strenuous duties; and probably the King's sister, Princess Amalia, helped too. Finally the King reluctantly gave his consent, and the Princess, to honour the composer, appointed him before his departure, conductor of her court. In March 1768 everything was settled and Emanuel took charge of his new duties. In many ways they resembled those of Sebastian in Leipzig; Emanuel was Cantor of the Latin school, the Johanneum, and musical director of Hamburg's five main churches. Like his father, he was only interested in the musical directorship, and fortunately he was able to free himself from teaching work at school. Telemann had paved the way by refusing to teach extra-musical subjects; Emanuel went one step further by having

---

[1] Schubuk was a town official in Hamburg. This postscript shows that Emanuel was already at that time in contact with influential persons in the city.

[2] Rolle was from 1741-46 viola player at Friedrich 'the Great's' court and subsequently organist at Magdeburg. His father, Christian Friedrich Rolle, organist of Quedlinburg, had examined the Halle organ together with Sebastian Bach in 1716; and in 1722, shortly before Sebastian did so, he applied for the Thomas Cantor's position in Leipzig.

[3] Little is known about Emanuel's physical condition. He mentioned to Forkel that in 1743 he had to take the waters at Teplitz because of his podagra. He is also reported to have found travelling to Potsdam on the very bad roads extremely strenuous. But as he was able to reach the age of 74 we may assume that his gouty condition was not too serious.

even the music lessons at the Johanneum taken over by a deputy whom he remunerated. Thus he was able to concentrate on the musical work of the churches, and this was indeed a big enough sphere of activities. The quantity of music offered was staggering; something like 200 musical performances[1] were given every year, among them no less than 10 Passions which would at times be crowded into 13 successive days, the same work being sung in sequence in all the churches of the town. To provide such an enormous output of music was no easy matter, and Telemann had probably enlisted not only Emanuel's help to solve the problem. His godson, on the other hand, relied heavily on music by Telemann, and more still on the works of his own father. Besides extensive duties as conductor and composer, the position entailed administrative work. All the honoraria paid to instrumentalists, vocalists, copyists, etc., passed through the music director's hands. Emanuel kept most meticulous accounts of such payments as well as of financial matters concerning himself, and, curiously enough, did not mind work of this kind. He had an excellent business head and everything connected with finances interested him. At times he jotted down characteristic aide-memoires in his account-book, such as the pleased comment 'the Dutch ducats were exchanged to me at a somewhat higher rate than the official one,' or the determined remark regarding payment he had received for a funeral music: 'henceforth *I* will fix the honorarium and bill it.' The income Emanuel derived from his church work was quite considerable. His daughter, after his death, made a detailed statement of the various items according to which he received a yearly amount of more than 1000 thalers,[2] plus a quantity of coal, and revenues from the sale of librettos to his compositions (on the exclusive handling of which he insisted with iron determination),[3] from funeral music, from testing applicants for the various organist's positions, from writing music for certain civic occasions etc., etc. His was a lucrative position, as everything had to be lucrative in this thriving centre of German trade, where money moved freely. Being money-minded was the natural thing in Hamburg. Here civic jobs were still being bought, as in Sebastian's time (cf. p. 159), here nobody saw anything offensive in the publication of a prayer-book offering devotional exercises alternating with quotations of the rates of exchange for the European currencies in the various capitals.[4] Emanuel felt quite at home in this peculiar atmosphere, and his ability to take an

---

[1] Cf. 'Acta die neueren Einrichtungen bey den Kirchenmusiken betreffend,' 1789-90.
[2] Cf. Miesner, 'Philipp Emanuel Bach in Hamburg.'
[3] He fought a spirited battle à la Sebastian with the printer, Meyer, and won.
[4] 'Geistreich Gebetbüchlein vor Reisende zu Land und Wasser.'

intelligent part in financial talks endeared him no less to the burghers than his sparkling wit and pleasant manners.

The financial improvement was not the only asset of the Hamburg position. Emanuel also felt relieved not to have to conform to court etiquette any more, not to have to wait for hours in the King's ante-chamber for a royal command, but to be a highly respected member of a prosperous community. He relished the 'air of cheerfulness, industry, plenty and liberty in the place, seldom to be seen in other parts of Germany' (Burney), and he was no less responsive to the city's lovely location. Reichardt, who met the Hamburg music director in 1774, liked to ramble with Emanuel round the town. He evidently had in mind these walks when he wrote in his *Briefe eines aufmerksamen Reisenden*: 'Round this great commercial city the scenery is of particular beauty and variety. The Elbe and the Alster with their wide expanses of water studded with sailing craft, and their charming shores present the finest views. A particular feature of the Alster, unique among all other rivers, is the huge reservoir it forms within the city, which is bordered on all sides by avenues inviting to very pleasant walks.'

Another attractive aspect of life in Hamburg was afforded by the wide circle of friends Emanuel made. All the eminent writers of the town were on excellent terms with the new music director: Lessing, now also a resident of Hamburg; the revered poet Klopstock and his second wife, who was an excellent singer; the great preacher, Christoph Christian Sturm[1] (cf. Ill. XVI), whose poems Emanuel set to music, as he did those of his other poet-friends, J. Heinrich Voss, Mathias Claudius, and Heinrich Wilhelm von Gerstenberg. Hamburg's intelligentsia accepted the genial and erudite musician with open arms. In the houses of professors J. Georg Büsch and Christoph Daniel Ebeling,[2] who lived in the same street as Emanuel, many delightful gatherings took place at which music was regularly performed. Comparing the social life of Emanuel with that of his father, we see how, in spite of holding similar positions, Sebastian was confined much more closely than his son to intercourse with his immediate colleagues. Various causes were responsible for Emanuel's different standing in the community: a general tendency of the time to remove former strict barriers between the different professions; the

[1] Sturm, pastor at St. Petri, had for several years been teacher and preacher in Halle, where he probably met Friedemann Bach.

[2] Büsch was professor of mathematics and a renowned writer on commercial subjects; Ebeling, professor of History and Greek, and translator of Burney's 'State of Music' into German. (Cf. Note 1, p. 337.)

academic education Emanuel had received, which gave him a certain status in the eyes of the intellectuals; and, most of all, Emanuel's natural social graces. Hospitality was in the Bachs' blood, and Emanuel, like his father, delighted in it; but while visiting musicians all flocked to the Thomas Cantor's house, few members of the University found their way to it. There was, on the other hand, no important writer or scholar in Hamburg who did not feel honoured by intercourse with Emanuel Bach. Distinguished visitors also came from out of town to meet him. One of these visits had far-reaching results. The Austrian Baron Gottfried van Swieten, while attached as ambassador to the Prussian court, had heard so much about Emanuel's art that he went to Hamburg to make the composer's acquaintance. He acquired various works by Sebastian and Emanuel and ordered symphonies from the latter; all of which he introduced in his Viennese concerts, to the delight of Mozart, on whom the Thomas Cantor's music made a profound impression.

It would be wrong to assume, however, that life in Hamburg had nothing but pleasant aspects for Emanuel. The great quantity of music played coupled with the City's unwillingness to spend much on production resulted in poor quality. As a report written after Emanuel's death put it:[1] 'The instrumentalists grew bored with so much playing, the singers became weary, hoarse, and even ill.' Burney, too, when visiting Hamburg in 1773, reported that he heard at St. Catherine's some very fine music by Emanuel 'very ill performed, and to a congregation wholly inattentive.' The composer, continues Burney, was well aware of these deficiencies, but put up with them because of the tranquillity and independence he was enjoying. Although this report sounds as if it might be somewhat exaggerated and is contradicted by other contemporary verdicts, such as that of Gerstenberg, who praised the music at St. Catherine's as 'delighting like the angels' harmony,'[2] there is certainly some grain of truth in it. Emanuel made a clear distinction between the music he composed or performed in the discharge of his duties, and that written for his own enjoyment. His official work at Hamburg belonged to the 'bread and butter' category, and fully aware of the limited resources at his disposal, he put up with the inevitably mediocre execution as long as he had a chance to do first-class music as well. To this second category belonged

---

[1] Cf. Note 1, p. 345.

[2] Similarly Georg Benda wrote to a friend on November 18, 1778: 'Recently I was surprised in a most pleasant manner at Vespers. I went to hear Bach's Michaelmas music. You may imagine whether I expected anything mediocre, knowing Bach had composed it. However, great though my expectations were, they were by far exceeded.' The work performed was the *Heilig* for 2 choirs (*Wq* 217). Cf. Miesner, *l.c.*

the subscription concerts he gave in Hamburg, in which he appeared as outstanding soloist or conductor.[1] Also of vital importance were the hours he spent improvising on his favourite Silbermann clavichord. Various contemporaries have given us enthusiastic reports on these improvisations, and they all leave in our mind the picture of a person possessed. 'In his free phantasies he was quite unique and inexhaustible. For hours he would lose himself in his ideas and in an ocean of modulations. His soul seemed to be far removed, the eyes swam as though in some ravishing dream, the lower lip drooped over his chin, his face and form bowed almost inanimately over the instrument.'[2]

It is interesting to note that both Friedemann and Emanuel felt this tremendous urge towards improvisation, in which they both excelled. But while the exaltation thus produced only increased Friedemann's inability to cope with reality, Emanuel had the rare capacity of keeping the two spheres of his existence neatly separated. The hours of ecstasy at the clavichord were vital to him, as they provided an outlet for his innermost artistic yearnings, but after such an experience he was able and willing to resume the extremely skilful handling of his every-day problems. In this dualism of his personality ensuring artistic as well as material success, Emanuel Bach had much in common with Joseph Haydn, to whom the elder master's works provided a decisive stimulus. We can well imagine how much they would have enjoyed each other's company, chuckling over the humorous sides of life, for which both possessed a keen perception, and delightedly sampling unusual foods, such as the larks that Emanuel had sent by the three-score from Leipzig. But they were never to meet, and young Haydn, rapturously playing Emanuel's Sonatas night after night on his worm-eaten clavier and discovering a new world in them, could not guess that this revered composer was an eminently practical man, shrewd, even hard in his business dealings.

Reports have been preserved which present Emanuel as a disagreeable miser, but these may be classed, together with stories of Friedemann's drunken bouts, as among the legends spread by the enemies whom such outstanding personalities were bound to make. The deprecatory remarks by Reichardt, for instance, may well have been caused by some unpleasantness which arose between Emanuel and the younger musician

---

[1] In 1773 he performed Handel's 'Messiah'; however, this was not, as it is sometimes claimed, the first performance of the work in Germany. Thomas Arne had already produced it in Hamburg on April 15, 1772. Cf. Sittard, 'Geschichte des Musik- und Konzertwesens in Hamburg,' 1898.

[2] Cf. Reichardt's Autobiography in 'Allgemeine Musikzeitung,' 16. Jhg. Another description is provided by Burney, l.c.

after the latter had contracted various debts. There is no doubt that Emanuel was as scrupulous in money matters as his father had been. He was brought up in a tradition of strict economy in financial matters and Hamburg's peculiar atmosphere further increased such tendencies. Thus he became an excellent business man, well able to achieve the best possible results by the sale of his works. Of any real avariciousness, however, we have no proof.[1] 'If Bach is miserly,' wrote a friend, G. F. E. Schönborn, to the Danish musician, N. Schiörring, 'I believe that his wife inoculated him with this habit, or rather that her failings are charged to his debit.' We have no means of checking this statement, but we might mention that in Johanna Maria Bach's social sphere the fate of women widowed in old age was a very sad one. The salary stopped a few months after the husband's death, insurances or pensions did not exist, and the scanty savings that a musician could as a rule accumulate were used up all too quickly. Naturally Emanuel's wife was anxious to be spared such hardship.

Like his father, Emanuel seems to have enjoyed a pleasant home life, but everything was on a more opulent scale than in the modest Thomas Cantorate. Burney praises the 'elegantly served dinner' he ate at Emanuel's house, and the beautiful, large music room, furnished with pictures of more than 150 eminent musicians, which his host had collected. We should like to think that the lovely room with its many books which we see in a drawing the painter August Stöttrup made of Emanuel, Sturm, and himself (Ill. XVI) is one in Emanuel's home. The portrait of the musician standing next to the pastor, Sturm, clearly reveals the dualism in Emanuel's nature. This elegantly dressed, rather stoutish person is very much a man of the world, enjoying the good things in life; the agile hands seem to express their owner's caustic wit and his temperamental way of speaking. The face, however, is full of longing and a poignant sadness. This sadness is also visible in a portrait painted in 1773 by the composer's godson, his Meiningen kinsman, Johann Philipp Bach (Ill. XXII).

In the following years an event in his own family greatly contributed to deepen the expression in Emanuel's eyes. The Hamburg music director had only three children: two sons and one daughter. It was one of the

---

[1] A letter Emanuel wrote to Forkel on June 20, 1777, has been repeatedly quoted as proof of his parsimoniousness. Telling Forkel of his anxiety about his younger son's grave illness in Rome, Emanuel mentions that he had to send him 50 ducats and would have to pay another 200 thalers to the doctors. We should not forget, however, that this was a business letter starting with an appeal to Forkel to collect, as rapidly as possible, subscriptions for Emanuel's new sonatas. The mention of the heavy expenditures for the ailing son was made to increase Forkel's zeal for obtaining these subscriptions.

tricks of a malicious fate that neither of the sons wished to be a musician. This had been a great blow to Emanuel, to whom the unbroken line of Bach musicians was a source of pride and delight, and who lovingly assembled material pertaining to the family history. But he had to get used to seeing the elder son become a lawyer, the younger a painter, and none of his children with offspring of their own to carry on the Bach tradition. His only consolation was in the decided aptitude which the second son showed for painting. When an authority like Adam Friedrich Oeser, the friend of Winckelmann and teacher of Goethe, had confirmed this, Emanuel felt great hopes for the youth's future, hopes that were cruelly crushed when the son, while working in Rome, succumbed to a fever at the age of 30. Emanuel announced this in a letter to his friend and publisher, Immanuel Breitkopf: 'Stunned by the tragic news of my beloved son's death in Rome, I can hardly put down these words. I know you will pity me. May God preserve you from similar pain!'

This happened in 1778, and thenceforward Death was a frequent visitor in the family. In 1781 there died Elisabeth Altnikol (cf. p. 200), a half-sister, for whom Emanuel cared greatly, and to whom he had frequently given financial help. A year later followed Sebastian's youngest son, the brilliant 'London Bach,' Emanuel's former pupil; while in 1784 it was Friedemann's turn. Emanuel himself had been seriously ill in 1782 when, as he wrote to Breitkopf, 'I barely escaped death, as the obnoxious influenza wanted to choke my throat.' He never recovered his strength and six years later, on December 14, 1788, he passed away, aged 74 years. The following day the 'Hamburger unpartheiischer Korrespondent' published an Obituary. 'He was one of the greatest theoretical and practical musicians,' maintained the author (probably Carl Friedrich Cramer), 'creator of the true clavier technique . . . unmatched on this instrument. Music loses in him one of its greatest ornaments and to musicians the name of Carl Philipp Emanuel Bach will always be a holy one. In his personal intercourse he was a lively, cheerful man, full of spirit and wit, gay and merry. . . .'

Emanuel's eldest son survived his father by only four months, dying at the age of 44. Now only two women were left, the widow and her daughter. They handled Emanuel's business as best they could, and when Frau Bach died in 1795, her daughter made a public announcement that she would carry on the paternal business, supplying the works of her father and grandfather. This she did up to 1804, when her name disappears from the Hamburg address books. During her lifetime, Emanuel's huge collection of music and pictures was sold by auction, and most of it came, through Georg Pölchau, librarian of the Berlin Singakademie, into the Prussian capital.

The catalogue for the auction has been preserved and constitutes an important historical document.[1] Most of the Bachiana which have survived were in Emanuel's possession. Proudly he used to exhibit to his visitors portraits of Hans Bach, 'the jester,' Ambrosius, his grandfather, and one of his own father painted in oils by Haussmann,[2] as well as the music of his ancestors, partly copied by his father. All these he treasured and handed down in good condition to posterity. Furthermore, if we take into consideration the fact that the family chronicle with Emanuel's own additions, the account of the Bachs' yearly meetings, and many data concerning Sebastian's teaching methods, character and works were all supplied to Forkel by the Hamburg music director, we realize how much the Bach research owes to Emanuel's deep family loyalty. No one who reads the loving comments on his father which he sent to Forkel in the years 1774-75 can doubt the son's attachment to Sebastian. In his youth, before he had quite established his own style, he may, out of a natural tendency towards artistic self-preservation, have avoided conceding to himself the full extent of his father's greatness. Later, however, he allowed himself to become fully aware of Sebastian's artistic stature. Emanuel was often blamed for offering for sale in September 1756 the plates of the Art of the Fugue. To us, who look on this sublime work with the greatest reverence, an act of this kind seems to reveal a sad lack of understanding and of filial piety. It should not be forgotten, however, that Emanuel decided on this action after the great war had broken out. He had to consider the possibility of a quick evacuation and felt anxious not to have a hundredweight of plates among his possessions. On the other hand, when peace was restored, it was he who was responsible for the publication of Sebastian's four-part chorales.

What Emanuel truly thought of his father is revealed in a most interesting letter to the editor of the *Allgemeine deutsche Biographie* published anonymously in 1788.[3] D. Plamenac proved in a fine study[4] that only Emanuel can have been the author of this penetrating comparison of Bach and Handel which was written in answer to a passage in Burney's account of the life of Handel. It reveals not only inside information on

---

[1] Reproduced by Miesner in *BJ*, 1938, 1939, 1940-48.

[2] According to recent research it seems likely that this was the copy Haussmann made in 1748, owned at present by Mr. William H. Scheide, Princeton, N.J., U.S.A. Cf. Raupach, 'Das wahre Bildnis J. S. Bachs,' Wolfenbüttel, 1950.

[3] Letter of February 27, 1788, Vol. 81, p. 295, Berlin, 1788.

[4] Cf. *MQ*, October 1949.

Sebastian's life available only to a member of the family, but also the deepest reverence and understanding of his art. Emanuel becomes particularly eloquent when he, the great master of keyboard music, discusses his father's contributions to this form. After praising Sebastian's fugues, which he finds superior to those of Handel, he continues: 'But what virtues Bach's other clavier works possess! What vitality, originality, and ingratiating melody do we find in them even to-day, when the singing style has been so greatly refined! What invention, what variety in different styles, the elaborate and the *galant*, the strict and the free! . . . This one presenting the utmost difficulties to skilled hands, that one in a style easily to be followed by the somewhat experienced amateur. How many able clavier players have received their training from these works! Was he not the creator of quite a novel treatment of keyboard instruments? Did he not bestow on them specific melodies, expression, and a singing style? He, who possessed the most profound knowledge of all contrapuntal arts (and even artifices) understood how to make art subservient to beauty.'

THE MUSIC OF CARL PHILIPP EMANUEL BACH

In his compositions Emanuel was stimulated rather than overawed by Sebastian's work. Only during his *first creative period*, the apprenticeship in Leipzig and Frankfurt (before 1738), did the son actually copy the father. For this phase we may take quite literally Emanuel's statement in his autobiography that Sebastian was the only teacher he ever had. Although most of these very early works were later revised by the composer, the frequent use of sequences, the rhythmic uniformity of the compositions and their heavy Baroque cadences follow the idiom of the Thomas Cantor.

When at the age of 24 Emanuel came to Berlin, his *second creative period* started and was to last until 1768. In this period of transition he soon established a new style of instrumental music, full of expressive power and passion. Even in the first great products of this period, the Prussian Sonatas, the subjective and highly emotional idiom of *Empfindsamkeit* (sensibility) is clearly noticeable. Emanuel adopted for his instrumental works elements from the *opera seria* of his time, such as recitatives, ariosos, and certain forms of aria accompaniments;[1] sometimes his sonatas appear like keyboard transcriptions of dramatic compositions. He had learned from his father that transplanting musical idioms from one medium

---

[1] Burney attributes this innovation particularly to the influence that Hasse's operas exercised on Emanuel. Cf. 'A General History of Music,' IV, p. 454.

XVI. C. P. E. Bach, Pastor Sturm and the Artist. Drawing by Andreas Stöttrup

XVII. Autograph of a 'Heilig' by C. P. E. Bach. In the last three measures starts a quotation from Johann Sebastian's 'Magnificat' ('Sicut locutus est')

to another could produce outstanding results. Nevertheless his technique of transferring elements of the dramatic vocal style into keyboard music had never before been used to such an extent and with equal success.[1]

Although Emanuel adopted the new language of *Empfindsamkeit* so enthusiastically, conservative elements are by no means lacking in his works. We still find in them his father's use of sequences; Emanuel employed the stepwise ascending and descending bass-lines of the Baroque period and, most of all, he maintained the idea of developing whole movements from a single subject. When the need arose, he wrote intricate canons and fugues, and while reserving his more daring experiments for his favourite instrument, the clavier, he fashioned his great choral work, the *Magnificat* of 1749, after Sebastian's composition on the same text. From his father Emanuel also inherited the pedagogic interests and talents. These, together with the tendency for theoretical speculation then prevailing in Berlin, induced him to publish his 'Essay on the True Art of Playing Keyboard Instruments,' one of the finest works of musical instruction and theory ever written. The *style galant*, which held so great a fascination for Emanuel's generation, meant almost as little to him as it did to his father and elder brother. As a rule it is confined to compositions of minor value written to please the King.

During the years Emanuel spent in Berlin, his artistic personality developed fully, and gradually the limitations of his position and the conservative attitude of his colleagues and his patron became unbearable to him. He was glad to exchange the narrowness of his activities in the Prussian capital for the greater spiritual freedom in the Hanse city. In his *third creative period* (Hamburg 1769-88) the quality of his output reached a climax. The six mighty collections of sonatas, rondos and fantasias 'for connoisseurs and amateurs,' which mark the peak of his keyboard music, were then published. Moreover, most of his choral compositions and his great symphonies were products of the Hamburg years. In the meantime, contemporary composers such as Gassmann, Haydn and Mozart, had adopted Emanuel's language not only in their clavier music, but also in quartets and symphonies. Bach, whose fame was constantly growing, felt the responsibilities of leadership. Though his works written in Hamburg speak the highly emotional language of the *Sturm und Drang* (Storm and Stress) dominating the literature of the period, they reveal at the same time a supreme mastery of all technical problems. The composer showed

---

[1] The occasional use of recitatives in keyboard music, however, antedates the work of Emanuel. Johann Krieger, Johann Kuhnau, Sebastian Bach and others employed it in some of their works.

z

but little interest in, or understanding for, the steady growth of classical feeling in music. On the other hand their passionate subjectivism links these Hamburg works with the newly rising trends of romanticism.

Compositions for the clavier form the core of Emanuel's production. In his lifetime more than a hundred sonatas, sonatinas, rondos, and fantasias were printed, together with an almost equal number of short character pieces, altogether about two thirds of what he wrote in this field. His contemporaries saw in Emanuel primarily the keyboard virtuoso and composer. Even in our days, most pieces by Emanuel available in modern editions are either solo works for clavier or compositions in which the keyboard instrument has an important part to perform.

A good example of Emanuel's youthful style is furnished by a Sonata in d (*Wq* 65/3) written in Leipzig in 1732.[1] In its first movement, an Allegro molto, the continuously repeated sixteenth motion in the right hand, sparingly supported by the bass, gives the impression of a Baroque 'solo,' accompanied by basso continuo. The slow middle movement seems to be modelled on the lines of Sebastian's Italian Concerto. In the son's work, too, solo sections alternate with tuttis of the full body of sound. However, the frequent use of the sentimental parallel thirds and sixths points to a new artistic conception. The finale in strict two-part style has the character of a gay Gigue with imitations.

Emanuel's clavier works written in Berlin display a very different aspect. The very first movement of the famous 6 *Prussian Sonatas* (*Wq* 48), which were printed in 1742 with a dedication to the King, has an old-fashioned beginning resembling a two-part invention. On the other hand the classical sonata-allegro form with a contrasting second subject, full development, and complete recapitulation is to be found here. The following Andante movement appears almost like an opera scene without

Ex. 81 Andante

text. How passionate is the bold skip of a diminished octave in its second bar (*Ex.* 81): and what wealth of powerful emotions is unfolded in the

[1] The work was revised in Berlin in 1744.

two 'secco' recitatives inserted into the arioso sections, for which the composer even provided the kind of basses customary in vocal music (*Ex.* 82). It is significant that in this movement which starts and ends in f,

no signature is used, in order to facilitate the notation of the quick key changes. The third movement of the Sonata is more conventional in form; it is a Vivace, in which the high tension of the Andante is resolved in care-free gaiety. All through this set and the 6 *Württemberg Sonatas* (*Wq* 49) published in 1744, are found the utterances of a revolutionary composer, who expressed emotions hitherto absent from keyboard music. Some of the most significant features of Emanuel's style are: a daring harmonic language with incisive dissonances and stunning chord-combinations; dramatic pauses, unexpected rests, alterations in tempo,[1] and sudden changes between major and minor modes, an effect often increased by varying dynamics and the use of different registers (*Ex.* 83). Typical of

the turbulent spirit of the composer are passages which appear to imitate orchestral sounds, as, for instance, in the first movement of the sixth Württemberg Sonata. Peculiar effects of colour are achieved by placing the two hands at a great distance from each other, thus producing a 'thinness' of sound which gives the music a transcendental character.[2]

Quite often it suited Emanuel to build a whole movement out of elements presented in the first measures. At the same time there is a

[1] In his 'Essay' (Part I, 3-28) Emanuel recommends for the Adagio in his sixth Württemberg Sonata a 'gradual and gentle acceleration to be followed shortly afterwards by a sleepy ritardando.'

[2] In the 19th century this peculiarity of Emanuel's style was completely misunderstood, and in his editions Hans v. Bülow found it necessary to thicken and coarsen the transparent texture of this music.

noticeable tendency to start the elaboration of the subject soon after its first statement, before the traditional development section is reached. It is interesting that these principles of a more retrospective character were to achieve tremendous importance for the works of Haydn and Beethoven, while Mozart, who preferred dualistic contrasts within his Sonata movements, was less susceptible to them.

No other work contributed so greatly to its author's fame as Emanuel's *Versuch über die wahre Art das Clavier zu spielen* ('Essay on the True Art of Playing Keyboard Instruments'[1]) published by the composer himself. The first part, printed in 1753, was reissued three times, and the second part published in 1762 twice in Bach's lifetime. The 'Essay' is mainly concerned with keyboard instruments, among which the expressive clavichord, particularly suited to the performance of emotional music, was closest to Emanuel's heart; but he was too broadminded and too practical, narrowly to limit his discussions. Not only the clavierist but any musician can benefit from the fine craftsmanship and clear logical thinking revealed in the work.

In this manual written after Sebastian's death, it is noteworthy how closely the son followed in the father's footsteps. For instance, in the chapter on Fingering he adopted Sebastian's use of the thumb, adding a wealth of important details, and he even did not completely discard his father's old-fashioned crossing of the 3rd over the 4th finger. Again, when dealing with ornaments and embellishment, Emanuel continued along the lines of the *Clavierbüchlein* of 1720, explaining at greater length trills, turns, mordents, etc. Thus the necessary basis was laid for a correct execution of Emanuel's own compositions, in which ornaments were never used merely to decorate a tune, but always formed an essential part of its melodic life. The writer's conceptions of the thorough bass and intervals were also firmly founded on his teacher's methods. Both rejected the theoretical and mathematical aspects of Rameau's famous '*Traité d'Harmonie.*' Father and son alike looked at the problem as teachers anxious to convey to growing musicians their own practical knowledge. Possibly the most individual section of the 'Essay' is the last chapter of the first part. In dealing with the problems of performance the master of *Empfindsamkeit* expressed his artistic creed: technical proficiency is not sufficient for the perfect execution of music; the player must transmit the whole emotional content of the composition to his audience.

Altogether, this is not a book of speculation, but the attempt of a composer and educator to guide his students in a practical manner to

---

[1] The work is available in an English translation with annotations, and a valuable ntroduction by W. J. Mitchell, New York, 1949.

better musicianship. It displays a freshness of approach and a clear simplicity of diction that will make the 'Essay' live long after the many similar books of the time have been forgotten.

To illustrate his point of view, Emanuel added in the edition of 1753 eighteen compositions which he called *Probestücke* ('sample pieces'; *Wq* 63), grouped together in six Sonatas. As if to make up for a certain inevitable pedantry in the textbook, he displayed in these examples all the shades of his emotional palette. No two of the movements of each separate Sonata are in the same key, and their subjective nature is stressed by such unusual headings as 'Adagio assai mesto e sostenuto' or 'Allegretto arioso ed amoroso.' The conclusion and climax of the whole set is formed by the beautiful *Fantasia in c*. In order to ensure complete rhythmic flexibility, Emanuel even omitted the bar lines in its improvisatory first and last sections. The striking emotional intensity of this Fantasia was felt so keenly by his contemporaries that Emanuel's friend, the poet W. Gerstenberg, made two attempts at transforming the purely instrumental number

into a kind of cantata by adding recitatives, one of which was based on Hamlet's monologue, the other on the last words of Socrates emptying the cup of poison (*Ex.* 84).

In 1760 Emanuel dedicated to Princess Amalia, the sister of the King, six *Sonaten mit veränderten Reprisen* ('with altered restatements'; *Wq* 50). They reveal his conviction that embellishments and ornaments form an essential part of the melody, and that it is not for performers arbitrarily to add ornaments in repetitions, according to the fashion of the time. He maintained this practice in many of his later compositions as well, as the following example from a Sonata printed in 1770 may illustrate (*Ex.* 85).

Ex. 85   *Sonata from „ Musikalisches Vielerlei "*

Among the great number of Sonatas for keyboard instruments written in Berlin are six Sonatas for the organ without pedal (*Wq* 70). Burney's report that Emanuel was not interested in the organ is fully confirmed by these works. Little in them suggests that they were intended for the king of instruments. This is ordinary clavier music, only of a slightly more conventional character.[1] Also the Concerto in C for unaccompanied clavier (*Wq* 112/1) published in 1765 is retrospective in its basic character. It follows closely the example of similar works by Sebastian and Friedemann, emphasizing the contrast between solo and tutti. Like Sebastian's Italian Concerto and Friedemann's Concerto in G it has the aspects of a keyboard arrangement of an imaginary orchestral work.

Every element of Emanuel's style in the Berlin period reappears in maturer and more concentrated form in the composer's masterwork, the six collections *für Kenner und Liebhaber* ('for connoisseurs and amateurs'; *Wq* 55-59, 61) published between 1779 and 1787. Here Emanuel displays the sureness of touch and the virtuosity of the mature master. Most of these compositions are sonatas which, as a rule, consist of three movements in closely related keys; but when the expressive content demands it the composer does not hesitate to use as unusual a key combination as

---

[1] Emanuel's only sonata for organ with pedal (*Wq* 70/7) is of a similar nature. To his pseudo-organ compositions belong also the 6 fugues (*Wq* 119) written between 1754-63, mostly for his learned friend, Marpurg's, collections. The compositions, while showing thorough contrapuntal knowledge, clearly display the composer's indifference towards the form of the instrumental fugue.

G-g-E for the successive movements. Occasionally the three movements shrink to two, connected by a few transitional measures, and even a complete integration of all movements into a single unit occurs, anticipating 19th-century tendencies. Beginning with the second collection, Rondos join the Sonatas. These compositions, which were particular favourites with Emanuel's contemporaries, are based on brief and deceptively simple subjects. The composer presents his ideas in ever new transformations, changing their pitch, dissolving them melodically, harmonizing them in different ways, and introducing unexpected rests and *rubatos*. His sudden changes between pianissimo and fortissimo, his crescendi ending up in piano, his diminuendi leading to a forte, as well as his ingenuity in offering ever new surprises to the delighted and amused listener clearly reveal an exquisite sense of humour. These rondos are the musical counterpart of his witty and spirited conversations, which made the great intellects of his time seek Emanuel's company. Into the three last sets Emanuel inserted Fantasias. Here we get a glimpse of what his improvisations, which made so tremendous an impression on his listeners, must have been like. Most of these compositions resemble in character the Fantasia in c, their recitatives and ariosos not following a strict rhythmic pattern. Only the last Fantasia in C presents a single idea in ever-changing garb, thus approaching Emanuel's Rondos.

In both his Berlin and his Hamburg years Emanuel wrote a substantial number of *short clavier pieces*. They frequently appear to be miniature editions of the larger forms, reduced not only in size but also in technical difficulty. Thus while the 6 Sonatas accompanying the first edition of the 'Essay' were most ambitious in their whole conception, the 6 *Sonatinas*, which the composer added in 1786 to a new edition of the book (*Wq* 63) are completely unpretentious. Each consists of only a single movement and rarely has more than 30 measures. Technically they are within the reach of any player of medium abilities. However, in spite of their almost aphoristic character, they are as carefully worked out as his larger compositions, and the heart-felt little Largo in E (*Wq* 63/8), for instance, is a piece of almost classical poise.

Among these short clavier pieces are numerous *Solfeggii*, prelude-like little fantasias, usually developed out of a single motive. It is interesting to compare the well-known Solfeggii in c (*Wq* 117/2), published in 1770, with similar compositions by Sebastian. While the piece is obviously based on forms the father liked to use, the strongly throbbing emotional life belongs to a younger generation.

Many Minuets (often appearing in pairs) and Polaccas are to be found in this group, the latter being free of the formal, even melancholy character they assumed for Friedemann. These are gay dances in 3/4 time approaching in character the polonaise of the 19th century.

To a special category belong the musical portraits and other pieces of programme music with descriptive titles (*Wq* 117). Emanuel gives us delightful little pictures of some of his lady-friends. A graceful Allegro in 6/8 time describes 'La Gleim' (cf. p. 342), a ceremonious minuet 'La Lott'; serious and melancholy (probably on account of the loss of her children) is 'La Stahl'; saucy and temperamental 'La Böhmer.' 'La Journalière' with its gay pralltrillers and 'La Capricieuse' with its merrily skipping dotted rhythms portray true daughters of Eve. 'La Complaisante' makes the listener wish to meet a lady so anxious to please. One of the most mature of these character-pieces is the 'Farewell to my Silbermann Clavichord' (*Wq* 66), composed in 1781 in the form of a rondo. A pupil of Emanuel, Ewald v. Grotthus, received from the composer a clavier made by the great Silbermann. Bach accompanied his instrument with a composition, thus proving, as he wrote to Grotthus, that 'it is also possible to write lamenting rondos.' Actually this composition is a stirring and passionate piece, growing out of the germ-cell of a single main subject, in which Emanuel's attachment to the clavichord finds heart-felt expression.[1]

In his *Chamber Music* Emanuel was not as progressive as in his clavier works. It seems likely that the first compositions the young artist wrote in this field attracted the attention of the Prussian Crown Prince and secured Emanuel the position he was to hold for almost thirty years. During this time most of Emanuel's chamber music was written for the King and his court, and the increasingly conservative leanings of the monarch forced the composer to renounce in them the more daring of his experiments. The situation changed when Emanuel moved to Hamburg. The former restrictions no longer existed, and the composer produced a number of instrumental ensemble works, almost equal in perfection to his keyboard music.

To the first period belong a number of 'solos' and 'trios,' as the composer called them in the traditional manner. The 'solos' are for (transverse) flute and bass or for oboe and bass; the 'trios' for flute, violin and bass or for violin and cembalo obbligato. Both in the choice of these forms

---

[1] Grotthus' musical answer 'Joy at receiving the Silbermann Clavier' is artistically of little significance.

and in their contents, Emanuel reveals himself as his father's faithful disciple. We find among these works sonatas in the four movements of the Baroque period, canonic episodes, concerto forms, and the whole harmonic language and bass lines of Sebastian's music.

In the chamber music works written in Berlin, the dependence on the past recedes only slowly. Again Emanuel writes 'solos' and 'trios'; in many of them the same key is preserved throughout, a feature pointing back to the suite of the 17th century. The different versions existing of most of the 'trios' also point towards the Baroque period. The lovely work in G, of 1754, for instance, is once scored for 2 violins and bass (*Wq* 157), then for flute, violin, and bass (*Wq* 152) and again for cembalo and flute (*Wq* 85).[1] On the other hand a leaning towards the *style galant* finds expression in the frequent prescription of the word *grazioso* in the tempo indications. To his former combinations of instruments Emanuel now adds some new ones, such as viola da gamba and bass, or harp and bass. The constant work with the King's excellent musicians helped to familiarize the composer with the technical possibilities of the instruments, and often to use them in a truly idiomatic manner. His viola da gamba sonatas, for instance, introduce arpeggios and even triple stops, while large skips in the solo parts of the flute works allowed the august performer to show off his technical skill.

It is significant that a Trio (*Wq* 161/1) of a clearly experimental character was not written for the King, but was dedicated to the young Count Wilhelm of Schaumburg-Lippe, the employer of Emanuel's half-brother, Friedrich. A definite programme dealing with different temperaments underlies this music, a subject popular in the 18th century.[2] The composer explains it in his preface with these words: 'An attempt has been made to express as far as possible through instruments, what otherwise is done much more easily through the voice and words. This is supposed to be a conversation between a Sanguine and a Melancholic who . . . endeavour to convince each other, until by the end of the second movement . . . the Melancholic gives in and adopts the other's point of view.' Emanuel portrays the argument through an intensive development of his subjects, and explains his procedure in a running commentary, using letters to refer to individual places in the score. He alludes, for instance, to a passage in the first movement with these words: 'At (h) Sanguine tries to

---

[1] Similarly the 2 trios printed in Bach's lifetime (*Wq* 161, published 1751) have, on the title page, an indication that one of the two melody instruments might be taken over by the right hand of the cembalist.

[2] Beethoven still had in his string quartet op. 18/6 a finale entitled 'La Malinconia.'

convert Melancholic. The latter begins to give in, but soon stops (i) and
has to take a full rest (k) to find his own self again (l). Impatiently Sanguine interrupts him, mockingly aping his ideas (m). . . .' (*Ex.* 86).

Ex. 86

Although other dramatic dialogues are found in Emanuel's chamber
music, he never again attempted to write a literary programme to a composition of his own, and in later years, even admitted the weakness of this
early experiment.

On the whole the chamber music of the Berlin years displays the
characteristics of a transitional phase, when the composer felt inclined to
try out the most varied devices. Side by side with compositions based on
the Baroque conception of using two melody instruments equal in range
and importance, we find trios in which the rigid balance between the upper
voices is abandoned. In *Wq* 156 and 160 for 2 violins and bass, the second
violin is clearly subordinated to the first. It usually accompanies in parallel
thirds and sixths, never competing on equal terms with the leading voices.
The same procedure may be noticed in the *Sinfonia a cembalo obbligato e
violino* (*Wq* 74), in which the right hand of the clavier dominates, while
the violin is used mainly as a filling and accompanying voice. All three
compositions reject polyphony and the concertante style and tend towards
the later type of clavier sonata with the accompaniment of a violin.

In the last twenty years of Emanuel's life his chamber music presents
a very different picture. The Baroque combination of two melody voices
and bass completely disappears, and chamber music employing a continuo
part to be realized by the performer is hardly to be found. The composer's
output includes several Duos, Trios, and 'Quartets' (*Wq* 79-80, 89-91,
93-95) for clavier obbligato with the accompaniment of string and,
occasionally, wind instruments. In the works for clavier and violin or
for clavier, violin and violoncello, compositions clearly meant for
amateurs, the keyboard instrument has constantly the lead; the violin as a
rule doubles the melody, the 'cello the bass, and either may be used to fill
in a middle part. Yet, in spite of the small role assigned to them, the

omission of these instruments would deprive the works of attractive effects of colour.

In some chamber music works the composer entrusts important tasks to the flute, the bassoon, the viola, and, in particular, the clarinet, the favourite of his later years. For all that, the clavier always stands in the centre of the Hamburg chamber music. Its part no longer results from the more or less mechanical combination of a violin melody with a supporting bass, as was the rule in the Berlin 'trios'; dynamic contrasts are now widely employed, and these chamber music works gradually become imbued with the strongly personal and unconventional character of Emanuel's keyboard compositions. The second and third of the 'Clavier-Sonatas accompanied by violin and violoncello' (*Wq* 91, published in 1777) contain gems unforgettable in their poignancy and emotional intensity. It is significant that the rondo, which had brought Emanuel so great a success in his works for solo clavier, now also appears in his chamber music. Its natural place is obviously the third movement, but in the highly unorthodox composition for cembalo obbligato, flute and viola (*Wq* 93), written in the year of Emanuel's death, it is used even for the first movement. This is a deeply felt, and most expressive composition, in which beauty of content is balanced by complete technical perfection. Rhapsodic elements are conspicuous in many of Emanuel's late chamber music works, and one of the finest Fantasias he wrote (*Wq* 80, composed in 1787) was conceived for clavier with the accompaniment of a violin. The composer headed it with the significant words *sehr traurig und ganz langsam. C. P. E. Bachs Empfindungen* ('very sadly and quite slowly; C. P. E. Bach's emotions'). Works of this kind (cf. also the poignant middle movement in *Wq* 95) seem to lead right to the threshold of Romanticism. On the other hand there is clear evidence that, near the end of his life, Emanuel was also under the influence of a composer who had learned a great deal from him in

Ex.87

earlier years. The last movement of the 'Quartet' in D for harpsichord, flute and viola (*Wq* 94) is spiritually akin to works by Joseph Haydn[1] (*Ex.* 87).

---

[1] Cf. E. F. Schmid's valuable study 'C. P. E. Bach und seine Kammermusik,' p. 147.

Short compositions of little technical difficulty, which are equal in craftsmanship and beauty to his larger works, are also to be found in Emanuel's chamber music. He wrote these precious miniatures for two to seven instruments. Particularly charming are the 12 *little pieces for two flutes (or violins) and clavier*, printed in 1770 (*Wq* 82). They consist of brief character sketches, usually of not more than sixteen measures, for all three instruments, alternating with movements in which the cembalo is not used. The latter are particularly attractive, but also trios, such as the sentimental Allegro (No. 1), the Minuetto in the *style galant* (No. 5), or the irresistible Polacca (No. 8), are of delightful grace and simplicity. Equally important are the six undated *little sonatas for clavier, clarinet and bassoon* (*Wq* 92), most of which also exist in arrangements for seven wind instruments. Emanuel achieved through soloistic treatment of the instruments a transparent chamber music style hardly surpassed in any of his larger works.

The composer's attitude in his *clavier concertos* is similar to that revealed in his chamber music. To the first period belong three concertos for cembalo and strings written in Leipzig or Frankfurt and revised in Berlin (*Wq* 1-3). Tutti and soli are short and supplement each other rather than compete in concerto manner. Contrapuntal texture is often used for the orchestral sections, and the accompaniments to the cembalo parts are rather powerful. Although the young composer is anxious to equip the soli with all the fashionable brilliance, the clavier technique discloses his lack of experience. A leaning towards the *style galant* is unmistakable, yet at the same time the son resorts repeatedly to a close imitation of his father's style.

The 38 concertos written in the Berlin years (*Wq* 4-40, 46)[1] conform to each other in basic elements. They are always in three movements, fast-slow-fast, each of them containing from three to five tutti. These ritornels differ widely in length; in their most expansive form they consist of an energetic first, and a contrasting, more tender second section, a group of sequences, and a coda resuming the ideas of the first section. The solos, which are frequently interrupted by short tutti episodes, are as long and even longer than the ritornels. They employ partly thematic material derived from the first tutti and partly new ideas, or else they accompany the

[1] A few more are preserved under Emanuel's name in old manuscripts, but their authenticity is not established.

orchestra with rich figurations. In movements with four ritornels the first solo has an exposition-like character, the second reminds us of a development, while the third restates ideas from the first two solos. In movements with five ritornels the two middle solos have the character of a development. All these features point towards the gradual transition from the old Vivaldi concerto form to the new sonata form. Although Emanuel's treatment of the solo instrument is growing more and more idiomatic, his style is not always appropriate to the clavier. It is worthy of notice that some of the concertos exist in versions in which the keyboard part is replaced by a stringed or a wind instrument. The Baroque practice of freely exchanging solo instruments in concertos obviously holds good for Sebastian's son. The Concerto in a of 1750 (*Wq* 26) for example, exists in three versions, for 'cello, flute, and harpsichord solo respectively. With minor changes in the figuration the composer cleverly adapts the part of the main instrument to the changing medium of woodwind, low-pitched string and keyboard instrument.[1]

Among the numerous remarkable works, the deeply passionate and exciting *Concerto in d* of 1748 (*Wq* 23) with the wide skips at the beginning (*Ex.* 88) deserves mention. Schering rightly points out that in its

Ex. 88

first and third movements a spirit reigns which reached its full growth in Beethoven's Vth and IXth symphonies. The middle movement of the Concerto in c of 1753 (*Wq* 31) is noteworthy. It contains instrumental recitatives of the solo instrument dramatically interrupted by the orchestra with a dynamic range from *pp* to *ff*, and repeated changes of tempo from adagio to presto. This highly romantic movement appears as a kind of over-extended introduction to the finale which is meant to follow instantly.

The *Sonatinas* (*Wq* 96-110) written between 1762 and 1764 may be considered as an attempt to leave the narrow confines of the Berlin musical

---

[1] Similarly the Harpsichord Concertos *Wq* 28, 29 also exist as flute and as 'cello concertos. *Wq* 39, 40 are to be found as oboe concertos. In *Wq* 34, 35 execution of the solo part on the organ is optional. At practically the same time (1756) Joseph Haydn wrote his concerto in C for organ or harpsichord with orchestra.

school, and to become familiar with different artistic trends. In these compositions which follow the style of the Austrian court composer, Wagenseil, and of the young Haydn, Emanuel no longer attempts to produce real concertos. These are suite-like divertimenti with a prominent clavier part, preserving the same key throughout each composition. In these forms variety is as great as was the standardization in the older concertos. While Wq 96 consists only of a theme with variations and an extensive finale, Wq 109 has no less than eight movements, I and IV being identical, III and V as well as VI and VIII closely interrelated. Other Sonatinas are in three movements with the slow one at the beginning, or with fast tempi in all three movements. They are mostly scored for one or two cembali with strings, 2 flutes and 2 horns. Wq 109 in D for 2 cembali uses in addition 3 trumpets, timpani, 2 oboes and bassoon. As in the Austrian divertimento, a gay and carefree mood prevails; major modes dominate, a dance-like character is emphasized in many movements, and we find the direction 'Alla Polacca' indicated among the finales.

The result of Emanuel's studies is noticeable in the ten concertos for one clavier, and one for two claviers written in Hamburg (Wq 41-45, 47). They belong to the best the North German school produced in this sphere of music. None of them exists in a version for any other instrument, and accordingly the keyboard part is completely idiomatic. The accompanying orchestra is, as a rule, that of the Sonatinas. Most movements are lacking in any real ending and lead immediately into the next one. The unity thus created is also emphasized by other methods. In the Concerto in G, belonging to the fine set published in 1772 (Wq 43), the first and second movements use the same introduction. In the magnificent Concerto in c from the same group, the last movement even employs thematic material from the first. This work is the only Concerto of Emanuel's in four movements, the third being a Minuet as in Austrian symphonies.

Fundamentally the old concerto form remains in force, but mighty inroads were made to meet the requirements of the new age. The plain song-form, the true rondo form which, unlike the Vivaldi form, always restates the main subject in the same key, and the classical sonata form with its basic dualistic and well-balanced construction left their imprint on these works. It is characteristic of the composer's progressive attitude that the second movement of the Concerto in F of 1772 replaces the traditional tutti at the beginning and end by unaccompanied soli of the clavier. Equally unorthodox is Emanuel's idea of writing out the cadenzas for all six concertos of the set, a method widely used in the 19th century.

The attitude of the aged Emanuel towards the concerto is perhaps best revealed by the *Double Concerto in E flat* (*Wq* 47) composed in Hamburg, possibly as late as 1788, the year of his death. It is written for two keyboard instruments,[1] one the old cembalo, the other the young fortepiano. Emanuel's feelings towards the latter were those of distrust. Although his father had used the fortepiano forty years earlier, Emanuel's Concerto in E flat is the only work in which he prescribed the instrument expressly. In its form the Double Concerto clearly reverts to the architecture of the Berlin years with its massive main tuttis, but the timid question uttered in piano by the violins at the beginning of the first movement is diametrically opposed to the traditional conception that a concerto ought to start with a forceful statement. This tutti also introduces a persuasive tune of the flutes in parallel thirds and sixths which has the character of a subsidiary subject in a sonata form, and the first idea of the finale has the sparkle of a composition by Haydn (*Ex.* 89).—Emanuel's last concertos,

in which all stylistic elements of his earlier works were amalgamated, contributed much to the fame of their author; in Northern Germany they were performed long after Emanuel's death, and were superseded only by Beethoven's compositions in this field.

No *symphonies* from Emanuel's first period are known. Eight compositions were written in Berlin (*Wq* 173-81) which, like most works from this period of transition, exist in different versions. The one in e of 1756, for instance, is preserved in a setting for strings only (*Wq* 177), another with horns, oboes and flutes (*Wq* 178), and a transcription for clavier (*Wq* 122/3). This might also have been due to the work's popularity, corroborated by as great an authority as Hasse who described it as 'an unequalled masterpiece.' It starts with a forceful, almost fierce movement, containing passages soaring upward like rockets, effective changes between major and minor, and sudden pianissimos framed by fortes. A most expressive transition leads to the middle movement

---

[1] Friedemann's only concerto for 2 claviers is in the same key of E flat.

(*Ex.* 90). This brief and more conventional piece is followed by a finale
which, with its jagged melodic lines, and its spirit of vehement determina-

tion, represents a tour de force of a highly emotional composer. But not
all the Berlin symphonies are on this high level, even the latest of the
period, *Wq* 181 in F of 1762, is rather old-fashioned in character.

The ten symphonies written in Hamburg consist of two sets: six
works (*Wq* 182) composed in 1773 for Gottfried van Swieten, Austrian
Ambassador to the court at Berlin, and four (*Wq* 183) published in 1780
with a dedication to Friedrich Wilhelm, Crown Prince of Prussia. Thus
these compositions established contacts with men who were to have
significant artistic connections with Haydn, Mozart, and Beethoven. In
the six symphonies of 1773 for strings and continuo[1] the old concerto
symphony of the Baroque period seems to be revived. There are neither
soloists nor ripienists, but each instrument serves in turn as a melodic
leader and an accompanist. Similar in character are the symphonies printed
in 1780 and scored for two oboes, two horns, strings, bassoon and cembalo. Impressive tutti alternate with delicate soli; even the virtuoso element is not completely missing and contemporary critics emphasized the
works' technical difficulty. Emanuel had apparently no use for the South
German innovation of including a Minuet in the symphony as a fourth
movement. All compositions are in three movements, fast-slow-fast, inter-
connected by modulating bridge passages. In the first symphony of 1780,
for instance, a dramatic transition connects the exciting initial movement
in D with the beautiful middle movement in E flat.

Reichardt, who attended a rehearsal of the six symphonies of 1773,
wrote in later years:[2] 'One heard with rapture the original and bold course
of ideas as well as the great variety and novelty in forms and modulations.
Hardly ever did a musical composition of higher, more daring, and more
humorous character flow from the soul of a genius.' Although Reichardt
was notorious for his exaggerations, this report gives an idea of the
general reaction to Emanuel's intense works, which were real products of

[1] Hugo Riemann, who first edited two of them, erroneously considered them as
string quartets.
[2] 'Allgemeine Musicalische Zeitung,' 1814.

the *Sturm und Drang* movement just then reaching its climax. The following set shows the same characteristics, although it is superior in artistic quality. Its four symphonies are imbued with a dramatic power unusual even among Emanuel's works. The mighty build-up towards a climax at the beginning of the symphony in D, the sinister chains of trills in the first movement of the E flat symphony, and the humorous finale of that in F leave indelible impressions in the mind of the listener. It is more than a mere coincidence that the finale of Beethoven's second symphony is melodically related to the beginning of this symphony in F, which is possibly the most attractive work of the set.

From a composer imbuing his instrumental works with so great an expressive power important contributions in the field of vocal composition may be expected, and indeed Emanuel's abilities in this respect far surpass those of his elder brother. He composed songs, arias, choruses, cantatas and oratorios both for sacred and secular purposes; but he never wrote an opera.

As a composer of secular songs or odes, as they were called at that time, Emanuel developed along the same lines as in his instrumental music. Up to the end his output showed a certain growth in quality and technical perfection. It was different, however, in the field of the sacred song. Owing to the royal free-thinker's aversion to church music, Emanuel wrote very few sacred works on the large scale at Berlin, but he found an outlet in the composition of outstanding religious songs. The situation changed as soon as he moved to Hamburg, where his new duties not merely allowed, but compelled him to write choral music for the church. During this period his interest was no longer engrossed in the smaller forms, and neither in style nor quality do the sacred songs written in Hamburg exhibit any improvement.

Little is known of Emanuel's work as a writer of *secular songs* in Leipzig or Frankfurt, but in his first years in Berlin he contributed to various collections, which, according to Marpurg, held the 'balance between too ornate and too plain a style,' and whose texts 'made the listener neither blush nor yawn.' These widely dispersed songs as well as a few new compositions were published by the composer in 1762 as *Oden mit Melodien* (*Wq* 199). The texts frequently introduce the fashionable shepherds and shepherdesses. These are clavier songs, in which the strophic form, customary at the time, prevails. The keyboard part is written out, and the

2 A

right hand doubles the vocal melody. Emanuel belongs to the first composers who introduced brief and purely instrumental ritornels into the
songs, preceding or interrupting the vocal sections. The finest of these
early songs (first published in 1741) is based on Marianne von Ziegler's
Eilt ihr Schäfer ('Hasten ye shepherds'). Emanuel uses the words of a
poetess who had already provided texts for his father's cantatas, and it is
worth mentioning that the same shepherd's song was set to music forty
years later by Joseph Haydn. Emanuel's composition in plain two-part
song form is quite charming and of classical simplicity. Equal in value are
Der Morgen ('The morning'), gay and unpretentious in the manner of a
hunting song, and the tragic lament *Die verliebte Verzweiflung* ('Love's
despair') in Emanuel's favourite key of c. Other songs in the collection of
1762, however, are conventional in their musical expression and devoid of
deeper feeling. The composer often transplants his keyboard style rather
mechanically to the song form and creates odes of instrumental rather than
vocal conception.

In the Berlin years a number of cantata-like songs were written, such
as the jolly drinking song *Brüder, unser Bruder lebe* ('Brothers, long live
our brother'; *Wq* 201), on words by Emanuel's friend, Gleim, in which
the lines are presented alternately by a group of merry guests and their
liberal host. In the same year 1766 Emanuel published *Phillis und Tirsis*
(*Wq* 232) for 2 sopranos, 2 flutes, and continuo, one of the most tender
and delicate miniatures the musical Rococo has produced. To the Hamburg period belongs *Selma* (*Wq* 236), a passionate soprano cantata set
with full orchestral accompaniment in 1770, but reduced for publication
in Voss' 'Musen-Almanach' of 1776 to the essential parts, soprano and
continuo. The same Almanach for the year 1782 contains the lovely song
Ich ging unter Erlen ('I walked beneath alders'; *Wq* 202/L), a gem of graceful simplicity. Quite different in character is the magnificent *Trennung*
('Separation'; *Wq* 202/O/4), in which sonorous octaves of the left hand

Ex. 91

imitate bells ringing a farewell (*Ex.* 91). The song assumes a weird
character when diminished and augmented intervals appear in the left

hand symbolizing the hopeless sadness of this scene of parting.[1] The very latest collection of Emanuel's odes (*Wq* 200), which appeared in 1789, one year after his death, shows both a greater depth of feeling and an increase in technical skill. The serious songs in particular sometimes foreshadow the art of Beethoven and Brahms. In *Nonnelied* ('Nun's song'), for instance, Emanuel avoids the traditional strophic form; the music of the five stanzas is beautifully differentiated, to achieve the effect of growing despair.

In the field of the *sacred song* Emanuel's output is inseparably connected with the work of Christian Fürchtegott Gellert (1715-69), whose importance for the lied of the 18th century can only be compared to Heinrich Heine's influence on that of the 19th century. Gellert's *Geistliche Oden und Lieder* of 1757 belong to the greatest poems written for the Protestant Church in the age of Rationalism. The poet indicated numerous chorale melodies to which his songs could be sung; nevertheless for more than seventy years composers competed in setting them to music. Half a century after their creation their noble sentiments still inspired compositions by Haydn and Beethoven. In 1758, one year after the publication of the texts, 55 Gellert songs appeared with Emanuel's music (*Wq* 194) and were so successful that five editions had to be printed in the composer's lifetime. Gellert himself, who stressed that 'the best song without its fitting melody is like a loving heart lacking its consort,' was deeply impressed by this music. In the preface to the collection Emanuel explained: 'When inventing the melodies, I considered as far as possible the poem as a whole. I say as far as possible since no expert can ignore the fact that not too much should be expected of a tune meant for more than a single stanza.' Though aware of these difficulties, Emanuel did not consider the expedient (later used in his secular songs) of altering the music in accordance with changes in the text, as this would have made the employment of his odes in the church service impracticable. It is true that *Du klagst* ('Thou lamentest') has two melodies, a sad one in c minor for the first five stanzas, and a more serene one in C major for the remaining nine stanzas; but this is an exception, and in some other songs discrepancies between music and text were not avoided. At times there is also a certain preponderance of the declamatory and arioso element, resulting in a neglect of simple melodic beauty. Besides, Emanuel again stresses the instrumental character, prescribing ornaments mainly meant for the keyboard which a singer would have difficulties in executing.

[1] Gustav Mahler may have known Emanuel's ode (which was first published in 1900); there is both in the poignancy of expression and the harmonic idiom a certain resemblance between the last movement of 'Das Lied von der Erde' and 'Trennung.'

These deficiencies, which the composer shares with most of the song writers of his time, are outweighed, however, by outstanding merits. The technical perfection, in particular the harmonic boldness and contrapuntal skill, is superb. The intensity of Emanuel's interpretation is revealed in most unusual prescriptions heading the songs, such as 'loftily and emphatically,' 'pompously,' 'magnanimously,' 'composedly.'[1] Among the finest songs of the set are *Demuth* ('Humility'), *Wider den Uebermuth* ('Against Pride'), *Der Kampf der Tugend* ('The struggle of virtue'), and the magnificent *Bitten* ('Prayers'), which may have induced Beethoven to use the same text (op. 48/1).

In 1764 there was published an Appendix to the Gellert songs (*Wq* 195) which contained, among others, the beautiful 88th Psalm, resembling in its powerful harmonic language Sebastian's chorales. The success of this song seems to have caused the composer to publish, in 1774, music to 42 of Cramer's sentimental German translations of the Psalms (*Wq* 196). While some of them do achieve the character of chorales, none reaches the virility and strength of the former work.

Two sets of *Geistliche Gesänge* by Sturm published in 1780-81 (*Wq* 197-98) seem to reflect, especially in the more tragic compositions, the vigorous personality of the librettist, who was Emanuel's personal friend (cf. p. 346). *Der Tag des Weltgerichts* ('The day of the last judgment'), with its threatening dotted rhythms in the left hand, and the moving *Ueber die Finsternisz kurz vor dem Tode Jesu* ('On the darkness shortly before Jesus' death'), both ending with the stirring invocation 'Have mercy on us,' belong to his most powerful settings. Unfortunately their spontaneity of expression is not maintained in other songs of the collection.

Of Emanuel's *larger vocal works* the majority were written in Hamburg to comply with the pressing needs of the day. As music director in one of the biggest North German cities he was expected to produce a continuous stream of *Singstücke für die Kirche*, as he called them in his autobiography. What counted was the quantity, not the quality of the output. The composer manufactured no less than 20 Passions, and various Cantatas for Christmas, Easter, Whitsuntide, St. Michael's Day, and certain Sundays. In addition he produced birthday and wedding cantatas, and compositions for the induction of a new pastor or the funeral of a mayor. Little among this music is of any importance. It is routine work using stereotyped

[1] 'Erhaben und nachdrücklich,' 'prächtig,' 'grossmütig,' 'gelassen.'

patterns: smooth opera recitatives, arias of a pale and insignificant lyricism, and homophonic choruses with infrequent polyphonic episodes. Often the composer borrowed from other works, arranged and transposed them, changed the texts, added a little of his own making and obtained with a minimum of effort a 'new' composition. In Emanuel's *Einchöriges Heilig* in C (*Wq* 218), for instance, a short and solemn introduction is followed by a fugue using music from Sebastian's *Magnificat* ('Sicut locutus').[1] His Cantata for the 16th or 24th Sunday after Trinity, of 1774,[2] even employs as first and last chorus the motet *Der Gerechte* by Johann Christoph Bach (cf. Ill. VI) leaving the five voice parts and the text of the original unchanged, but adding orchestral instruments. The rest of the cantata consists of recitatives and arias by Johann Christoph's great-nephew; Emanuel apparently did not mind the stylistic gap between the two sections of the work. In his St. Matthew Passions Emanuel borrowed no less than 3 chorales and 10 choruses from his father's St. Matthew Passion, besides one chorale each from Sebastian's St. John Passion, Christmas Oratorio, Cantatas 39 and 153. Compositions by Telemann were also frequently used for his Passions, in particular for those according to St. John. As a matter of fact not one of Emanuel's 20 Passions is a completely new composition. Possibly the most attractive sections in these pasticcios for the church are arrangements for chorus and orchestra which the composer made of his own sacred songs.

The question may well be asked why Emanuel, instead of plundering other works, did not provide his congregation with the great experience of occasionally hearing Sebastian's Passions as a whole. The reason for this, as we see it to-day, irreverent attitude may have been the Hamburg citizens' novelty-hunger. They would not have cared to hear a work composed some 50 years ago, while an adaptation of the kind Emanuel made might pass as a new composition.[3]

In his Autobiography Emanuel remarked that all through his life he had to write much in compliance with orders, while he found only limited time for composing after his own heart. In order to evaluate his greatness rightly, one must disregard such inferior works which were obviously written to satisfy pressing demands.

There is a small group of works, however, which were not written merely for Hamburg's churches, but for the large circle of Emanuel's admirers throughout the country. This handful of compositions gives a

---

[1] Cf. Karl Geiringer, 'Artistic Interrelations of the Bachs,' *MQ*, July 1950.
[2] Autograph University Library of Tübingen. The work is not mentioned in *Wq*.
[3] Cf. Emanuel's letter to G. M. Telemann, 'Allgemeine Musikal. Zeitung,' 1869.

good idea of the high standards Emanuel could reach in choral music if he gave of his best. The earliest work of this kind is the *Magnificat* (*Wq* 215) for solo voices, four-part chorus, flutes, oboes, horns, trumpets, timpani and strings, written in 1749, while he lived in Berlin. Winterfeld, that fine judge of Protestant church music, justly called it an 'anthology of various styles.' In fact we find French rhythms and Italian melodies of the kind used by Hasse in this work. Even more important is the son's dependence on Sebastian's model. The melodies to *Deposuit potentes* and *Fecit potentiam* practically quote the father's work, and the brilliant and fiery fugue *Sicut erat in principio* seems to revive experiences from Emanuel's student days. On the other hand, the homophonic choruses Nos. 1 and 4 and the expressive numbers for the soloists reveal the composer's progressive attitude. It is significant that themes similar to those used in the last movement of the *Magnificat* appear in the Kyrie of Mozart's *Requiem* (*Ex.* 92); this points once more to Emanuel's historic position as a link between Sebastian and the classical composers.

The *Passion Cantata* (*Wq* 233) of 1769-70 was, according to a notice in the *Nachlasskatalog*, derived from an earlier Passion from which the part of the Evangelist was omitted. Furthermore the work contains hardly any chorales, and exhibits the then fashionable, sentimental lyricism. The funeral music after the death of Jesus is orchestrated for flutes and muted strings to create a feeling of delicate suffering in the souls of the audience. The most famous number of the Cantata was the tenor aria in b of Peter ('Turn toward my grief'), which, according to Burney, who attended a performance, moved all the listeners to tears. The sensibility of Emanuel's Berlin colleague, Karl Heinrich Graun, whose 'Death of Jesus' (1755) belonged to the most successful works of the period, permeates the score. Even operatic elements, such as a rondo-like construction at the end of the work, find their place in the score. Yet Sebastian's spirit is not completely absent in this cantata. In the chorus 'Let us look up toward Jesus' the voices in unison present a chorale-like melody in long notes accompanied by the slow and solemn strains of the orchestra, producing an overwhelming picture of divine majesty and its reflection in the human soul.

Equally powerful and imbued with the Baroque spirit is the double fugue concluding this number.

The two-part cantata *Die Israeliten in der Wüste* ('The Israelites in the desert'; *Wq* 238) was written in the same year, 1769, but not published until 1775. It is altogether homophonic in its texture and completely undramatic. Nevertheless this score too contains remarkable details, such as the prayer of Moses in the form of an agitated accompagnato recitative repeatedly interrupted by frenzied interjections from the chorus. Another highlight of the work is the scene when Moses strikes the rock three times and water gushes forth. Here the murmuring runs of the violin accompanying the joyful song of the Israelites produce a highly colourful piece.

Whenever 'The Israelites' was performed in later years, the powerful *Heilig* (*Wq* 217) for two choruses, published in 1779, was chosen as a conclusion. In composing a German *Sanctus*, Emanuel followed old Protestant traditions also adopted by his predecessor, Telemann, and his brother, Friedemann. The beginning of the work is not very promising, for it starts with a rather playful 'Ariette' for soprano solo, which even ardent admirers of the composition felt to be out of place. Rochlitz omitted it altogether in his edition of the work, while Zelter arranged it for a separate third chorus. With the entrance of the main choral section, however, the work radiates dramatic energy and a fiery spirit. The music is entrusted to a 'chorus of the angels' and a second 'chorus of the nations,' which Emanuel, conforming to earlier conceptions of the Roman and Venetian school, endowed with contrasting tone-colours and posted in different parts of the church; at the beginning strings only are used as accompaniment for the angels, full orchestra with oboes, trumpets and timpani for the chorus of the nations. Three times each of the two groups enunciates the words: 'Holy is the Lord of Sabaoth.' A fugue of Handelian grandeur ensues which introduces the hymn 'Lord God, Thy praise we sing' as a powerful *cantus firmus* presented in unison by the chorus to the polyphonic accompaniment of the orchestra. Bold modulations (*Ex.* 93) and

the effective juxtaposition of sharply contrasting keys, to distinguish between celestial and terrestrial hosts, equip this music with an expressive power that was admired long after Emanuel's death. The more remote keys like C sharp, B and F sharp are usually reserved for the divine, the simpler D, G and C for the human chorus. There is a general tendency towards chromatic ascent, lifting the listener to higher and higher levels, until the whole octave is covered. With the *Heilig* Emanuel created a work untouched by the general decline in late 18th-century sacred music, and equal in importance to the finest of his compositions for the clavier. The public's response was most gratifying, and soon after the publication Emanuel could write to Breitkopf that his '*Heilig* like the Sonatas was selling as fast as the hot pastry in front of the Stock Exchange, where as a lad he had broken the neck of many an almond-cracknel.'

Emanuel's *Auferstehung und Himmelfahrt Jesu* ('Jesus' Resurrection and Ascension'; *Wq* 240), published in 1778, is based on a text by K. W. Ramler that was also set to music by Telemann and Zelter. The libretto introduces no Biblical characters and consists of lyrical observations only. Emanuel's music, however, adds vigour and fire to the sentimental words. The sinister orchestral introduction of violas and basses in unison ending in pianissimo seems like a dirge mourning the death of God's own Son. The first chorus rather timidly prepares for the miracle of the resurrection. It is followed by a magnificent recitative 'Judaea trembles,' in which earthquake and inundation reflect nature's reaction to the Lord's return. With the help of strings and timpani only the composer creates 'one of the most powerful recitatives written in Germany during the second half of the 18th century' (Schering). Among the arias the great bass solo 'Open, ye gates of Heaven,' with trumpets and horns, was particularly admired. Zelter omitted this aria from his own setting of Ramler's poem, explaining that Bach had composed it 'with such colossal grandeur and so divinely that any composer after him must fail in an equal attempt.' Similarly inspired are the great choruses of the work, especially its monumental finale, 'God is gone up,' with its almost Beethoven-like unison of the voices at the words 'God is the King' (*Ex.* 94) and its concluding free

fugue. The large dimensions of this chorus, which fills nearly one-third of the printed score, are meant to counterbalance the preponderance of solo numbers in Ramler's text. Between the works of Handel and Haydn few oratorios of equal significance were produced in Germany, and it is not hard to understand why Mozart felt induced to conduct the work in Vienna one year after its publication.

Unlike his elder brother, Emanuel took a vital interest in the idiom of his own time. The musical language of sensibility was of the utmost importance to him, but, as a true son of Sebastian, he spurned its shallow tearfulness and gave it depth and strength. Thus his works display genuine passion instead of the prevalent weak sentimentality, and in their emotional intensity they range close to the greatest products which the *Sturm und Drang* produced in the field of literature. Haydn, Mozart and Beethoven were deeply impressed by these compositions, which are progressive and conservative, soulful and vigorous, all at the same time.

THE BÜCKEBURG BACH
(JOHANN CHRISTOPH FRIEDRICH BACH)

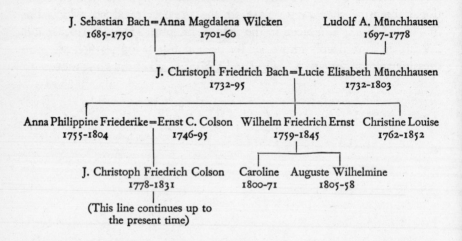

J. Sebastian Bach═Anna Magdalena Wilcken   Ludolf A. Münchhausen
1685-1750   1701-60   1697-1778

J. Christoph Friedrich Bach═Lucie Elisabeth Münchhausen
1732-95   1732-1803

Anna Philippine Friederike═Ernst C. Colson Wilhelm Friedrich Ernst Christine Louise
1755-1804   1746-95   1759-1845   1762-1852

J. Christoph Friedrich Colson Caroline Auguste Wilhelmine
1778-1831   1800-71   1805-58

(This line continues up to
the present time)

JOHANN CHRISTOPH FRIEDRICH BACH, born on June 21, 1732, the eldest son of Sebastian's second marriage to gain distinction, had, like his half-brothers, musical ancestors on both sides of the family. His mother, Anna Magdalena, was a professional singer herself; her grandfathers had been a town musician and an organist, while her father had served as a court trumpeter.

Friedrich received the usual excellent musical instruction from his father and planned to study law at Leipzig University, before starting a career as a musician. However, not long after he had become enrolled there, a chance came his way to be appointed to the court of the Count of Schaumburg-Lippe in Bückeburg, a little Westphalian town some 30 miles west of Hanover. Sebastian, at that time nearly blind and seriously ailing, felt this to be too good an opportunity to be missed, and so Friedrich left his father's house early in 1750, shortly before his 18th birthday.

How the youth got this position is left to guesswork. There may have been some connection between Sebastian and the Bückeburg court; for Count Albrecht Wolfgang of Schaumburg-Lippe was married to the widow of Prince Leopold of Anhalt-Cöthen,[1] the Princess for whom

---

[1] Cf. K. A. Varnhagen von Ense, 'Biographische Denkmale,' I, Berlin, 1824.

Sebastian had composed the Cantata *Steigt freudig in die Luft* (cf. p. 168). However, it seems more likely that it was Emanuel who helped his young half-brother. In 1748 Count Wolfgang died and was succeeded by his son, Count Wilhelm. Soon after ascending the throne, the new ruler went to Berlin to visit King Friedrich, with whom he shared a passionate interest in military problems and a genuine love of music. That he met the court accompanist is proved by Emanuel's dedication of 2 Trio Sonatas to the Count (cf. p. 361). The young ruler was anxious to cultivate the muses in his little court at Bückeburg, and to follow King Friedrich's example in having fine chamber music. He may have talked of his ambitions to Emanuel, who thus got an opportunity of recommending his half-brother. Anyway, by the time Sebastian's property was divided among his heirs, Friedrich Bach was mentioned in the acts as Chamber musician to his Excellency, the Count of Lippe.[1] The position was an excellent one for a beginner. Friedrich received a salary of 200 thalers, two-thirds of what Emanuel, 18 years older and a well-recognized composer and pianist, was paid at that time at the Prussian court. Bückeburg, a town of some 6000 inhabitants, could not, of course, offer the artistic and intellectual stimulus of Berlin, but it was beautifully located, and the impressionable young Friedrich must have loved the enormous oak and beech forest nearby, the 'boldest, most German, and most romantic landscape in the world' (Herder).[2] Moreover there could not be any dullness at the court of a man whom even Goethe called 'extraordinary.' 'His was a queer appearance,' wrote the Swiss physician, J. G. Zimmermann,[3] 'because of the heroic proportions of his body, his flying hair, and his unusually long and lanky person. But on approaching him, one felt differently: grandeur, acumen, nobility, deep observation, goodness and calm were eloquent in his face.' Intensely ambitious, endowed with a tremendous aptitude for physical activity, and a keen intellect, the Count, who was a second son, originally concentrated all his great gifts on military exploits. When, on the death of his elder brother, he was called upon to rule over his subjects, he wanted to prove that he could make of the small principality a model of military preparedness, economic well-being, and high culture. His first step was to introduce universal military training, which was something unheard-of at that time; subsequently he organized an equally novel insurance scheme

---

[1] The Bückeburg City Council invited him in the summer of 1750 to appear in the City Hall in order to take possession of a clavier from his father's legacy.

[2] Cf. R. Haym, 'Herder nach seinem Leben und seinen Werken dargestellt,' Berlin, 1877-85.

[3] 'Ueber die Einsamkeit,' Zürich, 1756.

for his subjects, reclaimed desert soil, created settlements for military veterans in the huge forests, took proper care of orphans and destitute people, and, best of all, contrary to the tradition at his court, he managed to carry out his great schemes without undue taxation of his people.

In the realm of music, Count Wilhelm, who often conducted his own orchestra, greatly admired the Italian style. He engaged, probably simultaneously with young Bach, two Italians for the leading positions: Angelo Colonna as concert-master and Giovanni Battista Serini as composer. At first Sebastian Bach's son was merely a member of the orchestra, and it was his main concern to become thoroughly familiar with Italian music. This he evidently achieved to the satisfaction of the Count, who presented him in 1755 with a large and beautiful garden situated outside the city wall. It is probable that this was intended as a wedding gift, for in the same year Friedrich married Lucia Elisabeth Münchhausen, daughter of a colleague in the court orchestra. Lucia, born in the same year as her husband, 1732, was a professional musician. She had received singing lessons from Serini and was engaged by the Count as court singer at a yearly salary of 100 thalers. In wedding a singer, whose ancestors had through three generations served as court musicians or organists, and in taking this step at the age of 23, Friedrich followed closely his father's example, the only one of Sebastian's sons to do so. However, Lucia Bach was more fortunate than her mother-in-law; she did not have to give up her artistic work, like Anna Magdalena, but continued to earn a salary up to her death at the age of 71.

One year after the wedding Fate intervened to bring about a change in Friedrich Bach's status: war broke out, the war that was to last for seven years. The two Italian musicians left the court; no replacement was made, and Friedrich as a matter of course took over both their duties. This did not mean too much at the moment, for the Count's military ambition was aflame, making him neglect everything else. He concluded an alliance against France with Hanover and England (a country to which he was deeply attached as he was born and educated there) and in the following years was absent from Bückeburg for long stretches of time, winning laurels that brought him the title of British field-marshal. Yet he did not quite forget his musicians, and in 1759, when Friedrich's first son was born, the Count stood godfather to him, and now confirmed Bach's engagement as concert-master, allowing him a salary of 400 thalers, twice his initial honorarium. This was welcome indeed to the Bachs, for war was having its disastrous effect on living conditions in the little state, which, owing to its ruler's allegiance to England, repeatedly suffered occupation by French troops. At last peace was concluded, and in November

1763 the Count returned, after winning outstanding victories as Commander-in-Chief and reorganizer of the Portuguese army. He now threw himself with all the zest of his vigorous nature into civil tasks. He took a lively interest in the music at his court and, thanks to his encouragement, Friedrich Bach was able to establish in little Bückeburg a musical repertoire that could well stand comparison with that of much larger courts. Performances took place regularly twice a week, but in addition special events were celebrated through the presentation of oratorios, symphonies, etc., and Bückeburg could pride itself on acquiring important musical novelties almost as soon as they came out. By degrees the preponderance of Italian music gave way to somewhat greater variety, and works by Gluck, Haydn, and members of the Mannheim school were occasionally played under Friedrich Bach's direction.

The intellectual life at the court received stimulation through the arrival in 1765 of a gifted young philosopher, Thomas Abbt. The Count especially enjoyed talking to so congenial a spirit and Abbt could report to his friend, Moses Mendelssohn: 'If you heard the Count recite at table whole passages from Shakespeare with the deepest sentiment, and listened to him in a starry night discoursing with the profoundest philosophy on mankind's most important problems, you would revere him.' It is probable that Friedrich Bach also had some intercourse with Abbt, who as a former lecturer at Halle would have known Friedemann Bach. He must have deeply regretted Abbt's sudden death in 1766, which was a terrible blow to the Count.

An event of this kind, and the ensuing gloom at court, made Friedrich realize how everything at Bückeburg depended on the mood of a single person. He began to consider the advantages of life in a big city, and when he heard of Telemann's death in Hamburg he applied for this important position, probably not aware that his brother Emanuel was doing the same. The elder Bach, who enjoyed a much higher reputation, was chosen, and it is evidence of Friedrich's fine character that he did not grudge his half-brother this good fortune. Their relations were, as ever, very cordial, and many of Emanuel's works found their way into the Bückeburg library. The Hamburg venture at least brought Friedrich a little financial improvement, for the Count granted him an additional 16 thalers a year. He now received 416 thalers per annum plus 60 th. *Tafelgeld* (compensation for the meals he was entitled to receive at court), besides a supply of wood; to this could be added the 100 thalers earned by his wife. Although this was by no means an ample sustenance for a couple raising 9 children, they could manage on it in a provincial town. For some reason the firewood allocated to him was reduced in 1771, whereupon he wrote to the Count that under present conditions he could heat but one stove in his house and so he was forced to compose in a room crowded with the whole family. The Count thereupon granted him the former quantity, but this, together with the salary established in 1768, was the highest remuneration Friedrich ever earned, and he had to make the best of it. There were other compensations at Bückeburg. At court the influence of the Count's young wife was steadily increasing, an influence beneficial to everyone around her. The Count had proposed to Countess Maria Eleonore, a distant relative of his, after merely seeing her picture, and he married her when she was 22 and he 41. The experiment turned out surprisingly well, for the Countess possessed not only charm, but the most loving nature. Deeply religious and very sensitive to beauty in any form, she was an ideal audience for an earnestly striving composer. How greatly Friedrich must have cherished a letter like the following, dated April 25, 1774, which the Countess wrote to him after he had thanked her for a gift!

'To accept the trifle I sent you so kindly, honours your character as much as does every composition with which you lift our hearts and make us capable of nobler sentiments and actions. The first thanks are therefore due to yourself. I did no more than show you, from a distance, that I am perhaps a not quite unworthy listener to your admirable songs; a fine aim, but how little compared to *what you give us*. If Nature had bestowed on me more courage and a better voice, I should already be chiming in your choirs—but what is impossible here, I hope to achieve in a better world with the great Hallelujah, for which you prepare us, and of which you offer us many a blissful foretaste. May all the blessings of heaven descend on you and your dear family!'

The Countess' intensely emotional language is typical of the era of sensibility in which the letter was written; the humility in her intercourse with a court employee, however, was something very rare in that period of enlightened absolutism. How unusual it was is best revealed by Friedrich's own letters to the Count, which he used to conclude with the words: 'I am dying in deepest reverence.'

The radiance which Countess Maria shed on Friedrich's creative work was further increased by the arrival of a most outstanding personality. Johann Gottfried Herder (b. 1744), already famous as writer and critic, was engaged in 1771 as court pastor and consistorial counsellor, to provide for the Count the intellectual companionship which he lacked since Abbt's death. Herder stayed at Bückeburg for five years, and though he himself spoke of this period as his 'exile,' it certainly marked the climax in Friedrich Bach's artistic life. Herder, who loved music passionately and knew a great deal about it, had probably met Emanuel Bach while visiting in 1769 their common friend, Lessing, in Hamburg. Finding Emanuel's brother in Bückeburg was most welcome to him, for he was deeply interested in the problem of how to establish a just equilibrium between words and music, and he now had a chance to conduct his experiments together with Friedrich Bach. Herder wrote various texts for cantatas, Biblical oratorios, and a music drama, and the Bückeburg concert-master set them to music, after discussing every detail with the eminent librettist. Friedrich threw himself with the greatest zest into this work. How much it meant to him is suggested in a letter written by the Countess to Herder about his new poem, *Die Kindheit Jesu*, which Bach had not yet seen. The composer was at that time deeply dejected by the death of his little son, Ludolf Emanuel. Three days after the funeral,[1] the Countess wrote: 'How I wished that our good Bach might start on this beautiful task! I feel that at a time like this it would soothe his deep grief and make him again the comfort of his family.' Herder complied, and Friedrich's composition was performed a month later and received with genuine admiration.

The years with Herder were indeed a golden, fruitful time for the composer. The poet, however, became restless in the provincial town, longing for more congenial duties and intercourse with the greatest minds of his time, and in 1776 he accepted a call from Goethe to Weimar. Even before his departure, the frail Countess succumbed to an old ailment on her 33rd birthday. Her husband, left alone without children or close relatives, could not get over his loss, and a year later he followed his beloved wife. Thus by September 1777 Friedrich Bach had lost the patron whom he had devotedly served for twenty-seven years, and the two persons who had most deeply inspired his creative work.

All the light seemed to have gone out of his life at Bückeburg and longing for a change obsessed him. Fortunately the duty he owed to his eldest son offered at least a temporary release from his work at court. Wilhelm Friedrich Ernst Bach, the Count's godson, then aged 18, had developed into a fine musician, and the father felt that, to attain full mastery of his art, the youth needed the artistic experiences offered by a musical centre. Why not entrust him to his uncle Christian, who was tremendously successful in London? Christian, who had probably visited Friedrich

---

[1] The letter is dated January 5, 1773, while the funeral took place on January 2, 1773. Cf. C. U. von Ulmenstein in *AfMf*, IV, 1939.

some years previously when performing an opera in Mannheim, agreed, and Friedrich for the first time in his life got leave to travel to England, taking young Wilhelm with him. The trip, which began in April 1778 and lasted for about three months, certainly supplied him with the tonic he needed; it was a time overflowing with artistic stimulation. On the way the travellers visited Emanuel in Hamburg, and Wilhelm had an opportunity of appearing in public as a pianist. In London they arrived just in time to attend performances of Christian's new opera *La Clemenza di Scipione*, for which a brilliant cast had been secured. There were also other operas, oratorios, and the concerts which Christian gave with Abel in the newly erected, sumptuous Hanover Square rooms, Vauxhall—in short, the dazzling array of talent offered to London audiences at the height of the season. We can imagine that Friedrich and Wilhelm were fascinated. In other respects the time for their visit was not too well chosen. Christian was going through a period of bad luck, having been robbed of £1200 by a fraudulent housekeeper, whom he had trusted with the payment of bills. Furthermore there was a certain upheaval in his own establishment, as he was on the point of giving up his house in Richmond. However, taken as a whole, it must have been a most stimulating time for Friedrich, who became infected with his brother's enthusiasm for the new keyboard instrument, the pianoforte, and bought one for himself.

When he returned to Bückeburg (while Christian went to Paris, to prepare the presentation of his *Amadis des Gaules*), this instrument and the great amount of new music he had acquired on his trip were the bright points in an otherwise depressing existence. To adjust himself to Bückeburg after London was no easy task, especially under a new ruler, Count Philipp Ernst, who, after succeeding to the throne, promptly reduced Bach's salary, cutting off the additional 16 thalers which Friedrich had received since 1768. Nevertheless the music played at Bückeburg remained at its high standard, and Friedrich's orchestra ranked among the best in Germany.[1] Friedrich, influenced by his brother's admiration for Mozart, introduced the latter's works, and subsequently performed the opera *Die Entführung aus dem Serail*.

A spirit of enterprise reveals itself also in a publishing venture started in 1787. Friedrich announced his plan to present a quarterly publication with various works of his own, and so attractive did his proposed *Musikalische Nebenstunden* sound that he succeeded in securing more than 400 subscribers from all parts of Germany. Through 1787 and the beginning of 1788 he published four instalments containing sonatas and short

[1] Cf. Forkel's 'Musikalischer Almanach auf das Jahr 1782.'

pieces for the clavier, violin sonatas, songs, arias, solo cantatas, and a symphony in piano reduction. Except for a song by his son and one or two pieces by high-ranking personalities he knew, the works were all composed by him. As he remarked in his preface, he attempted to 'offer to both the more experienced player and to the beginner music likely to entertain.' The preface is followed by valuable directions as to the execution of musical ornaments. In this publication Friedrich clearly attempted to match his brother Emanuel's business acumen, but it must regretfully be stated that the extension of the project beyond the first year, which the composer had contemplated, did not materialize.

In 1787, after a reign of ten years, Count Philipp Ernst died, leaving an heir only two years old, for whom his mother, the music-loving Countess Juliane, assumed the regency. In her, Friedrich recaptured something of the understanding attitude he had so greatly appreciated in the unforgettable Countess Maria. The new patroness found time for a daily piano lesson from Bach; and frequently undertook a solo in an oratorio performance. Thus Friedrich's last years of service were spent in an atmosphere of great esteem and friendliness. A very pleasant relationship was also established with Herder's successor as consistorial counsellor. This man, by the name of Horstig, wrote an obituary notice after Friedrich's death characterizing the musician as an artist and man, and lovingly describing the hours they spent together. 'Never will I forget,' remarked Horstig, 'this blissful time. With what boundless kindliness did he entertain me for hours on his instrument! How quickly did the evening pass in his instructive company, and midnight was reached before we knew it. How gladly did he examine my attempts at composition . . . and how he encouraged me to acquaint him with the most expressive pieces out of the stock of my own poetic ventures and those of others.'

The evening sessions must have meant much to Horstig, and hardly less to his genial host. The stimulation derived from conversation with a genuine lover of the arts was just what the ageing musician needed at a time filled with sad events. It was Friedrich's fate to see all his brothers pass away before him; first the youngest of them all, Christian, with whom he felt so close an affinity since their London meeting; next Friedemann, and four years later his beloved Emanuel. Deeper still was the grief caused by witnessing the decline in the young generation. Emanuel's painter son died before his father, and when the other son of the Hamburg Bach passed away in 1789, Friedrich, as he wrote to his publisher, Immanuel Breitkopf, was 'so cast down and stunned that he could only by and by begin to think again.' It was tragic indeed for one so proud of the family tradition to see the Bach dynasty's only hope of survival in his own son, Wilhelm Ernst, who so far had not married. The best antidote to such depressing thoughts was work, and 'although' (as Horstig writes) 'most of his compositions remained locked in his desk, like the silkworm he never tired of spinning his cocoon up to the last days of his life.' Nor was there any slackening in the quality of his work. As late as August 1794 he completed one of his largest and most progressive compositions, a Symphony in B flat.

Anna Magdalena Bach's children were not fated to attain a very great age; while both Friedemann and Emanuel died at the age of 74, Friedrich was struck down by an 'acute chest-fever' a few days before his 63rd birthday, on January 26, 1795.

By Friedrich more than by any other son of Sebastian, the old Bach tradition was faithfully upheld. Serving through all his life at the same small court, marrying in youth, raising (and losing) a great number of children—all this is what a Bach musician did a hundred or more years earlier. We may assume that Friedrich was reasonably happy in so restricted an existence, and only at rare intervals felt the ambition to change it. To him life in provincial Bückeburg did not seem too monotonous, for his intense creative activity afforded all the adventures and excitement that he needed.

THE MUSIC OF JOHANN CHRISTOPH FRIEDRICH BACH

His creative output can be divided into three periods. No work of his early youth seems to have survived. The very few compositions known to-day from the first years spent at Bückeburg display interest in the light and graceful idiom of the *style galant*. In the works written after 1765 (they are mainly vocal compositions) the influence of Italian music, prevailing at the Bückeburg court, is noticeable, but it is partly counteracted by the admiration Friedrich felt both for the art of the Berlin school and for the intricate polyphony of his father's music. Consequently the works from this period of transition display a slightly contradictory character. In the music written after 1780 (mostly instrumental compositions) the influence of Graun and Emanuel is gradually replaced by that of Christian Bach. The divergencies between Southern and Northern art apparent in the earlier works disappear. Friedrich's music becomes more homogeneous, assuming increasingly a serene and singing quality. He grows familiar with the style of Mozart and Haydn and approaches the ideals of classical simplicity, charm, and balance.

Music for the *clavier* had the same great significance for Friedrich Bach as for his brothers. He was famous as a performing artist, and Forkel's Almanac for the year 1782 states that when playing on a keyboard instrument 'he hardly knew the meaning of difficulties.' The necrologue praises the 'unprecedented nimbleness of his fingers and the accuracy of his performance, revealing the master in every chord.' An interesting selection of his early works for clavier can be found in *Musikalisches Vielerley*, edited in 1770 as a sort of family enterprise by Emanuel, containing not only the Hamburg Bach's own compositions, but also pieces by the 'Capellmeister Bach in Eisenach' (Johann Ernst) and by the 'Concertmeister Bach in Bückeburg.'[1] Friedrich's two sonatas in this set (*Sü* IV/4 and 5) display the transition from the *style galant* in its conventional aspects to the more substantial idiom of Emanuel. This is richly ornamented, graceful music, without a deeper emotional content, yet with careful dynamic indications including all shades from *pp* to *ff*, and extended development sections. The composer's strong interest in Italian music is revealed by the attractive *Andante alla Siciliana*, the middle movement of the Sonata in C. The *Menuetten zum Tanz* ('Minuets to be danced'; *Sü* IV/10 and 12) and the *Alla Polaccas* (*Sü* IV/13 and 14) in *Musikalisches Vielerley* are short, unpretentious pieces of the kind the 20th century would call utility music.

In 1785 *six easy sonatas for the clavier or pianoforte* (*Sü* IV/1) were published, followed in 1787 by Friedrich's collection *Musikalische Nebenstunden* which contained three sonatas (*Sü* IV/6 and 7), a sonatina,[2] and numerous shorter pieces. In 1789 a set of *three easy sonatas for the clavier or pianoforte* (*Sü* IV/2) concluded the series of Friedrich's keyboard compositions that were printed in his lifetime. It is significant that the composer stressed the simple nature of his music. These are compositions for amateurs making no undue demands on the fingers or minds of the performers. In the slow middle movements in a minor key the spirit of sensibility is prevalent, but in the first movements and in particular in the gay rondo finales the more flexible idiom of the London Bach dominates. Although Friedrich does not exclude the use of earlier keyboard instruments, this music is primarily meant for the pianoforte, whose

---

[1] The absence of compositions by Friedemann Bach is highly significant. Evidently Emanuel could not count on a punctual delivery of manuscripts from his elder brother.

[2] *Sü* does not know the third and fourth parts of *Musikalische Nebenstunden*, so he fails to list the Sonata No. 3 in F as well as the Sonatina in a.

singing quality and full tone are here admirably utilized. A simple folk-songlike quality and some of Mozart's sweetness, warmth and sparkle may be found in this music. It is interesting that the Allegro in G with 18 variations (*Sü* IV/8), which Hugo Riemann published from the manuscript in the Berlin Library, is based on the theme *Ah, vous dirais-je, Maman,* which young Mozart also used in a set of piano variations (K. 265). The Rondo of the Sonata in A (*Sü* IV/2) of 1789 is more in the vein of Haydn, a touch of piquancy being introduced through the combination of contrasting rhythms in the two hands (*Ex.* 95). The little character

pieces of the *Musikalische Nebenstunden* (*Sü* IV/16) also exhibit more variety than those of the earlier collection. Next to Minuets and Polonaises, they include *Villanelle, Angloises, Schwäbische, Solfeggii,* Marches and Scherzos.

Like Emanuel, Friedrich was not really interested in the *organ*. The only work of his which was probably meant for the king of instruments is a *Fughette* (*Sü* IV/27), which he wrote into a friend's album. The theme employs the letters of the composer's name: H(ans) C(hristoph) F(riedrich) B(ückeburger) BACH (*Ex.* 96). In doing so, Friedrich may have

remembered his father's use of the family name in the Art of the Fugue.— Friedrich belonged to the early composers of music for *piano duet*. Maybe it was again his younger brother who started him on this venture (cf. p. 421). His first sonata in A written in 1786 (*Sü* IV/17) consists of two movements (Allegro con spirito–Rondo, Allegretto), while the second one in C of 1791 (*Sü* IV/18) has the three movements fast-slow-fast of his sonatas for twohands. This again is educational music, meant primarily for players of limited technical proficiency. Although the parts of the two pianists sometimes double each other in a somewhat mechanical manner, Friedrich manages to produce ingratiating and effective music. With a

little skill and strict observance of the dynamic signs players can awaken
these humble duos to sparkling freshness.

His *chamber music* is as pleasant and unassuming as his compositions
for the clavier. The collection *Musikalisches Vielerley* contains significant
examples of his *earlier art*. A Sonata for 'cello and figured bass in A (*Sü*
V/4) consists of an introductory Larghetto, an Allegro in sonata form and
a concluding Tempo di Minuetto. Its lovely cantilenas allow the string
instrument to display a certain amount of technical brilliance. A Trio for
flute, violin and bass in the same key (*Sü* V/9) was composed in 1763,
possibly in honour of the return of Count Wilhelm from the Seven Years
War. According to a note in the nicely printed volume it can also be performed by flute and clavier only. In this case the clavierist plays the violin
part with his right hand, a procedure well known to Sebastian and
Emanuel. The numerous imitations used in the first Allegretto (*Ex.* 97)

give a retrospective character to this work, while the delicate flute solos
of the middle movement strike a note of sensibility which was becoming
fashionable at that time. A second so-called 'Trio' in the collection, in E
flat (*Sü* V/8), is designed for clavier with violin (*or* flute). In this work the
performance by three instruments is no longer optional. Friedrich writes
a real keyboard part with chords in both hands, which excludes the
possibility of a melody instrument taking over the right hand. The very
extensive development section in the first movement, a device for which
Friedrich showed a predilection, and the use of the sonata form in the
graceful Tempo di Menuetto of the finale, give the composition a character
of solid craftsmanship.

To the same period belong *six quartets for transverse flute, violin,
viola and figured bass*, dedicated to Count Wilhelm and printed in parts
by M. C. Bock in Hamburg (*Sü* V/13). An invitation to subscribe to the
works mentions the end of 1768 as the prospective date of publication
though they were probably written at an earlier date. These are pleasant

compositions in a light and gay Italian style. They are in two moderately fast movements, the first in a primitive sonata form, the second in da capo form, either a Minuetto or a 'Scherzo' in 2/4, clearly expressing the Rococo spirit. In all six quartets the flute dominates; possibly the Count, imitating Friedrich 'the Great' in this respect too, played the part himself. Yet the violin, the viola, and even the bass actively participate in the presentation of the melodic material. This bass is accurately figured, showing that Friedrich counted on the inclusion of a harpsichord, but as the middle parts are so carefully worked out, in most cases the 'cello alone would be sufficient. Distinctive skill in handling the chamber music style and a youthful spontaneity of expression make this early set very attractive.[1]

A collection of *six sonatas for clavier with the accompaniment of a flute or violin* printed by G. F. Hartknoch in Riga, 1777 (not in *Sü*)[2] has so far been overlooked by research students. Yet the sonatas are among the most significant chamber music works Friedrich wrote before he reached full artistic maturity. The title of the work is not quite accurate, as the flute (violin) has important solo parts, and for most of the time it is an equal partner in the musical elaboration. Particularly attractive are the middle movements. In the first sonata a complete solo cantata with ariosos and numerous secco recitatives seems to be transplanted into the medium of chamber music. The flute intones moving cantilenas, again and again interrupted by dramatic solo episodes, in which both voice part and accompaniment are given to the keyboard instrument. Thus Friedrich shows himself fully conversant with the peculiar style of Emanuel's clavier music. The sentimental leanings of the period are reflected in the 'Andante Amoroso' of the sixth sonata, while the inclusion of an 'Andante alla Polacca' gives a touch of piquancy to three other works. Occasionally, as in the Andante of No. 5, we seem to be almost on the threshold of classicism (*Ex.* 98).

Ex 98   Andante

Figured bass parts which are now and then found in these sonatas no longer appear in the *String Quartets* (not in *Sü*), which Louis Dutten-

---

[1] In 1925 the quartets were edited by Schwedler and Wittenbecher in an arrangement for flute and clavier (Zimmermann, Leipzig).

[2] A copy of the work is in the Library of Congress in Washington.

hofer edited from unidentified sources. The melodic language is gentle and imbued with Rococo grace. These quartets in three movements seem like preparatory studies to the great clavier trios which Friedrich was subsequently to write. The two violins share the melodic material, which they often present in alternation, with the viola following one of their parts in thirds and sixths. If a clavierist were to play the 'cello part with the left hand and the viola or one of the violin parts with the right hand, the result would be one of Friedrich's clavier trios. There is warmth and tenderness in these quartets coupled with good workmanship.

Among the chamber music works of Friedrich's *maturity* there are two sonatas for clavier and violin, published in *Musikalische Nebenstunden* (*Sü* V/2),[1] and a fine sonata for 'cello and clavier (*Sü* V/3) written in 1789. The latter is a delightful composition, using the string instrument as a singer of lovely tunes. The character of the old 'trio' is only occasionally noticeable, while in general a more homophonic style prevails in which the piano supports and accompanies the 'cello. Among the three movements the concluding Rondo Allegretto is particularly attractive; its main theme sounds like a merry tune sung by university students (*Ex.* 99).

Ex. 99

In the *trios for clavier and two melody instruments* the composer's preference is for the combination of flute, violin and clavier, or violin, viola and clavier, while the clavier trio with violin and 'cello, to which the future was to belong, appears only once in his chamber music (*Sü* V/7). Old-fashioned are also the thumping harpsichord basses and intricate ornaments which Friedrich sometimes uses in his slow movements. However, polyphony is completely ignored; there is very little crossing of the two melody instruments and quite often they proceed in parallel thirds and sixths. The clavier part is almost completely written out and hardly any addition by the performer is needed. On the contrary, the insertion of filling voices might damage the fine balance which the composer succeeds in establishing between the two melody instruments as one group and the soprano and bass parts of the clavier as the other. Broken

---

[1] *Sü* lists only the first of the two violin sonatas.

chords and 'Alberti basses,' typical of pianoforte technique, are quite numerous, and a sweet and singing quality is evident not only in the melodies but also in runs and passages. In the delightful trio in G for violin and viola (*Sü* V/10) or the charming trio in C for flute and violin (*Sü* V/12) we have works of an artist who opened his heart wide to classical beauty, although he neither wished nor attempted quite to abandon the devices of his earlier training.

The climax of Friedrich's production in the field of chamber music was reached in his *Sextet in C* (*Sü* V/14) and *Septet in E flat* (*Sü* V/15). The former, written for pianoforte, 2 horns, oboe, violin, and violoncello,[1] is probably a product of the eighties, while the latter, a work for 2 horns, oboe, 2 clarinets and 2 bassoons, is dated 1794. In the Sextet the spirit of the trio is still noticeable. The piano often has extensive rests, thus allowing the strings and the oboe to proceed on their own. This is clever and delicate music full of sparkle and wit in which the composer comes surprisingly close to the style of Haydn and Mozart. Passages like *Ex.* 100 show a clear affinity to the language of the Austrian masters. The

demands made on the proficiency of the players clearly demonstrate the high standards of the Bückeburg musicians. In this respect the Sextet and Septet are in marked contrast to Friedrich's clavier works, which, for the sake of wider distribution, dispensed with any greater technical difficulties.

Most of Friedrich's *Clavier Concertos* were composed during the last fifteen years of his life. To the seventies or early eighties of the 18th

---

[1] The Sextet was printed by André as a work of 'Giov. Christ. Bach.' An English arranger, J. Christian Luther, took it for a composition of Johann Christian Bach and presented it under that name in a version for clavier and violin. Terry (302 and 310/2) accepts the authorship of Christian, ignoring the fact that the Berlin Library owned the autograph parts of the Sextet in the hand of Johann Christoph Friedrich Bach.—This autograph set of the work contains also a viola part which is identical with that of the 'cello, though sometimes an octave higher. It seems most likely that this viola part was meant to replace the 'cello part, if the bass instrument was not available; but it is hardly to be assumed that the composer wanted the two instruments used together. This method is unfortunately adopted in Schünemann's edition of the work, which is therefore entitled 'Septet.' The very frequent unison passages resulting from this procedure affect the work's chamber music character.

century belongs the Concerto in E for cembalo (*Sü* IV/19), the only one of these works in which the accompanying orchestra is limited to strings. During the late eighties and the nineties five more concertos made their appearance. Two of them were designated by the composer himself as works for harpsichord or fortepiano, and in all these works the use of 'Alberti basses' and other pianistic devices emphasize Friedrich's progressive attitude. Nevertheless, he still practises the habit of the early 18th century of using the solo instrument also as a filling continuo instrument in the tutti sections. Flutes and horns or oboes and horns are employed in all these compositions mostly as reinforcement, and only rarely to execute a solo. The concertos are in three movements (fast-slow-fast), with a gay rondo as finale. In the concerto in E flat (*Sü* IV/24) of 1792, the first Allegro is dramatically interrupted by a little Andante episode. This work and the concertos in D (*Sü* IV/20) and A (*Sü* IV/21) might still be used in our time as preparatory studies to the concertos of Mozart.[1]

Fourteen *Symphonies* by Friedrich are known.[2] Four of them (*Sü* VI/1-4) are in three movements and typical works of the pre-classical school, influenced by Emanuel and by West- and South-German composers. The orchestra is small; to the strings are added two horns, or two flutes and two horns, and a harpsichord is needed as a continuo instrument. The autograph parts of one of these works (*Sü* VI/1) bears the date 1770, and the other three may be products of approximately the same time. The most significant sections of these symphonies are the highly emotional middle movements. The tide of sensibility which was swaying artistic minds all over Europe made itself felt in these works as well.

Ten more symphonies (*Sü* VI/5-14) have been preserved, all of them in autographs bearing a date. The earliest was written in 1792, the latest in August 1794, five months before the composer's death. With the exception of the very last one, the symphonies are scored for oboes, horns and strings, to which in two cases (*Sü* VI/5-6) two bassoons are added. Most of these works have figured basses and obviously the composer still expected the participation of a harpsichord. In this connection it should not be forgotten that even Haydn's London symphonies were conducted from the cembalo. Friedrich's Symphony in B flat of 1794 (*Sü* VI/14) is the only work to dispense with a keyboard instrument, and the composition also employs the somewhat unusual orchestration of flute, 2 clarinets,

---

[1] The Double Concerto for viola and harpsichord in E flat (not in *Sü*) recorded by Polydor is of doubtful authenticity.

[2] The fourth part of *Musikalische Nebenstunden* contains a further symphony in D in a reduction for clavier (not in *Sü*). An orchestral score of this work is not known.

bassoon, 2 horns and strings. Each of the ten symphonies is in four movements: a Largo or Adagio, sometimes in the minor mode (*Sü* VI/9-10),
dramatically prepares for the first Allegro, which is always in a major key;
the simple and charming second movement is an Andante or Andantino,
usually entitled 'Romanza'; and an unassuming Menuetto, gay and like a
folkdance, leads to the Rondo finale. In these spirited last movements the
melodic invention is not unlike that in Haydn's Paris symphonies, while
the clever and witty retransitions to the main theme point to a thorough
study of Emanuel's Rondos. Friedrich likes to shape these finales into
character pieces. He gives them, for instance, the name 'Rondo Scherzo'
or 'Rondo Scherzando,' and in the C major symphony of 1794 (*Sü* VI/11)
there is a 'Rondo Musette' (cf. Haydn's 'L'Ours'). Particularly delightful
is the very last symphony in B flat, which captivates through folksonglike
melodies, robust rhythm, and colourful orchestration. The ideas are skilfully divided between different instrumental groups, often in effective
dynamic contrast (*Ex.* 101). No other of Friedrich's symphonies so well

deserves to be revived to-day as this, his last work in the field, a composition full of vigour and rich emotional life.

    Neither in his symphonies nor in any other of his instrumental works
was Friedrich Bach a pioneer. He was satisfied to follow the paths shown
by more progressive minds; yet his contributions are by no means insignificant, and his music always reveals character, freshness of invention, and
technical skill.

    In his *vocal output* Friedrich was perhaps more versatile than in his
instrumental work. Almost every type of composition from sacred and
secular song to oratorio and opera[1] was cultivated by him. In the year

---

[1] Of the two operas 'Brutus' and 'Philoctetes' (*Sü* I/1-2) written in 1774, only the
text is known; the music is lost. Of the 'Duodrama' *Mosis Mutter und ihre Tochter* (*Sü*
I/3) few parts have survived; these do not give a clear idea of the score.

1773 the first collection of musical settings to *Geistliche Lieder* by the Copenhagen pastor, Balthasar Münter, was printed in Leipzig. It contained works by different composers, among them six songs by Emanuel and five by Friedrich Bach (*Sü* III/8). Although the compositions of the Bückeburg concert-master are not particularly inspired and indeed are weaker than most of the other contributions to the volume, Münter entrusted a second collection entirely to Friedrich (*Sü* III/9). It was printed in the following year and contains 50 songs, far superior in quality to the composer's works for the first collection. In these sacred songs he closely follows the style of his brother's Gellert odes. They are simple and noble in character and unconventional in their harmonic language. The melodies are dignified, although there is a certain disregard for the accents of the text. The impressive No. 44, *Lied im Winter* ('Winter song') anticipates in its majestic grandeur the spirit of Haydn's vocal quartets (*Ex.* 102).

Beautiful too is the 'Communion song,' No. 9, and the humble and submissive *Bussgesang* ('Song of Penitence'), No. 33. In these compositions the strong religious feeling of the Bachs manifests itself in its old fervour.

Friedrich's secular songs were all printed in the two collections *Musikalisches Vielerley* (1770) and *Musikalische Nebenstunden* (1787-88). The earlier set still contains a dance song (*Sü* III/14) displaying the instrumental character predominant in the secular songs at the beginning of the century. An abundance of pedantic ornaments mars other pieces, but on the whole these compositions are pleasant, their main distinguishing feature being a delightful sense of humour. In *Die Zeit* ('Time'; *Sü* III/12) Friedrich realistically describes the contrast between the boredom caused by elderly ladies and the entertainment provided by young girls. *Der Kranke* ('The invalid'; *Sü* III/18) from the later set implores God to make water taste better, since wine is so bad for the health. Drinking songs are set to music with real gusto. *Rheinweinlob* ('Praise of the Rhine wine'; *Sü* III/23), for instance, is artless and folksonglike. Friedrich, who in his earlier songs clearly depended on the past, in the later compositions shows a most gratifying naturalness and directness of expression.

Several *monodramas* for solo voice, strings and harpsichord lead from the songs to the composer's larger vocal works. Probably the earliest of these solo cantatas is *Cassandra* (*Sü* III/4)[1] for contralto, on an Italian text. In a long-winded monologue Cassandra, the daughter of Priamus, describes the tragedy of the Trojan war, bewailing the destruction of the city and the death of Hector, its greatest hero. Friedrich's work is a very dramatic composition, similar in character to scenes in contemporary operas of Hasse and Jomelli. Secco recitatives are completely avoided, and accompagnato recitatives of great expressive power alternate with arias in which the composer strives to achieve formal variety. The very passionate character of the work, with its sudden changes in tempo and dynamics, and the frequent use of minor keys point to the idiom of *Empfindsamkeit*, which reached its greatest vogue in Germany around the year 1770. It is significant that the last number of the cantata is not an aria, but a recitative concluding with the stirring measures in *Ex*. 103. The

origin of 'Cassandra' in the early seventies seems to be corroborated by a letter Herder wrote to his fiancée soon after his arrival in Bückeburg, mentioning an invitation to attend the performance of an Italian cantata Cassandra at court.[2] Although the accompanying orchestra consists of few instruments only, Friedrich obtains a certain amount of colouristic variety through the occasional use of obbligato violin and 'cello as well as a completely elaborated cembalo part to replace the figured bass. Surprising effects approaching the setting in a clavier trio are thus achieved.

The remainder of Friedrich's solo cantatas use German texts. The most successful of these was *Die Amerikanerin* ('The American girl'; *Sü* III/2) published in 1776. In this work Gerstenberg, the author of the poem, set out to describe the simple and strong emotions of children of nature such as he believed the inhabitants of the new world to be. A lover im-

---

[1] It is preserved in MS. in the Bibliothèque du Conservatoire, Brussels.

[2] Cf. M. C. von Herder, 'Erinnerungen aus dem Leben J. G. von Herders,' Tübingen, 1820, p. 206.

patiently awaits the arrival of his sweetheart. He is afraid she might have
been killed by wild beasts and he decides rather to share death with her
than to live on alone. It fits the sentimental character of the text that the
young man who expresses his deep love for the girl, Saide, is sung by a
soprano voice. The music of the cantata is gentle and graceful. In the
accompagnato recitatives the composer provides a delightful expression
for the 'brook winding through the golden sand,' but he is rather helpless
when he has to represent the 'blood-thirsty tiger,' an animal with which
Gerstenberg presumed America to be infested. The very last number
depicts the lover's longing for death in a slow dance of serene beauty (*Ex.*
104) in which the spirit of Gluck's description of the Elysian fields seems

to be captured. It is not surprising that this tearful subject, with its
Rousseau-like touch interpreted by the composer in a congenial spirit,
should have appealed to music lovers in the period of sensibility. Its
success is apparent from the fact that both full score and piano reduction[1]
were published by Friedrich Bach himself.

In the year 1786 another soprano cantata, *Ino* (*Sü* III/3), was offered
to the public. Here Friedrich used a text which had also been set to music
by Telemann and Sebastian Bach's pupil, Kirnberger. Ramler's libretto
deals with a subject from Greek mythology, the story of the unfortunate
Ino, whose husband, afflicted by an irate Goddess with madness, kills his
own son and threatens to murder his wife. To escape him, Ino jumps into
the sea clasping her youngest child in her arms, and both are transformed
by a compassionate God into sea deities. Among the three settings of the
poem, Friedrich's is by far the finest. Its great accompagnato recitatives
show more cohesion, more vigour and strength than those of the *Amerikanerin*, and replace sensibility by dramatic tension. Ino's frantic flight
from cliff to cliff, her subsequent exhaustion, and the screaming and
panting of her husband, Athamus, trying to reach her, create an atmosphere of breathless suspense which reaches its climax in her desperate leap
into the abyss. Masterly is the transformation of this scene of horror to the
serenity of the peacefully rippling waves. This striking episode foreshadows in more than one respect the cantata *Arianna a Naxos*, with
which Joseph Haydn was to win so great a success a few years later.

[1] In the second part of *Musikalische Nebenstunden*, 1787.

Friedrich's cantata *Pygmalion*, again on words by Ramler (*Sü* III/1), for bass or contralto remained in manuscript. The cantata *Prokris und Cephalus* (not in *Sü*) for soprano is only known from a reduction for clavier, published in the third part of *Musikalische Nebenstunden* (1787). Strictly speaking this is not a solo cantata since, for a short time, Prokris and Cephalus simultaneously sing different notes. Friedrich may have been inspired to write this German work when he saw his brother Christian's Italian cantata of 1776 in London; it dealt with the same subject, though it was set for three voices (cf. p. 443). However, a direct musical connection between the two cantatas is not noticeable, the later work being simpler in its melodic language and more compact in its formal construction. Most of its story is told by a narrator, whereas Christian's cantata has the character of a miniature opera.

The constant connection with Emanuel led Friedrich to arrange three of his brother's Gellert Odes for a simple four-part mixed chorus (*Sü* II/16-18).[1] He also adapted two of his own sacred songs on texts by Münter for soprano, alto, tenor and bass (*Sü* II/15 and 19).

Of greater significance than these little arrangements are two four-part motets in which Friedrich skilfully adopted his father's style. *Wachet auf, ruft uns die Stimme* ('Sleepers wake'; *Sü* II/14) begins with a melody and rhythm similar to Sebastian's violin concerto in E (*Ex.* 105), and an

instrumental character prevails throughout the composition. The resemblance to the father's works goes further still. *Wachet auf* is a chorale motet, using both the text and the melody of this great Protestant hymn. In the first stanza the tune is treated as a *cantus firmus* in the soprano, a technique to be found in the first chorus of Sebastian's cantata No. 140 based on the same chorale. Near the end of the motet the hymn is presented in simple

---

[1] They are *Weynachtslied*, *Dancklied*, and *Der thätige Glaube* (*Wq* 194/5, 8, 11). *Sü* erroneously considered these arrangements, which are preserved in Friedrich's autograph, as original compositions of the Bückeburg Bach.

chords, and this time the harmonization is literally taken from the father's cantata. Nevertheless Friedrich's motet is far more than a mere imitation. The development of the chorale melody which precedes and follows the entrance of the *cantus firmus* in the first stanza displays spirit and great technical skill. Even more effective is the treatment of the second stanza which introduces valuable new melodic material. A beautiful Adagio gradually reverting to the hymn tune leads to the chorale harmonization, while a compact and brief fugue serves as a coda. There is joyful ardour, strength, and fire in this score which makes the motet one of Friedrich's most remarkable creations.

On the same high level stands the second motet, *Ich lieg und schlafe* ('I lay me down and sleep'; *Sü* II/13), the autograph of which is dated 1780 (when *Wachet auf* was also composed in all likelihood). In *Ich lieg und schlafe* Friedrich, like many of the older Bachs, combines a Bible text with a chorale. Deeply moving is the beginning using Psalm iv, 9, which occasionally introduces an almost Mendelssohnian idiom (*Ex.* 106). In

the middle of the movement the soprano enters with the chorale 'There is still rest' as *cantus firmus*, while the lower voices continue singing the Bible text. Fugue and chorale harmonization again conclude this significant work, in which Friedrich infuses the great Bach traditions with stylistic elements of his own time.

On August 15, 1769, according to the testimony of the original manuscript in the Bibliothèque du Conservatoire, Brussels, Friedrich's first work for soloists, chorus and orchestra, the cantata *Der Tod Jesu* ('The Death of Jesus'; *Sü* II/1) was concluded. In using Ramler's poem the Bückeburg composer chose a text that had been made famous through the setting by Carl Heinrich Graun in 1755.[1] Ramler's libretto was 'far removed in spirit and insight from the Bible. It depicted the Passion of the Lord in a series of touching, tearful, and lamenting pictures equipped with edifying running comments.'[2] The music Graun wrote to these words included a number of solid fugues, yet it was basically conceived in an

---

[1] Also among the composers of the text was Telemann. Cf. Hans Hörner, 'G. Ph. Telemanns Passionsmusiken,' Leipzig, 1933.

[2] Paul H. Lang, 'Music in Western Civilization,' New York, 1941, p. 502.

operatic manner. Friedrich Bach, owing to his lack of experience in this
field, took the Berlin composer's work as a model, but at the same time
made ample use of the paternal heritage. Graun's cantata has no overture
but begins with the Passion chorale. The Bückeburg concert-master
followed his example and presented the hymn in the same key of c. Most
of the harmonic progressions, however, were taken from Sebastian's St.
Matthew Passion (No. 72). A similar attitude is revealed in the remainder
of the cantata. In corresponding sections Friedrich often adopted Graun's
tempo markings, keys, and time signatures, including the very changes in
these devices. Even direct melodic resemblances are to be found, as for
instance in the bass recitative *Jerusalem voll Mordlust ruft* ('Jerusalem for
slaughter thirsting') and in the ensuing bass aria *So steht ein Berg Gottes*
('As stands a lofty mountain'). In the harmonization of the chorales, however, Friedrich keeps looking to his father for guidance. *Wen hab ich
sonst* ('Whom have I, Lord') has a certain resemblance to No. 16 in the St.
Matthew Passion, and the chorale *Ich werde dir zu Ehren* ('I will in Thine
honour') is practically identical with No. 3 in Sebastian's work.

But Friedrich does not content himself with mere imitation. His text
is not quite the same as that used by Graun. Several numbers of the earlier
work are either replaced by other pieces or completely omitted in the
Bückeburg composer's cantata. Fugues and polyphonic texture play a
much smaller part, and there is more warmth and tenderness in Friedrich's
work. It is characteristic that a duet for which Graun prescribes *grazioso*
bears in the later cantata the indication *amoroso*. Friedrich's work
occasionally displays an expressive strength (*Ex.* 107) quite foreign to the

shallow brilliance of the earlier composition. Real force and imagination
are to be found in the chorus, *Herr, höre die Stimme* ('Lord, hearken to the
voice') using a text missing in Graun's cantata, and when Friedrich replaces the sentimental words of his time by the powerful language of the
Revelation ('Blessed are the dead which die in the Lord from henceforth'),
he feels inspired to write a fugue of real strength and dignity.

Some of Friedrich's finest choral works were composed on texts by

XVIII. Johann Christian Bach by Thomas Gainsborough

XIX. Autograph of J. Christian Bach's Clavier Concerto in B flat major. In the lower right corner Christian wrote: 'I, I made this concerto; isn't that beautiful?'

the great writer and theologian, Johann Gottfried Herder (cf. p. 383). The cantata *Michaels Sieg. Der Streit des Guten und Bösen in der Welt* ('Michael's victory. The struggle between good and bad in the world'; *Sü* II/8) deals once more with a subject dear to the Bachs. Both Johann Christoph (13) and Sebastian had treated it in immortal cantatas. Herder, who had a deep insight into the possibilities of vocal composition, prescribed at the beginning a rondolike construction in which stanzas of a hymn alternate with choruses on Bible words. He demanded the first chorus to be presented 'like a distant thunderstorm,' the second 'stronger and more violently,' the third in a 'most powerful manner.' And like Joseph Haydn working on his 'Creation' and 'Seasons,' Friedrich Bach allowed himself to be guided by the shrewd suggestions of his librettist, thus building up towards an effective climax. The following accompagnato recitative and coloratura aria come close to the fashionable Italian style, while the end of the work reverts to the technique of the beginning. In the concluding section, the melody to 'A mighty fortress' separates different choruses of praise and triumph. Unfortunately the tune which Friedrich gave to the words of the 'loud voice in heaven' does not do justice to the powerful language of the Revelation. A comparison with Sebastian's melody to the same text makes the inadequacy of the later version still more apparent (*Ex.* 108).

Ex. 108

Friedrich Bach: Michaels Sieg

Nun ist das Heil, und die Kraft, und das Reich und die Macht un - sers Got - - tes

Sebastian Bach: Cant. 50

Nun ist das Heil, und die Kraft, und das Reich und die Macht un - sers Got tes sei..

A curious instance of co-operation between different Bachs is to be found in another *Michaelis-Cantata* (*Sü* II/9).[1] This interesting manuscript, which was found among the music left by Emanuel, bears the initials of two of its authors 'J. C. F. B. & C. P. E. B.' (Johann Christoph Friedrich Bach and Carl Philipp Emanuel Bach) and the remark 'the bass accompaniment is by C. P. E. Bach.' Obviously the Bückeburg composer wanted to help out his brother and supplied him with a cantata he had arranged for St. Michael's Day. It consists of three numbers of Friedrich's cantata *Michaels Sieg* and an equal number of pieces which he seems to

---

[1] *Wq* (246) lists it with a different beginning to the text. The date, 1772, which he gives is obviously wrong. According to the list of Emanuel's estate the work belongs to the year 1785.

have written especially for this work. Emanuel's contribution was probably not confined to revising the bass accompaniment. Near the end, a chorus *Heilig* is mentioned in all parts, but no music for it is given. It seems most likely that at this place the Hamburg Bach inserted the short *Heilig* for a single chorus (*Wq* 218), which has the same orchestration for strings, 2 oboes, 3 trumpets and kettledrums as the *Michaelis Cantata*, and, moreover, was preserved among Emanuel's property in the same package of music. But even in this *Heilig* the aged composer did not unduly exert himself, for he chose his father as a collaborator. After 15 measures of introduction written by the Hamburg Bach, the fugue *Sicut locutus est* from Sebastian's *Magnificat* is employed furnished with a new text (Ill. 373). Since the words of this composite cantata were in all likelihood written by Herder, four great minds seem to have contributed to the *Michaelis Cantata*.

Among Friedrich's chief works are included the two oratorios *Die Kindheit Jesu* ('The childhood of Jesus'; *Sü* II/3) and *Die Auferstehung Lazarus* ('The raising from the dead of Lazarus'; *Sü* II/3), both composed in 1773. Herder, who wrote the texts for these two works, follows on the whole the ideas of Ramler and Gerstenberg. His poems are not meant as dramatic accounts of soul-stirring events, but rather as lyric descriptions of sentiments and feelings evoked by those events. Although the poet keeps closely to the original text of the Bible, the person of the *historicus*, telling the story, is abolished and wherever there is a chance the poem turns from the specific narrative to general observations. As in the cantata, *Michaels Sieg*, Herder attempts to build up larger units out of individual numbers, achieving rondo-like forms, and he guides the composer with the help of minute instructions. In the *Kindheit Jesu*, for instance, after the annunciation by the angel he demands: 'Celestial music in the distance, without words.' Exclamations by one of the shepherds are followed by the direction: 'Celestial music closer, still without words.' A second and a third episode between the shepherds is inserted before 'the full chorus of the angels sets in with words.' Friedrich responded by scoring the same tune first for muted strings, then for strings without mutes, a third time for strings reinforced by flutes and bassoons, and finally for full chorus and orchestra, this time including horns. Herder's libretti are not to be considered as poetical works in their own right. A characteristic feature of his texts is the occasional use of incomplete sentences, which he called 'hieroglyphs.' They are meant to inspire the composer and to create a certain atmosphere, but not to express a clear meaning. For instance, one of the shepherds in the 'Childhood of Jesus' stammers: 'O brethren, are

we? imagine? hear? see?' which apparently stands for: 'O brethren, are we
in heaven? Did we imagine the celestial vision or did we hear and see it?'

To these texts written at the height of the era of sensibility Friedrich
composed music faithfully reflecting the character of the libretti. His
models are the cantatas of Graun, Emanuel's vocal compositions, and
possibly, to some extent, the oratorios of the Neapolitan school. A gentle,
folksonglike character prevails in the melodies and the da capo form is
employed not only in arias but also in choruses. The architecture of the
oratorios is clear and convincing. Friedrich uses his resources economically and builds up effective climaxes. The first half of 'Lazarus,' for
instance, is scored for strings only; flutes join in later and, near the end,
oboes and horns. It is characteristic of the composer's attitude, however,
that the last number of the oratorio is not a jubilant chorus but a deeply
felt aria in f, ending in a pianissimo. Nor do the two oratorios start with a
chorus or with an instrumental overture. Ariosolike introductory numbers
enhance their more intimate chamber music character. In both compositions ample use is made of chorales, the harmonizations of which Friedrich liked to borrow from his father's works. In the 'Childhood' the
beautiful visionary recitative of Simon 'The spirit moves me! I see, I see'
is both preceded and followed by a stanza from the chorale 'In Peace and
Joy I go my way,' taken from Sebastian's Cantata No. 83. In 'Lazarus'
the hymn 'When comfort and salvation fade away,' originates with Cantata No. 86. However, the Baroque grandeur of Sebastian's chord-
progressions seems somewhat incongruous in these works, conceived as
they are on a much smaller scale. The highlights of Friedrich's scores are
such artless and deeply felt pieces as the folksonglike shepherds' song, the
jubilant final chorus of the 'Childhood,' or the dialogue between grieving
Mary and Martha who tries to console her, in 'Lazarus.' We can well
imagine that works of this kind filled a real need for sentimental souls.
When Countess Maria first heard the 'Childhood,' she was, as she wrote,
'transported by this heavenly music.' And even to-day the gentle charm
of Friedrich's oratorios captivates our hearts.

THE MILAN AND LONDON BACH [1]
(JOHANN CHRISTIAN BACH)

JOHANN CHRISTIAN, youngest son of Sebastian Bach, born in Leipzig on September 5, 1735, spent his childhood and adolescence in not too cheerful an atmosphere. The glorious music making at home that Sebastian's elder children so much enjoyed had diminished since Friedemann, Emanuel and Bernhard left Leipzig, for now the household was made up of half-witted Gottfried, little Friedrich and Christian, as well as their sisters and the parents. Moreover, shortly after Christian's birth, Sebastian went through a phase disturbed by violent conflict. For years a feud with Christian's godfather, rector J. August Ernesti, raged with unabated vehemence at the Thomas school, casting a gloom on everybody. Although not defeated, Sebastian emerged from the controversy a greatly embittered man who took less and less interest in his official work, and withdrew as much as possible into a world of his own. When Christian was still a young boy, his father's health began to decline, and the family had to watch helplessly the agony suffered by a highly active man who was losing his sight.

As a child, Christian was naturally unable to understand all that was going on at home, but he could not help being affected by the prevailing tension and bitterness. From such experiences was born a firm resolve not to lead a life like that of his father. Naturally he intended to be a musician; there was no doubt about that in his or in his father's mind. But he would not be tied to a church, be poorly paid, and even less appreciated by a straight-laced and inartistic city council. Surely there must be a way to win fame and wealth as a musician. Vague dreams of that kind were further strengthened when Christian, before he reached his 15th birthday, lost his father. It was shocking to see what little material wealth had been accumulated in a life of ceaseless industry and most rigid economy. When Sebastian's entire property had been divided between the widow and the children, Christian's worldly goods amounted to 3 claviers his father had given him personally, a few of Sebastian's linen shirts, 38 thalers, and the prospect of a share in the proceeds from the sale of some valuables which his mother was to undertake. Staying on in Leipzig with his sisters was

[1] For Genealogical Table see p. 464.

out of the question; he needed expert training to achieve the mastery which alone could fit him for the career of which he dreamed. Fortunately Emanuel offered to take the young half-brother, whom he hardly knew, into his home in Berlin. Thus Christian was privileged to work with one of the foremost clavier players of the time, who was beginning to win equal fame as a teacher too. Eagerly Christian threw himself into his studies and under Emanuel's guidance he developed into a virtuoso of the first rank. Instruction in musical composition, which he had received in Leipzig, was continued and he wrote various works, mainly clavier concertos, which made the warmth of the reception Christian was already accorded in Berlin quite understandable. But Emanuel's training, outstanding though it was, did not prove the most decisive influence on his young charge. In Berlin, operatic performances, which the King had inaugurated on the most brilliant scale, were at that time reaching a peak. Admission to the opera was free to any person decently dressed; Christian naturally made the most of this opportunity, and became thoroughly familiar with operas in the Italian style written by such successful German composers as Hasse, Graun, and Agricola. A new world opened to the youth, into which he entered with the utmost delight. Emanuel also had been greatly influenced by Italian operatic music, which had stimulated him to make bold experiments in keyboard composition, leading to an entirely new pianistic idiom. In Christian, however, the effect of Italian art reached far deeper. For him there was no question of adapting the operatic style to a new medium, for he did not feel that distrust of opera which Sebastian's elder sons owed to their upbringing, and could never quite overcome. Christian had naturally not been as strongly influenced by his ailing father; he had not the slightest prejudice against opera, and the conviction grew in him that this was the field in which he could win laurels. But first it was imperative to study Italian opera in its homeland. So, while Emanuel was trying to find a good position for his brother as an organist or cembalist, Christian investigated every conceivable means of going to Italy. It was no easy task, for he had no material resources and depended on his brother, who certainly did not take too sympathetic a view of so fantastic a project which defied the good old Bach tradition. But Christian did not give up. He had inherited from his father a dogged determination to carry out what he thought best, and this, combined with resourcefulness, talent and charm, made him eventually succeed. It is not known with any certainty how he achieved it, but according to the reports of several writers he joined an Italian prima donna returning to her country. Anyway, in 1754 or 1755, at the age of 20, he left his brother, severing all ties with the Bach family, and with his country as well; he was to revisit it only for short appearances as a guest. Henceforth it was entirely up to him whether success or failure would come his way.

When the French scholar, J. J. L. de Lalande, visited Italy at about that time, he wrote:[1] 'It seems that in this country the very skins of the timpani are more tender, harmonious and sonorous than in the rest of Europe; the nation itself is a singing one. The gestures, the inflection of the voice, the rhythm of the syllables, the conversation—all breathes music there.' Christian Bach, accustomed to the harsh sounds of the German language as spoken in Prussia, and to the formality of Prussian manners, may have been even more delighted than the Frenchman. He absorbed it all with the greatest ease, and in a surprisingly short time the offspring of Thuringian musicians, who through generations had kept so loyally to this small section of Germany, had become thoroughly Italianized. He called himself Giovanni Bach; he spoke and wrote Italian quite fluently; and not long after his arrival he even gave up the faith of his fathers and became a member of the Roman Catholic church. This latter step, deeply resented by his brothers, was due not so much to a spiritual conversion as to practical considerations. He was eager to adapt himself in all respects to the prevailing attitude; moreover adherence to the Roman Catholic faith was, as his friends pointed out, the *conditio sine qua non* for any good appointment. Giovanni, to whom religion did not mean much, had no qualms in following such advice, and the fact that he thus cut himself off completely from what had been the pivot of his father's work, did not matter to the youth in the least.

This desire to take root in Italy could not fail to bear results. Giovanni had the good fortune to become the protégé of a wealthy Italian nobleman, Count Litta of Milan, who not only engaged the promising musician for his private orchestra, but enabled him to continue extensive studies. The relationship between the two men was of the friendliest nature, which speaks as much for the generous young Count as for the recipient of such favours. It seems that neither Sebastian nor any other of his sons ever received as much affection and help from an employer as that which fell to Giovanni. He certainly had the gift of making friends, and there was in his nature an adaptability and easy charm not often to be found among the Bachs that was probably inherited from his mother. Thus we see him establish a second highly important connection in the person of Padre Giovanni Battista Martini of Bologna. Studying with this outstanding scholar and foremost authority on musical theory seemed imperative to

[1] 'Voyages en Italie,' Venice, 1769.

Count Litta, and Giovanni gladly availed himself of the Count's introduction and frequently stayed in Bologna for long periods of instruction.
During the interludes he sent Martini his compositions for correction,
corresponding with him about minute details of contrapuntal technique
with an assiduity and zeal that reminds us strongly of young Sebastian
Bach. This fruitful intercourse lasted for several years and the Count
showed his gratitude by sending the Padre various gifts ranging from a
consignment of 28 lbs. of home-made chocolate to rare books, which the
scholar acknowledged with the remark that 'Bach himself was his highest
reward.' Under Martini's guidance the young composer wrote various
works of church music for Milan, and on August 13, 1757, for instance,
the Count could write exultantly that the leading critics had praised his
'beloved Giovannino's' *Officio* and *Messa di Requiem* as 'correct, impressive, clear, eloquent, and deliciously harmonious.'

It seems strange at first sight that young Giovanni, who had shunned
a church position in Germany, should now give so much time to composing for an Italian church. This was due to Count Litta's plan of establishing him as organist of the Milan Cathedral, a 'nice little post,' as he put
it, and 'an excellent support in old age.' It was therefore important
for Giovanni to show himself fully conversant with liturgical composition, and make a name for himself in influential clerical circles. Bach
followed the Count's lead with the best of grace, throwing himself into
the work with the greatest vigour, for any composition he undertook
seemed valuable to him from the standpoint of new experience. Litta's
prestige eventually brought him the coveted goal. In June 1760 the aged
organist of the *Duomo* agreed to surrender his position to Bach, and the
authorities gave their consent to this transaction. A good and by no
means strenuous post bringing an income of 800 lire had thus fallen into
Giovanni's lap, and as he continued to work and compose for Count Litta,
he was not at all badly off. The gain of such financial security, however,
made no difference to Bach's attitude, and he had no intention whatever
of peacefully settling down in Milan. He never lost sight of his real ambition, and even when engaged in serious studies with Martini, he had
always left a path free towards satisfying this deeply-rooted desire. As
early as January 1757 we see him writing to the Padre from Naples, where
he stayed until rejoining his master at Easter; and it seems likely that such
visits to the most important operatic centre of the country were repeated
on various occasions. What he did in Naples is unknown; maybe he
wanted to study opera at its source by attending the performances at the
Teatro di San Carlo, revelling in its orchestra of 80 musicians, and its

world-famous singers. But whatever was his method of learning, it proved
truly fruitful. In 1758 he submitted to Martini an *Aria cantabile* of his
composition, which an altist from Bologna had to sing every night at the
Milan opera house. Similar efforts no doubt continued (although no trace
of this music has been preserved), and gradually Giovanni won a reputation as a dramatic composer. Thus it came about that in the very month
he assumed his duties at the Cathedral, he had to leave Milan in order
to test two singers engaged for the Teatro Regio of Turin. This he did
because he had been commissioned to write a composition for this distinguished opera house to be performed in the coming Carnival. The opera,
Artaserse, was duly presented in 1761 and the success must have been
great, for Giovanni was now honoured with an invitation to compose
another work for the Teatro di San Carlo in Naples. *Catone in Utica* was
performed in the same year and pleased so well that in spite of the Italians'
'rage of novelty' (Burney), it was played again in 1764. Moreover, San
Carlo, impressed by Bach's brilliant success, commissioned another work
from him and in January 1762 his *Alessandro nell' Indie* earned similar
applause.[1]

Familiar though Bach was with Naples from former visits, he must
have experienced a peculiar thrill in having his own work played in this
immense theatre, which a very critical visitor, Samuel Sharp, with typical
British reserve described as 'perhaps almost as remarkable an object as
any man sees in his travels.'[2] By that time Bach had probably become
inured to the outrageous behaviour of the audience, the description of
which any present-day opera lover cannot read without shuddering.
During the performance, constant visiting and loud conversation in the
boxes, which served the impoverished Italian aristocracy as a substitute
for parties at home, were just as common as applause to favourite singers
during the whole time they sang, with the men in the pit increasing the
effect of their shouts by striking the benches with long sticks. How any
music could be heard and appreciated in this pandemonium is beyond our
understanding.

Nevertheless Giovanni spent glorious months in Naples, basking in
his success, and he was extremely reluctant to return to the organ-loft. He
had been absent for a whole year, leaving the discharge of his duties to a
substitute, and Count Litta, who had to hear various not unjustified criti-

---

[1] In it appeared the great tenor, Anton Raaf, for whom Bach wrote one of his most
beautiful arias, 'Non so d'onde viene.' Raaf subsequently sang the title role in the first
performance of Mozart's 'Idomeneo.'
[2] Cf. Samuel Sharp, 'Letters from Italy,' London, 1767.

cisms of his protégé's behaviour, was getting restive. Martini was so fine a musician and so observant a man that he realized the irresistible force drawing his pupil away from church music. But his attempts to intercede with the Count failed; finally Bach realized that he had to comply with his benefactor's wish, and he returned to Milan in April 1762. He was not fated to stay there too long. Reports of his outstanding success on the musical stage had travelled beyond Italy. In London Colomba Mattei, *impresaria* of the King's Theatre, was in urgent need of a maestro who would add glamour to the institute and thus ease her great financial difficulties. Bach seemed the very man for her, and she offered him a position as official composer to the King's Theatre for the season from November 1762 to June 1763. This was indeed a tempting proposition. The maxim put forth by Samuel Sharp,[1] 'An excellent performer, if he is well advised, will certainly set out for England, where talents of every kind are rewarded tenfold above what they are at Naples,' reflected the prevailing opinion. Bach was no exception and felt most eager to try his luck with a British audience. Even his protector could not deny the validity of Giovanni's arguments, and thus the Milan church organist after serving for a few months set out for England.[2]

Although engaged for a theatre devoted exclusively to Italian opera, Bach did not attempt to appear as an Italian in England; he was announced in the programmes as Mr. John Bach, a 'Saxon Master of Music' or a 'Saxon Professor.' This is significant of the conditions then prevailing in England. The reigning house had come from Hanover only 48 years previously; King George III's own grandfather had been born in Germany; and there

[1] *l.c.*

[2] Terry's report in his Biography of the composer that Christian first travelled from Milan to the court of Strelitz in North-Eastern Germany, where he was handed a travelling stipend of 100 thalers for his journey to London, is based on the assumption that a receipt for this amount bearing the signature of Bach, which was found in the Mecklenburg-Strelitz archives but not actually seen by Terry, was signed by Christian. Miesner in *BJ*, 1937, contends that the signature is that of Emanuel Bach, a point which has much in its favour. It seems very unlikely that Christian would have made this tremendous detour on his journey from Milan to London, especially as he would have had to go through territory in which the war was still raging. Emanuel, on the other hand, like other prominent Berlin musicians, was in close contact with Joh. Wilhelm Ludwig Hertel, conductor of the Strelitz court, and had a standing invitation to play there. In 1762 he seems to have done so. Maybe his visit was in some way connected with Christian Bach. The latter was to be appointed music master to Sophie Charlotte of Mecklenburg-Strelitz, who had recently married King George III of England, and was anxious to secure a German music teacher. The purpose of the payment is, however, as yet quite unclear. It may have been paid to Emanuel with the instruction to pass it on to his brother, or it may have been meant for Emanuel himself in remuneration for his services. The latter theory seems more likely, as Christian's appointment to the English court was not made until the end of 1763.

was still a close contact with that country, where the English King retained influence in his capacity as Elector of Hanover. The emotional ties with Germany were even stronger for the Queen, who in 1761, at the age of 18, had left the small court of Mecklenburg-Strelitz to marry George III, and was only gradually adapting herself to English ways. To be a German musician was, in her eyes, a definite asset and one which John Bach was glad to possess. Yet his situation was an ambiguous one. At the King's Theatre the Italian musicians had long reigned supreme; some of them were apt to watch with misgivings and jealousy the success of a German composer in their very own field, and would fight him with any weapons they could get hold of. If we add to this conflict the maze of intrigue through which anyone connected with the theatre has to find his way, we can well imagine that John Bach had not chosen an easy life when he accepted Signora Mattei's call. Sometimes he may have thought with longing of the peaceful organ-loft he had abandoned in Milan.

He planned to compose a serious opera for the theatre, but when he became acquainted with the singers at his disposal, he was dismayed by their mediocrity. So much depended on the first impression he would make in London that he was loath to entrust his reputation to such a cast. Thus he first presented various pasticcios made up of music by different composers, pondering meanwhile how to solve his own problem. Finally he found a way out. An Italian singer, Anna Lucia de Amicis, had done extremely well in comedy roles, and he decided to try her out in a serious part. The experiment proved highly successful, and when in February 1763 Bach performed his new drama *Orione*, it created a veritable sensation. 'Every judge of music perceived,' as Burney reports, 'the emanations of genius throughout the whole performance.' The royal couple, who had honoured the première with their presence, liked *Orione* so much that they attended the second performance as well, although this took place on a Tuesday, a day on which the society snobs considered it unfashionable to visit the King's Theatre. But be it Tuesday or Saturday, the house was crowded whenever Bach's opera was played, and a collection of 'Favourite Songs' from *Orione*, which the enterprising firm of Walsh published a few weeks after the première, had excellent sales. In May of this year, after *Orione* had been performed 13 times, Bach presented his *Zanaida*, with the same outstanding prima donna, and the response of the audience was just as enthusiastic.

In spite of all this John Bach's contract with the King's Theatre was not renewed for the coming year. Signora Mattei, weary of the countless problems besetting an *impresaria*, decided to return to Italy, and in her stead two other Italians, the singer Mingotti and the violinist Giardini, took over. Having no liking for the Saxon master, they engaged an Italian composer. Giardini especially was anti-German, and it is known that as an old man he refused to meet Haydn, 'that German dog'; which feelings Haydn reciprocated by noting in his diary that 'Giardini played like a pig.'

But John Bach could not be kept away for good from the domain of opera, and in 1765 and 1767 two new dramatic works of his were presented at the King's Theatre. The royal couple fully supported 'their trusty and well-beloved Bach,' as he is called in a royal decree granting him certain printing privileges, to safeguard him against unauthorized publications of his works; indeed they were responsible for his not returning to Italy at the end of the first London season. In the same year he was appointed Music Master to the Queen at a salary of £300, a position he retained until his death. Bach's duties at court were manifold. He gave regular lessons to the Queen, whose genuine love of music is proved by the report that on the voyage to England she bravely bore the horrors of a terrible storm by playing constantly on her beloved harpsichord.[1] Contemporaries praised her 'sweet and correct singing,' while Haydn in 1791 found her achievements on the clavier 'quite good—for a queen.' Occasionally John Bach was also required to accompany the King's flute-playing, and will have remembered his brother Emanuel's similar experiences in Potsdam. Then there were the royal children to be taught too, which, as the years went by, meant a good deal of work, as Queen Charlotte by the time she was 30 had borne her husband ten children. Still, the music master may have rather enjoyed working with these princes and princesses who made the great Gainsborough, when he painted their portraits, 'all but raving mad with ecstasy in beholding such a constellation of youthful beauty.'[2] Some of them had real talent, especially the Prince of Wales, whose 'extraordinary love of music' was later so favourably to impress Haydn.

In the first year of his service at court John Bach had the pleasure of arranging for the appearance at Buckingham House of that unique youthful prodigy, Wolfgang Amadeus Mozart, aged 8, and his sister, Nannerl, who in April 1764 arrived in London. John Bach was fascinated by Wolfgang; they became great friends and liked doing stunts together before an enraptured audience. He would, for instance, have Wolfgang on his lap

[1] Cf. John Heneage Jesse, 'Memoirs of the Life and Reign of King George III,' London, 1867.
[2] Cf. Henry Angelo, 'Reminiscences,' London, 1828-30.

while they played the harpsichord together, alternating after every bar; or they would compose a fugue, Bach starting, Mozart completing it. For the child genius, the association with John Bach was of the greatest artistic significance, and his compositions clearly show the tremendous influence the mature composer exercised on him.

Naturally the Queen's music master was in great demand for the instruction of the high nobility, and before long he established many lucrative and pleasant connections with the British aristocracy, who even admitted him to their social life. London was then a gay and stimulating place to live in, at least if one belonged to the privileged class. Countless amusements, routs, and masked balls followed each other with hardly a pause. The centres of diversions were 'sweet, charming, elegant, delicious' Ranelagh Gardens, to which, in the opinion of the Londoners, 'Paradise itself could hardly be equal,'[1] and Vauxhall, a veritable fairyland with its myriads of coloured lights, lovely flowers, and the splendid music hall decorated by Hogarth. Persons interested in the cultivation of the mind could find in the London of the late 18th century plenty of parties where intelligent discussions were the main feature. Into this society, 'hooped and caparisoned, plumed, powdered, pigtailed, fruit and pompons piled on huge coiffures, knee-breeched, snuff-boxed, incomparably conversing',[2] John Bach fitted perfectly. His gaiety, charm, and poise were spiced by a keen wit, a talent for *bons mots*, and thus he was at home in fashionable assemblies as well as in the new Blue Stocking Clubs or among the prominent artists of his time, such as Gainsborough, Cipriani, Zoffany. He became accustomed to a rather luxurious way of living, and, not unmindful of the rigid economy he had watched in his father's house, he derived satisfaction from spending money freely. John Bach was most elegantly dressed, as we see from the beautiful portraits Gainsborough painted of him,[3] and he had his own fine carriage to take him from one high-born pupil to the other. An indication of his amiable disposition is the fact that he had the same coachman through all the years in London, and that this faithful servant, out of loyalty to his deceased master, followed Bach's widow to Italy.[4]

In spite of a whirl of social engagements, Bach was prodigiously active

[1] Cf. Henry Fielding, 'The History of Amelia,' London, 1752.

[2] Cf. Rose Macaulay, 'Life Among the English,' 2nd. impr., London, 1946.

[3] One he sent, following his former teacher's request, 'as a small token of his heavy debt' to Padre Martini, who owned a collection of pictures of famous musicians. It is still preserved in the Liceo Musicale, Bologna.

[4] Cf. 'Court and Private Life in the Time of Queen Charlotte, being the Journals of Mrs. Papendiek,' London, 1887.

in various fields. He not only composed serious operas, but contributed to comic works performed at Covent Garden, and supplied the Vauxhall concerts with many delightful arias, which brought laurels to his favourite pupil, Mrs. Weichsell.[1] Instrumental music was constantly composed and published by him, including clavier works, chamber music and symphonies; Burney, for instance, found the latter his most outstanding compositions. In spite of all his creative and instructive activity, he was still able to devote a great deal of energy to his work as a performing artist and concert manager. In the second year of his stay in London he inaugurated, together with Carl Friedrich Abel, a subscription series of concerts that was continued up to his death. The connection between the Bachs and Abels dated back to Sebastian's stay at Cöthen, when Christian Ferdinand Abel worked under him as an excellent violinist and violist. The elder Abel's son, Carl Friedrich, studied with Sebastian at Leipzig, if we may believe contemporary reports,[2] and was subsequently engaged as viola da gamba player to the Dresden court orchestra. Ten years later he went to London, where his admirable playing won him general acclaim and an appointment as chamber musician to Queen Charlotte. Burney in his 'General History of Music' wrote of Abel: 'He had a hand which no difficulties could embarrass, a taste most refined and delicate, and a judgment so correct and certain as never to let a single note escape him without meaning.' An intimate friendship developed between John Bach and Friedrich Abel. For many years they shared an apartment and frequented the same circle of friends. The artistic fruit of this most congenial association was the institution of the Bach-Abel concerts, fifteen of which were offered every season; for many years they ranked among the chief entertainments in the field of music. Both Bach and Abel appeared in them as composers, soloists and conductors, adding as further attractions eminent guest artists such as the singers Mrs. Weichsell and Cecilia Grassi, the great oboist, J. C. Fischer (son-in-law of Gainsborough), and the excellent violinist, Wilhelm Cramer, from Mannheim. Another German guest, J. B. Wendling, first flutist of Mannheim's famous orchestra, was probably responsible for an invitation to Bach which the latter may well have considered the peak of his achievements. In 1772, ten years after his arrival in London, John Bach's success in the field of serious opera was given full recognition when he was asked to compose a music drama for Mannheim, capital of the Palatinate, to be given at a gala performance in

---

[1] She was the mother of the great singer, Elisabeth Billington, model of Reynolds' St. Cecilia, who was so greatly admired by Haydn.

[2] No evidence to this effect has been found in the records of the Thomas school.

honour of the Elector's birthday. It was not the first time that one of the
composer's dramatic works was played in Germany. In 1766 and 1768 his
Catone in Utica had been presented at the court of Braunschweig (cf. p. 467)
and Prince Ferdinand had been so deeply impressed that he granted
the composer a pension for life.[1] Yet the call from Mannheim was of quite
a different order. At that time, this German city was considered one of the
most important musical centres as the Elector Karl Theodor had spared
no expense or effort to secure first-class singers, and to build up an
orchestra of the finest players (an 'army of generals,' as Burney termed it),
which was generally considered the best in Europe. To compose for so
outstanding a group of artists seemed like the fulfilment of the dreams that
had made young Christian escape from Germany to Italy. Now he could
triumphantly return to his native country, with the prestige of having won
a distinction greater than any accorded to his brothers. In November 1772
his opera, *Temistocle*, was performed by a brilliant cast, including the
great tenor, Anton Raaf, who ten years earlier had won laurels in Naples
with Bach's opera *Alessandro nell' Indie*. The artistic glamour was
matched by the outward pomp necessitated by the presence of a great
number of exalted personages, and the evening constituted an unforgettable event in John Bach's career. Altogether the time spent in Mannheim
was a most exciting one. Something in the atmosphere of the town, where
music reigned supreme, must have been conducive to romance. Mozart,
when he visited it in 1777, trying to gain a position in the Elector's
orchestra, fell in love twice, his first infatuation for Rose Cannabich being
superseded by the deeper and more lasting emotion for Aloysia Weber.
Bach, who had so far been a confirmed bachelor, unresponsive to the
lovely prima donnas with whom he was working, was captivated by
beautiful Augusta Wendling, the young daughter of his host, and he
proposed to her. She refused to marry a man 20 years her senior, but later
did not mind becoming the mistress of the Elector, who was even 9 years
older than Bach. Her contemporaries describe her as a very cold character,
so one need not pity Bach too much for not winning her hand. But, when
living with the Wendling family, he felt that a home of one's own had
definite advantages, and so, after his return to London, he looked around
for a suitable wife, and found her in the Italian singer, Cecilia Grassi,
whom he had known for years. They were married in 1773, the bridegroom being 38, the bride 27. Cecilia was not beautiful, but she was a fine
musician, whose 'truth of intonation, plaintive sweetness of voice, and

---

[1] Cf. Miesner in *BJ*, 1936. Miesner also points out that Bach's Trio op. 2 was dedicated
to Princess Augusta of Braunschweig-Lüneburg.

innocence of expression' Burney praised; and she could help her husband a good deal with his voice pupils.

Bach's success was not forgotten in Mannheim, and the next year his *Temistocle* was performed there again, the composer, however, being too busy in London to attend. It was only four years later, in 1776, that he was able to visit the town again, and for this occasion he wrote a new opera *Lucio Silla*. Although the cast was almost identical with that of *Temistocle*, the reception was less enthusiastic. New trends towards establishing a national German opera had been steadily gaining in strength, and Bach's work belonged to the very last Italian operas performed in Mannheim. Soon after *Lucio Silla*, Holzbauer's German opera *Günther von Schwarzburg* had a brilliant success there. It is noteworthy that Holzbauer, who was born in 1711 and had up to then only composed Italian libretti, responded to the new national feeling, while Bach, although much younger, did not consider such a move.

A great challenge was set him, when he was commissioned in 1778 to write an opera for Paris, where the war between the adherents of Gluck and Piccini was raging with furious vehemence. According to Baron Grimm both camps in Paris were disappointed by the new opera *Amadis des Gaules*; the Piccinists found Bach's work too heavy and not charming enough, while the Gluckists felt it to be as outdated as Piccini's products.

For a considerable time Bach had had no connection with the King's Theatre in London, probably because he was tired of the Italian clique's intrigues against him. As long as he was extremely successful as organizer of concerts, performer and teacher, he held himself aloof, seeing no reason why he should put up with his colleagues' cabals. In 1778, however, he felt it necessary to return to the scene of his former triumphs and to present a new opera, *La Clemenza di Scipione*, for at that time he was sincerely anxious to improve his standing in London. Various events had contributed to a decrease in his popularity there. In the field of teaching, his position at the very top of the profession had been undermined by the great Italian singer, Venanzio Rauzzini, who came to London in 1774 and drew fashionable pupils like a magnet; a still more serious rival was the German pianist, Johann Samuel Schroeter,[1] whom Bach himself had introduced to the London public in 1772 and afterwards advanced in every

---

[1] He was the son of an oboist, and the brother of the great singer and actress, Corona Schroeter, who from 1776 worked at Weimar in close co-operation with Goethe, creating the part of Iphigenia and others. Schroeter's aristocratic widow, a few years after her husband's death, fell in love with Haydn, who declared he would have married her, had he been free.

conceivable way, even helping him with his compositions. Schroeter, 15 years younger than his benefactor, was before long considered the foremost pianoforte player in the capital, and, what was worse, 'this fascinating, fawning, suave teacher for the belles'[1] was in the greatest demand for instruction. Bach's income dwindled, and he suffered a terrible blow to his pride. Retrospectively, it seems tragic that what hurt Bach so deeply was to stop of its own accord a few years later; for Schroeter married a high-born pupil and had to promise his new relatives not to appear in public any more. Besides, his health was undermined and he was to die in 1788, at the age of 38. But all this Bach could not foresee, and the eclipse of his fame through Schroeter brought him great suffering. Moreover, he had to bear the consequences of too ambitious a scheme. In 1775 the Bach-Abel concerts, which had formerly taken place in Carlisle House and subsequently in Almack's Assembly rooms, moved to extremely stylish quarters. A new building had been erected in Hanover Square, the freehold of which was bought jointly by Bach, Abel, and Sir John Gallini, a wealthy dancing master. The beautiful concert hall, adorned with pictures by Gainsborough and Cipriani, represented a *ne plus ultra* in splendour, and an aristocratic lady describing it to her son wrote approvingly: "Tis a great stroke of Bach's to entertain the town so elegantly.' It was indeed a bold stroke, too bold for John Bach's resources. He found it difficult to pay back the loans he had contracted for the project, and after two years of struggle he had to dissolve the partnership with Gallini, who remained sole owner and merely rented the hall to Bach. Even then his former financial security was not regained. The London music lovers, who had attended the Bach-Abel concerts for so many years, were eager to hear something different, and when the novelty of the Hanover Square rooms wore off, they preferred other attractions. Thus the revenues from these concerts dwindled to only a fraction of their former size, and the Earl of Abingdon, a patron of music, had to give financial assistance to keep the series going.

All these were great setbacks, to be sure; yet the situation was one that a man of only 46, endowed with talent, ambition, and diligence, could have mastered in some way. A decisive break with the old routine was imperative, both in Bach's artistic contributions and in his luxurious way of life. John Bach, however, lacked the will-power for such reforms. He had not inherited his father's fighting power to any extent. While difficulties stimulated Sebastian, they proved overpowering to his youngest son. The constant worries had a serious effect on his health, and after he had

[1] Cf. Papendiek, *l.c.*

appeared in May 1781 in his last concert of the season, he suffered a break-down. A removal to the country did not bring the hoped-for improvement; indeed in November he felt it necessary to make his will. He steadily grew weaker, and on New Year's Day, 1782, he breathed his last.

The funeral, which took place on January 6, proved the shockingly short memory of the Londoners who, after only a few months, had all but forgotten their former favourite. No more than four friends were present to render the last honour to John Bach. Among his creditors pandemonium reigned. It was found that he had left debts amounting to £4000, and every bit of his property had to be sold. Thus, in spite of distinguished successes and an income reaching figures his father had never hoped for, John Bach left his widow even less than Sebastian had bequeathed to Anna Magdalena. However, John Bach's royal patron acted much more generously than the Leipzig city fathers. The Queen paid for the funeral of her music master and allowed the widow £100 for the return trip to Italy, as well as a yearly pension of £200. On the other hand, even before John Bach was buried, an official decree was issued appointing Schroeter his successor at court.

The life of this youngest son of Sebastian differs in many respects from that of his brothers; there was more adventure in it, more of acclaim and dazzling success; a larger income and more debts, and also more enjoyment of a luxurious life. For a top-ranking musician, existence in London was brimful of stimulation, commotion, and tension; not for a moment could one afford to relax. One had to watch out to avoid falling victim to the intrigues of ambitious colleagues, and one had, through most strenuous work, to satisfy the voracious novelty-hunger of the audience. For over a decade John Bach succeeded in reigning supreme in the British capital. With his early death he paid the price for a life of glamour and excitement.

THE MUSIC OF JOHANN CHRISTIAN BACH

Like his brother Emanuel, Johann Christian offered a sizable contribution to the growth of the Viennese classical style. The work of the Berlin Bach made a deep impression on young Haydn, who learned from it expressive subjectivity and the art to develop a theme until its possibilities were exhausted. A similar or even greater influence was exercised by Christian Bach on young Mozart. 'Bach,' as Burney remarks,[1] 'seems to

[1] 'General History of Music,' IV, 483.

2 D

have been the first composer who observed the law of contrast as a principle. Before his time, contrast there frequently was in the work of others, but it seems to have been accidental. Bach in his symphonies and other incidental pieces as well as his songs, seldom failed, after a rapid and noisy passage, to introduce one that was slow and soothing.' This principle, as well as Christian's tendency to create graceful yet tender melodies, encouraged similar trends in Mozart's own creative output. There were few contemporary artists for whom the young master from Salzburg felt so much love and admiration. From their first meeting in London in 1764, when the boy of eight played duets with the music master to the British Queen, to their reunion in Paris, fourteen years later, and finally to the day in 1782 when Wolfgang wrote to his father: 'the English Bach is dead . . . a sad day for the world of music,' Mozart's loyalty to his elder friend did not waver.

Not much is known about Christian's period of artistic preparation. Like his brothers, he studied as a child under his father. But before he reached an age when the instruction of the greatest teacher of the time could be fully utilized, Sebastian was ailing and finally died. Young Christian then went as a kind of fosterchild to Emanuel in Berlin. There is no doubt that he soon succumbed to his half-brother's personality. The passionate subjectivism of Emanuel's clavier style is mirrored in the few compositions by Christian which we know to have been written in Berlin. But the youth was by no means a mere imitator of Emanuel's music. He had not forgotten what his father showed him, and his own predilection for the larger forms and ensembles asserted itself. Thus the earliest works by Christian were written for the clavier but with the accompaniment of strings. They are not sonatas for a single instrument, but concertos conceived on a larger scale.

The period of transition in Christian's creative output started in 1755 with his sojourn in Italy. The romantic fervour of the earlier works is still alive in the compositions he wrote after he left his brother's house. It is characteristic that in particular the soulful and expressive music of Tartini left its imprint on his work. The young man felt, however, that his technical training was still inadequate, and he gladly availed himself of the opportunity to become a pupil of Italy's greatest music teacher, Padre Martini. Giambattista Martini of Bologna was a fine violinist, an excellent player of keyboard instruments, an accomplished mathematician, a successful composer and music historian, and the undisputed authority in the field of counterpoint. Under his guidance the descendant of stout Protestant organists and cantors wrote numerous works of Latin church music and even became a member of the Catholic Church. The solid technical training which the Padre gave him remained the firm foundation on which his whole creative work of later years was built.

After a few years in Italy, Christian turned to a field of music which the other Bachs had always held in contempt, while being secretly somewhat attracted by it. He became a successful opera composer who saw five of his musical dramas performed within two years. The Neapolitan opera brought young Bach into contact with light, carefree, uncomplicated and melodious music, and it must be considered as his great achievement that he succeeded in bringing to a complete fusion the different artistic experiences he had had up to that time. Out of the solid earthiness of the Bachs, the passionate expressiveness of *Empfindsamkeit*, the playful world of make-believe of the stage, and the sweet tunefulness of Catholic church music, the pupil of Padre Martini created a kind of music that was noble and yet light, technically competent, yet free of ponderousness.

The full artistic maturity which Bach thus achieved at the age of 27 coincided with his call to England. It is not surprising that his specific brand of what we might call early classicism, with its mixture of German and Italian elements and equal accomplishments in the field of vocal and instrumental music, made him one of the most successful composers of his time. His works were performed all over Europe, and publishers of different countries vied with each other in reprinting them.

It seems, however, that this last son of Sebastian's had neither the moral nor the physical fibre to resist the contaminating effect of excessive popularity. During the twenty years the composer spent in London (1762-1782), his artistic growth almost came to a standstill. In many details the works of the seventies were superior to those of the sixties, but a basic change is not to be noticed. For this reason, quite gradually, the compositions of this favourite among musicians appeared to be outmoded. Neither in form nor content, nor in power of expression did he reach the supreme perfection of the classical style as developed by Haydn and Mozart. It was the tragedy in the career of Christian Bach that at a comparatively early age he came almost to the threshold of the promised land, stopped there, confused by the praise of his admirers, and died before he had a chance to take the last and decisive step.

It is characteristic of the progressive attitude of the young composer that he wrote hardly any works for *clavier solo*, as long as only the older forms of the keyboard instruments, harpsichord and clavichord, were available to him. This attitude changed in London, where Bach had a chance to try out the new fortepiano, with its flexible tone, on which not only sudden dynamic contrasts, but even crescendi and decrescendi were possible.

We must regret that Christian did not cultivate the keyboard instrument to a greater extent during his first two creative periods, for the sonata in c, published as op. 5/6 (*T* 339), which we can attribute with certainty to the Italian sojourn, belongs to his most significant compositions. The passionate character of the impressive prelude in ternary form which opens the sonata points to the influence of North Italian violin music, proving at the same time how well Bach remembered, even in Italy, his half-brother's artistic language. The force of this grief-stricken Grave at times foreshadows Beethoven's music. The following fugue, with its somewhat conventional subject, displays an imposing array of contrapuntal devices; it shows that the pupil had put Padre Martini's instruction to good use. The fine stretto near the end, in particular, reveals the composer as a craftsman worthy of the name of Bach (*Ex.* 109). A gavotte-

like Allegretto of somewhat stilted grace concludes this remarkable composition which was apparently written between 1757 and 1760, before the composer adopted the Italian *bel canto* also for his instrumental style.

The remaining five sonatas in opus 5 (*T* 338-39), published around the year 1768, are obviously products of the London years. They show the sweetness and grace of expression, the warm melodious sensuousness that fascinated little Mozart. In particular the gentle charm and noble diction of the E flat Rondo finale in No. 4 deeply impressed the susceptible boy. It is interesting to note that Wolfgang, who played the Sonatas while they were still in manuscript, in 1765 arranged three of them (Nos. 2, 3, 4) as concertos by adding an accompaniment for 2 violins and bass (K. 107). As Alfred Einstein points out, the young genius seems to have performed these concertos not only on the way home from London, but also in later years; the cadenzas he added are obviously in a more mature handwriting than the rest of the score.

The title-page of the sonatas op. 5 bears the indication '*pour le clavecin ou pianoforte*,' but there can be no doubt that Bach had the modern instrument primarily in mind. The Alberti basses, arpeggios, and melodious passages of these compositions are conceived with a view to performance on the pianoforte, and the beautiful Adagio of No. 5 could never unfold its ingratiating cantilena on the rigid and unbending harpsichord.

John Bach's later clavier compositions, although possibly superior in quality, reveal no change in style. The six sonatas op. 17 published around 1779 (*T* 341-42), are in two or three movements like those of the earlier set. They display once more the typical mixture of brilliance and elegance with the *bel canto* and the homophonic idiom of the Italian opera, which was the trademark of his London music. Both the op. 5 and op. 17 have as a first number a sonata which even a beginner could play; but whoever bought the sets on the strength of these first compositions would soon discover that in the following pieces the arpeggios in both hands, the fast runs, trills and other ornaments could only be adequately performed by an expert. Christian is at his best in the noble Andantes in E flat (a key in which he wrote some of his most beautiful slow movements) of his sonatas op. 17 Nos. 2 and 6. The Prestissimo in c which concludes No. 2 shows a sense of humour and wit far superior to the frothy routine gaiety in the London clavier music of the time.

In the course of his educational activities Bach may often have found opportunities to accompany a pupil on the same instrument or on a second clavier. Around 1774 he even played *clavier duets* in public, with an infant prodigy only six years old who was later to become Mrs. Billington, one of the greatest English singers. The success of this enterprise encouraged Bach to publish original compositions for two performers, and he thus became one of the initiators of a new type of clavier music. Several works *a due cembali obbligati* or 'for two performers on one pianoforte or harpsichord' were published around 1779. The duet op. 15/5 for 2 harpsichords (*T* 340) is probably an earlier work written during the first years of Bach's stay in London. Here the performers have to be satisfied with frequent echo effects or playing in parallel thirds or sixths. The piano duets for a single instrument op. 15/6, op. 18/5 and 6 (*T* 340, 343, also 351-52) seem to be of a somewhat later date. They ingeniously explore the possibilities of the new genre. Although they are in two movements only, they are conceived on a larger scale and sometimes achieve an almost symphonic character. For once, these compositions display a new and progressive trend which pointed the way to a younger generation.

Two of these piano duets were included in a collection (published in 1780; *T* 350-52) of a decidedly educational character. It contained, moreover, a set of 4 'progressive lessons for the harpsichord or pianoforte,' carefully graded compositions for the keyboard, none of which presents great technical problems. To the same field belongs the *Méthode ou Recueil de connoissances élémentaires pour le Forte-Piano ou Clavecin* published by Leduc, Paris, which Bach wrote together with Pasquale Ricci for pupils of the Naples Conservatory (the exercises are therefore provided not only with French but also with Italian annotations). The manual deals with the elementary problems of piano playing in 12 chapters. Of special interest are the sections treating tempo and ornaments, which reach even beyond the information provided in Emanuel's 'Essay.' The second part contains six music numbers, each in three movements, which also appeared separately, one year after Christian's death, under the significant title of '6 Progressive Lessons . . . composed by Mr. Bach, master to the celebrated Mr. Schroeter' (*T* 349-50). The shrewd publisher ascribed them, however, to the wrong Bach, for these numbers are the illustrations which Emanuel provided for his 'Essay' (*Wq* 63); they were reprinted in the *Recueil* without mention of the composer's name.[1]

The numerous little exercises contained in the first part of Ricci's and Christian Bach's manual are, for the convenience of the instructor, provided 'with the accompaniment of a flute or violin.' As some teachers preferred to join their pupils in playing on the keyboard instrument itself, while others chose to accompany them on the violin, it became a habit with Christian Bach to combine, in a single set, piano duets and *duets for clavier and violin*. Twenty-nine such duets for a keyboard and a melody instrument were printed during the latter part of Christian's life or shortly after his death. They were usually dedicated to society ladies, and the absence of technical difficulties as well as the 'address' of their smoothly flowing idiom is sure to have appealed to the fair dedicatees. How very popular they were with musical amateurs can be seen from the fact that no less than seven contemporary editions exist of the first set of sonatas for clavier and violin published in 1773 as op. 10 (*T* 322-23), and printed not only in London but also in Vienna,[2] Paris and Amsterdam. The compositions are all in major keys, using not more than three sharps or flats. The first movement is in a rudimentary sonata form with an energetic, some-

---

[1] Terry, who even reprints a complete Menuet (pp. 136-7), considers them as compositions by Christian, overlooking their obvious stylistic relationship to other works of Emanuel Bach.

[2] The Viennese edition gives them the traditional title 'Trio.'

what conservative first subject, a singing, rather Mozartian subsidiary theme, and a whimsical, often folksonglike concluding subject. After occasional half-hearted attempts to develop the first subject and to introduce remoter keys, the incomplete recapitulation sets in with the subsidiary subject. The second movement is usually an Allegretto or 'Tempo di Minuetto' in simple da capo form, or in rondo form with two episodes.

As an acknowledgment of his indebtedness to the Bach family and especially to his father, Christian based the main subject of the first Sonata for clavier and violin that he published (op. 10/1), on the beginning of the first partita in Sebastian's *Clavier Übung*. The son somewhat changed the rhythmic aspect of the tune and broke up the flow of the Baroque melody into a clear-cut 4-measure phrase. Nevertheless, the whole first section, in which the subject is even given to the left hand of the clavierist (a procedure hardly ever used in Christian's later sonatas), discloses the influence of the father's music. However, the character of the second subject and the use of the violin as a filling middle part, being given lower notes in passages of parallel thirds and sixths, point to a post-Baroque composition.

It greatly contributes to the attraction of these sonatas that the violin is not always condemned to a purely accompanying function. Little echo effects or imitations are occasionally entrusted to it; in the finale of No. 2 it has a long solo in which the clavier serves mainly as support, and in the third sonata of the set it plays by itself temporarily while the piano takes a rest.

Bach's later duets are basically similar to the compositions in op. 10. However, a flute may be substituted for the violin, which makes the melody instrument even less suitable to perform a low-pitched middle part. Quite often the wind instrument dominates (cf. op. 16/2, T 325), and occasionally a spontaneous dialogue develops between flute and clavier. It would not seem impossible that these compositions reflect a study of the fine violin sonatas by Christian's kinsman, Johann Ernst (cf. p. 456).

Like his two brothers, Friedemann and Emanuel, Christian also wrote works for two melody instruments without bass. Approximately in 1775 six *duets for two violins* were published in London without opus number (T 335-36). These are suite-like little works of a casual character consisting of two or three movements in a basically homophonic idiom. To the violinist who is only a beginner they offer melodious and uncomplicated exercises.

A number of *trios* in the traditional combination of 2 violins and bass

(T 317-21) has been preserved in manuscripts which are sometimes inscribed *Del Signore Bach in Milano*. It would seem that the majority of these compositions were written before Bach came to London. In their melodies as well as in the arrangement of movements the influence of the Italian *sinfonia* may be detected;[1] they display the scattered polyphonic elements characteristic of the phase of decline in the trio sonata, and such headings as *Affettuoso, Minuetto grazioso*, or *Allegrino prezioso* (T 318/1) point back to the model of Emanuel.

Probably belonging to the end of Bach's stay in Italy are six trios or *nocturnes* op. 4 for two violins and viola or Basse obligé (T 314-16), first printed around 1765 in Paris,[2] later reprinted in London and Amsterdam. Although the use of a filling keyboard instrument is still left to the discretion of the performer, these are actually string trios in the modern sense. They make, as the preface to the new edition of the New York Public Library aptly remarks; 'excellent diversion for quartet players when the 'cellist is late.' The viola is by no means used merely as a supporting bass. Not infrequently solo passages are entrusted to it, and Bach does not hesitate to let it cross parts with the violin. Each work starts with a slow movement followed by a minuet with trio, while fast sections are missing altogether. Owing to the peculiar combination of instruments, these compositions have an insubstantial and delicate character quite unusual in the music of the time.

A third type of trio was published by the composer himself in 1763 as his op. 2 (T 313-14). These six compositions are for the harpsichord, 'accompanied' by violin or flute and 'cello. The role the violin plays in these trios is very similar to that in the sonatas for clavier and violin. The string instrument is not always allotted a subservient part; solos are allowed it and occasionally there is a brisk exchange of questions and answers between the harpsichord and the violin. The 'cello, however, is inextricably bound to the harpsichord bass, which makes the need for its participation rather questionable. This may have induced Bach, in later years, to write instead of trios, sonatas for clavier and violin, which dispense altogether with a 'cello part.

In John Bach's *quartets* for flute, violin, viola and 'cello some of the features of the old trio sonata may be detected. The two top parts gaily alternate or join forces, the viola, which is not often allowed to share in the thematic elaboration, serves as a filling middle voice, and the 'cello

---

[1] In T 321/1, the only Trio sonata in more than 3 movements, the Andante in B is obviously a foreign body which does not belong to the composition.

[2] The first edition erroneously designates them as op. 2.

provides a kind of continuo bass as foundation. It would be easy to transplant viola and 'cello to a harpsichord and thus to re-create the traditional trio sonata. As a matter of fact the few compositions of this genre which were published in Christian's lifetime—six quartets op. 8 printed around 1775 (*T* 306/7) and three quartets issued in 1777 together with works by Abel and Giardini (*T* 309)—seem to be comparatively early works written shortly before or after the composer moved to London. They consist of the typical two movements, the first either fast or slow, the second a minuet or rondo of the kind to be found in so many of the chamber music works of his maturity; however, a certain tenderness and subjectivity, a romantic leaning towards an ardent sensibility, seems like an echo of impressions Christian had gathered in earlier years. Four other quartets, 'two for Two Flutes, Tenor [viola] and Violoncello, one for Two Flutes, a Violin and Violoncello, and one for a Flute and Hoboy, or Two Flutes, a Tenor and Violoncello,' published posthumously as op. 19 (*T* 307-8) show the more polished elegance of John Bach's later works. They have the three movements of his symphonies, and the intimate character of chamber music gives way to more conventional forms conceived on a larger scale.

The climax of Christian's chamber music is reached in his *quintets* op. 11 (*T* 303-4) which were written and published in the seventies. In these works, scored for flute, oboe, violin, viola and bass, the composer reveals himself as a master at the peak of his creative power, overflowing with inspiration. Well aware of their value he dedicated them to the Elector Palatine, wishing to keep up friendly relations with this influential patron of the arts for whom he wrote the operas *Temistocle* and *Lucio Silla*.

Mrs. Papendiek relates in her memoirs that Christian, one summer day, had been in a great hurry to get a new piece of music ready for a forthcoming rehearsal. He quickly went to work, and while he produced the score, two copyists, standing behind him and looking over his shoulders, wrote out the parts. The composition thus created was the 'enchanting first movement' of the quintet in E flat (op. 11/4). If this anecdote, which reminds us of similar stories connected with the name of Mozart, is based on fact, Bach had the composition finished in his mind before he brought the first note to paper. There is no fumbling or improvising in any of these six quintets. They are finely chiselled gems, every delightful detail of which is most carefully planned. Characteristically enough, Christian's interest in the old trio is noticeable even here. He likes to subdivide his instruments into two groups: a trio of two melody instruments and bass which is presently opposed by another of the remaining two instruments

plus bass (*Ex.* 110). Particularly intriguing effects result from the alternation of wind and stringed instruments. As in the quartets, the bass does

not participate in the thematic elaboration, being a typical supporting
continuo. Its equipment with figures, however, may be a mere concession
to the wishes of the publisher, as a filling harpsichord part is not really
necessary, and may even produce an effect of thickness and heaviness fatal
to a work of so superbly transparent a texture.[1]

The discussion of Christian's chamber music can most fittingly be
concluded with the remarks Leopold Mozart made in 1778 in a letter to
his son, who had just renewed the acquaintance with Bach while they were
both in Paris. 'Write something new—short, light, and popular. Consult
with an engraver to find out what he would like best. Perhaps easy
quartets. . . . Do you believe perhaps that you lower your standards by
writing such music? By no means! Did Bach in London ever publish anything else? The small is great, when it is composed in a natural, fluent and
easy manner and is worked out soundly. . . . Has Bach debased himself by
so doing? By no means! The solid texture and structure, the continuity:
these distinguish the master from the bungler, even in trifles.'

The *clavier concerto* belongs to Christian's favourite forms. Like his
father and his brother, Emanuel, he was a born player of keyboard instruments, but the brilliant and competitive concerto would appeal to his
sense of drama and showmanship more than the intimate sonata. Among
the very earliest works he wrote in Berlin are a number of clavier concertos, and when he moved to London the op. 1 with which he introduced

---

[1] The *Sei Sinfonia* [*sic!*] *pour deux Clarinettes, deux Cors de chasse et Basson* (*T* 285)
published by Longman & Broderip are of little artistic interest. Their unusual combination
of instruments seems to indicate that they are arrangements. The Sextet op. 3 listed by
T (302) is not by Christian but by Friedrich Bach (cf. p. 392).

himself to the musical world in the British capital was a set of six concertos. In all, close to forty concertos for the clavier obbligato are known, originating from every phase of Christian's creative activity.

At least six of the concertos preserved in manuscript in the *Westdeutsche Bibliothek*, Marburg, were composed while Christian lived in his brother's house. The formal construction is similar to that in Sebastian's Italian Concerto, and the clavier parts occasionally reveal a faithful student of the father's Inventions (*Ex.* 111). On the other hand, the

Concerto in E, first movement

brother's work is unmistakably the model. The concerto in f (*T* 301/17) bears the inscription *riveduto dal Sign. C. P. E. Bach* (revised by Mr. C. P. E. Bach) and that in A (*T* 300/12) shows, in its middle movement, the recitative sections so often used by Emanuel. The five works preserved in Christian's own handwriting (*T* 298/1-4, 299/5) display emphasis on homophony, passionate subjectivism, and a rather melancholy yearning which point to the new artistic ideals. Two of these are in a minor mode (which the mature composer employed but rarely) and the middle movements bear such telltale inscriptions as *Adagio affetuoso con sordini* or *Andante e grazioso con sordini*. On the much corrected manuscript of the concerto in B flat (*T* 298/1) the youth scribbled with naïve pleasure in his own achievements: *Ich habe ich dieses Conc. gemacht, ist das nicht schön?* ('I, I made this concerto; isn't that beautiful?') (Ill. XIX). He had indeed every reason to be proud of these early creative attempts. They reveal remarkable talent, and the most advanced pieces—the concertos in E and G (*T* 298/4, 299/5)—already show, in their architecture, most of the features of Christian's mature concertos.

Two concertos in E flat and A published around 1770 by G. F. Hartknoch in Riga (*T* 297) lead to Christian's Italian period. The frequent unisons of the full orchestra, particularly at the end of phrases, give the first an almost Baroque character. In its finale the initial motive of the main theme is used throughout the movement to enrich the rhythmic and harmonic structure. It is one of Sebastian's and Emanuel's devices which Christian employs here, a device which was later to find its rebirth in a somewhat different form in the quartets and symphonies of Haydn and Mozart. The sudden contrasts in emotional content and the frequent dramatic fermatas show how close Christian still was to the world of sensibility. At the same time, however, the warmth and splendour of his broadly contoured melodic lines, particularly in the first movement of the concerto in A, and the romantic sensuality of the beautiful slow middle movements in both works, disclose the vital influence which the Italian scene exercised on the impressionable mind of the young artist.

A concerto in E (*T* 300/13), the manuscript of which is inscribed *dell' Sign. Bach in Meiland*, was probably written towards the end of the composer's stay in Italy. The middle movement again introduces a lovely cantilena such as only a composer familiar with the art of *bel canto* could conceive, while beautiful modulations of the kind he had learned from his brother Emanuel add depth to the harmonic language. In the tutti sections of the first movement a thematic duality, merely implied in earlier works, is fully developed. Two strongly contrasting subjects, an energetic and vigorously rhythmic first theme and a sweetly singing second one, are now in evidence, and the solo instrument adapts them to a more clavieristic language. This work, which also belongs to the first compositions by Christian to be presented in a modern edition, shows the 'Italian Bach' at his best.

The six Concertos op. 1 (*T* 292-93) which Christian published in 1763, shortly after his arrival in London, are dedicated to the English Queen, and they are typical of the works of a fashionable composer aiming to please a wide circle of amateurs. In various ways he is limiting his resources. The former accompanying body of a string quartet has shrunk to two violins and 'cello; the three movements, hitherto the rule, are replaced in four works by two movements, with a minuet or dance-like piece as finale. The spirit of competition between solo and tutti prevailing in his previous concertos is replaced by a more symphonic handling of the two factions, which, instead of fighting, gracefully relieve each other. These concertos are easier to perform than the earlier works, and the more ambitious devices such as crossing hands or big leaps are almost entirely eliminated. The technical requirements always stay within the range of the average amateur; more than two voices are rarely used, and the thinness and transparency of the setting balances the equally light body of the accompanying instruments. With regard to construction, these concertos show a decisive change. Tartini's concerto form with its four tutti interspersed by three soli, traditional in older works, is no longer predominant. There is a clear advance towards the sonata-concerto form, with its three main sections and thematic dualism in the exposition. The style is quite homophonic and strongly melodic, avoiding deeper emotions. Yet these works do not display the superficiality of the *style galant*. There is warmth in their gaiety, and a streak of darker hue is intertwined with their brilliance, that combination which exercised so irresistible an appeal on young Mozart. No. 6 has, in honour of the august dedicatee, a set of variations on 'God save the King,' and the variation form, in which Christian never showed himself to best advantage, is treated here with the utmost simplicity so as not to overtax the imagination of the royal recipient.

The six concertos which were published around the year 1770 as op. 7 (*T* 293-94) are closely related to opus 1. The set contains two concertos in three, and four in two movements, and even the dedication to the Queen of England is the same. Burney's words that Christian's clavier compositions were 'such as ladies can execute with little trouble' may be applied to the two sets of clavier concertos just as well as to his sonatas for violin and clavier. The great innovation is mentioned in a brief remark in the title: *Sei Concerti per il Cembalo o Piano e Forte*. Bach, who in 1768 was the first to play a solo on a pianoforte in public, meant these works not so much for the old harpsichord, with its rigid tone quality, as for the modern pianoforte on which a cantilena can be performed with all necessary dynamic shadings. The gay, gentle, light, and singing music of this set with the frequent Alberti basses (*Ex.* 112) is primarily written

for a clavier instrument which shares its expressive qualities with the old clavichord, without, however, suffering from the latter's extreme weakness of tone. 'Mozartisms' are constantly to be found. When arpeggios of the clavier accompany the leading voices in the strings, when whimsical little motives are gaily skipping back and forth between the two contestants, we are reminded of later works by the Salzburg master. A comparison of this kind is highly revealing, as it shows how much the younger composer received from his model, and yet how tremendously he outdistanced him. Although all the concertos of this set have merits, a few deserve special mention.

In the *Allegretto con spirito* forming the first movement of No. 3 in D, the teasing question and blustering answer of the subsidiary subject

(*Ex.* 113) testify to the composer's delightful sense of humour. The
Allegretto in rondo form, serving as the second and last movement of this

concerto, is of a particularly transparent texture, displaying at the same
time a very solid construction. The middle movement in c of No. 5, with
its sweetly melancholic melodies and gently running passages, is genuine
pianoforte music; the brief and effervescent last movement achieves
brilliance, in spite of its few technical difficulties. Such pieces, perfectly
suited as they are to the student who has not yet reached full mastery of
the instrument, pieces that sound more difficult than they really are, make
us understand Bach's tremendous vogue as a piano teacher.

Even the third set of six concertos published in 1777 as op. 13 (*T* 295-
296) is, basically, not very different from his op. 1, printed 14 years earlier.
The same harmonic-homophonic style prevails, and the keyboard instrument maintains the traditional role it had held since the days of Sebastian
Bach: at one moment it serves as a member of the orchestra, for which it
provides the filling continuo, at the next it is the glamorous soloist to
whom all others bow. The old proportion of one to two is maintained;
two of the six works are in three movements, the four others in two movements. Although the set is not dedicated to the Queen this time, it is
again inscribed to a lady, a Mrs. Pelham. Yet these compositions have
gained in breadth and depth of conception; they mark not only the conclusion but the climax of Bach's production in this field. It is noteworthy
that the use of oboes and horns 'ad libitum,' in addition to the previous
string trio, is suggested. The composer feels that a more powerful
orchestral body is desirable to give suitable expression to the more significant content of the concertos. Possibly the finest works of the set are the
two concertos in three movements. In No. 2 in D, the Andante serving
as a middle movement is not free from operatic elements. Some of the
passages sound as if they were meant for a coloratura soprano rather than
for a keyboard instrument; but the healthy melodic invention inspired by
folksongs cannot but captivate the listener. The same folkloristic elements
are also noticeable in the melodies of the rondo finale of this concerto; and
in No. 4 in B flat even a real Scottish tune makes its appearance. The last
movement introduces variations on the popular folksong 'The Yellow-
Haired Laddie.' When Haydn came to England he was so interested in

this concerto, which had quickly become a favourite with the English public, that he transcribed it in 1792 for piano alone.[1] The Viennese composer, who at that time started to arrange Scottish songs, seems to have used Christian's composition as a kind of model when he wrote his own variations on Scottish folksongs.[2]—John Bach's piano concertos op. 13, with their superb craftsmanship and charm, seem to be like musical counterparts to the delightful portraits of fashionable society ladies which were produced simultaneously by Gainsborough and Reynolds.

Of Christian's numerous *symphonies* more than forty were printed in his lifetime. Basically the works belong to three categories: the overtures originally written as introductions to operas, the symphonies meant for concert performances, and the *symphonies concertantes*, which combined elements of the concerto with those of the symphonies. Since overture and symphony were structurally alike, and both closely related to the *symphonie concertante*, it seems best to discuss all three types together.

In his symphonic output, as in all his works, John Bach combines features of Italian and of German music. He paid regard to both the Italian comic opera's loosely built overture in a single movement, and to the *opera seria's* more solidly constructed overture in 3 movements which contained, in embryonic form, all the elements of the future symphony. Of equal importance, however, were the Mannheim symphony, with its abrupt changes in emotional content and its striking orchestral effects, and the Vienna symphony, which combined features of Tartini's concerto form with those of the Italian overture, adding also folkloristic elements out of its own native soil.[3] Christian allowed himself to be influenced by each of these forms, alternately approaching one or the other more closely, without showing a definite preference. It is also significant of his artistic personality that no real stylistic evolution can be traced in his symphonies. His most mature works in this field, although far superior in quality to his youthful compositions, yet revert to them in some respects.

His first two symphonies, the overtures to the operas *Artaserse* and

[1] On the other hand, Christian made a piano arrangement of Haydn's Symphony No. 62 of 1777 in D, which was published by Sieber in Paris (*T* 352).

[2] Cf. Karl Geiringer, 'Haydn and the Folksong of the British Isles,' *MQ*, 1949.

[3] Cf. Fritz Tutenberg, 'Die Sinfonik Joh. Christian Bachs,' Wolfenbüttel, 1928.

Catone in Utica (*T* 272/3, 277/6) probably belong to the year 1761.[1] The formal aspect of these works, scored for 2 oboes, 2 horns and strings, is typical of the overture to the Neapolitan *opera seria*. A fast movement, with a slightly contrasting second subject, but lacking any real development, is followed by a simple Andante for strings only. The finale, approaching the rondo form, assumes the tempo, key and orchestration of the first movement. Bach's own style comes to the fore in the sweet and noble melodies of the Andantes with their carefully worked out accompanying parts, disclosing the thorough training Christian had received from Padre Martini. Of equal significance is the 'Andante grazioso' for strings and flutes, the second movement in the overture which Bach wrote in 1763 to Galuppi's *La Calamità de' Cuori* (*T* 272/2b). The attractive and unconventional harmonization gives this instrumental aria a subtle flavour pointing almost beyond the classical period (*Ex.* 114).

The 6 symphonies published in 1765 as op. 3 (*T* 262-63) were written for the concert hall, probably for the composer's own subscription series. While they reveal the typical aspects of the opera overture, and their use of wind instruments as filling and reinforcing voices in the tutti sections is a common feature of this form, the musical texture is on a somewhat higher level. Chromaticism colours the voices, greater care is given to musical phrasing, and features of German folklore occasionally appear in the melodies. The music critic of the *Hamburger Unterhaltungen* apparently referred to this mixture of different elements when, in 1766, he wrote of the symphonies: 'If the name of the composer were not expressly mentioned, one would think that he is an Italian. The first movements are fiery and good Italian pieces. However, certain episodes appear to us to be hurried and rugged.' Particularly attractive are Nos. 3 and 4 of the set. The former has as middle movement an Andantino of a delightfully archaic, sarabande-like character. The latter uses as third movement a Tempo di Minuetto in rondo form, a type of finale that was to become a favourite with Christian. No. 1 is significant for another reason. George

---

[1] The two operas were first performed in that year. Gerber's report in 'Lexicon der Tonkünstler,' Leipzig, 1790, I/34, that *Catone* was produced as early as 1758 in Milan, does not seem to be correct.

de St. Foix pointed out that Mozart's Symphony in D (K. 19), composed in 1765 in London, is completely fashioned after this work, and is in the same key.

There is a strong resemblance between Bach's thirteen symphonies op. 6, 8, and 9[1] (*T* 264-69/3). In fact, two of the symphonies of op. 6 were reprinted in op. 8. The exact years of composition or publication of these works are not known, but op. 6/1 exists in a manuscript dated 1764, while op. 6/6, for reasons to be discussed later, may be considered as a product of the years 1771 or 1772. The other symphonies of this group may well have originated in the intervening years. The general aspects of these works are still those of the earlier symphonies and overtures. The basis of the formal construction has not changed; unisons between the two violins are not infrequent, and repeatedly the use of a continuo instrument seems necessary to fill gaps between melody and bass. The inclusion of two separate viola parts in the symphony in D, op. 6/2, which provides an unusual timbre in the orchestration, may also be considered as a retrospective feature. On the other hand there is no lack of progressive trends either. Interesting development sections are now included in some of the movements (cf. op. 6/1), and more regard is paid to the potentialities of the wind instruments. In op. 9 a chorus of two oboes and two horns frequently alternates with the string quartet, an antiphonal technique which foreshadows the use of two orchestras in Bach's op. 18. At the same time the musical content has gained considerably in significance. Op. 6/3 belongs to the composer's best symphonies. The unruly and whimsical second subject of its delightful finale displays a rhythmical refinement but rarely to be found in works of the time (*Ex.* 115). Equally dashing and

Ex. 115

high-spirited is the bourrée-like last movement of op. 9/3, while the finale of op. 8/4, a Tempo di Minuetto, shows a healthy earthiness to which the nostalgic sweetness of the ensuing trio provides an effective contrast. Somewhat similar in character is the last movement of op. 9/2, a symphony which must have been very popular with 18th-century audiences, since numerous old prints and manuscripts of the work have survived. Its most attractive part is the middle movement, *Andante con sordini* in c, in which a tender and melancholy song by the muted first violins is

---

[1] Op. 9 was later republished as op. 21.

delicately accompanied by plucked strings. Here, in a manner which is
Christian Bach's very own, sensuous Rococo music is pervaded by a
feeling of sadness and nostalgia.

Quite different from the rest of the symphonies is op. 6/6 in g. It
clearly shows the influence of the 'Storm and Stress' movement which
affected the leading musicians of Germany and Austria in 1771 and 1772.
Both Haydn and Mozart, besides composers of lesser significance, were
struck by this 'romantic crisis' as Th. de Wyzewa termed it. Christian's
symphony displays an unrestrained emotionalism and passionate subjectivity well known to us from Haydn's 'Farewell' and 'La Passione'
symphonies. The first and last movements are stormy in character, with
harsh dissonances and sudden dynamic contrasts. In the *Andante più tosto
Adagio* serving as a middle movement, noble melodies are supported by
expressive harmonies. Significant is the Beethovenian crescendo at the
end, leading into a piano, and fading away in a mysterious pianissimo
(*Ex.* 116).

In approximately the same years during which op. 6, 8, and 9 were
created, Bach wrote three symphonies showing certain influences of the
suite and the concerto. In these works, which appear like late offspring of
the Baroque concerto grosso, the composer was more concerned with the
colouristic possibilities offered by the alternation of soli and tutti than
with a real display of technical brilliance. The contemporary publishers
emphasized the mixed character of these works by calling some of them
Concert ou Symphonie (*T* 284/3) or *Symphonie Concertante* (*T* 284/1 and
2). The rich possibilities provided by the combination of from two to
four solo instruments (two violins—oboe and 'cello—violin and 'cello—
violin, viola, oboe, and 'cello) greatly stimulated the composer's imagination, and some of the finest instrumental music he wrote at that time is
to be found among these concerted symphonies.

The *Symphonie Concertante* in A with violin and 'cello solo (*T* 284/2)
belongs to the very small number of symphonic works by Christian Bach
in two movements only. The initial *Andante di molto* combines features of
an introductory movement with those of a centrally placed one. The
sensuous grace and beauty of sound in this enchanting idyllic scene make

it a veritable gem among the composer's instrumental works, and it is not surprising that it had a particular appeal to Mozart (cf. the *Incarnatus* in the Mass in c). The second movement is a kind of gavotte in the rondo form so often used by the composer. Here Bach conjures a delicate Rococo pastel complete with shepherds and shepherdesses dancing shyly to the tune of a musette (*Ex.* 117).

Compared with this composition, the *Concert ou Symphonie* in E flat (*T* 284/3) is more symphonic in character and more closely knit. Here the initial Allegro, whose gentle sweetness seems to cover hidden fires, is the most striking movement. The rapturous Andante using an oboe obbligato instead of two solo violins employed in the other movements, intones a typical Italian tune of the time, somewhat reminiscent of Gluck's aria *Che farò senza Euridice*[1] in *Orfeo*. In the robust concluding Tempo di Minuetto the earthy spirit of Haydn's rustic dances may be found.

In the *Symphonie Concertante* in G (*T* 284/1) all the instruments of the orchestra are called upon in turns to serve as soloists and then again as ripienists. The technique is not quite unlike that found in Vivaldi's and Sebastian Bach's orchestral concertos. The scoring with its four violin[2] and two viola parts is rich and mellow, and the texture is loosened up through interesting imitations. The spirit of the work is gay, optimistic, and unsophisticated. Instead of the traditional rondo, a brisk menuetto in simple da capo form serves as a finale.

The climax of Bach's output in the symphonic field was reached with his opus 18 (*T* 269-71) published by William Forster in London shortly before the composer's death. It comprises opera overtures as well as concert symphonies probably composed between 1772 and 1777. Three numbers of the set (Nos. 2, 4, 6) are for ordinary orchestra; the remaining three for double orchestra. In the latter, the technique of the *symphonie*

---

[1] A melody similar to the above-mentioned Gluck aria also occurs in the introductory Adagio of Haydn's Symphony No. 11, composed in 1763. The Austrian composer wrote numerous works in the sixties related to Christian's *symphonies concertantes*.

[2] Not three violins, as the title and, following it, Terry, erroneously state.

concertante is resumed on a larger scale. The composer again reverts to the concerto grosso type, using two different groups of instruments—strings, oboes, bassoons, and horns in the first orchestra; merely strings and flutes in the second. These forces compete with each other, and the resulting colouristic possibilities concern Bach more than structural problems. In regard to the evolution of the classical symphony, these works do not offer any new contribution. The development of the thematic material is limited in scope, while in harmony and rhythm little progress is noticeable. The melodic invention, however, is superb; the beauty, warmth and sparkle of these broadly contoured tunes secure them a special place within the realm of preclassical music. The solidity of Padre Martini's training is still exercising its effect: in the first movement of No. 1, for instance, we find a striking combination of two ideas, the first orchestra intoning the energetic main subject, while the second simultaneously sings a caressing melody which forms part of the subsidiary theme (*Ex.* 118).

The spirit of the concerto is particularly evident in No. 3, the Overture to *Endimione*, in which the competing violins force each other to reach the highest registers. The viola, too, sheds its traditional stupor and contributes vigorously to the thematic elaboration. Even 'cello and bass are occasionally separated. In No. 5, striking contrasts may be observed in the use of the instrumental groups. In the first movement the strings are dominant and the wind instruments merely fill in, in the manner of the earlier symphonies; the last movement, however, presents a concerto-like interchange of ideas between flutes and oboes against the background of accompanying strings.

While these three works clearly belong to a side-line in the field of symphonic music, the remaining three come much closer to the average symphony of the time. No. 2, the overture to *Lucio Silla*, scored for full orchestra including clarinets (a remnant from the opera version) is one of the finest orchestral works Bach composed. The light, entrancing charm of the scintillating first movement is effectively contrasted by a solemn Andante which, in spite of its lofty character, shows traces of the composer's sensuous, mundane disposition. The rondo finale is irresistibly dashing, and the transparency of the 'broken work' employed serves to prove how closely Bach at times approached the classical style.

Not quite on the same high level are Nos. 4 and 6, which reveal the composer's brilliant wit rather than emotional intensity. No. 6, for once, is in four movements: Allegro–Andante–Allegretto–Allegro. It may be doubted whether the gavotte-like Allegretto originally formed part of the composition; yet it fits in well, as it increases the gay and carefree character of the work. Possibly the best movement is the finale with its formally concise construction and transparent orchestration. No. 4 has a particularly festive character, employing trumpets and timpani in addition to the usual instruments. Its attractive Andante was originally used in the overture to the opera *Temistocle* (1772). However, Bach eliminated the *clarinetti d'amore* from the concert version as these instruments were difficult to obtain in a symphony orchestra. In the first movement the rude *sforzando* answers to the teasing questions played piano by the violins (meas. 43-51) appear like an episode from an *opera buffa*. Yet, for all its effervescence, there is solidity of texture in this work, and details such as the spirited imitations in the finale reveal the hand of the master (*Ex.* 119).

To conclude this survey of Bach's instrumental works, it ought to be emphasized that there is always a fine balance between the means employed and the significance of the music. The works for bigger ensembles display the most genuine inspiration and are worked out with particular care. Thus Bach gives his best in the quintets, the largest among the chamber music works, and in the great orchestral compositions.

Christian's *church music*[1] consists almost exclusively of Latin compositions meant for the Catholic service. They belong to two completely

[1] The manuscripts are mainly preserved in the British Museum and in the Benedictine Monastery of Einsiedeln. The valuable autographs dated 1757-60 which were owned by the Staats- und Universitätsbibliothek Hamburg (MS. ND, VI, 540, vols. I-IV) were sent during the war to the Eastern part of Germany. According to a letter dated February 8, 1952, received from the Hamburg library, they were seized by the Russian authorities and their whereabouts is unknown.

different groups. Some of them are arrangements of numbers from Bach's operas and cantatas, often done in a more than superficial manner, and in all likelihood not by the composer himself. The poet J. J. W. Heinse apparently had such pieces in mind when he stated in his novel, 'Hildegard von Hohenthal' (1795-96), that John Bach wrote them 'while drinking champagne and burgundy . . . and without a spark of faith.' Of much greater significance are the original compositions written in Italy between 1757 and 1762. They comprise among others the following works: a *Dies Irae*, 2 *Gloria in excelsis*, 3 *Lezioni del offizio per gli morti*, 2 *Magnificat*, a *Miserere*, a *Salve Regina*, 2 *Tantum Ergo*, and 2 *Te Deum*. They are scored for solo voices with instruments or for full chorus and orchestra. If texts of a particular force or splendour are interpreted, as in the *Dies Irae, Magnificat*, or *Te Deum*, the composer employs a double chorus of 8 voices. The standard orchestra used in his church compositions consists of strings, oboes, horns and organ, while in compositions of a more brilliant nature trumpets replace the horns or are added to them.

Christian's technique of employing the different choruses of voices and instruments in an antiphonal manner points to Venetian and Roman models which had dominated Italian church music since the 17th century. The texture of his works is as solid as may be expected from a son of Sebastian who had studied with Italy's greatest teacher. Christian's simple harmonic language assumes an almost Baroque impetus through the

competent use of briskly moving parts (*Ex.* 120). At the same time the inclusion of arias and duets, the vocal brilliance expected of the soloists, and other operatic elements point to the strength of Neapolitan influences. Although the composer considered himself by no means an accomplished artist, and sent the works, accompanied by humble letters, to Padre Martini for correction, these church compositions were liked and even admired by his contemporaries. They helped Bach to obtain the coveted position of organist at the Milan Cathedral, and the *Te Deum* of 1758 (*T* 210/2) was described by C. F. D. Schubart as 'one of the most beautiful we have in Europe.'

In 1761 Bach at last reached the artistic goal that had induced him to leave Germany and to travel to Italy. His first *opera*, *Artaserse*, was performed at the Teatro Regio in Torino, and within a few months two more of his works for the stage, *Catone in Utica* and *Alessandro nell' Indie*, were given in one of Italy's foremost opera houses, the Teatro San Carlo in Naples. Obviously the young organist of the Milan Cathedral was attempting to follow in these compositions the style of his Neapolitan colleagues as closely as possible. Ensemble numbers are infrequently used; the arias are primarily meant to please the ear and abound in luxurious coloratura, while accompagnato recitatives presented against the background of a full orchestra are very rare. The only significant specimen of the kind in the third act of '*Catone*' is so extravagantly orchestrated that its instrumental garb seems to have been borrowed from a concerto or divertimento. On the other hand, the main exponents of the plot, the secco recitatives, accompanied by basses and harpsichord, are executed in the most perfunctory manner. Nevertheless the composer's human and environmental background is noticeable in these operas. As Hermann Abert, in a fine article on Christian's operas, pointed out: 'In the robust, unaffected sturdiness of his music, influences of the Thuringian Bachs survive.' A careful, always interesting orchestration reveals the German artist, while the noble tenderness of the melodies, which are often flavoured by chromatic passing notes, are remnants from Christian's period of romantic subjectivity. These features, combined with the buoyant and sanguinic style of the Neapolitan opera, produced a mixture the attraction of which young Mozart found hard to resist. The tenor aria from the third act of '*Alessandro*' (*T* 214-19), which he heard in London, was a favourite piece of the eight-year-old boy, and even as late as 1778 Mozart wrote to his father from Paris: 'As an exercise I set to music the aria *Non so d'onde viene*, which Bach had composed so beautifully; my reason was that I know Bach's piece so well, like it so much and have it always in my ears.' Christian himself was very much attached to this piece. He used it in London twice for 'pasticcios' (operatic works employing music by more than one composer), and many years later, possibly for Anton Raaf's Paris debut in 1778, he took it up again, this time giving it the smooth elegance of line characteristic of his mature works, while reducing its emotional intensity (*Ex.* 121).

Ex. 121

Altogether the operas written in Italy display a warmth of feeling and an almost romantic fervour—as revealed, for instance, in the entrancing duet in E, *Se mai turbo* from '*Alessandro*' (*T* 213/5)—such as only an ardent young artist can muster.

The number of works for the stage that Bach wrote during his period of maturity is comparatively small. In addition to his contributions to several pasticcios, he composed 5 operas performed in London, 2 written for Mannheim, and 1 for Paris, viz.:

> *Orione.* London, 1763.
> *Zanaida.* ,, 1763.
> *Adriano in Siria.* London, 1765.
> *Carattaco.* ,, 1767.
> *Temistocle.* Mannheim, 1772.
> *Lucio Silla.* ,, 1776.
> *La Clemenza di Scipione.* London, 1778.
> *Amadis des Gaules.* Paris, 1779.

Again, there is no basic difference between these and Bach's earlier works. They are all *opere serie*, clearly showing the limitations in the composer's gifts for dramatic expression. His attempts to portray heroic feeling or real tragedy seem hollow and artificial; violent emotions assume an almost bombastic character, while he is singularly successful in his endeavours to express delicate, sweet, sad, noble, and tender sentiments. Christian's mature operas reveal an advance in technical refinement, but romantic exuberance is not as strongly in evidence as in the earlier works.

The number of accompagnato recitatives gradually increases; they are particularly frequent in the operas of the seventies, *Lucio Silla* and '*Amadis*' providing the best examples. In the arias the element of contrast is stressed, which is so significant a feature of his instrumental music. The variety of forms employed in these solo numbers is very great. Christian uses not only different three-part but also rondo structures. The last operas in particular contain a very attractive type of rondo consisting of fast and slow sections that take up themes already used in the preceding recitative (cf. the aria *Nel partir* in *La Clemenza di Scipione*, *T* 230/17). In the works of the seventies, recitatives and arias are blended with great skill into effective scenes of a homogeneous structure. The composer frequently uses a concertizing flute, oboe, or bassoon in conjunction with a solo voice and thus creates, as his father did, a kind of duet between the singer and the instrumentalist. He writes completely idiomatic music for either; the flutist or oboist, who is even provided with the opportunity for inserting a cadenza into the introductory ritornel, finds his part as rewarding as the singer does. A decidedly progressive feature of John Bach's operas is the use of clarinets, which he introduced in 1763 (*Orione*). He employs them, for instance, to emphasize an other-worldly atmosphere (such as in the *ombra* scene of *Lucio Silla*, *T* 232/5), or even, in the romantic way, to express longing. In *Temistocle* of 1772 he goes one step further, prescribing *clarinetti d'amore*, whose tone, thanks to the pear-shaped bell, was free from harshness.

In the operas of the seventies, ensemble numbers and choruses gain more and more in importance. In the manner of the French opera, a kind of large form is achieved by the repetition of choruses alternating with solo numbers. Near the end of an act an uninterrupted sequence of accompagnatos, solos and ensembles, and a gradual increase in the number of performers, create a sort of opera finale. The predominantly lyric character of such forms reveals, however, that Christian is more concerned with musically rounding off the act than with building a dramatic climax (cf. the end of *Temistocle*, *T* 241).

In a work of the seventies we observe a close affinity to operatic compositions by outstanding German masters. *Lucio Silla*, written for Mannheim, uses a libretto composed two years earlier by Mozart. Possibly the traditional procedure was this time reversed, and Christian was somewhat influenced by his young friend. The love duet in the first act shows, as Abert pointed out, a certain resemblance in architecture to that in Mozart's opera. Bach's intimate knowledge of Gluck is apparent in the tragic strains of the first act. Although in 1770 he had not hesitated to spoil Gluck's masterwork, *Orfeo*, through the addition of seven numbers of his own, he later showed himself impressed by the operatic reformer's ideas. This attitude is most evident in Christian's French opera, *Amadis des Gaules*, especially so in the recitatives entrusted to the full chorus and in the powerful scene of Oriane deploring the death of Amadis (missing in *T* after 216/12), in which the composer for once approaches an expression of grandeur and pathos. '*Amadis*' shows the London Bach earnestly bent on pleasing a French audience. He employs a French libretto adapted from a text Lully had set to music in 1684. The arias are conceived on simple lines, using hardly any coloraturas. Moreover, the composer includes numerous ballets in his score and, dispensing altogether with secco recitatives, has the very large orchestra accompany the entire work. '*Amadis*' was performed seven times only, mainly on account of its insipid libretto which had been awkwardly cut down from Lully's five acts to three. Yet the work must have interested the Parisians, as the full score presently appeared in print, and the composer was invited to write another opera. But all such plans were thwarted by his premature death.

Looking at Bach's operatic output as a whole, we might find the key to its evaluation in a remark by Burney. After the lukewarm reception of the opera *Adriano in Siria* in London, the great historian remarked that its songs were 'found, as detached airs, excellent, though they had been unfortunate in their totality.'[1] It cannot be denied that Christian Bach's dramatic works suffer from the weakness inherent in his Neapolitan models. The individual numbers are not welded together by the dramatic spirit that transforms a sequence of musical pieces into a real opera. Thus, the only member of the Bach family to work consistently in the field of opera was unable to make a contribution of lasting value to the form. There is a remarkable resemblance between Christian's serious operas and those of his contemporary, Joseph Haydn. They both produced beautiful pieces of music, but no real drama.

It is significant that the London Bach was always willing to write individual scenes of a dramatic character for the concert performances of his friends. Ludwig Landshoff, who has greatly promoted our knowledge of Christian's music by presenting some of his most important compositions in modern editions, reprinted two such arias (*T* 250, 251/8) written for the castrato Tenducci. One of them, *Rinaldo ed Armida*, has a delightful oboe part destined for the famous oboist, Joh. Christian Fischer; the

---

[1] *l.c.*, IV, 487.

composition enjoyed a tremendous vogue during the 18th century and was even transcribed for glass harmonica.

John Bach's various cantatas, and his only oratorio *Gioas*, might also be considered as byproducts of his activity as an opera composer. They all use Italian words, and the libretti are similar to those of Neapolitan operas, though, in the case of the cantatas, on a much smaller scale. A good example is offered by *Cefalo e Procri, Cantata a tre voci*, composed in London, 1776 (not contained in *T*).[1] According to the testimony of the autograph, preserved in the Library of Congress in Washington, the part of Cefalo was written for the male soprano, Signore Savoi, who belonged to the busiest singers of Italian opera in London. Procri was meant for a woman soprano, Cecilia Grassi, Bach's wife, and the third character, Aurora, was composed for Signora Sales, a contralto. Cefalo and Aurora have one aria each, while the composer favoured his spouse with two. In the first, her voice is competing with a violino principale, treated so brilliantly that the ritornel before the entrance of the singer assumes the character of a violin concerto. The second aria has an obbligato bassoon, and the coarse, somewhat humorous tone of the bass instrument provides an admirable contrast to the light and sweet timbre of the soprano voice. There is also a rather superficially constructed instrumental introduction to the whole cantata, as well as a number of secco and accompagnato recitatives, which are at times thematically connected with the following aria; a terzetto of all three singers concludes the work. Christian Bach here gives us frothy and colourful music providing ample opportunity for the performers' fingers and larynx, music which the connoisseurs of London's concert hall must have enjoyed as exquisite titbits, only to forget them the next moment. Possibly the most remarkable piece of the score is the accompagnato recitative of Aurora in e. Here Bach displays all his gifts of orchestration to describe the spectacle of the sunrise. He uses the method of the 'steamroller,' with which he had probably become familiar in Mannheim: a motive is gradually carried upwards with a simultaneous increase in volume, while a pedal point bass serves as an immovable foundation. At first one violin enters, then a second; the flutes join in with playful tunes, the clarinets follow with a little wail, then comes the bassoon and finally the horns. The full orchestra is united in a mighty crescendo and at the climax of the forte the voice of Aurora comes in. Haydn may have had a chance to study Bach's score while he was in

[1] Only the recitative and aria of Aurora from this cantata are listed by *T* (247-48) in a manuscript of the British Museum and a contemporary print (transposed one whole tone up).

London. His own description of the sunrise in the 'Creation' and 'Seasons,' although far superior in expressive power, also makes use of a gradually rising melodic line combined with a crescendo effect.

It is characteristic that Bach's 'Serenata a quattro' *Endimione* (1774; *T* 248-49) and his only oratorio, *Gioas, Re di Giuda* (1770, *T* 226-27) are both based on texts by Metastasio, the greatest librettist of the Neapolitan opera. In spite of its numerous choruses, this oratorio is, as Terry aptly remarks, nothing but 'an unacted opera on a biblical subject.' Very little in this score points to the fact that it was written for an audience familiar with the works of Handel.

While Bach felt no need to adapt his style to that of the *genius loci*, his attitude was different with a number of small songs for voice and orchestra composed to English texts. For the popular outdoor evening concerts at Vauxhall he wrote most successful compositions, three sets of which, containing four songs each, were published in his life-time. Welsh, Irish, and Scottish folksongs were often heard in these recitals, and the numbers which Bach contributed show a curious blending of the music of the British Isles with Italian virtuosity (*Ex.* 122). The rollicking tunes

Ex. 122   *In this Shady Blest Retreat*

tell___ the love.ly charm.er near, tell the love.ly charm_____er, the love.ly charm.er near.

which Bach offered at the Vauxhall concerts (in particular 'Ah seek to know,' *T* 255/2) prove how thoroughly he enjoyed the atmosphere of this unique amusement-park. Like Joseph Haydn he succumbed to the delights of this garden, which Boswell described as 'a mixture of curious show, gay exhibition, music . . . not too refined for the general ear and, though last, not least, good eating and drinking.'

TWO PAINTERS AT MEININGEN
(GOTTLIEB FRIEDRICH AND JOHANN PHILIPP BACH)

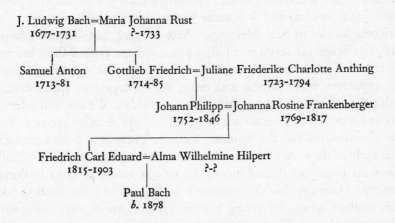

J. Ludwig Bach=Maria Johanna Rust
1677-1731   ?-1733

Samuel Anton   Gottlieb Friedrich=Juliane Friederike Charlotte Anthing
1713-81   1714-85   1723-1794

Johann Philipp=Johanna Rosine Frankenberger
1752-1846   1769-1817

Friedrich Carl Eduard=Alma Wilhelmine Hilpert
1815-1903   ?-?

Paul Bach
b. 1878

WHEN Ludwig Bach died in 1731 at Meiningen, neither of his two sons was able to succeed the father as court conductor. Both Samuel Anton (b. 1713) and Gottlieb Friedrich (b. 1714) were too young for so responsible a position; besides, although they were proficient organists, their interest was not centred in music. The elder went to Leipzig University, studying law simultaneously with his kinsman, Philipp Emanuel Bach, and enjoying the hospitality so unstintingly offered by Sebastian and Magdalena Bach. On his return to Meiningen in 1735, Samuel Anton was employed in various capacities in the court offices until he rose, in 1777, to the post of secretary, which he held up to his death in 1781. For some time he also acted as court organist. So did his brother, Gottlieb Friedrich, for whom musical work was again but a sideline. Gottlieb's main profession was that of painter, and as such he was, in 1745, officially appointed to the Meiningen court. Such dual interests had already been entertained by an uncle, Nikolaus Ephraim Bach (cf. p. 108), who instructed the court employees at Gandersheim in both painting and music. On the other hand, Gottlieb's maternal grandfather was the architect, Samuel Rust, who, together with J. Peter Rust (probably a brother), had played an important part in the erection of the castle of Elisabethenburg. The mixture of such strains from both sides produced a decided leaning towards the graphic

arts in Johann Ludwig Bach's second son, and it revealed itself also in
Samuel Anton, who painted miniatures too. On the other hand, Gottlieb
Friedrich did not quite disown the old Bach heritage; he was not only a
competent organist and pianist, but also tried his hand at composing.[1]

Gottlieb, who died in 1785, left three sons, two of whom were
Protestant ministers, while the youngest, Johann Philipp (b. 1752), became a highly successful painter. Philipp's portraits, especially his pastels,
won great acclaim, and it became the fashion for each member of the
princely houses of Saxe-Meiningen, Saxe-Coburg, Saxe-Hildburghausen,
etc., to engage his services. Philipp possessed the typical Bach industry;
he travelled from one little court to the other, producing likenesses of all
its important personalities, and once, while staying at Rudolstadt, he
painted no less than 23 portraits within 10 weeks. We are well informed
about his activities because for 50 years he kept detailed accounts of all
his commissions and the resulting income. These neat books remind us
definitely of the very business-like manner in which his godfather, Philipp
Emanuel Bach, handled all money matters. It would be quite in keeping
with the Hamburg Bach's character if he had urged his godson to adopt
this method when the young painter visited him in 1773 and painted
Emanuel's picture. The constant flow of orders did not make Philipp Bach
a wealthy man, as he charged very modest fees, but it kept him very happy
and active and was apparently just what he needed, for the painter lived
to the age of 94, generally admired as the oldest citizen of Meiningen.
Besides his painting, he still found time to hold the position of court
organist and to play an active part in the local rifle association. When he
had been its member for 60 years, the whole city joined in celebrations,
and a Meiningen newspaper published this verse in his praise:[2]

> Happy is indeed the artist
> When he paints the fairest, smartest,
> Sweetest women by his skill;
> Draws the soul behind their features,
> Making thus the lovely creatures
> Smarter, fairer, sweeter still.

On that day Philipp was driven in state through the town, accompanied
by a music band and the members of his club resplendent in uniform;

---

[1] Cf. Pusch, 'Meiningen und die Meininger Bach'schen Nebenlinien.' Thüringer
Fähnlein, 1935, and 'Neue Beiträge zur Geschichte des deutsches Altertums,' 19. Lief.
Meininger Pastellgemälde von E. Doebner und W. Simons, Meiningen, 1904. See also
Conrad Freyse, 'Unbekannte Jugendbildnisse Friedemann und Emanuel Bachs,' in
'Wissenschaftliche Bachtagung,' Leipzig, 1950.

[2] 'Meininger Volksblatt,' 1835, No. 33, p. 141. English version by Henry S. Drinker.

young girls lined the streets through which he passed, throwing flowers at his feet, and cannon shots were fired before the festive dinner in his honour started.

Philipp's robust vigour was handed on to the following generations. At the age of 63 he had a son, Friedrich Carl Eduard, a ducal forester, who reached the age of 88 and, again at the age of 63, produced a son. The latter, Paul Bach (b. 1878), a fine musician and gifted painter,[1] is still living at Eisenach, and owns an exquisite little gallery of paintings by his grandfather and great-grandfather. His daughter, Annemarie, has inherited the artistic talent so strong in this branch of the family.

THE WORKS OF GOTTLIEB FRIEDRICH AND JOHANN PHILIPP BACH

Of the two great painters produced by the Meiningen branch of the family, the elder, Gottlieb Friedrich, shows in his work the main trends of Rococo art. As compared to the stately and pompous Baroque, it appears as lighter and more intimate. In painting, this new conception often brought about a reduction in physical size. The monumental and imposing canvases and frescoes which we have come to associate with dynastic pretensions gave way to smaller and daintier renderings. The ultimate result of this process of diminution was the miniature, a form of art in which Gottlieb Friedrich produced some of his finest works. These miniatures were done in pastel rather than in the traditional oil medium, a change which again reflects Rococo tendencies towards airiness and charm. The employment of this unstable, powderlike medium must be considered as a symptom of the new mode of thinking, the artist's reaction to the demands of his time.

Gottlieb Friedrich, who was primarily a portrait painter, seems to have looked up in particular to the French artist, Quentin de la Tour, whose example he followed with considerable fidelity. Like him, the Meiningen artist observed his subjects closely, earnestly bent upon rendering an honest, true likeness; he frequently produced remarkable characterizations that are not devoid of decorative quality. Like de la Tour, the German painter was adept at employing subtle colour and light effects resulting in a pleasing and accomplished, if somewhat ephemeral art.

[1] The present author owns four delightful, tiny oil paintings of the Bach house which Mr. Paul Bach made for him. (See Ill. XII.)

However, Gottlieb Friedrich was not satisfied merely to take over the Rococo formula from his French model; he was anxious to adapt the international style to his own native background. He seems at his best in those portraits in which he relinquishes the fashionable playfulness in favour of deeper penetration, a refusal to flatter, and a good measure of merciless realism. An excellent example is offered by the triple portrait of the Duchess Philippina Elisabeth Caesar of Saxe-Meiningen, her daughter, and a lady-in-waiting, painted in 1759 and preserved in the Meiningen city hall. The haughty sulkiness of the three women is depicted with pitiless objectivity. They look stiff, unapproachable, and somewhat uncomfortable in their pompous attire, reproduced with scrupulous care by the painter. It might be considered as a proof of the artist's subtle sense of humour that there seems to be a certain resemblance between the august lady and the undersized pug dog at her feet. The pastel of the Meiningen kitchen clerk Weissenborn shows a man with a narrow head, pinched mouth, and anxious mien scraping away on a 'cello. A scarf round the neck and a cap seem to be intended to protect him from any breath of fresh air, and the curiously flat technique employed in the little painting contributes to create the likeness of a rather humdrum philistine.

Gottlieb Friedrich displayed his art to best advantage in the miniatures he painted of himself and the members of his family. The self-portrait (Ill. XX) shows a man immaculately dressed according to the fashion of his time, with a sensitive face and tired, rather disillusioned eyes. It is a noble and delicate painting of a wise, though not particularly energetic man, who may have been not too happy in his role as son of a great father and father of an outstanding son.

As Gottlieb was only 17 years old when Johann Ludwig died, the fine pastel which the son painted of his father may have been created in later years from memory, or from earlier portraits. This miniature (Ill. X) formed part of Philipp Emanuel's extensive pictorial collection and later became the property of the Berlin Library. It shows a handsome gentleman with large dark eyes, sensuous mouth, and the fleshy chin of the Bachs. The highly intelligent face is that of a person who enjoys the luxuries of life; looking at him we can well understand Johann Ludwig's artistic leanings towards Italian music.

One of the finest and most significant portraits by Gottlieb Friedrich is that of his kinsman, Johann Sebastian (Frontisp.). It is to be assumed that this is the picture to which Emanuel referred in a letter of 1775 addressed to Forkel as 'a beautiful original pastel, a good likeness.' According to a tradition well established in the Meiningen branch of the Bach family,

xx. Gottlieb Friedrich Bach. Self-portrait. Pastel

xxi. Johann Philipp Bach. Self-portrait. Pastel

Gottlieb Friedrich Bach, during a visit to Leipzig, made this portrait of his eminent cousin and presented it to Sebastian, from whom Emanuel inherited it. Subsequently it was exchanged by the owner, who possessed the large Haussmann painting of his father, against the pastel of Johann Ludwig Bach; and thus it came about that Sebastian's portrait was returned to the artist, in whose family it has remained up to the present day.[1] Like other pastels by Gottlieb Friedrich Bach, this portrait is not signed. However, its small size, the predominant use of the painter's favourite colour, a brilliant cobalt blue, and in particular the realistic conception of the picture, are distinctive characteristics of Friedrich's art. The beautiful courtier's redingote Sebastian is wearing contrasts with the sober garments depicted in the Haussmann portraits, and might supply a clue to the time when the pastel was done. Sebastian received the title of Court Composer to the Elector of Saxony on November 28, 1736, and it seems likely that the pastel was painted in celebration of this important event, the new Electoral court composer being shown in his official attire. If Gottlieb Friedrich had no other claims to fame, this highly expressive likeness of the Thomas Cantor which greatly enriches our extremely meagre stock of authentic Bach pictures would be sufficient to establish the painter among the significant portraitists of the time.

Johann Philipp, Gottlieb's son, lived much longer and was far more successful than his father. He was born in 1752, one year after Handel wrote his oratorio *Jephtha*; when he died 94 years later, Wagner was already engaged in composing his *Lohengrin*. We know of numerous drawings and oil paintings as well as nearly a thousand pastels which the artist produced. Among them are more than a hundred portraits of members of princely houses, and even one of a Meiningen Princess who later became Queen of England.

As a young man Johann Philipp assisted his father. The works he produced at that time are very similar to those of Gottlieb, and it is not surprising that the two pastels he made in 1773 of his godfather Emanuel Bach were for a long time considered as works of the older painter. The very realistic reproduction of the composer's heavy features, the painter's trick of using a dark background for the lighted side of the head and a light background for the shadowed part of the face, the loving care with

[1] Cf. Karl Geiringer, 'The Lost Portrait of J. S. Bach,' Oxford University Press, New York, 1950.

2 F

which the material of Emanuel's suit is painted: all these features might equally well point to the father's authorship as to that of his young son. It is only from an entry Emanuel made in the Genealogy he sent to Forkel that we know who the real author of the pastel is. Emanuel wrote: 'Both father and son are excellent portrait painters. The latter visited me last summer and painted my portrait, catching the likeness extremely well.' Apparently the young artist gave one copy to Emanuel, while he kept the second one for himself.[1]

Gradually Philipp's paintings began to differ from those of his father. The first sign of emancipation may be found in the silver-grey hue he gave to some of his portraits. His amazing technical virtuosity is revealed in the portrait of a Freiin von Stein, where he succeeded in painting the sheen of the skin and of a pearl-necklace as they appear through the gauze draped around the lady's neck.

Before long he created portraits that clearly indicate the influence of English painters; we find the same swift brushstrokes, the same mannered elegance and aristocratic pretentiousness which was developed by Gainsborough and Reynolds. Finally, in the painter's maturity, we observe a distinct turn towards a classical mode of expression. Philipp assumed a simplified and more severe idiom, supplanting the rhythmical animation of his earlier works by a wider use of the straight line, and reducing the vivid colours of the past in favour of an enforced restraint. At the same time he managed, better even than his father, to reveal the character of the person he portrayed. A good example of this mature style is offered by his self-portrait (Ill. XXI). Here all is understatement. The posture of the simple and unaffected man soberly looking at us is rather stiff and awkward. The artist scrupulously avoids any romantic self-glorification and goes out of his way to achieve complete truthfulness. The painting on which he is working in the self-portrait is a likeness of his second wife, Johanna Rosine (b. 1769). This pastel is also preserved and it shows a light, gay, and affectionate treatment quite different from the pedantic and somewhat formalistic attitude the painter assumed in the former work. In portraying his spouse Philipp does not restrain his emotions, and he succeeds in producing a character-study of a sweet, warm-hearted, and motherly woman. In spite of ceaselessly devoting himself to portraiture, Philipp did not succumb to the danger of establishing a monotonous routine; he found a fresh approach to every new task, which proves the greatness of his artistic personality.

[1] The former became the property of the Berlin Library, while the latter remained in the family of the painter and belongs to-day to Mr. Paul Bach. (Cf. Ill. XXII.)

BACHS AT EISENACH
(JOHANN ERNST AND JOHANN GEORG BACH)

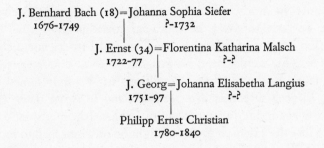

J. Bernhard Bach (18)=Johanna Sophia Siefer
1676-1749 | ?-1732

J. Ernst (34)=Florentina Katharina Malsch
1722-77 | ?-?

J. Georg=Johanna Elisabetha Langius
1751-97 | ?-?

Philipp Ernst Christian
1780-1840

THE tradition started in 1665 was continued through the 18th century, and again one of the Bachs was sitting on the organist's bench of the *Georgenkirche* in Eisenach. The great Johann Christoph (13) had been succeeded by a cousin, Johann Bernhard (18), and when the latter died in 1749 the position fell to Bernhard's eldest son, *Johann Ernst* (34), born in 1722. The young organist, who had been trained by his father and by his kinsman, Sebastian Bach (cf. p. 200), was highly qualified, not only for musical work. He had also studied law at the University of Leipzig, and although he probably did not finish the course, having been forced to return to Eisenach at the age of 19, he was anxious to put his legal training, too, to the best possible use. Duke Friedrich III of Gotha, who at that time ruled Eisenach, granted him permission to establish himself as a barrister for the so-called 'lower court,' but Ernst was not satisfied with this solution, claiming that most clients preferred to engage the services of a 'court counsel' (*Hofadvokat*), who had admission to all the courts. He made applications to the Duke in 1749 and 1750, in which he forcefully explained that the rank of 'Court Counsel' was granted to other, newly appointed barristers, while 'his humble self was more and more incurring bad credit, scorn and oblivion.' The Duke, however, was not persuaded and rejected Ernst's plea with the remark that the 'position of Court Counsel was not well compatible with the functions of an organist.' Various reasons may have been responsible for this decision, such as the difference in social status between the two positions, Ernst's very brief University training, and, on the other hand, the young man's decided

451

artistic gifts, which made the neglect of his musical duties for those of a barrister not at all desirable. Thus Ernst had to accustom himself to the idea that his ambitions in the field of law practice would not be fulfilled in Eisenach. Henceforth he abandoned work as a lawyer, giving all his energy to musical activities. The result became apparent before long. In Weimar a young prince, Ernst August Constantin, was growing up; by the time he was of age he would rule Weimar and Eisenach.[1] Constantin was interested in music, which he studied with Sebastian Bach's pupil, J. Kaspar Vogler. Moreover, he was aware that his wife-to-be, Princess Anna Amalia, a niece of Friedrich 'the Great' of Prussia, and a composer in her own right, would insist on first-rate musical performances at her court. Thus a reform of musical conditions in Weimar seemed imperative. The Prince's attention had been directed to Ernst Bach when the latter dedicated to him, in 1749, a set of Fables charmingly set to music, and he felt that the Eisenach organist might be the right man to reorganize the music at Weimar. Ernst was requested to work out plans for an enlarged and improved court orchestra which was not, however, to entail an expenditure higher than 2500 thalers. As a precautionary measure the renowned court conductor of Gotha, Georg Benda,[2] was asked for his opinion also. Benda flatly declared that the establishment of a good orchestra on such a budget was out of the question. But Ernst Bach, with the typical thriftiness of the Bachs, found a solution and offered a budget of 2410 thalers. Being familiar with the qualifications of all the musicians in Weimar, he suggested how each could best be employed; and in his plan he included the regular participation of court trumpeters, and various lackeys and officials for whom no additional salary would have to be paid. His plan was accepted, and when Prince Constantin took over the government one of his first acts was to sign, on February 3, 1756, a decree appointing Ernst Bach Princely Saxon Court Conductor—a position to which his teacher and kinsman, Sebastian Bach, had vainly aspired forty years earlier. Ernst received a salary of 400 thalers, as he had budgeted it in his own plan, and he was allowed to retain his position as Eisenach's town organist, being expected to provide a substitute whenever he was absent from the city. A very busy time followed, for, according to Ernst's remark in an application, 'there was always something new to compose for His as well as for Her Grace.' Moreover, he was expected to provide

---

[1] The principality of Eisenach had, owing to the lack of a male successor, been united in 1741 with Weimar.

[2] Georg Benda was, for several years, a colleague of Emanuel Bach at the court of Friedrich 'the Great.'

musical entertainment twice every day, and very often a third time for special academies. Yet Ernst found time to attend to the needs of his subordinates, and in lengthy petitions he attempted to secure small additions to their regular fee for special services, such as, for instance, a bottle of wine to a player employed at dances.

This strenuous, though rewarding, work lasted for two years only. In 1758 Prince Constantin died suddenly, and his widow, at the age of 19, was left with two infant sons, for whom she took over the government. Ambitious musical schemes had to be dropped, as it was Princess Amalia's main concern to rule with the greatest possible economy, in order to hand over a financially stable Principality to her elder son when he came of age. Thus the Weimar orchestra ceased to exist. To express her esteem for Ernst Bach, however, the Princess allowed him to retain his title and paid him a pension for the rest of his life.

Ernst mourned his patron deeply and wrote a fine cantata for his funeral service. Henceforth he concentrated on his work in Eisenach, where in 1765 he was appointed *Kastenverwalter*, a kind of book-keeper to the church, receiving a third income from this source. As some of his compositions also appeared in print, his financial position was a satisfactory one, and Emanuel had reason to remark in the Genealogy that Ernst 'was working very happily and quietly as an organist in Eisenach.'

The private life of the composer seems to have developed on traditional Bach lines. In 1750 he married the daughter of a pastor and had 8 children, among them 7 sons. While most of them showed no inclination for the family's traditional profession, he had the joy of seeing the eldest, *Johann Georg* (b. 1751), follow in his footsteps, studying both music and law, with the reasonable hope of succeeding him. This indeed happened on Ernst's death in 1777, and Georg held the post for twenty years.[1] All the ambitions which Ernst had entertained were fulfilled in this son, who was appointed Court Counsel and eventually also Imperial Notary, yet retained his father's office of organist and *Kastenverwalter*. When he applied in 1793 for the vacant post of Chamberlain in the Eisenach Council, the authorities granted his request because he was 'a highly experienced, active and honest man'; but they suggested that, as a member of a Noble Council, it would be advisable for him to resign his post of town organist. Georg, proud of his family's distinguished service in this field through more than a hundred years, did not like to see anybody but

[1] This refutes Emanuel Bach's remark in the Genealogy that 'Ernst's sons were presumably unmusical.' Cf. H. Kühn, 'Vier Organisten Eisenachs aus Bachischem Geschlecht,' in 'Bach in Thüringen,' Berlin, 1950.

a Bach hold this position. He suggested therefore that he be allowed to retain the work and provide a substitute, whenever necessary, until his son, Philipp Ernst Christian, then aged 13, who showed 'an extraordinary leaning toward music,' would be ready to become organist. This plan was adopted; but as Georg died in 1797, when his son was not yet 17, the position fell to an older, more experienced man, and the name of Bach disappeared from the musical annals of Eisenach.[1]

We do not know whether there was any creative talent in the last of the four Bach organists of Eisenach. There is no doubt, however, that Georg's father, Johann Ernst, possessed such gifts to a very great extent and was highly thought of by his contemporaries. In 1758 he was invited to write a preface to an important work of musical theory, Adlung's *Anleitung zu der musikalischen Gelahrtheit*; and when a collection of contemporary clavier sonatas was published in Nuremberg soon afterwards, Ernst and his kinsman, Emanuel Bach, were the only composers represented by two works, while so well known an artist as Georg Benda had to be satisfied with the inclusion of a single piece. On the other hand, a church superintendent, by the name of Christian Köhler, in a preface to an *Eisenacher Gesangbuch* ('Book of church hymns') he published in 1776, mentioned that 'Conductor Bach had been granted by God a particular gift for church music,' and that one expected from him 'with longing, a delicate, moving, and expressive music for the whole church year, which would displace the shouting, noise and roaring in our temples.' This wish could not be fulfilled, however, as Ernst Bach died one year later, at the age of 55.

THE MUSIC OF JOHANN ERNST BACH

The number of his compositions known to-day is unfortunately rather small. It seems that he wrote by no means as many works as his kinsmen in Hamburg and London, and even this modest output was apparently not preserved in its entirety. Nevertheless two significant facts emerge from an analysis of the compositions which are still available. Johann Ernst was one of the most talented men of the younger generation of Bachs, and he belonged to the first artists who attempted to distinguish between secular and sacred music, using a different approach to each of

---

[1] Georg's son became an *Oberamtskopist* (a kind of city clerk), while one of his daughters married Deacon Johann Wilhelm Victor Kühn, from whom Hermann Kühn, author of the above-mentioned study, was descended.

them. In his sacred compositions Ernst started out as a follower of his great teacher, Sebastian Bach. During the late thirties and forties of the 18th century he was under the spell of the Thomas Cantor's artistic personality. The works of the fifties and early sixties show a somewhat different character. While keeping up the artistic traditions of the Baroque period, they make increasing use of the new idiom of *Empfindsamkeit*. Henceforth he followed in his cantatas and in his oratorios the lead of Karl Heinrich Graun, who was a master of sacred music, expert in the field of contrapuntal art, but at the same time a champion of the new 'language of the heart.' Quite different was the Eisenach composer's approach to secular music. Here he adopted a progressive form of the *style galant*, light, graceful and entertaining in character, worked out with solid craftsmanship, and imbued with a warmth of feeling which reveals his familiarity with the idiom of sensibility.

No trace can be found of the 'many symphonies' which, according to Gerber, Ernst Bach wrote for the princely court. All the instrumental compositions that survived are either for a keyboard instrument or for clavier and violin.

The chorale prelude *Valet will ich Dir geben* and the fantasia and fugue in d with its numerous references to 'manual' and 'pedal' are obviously meant for the organ. The two fantasias and fugues in F[1] and a are primarily conceived for the organ, but may also be performed on a stringed keyboard instrument. On the other hand, the sonatas in F and G which were published around 1760 in Nuremberg in the fifth part of Ulrich Haffner's *Œuvres mêlées*, as well as the sonata in A, are written for the harpsichord.

Ernst's *fantasias* reveal the inner bond between the Baroque toccata style and the expressive language of the age of sensibility. These preludes, with their broken chords and runs, their frequent changes of rhythm and tempo, their succession of recitative and arioso sections, point back to similar pieces by Sebastian Bach and the Viennese masters, Fux and Froberger, but there is also an undeniable kinship with the imaginative idiom of Emanuel Bach. The four-part *fugue* in d is not equal in significance to the high-spirited fantasia that precedes it. Its heavy and somewhat monotonous ricercar theme and the absence of modulations seem to indicate that Ernst wrote the work in his student years. The fine three-part fugue in F of 1770 is on a completely different level. Its smooth harmonic language, enriched by colourful chromaticism, and the well-

---

[1] The Fantasia and Fugue in F was published by Emanuel Bach in 1770 in his *Musikalisches Vielerley*.

planned succession of keys contribute towards creating a movement that
is bound to hold the listener's attention, in spite of the fact that the contrapuntal elaboration is not very impressive.

The texture in the *sonatas for the clavier* is completely homophonic,
and they explore the possibilities of the keyboard instrument with great
skill. A certain stylistic prolixity (the Sonata in G is in four movements)
points to the composer's lack of experience, and an occasional passage of
an improvisatory character, to the admiration he felt for the work of his
cousin, Emanuel. The compositions are light and gay in character, and in
their melodic language clearly influenced by Italian models; at the same
time the superficiality so often to be found in contemporary clavier music
is successfully avoided. Rhythmic diversity, a characteristic feature of
Ernst Bach's music, distinguishes the sonatas, and the composer endeavours to develop the different ideas thoroughly. The *Minuetto con
Variazioni* of the Sonata in G so successfully avoids the purely ornamental
variations of the time that, from a technical point of view, the composition
almost seems to have been written two decades too late—or too early.

The *sonatas for clavier and violin* appear like a sequel to the harpsichord sonatas. The first three were published by Griessbach in Eisenach
in 1770 and reprinted in 1780. A second set of three appeared in 1772.
They all display the three movements, fast-slow-fast, of the Italian *sinfonia*, and, in accordance with Emanuel's tendencies towards stronger
unification, the second movement often ends with a half cadence leading
straight into the finale. These sonatas are altogether briefer and more
condensed, avoiding the youthful diffuseness of earlier works. The title-
page no longer bears the standard reference to the 'accompaniment' of the
violin. Keyboard and stringed instrument begin to emerge as equal
partners; mere doubling in unison of the right hand of the clavier by the
violin is hardly ever to be found; and violin and clavier often indulge
in spirited dialogues (*Ex.* 123). Ernst endeavours to write idiomatic music

for either partner, as the long-held violin notes which accompany
brisk figurations of the keyboard instrument testify. His clavier was prob-

XXII. C. P. E. Bach. Pastel by Johann Philipp Bach, 1773

ably the harpsichord, but cantabile sections in the slow movements, and an occasional use of Alberti basses, betray the interest he took in the possibilities of the new pianoforte with its more flexible tone. These pieces present merry, often humorous music, full of life and ingenuity, avoiding the shallow gaiety which so often mars the products of the *style galant*. Between Sebastian Bach and Mozart few violin sonatas of equal significance were written.

The great success of these works was denied to another composition by Ernst Bach, which to-day is considered one of his main achievements. In 1749 Ulrich Haffner published the 'first part' of *Sammlung auserlesener Fabeln* ('Anthology of selected fables') by the Eisenach composer. The second part that was apparently to follow these eighteen songs never appeared in print. To make up for this omission the Nuremberg firm printed at a later date Ernst's two clavier sonatas.[1]

It proves the sound artistic judgment of Ulrich Haffner that he was willing to publish this work by a young and unknown composer. But it is not altogether surprising that the musical public was less enthusiastic in its reaction to the composition. The cool reception was probably due not to the fact that Ernst's songs were partly conceived along instrumental lines, that the rhythm of the music often did not conform to that of the text, and that awkward coloraturas as well as big skips were in evidence; all this was by no means unusual in the German lied of the time. It seems far more likely that the almost revolutionary character which Ernst's Fables showed in some respects was responsible for their lack of success. Instead of using the fashionable poems of the time, endowed with French grace and wit, Ernst Bach chose the more substantial and solid fables of Gellert and his followers, which had not yet won real acclaim. In setting them to music, he imbued them with genuine warmth and vitality. He attempted to depict nature in a manner which had been explored before in Handel's oratorios, but was almost unknown in the German lied. The

singing of a nightingale, the hooting of an owl, or the buzzing of bees (*Ex.* 124) were described through voice or keyboard instrument, and

[1] In 1910 Hermann Kretzschmar presented the Fables with a comprehensive preface in vol. 42 of *DDT*.

under the composer's hands the stilted and pedantic texts were transformed into genre paintings sparkling with life and humour. A further breach with tradition was accomplished through Ernst's habit of altering his composition should the same tune not be appropriate to all the verses of a poem. If he felt, after a few strophes, that the original melody no longer did justice to the changing mood of the text, he produced a second, and possibly later, a third and a fourth setting, revising voice part and accompaniment, key, rhythm and tempo as far as necessary. This procedure greatly added to the variety of the Fables and foreshadowed the musical ballad of a later period which did away with the strophic form. The most noteworthy innovation in the Fables concerned the treatment of the figured bass. If the problems connected with the realization of the continuo seemed too difficult, the composer provided the right hand of the clavier part too, thus creating accompaniments which, in 1749, appeared rather modern. On the whole, the Fables constitute an important milestone in the evolution of the Rococo song, which had been shaped by such composers as Telemann and Valentin Görner. Whatever the response of the general public, the princely patron to whom the Fables were dedicated appreciated their merits; it was mainly on the strength of this bold creative venture that the composer was awarded the post of Weimar court conductor.

A fine cantata celebrating the birthday of Duke Friedrich III of Gotha was probably written during the early fifties. Here, for once, a secular work in its recitatives, arias and choruses, resembles Ernst's church music, and the composer may have used it, with a slightly changed text, also as a piece of sacred music. It should be noticed that in the extensive first number the different stanzas of the chorus are interrupted by recitatives; thus a rondo-like form is constructed such as Gluck liked to use in his operas.

In the interesting preface which Ernst wrote in 1758 to Adlung's *Anleitung zu der musikalischen Gelahrtheit*, the composer expressed his concern over the decline of church music in his time. Undoubtedly he himself did his best to stop a further deterioration of the form, and Spitta is right in considering Ernst as one of the foremost German composers of sacred music in the generation following Johann Sebastian.

Only a handful of his vocal compositions for the church were preserved and, with a single exception, they all remained in manuscript. There is a short Mass, consisting of *Kyrie* and *Gloria* only, a German *Magnificat, Meine Seele erhebet den Herren* ('My soul doth magnify the Lord'), several cantatas, among them the funeral cantata for Duke Ernst

August Constantin written in 1758, and the *Passionsoratorium* of 1764.[1] In these compositions conservative and progressive elements are united in a significant whole. The chorale is the lifeblood of Ernst's church music, as it was for his great kinsman. It is true that his harmonizations of the hymn tunes display the simplicity of a later period and are lacking in the expressive strength of Sebastian's chorales. But Ernst never forgot the rich potentialities of the chorale cantata and its related forms, with which he had become intimately acquainted during his stay in Leipzig. His *Kyrie and Gloria* in D may have been fashioned after Sebastian's short Mass in the key of F. The Thomas Cantor used as a *cantus firmus* the German chorale *Christe du Lamm Gottes* (cf. p. 239), while the Eisenach composer based his work on the hymn, *Es woll uns Gott gnädig sein* ('God have mercy on us'). Strangely enough, the Mass of the younger composer is stricter and more retrospective in character than Sebastian's work. It has the character of a motet, dispensing with all instruments except those needed for the realization of the figured bass. Each verse of the hymn is presented in long notes by one of the four voices and surrounded by little fugatos, a technique used in Pachelbel's organ chorales. The *Kyrie* is based on the first half of the melody, the *Gloria* on the second. This powerful and joyous work may be considered as one of Ernst's first larger compositions for the church, and it was probably written during, or soon after, his apprenticeship in Leipzig.[2]

In the composer's *Magnificat* the procedure is reversed. Its text is in German, but the tune of a Latin *Magnificat* is employed as a *cantus firmus*. Short fugatos presented by soprano, alto, tenor, and bass voices are introduced in the first number, while a second bass adds, in long notes, the individual lines of the Virgin's song of praise. Once more Ernst Bach demonstrates his admiration for Pachelbel's technique, although he assumes a more progressive attitude by keeping the themes of the fugatos independent of that of the *cantus firmus*.

Particularly important is the use of the chorale in Ernst's cantatas. It is played by instruments alone, or used in versions for chorus and independent orchestra; it appears in antiphonal combinations with solo voices, in recitatives, in arias, or in plain harmonization. There is hardly a single form employed by the Thomas Cantor in his chorale cantatas of the Leipzig period which was overlooked by his pupil. In *Mein Odem ist schwach* ('My breath is corrupt'), for instance, Ernst creates a kind of rondo

---

[1] It was reprinted in vol. 48 of *DDT*.

[2] Ernst's copies of 12 of Sebastian's keyboard arrangements of various concertos probably belong to this period too.

form through the alternations of numbers based on the hymn tune with others that are freely invented. At first a solo bass and the chorus, presenting the harmonized chorale, perform one of these deeply moving dialogues well known to us from the cantatas of young Sebastian. After a passionate da capo aria by the soprano, the chorale appears once more in simple harmonization. A vigorous fugue of the four voices leads to the third entrance of the hymn tune, in which soprano and bassoon in octaves present the *cantus firmus* to the accompaniment of woodwind and plucked basses; while a second fugue on the impressive subject (*Ex.* 125) con-

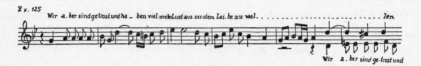

cludes the work. As this number ends with a half-close on the dominant of the main key, it seems likely that, at the service, a verse of the hymn was still attached.

In other respects too the composer's works for the church reveal the influence of his great teacher. Ernst's *Passionsoratorium* reminds us of Sebastian's St. Matthew Passion when, at the words of Christ, the dry recitative is transformed into an arioso in which strings add solemn beauty to the utterances of the Lord. And all through the Eisenach composer's sacred music the same fervent longing for death finds expression which represents so characteristic a trait in the work of his kinsman.

Ernst revives a feature of the Baroque period in another small detail. His setting of Psalm vi, *Ach Herr, straf mich nicht in deinem Zorn* ('O Lord, rebuke me not in Thine anger') begins, like the works of previous generations, with the reiterated first short exclamations: *Ach, ach; Herr, Herr, Herr, Herr.* All through the first movement the exclamation *Herr, Herr!* is repeated, providing the invocation with an excited, almost feverish urgency.

Fugues are frequent in Ernst's church music. They start with impressive, broadly contoured themes, but before long they fall, as Hermann Kretzschmar shrewdly remarks,[1] into 'a comfortable homophony, occasionally spiced with suspensions; and when approaching the climax, they resort to motivic repetition, to sequences, grand pauses and other dramatic devices.' In such pieces the Janus nature of Ernst's art is parti-

[1] *DDT* 42/XIII.

cularly noticeable: his attempt to keep up with tradition, and yet to write compositions which fully belong to the time in which they were created.

Most of Ernst Bach's sacred cantatas clearly display the ardent subjectivism characteristic of the period of *Empfindsamkeit*. In his German *Magnificat* for instance, more than half the numbers are in the minor mode, and a dark and impassioned mood seems to prevail. The Canticle of the Virgin, with its jubilant praise of the Lord, does not offer any clue to this attitude, nor would it seem justified to attribute it to any tragic experiences the composer underwent while writing the *Magnificat*. In general, 18th-century compositions may not be regarded as 'confession-music' of the kind the 19th century produced. Ernst Bach had discovered the vast field of musical expression in darker hues and felt tempted to use them even in this composition.

Syncopations are almost a trademark with this composer, imbuing his church music with a feeling of restless excitement and impatience. Chromaticism plays a big part in his melodic language and progressions like those in *Ex.* 126 from the cantata *Mein Odem* are very frequent in his

music. Ernst is fond of bold modulations as well as of sudden changes of tonality. The first arioso in the *Passionsoratorium*, for instance, begins in c, turns with the help of enharmonic changes to f sharp (*Ex.* 127), proceeding

through g and d to the concluding key of F. In other movements too the concluding key is often different from that used at the beginning. The composer takes special care clearly to indicate the tempo he requests, and in the cantata *Kein Stündlein geht dahin* ('No hour passes') he even prescribes the desired mood in a chorus with the word 'freudig' ('joyfully'), a German translation of the conventional Italian 'Allegro.' Ernst's dynamic range shows the greatest variety, and in certain pieces changes between *f*, *p* and *pp* occur almost from measure to measure. The expressive character of the church music is increased through the almost inexhaustible colouristic variety it offers. In the cantata, *Der Herr ist nahe* ('The Lord is nigh'), which served as funeral music for Duke Ernst Constantin,[1] the first chorus is scored for flutes, strings *con sordini*, and plucked basses. With its strange rhythm of 3/8 it assumes the weird character of a medieval dance of death. The following da capo aria in Adagio tempo has an unusual tenderness, with two solo violins accompanying the soprano voice besides the traditional string orchestra. In a chorus near the end of the *Passionsoratorium* the full orchestra of flutes, oboes, horns and muted strings is used piano and pianissimo in an unusual and exciting manner to prepare the listener for the supreme tragedy of the Lord's passing. On the other hand, the oboes and horns add brilliance to the powerful chorus No. 5, with the following fugue, in the cantata *Herzlich lieb hab ich dich* ('Dearly do I love thee'). The cantata *Die Liebe Gottes ist ausgegossen* ('The love of God is shed abroad') begins with a 'Concerto,' in which a richly ornamented obbligato organ part competes with horns and strings. Eventually the chorus enters, but the instruments pursue their cheerful game in brisk figuration, describing the unending flow of God's love throughout the world. Even in the ensuing da capo aria for soprano the part of the 'organo concertato' is carried on. Sebastian Bach had already written cantatas with an organ obbligato part, but Ernst's composition is closer in technique and spirit to younger works such as Joseph Haydn's 'Organ solo Mass' of 1766.

The succession of the individual numbers in the Eisenach composer's church music is both imaginative and unconventional. In a manner which he may have copied from Italian models, secco and accompagnato recitatives are freely mixed, and he achieves most poetical effects by letting ariosos or arias merge into choral numbers. In the cantata, *Kein Stündlein geht dahin*, the text of which uses several quotations from the Bible also employed later by Brahms in his 'Requiem,' the contralto, for instance, sings of pain, anguish and torment, while the chorus answers with the words of Isaiah, 'As one whom his mother comforteth, so will I comfort you.' Later, a single voice cries out to Jesus to help him in his hour of need and death, whereupon a choral fugue replies: 'And the ransomed

---

[1] Eitner, 'Quellenlexikon,' assumes that the cantata *Kein Stündlein geht dahin* was written for the Duke's funeral service. However, the MS. score (p. 403) of the Marburg (formerly Berlin) Library indicates on the title-page of the cantata, *Der Herr ist nahe*, in the hand of a 19th-century writer: 'aus der Trauermusik auf Herzog Ernst Constantin' (from the funeral music for Duke Ernst Constantin).

of the Lord shall return, and come to Zion with songs and everlasting joy upon their heads: they shall obtain joy and gladness, and sorrow and sighing shall flee away' (*Ex.* 128). In the German *Magnificat,* the Eisenach

composer employs the alternation of solo voice and chorus in a manner that points most significantly into the future. The last movement uses four soloists in turns with the tutti of all the singers. Here the chorus is confronted by the solo quartet in the same manner as that which was later so successfully employed by Mozart, and especially by Haydn.

There has been a certain tendency to stress the contributions of pre-classical composers to the instrumental field. It is hardly less important to establish the links which connect the Baroque and the classical idiom in the realm of vocal music. The compositions of Johann Ernst Bach will have to be remembered in this connection.

SEBASTIAN'S CHILDREN AND THE BACH FAMILY

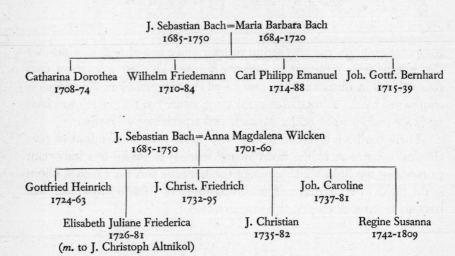

J. Sebastian Bach=Maria Barbara Bach
1685-1750 · 1684-1720

Catharina Dorothea 1708-74 · Wilhelm Friedemann 1710-84 · Carl Philipp Emanuel 1714-88 · Joh. Gottf. Bernhard 1715-39

J. Sebastian Bach=Anna Magdalena Wilcken
1685-1750 · 1701-60

Gottfried Heinrich 1724-63 · J. Christ. Friedrich 1732-95 · Joh. Caroline 1737-81

Elisabeth Juliane Friederica 1726-81 (*m.* to J. Christoph Altnikol) · J. Christian 1735-82 · Regine Susanna 1742-1809

TO obtain the proper perspective, we must once more return to the year 1750. After Sebastian's death his widow, aged 49, declared her firm intention not to marry again. We can well understand that after living for 29 years with Sebastian Bach and unceasingly giving him of her devotion and loyalty, she felt emotionally unable to adapt herself to another husband. Anna Magdalena made this decision although she must from the outset have been aware of her insecure financial position. Thanks to rigid economy, Sebastian had been able to leave an estate which was not inconsiderable according to the standards then prevailing for a church musician, but there were nine children who each claimed part of the property, and as no will had been left, one-third was allocated to the widow, while the other two-thirds were evenly divided among the progeny. Before the official evaluation and allocation by the curators was undertaken, the two eldest sons took possession of that part of their father's music, books, and pictures which seemed useful to them, and the youngest, Christian, retained—against some opposition from his brothers —three claviers his father had given him. The property to be divided was valued, after the deduction of some debts, at 1007 thalers, and of it the widow received a mining share, some bonds from debtors, who may

XXIII. Wilhelm Friedrich Ernst Bach. Oil-painting

I. S. BACH.

XXIV. The painter J. S. Bach II, son of C. P. E. and grandson of Johann
Sebastian Bach

never have paid off, and various valuable instruments, silver and jewelry, with a view to selling them. All the male members of the family moved away. Half-witted Gottfried went to Naumburg with his brother-in-law, J. C. Altnikol, while young Christian was taken by Friedemann to Emanuel, who had offered to give him a home and further musical training. Four female Bachs remained in Leipzig: the widow, her unmarried stepdaughter, Catharina, aged 42, and her two young daughters, Caroline, aged 13, and Susanna, aged 8. To provide for them proved anything but easy. The Leipzig authorities allowed Magdalena the traditional half-year's salary, but as they deducted an excess payment her husband had received 28 years before, she was only paid twice 21 th. 21 gr., plus 11 th. 12 gr. for candles, and a certain amount of grain. The apartment in the school had to be vacated by February 1751, and a desperate struggle began to make ends meet; every saleable object had to be disposed of. Magdalena managed, for instance, to sell what music of Sebastian's was still in her hands to the Council, which paid her for it 40 th. 'in view of her impoverished state.' Eventually all her resources were exhausted and she had to subsist on the town's charity. When she passed away in 1760 at the age of 59, worn out from worries, the Thomas Cantor's widow was as an 'alms-woman' given the lowest-class funeral.

Nobody can help feeling shocked by the fate of Sebastian's beloved wife. The strict economy to which they had always adhered and the good business sense that Bach possessed had been of no avail. Magdalena, who had given up her own career and through many years of married life ceaselessly toiled on behalf of her big family, did not have means enough for even the most modest existence; and the sons, who owed her so much, did not intervene to save her from the ignominy of depending on the charity of the very same city officials against whom her husband, the Royal Polish and Electoral Saxon Court composer, had stood up with so much spirit. And this happened while three Bach sons were holding adequate positions, and a fourth was beginning to win success in Italy. Her own son, Friedrich, was particularly praised in a Necrologue for 'his goodness of heart and uprightness of principles'; yet he let his mother suffer like that.

To understand this perplexing behaviour of Sebastian's sons, we should bear in mind the geographic dislocation of the family, which was effecting a loosening of the old blood-ties. The Bachs of preceding generations had lived in Thuringia close to each other. Travelling from Erfurt to Arnstadt or Eisenach was not difficult, and if money was lacking, one could even walk from one Bach centre to the other. Thus there was continuous intercourse between the kinsmen. Messages were transmitted through visiting friends or colleagues, and in this way the Bachs were well aware of what was happening to their relatives and could intervene when necessity arose. Ambrosius Bach, for instance, felt compelled (in spite of his modest income) to have his mother-in-law and his half-witted sister stay with him. In Weimar Sebastian had a sister of his wife's as well as two nephews in his home. They may have been more hospitable and more family-minded than the later generation; but above all they were in close contact with their kinsfolk.

For Sebastian's children conditions had greatly changed. There were considerable distances between Halle, Bückeburg, Berlin, and Leipzig, not to speak of Milan. The sons certainly had no opportunity to visit Magdalena and her daughters, as pleasure trips were a luxury they could not afford; on the other hand it is doubtful whether the women in Leipzig attempted to carry on a correspondence with them. Thus the men were not aware of the difficulties their relatives had to face, and, engrossed in their own problems, they did not give much thought to their womenfolk in Leipzig. Soon after Sebastian's death Friedemann, at the age of 41, started matrimonial life; young Friedrich had to establish himself in his new position; and Emanuel felt he was doing his share by providing for Christian. When the war broke out in 1756, Leipzig became enemy territory to residents in Bückeburg, Halle, and Berlin, and communication with it very difficult. It seems unlikely that Magdalena could have reached Sebastian's sons with an appeal for help, and it would have been difficult for them to send her money had they wished to do so. Thus various circumstances combined to make poor Magdalena's last years very tragic ones.

What happened to her daughters afterwards is not known. We learn from Emanuel's letters to his publisher, Immanuel Breitkopf, that he regularly sent money to his sister, Elisabeth Altnikol, a widow since 1759, and it is possible that these payments were also meant for Catharina, Caroline, and Susanna Bach. The other brothers may have helped too, but no records to this effect have been found as yet. The darkness surrounding the fate of Sebastian's daughters is only dispelled in 1800. By that time all of the Thomas Cantor's children had died, except the youngest, Susanna, then 58 years old and apparently ailing and unable to work. Friedrich Rochlitz, editor of Breitkopf's *Allgemeine Musikalische Zeitung*, found out about her desperate situation and published the following appeal, interesting as the first public reference to the Bach family:[1] 'Hardly did I

---

[1] Forkel's Biography, which included all the information on the family he had received from Emanuel, was published two years later.

ever seize my pen as gladly as now; for never before was I as firmly convinced of doing something useful. The Bach family which for two centuries has given to Germany (and not to her alone) masters and masterworks—the family from which descended Sebastian Bach, greatest harmonist of our century . . . ; Emanuel Bach, following his father in teaching and composition, a master whose pupil in many important respects every really fine pianist admits himself to be (as Mozart did); Friedemann, renouncing everything, equipped and blessed with nothing but a towering imagination, finding his whole life in the depths of his art; Christian who cultivated the flowers of gracefulness and *galanterie* in the classic soil—this family is extinct except for one daughter of the great Sebastian. And this daughter is starving! Very few know it, for she cannot —and she must not—beg for alms. . . . If everyone who learned from the Bachs gave just a trifle, how carefree would the good woman's last years be!' At first the response to Rochlitz's plea was not too good. Sixteen people sent contributions amounting to 96 thalers. For Susanna Bach this was, however, a sizeable amount, and she expressed deeply-felt thanks to the donors. When Beethoven read her acknowledgment in the magazine, he was shocked by the small returns, and in his circle of friends a new collection was started by the piano-builder, Andreas Streicher, which yielded 256 thalers. Henceforth Sebastian's youngest daughter enjoyed a modest security, until she closed her eyes in 1809.

Between Sebastian's sons the contact was not a very close one either, owing to differences in temperament as well as in age. Friedemann seems to have kept very much to himself. While they were all still at home, he was generally considered as the most promising of Sebastian's sons, and even later Emanuel declared that his elder brother was best qualified to carry on the tradition established by their father. On the other hand, Emanuel certainly had more success in life, and he therefore felt obliged to help Friedemann financially. Eventually he became discouraged, however, by Friedemann's inability to solve his own problems and his tendency to drift, traits which a man of Emanuel's practical sense and purposefulness could not comprehend. The elder brother on the other hand did not find Emanuel's music substantial enough, and condescendingly spoke of these works as 'nice little things.' As to his half-brothers, there is no evidence that Friedemann maintained contact with them. Christian's success must have filled him with contempt, and he may have resented the fact that shortly before he failed to secure the organist's position in Braunschweig, Christian's opera *Catone in Utica* had given such pleasure there that the Duke had rewarded the composer with a pension for life. The remark regarding Christian which Friedemann ascribed to Sebastian rather reflects his own attitude. In a conversation with Cramer he claimed that his father had paraphrased a line from a well-known Gellert fable, saying: 'For Christl I am not afraid, he will succeed through his stupidity.'[1] We don't know how he felt about Friedrich Bach, his other half-brother, but may assume that he found him less offensive, if not very interesting. Emanuel had a very different attitude. He kept up a regular correspondence with Friedrich, had the Bückeburg conductor contribute to his *Musikalisches Vielerley*, and performed Friedrich's cantata *Ino*. They exchanged their compositions and tried to help one another by collecting subscribers for each other's publications. In one respect Emanuel envied his half-brother. In the Genealogy of the Bach Family which he sent to Forkel, he inserted this note about Friedrich: 'has a musical wife and children who are musical'; we can read between the lines Emanuel's sadness not to have been as fortunate himself. Regarding Christian, his former pupil, Emanuel's feelings were rather mixed. In the Genealogy he jotted down this remark for Forkel: 'Is now in England in the service of the Queen—*inter nos* he has acted differently from our honest Veit.' The difference between him and their ancestor, the miller, Veit Bach (cf. p. 7), was twofold: Christian had risen to a high social status, a rise which filled the worldly Emanuel with pride; yet he resented the fact that Christian, unlike Veit, had not stoutly adhered to Protestantism and even suffered for it, but had become a Catholic when reasons of expediency demanded it. In artistic matters also the 21 years that separated the two brothers made themselves keenly felt (while they made very little difference in Emanuel's relation with Friedrich, who was only 3 years older than Christian). A conversation between Emanuel and the poet, Mathias Claudius, reported in a letter to Gerstenberg,[2] shows this very clearly. Claudius, when asked about music in Copenhagen, said: 'Schobert and your brother [Christian] are the favourites; *you* don't please them particularly,' whereupon Emanuel remarked: 'There is nothing behind my brother's compositions. They leave the heart empty.' We don't know Christian's attitude to his former teacher. The remark attributed to him: 'my brother lives to compose, while I compose to live,' if authentic at all,

---

[1] Gellert's poem was published in 1748. Sebastian could therefore have made this remark only in the two years preceding his death. At that time Friedemann was in Halle and it is doubtful whether he had a chance to visit his father. The present author is inclined to place into the same category Sebastian's alleged remark about Emanuel's music, that—like Prussian blue—it would soon fade.

[2] Cf. Bernhard Engelke, 'Gerstenberg und die Musik seiner Zeit,' in Zschr. d. Ges. f. Schlewswig Holstein. Geschichte, 1927.

may have been made mainly for the sake of the *bon mot*. At all events, in his own treatise on the fortepiano Christian showed what a lasting impression he had received from the 'Essay' written during his stay with Emanuel in Berlin. The Bückeburg brother's artistic personality was not sharply enough outlined to provoke friction. Like Emanuel, Christian got on well with him. One of the highlights of modest Friedrich's existence was the visit he paid to his famous London brother in 1778. Christian showed himself very hospitable and he had his nephew, Wilhelm, stay with him to be trained as a piano virtuoso.

The divergences in the brothers' relationships clearly reflect very different individualities. Comparing Sebastian's sons of his first with those of his second marriage, we see how great an influence was exercised by the mothers. In Friedemann and Emanuel the Bach heritage was much more in evidence than in Friedrich and Christian. We may even go so far as to see in a culmination of certain family traits one of the reasons for Friedemann's tragic existence. Stubbornness, lack of tact, and a tendency to choose the hard instead of the easy way characterize the majority of the Bachs. Friedemann may have inherited this disposition not only from his father, but also from his mother. We are unfortunately without any information about Barbara Bach's nature, but we know how unhappy was the life of her uncle, the great Johann Christoph (13), because of these very 'Bachian' traits. In Friedemann the double heritage appeared in over-size proportions as an inability to gauge other people's reactions and an ever increasing unwillingness to be conciliatory in minor matters, such as teaching or performing to important personages who could greatly have helped him.

In Emanuel these family traits are much less noticeable. 'Bachian,' however, are his inability sufficiently to flatter the Prussian King, and his independent spirit which made him prefer bourgeois Hamburg with its mediocre performances to the glitter of the etiquette-bound Prussian court. To his mother's line he probably owed a certain serene acceptance of life as it is and a sense of humour, traits found in his maternal great-grandfather, Heinrich.

Of Barbara's ill-fated third son, Gottfried Bernhard (47), we do not know enough to obtain a clear picture. Yet the antagonism of his superiors, together with the young man's inability to make ends meet, which forced him into debt, sound like an echo of what happened to his maternal great-uncle, Johann Christoph (13).

Sebastian's second wife, like his first, had three sons who survived infancy. Again one of them (curiously enough also bearing the name of

Gottfried), in spite of musical talent, was not destined to be successful. Gottfried Heinrich, the first-born, was feeble-minded, as his great-aunt, Dorothea, a sister of Ambrosius Bach, had been. As to the two others, they certainly were of a much more pliable disposition than Barbara Bach's offspring. Friedrich managed to retain the same position through his whole professional life—a period of 45 years—serving under three different personalities, with all of whom he maintained harmonious relations, in this respect reminding us of Joseph Haydn, born in the same year. His brother Christian, as a youth, gave up most of the tenets held by the family. He left his fatherland, was converted to the Catholic faith, and was the first of the Bachs to win fame on the operatic stage. Yet even in this mundane darling of London society Sebastian's heritage was at work, revealing itself in Christian's prodigious industry and in his endeavours to give warmth and substance to frothy Rococo music. In later years he too developed a certain stubbornness, for, not unlike his father, he clung for almost 20 years to the same form of music, closing his eyes to the victorious rise of new trends.

Thus in one way or another Bach family traits are noticeable in each of Sebastian's sons, although they are far more pronounced in the children from his first marriage.

TWO GRANDSONS OF SEBASTIAN
(JOHANN SEBASTIAN II AND WILHELM FRIEDRICH ERNST BACH)

WHEN, on September 26, 1748, the third child of Emanuel Bach was christened, no less than six aristocrats acted as godfathers or godmothers. There were two margraves, Friedrich Heinrich,[1] and Carl von Brandenburg-Schwedt; two ministers of state, Count Keyserlingk and von Happe; the widow of a General von Meyer, as well as her daughter, wife of Emanuel's friend, Friedrich Wilhelm von Printzen (cf. p. 342). This illustrious array of godparents proves Emanuel Bach's high prestige in Berlin; it reveals, moreover, the great hopes Emanuel entertained for this his second son. To promote the child's worldly success, the father secured the patronage of high-born lovers of music; to lead him in the right direction, he had him christened Johann Sebastian, although none of the godfathers bore the latter name. As Emanuel explained at one time to Rochlitz,[2] it was his ambition to 'transmit through this son to the world all that he had learned from his great father and what he had subsequently discovered himself.' To be entrusted with a mission of such magnitude proved no small burden for the youth, and Emanuel's son responded in typical Bach fashion: he rebelled. He did not attempt to become another Sebastian, and in order to proclaim his attitude to the world he discarded the name of his grandfather, substituting 'Samuel' for 'Sebastian' in his signature. Although his interests were dominated by the Muses, he did not feel drawn to composition, but showed instead a passion for drawing and painting. This, he decided, was to be his profession. Emanuel was shocked and distressed and tried every conceivable method to bring Hans, as he liked to call the boy, to his senses. It was of no avail. Though as a rule the gentlest of persons, the youth could be as stubborn as his grandfather, and nothing would shake his determination to become a painter. At last, at the age of 22, he was allowed to go to Leipzig to work with Friedrich Oeser,

---

[1] Margrave Friedrich Heinrich was the nephew of the recipient of Sebastian's 'Brandenburg Concertos.' Emanuel remained in contact with his son's godfather even after he left Berlin. In 1780 the composer dedicated to Margrave Friedrich Heinrich his second collection of *Sonaten für Kenner und Liebhaber*.

[2] Cf. Allgemeine Musikal. Zeitung, II, p. 829.

director of the Academy, who had expressed to Emanuel a very favourable verdict of the young man's talent. In Leipzig several aunts of Hans were still living, but none of them was comfortably enough off to offer the art-student a home. He therefore boarded with the engraver Stock, a young, highly skilled craftsman, who had two years earlier taught young Goethe how to cut in wood and copper. Hans Bach naturally received similar instruction, and as Stock's modest rooms were located in the attic of the 'Silver Bear,' a dwelling that also housed J. Gottlob Immanuel Breitkopf and his distinguished music publishing firm, the arrangement suited Emanuel very well. He had for some time co-operated very pleasantly with the publisher, whom he respected highly; now he could entrust him with paying out his son's quarterly allowance—amounting to 50 thalers—and ask him to keep an eye on the young artist. At that time the portrait of the painter may have been created which shows a delicate and dreamy youth entirely absorbed in the book he is reading (Ill. XXIV). (The way he strains his eyes and holds the book rather close to them seems to indicate the affliction from which his grandfather also suffered.) While at Leipzig Hans fell seriously ill (a further resemblance to Goethe's life in this city) and was nursed with loving care by the Breitkopfs, who became his good friends. A correspondence was conducted between them after Hans had moved to Dresden for further studies, and it is significant that the painter asked to have Breitkopf's lists of novelties mailed to him regularly. Apparently he was not as uninterested in music as he pretended. But his heart was in painting and his greatest desire was to visit the Mecca of artists, Italy. His father apparently did not raise objections. He had by now accepted the inevitable and wanted his Hans to enjoy the very best training an artist could receive. Thus the painter was enabled to travel to Rome, where, except for one visit to Hamburg, he stayed for several years. It was a glorious time, overflowing with artistic stimulation and warmed by the friendship of fellow artists, who fell under the spell of this 'calm, pure soul, this man of rare nobility' (Rochlitz). Among them was the painter, J. Friedrich Reifenstein, who, several years later, was to accompany Goethe on sight-seeing expeditions. It was Reifenstein who 'acted like a father'[1] when Hans was again attacked by grave illness. This time, however, all the friend's efforts were in vain, and on September 11, 1778, a few days before his 30th birthday, Johann 'Samuel' breathed his last.

Nineteen years later a Hamburg writer by the name of Dr. F. J.

---

[1] Letter of Emanuel to Oeser, dated August 11, 1777.

Lorenz Meyer, who had been with him in Rome, inserted a paragraph on the painter into his book *Darstellungen aus Italien*, which reveals how deeply the artist had impressed those who knew him. 'He died,' wrote Meyer, 'from a disease neglected by himself and wrongly treated by the ignorant Roman medicos. His friends lamented an eminent and spirited artist as well as one of the finest of men, and they spoke with admiration of his calm steadfastness when confronted with death in its most painful form.[1] Well enough known are his merits as an accomplished landscape-painter, the high flight of his poetic mind in his own composition, the happy closeness and verity in his imitations of nature, the vigour and decisiveness in elaboration, and his exquisite taste, especially in the combination and drawing of groups of trees.'

The work of the young artist reflects the period of peaceful co-existence of Rococo and Classicism, before the latter achieved undisputed domination. Samuel's 'Ideal Landscape' in the Hamburg Museum illustrates this double allegiance. For in it a Roman aqueduct and a Corinthian temple acknowledge the archaeological derivation of Winckelmann's age, while leisurely and graceful personages lose themselves in the caressing foliage of a cultivated park, much as Watteau's characters had done in the early days of Rococo (Ill. XXV). At the same time, the 'Ideal Landscape' bears witness to a third element which was destined to come to full fruition in the 19th century. A romantic presentiment breathes from the trees surrounding a lonely pond, beckons to us from the isolated height of the temple structure, and is expressed in a total mood pregnant with sentimental implications. Similarly Hans' drawing of a mill (in the Vienna Albertina) shows a decrepit building, with broken walls and holes in the roof, against a wild and desolate landscape and a strangely lighted sky revealing nature on the verge of a storm—a highly emotional composition full of dramatic, even realistic accents (Ill. XXVI).

It is frequently maintained that Classicism, however propagated by Winckelmann and Goethe, is truly comprehended only by the Latin race, whereas the mystic largeness and the sentimental content of Romanticism are grasped most readily by the Germans. If this be so, Johann Sebastian Bach II surely serves as a case in point; for, like his contemporaries, the German Oeser and the Swiss Gessner, he was able to imbue his work with the subtle plastic gradation, the rich colouristic and tonal quality, and above all with the obvious emotional implications

---

[1] Emanuel, too, in a letter dated June 20, 1877, to Breitkopf, emphasizes the 'terribly painful' nature of Hans' disease, from which he had been suffering for 5 months. This agony was to continue for more than a year, until Hans was released by death.

through which Romanticism reveals nature as a repository of human sentiment.

Among the Thomas Cantor's sons the 'Bückeburg Bach' showed the least ambition. He was the only one to keep the same position throughout his life, and he seems to have been but little tempted by the fascination of life in a great musical centre. These character-traits occur even more strongly in his eldest son, *Wilhelm Friedrich Ernst*, born in 1759. Artistically Wilhelm may have been well qualified for the career of a concert-pianist, but he lacked the showmanship necessary to achieve real success.

As the eldest son in a family of which both father and mother were professional musicians, he was as a matter of course trained for similar work. When his father felt that he had taught the son everything within his power, he took him in 1778 to London, where uncle Christian could give Wilhelm's style the last polish and start him on a professional career. For three years the youth stayed in London, and at that time, stimulated by the British capital's teeming musical life and especially by his uncle's brilliant art, he may have come as near to virtuosity as his nature would allow. At the same time he must have gained teaching experience by helping his uncle and aunt with their students. But on New Year's Day 1782, Christian was tragically felled by illness and disillusionment. The creditors seized all his possessions, his home was broken up, his widow moved to Italy, and there was no way for Wilhelm to stay on in London. After attending the auction of all his uncle's belongings and buying with his meagre savings a portrait bust of Christian, Wilhelm started on his way home, travelling through France and Holland and supporting himself as a pianist and organist. This kind of life did not suit him, however, and when the opportunity presented itself, he settled down as music director in the Westphalian town of Minden, near his native Bückeburg. Maybe his father had been instrumental in securing the position; anyway it is significant that in Friedrich Bach's series *Musikalische Nebenstunden*, consisting principally of his own works, a song by a titled lady from Minden is included. But Wilhelm was not to remain at Minden for long. Chance would have it that in 1786 Friedrich Wilhelm II, successor to Friedrich 'the Great,' paid a visit to this town. A cantata by the music director was performed in honour of this event, and the monarch was most favourably impressed by the work. The name of Bach was of course well known to him, and as recently as 1780 Emanuel had established a connection by dedicating four symphonies to Friedrich Wilhelm, who was at that time still Crown Prince. Now that the King had met the younger Bach, he felt inclined to engage him for Berlin. On July 11, 1789, Friedrich Bach could report to his publisher-friend, Breitkopf: 'My son is now in Berlin and is doing quite nicely. He entertains hopes of being admitted to the King's band. So far he has received from the Queen a monthly salary of 40 th. for teaching.' The Queen, whom he served as conductor and teacher, was Elisabeth Christine, widow of Friedrich 'the Great'; when she died in 1797 Wilhelm Bach took over a similar office with young Queen Luise, wife of Prussia's new ruler, Friedrich Wilhelm III (who succeeded his father in the same year, 1797), serving also as an instructor to the royal children.

Wilhelm Bach must have found life in the Prussian capital very different from that in provincial Minden. Music played a great role there, for King Friedrich Wilhelm was intensely interested in it, and was an excellent 'cellist himself. In the very year Wilhelm Bach was appointed, Mozart paid a visit to Berlin in order to attend performances of his opera *Die Entführung aus dem Serail*, and he expressed his admiration for the Prussian King by dedicating to the monarch his last 3 quartets. Seven years later Beethoven was received there with great enthusiasm and held the Berlin music lovers spellbound with his fantasies on the pianoforte. Most likely the royal music teacher, Wilhelm Bach, was able to hear the young genius. One of the Princes, the highly gifted Louis Ferdinand, became very friendly with Beethoven, who paid him this compliment: 'Louis Ferdinand played not royally nor princely, but like a genuinely fine pianist.' If the Prince, like the other royal children, received instruction from Wilhelm Bach, the teacher will have been pleased by the verdict, while feeling at the same time rather shocked at Beethoven's unconventional way of expressing himself. Wilhelm, reared at the Bückeburg court, where the word of the Count was law to everybody, could never have uttered any remark of this kind to his royal pupils. Yet in his modest and unassuming way he obtained good results. After one of the princesses, Friederike Charlotte Ulrike, was married to the Duke of York, Haydn had occasion to make music with her and he praised her playing on the piano and her singing. Another pupil, Prince Heinrich, became so attached to his music master that on moving to Rome he arranged that a yearly pension of 300 thalers should henceforth be paid to Wilhelm Bach. This enabled the musician to retire from court work when his royal mistress died in 1810. Teaching, combined with composing (which, however, rarely led to publication), seems to have fully satisfied him. No reports of any public appearance have been preserved and it may well be that the tremendous impression made on him by Beethoven's playing had discouraged Bach once and for all from ventures in this field. He was a shy person, and, except for membership in a masonic lodge, he did not take part in the social and intellectual life of the capital as his uncle had done. That even as a young man he would have preferred a life like his father's is revealed by the application for Friedrich's former position which he sent to Bückeburg on November 21, 1795, after the death of his father's immediate successor. He was too late, however; for the duties had already been conferred on concert-master Wagny. The ruling Countess regretfully explained this, adding a remuneration for the composition he had sent her, and remarking that she would never have assumed he was willing to 'exchange his pleasant and favourable situation in Berlin for the less lucrative one at Bückeburg.'

Where matrimony was concerned, Wilhelm did not imitate his father's example. He was 39 when he married in 1798; and his partner, the daughter of a hairdresser, was 19. Their happiness did not last long. After giving birth to two daughters, the young wife died of scarlet fever, before she was 21 years old. The widower had to provide for the two infant girls, and so nine months later he married again, choosing this time a woman of 28 who was to remain his faithful companion through his long life. The Bach couple seems to have led a rather secluded but comfortable existence with little to worry them. Both enjoyed excellent health. Wilhelm, deviating in this respect from most of his kinsmen, was 86 when he died,[1] and his wife even reached the age of 88. Two years before his death Wilhelm was granted a very wonderful experience. He was the only member of the Bach musicians who was privileged to witness the rediscovery of Sebastian Bach, leading to the solemn inauguration of the Leipzig monument on April 23, 1843. Robert Schumann reported this memorable event in his *Neue Zeitschrift für Musik* with these words: 'The celebrated hero of the day, apart from Bach, was his only surviving grandson, a very old man, yet vigorous, with snow-white hair and expressive features. No one had known of him, not even Mendelssohn, who had lived for so long in Berlin and certainly would have eagerly followed up anything connected with Bach—and this man had been there for more than 40 years! About his circumstances no particulars could be ascertained, except that he was conductor to the wife of King Friedrich II, and later received a pension assuring him a carefree existence. Let us honour the worthy head bearing so sacred a name!' At the Leipzig celebration Wilhelm Bach was accom-

[1] The date of 1846 on his tomb is not correct. He died in 1845. Cf. Hey in *BJ*, 1933.

panied by his aged wife and two daughters, but his only son had not survived infancy, and so there was no one to carry on the name of which he felt so proud. After his death in 1845 one of his daughters married, but she had no children and thus Wilhelm's line of the family expired.

THE MUSIC OF WILHELM FRIEDRICH ERNST BACH

Outwardly, the lives of the two artistically-minded grandsons of Sebastian seem diametrically opposed. Sebastian II never secured a position in his field and died at the age of 30; Wilhelm received a good appointment at the Prussian court and lived to be 86, thus reaching an age not attained by any other member of this branch of the family. Yet artistically their careers bear a certain resemblance. Wilhelm's style was formed during the decisive years he spent in London with his uncle. There he adopted an idiom of early classicism which had not yet entirely outgrown the somewhat stiff grace of Rococo music. The Andante con moto in B flat in his *Grande Sonate pour le Pianoforte*, which he performed on December 6, 1778, in the Hanover Square concert hall, shows the youth of 19 to be a disciple of his brilliant uncle (*Ex.* 129). He maintained a

musical language of this type more or less throughout his long life. Artistically he never fully matured; he ignored the tremendous changes music was undergoing from the hands of Beethoven, Schubert, Schumann, and Chopin, and he did not even follow the romantic trends revealed in the later works of Mozart and Haydn. Although the exact dates of composition can be ascertained for only a few of his works, it appears that his style underwent hardly any changes and that long before he died his creative urge ran out. He gave his best while his father and his uncle were still alive, but when he was the only Bach left to carry on the family tradition he felt this to be so crushing a responsibility that it stunted his creative faculties.

Only a comparatively small number of his works was printed in his lifetime, such as the piano score of his successful cantata *Westphalens Freude ihren...geliebten König...zu sehen* (Bösendahl, Rinteln, 1791), which led to his appointment in Berlin; 6 trios for clavier, violin, and 'cello (Preston, London, *ca.* 1785); 12 *grandes variations pour piano* (Schlesinger, Berlin); a selection of German and French songs and ariettes dedicated to the Prussian Queen (published by the composer himself), and the *Rheinweinlied* (Werckmeister, Berlin). The majority of his compositions were preserved in manuscript in Berlin and in the British Museum, which in 1883 purchased from C. Zoeller a large amount of Wilhelm's music, mostly in the composer's own hand.

Wilhelm Bach avoided the larger forms of composition. Unlike his uncle Christian, he wrote no operas,[1] and his secular and sacred cantatas are all on a very modest scale.[2] His output includes works for piano solo, various chamber music, a ballet, concertos for one and two pianos, symphonies, songs, duets, choruses, and short cantatas. Many are brilliant concert pieces meant to allow a soloist to exhibit a maximum of technical virtuosity, such as the 2 rondos for soprano and orchestra, '*L'amour est un bien suprême*' and *Ninfe se liete*, which in the solo part contains passages of breath-taking difficulty (*Ex.* 130.) Others are simple educational pieces

written for amateurs of very limited technical abilities. The Sonata in C for violin and piano which the composer designates as 'Sinfonia' (probably to make the performing pupils feel more important) has four movements, but its naïve and rather primitive language does not do justice to the pompous title and the over-extended form. The work which starts as follows (*Ex.* 131) bears a close resemblance to educational music by Clementi, Kuhlau, and others, written around the turn of the century. Even the orchestral Symphony in G composed in Berlin is of a similar character. It is in 3 movements (without Minuet), the best of which is the last Allegro in 6/8, a gay hunting scene. This work too is very easy to perform and was probably meant for an amateur group. A third category comprises short pieces for mixed or male chorus with or without soloists,

---

[1] Terry's assumption in Grove's 'Dictionary,' 3rd ed., I, p. 179, that his 'Columbus or the discovery of America' was a *scena* from an opera, is erroneous. This is a ballad-like short cantata complete in itself.

[2] The oratorio *Die Kindheit Jesu* attributed to him in the catalogue of MSS. of the British Museum is the work of his father (cf. p. 402).

evidently intended for 'Liedertafeln' and other choral groups of untrained music lovers. The range of emotions covered here is very wide. A good

example of the serious works is offered by the *Vater unser* ('Lord's Prayer') for tenor and bass with chorus and orchestra. The soloists take turns in praising the Lord, and each section is concluded by a line from the Lord's Prayer sung by the chorus. This work is built up towards a climax through the entrance of timpani and trumpets at the words 'for Thine is the kingdom, and the power, and the glory'; it displays a pleasing warmth and fervour. Conceived along similar lines is the ballad *Columbus oder die Entdeckung von America* ('Columbus or the discovery of America') for tenor solo, bass solo, chorus, and a group of wind and string instruments; in it Wilhelm's favourite device of enhancing the expressiveness through added trumpets and timpani occurs when land is sighted by the mutinous sailors. Another work for solo voices and chorus, this time, however, with the accompaniment of piano, is *Erinnerung an Schillers Sterbetag* ('In memory of Friedrich Schiller's death in 1805'), the harmonic and melodic language of which reveals a timid approach to Romanticism. On the other hand, there is a multitude of humorous, even burlesque pieces, among them the *Concerto buffo*, in which various toy instruments are presented. In the 'duetto comico' *Der Dichter und der Komponist* ('The poet and the composer') for three voices and piano, a poet and a composer converse about the creative process and are again and again rudely interrupted in their big-sounding orations by a peddler advertising 'Limburg cheese,' 'apples,' 'berries,' and, as a final iniquity, 'sour pickles.' In a remark on the score Wilhelm Bach stresses that the Berlin dialect should be used for the peddler's utterances. The kind of entertainment which Wilhelm provides here makes us think of the 'barbershop quartets' of a later time.

A similar sense of humour is revealed in the *Dreyblatt* ('Trefoil') for piano six hands. In a note on the title-page of the composition Wilhelm remarks: 'the gentleman playing the middle part should sit a little further back than the two ladies on either side of him. Their arms must be held above his own.' As a matter of fact, the piece is written in such a way that it is the man in the centre who plays, with his right hand, the highest and, with his left, the lowest notes of the composition.

His *Lieder* show the simple, pre-romantic character of compositions written in the seventeen-eighties. Wilhelm composed not only to German, but also to French and Italian texts. For pieces in a more brilliant idiom he preferred foreign languages, which he used with great ease. While the scholastic education given him in Bückeburg bore good fruit in this respect, the special training he received from his father left a surprisingly weak imprint, and there is not much of musical craftsmanship to be noticed in the majority of his works. The *Allegro fugato* that concludes a Divertimento for piano duet, for instance, uses a weak and repetitious theme rather unsuitable for contrapuntal elaboration (*Ex.* 132) that would not have seemed acceptable to the older Bachs.

The British Museum preserves among Wilhelm's manuscript works a Sextet in E flat for clarinet, 2 horns, violin, viola, and 'cello. The name of the composer is not mentioned, but as it is in his own hand and as the collection of Wilhelm's music contains works of a similar character, we are justified in assuming it to be a product of the same author. This is real chamber music, affording good opportunities for each of the six players and written in a transparent and highly effective style. In particular, the rondo finale with its main subject in the character of a German peasant dance (*Ex.* 133) shows vigour and spirit. Wilhelm's music, for once

neither fettered by the demands of exacting virtuosi nor by those of incompetent amateurs, here assumes a solid and pleasing character, not too often apparent in his works.[1] As a rule the artistic personality of Sebastian's grandson shows but few of the characteristic features of the Bach musicians.

[1] Among his more attractive works of chamber music the little Trio in G for two flutes and viola should be mentioned which was edited by Rolf Ermeler in the collection 'Hortus Musicus.'

xxv. J. S. Bach II. 'Ideal Landscape.' Oil-painting

XXVI. J. S. Bach II. 'Landscape with mill.' Drawing

EPILOGUE

THE two grandsons of Sebastian Bach may well be considered as typical of the seventh generation counting from Veit, the miller. Physically and artistically the strength of the family was ebbing away; the gifted Johann Sebastian II died at the age of 30, before he was able to create real master-works, while Wilhelm Friedrich Ernst never developed artistic maturity and wrote in a superficial style strangely unfit for a Bach. Nor was the picture different with other grandsons of Sebastian, most of whom did not survive infancy. What the Bückeburg Bach had felt so deeply was in a certain sense true: the Bachs were dying out. However, in Friedrich Bach's very own progeny some survival took place. His eldest daughter, Anna Philippine Friederike, in 1776 married Lieutenant Ernst Carl Colson. They had five children, who for the greater part showed typical symptoms of degeneration. Indeed one of them, Wilhelm Friedrich (1781-1809), was an epileptic who never held a profession; he had an illegitimate son, Wilhelm Ernst, who at the age of 15 committed suicide by hanging himself. The eldest of Friedrich Bach's grandsons, however, named Johann Christoph Friedrich after his grandfather (1778-1831), escaped the lack of vitality prevalent in the others. As a young man he had to leave Bückeburg because of some kind of trouble with the authorities; this led to a quarrel with his mother as well, and hence he supported him-self as tutor for mathematics (an interest he shared with some of his greatest kinsmen) in aristocratic families of eastern Germany. At the age of 35 he married Josepha Schiweck, had six children, all of whom had numerous offspring too. This branch of the family began modestly, earning their living as farmers or artisans, with some of the younger generation rising to the position of teachers. In 1939 28 grandsons and 52 great-grandsons of Friedrich Colson could be traced, some of them carrying Polish names. Thus the blood of Sebastian Bach is still alive in various families of Silesia and Poland.[1] They are all Roman Catholics, like their ancestor, Ernst Carl Colson.

It is interesting to note that while the most prominent branch of the

[1] Terry's statement 'since 13 May 1871 Bach's blood has ceased in mortal veins' (cf. 'Bach. The Historical Approach,' 1930) can therefore no longer be upheld. See Ulmenstein in *ZfMw*, 1939.

Bach tree was extinguished or degenerated in the seventh generation other, less important lines continued to flourish for some time. This applies to the Meiningen branch (cf. p. 447), which is still in existence to-day, and to the Ohrdruf line, which supplies good examples of the unassuming, deeply religious, hard-working type of Bach musician.

Ambrosius' eldest son, Johann Christoph (22), came to Ohrdruf in 1690, and it was in this little town that the orphaned Sebastian went to school for five years, receiving a thorough musical training from his brother. When Johann Christoph died in 1721, at the age of 50, his widow was badly off. Her husband had not earned enough to be able to save anything worth speaking of, and of her five sons, only the eldest, Tobias Friedrich[1] (40; 1695-1768), was supporting himself as Cantor of Udestedt, while the two youngest, aged 14 and 8, would still be financially dependent for quite a while. There were also three daughters to take care of. Frau Bach's problems were solved in the traditional manner. Her second son, Johann Bernhard (41; 1700-43), who had been studying with his uncle Sebastian at Weimar and Cöthen, serving also as a copyist, was appointed his father's successor as organist of St. Michael *propter merita defuncti patris*; and as he did not marry until ten years later, he was able to help his family. The third son, another Johann Christoph (42; 1702-56), applied, when an opening occurred, for the position of Cantor at Ohrdruf; he stressed the benefit his mother would thus derive, who 'had been living for eight years as a poor widow with so many children unprovided,' and he got the post. The fourth son, Johann Heinrich (43; 1707-82), received his uncle Sebastian's help, for shortly after the latter had moved to Leipzig the youth was enrolled in the Thomas school; subsequently he became Cantor at Oehringen. (That he as well as his elder brother, J. Christoph, were active composers is revealed by a festive cantata which these two brothers wrote together in celebration of the nuptials of a Count of Hohenlohe and a Saxon Princess.) Johann Andreas (44; 1713-79), the youngest offspring, first felt tempted to try a more adventurous life, and joined the army as a musician; eventually he, too, returned to his native town, serving as organist of the Trinitatis Church, and on the death of his brother Johann Bernhard in 1743 as the latter's successor. Apparently he rendered very satisfactory service; for it is significant that at his wife's funeral the bells were rung for a quarter of an hour 'because of the husband's special merits and outstanding artistic achievements.' In the

---

[1] Tobias Friedrich Bach first served as Cantor at Gandersheim, co-operating with his kinsman, Nikolaus Ephraim Bach (cf. p. 108); subsequently he was appointed in the same capacity at Pferdingsleben, and from 1721 to his death in 1763 at Udestedt.

following generation the Ohrdruf Bachs continued holding the positions of Organist and Cantor respectively, while other members served in schools or churches. The Organist, Andreas, was succeeded by his son, Johann Christoph Georg (1747-1814); and strangely enough father and son had the same tragic experience, when their church was destroyed by fire, first in 1753 and, after its restoration, a second time in 1808. (St. Michael's was finally hit by bombs in 1945, on which occasion a valuable library went up in flames.) A few years after Georg's appointment, his cousin, Philipp Christian (1734-1809) became Cantor, because, as is mentioned in the minutes of the Council, 'none of the other candidates had similar qualifications, especially with regard to music.' However, Philipp's interests were primarily in the field of theology, which he had studied in Jena. In 1772 he became pastor in a nearby town, whereupon his brother, Ernst Carl Gottfried (1738-1801), succeeded him as Cantor in Ohrdruf. The latter's son, Carl Christian (1785-1859), who—incidentally, like his kinsman, Sebastian Bach, married a cousin—chose the ministry and became an outstanding preacher and superintendent. Thus the Bach musicians proper ceased to work in Ohrdruf in 1814, but they continued to be active as teachers or pastors in this district and the line is now in its twelfth generation.

The Ohrdruf branch was also instrumental in carrying on the Bach tradition in Erfurt, where the family had served since 1635. The last Bach employed as director of the town band was Johann Christoph (19), born in the same year as Sebastian. His sons all chose the teaching profession, and moved away from Erfurt; so, on Johann Christoph's death in 1740, a son-in-law, Christoph Müller, was given the position. Moreover another Bach, Johann Günther (33; 1703-56), a great-grandson of Johann (4), joined the band as viola player and tenor singer. At about the same time a member of the Ohrdruf branch, Tobias Friedrich (b. 1723), worked as Cantor in Erfurt. His robust, typically Bachian sense of humour is expressed in a verse which the Cantor wrote at the age of 80 with a firm hand into the 'friendship-book' of a young relative who was paying him a visit:

> A Bach am I, and love my beer,
> But I must die, like others here!
> Yet while I live, a Cantor, I
> Gain profit when the others die.[1]

With Tobias Friedrich, who lived to be 90, the line of Bach musicians in Erfurt came to an end in 1813. Yet the name maintained its distinction in the district, for in the nearby village of Bindersleben there worked at that

[1] English translation by Henry S. Drinker.

time another gifted man of this name, again a Johann Christoph Bach (1782-1846), who was descended from a branch of the family that can be traced back to the year 1650, although no relationship to Veit, the baker, could be established. This Johann Christoph, who incidentally studied music with Sebastian Bach's latest pupil, J. Christoph Kittel, was an outstanding organist and choir director, and various compositions by him were published in Erfurt. Musical talent remained apparent in his descendants, and a grandson, Ernst Louis Heimann, enjoyed a fine reputation as Organist and *Regens chori*.

The fascination which genealogical research has exercised in recent times on the minds of the German people was responsible for the unearthing of many more Bach branches not descending from Veit, the baker.[1] Under the leadership of a retired teacher, Arthur Bach of Arnstadt, the Bachs were organized into a kind of society. The old institution of the annual family day, reported by Forkel (cf. p. 79), was revived, and thanks to a *Mitteilungsblatt* (journal) published since 1937 by the *Bach'scher Familienverband für Thüringen* (Bach Family Association for Thuringia) the Bachs kept each other informed of new genealogical discoveries as well as of weddings, christenings, deaths, appointments, etc. occurring in the clan. The Second World War put an end to the activities of this association, and it seems that it lost its most active members partly through death, partly through emigration. Yet those surviving in Germany still proudly cherish their heritage, and it would not be surprising if the Bach Family Association came to life again before long.

The 20th-century Bachs are, however, no longer professional musicians. Making music or painting is for them merely a pleasant hobby, and their activities therefore do not concern us here. Even such branches as the 18th-century Ohrdruf Bachs are for us of minor interest, for it should be borne in mind that carrying on a musical profession through several generations was by no means a rarity. A historian has figured out[2] that there are for instance 37 Thuringian families which produced two or more good musicians. The question therefore arises how it came about that the descendants of Veit, the baker, succeeded in surpassing those others not only in quantity and length of their reign, but, most of all, in artistic quality. In all these respects the Bachs may be termed unique and they were far superior to as outstanding a family as the French Couperins, who

---

[1] Quite a few Bachs were found in Bonn a.Rh., who worked as pianists, violinists, or church musicians, among them Ferdinand Bach (b. 1837), who at the age of 20 became a member of Joseph Joachim's quartet, but passed away a year later from typhus.

[2] Wilhelm Greiner, 'Die Musik im Lande Bachs,' Eisenach, 1935.

from the 17th to the 19th century produced in an unbroken line distinguished organists and pianists as well as some fine composers.

While it would be difficult to give definite reasons for the singular achievements of the Bachs, we might point to a few factors which worked in their favour. Theirs was a fighting spirit that thrived on difficulties. The greater the challenge, the fiercer was their determination to meet it nobly. Thus it happened that in the most tragic period of German history the Bachs were able to establish a tradition of fine, in some cases even of outstanding, musical accomplishments. Most helpful was also the family solidarity among the Bachs. Their homes as well as their rich fund of practical experience as musicians stood at the disposal of their kinspeople; as a unity they were able to weather economic storms which would have destroyed the single individual. They often married women who were descendants of musical families, and thus the artistic talent from two different sources was accumulated. It also seems that various national strains were combined in them to great advantage. Veit, the founder of the musical dynasty, may have handed on a mixed German-Magyar inheritance derived from his own or his wife's ancestry. While this is only conjectural, we are on firmer ground looking at Sebastian Bach's direct forebears. Only one of his grandparents was a Thuringian. His paternal grandmother came from a district in Saxony partly inhabited by Lower or North Germans and brought him some characteristics of this people; to her he may have owed his leanings towards Northern music which caused him to choose Lüneburg and Lübeck as places of study instead of Italy. His mother's family, though of Thuringian origin, had lived for several generations in Lower Silesia, which again has a mixed population. This heritage of mingled nationalities was at work in the production of the immortal genius. It should also not be forgotten that although among Sebastian's near relatives were some very fine composers, his own father did not exhibit any creative gifts, and probably this was true of his grandfather, Christoph Bach, as well. The musical inheritance thus accumulated in two generations triumphantly burst forth in Sebastian, who, on the other hand, had received emotional depth and a trend towards mystic ecstasy from the Lämmerhirts. The importance of his mother's family is also illuminated by another fact. His father, J. Ambrosius, had a twin brother, J. Christoph (12); these twins were so much alike that even their own wives could not distinguish them, and also as musicians they were not to be told apart (cf. p. 65). Yet the descendants of these twins bore no resemblance whatever, and while J. Christoph's son, J. Ernst (25), was an organist of mediocre talent, J. Ambrosius was the father of J. Sebastian.

While the achievements of this greatest Bach appear like the logical climax to which the work of his ancestors had led, his children present a baffling phenomenon indeed. As a rule genius does not produce progeny endowed with outstanding creative gifts. But in spite of Sebastian's titanic contributions to music, two of his sons were leaders in the music of their time, while two others revealed substantial talent. We must just accept the family's unique position in this respect, without attempting to produce sufficient reasons for it. However, it should be remembered that exceptionally fortunate conditions were created by Sebastian's choice of spouses, both wives being descendants of a long line of musicians and singers in their own right.

It may also help if one tries to visualize these various composers within the general artistic conditions of their time. In the 17th century Baroque art slowly gathered momentum, carrying the Bach musicians on the crest of this wave. The closer we approach Sebastian, the more significant we find the artistic achievements of his kinsmen. The starting-point for the greatest Bach was an extremely high one; not only his own relatives but musicians all around him produced works of a very elevated standard. From a general artistic level of such altitude Sebastian's genius carried him to supreme achievements in the Baroque era.

Sebastian's sons were by no means endowed with similar creative gifts. But when they were at work, in that transitional phase between the Baroque and Classical periods, the general musical standard had somewhat declined and Emanuel's as well as Christian's talent, though vastly inferior to that of their father, was sufficient to secure them leadership.

The chronicler investigating the history of the Bach family feels very much like a mountain climber. Slowly he ascends to a high plateau affording some enchanting views; proceeding across it he comes to a tower of the most generous proportions, the highest gallery of which seems to reach right into the sky and offers vistas of breath-taking splendour. Henceforth he continues along the wide, pleasant expanse of the plateau which discloses ever new attractions, and only after a long walk he descends on a steep trail into the valley. Looking back from a greater distance he might find the outlines of the mountainous plateau somewhat blurred, but the tower will still stand out in all its glory.

GENEALOGICAL TABLE OF THE BACH MUSICIANS
(DESCENDANTS OF VEIT BACH, THE MILLER)

IN the following list the unwieldy genealogical trees have been replaced by the space-saving device of the decimal system to indicate the relationship between the different members of the Bach family. Accordingly the name of Veit, the baker, is preceded by a 1, that of his brother Caspar by a 2. Veit's two sons, Johannes and Lips, are given 11 and 12 respectively, and Caspar's five sons 21, 22, 23, 24, 25.

The three sons of 11 Johannes are 111 Johann, 112 Christoph, and 113 Heinrich. Lips' only son is 121 Wendel. The three sons of 111 Johann are shown by 111.1, 111.2 and 111.3, those of 112 Christoph with 112.1, 112.2, and 112.3.

The number of digits in an italicized number indicates therefore how many generations the person is removed from the founder of the family (112.24 J. Sebastian, for instance, belongs to the fifth generation counting from Veit). By omitting the last digit from an italicized number we receive that assigned to the person's father, by removing the last two digits that of his grandfather (112.24 J. Sebastian is the son of 112.2 J. Ambrosius and the grandson of 112 Christoph).

If two italicized numbers are identical except for the last digit, the two men referred to are brothers; if the numbers are identical in all but the last two digits, the persons are cousins. (112.24 J. Sebastian is a brother of 112.23 J. Jakob; the two men are cousins of 112.31 J. Ernst.) Other relationships can easily be worked out.

The name Johann preceding a middle name is abbreviated into J. Numbers in ( ) following a name are those of J. Sebastian's *Ursprung der musicalisch-Bachischen Familie*. The reader will notice that our system leads to a succession of names identical with that achieved in J. Sebastian's Genealogy, although our list is naturally larger. There is one slight discrepancy, however: No. 51 of J. Sebastian's list was omitted by us, as the J. Christoph mentioned under this number did not exist.

No attempt towards completeness has been made. Those who died at an early age, the female members of the family, and the non-musicians, were as a rule omitted.

1	Veit (1), the baker, Wechmar, ?-1619.
2	Caspar, town musician, Gotha, Arnstadt, ca. 1570-ca. 1642.
3	Hans ('The jester'), Nürtingen, 1555-1615.
11	Johannes or Hans (2), musician, Wechmar, ?-1626.
12	Lips (3), carpetmaker, ?, ?-1620.
21	Caspar, musician, Arnstadt, ca. 1600-?.
22	Johannes, musician, Arnstadt, 1602-32.
23	Melchior, musician, Arnstadt, 1603-34.
24	Nicol, musician, Arnstadt, 1619-37.
25	Heinrich, blind, Arnstadt, ?-1635.
111	Johann (4), town musician and organist, Erfurt, 1604-73.
112	Christoph (5), town and court musician, Arnstadt, 1613-61.
113	Heinrich (6), organist, Arnstadt, 1615-92.
121	Wendel, farmer, Wolfsbehringen, 1619-82.
111.1	J. Christian (7), director of town band, Erfurt, 1640-82.
111.2	J. Egidius (8), director of town band, Erfurt, 1645-1716.
111.3	J. Nikolaus (9), town musician, Erfurt, 1653-82.
112.1	Georg Christoph (10), cantor, Schweinfurt, 1642-97.

112.2	J. Ambrosius (11), town musician, Eisenach, 1645-95.
112.3	J. Christoph (12), town musician, Arnstadt, 1645-93.
113.1	J. Christoph (13), organist, Eisenach, 1642-1703.
113.2	J. Michael (14), organist, Gehren, 1648-94.
113.3	J. Günther (15), organist, Arnstadt, 1653-83.
121.1	Jakob, cantor, Ruhla, 1655-1718.
111.11	J. Jakob (16), town musician's journeyman, Eisenach, 1668-92.
111.12	J. Christoph (17), cantor, Gehren, 1673-1727.
111.21	J. Bernhard (18), organist, Eisenach, 1676-1749.
111.22	J. Christoph (19), director of town band, Erfurt, 1685-1740.
111.31	J. Nikolaus (20), barber and surgeon, Königsberg, 1682-after 1735.
112.11	J. Valentin (21), cantor, Schweinfurt, 1669-1720.
112.21	J. Christoph (22), organist, Ohrdruf, 1671-1721.
112.22	J. Balthasar, trumpeter, Cöthen, 1673-91.
112.23	J. Jakob (23), court musician, Stockholm, 1682-1722.
112.24	**J. Sebastian (24), 1685-1750.**
112.31	J. Ernst (25), organist, Arnstadt, 1683-1739.
112.32	J. Christoph (26), organist, Blankenheim, 1689-1740.
113.11	J. Nicolaus (27), organist, Jena, 1669-1753.
113.12	J. Christoph (28), clavier teacher, England, 1676-?.
113.13	J. Friedrich (29), organist, Mühlhausen, 1682-1730.
113.14	J. Michael (30), organ builder, Stockholm ?, 1685-?.
113.21	Maria Barbara, m. J. Sebastian, 1684-1720.
121.11	J. Ludwig, court conductor, Meiningen, 1677-1731.
121.12	Nikolaus Ephraim, intendant and organist, Gandersheim, 1690-1760.
121.13	Georg Michael, cantor, Halle, 1701-77.
111.121	J. Samuel (31), musician, Sondershausen, 1694-1720.
111.122	J. Christian (32), musician, Sondershausen, 1696-?.
111.123	J. Günther (33), teacher and musician, Erfurt, 1703-56.
111.211	J. Ernst (34), organist and conductor, Weimar, Eisenach, 1722-77.
111.221	J. Friedrich (35), schoolmaster, Andisleben, 1706-43.
111.222	J. Egidius (36), schoolmaster, Gross Munra, 1709-46.
111.223	Wilhelm Hieronymus (37), 1730-54.
112.111	J. Lorenz (38), organist and cantor, Lahm, 1695-1773.
112.112	J. Elias (39), cantor, Schweinfurt, 1705-55.
112.211	Tobias Friedrich (40), cantor, Udestedt, 1695-1768.
112.212	J. Bernhard (41), organist, Ohrdruf, 1700-43.
112.213	J. Christoph (42), cantor, Ohrdruf, 1702-56.
112.214	J. Heinrich (43), cantor, Oehringen, 1707-82.
112.215	J. Andreas (44), organist, Ohrdruf, 1713-79.
112.241	Wilhelm Friedemann (45), the 'Halle Bach,' 1710-84.
112.242	Carl Philipp Emanuel (46), the 'Berlin or Hamburg Bach,' 1714-88.
122.243	J. Gottfried Bernhard (47), organist, Mühlhausen, 1715-39.
112.244	Gottfried Heinrich (48), mentally deficient, 1724-63.
112.245	Elisabeth Juliane Friederica, m. J. Christoph Altnikol, 1726-81.
112.246	J. Christoph Friedrich (49), the 'Bückeburg Bach,' 1732-95.
112.247	J. Christian (50), the 'London Bach,' 1735-82.
112.248	Regine Susanna, J. Sebastian's youngest child, 1742-1809.
113.111	J. Christian (52), theologian, Jena, 1717-38.
113.121	J. Heinrich (53), clavierist, ?-after 1735.
121.111	Samuel Anton, organist and court official, Meiningen, 1713-81.
121.112	Gottlieb Friedrich, organist and painter, Meiningen, 1714-85.

121.131   J. Christian, clavierist, Halle, 1743-1814.

111.211.1   J. Georg, organist and lawyer, Eisenach, 1751-97.

111.221.1   J. Christoph, Andisleben, 1736-1808.

112.112.1   J. Michael, music theoretician, composer, lawyer, Güstrow, travelled to U.S., 1754-?.

112.211.1   Tobias Friedrich, cantor, Erfurt, 1723-1813.

112.212.1   J. Wilhelm, gold lace maker, Ohrdruf, 1732-1800.

112.213.1   Philipp Christian, cantor and minister, Werningshausen, 1734-1809.

112.213.2   Ernst Carl Gottfried, cantor, Ohrdruf, 1738-1801.

112.213.3   Ernst Christian, cantor, Wechmar, 1747-1822.

112.215.1   J. Christoph Georg, organist, Ohrdruf, 1747-1814.

112.241.1   Friederica Sophie, m. J. Schmidt in 1789, 1757-1801.

112.242.1   J. August, lawyer, Hamburg, 1745-89.

112.242.2   J. Sebastian (J. Samuel), painter, Rome, 1748-78.

112.245.1   Augusta Magdalena Altnikol, m. E. F. Ahlefeldt, sealing-wax maker, 1751-1809.

112.245.2   Juliane Wilhelmine Altnikol, m. F. A. Prüfer, printer, 1754-1815.

112.246.1   Anna Philippine Friederike Bach, m. Lieut. W. E. Colson, 1755-1804.

112.246.2   Wilhelm Friedrich Ernst, court cembalist, Berlin, 1759-1845.

121.112.1   J. Philipp, organist and painter, Meiningen, 1752-1846.

121.112.2   Samuel Friedrich, minister, Neuhaus, 1755-1841.

111.211.11 Philipp Ernst Christian, city clerk, Eisenach, 1780-1840.

121.112.11 Friedrich Carl Eduard, ducal forester, 1815-1903.

121.112.111 Paul, post official Eisenach, b. 1878.

BIBLIOGRAPHY

A Selection of Literature on Members of the Bach Family

(For list of abbreviations see p. xv)

ABERT H. *Joh. Christian Bachs italienische Opern und ihr Einfluss auf Mozart, ZfMw*, I, 1919.

ADLUNG J. *Anleitung zu der musikalischen Gelahrtheit.* Erfurt, 1758.

—— *Musica Mechanica Organoedi* (1768). Reprint by Christhard Mahrenholz. Kassel, 1931.

ALBRECHT H. and BACH A. *Die Bache in Arnstadt.* Mitteilungsblatt des Bach'schen Familienverbandes für Thüringen. Arnstadt, 1938.

ALDRICH P. *Ornamentation in J. S. Bach's Organ Works.* New York, 1951.

ARNSTADT. *J. S. Bach und seine Verwandten in Arnstadt*, ed. by F. Wiegand. Arnstadt, 1950.

BACH C. P. E. *Versuch über die wahre Art, das Clavier zu spielen.* Berlin, 1759, 1762. Reprint by Walter Niemann, 5th ed. Leipzig, 1925. English translation by William J. Mitchell, New York, 1949.

Bach Gedenkschrift. Compiled by the 'International Bach Society,' ed. by K. Matthaei. Zürich, 1950.

Bach Jahrbuch. Leipzig, 1904-50.

Bach in Thüringen. Gabe der Thüringer Kirche an das Thüringer Volk zum Bach Gedenkjahr 1950. Berlin, 1950.

BEAULIEU-MARCONNAY C. VON. *Ernst August, Herzog v. Sachsen-Weimar.* Leipzig, 1872.

BECHSTEIN L. *Aus dem Leben der Herzöge von Meiningen.* Meiningen, 1856.

BERNHARDT R. *Das Schicksal der Familie Bach.* Der Bär, 1929-30.

BERTHOLD O. *Das Leben in der Thomasschule zur Bachzeit.—J. S. Bach. Das Schaffen des Meisters im Spiegel einer Stadt.* Leipzig, 1950.

BESCH H. *J. S. Bach. Frömmigkeit und Glaube.* Band I. 'Deutung und Wirklichkeit,' 2nd ed. Kassel, 1950.

BESSELER H. and KRAFT G. *Johann Sebastian Bach in Thüringen.* Erfurt, 1950.

BITTER C. H. *C. P. E. und W. Fr. Bach und deren Brüder.* Berlin, 1868.

—— *Johann Sebastian Bach*, 2nd ed. Berlin, 1881.

—— *Die Söhne Sebastian Bach's* in 'Haldersee: Sammlung Musikalischer Vorträge.' Leipzig, 1884.

BLUME F. *Die evangelische Kirchenmusik.* Berlin, 1931.

—— *Two Centuries of Bach. An Account of Changing Taste*, transl. by S. Godman. New York, 1950.

—— *J. S. Bach*, article in 'Die Musik in Geschichte und Gegenwart.' Kassel, 1949.

BOJANOWSKI P. VON. *Das Weimar J. S. Bachs.* Weimar, 1903.

BORKOWSKY E. *Das alte Jena und seine Universität.* Jena, 1908.

—— *Die Musikerfamilie Bach.* Jena, 1930.

BOUGHTON R. *Bach, the Master.* New York, 1930.

BRANDTS-BUYS H. *Het wohltemperirte Clavier.* Arnhem, 1944.

BÜCKEN E. *Der galante Stil. ZfMw*, VI. 1923-24.

BUKOFZER M. *Music in the Baroque Era.* New York, 1947.

BURNEY CH. *Musical Tour, or Present State of Music in France and Italy.* London, 1771.

—— *The Present State of Music in Germany, the Netherlands and United Provinces.* London, 1773.

—— *General History of Music.* London, 1776-89.

CART W. *J. S. Bach 1685-1750*, étude. Lausanne, 1946.

CHERBULIEZ A. E. *Carl Philip Emanuel Bach.* Zürich, 1940.

—— *Johann Sebastian Bach, sein Leben und sein Werk.* Olten, 1946.

CHRYSANDER F. *Briefe von C. Ph. E. Bach und G. M. Telemann.* Allg. Musikal. Ztg. IV,1869.

—— *Eine Klavierphantasie von C. Ph. E. Bach.* Vierteljahrsschr. f. Musikwissensch. VII, 1891.

CRAMER H. *Die Violoncell-Kompositionen Ph. E. Bachs.* Allg. Musikzeitg., 1930.

DANCKERT W. *Beiträge zur Bachkritik.* Kassel, 1934.

DAVID H. T. *Kritischer Anhang zu Bachs Kunst der Fuge.* Jahrbuch Peters, 1927.

—— *J. S. Bach, die Kunst der Fuge.* Leipzig, 1928.

—— *J. S. Bach's Musical Offering. History, Interpretation and Analysis.* New York, 1945

—— and MENDEL A. *The Bach Reader.* New York, 1945.

DAVISON A. T. *Bach and Handel.* Cambridge, 1951.

DEHNERT M. *Das Weltbild J. S. Bachs.* Leipzig, 1948.

DICKINSON A. E. F. *The Art of Bach.* London, 1936.

DIECK W. *Die Beziehungen der Familie Bach zu Erfurt.* Thüringer Allgem. Ztg., 1935.

DIETRICH F. *J. S. Bachs Orgelchoral und seine geschichtlichen Wurzeln.* BJ, 1929.

—— *Analogieformen in Bachs Tokkaten und Präludien für die Orgel.* BJ, 1931.

—— *Geschichte des deutschen Orgelchorals im 17. Jhdt.* Kassel, 1932.

DÜRR A. *Studien über die frühen Kantaten J. S. Bachs.* Leipzig, 1951.

EHRHARDT P. *Gisela Agnes-Bach; Bilder aus Köthens Vergangenheit.* Köthen, 1935.

EHRICHT K. *Die zyklische Gestalt und die Aufführungsmöglichkeit des III. Teiles der Klavierübung von Joh. Seb. Bach.* BJ, 1949-50.

ENGEL H. *J. S. Bach.* Berlin, 1950.

FALCK M. *Wilhelm Friedemann Bach.* Leipzig, 1913.

FIELD L. N. *J. S. Bach.* Minneapolis, 1943.

FINLAY J. *J. S. Bachs weltliche Kantaten.* Göttingen, 1950.

FISCHER E. *J. S. Bach.* Bern, 1948.

FISCHER K. *Das Freundschaftsbuch des Apothekers F. Thomas Bach.* BJ, 1938.

FISCHER M. *Die organistische Improvisation im 17. Jhdt. dargestellt an den '44 Chorälen zum Präambulieren' von Joh. Christoph Bach.* Kassel, 1929.

FISCHER W. *Zur Chronologie der Klaviersuiten J. S. Bachs,* in Musikwissensch. Kongressbericht. Basel, 1925.

FLORAND F. *Jean-Sébastien Bach; l'œuvre d'orgue.* Paris, 1947.

FLUELER M. *Die norddeutsche Sinfonie zur Zeit Friedrichs des Grossen und besonders die Werke Phil. Em. Bachs.* Berlin, 1908.

FOCK G. *Die Wahrheit über Bachs Aufenthalt in Lüneburg.* Hamburg, 1949.

—— *Der junge Bach in Lüneburg.* Hamburg, 1950.

FORKEL J. N. *Ueber J. S. Bachs Leben, Kunst und Kunstwerke.* Reprint of the edition of 1802. Kassel, 1950.

FREYSE C. *Eisenacher Dokumente um Sebastian Bach.* Leipzig, 1933.

—— *Das Bach-Haus in Eisenach.* BJ, 1939, 1940-48.

FRIEDLAENDER M. *Das deutsche Lied im 18. Jahrhundert.* Leipzig, 1902.

FROTSCHER G. *Geschichte des Orgelspiels und der Orgelkomposition.* Berlin, 1935.

—— *J. S. Bach und die Musik des 17. Jhdts.* Wädenswil, 1939.

FULLER-MAITLAND J. A. *The Age of Bach and Handel* (Oxf. Hist. of Music, IV). Oxford, 1902.

FÜRSTENAU M. *Zur Geschichte der Musik und des Theaters am Hof zu Dresden.* Dresden, 1861-62.

GEBHARDT H. *Thüringische Kirchengeschichte.* Gotha, 1881.

GEIRINGER K. *Die Familie Bach.* Wien, 1936.

—— *Artistic Interrelations of the Bachs.* MQ, 1950.

—— *The Lost Portrait of J. S. Bach.* New York, 1950.

GRACE H. *The Organ Works of Bach.* London, 1922.

GRAESER W. *Bach's Kunst der Fuge. BJ*, 1924.

GREINER W. O. L. *Die Musik im Lande Bachs. Thüringer Musikgeschichte*, Eisenach, 1935.

—— *Erbbiologische Beobachtungen aus der thüringischen Geistesgeschichte.* Thüringer Monatsblätter, 1935.

GRESKY H. *Ein unbekannter Arnstädter Bach.* Beilage zum 'Arnstädter Anzeiger,' 1935.

GREW E. and S. *Bach.* London, 1947.

GROHMANN, A. VON. *J. S. Bach.* Heidelberg, 1948.

GURLITT W. *J. S. Bach. Der Meister und sein Werk.* 3rd ed. Kassel, 1949.

HAMEL F. *Johann Sebastian Bach. Geistige Welt.* Göttingen, 1951.

HARTUNG O. *Geschichte der Stadt Cöthen.* Cöthen, 1900.

HASE H. VON. *C. P. E. Bach und J. G. I. Breitkopf. BJ*, 1911.

HASSE K. *J. S. Bach.* Leipzig, 1946.

HAYM R. *Herder nach seinem Leben und seinen Werken dargestellt.* Berlin, 1877-85.

HELMBOLD H. *Bilder aus Eisenachs Vergangenheit.* Eisenach, 1928.

HERTEL L. *Neue Landeskunde des Herzogtums Sachsen-Meiningen*, Heft 9. Hildburghausen, 1903-4.

HERTZBERG G. F. *Geschichte der Stadt Halle an der Saale*, III. Halle, 1893.

HERZ G. *J. S. Bach im Zeitalter des Rationalismus und der Frühromantik.* Bern, 1936.

—— *A 'New' Bach Portrait. MQ*, 1943.

—— *Bach's Religion.* Journal of Renaiss. and Baroque music, 1946.

HEY G. *Zur Biographie J. Friedrich Bachs und seiner Familie. BJ*, 1933.

HINDEMITH P. *Johann Sebastian Bach. Heritage and Obligation.* New Haven, 1952.

HOFFMANN H. J. K. *Die norddeutsche Triosonate des Kreises um J. G. Graun und C. P. E. Bach.* Kiel, 1927.

HUGHES R. D. *The French Influence on Bach.* Thesis, Harvard Univ., 1926.

HULL A. E. *Bach's Organ Works.* London, 1929.

HULSHOFF L. G. *De zes suites voor violoncello solo van J. S. Bach.* Arnhem, 1944.

JANSEN M. *Bachs Zahlensymbolik an seinen Passionen untersucht. BJ*, 1937.

JESSE J. H. *Memoirs of the Life and Reign of King George III.* London, 1867.

KELLER H. *Unechte Orgelwerke Bachs. BJ*, 1937.

—— *J. S. Bach. Der Künstler und sein Werk.* Lorch, 1947.

—— *Die Orgelwerke Bachs.* Leipzig, 1948.

—— *Die Klavierwerke Bachs.* Leipzig, 1950.

KINSKY G. *Pedalklavier oder Orgel bei Bach.* Acta Musicologica. Copenhagen, 1936.

—— *Die Originalausgaben der Werke J. S. Bachs.* Wien, 1937.

KRETZSCHMAR A. F. H. *Geschichte des neuen deutschen Liedes.* Leipzig, 1912.

—— *E. Bachs und V. Herbings Lieder.* Introd. to *DDT*, vol. 42.

KÜHN H. *Aus der Eisenacher Zeit J. Ambrosius Bachs.* Thüringer Fähnlein, 1935.

KURTH E. *Grundlagen des linearen Kontrapunkts.* Bern, 1916.

LÄMMERHIRT H. *Bachs Mutter und ihre Sippe. BJ*, 1925.

LANG P. H. *Music in Western Civilization.* New York, 1941.

LAUX K. *Der Thomaskantor und seine Söhne.* Dresden, 1939.

LINDAU M. B. *Geschichte der kgl. Haupt- und Residenzstadt Dresden.* Dresden, 1885.

LINNEMANN G. *Celler Musikgeschichte.* Celle, 1935.

LÖFFLER H. *Nachrichten über die St. Georgen-Orgel in Eisenach.* Zschr. f. evangel. Kirchenmusik, IV, V, 1926-27.

—— *Bache bei Seb. Bach. BJ*, 1949-50.

LUNOW A. *Einführung in die Kunst der Fuge.* Hamburg, 1950.

MATTHAEI K. Cf. *Bach Gedenkschrift.*

MENDEL A. See DAVID H. T.

MENKE W. *History of the Trumpet of Bach and Handel.* London, 1934.

MERSMANN H. *Ein Programmtrio K. Phil. Em. Bachs. BJ*, 1917.

MIESNER H. *Philipp Emanuel Bach in Hamburg.* Leipzig, 1929.

—— *Mitteilungen über die Familie Friedrich Bachs. BJ*, 1931.

—— *Ungedruckte Briefe von Phil. Emanuel Bach. ZfMw*, 1932.

—— *Urkundliche Nachrichten über die Familie Bach in Berlin. BJ*, 1932.

—— *Beziehungen zwischen den Familien Stahl und Bach. BJ*, 1933.

—— *Graf v. Keyserlingk und Minister v. Happe. BJ*, 1934.

—— *Aus der Umwelt Phil. Emanuel Bachs. BJ*, 1937.

—— *Phil. Emanuel Bachs musikalischer Nachlass. BJ*, 1938, 1939, 1940-48.

MITCHELL W. J. *C. P. E. Bach's Essay. MQ*, 1947.

MOSER A. *Zu J. S. Bachs Sonaten und Partiten für Violine allein. BJ*, 1920.

MOSER H. J. *Johann Sebastian Bach.* 2nd ed. Berlin, 1943.

MÜHLFELD, C. *Die herzogliche Hofkapelle in Meiningen.* Meiningen, 1910.

MÜLLER v. ASOW E. and H. *J. S. Bach, Briefe. Gesamtausgabe.* 2nd ed. Regensburg, 1950.

MÜLLER-BLATTAU J. *Genealogie der Musikalisch Bachischen Familie.* Kassel, 1950.

MÜLLER K. F. *J. S. Bach. Eine Würdigung seines Lebens und Schaffens.* Wien, 1950.

NEUMANN W. *J. S. Bach's Chorfuge.* Leipzig, 1938.

—— *Handbuch der Kantaten J. S. Bachs.* Leipzig, 1947.

NEWMAN, W. S. *The Keyboard Sonatas of Bach's Sons.* Proceedings of Music Teachers National Association, Pittsburgh, Pa., 1951.

NOHL, K. F. L. *Musikerbriefe.* Leipzig, 1873.

OERTEL A. *Festschrift zum Bachjahr 1950 hg. vom Bach Ausschuss der Stadt Ohrdruf.* Ohrdruf, 1950.

OLEARIUS J. G. *Begräbnispredigt auf Heinrich Bach*, publ. by R. Eitner, Monatshefte f. Musikgeschichte, 1875.

PAPENDIEK. *Court and Private Life in the Time of Queen Charlotte.* London, 1887.

PARRY C. H. H. *J. S. Bach.* London, 1909.

PAUMGARTNER B. *J. S. Bach. Leben und Werk*, I. Zürich, 1950.

PIRRO A. *L'orgue de Jean-Sébastien Bach.* Paris, 1895.

—— *J. S. Bach*, Paris, 1907.

—— *L'esthétique de Jean-Sébastien Bach.* Paris, 1907.

PITROU R. *Jean-Sébastien Bach.* Paris, 1941.

PLAMENAC D. *New Light on the Last Years of Carl Phil. Eman. Bach. MQ*, 1949.

POHL C. F. *Mozart in London.* Wien, 1867.

POTTGIESSER K. *Die Briefentwürfe des J. Elias Bach.* 'Die Musik,' 1912-13.

PREUSS H. *Dürer und Bach.* Gütersloh, 1935.

PUSCH. *Meiningen und die Meininger Bach'schen Nebenlinien.* Thüringer Fähnlein, 1935.

RAUPACH H. *Das wahre Bildnis J. S. Bachs.* Wolfenbüttel, 1950.

RAUSCHENBERGER W. *Die Familien Bach.* Frankfurt a. M., 1950.

REESER E. *The Sons of Bach.* Amsterdam (no date).

REICHARDT J. F. *Briefe eines aufmerksamen Reisenden, die Musik betreffend*, 1774-76.

RIEMANN H. *Die Söhne Bachs* in 'Präludien und Studien,' 1895-1900.

RIEMER O. *Johann Sebastian II.* Musica 7/8, 1950.

RITTER A. G. *Zur Geschichte des Orgelspiels im 14.-18. Jhdt.* Leipzig, 1884.

ROCHLITZ F. *Für Freunde der Tonkunst*, IV. Leipzig, 1832.

ROETHLISBERGER E. *Le Clavecin dans l'œuvre de J. S. Bach.* Geneva, 1920-21.

ROLLAND R. *Voyage musical au pays du passé.* Paris, 1920.

ROLLBERG F. *J. Ambrosius Bach. BJ*, 1927.

—— *J. Christoph Bach. ZfMw*, XI, 1928-29.

—— *Wo stand J. S. Bachs Geburtshaus?* Eisenacher Ztg. Oct. 10, 1929.

—— *Von den Eisenacher Stadtpfeifern*, Verein f. Thür. Geschichte und Altertumskunde. Jena, 1932.

ROLLBERG F. *Jakob Bach, Kantor und Knabenschulmeister in Ruhla*. Thüringer Fähnlein, 8, 1933.

—— *Aus der Heimat und dem Familienkreis des Jenaischen Organisten J. Nikolaus Bach.* Jenaische Ztg., No. 88, 1933.

—— *Die Geschichte der Eisenacher Kantoren*. Aus Luthers lieber Stadt, 1936.

ST. FOIX, G. DE. *A propos de Jean-Chrétien Bach*. Revue de Musicologie, X, 1926.

SCHÄFER F. *Der Organist J. Christoph Bach und die Eisenacher Münze*. Luginsland, 1929.

SCHEIBE J. A. *Critischer Musicus*. Leipzig, 1745.

SCHENKER H. *Ein Beitrag zur Ornamentik als Einführung zu Phil. Em. Bach's Klavierwerken*. Wien, 1908.

SCHERING A. *Bach und das Schemellische Gesangbuch. BJ*, 1924.

—— *Kleine Bachstudien. BJ*, 1933.

—— *J. S. Bachs Leipziger Kirchenmusik*. Leipzig, 1936.

—— *Zur Markus-Passion und zur 'vierten' Passion. BJ*, 1939.

—— *Bach und das Musikleben Leipzigs im 18. Jhdt.* Leipzig, 1941.

—— *Das Symbol in der Musik*. Leipzig, 1941.

—— *Ueber Kantaten J. S. Bachs*, with preface by F. Blume. Leipzig, 1942.

SCHMALZ T. *Denkwürdigkeiten des Grafen Wilhelm*. Hannover, 1783.

SCHMID E. F. *C. Ph. E. Bach und seine Kammermusik*. Kassel, 1931.

—— *Joseph Haydn und Carl Philipp Emanuel Bach. ZfMw*, 1932.

SCHMIEDER W. *Thematisch-systematisches Verzeichnis der musikalischen Werke J. S. Bachs*. Leipzig, 1950.

SCHMITZ A. *Die Bildlichkeit der wortgebundenen Musik J. S. Bachs*. Mainz, 1950.

SCHNEIDER M. *Thematisches Verzeichnis der musikalischen Werke der Familie Bach. BJ*, 1907.

SCHÖKEL H. P. *J. Christian Bach und die Instrumentalmusik seiner Zeit*. Wolfenbüttel, 1926.

SCHRADE L. *Bach: the Conflict between the Sacred and the Secular*. Journal of the History of Ideas, 1946.

SCHREYER J. *Beiträge zur Bachkritik*. Leipzig, 1910-13.

SCHUMM O. *Hof- und Stadtorganist J. Christoph Bach zu Eisenach*. Luginsland, 1927.

SCHÜNEMANN G. *J. Christ. Friedrich Bach. BJ*, 1914.

—— *Friedrich Bachs Briefwechsel mit Gerstenberg und Breitkopf. BJ*, 1916.

SCHWARZ M. *J. Christian Bach. Sein Leben und seine Werke*. Leipzig, 1901.

SCHWEBSCH E. *J. S. Bach und die Kunst der Fuge*. Stuttgart, 1931.

SCHWEITZER A. *J. S. Bach*. Paris, 1905; Leipzig, 1908. English translation by E. Newman, London, 1912, revised ed. 1952.

—— *Der für Bachs Werke für Violine solo erforderte Geigenbogen*. Bach Gedenkschrift, 1950.

SEIFFERT M. *Geschichte der Klaviermusik*. Leipzig, 1899.

—— *Sebastian Bachs Bewerbung um die Organistenstelle an St. Jakobi in Hamburg 1720.* Archiv. f. Musikwissenschaft III, 1921.

SHANET H. *Why did J. S. Bach transpose his arrangements? MQ*, 1950.

SHARP S. *Letters from Italy in the years 1765 and 1766*, 2nd ed. London, 1767.

SITTARD J. *Geschichte des Musik- und Konzertwesens in Hamburg*. Hamburg, 1890.

SMEND F. *Bachs H-moll Messe. BJ*, 1937.

—— *Neue Bach-Funde. AfMf*, 1942.

—— *Bachs Markus-Passion. BJ*, 1940-48.

—— *J. S. Bach: Kirchenkantaten*. 6 vols. Berlin, 1948-49.

—— *Johann Sebastian Bach bei seinem Namen gerufen*. Kassel, 1950.

—— *Bach in Köthen*. Berlin, 1951.

SOUCHAY M. A. *Das Thema in der Fuge Bachs. BJ*, 1927, 1930.

SPITTA P. *J. S. Bach*. Leipzig, 1873-80. Engl. ed. transl. by Clara Bell and J. A. Fuller-Maitland. London, 1884-85, repr. 1951.

SPITTA P. *Ueber die Beziehungen J. S. Bachs zu C. F. Hunold und M. v. Ziegler.* Historische und philologische Aufsätze. Berlin, 1884.

—— *Musikgeschichtliche Aufsätze.* Berlin, 1894.

STEGLICH R. *Karl Phil. Eman. Bach und der Dresdner Kreuzkantor G. A. Homilius. BJ,* 1915.

—— *Johann Sebastian Bach.* Potsdam, 1935.

—— *Wege zu Bach.* Regensburg, 1949.

STUDENY B. *Beiträge zur Geschichte der Violinsonate im 18. Jhdt.* München, 1911.

SZABOLCSI B. *Europai virradat. A klassicus zene kialakulasa Vivalditol Mozartig.* Budapest, 1949.

TERRY C. S. *The Orgelbüchlein.* Musical Times, 1917.

—— *J. S. Bach, Cantata texts.* London, 1926.

—— *Bach: a Biography.* London, 1928.

—— *John Christian Bach.* London, 1929.

—— *The Origin of the Family of Bach Musicians.* London, 1929.

—— *Bach: the Historical Approach.* New York, 1930.

—— *Bach's Orchestra.* London, 1932.

THIELE E. *Die Chorfugen J. S. Bachs.* Bern, 1936.

THIELE G. *Die Familie Bach in Mühlhausen.* Mühlhäuser Geschichtsblätter, 1920-21.

TIERSOT J. *J. S. Bach.* Paris, 1934.

TOVEY D. F. *A Companion to The Art of Fugue.* London, 1931.

TUTENBERG F. *Die Sinfonik J. Christian Bachs.* Wolfenbüttel, 1928.

ULDALL H. *Das Klavierkonzert der Berliner Schule and ihres Führers Philipp Emanuel Bach.* Leipzig, 1927.

ULMENSTEIN C. U. v. *Die Nachkommen des Bückeburger Bach. AfMf,* 1939.

VETTER W. *Der Kapellmeister Bach. Versuch einer Deutung.* Potsdam, 1950.

VETTER W.-MEYER E. H. *Bericht über die wissenschaftliche Bachtagung.* Leipzig, 1951.

VRIESLANDER O. *C. P. E. Bach als Klavierkomponist.* Dresden, 1922.

—— *C. P. E. Bach.* München, 1923.

—— *C. P. E. Bach als Theoretiker,* in 'Von Neuer Musik.' Köln, 1925.

WACKERNAGEL P. *J. S. Bach, Brandenburgische Konzerte.* Berlin, 1938.

WEISSMANN A. *Berlin als Musikstadt.* Berlin, 1911.

WENK A. *Beiträge zur Kenntnis des Opernschaffens von J. Christian Bach.* Unpublished dissertation. Frankfurt/Main, 1932.

WENNIG E. *Chronik des musikalischen Lebens der Stadt Jena.* Jena, 1937.

WERKER W. *Studien über die Symmetrie im Bau der Fugen und die motivische Zusammengehörigkeit der Präludien und Fugen des Wohltemperierten Klaviers von J. S. Bach.* Leipzig, 1922.

WETTE G. A. *Historische Nachrichten von der berühmten Residenzstadt Weimar.* Weimar, 1737.

WHITTAKER W. G. *The Bachs and Eisenach* in 'Collected Essays.' London, 1940.

WIEGAND F. Cf. Arnstadt.

WIEN-CLAUDI H. *Zum Liedschaffen C. P. E. Bachs.* Reichenberg, 1928.

WINKLER H. A. *Die Bachstätte in Eisenach; der Streit um J. S. Bachs Geburtshaus.* Flarchheim, 1931.

WINTERFELD C. VON. *Der evangelische Kirchengesang und sein Verhältnis zur Kunst des Tonsatzes.* Leipzig, 1847.

WUSTMANN R. *J. S. Bachs Kantatentexte.* Leipzig, 1913.

ZELTER C. F. *K. F. C. Fasch.* Berlin, 1801.

ZILLER E. *Der Erfurter Organist J. Heinrich Buttstädt.* Halle, 1935.

INDEX OF PERSONS AND PLACES

INDEX OF COMPOSITIONS
BY MEMBERS OF THE BACH FAMILY

GEORGE ALLEN & UNWIN LTD
London: 40 Museum Street, W.C.1

Auckland: Haddon Hall, City Road
Sydney, N.S.W.: Bradbury House, 55 York Street
Cape Town: 58–60 Long Street
Bombay: 15 Graham Road, Ballard Estate, Bombay 1
Calcutta: 17 Chittaranjan Avenue, Calcutta 13
New Delhi: Munshi Niketan, Kamla Market, Ajmeri Gate, New Delhi 1
Karachi: Haroon Chambers, South Napier Road, Karachi 2
Toronto: 91 Wellington Street West
Sao Paulo: Avenida 9 de Julho 1138–Ap. 51

also by Karl Geiringer

BRAHMS: His Life and Work

Demy 8vo   Revised and Enlarged 2nd Edition   21s. net

'The best existing book on Brahms. Not only has the author had access to a mass of material in the shape of hitherto unpublished letters, but he has known how to assemble it in an interesting and readable form. One may not always agree with his conclusions, but it is impossible not to respect his judgment, either of the man or of the music, to which ample space is devoted.'   *New Statesman and Nation*

'Much of the new material is of rare value, for it throws light on aspects of the composer's life that have been treated cursorily by previous biographers . . . However well informed readers may already be, they will learn something from this fine study of Brahms as man and musician.'   *Manchester Guardian*

HAYDN: A Creative Life in Music

Demy 8vo   Illustrated   21s. net

'At last a really substantial study of Haydn and his music has been published. I have little doubt that it will become the standard life in English . . . Dr. Geiringer happily combines scholarship with a considerable literary gift.'   *Penguin Music Magazine*

This book gives many facts generally unknown regarding the family and youth of the master. It not only introduces new material, but arranges it in such a way as to produce a picture of the unconventional and eternally young personality of the man who is so deceptively known as 'Papa Haydn.' The composer is seen to be not the simple-minded peasant but a man who, although earth-bound in his healthy humour and humbly religious, is fully aware of his standing as an artist.

MUSICAL INSTRUMENTS: Their History from the Stone Age to the Present Day

Demy 8vo   2nd Edition 3rd Impression   25s. net

' . . . very valuable book . . . a work of reference without parallel in the English language . . . Indeed, one is left with a doubt which to admire more, the extent of Dr. Geiringer's learning or the sense of proportion which controls it.'   *Times Educational Supplement*

GEORGE ALLEN AND UNWIN LTD

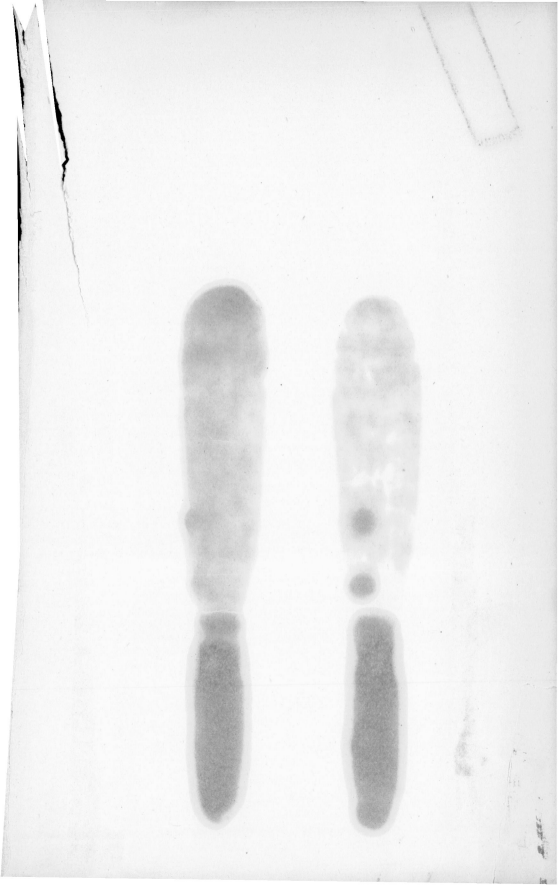